ABSOLUTELY POSTCOLONIAL

M. **, V ıÑ

ANGELAKIHUMANITIES

editors
Charlie Blake
Pelagia Goulimari
Timothy S. Murphy
Robert Smith

general editor
Gerard Greenway

Angelaki Humanities publishes works which address and probe broad and compelling issues in the theoretical humanities. The series favours path-breaking thought, promotes unjustly neglected figures, and grapples with established concerns It believes in the possibility of blending, without compromising, the rigorous, the well-crafted, and the inventive. The series seeks to host ambitious writing from around the world.

Angelaki Humanities is the associated book series of

ANGELAKI – journal of the theoretical humanities

ANGELAKIHUMANITIES

ABSOLUTELY POSTCOLONIAL

writing between
the singular and the specific

peter hallward

MANCHESTER UNIVERSITY PRESS

MANCHESTER AND NEW YORK

distributed exclusively in the USA by Palgrave

The right of Peter Hallward to be identified as the author of this work has been asserted by him in accordance with the Copyright, Designs and Patents Act 1988

Published by Manchester University Press
Oxford Road, Manchester M13 9NR, UK
and Room 400, 175 Fifth Avenue, New York, NY 10010, USA
www.manchesteruniversitypress.co.uk

Distributed exclusively in the USA by
Palgrave, 175 Fifth Avenue, New York NY 10010, USA

Distributed exclusively in Canada by
UBC Press, University of British Columbia, 2029 West Mall,
Vancouver, BC, Canada V6T 1Z2

British Library Cataloguing-in-Publication Data
A catalogue record for this book is available from the British Library

Library of Congress Cataloging-in-Publication Data
A catalog record for this book is available from the Library of Congress

ISBN: 0 7190 6126 1 paperback

ISBN 13: 978 0 7190 6126 4

First published 2001 by Manchester University Press

First digital paperback edition published 2007

Printed by Lightning Source

CONTENTS

contents

contents

ABBREVIATIONS

ALS   Said, Edward. *After the Last Sky. Palestinian Lives.* NY: Pantheon, 1986

BO   Sarduy, Severo. *Barroco* Buenos Aires: Sudamericana, 1974, references are to the collected volume *Ensayos generales sobre el barroco* (Mexico. Fondo de Cultura Economica, 1987). Trans. Carol Maier as *Written on a Body.* NY. Lumen Books, 1989. Except (where indicated) for occasional references to additional material in the French edition of *Barroco* (Paris. Gallimard, 'Folio', 1991).

BR   Johnson, Charles. *Being and Race. Black Writing Since 1970.* London: Serpent's Tail, 1988.

BV   Said, Edward et al. *Blaming the Victims. Spurious Scholarship and the Palestinian Question.* London: Verso, 1988.

CB   Sarduy, Severo. *Cobra* Buenos Aires: Sudamericana, 1972. Trans. Suzanne Jill Levine in joint volume *Cobra* [1975] and *Maitreya.* Normal, Ilinois. Dalkey Archive Press, 1995.

CC   Glissant, Edouard. *La Case du commandeur.* Paris. Seuil, 1981.

CI   Said, Edward. *Culture and Imperialism.* London. Chatto & Windus, 1993.

COL   Sarduy, Severo. *Colibri.* Barcelona: Editorial Argos Vergara, 1984.

CPR   Spivak, Gayatri. *The Critique of Postcolonial Reason. Toward a History of the Vanishing Present.* Cambridge Harvard University Press, 1999

CPT   Mongia, Padmini, ed. *Contemporary Postcolonial Theory. A Reader* London Arnold, 1996.

CR   Dib, Mohammed. *Cours sur la rive sauvage.* Paris: Seuil, 1964.

CvI   Said, Edward. *Covering Islam How the Media and the Experts Determine How We See the Rest of the World.* NY Pantheon, 1981

CY   Sarduy, Severo. *Cocuyo.* Barcelona· Tusquets, 1990.

DA   Glissant, Edouard. *Le Discours antillais.* Paris: Seuil, 1981.

DB   Dib, Mohammed *Dieu en barbarie* Paris. Seuil, 1970.

DD   Dib, Mohammed. *Le Désert sans détour.* Paris: Sindbad, 1992.

DS   Sarduy, Severo. *De donde son los cantantes.* Mexico: J. Mortiz, 1967 Trans.

Suzanne Jill Levine as *From Cuba With a Song* [1972]. Los Angeles. Sun & Moon Press, 1994.

DSR   Dib, Mohammed. *La Danse du roi*. Paris. Seuil, 1968.

EA   Dib, Mohammed. *Un Eté africain*. Paris: Seuil, 1959.

ES   Sarduy, Severo. *Escrito sobre un cuerpo*. Buenos Aires: Sudamericana, 1969; references are to the *Ensayos generales*.

FB   Gates, Henry Louis Jr. *Figures in Black. Words, Signs, and the 'Racial' Self*. Oxford. Oxford University Press, 1987.

FG   Johnson, Charles. *Faith and the Good Thing*. NY: Atheneum, 1974.

GM   Dib, Mohammed. *La Grande maison*. Paris: Seuil, 1952.

GS   Sarduy, Severo. *Gestos*. Barcelona: Seix Barral, 1963.

HB   Dib, Mohammed. *Habel*. Paris: Seuil, 1977.

HEG   Glissant, Edouard. *Horizons d'Edouard Glissant, Colloque*. Paris: Universities of Pau and Porto, 1992.

IM   Dib, Mohammed. *L'Infante maure*. Paris. Albin Michel, 1994.

IN   Dib, Mohammed *L'Incendie*. Paris: Seuil, 1954.

IOW   Spivak, Gayatri. *In Other Worlds: Essays in Cultural Politics*. London: Routledge, 1988.

IP   Glissant, Edouard. *L'Intention poétique*. Paris: Seuil, 1969.

IPD   Glissant, Edouard. *Introduction à une poétique du divers*. Paris: Gallimard, 1996.

LC   Bhabha, Homi. *The Location of Culture*. London: Routledge, 1994.

LZ   Glissant, Edouard. *La Lézarde*. Paris: Seuil, 1958.

MaT   Dib, Mohammed. *Le Métier à tisser*. Paris: Seuil, 1957.

MC   Dib, Mohammed *Le Maître de chasse*. Paris. Seuil, 1973

ME   Said, Edward. *Musical Elaborations*. London: Chatto & Windus, 1991.

MH   Glissant, Edouard. *Mahagony*. Paris. Seuil, 1987.

MM   Glissant, Edouard. *Malemort*. Paris Seuil, 1975.

MPg   Johnson, Charles *Middle Passage* [1990]. London Pan Books, 1991.

MT   Glissant, Edouard *Monsieur Toussaint*. Paris: Seuil, 1961; 2nd ed., 1986.

MY   Sarduy, Severo. *Maitreya*. Barcelona: Seix Barral, 1978. Trans. Levine [1987] in joint volume with *Cobra*. Normal, Illinois Dalkey Archive Press, 1995

NI   Sarduy, Severo. *Nueva inestabilidad* Mexico: Vuelta, 1987, references are to the *Ensayos generales*

NM   Dib, Mohammed. *Neiges de marbre* Paris Sindbad, 1990.

OR   Said, Edward *Orientalism* [1978] Harmondsworth Penguin, 1995

OT   Johnson, Charles *Ox-Herding Tale*. NY. Grove Press, 1982.

OTM   Spivak, Gayatri. *Outside in the Teaching Machine*. London. Routledge, 1993

P&S   Said, Edward. *The Pen and the Sword Conversations with David Barsamian* Edinburgh AK Press, 1994.

PC   Glissant, Edouard. *Poésie complète*. Paris: Gallimard, 1994.

PCC   Spivak, Gayatri. *The Post-Colonial Critic*. London: Routledge, 1990.

PcD   Said, Edward. *Peace and Its Discontents: Gaza-Jericho 1993-1995*. London. Vintage, 1995.

PCQ   Chambers, Iain, and Lindia Curi, eds. *The Post-Colonial Question. Common Skies, Divided Horizons*. London: Routledge, 1996.

PD   Said, Edward. *The Politics of Dispossession. The Struggle for Palestinian Self-Determination 1969-1994*. London: Vintage, 1995.

PP   Sarduy, Severo. *Pájaros de la playa*. Barcelona: Tusquets, 1993.

PR   Glissant, Edouard *Poétique de la Relation*. Paris: Gallimard, 1990.

QP   Said, Edward. *The Question of Palestine* [1979]. NY: Vintage, 1992.

QS   Glissant, Edouard. *Le Quatrième siècle*. Paris. Seuil, 1964.

QSS   Dib, Mohammed *Qui se souvient de la mer*. Paris: Seuil, 1962.

RI   Said, Edward. *Representations of the Intellectual*. London: Vintage, 1994.

RJ   Sarduy, Severo. *El Cristo de la rue Jacob*. Barcelona. Edicion del Mall, 1987. Trans. Levine and Maier as *Christ on the Rue Jacob*. San Francisco: Mercury House, 1995.

SA   Johnson, Charles. *The Sorcerer's Apprentice. Tales and Conjurations*. NY: Atheneum, 1986.

SC   Glissant, Edouard. *Soleil de la conscience*. Paris: Seuil, 1956.

SE   Dib, Mohammed. *Le Sommeil d'Eve*. Paris: Sindbad, 1989.

SI   Sarduy, Severo. *La Simulacion*. Caracas: Monte Avila, 1982; references are to the *Ensayos generales*. Where there is a second page reference it refers to the several translated chapters of *Simulacion* appended to Maier's translation of *Escrito sobre un cuerpo*.

SM   Gates, Henry Louis Jr. *The Signifying Monkey. A Theory of African-American Literary Criticism*. Oxford: Oxford University Press, 1988.

SR   Landry, Donna and Gerald Maclean, eds. *The Spivak Reader*. London: Routledge, 1996.

TL   Dib, Mohammed. *Tlemcen ou les lieux de l'écriture* Paris: Editions de la Revue Noire, 1994.

TM   Glissant, Edouard. *Tout-monde*. Paris: Gallimard, 1993.

TO   Dib, Mohammed. *Les Terrasses d'Orsol*. Paris. Sindbad, 1985

TTM   Glissant, Edouard. *Traité du tout-monde*. Paris. Gallimard, 1997.

WLT   *World Literature Today*

WTC   Said, Edward. *The World, The Text, and the Critic*. Cambridge: Harvard University Press, 1983.

PREFACE

Not so long ago, theoretical insight was usually defended in terms of its universal inclusiveness or powers of generalisation. It used to be that any theory worth the name – say a theory of evolution or class conflict, a theory of the unconscious or of signification – shared something of the ambition and scope associated with the theories that marked the scientific revolution of the seventeenth century. What distinguished such a theory from a careful observation or a rigorous process of induction was its attempt to provide general terms for the distinction, classification and explanation of *all* the phenomena that fell within its conceptual horizon.

Readers familiar with postcolonial theory, by contrast, will know that one of its peculiarities is its own apparent resistance to distinction and classification. Postcolonial theory often seems to present itself precisely as a sort of general theory of the non-generalisable as such. On the one hand, it certainly claims an almost global jurisdiction. Definition of the domain in terms of a vague reference to colonialism and its aftermath justifies a purview scarcely less inclusive, both historically and geographically, than that of something like the study of everything affected by modernisation and its consequences.[2] On the other hand, there is no more characteristically postcolonial an interpretation than one which strives to ward off the application of generalisable categories. The signature postcolonial concepts – the hybrid, the interstitial, the intercultural, the in-between, the indeterminate, the counter-hegemonic, the contingent, and so on – are so many attempts to evoke that which no concept can 'capture'. Spivak's aversion to 'general intelligibility, general or universal equivalences' is typical of the field as a whole.[3]

The present book begins with a refusal to go along with this understanding of postcolonial theory. A theory which does not offer some general degree of clarity and distinction is no theory at all. What follows, then, is an exercise in *discrimination*, but one which tries to take the postcolonial challenge seriously: I have tried to isolate a distinctly postcolonial domain, in terms that border the very limits of distinction itself. I propose to name these limits 'singular' and 'specific'. As used in this book, the words singular and specific designate two abstract poles of distinction, i.e. two fundamentally divergent conceptions of individuation and differentiation. Roughly speaking, a singular mode of individuation proceeds internally, through a process that creates its own medium of existence or expansion, whereas a specific mode operates, through the active negotiation of relations and the deliberate taking of sides, choices and risks, in a domain and under constraints that are external to these takings. *The specific is relational, the singular is non-relational.* (I develop this somewhat idiosyncratic distinction of the singular and the specific in my introduction.) My argument will be that postcolonial discourse, despite certain thematic first impressions, is best interpreted as an essentially singular or aspecific enterprise. This interpretation will allow, I think, for a relatively precise description of such discourse in terms that acknowledge or even foreground its resistance to distinctly specific understandings of individuality and difference. It's on this basis that I will mount a sustained critique of the postcolonial and of the singular more generally, while admitting that any viable theory of the specific (which is to say: any theory that allows for the *situated* articulation of genuinely universalisable principles) can only be developed in direct confrontation with the singular configurations active in its time.

The adjective 'singular' should evoke here some of its French associations with what is remarkable, uncommon and extreme (as in the adverb *singulièrement*), as well as its primary meanings of unique or one. I will use the word exclusively to describe configurations or procedures that are exceptional and solitary in the strictest sense – configurations or procedures that are truly one of a kind, that must ultimately be thought as self-constituent, as self-conditioning and self-regulating. As in every singular configuration, logics defined here as postcolonial will eventually defy modulation or mediation. As in every singular configuration, a distinctly postcolonial procedure will operate without criteria external to its operation. And ultimately, it will act even in the absence of *others* as such. Singular configurations replace the interpretation or representation *of* reality with an immanent participation in its production or creation: in the end, at the limit of 'absolute postcoloniality', there will be nothing left, nothing outside itself, to which it could be specific.

The issue here is not simply a matter of critical terminology. What is at stake is nothing less than the global and *contemporary* discrimination of fundamental approaches to our general conceptions of agency and context, self and other, politics and particularity. This book aims to demonstrate that recent 'singularisations' of these conceptions add up to form a striking (though not exclusive) tendency in contemporary literature and theory. The term 'postcolonial', in my opinion, cannot coherently be used to describe anything else.

Why not? In the first place, because I take seriously the recent suggestion that 'postcolonial studies has no definable *object*'.[4] As Parry observes, the term postcolonial implies a 'constant slippage between significations of an historical transition, a cultural location, a discursive stance, and an epochal condition'.[5] We must accept that there is no viable way to arrange these disparate components as an *objectively coherent* field of study. Like Shohat and Ahmad, I see the problems involved in risking a definition of certain sorts of writing as 'generically postcolonial' to be insurmountable: it is all too easy to pick out even a small sample of cases chosen from diverse times and places to show that no one term is adequate to include them all.[6] Though recent surveys do spend a great deal of time and effort deciding which people, places and times qualify for inclusion under the postcolonial umbrella, in the end, the attempt to determine what qualifies as objectively postcolonial can only turn into a futile argument over the authenticity of certain cultural identifications and the relative importance of various indicators of dispossession and complicity. The ensuing 'debates' are unworthy of academic attention.

The immediate consequence is perfectly clear: 'postcolonial' must be reserved for a strictly *subjective* application. In this era that can be trivially (and in actual fact only partially) identified as 'after-colonialism', *anybody* can be postcolonial in the sense suggested here, provided that they conceive things in essentially singularising terms. North Americans, say, can indeed be as postcolonial as anyone else – but not because of their own distant colonial relations with Britain, France and Spain. By the same token, however, it is much too simple merely to dismiss postcolonial theory as the parochial concern of a few privileged Western academics, a theory that 'can at best describe the little family quarrel between the white peoples of what is now an extended First World.'[7]

In the second place, only a singular understanding of the postcolonial provides a fully viable way of distinguishing it from its most obvious terminological rival, *anti-* or *counter*-colonial.[8] Remember that local variations notwithstanding, every colonial relationship presumes that 'a clear-cut and absolute hierarchical distinction should remain constant between ruler and ruled' (Said).[9] If 'between coloniser and colonised there is room only for forced labour, intimidation, pressure, the police, taxation, theft, rape' and other forms of exploitation (Césaire),[10] then a counter-colonial writer will recognise the need to preserve, through to the successful completion of any liberation struggle, 'the primary Manicheism which governed colonial society' (Fanon).[11] Counter-colonial writing assumes a world of constituent antagonisms and sharply demarcated interests; it is militant and partisan by definition. Its fundamental terms – engagement, position, mobilisation – are necessarily *specific* or relational rather than singular in their orientation.

Whereas both colonial and counter-colonial configurations operate in the medium of division and conflict, the postcolonial is generally associated with a more consensual, more harmonious domain of 'multiple identity, travelling theory, migration, diaspora, cultural synthesis and mutation [...]. The postcolonial is an open-ended field of discursive practices characterised by boundary and border crossings.'[12] As a rule, no singular configuration can tolerate borders, either internal or external. By the same token, nothing is more obviously opposed to singularity than a duality, and nothing is so typically and so insistently postcolonial as the refusal of all binaries.[13] Postcolonial critics go to remarkable lengths to avoid any 'simplistic' configuration of antagonism and engagement, to block any application of the rules of classical logic – any foreclosure of an excluded middle – to political situations.[14] Where the counter-colonial Césaire once saw 'cultures trampled underfoot' and 'extraordinary possibilities wiped out',[15] today's postcolonial critics generally survey, in whichever direction they turn, a more serene spectacle of syncretic transformation and hybrid intermingling.[16] And while some Marxist critics of the postcolonial may exaggerate its complicity with transnational capital, it is certainly true that postcolonial theory, like the postmodernism which inspired several of its most essential concepts, could only develop and grow in the place left empty by the demise of organised radical politics and the defeat or perversion of national liberation movements in exploited countries all over the world.[17] Very precisely, 'in relation to the global human condition of inequality, the [postcolonial] hybridisation perspective releases reflection and engagement from the boundaries of nation, community, ethnicity, or class':[18] it releases engagement, in other words, into something like thin air.

This is not to say that all writing or discourse produced in circumstances affected in some way by colonialism must necessarily be classified as *either* counter- or post-colonial.[19] That would be to concede rather too much to the grandiose ambitions of the colonisers themselves. Simply, insofar as we *are* determined to retain a reference to colonialism as a classifying principle then the least we can do is avoid blurring the difference between counter- and post-. Surely we don't need a *post*colonial theorist to tell us that colonialism installed an 'ambivalent and symbiotic relationship between coloniser and colonised',[20] if we recognise from the beginning that *all* human relations are to some degree ambivalent and symbiotic, that every subject is constitutively related to its others. (As we shall see, only on that condition can we describe the subject as a 'specific' subject at all.) What is remarkable is that postcolonial theory should so often have argued that the colonial relationship is especially 'ambivalent and symbiotic' rather than minimally or trivially so. Like Parry and her allies, I see the specifically colonial relation as an emphatically divisive and exploitative one, and understand colonialism to be less a matter of 'interstitial agency' than the product of 'military conquest, massacres and dispossession, forced labour, and cultural repression...'.[21] And like Fanon, I believe that every emancipatory process, every emergence of a *new* figure of universality, must begin as no less divisive: there can be no new mobilisation of the universal interest that does not immediately threaten particular privileged beneficiaries of the old status quo. That we *are* relational in no way determines the kinds of (political or ethical) relations we should pursue.

As anyone who has followed the ups and downs of postcolonial criticism will know, the category has generally been attacked for (a) being Eurocentric in its historical frame of reference and (broadly postmodern) theoretical orientation, (b) being indifferent to the particularity of distinct historical sequences and situations, and (c) privileging cultural, linguistic and rhetorical issues over social, historical and economic concerns. My own critique aims to be more sharply focused and more conclusive. The wager of this book is that the fundamental orientation of distinctly postcolonial configurations – including theories that, like Glissant's 'poetics of Relation' or Bhabha's 'enunciation' of difference, seem to foreground an explicitly relational dimension – is best described as at least tendentially singular or non-relational. Rather than debate the question of centre and periphery, then, I will identify the postcolonial orientation with a refusal of any identifiable or precisely located centre, in favour of its own self-regulating transcendence of location. Rather than echo the facile denunciation of binaries, I will seek to distinguish between 'specific' and 'specified' conceptions of difference. Rather than decide the tired contest of textualist against materialist conceptions of history, I will suggest that the postcolonial asserts an ultimately univocal coherence on a plane of consistency above and beyond this very distinction. And rather than add my voice to the chorus calling for an ever more specific form of postcolonial theory, one ever more attuned to the particularity of discrete sequences, I will claim that the singular orientation of the postcolonial undermines its every aspiration to specificity in advance.

Committed postcolonialists are likely to be so resistant to this characterisation of their orientation that it may be worth providing, at the outset of this study, a very brief sketch of four fairly well-known illustrations of the trend: Homi Bhabha's survey of 'postcolonial criticism' (1992), Achille Mbembe's portrait of the 'postcolony' (1992), Edouard Glissant's recent elaboration of a 'poetics of diversity' (1996), and Wilson Harris' elusive investigations into the mysterious 'mutuality of universal character'.

(a) Bhabha's hugely influential work is geared towards 'the emergence of an "interstitial" agency that refuses the binary representation of social antagonism.'[22] His understanding of postcolonial theory centres on the 'hybrid location of cultural value – the transnational as the translational', in an environment of generalised 'aporia, ambivalence, indeterminacy'.[23] The time and space of this hybrid sphere are 'the contingent and the liminal' (445), the dimensions of a movement characterised by 'migration, diaspora, displacement, relocation' (438). The properly 'post-'colonial moment, with Bhabha, is not a time of decision or mobilisation so much as the 'time-lag' opened up by the very 'enunciation' and dis-placement of ambivalence as such, an ambivalence that relates to nothing outside the field of its own articulation. As I will suggest in more detail in my first chapter, Bhabha's torturous formulations arguably provide some of the *clearest* illustrations of the fundamentally singular or self-constituent aspect of postcolonial theory.

(b) What Mbembe calls the 'postcolony' exists in a situation of 'extraordinary fluidity and equivocation'.[24] It coheres as a 'chaotic plurality' without any general coordination or principle; its daily operation resembles a macabre carnival of derision and excess. Mbembe's 'basic argument is that, to account for both the imagery and efficacy of postcolonial relations of power, we must go beyond the binary categories used in standard interpretations of domination (resistance/passivity, subjection/autonomy [etc.]). These oppositions are not helpful.'[25] For 'the postcolonial relationship is not primarily a relationship of resistance or of collaboration, but is rather best characterised as a promiscuous relationship: a convivial tension' that leaves 'both [sides] impotent' (5), in a state of 'mutual powerlessness' (11). Because the postcolony spontaneously generates a multiplicity of 'improvised' identities (2), its rule is essentially 'theatrical', 'magical', or 'baroque'. The postcolony leaves little place for relations of 'resistance and disjunction. Instead the emphasis should be upon the logic of conviviality [...], which inscribes the dominant and the dominated in the same epistemological field' (14) and ensures 'the mutual "zombification" of both the dominant and those whom they apparently dominate' (5).

(c) Glissant's version of 'creolisation comprehends and moves beyond all possible contraries'.[26] Drawing like so many postcolonial theorists on the work of Deleuze and Guattari, Glissant conceives of the world as a singular 'rhizome' (133), and 'in the rhizome of the totality-world, the notions of centres and peripheries are obsolete' (137). What has replaced such contrary notions is a kind of universal 'erratics', an anti-systemic celebration of 'chaos' and *'errance'*. Glissant's Whole-world [*Tout-monde*] can only be a 'chaos-world' (37, 43), a 'completely erratic' anti-system. 'What makes the *Tout-monde* is not cosmopolitanism, absolutely not' (89), but rather the deterritorialising exuberance of chaos itself. The 'erratic dimension has become the dimension of the *Tout-monde*' and 'today's *errances* no longer seek to establish a territory' (87-88). Why should they? There is no need for territorial security since – as the inhabitants of *systematically* exploited countries may be surprised to learn – 'absolute [...] unpredictability is the law as regards the relations between human cultures' (88, 85). The later Glissant's characteristically postcolonial vision has as its immediate implication the renunciation of Marx's famous eleventh thesis on Feuerbach: we must 'renounce the capacity to change the world. Because to change the world to give the world a future, that is, to predict it' (101). Glissant's preferred alternative is to go with the flow: 'We live in a time in which we can no longer impose conditions on the world' (132).

(d) The notoriously complex work of Guyanese novelist Wilson Harris deserves to be read, in my view, along similarly singularising lines. Harris everywhere attacks the 'conquistadorial' legacies of an aggressively isolated individuality, 'territorial imperatives', and a 'dead-end realism, a realism made narrow by egocentric histories that need to be creatively disrupted by pressures of infinity within the womb of space.'[27] Only such un-mediated exposure to 'untamed infinity' can illuminate what Harris calls 'the lightning mutuality of universal character', guide 'the creation of Man as spark of untameable cosmos' and reveal 'glimpses of naked spirit in degrees of rich counterpoint with unravelled shapes of realities'. Only the singularly 'seminal force of arbitrating genius' can successfully 'link sparks or evolutionary points within the bloodstream of space' and thus tap into 'the essence of life' grasped as pure fusion of the 'instinctive' and the 'imaginative' in a single cosmic vitality.[28] Believing that fundamental 'nature overlaps with the Creator, with deity', Harris thus strives to write 'some ultimate embrace, in which one is taken up by what cannot be tamed or domesticated in nature, and taken through into other dimensions'.[29] As we shall see, Harris anticipates Deleuze in his intuition of the 'immaterial and untameable foundations to the cosmos or to a universe composed of fabrics of mobility akin to thought'. These fabrics can be grasped only through quasi-miraculous artistic images, operating as so many 'catalyst[s] of discovery [...]. Each image confesses to textures which make paradoxically real a universe ceaselessly subject to qualities of alteration within creator and created [...], within a riddle of unfathomable being or timeless moment'.[30] This is a description that can be applied amost *tel quel* to the imagery of Sarduy, Johnson or the later Dib: the creative power of such images stems less from the cumulative impact of complex interactions between their semi-autonomous constituent elements than from their immediate exposure to the singular vital energy that infuses the cosmos as a whole, in its 'untamed infinity'.

In my first chapter, I will try to demonstrate that these four examples, far from being isolated cases, are indeed typical of a more general tendency.

To define the postcolonial as subjective, singular and non-relational in this sense is of course quite considerably to restrict its usage. This is, I think, a price well worth paying. A concept that cannot serve to make distinctions across otherwise highly comparable situations is of no use at all. 'Absolutely postcolonial', more precisely, will imply two closely related things. First, I use the phrase to describe writers whose work moves *almost unreservedly* beyond a relational conception of individuation and differentiation. This applies as much to an American (Charles Johnson)[31] whose enslaved ancestors never experienced colonisation in the strict sense, as to a Cuban (Severo Sarduy) for whom the struggle against a residual colonialism was an originally enabling condition of his writing; as much to a Martinican (Edouard Glissant) whose youngest compatriots are likely to inherit an ongoing colonial status, as to an Algerian (Mohammed Dib) for whom military victory against one of the most vicious of colonial regimes was to mark a decisive shift in aesthetic priorities. Second, it suggests that the way these writers move beyond the colonial divide involves, in some fashion, recourse to an absolute rather than relative mechanism of transcendence. Only an 'absolutely postcolonial' orientation tends towards the (ultimately unattainable) pole of a *totally singular* configuration of reality.

What follows will defend these arguments in four unequal parts. The introduction will distinguish between the singular and the specific in the broadest sense feasible, making only peripheral reference to the postcolonial situation *per se*. Next, the opening chapter will explore the singularising tendency in major strands of postcolonial theory, along with some of the problems encountered in pursuit of a theory of the specific as such. The peculiarity of Edward Said's position, straddling as it does the theoretical frontier between the singular and the specific, will merit particular attention. The third and most substantial stage of the argument, in chapters 2 through 5, provides readings of four of the most significant writers whose work illustrates this singularising trend, as well as (with Dib and Sarduy) its partial qualification. And at appropriate moments between the chapters, I develop in a series of excursuses some of the broader theoretical implications of the argument: I take issue with postcolonial interpretations of globalisation and the nation-state, and try to sketch workable formulations of the universal and the specific.

The guiding principles of this book can now be summarised (rather than defended) as follows:

(a) We need to bridge the ever-growing gap between theories of literature on the one hand and the detailed reading of literary texts on the other – without simply turning our backs on the theoretical project itself.[12] Postcolonial writing is indeed worthy of *systematic* and thorough interpretation, but such interpretation can only proceed on the basis of an unapologetically contemporary theoretical framework.

(b) We need to attempt an ambitious and systematic answer to the rhetorical question so often asked in recent theory: how to situate oneself in the global 'configuration of transnational power and culture without being trapped by a deadened nativism?'[33] There is general agreement that we must move beyond an insufficiently specific notion of hybridity or pure difference on the one hand, and an excessively specified notion of community or essence on the other. But the diagnosis remains vague, and the proposed remedies still more so. This is the problem I will try to address with my reconceptualisation of the specific at various points in this book. The specific is emphatically not synonymous with the simply particular, intrinsic, or local. A viable theory of the specific requires, as I have already suggested, its strict equation with the domain of *active* (or *subjective*) relationality as such. Just how exactly this distinguishes the specific from the singular transcendence of relation on the one hand and a specified reification of relation on the other, is something I will go to some trouble to explain.

(c) We need to resist the temptation pre-emptively to *orient* such relations in a particular direction, be it through the invocation of some transcendent telos (the risk variously run by Habermas, Taylor and the Marxist anti-postcolonialists) or through the presumption of a dynamic tendency immanent to the workings of relation itself (as with Glissant or Deleuze). In particular, we must not attempt to derive an inherently or automatically progressive politics of relation from the theoretical category of the specific as such. There is nothing 'in' relationality that determines whether social relations, for instance, are to be governed by race, or caste, or wealth, any more than by principles of civic responsibility, generic equality, or collective solidarity.

(d) Against the predominant tendency of cultural studies in general and of postcolonial criticism in particular, we need therefore to make and preserve a sharp conceptual *break between culture and politics*. The idea of a 'cultural politics' is a disastrous confusion of spheres. If politics is to mean anything at all, it should apply only to the domain of strictly in-different principles: principles of justice and equality, principles that apply to all relations without discrimination. As the philosopher Alain Badiou argues with particular force, progressive politics depends not on the benevolent recognition of the substantial attributes of a particular community or culture but on the militant assertion of universal principles that brook *no* qualification. As far as the political pursuit of justice is concerned, we need to find the courage to accept that the whole ethico-culturalist 'predication based upon recognition of the other must be purely and simply abandoned. For the real question – and it is an extraordinarily difficult one – is much more that of recognising the Same',[34] i.e. the austere in-difference of egalitarian justice itself. As a matter of universal principle, it is *everyone* who deserves security, legal protection, access to health and education, and so on. The ramified interpretation of cultural differences belongs on another discursive plane. If there is a task specific to politics, it must be to articulate and impose collective principles that break with the infinite complexities and complicities of history, the interminable 'negotiations' of culture and psychology. And thereby to allow something *else* to take place.

By contrast, every postcolonial theory (and also, most of the broadly Marxist *anti*-postcolonial theories) tends toward or asserts the confusion of politics and culture. This confusion generally leads, among other things, to a critique of the nation-state as the effect of a sinister and aggressive cultural nationalism. It is only the principled distinction of culture and politics that will allow for that reaffirmation of the nation-state essential, I will go on to argue, for any effective conceptualisation of a progressive political practice.

(e) By the same token, we must abandon any attempt to prescribe, at the level of general theory, a particular political agenda for art and literature. Neither politics nor art has anything to gain, today, from a general didactic coordination à la Brecht or Sembène – such coordination can be defended only in quite *specific* circumstances. After a sequence of ultimately unsustainable theoretical attempts to blend literature and politics in a single vanguardism (surrealism, existentialism, situationism, *Tel Quel*...), it is time to recognise that the evaluation of literature is essentially indifferent to politics as such. What is distinctive about literature is its capacity to invent new ways of using words (new in either form or practice, or both), at a disruptive distance from inherited norms and expectations – in other words, its capacity to provoke people to *think*, rather than merely recognise, represent or consume. To be sure, these new ways of using words may have an indirect political effect, but there is no theoretical justification for claiming that they *should* always have such an effect. Literature and politics can both be revolutionary, but only within the limits of their own field.[35]

(f) Acknowledgement of the essentially relational basis of human experience must not be confused with the recognition of some sort of empirical regularity but understood as a properly *transcendental* condition of all human experience (i.e. as transcendental in a very crudely Kantian sense).

'Transcendental' will describe here those capacities people require and cultivate so as to exist as beings-in-relation (including language, agency, imagination, consistency, and so on). The early Heidegger identified a number of these capacities; others have been emphasised, in different ways, by thinkers as varied as Bakhtin, Habermas, and Bourdieu, as well as a small army of cognitive scientists. And unless we are prepared to deny *any* application of evolutionary explanation to the basic operations of the mind (sensory perception, language-capability, problem-solving intelligence, etc.), we have nothing to lose by interpreting such capacities as *species* attributes, i.e. as aspects of a human 'nature' in a fairly strong sense of the word.

Use of the word 'universal', however, should be limited to the register partially invoked in the previous point. 'Universal' applies to concepts whose reach is properly meta-specific but not singular. 'Universal' applies to principles prescribed as directly valid for all relations contested within a particular situation, and as at least indirectly valid for *all* relations of the same type. Such principles articulate, in direct competition with more or less explicitly 'particularist' configurations, the way we determine the link *between* the transcendental (i.e. relationality) and the specific (i.e. particular relations). The prescription of a universal is always specific to a particular situation and only 'applies' if it continues to hold, in active practice, *for* that situation. But the ultimate horizon of its application is not itself limited, at least in principle, to relations within the situation. Most prescriptions of an end to racial discrimination, for example, have for obvious reasons been made from within the thoroughly particular situation of those who suffer such discrimination. But unless their justification is directly linked to the revaluation of particular, specified racial qualities, they can and should apply indifferently, to all people *qua* people.

This book proposes, then: the delimitation of a singular or non-relational postcolonial paradigm from a specific or relational understanding of difference and individuation; a sharp distinction of politics from culture, together with a re-affirmation of the limited autonomy of the literary sphere; an insistence on the partial transcendence in all creative expression of the immediately specifying characteristics of race, gender, and ideology; recognition of certain transcendental features of a relational human nature; rehabilitation of a prescriptive, situated conception of the universal that avoids its confusion with the contingent emergence of empirical tendencies or totalities. It frames these theoretical arguments in the order and terms suggested by a sustained reading of four of the most influential yet strangely neglected figures in what can quite *precisely* be called postcolonial literature.

ACKNOWLEDGEMENTS

An earlier version of this book was submitted as part of a dissertation supervised by Christopher Miller and Vera Kutzinski; I'm grateful for their help and forbearance during what turned out to be a somewhat demanding research project. Gordon Lafer, Kenneth Haltman, Caitlin DeSilvey, Brice Halimi and Jean-Philippe Narboux provided inspiration, criticism and friendship along the way.

My years as a graduate student were indelibly marked by the commitment and example of those involved with GESO and Mad Mare's Farm.

Mohammed Dib and Charles Bonn made valuable suggestions at an especially delicate moment in my work. The comments of Paul Gilroy and Margery Sabin subsequently encouraged me to reshape the entire project; Sinéad Rushe helped refine the final version of chapter 5, as did Nick Harrison the introduction and first chapter. I'm indebted to my colleague Patrick ffrench for reading through the whole text, and to Sara Peacock for copy-editing so bulky a manuscript with such care and good cheer.

About half of chapter two first appeared as an article on Edouard Glissant in the *Yale Journal of Criticism*, volume 11 (Autumn 1998), and some sections of the introduction are reworked from an article entitled 'The Singular and the Specific: Recent French Philosophy,' published in *Radical Philosophy* number 99 (January 2000). I'm grateful to these journals for permission to reprint.

This book could not have been written without doctoral funding from the Andrew W. Mellon Foundation and post-doctoral funding from the Social Sciences and Humanities Research Council of Canada; it would not have been published without the enthusiasm of Gerard Greenway, Pelagia Goulimari and the other members of the Angelaki Humanities board.

I dedicate this book to Sinéad, for every reason under the sun.

INTRODUCTION

SINGULAR OR SPECIFIC?

The One, which every philosophy would like to express, [is] beyond being.[1]

This book begins with a broad question prompted by perhaps the most salient characteristic of contemporary literature and philosophy – the assertion of an essential heterogeneity or plurality of subject positions. Are these positions to be read as so many *specific* perspectives defined in some sense through their relations *with* each other? Or are they to be understood rather as the *singular* modes of one self-differing force – fragments, that is, of a single immanent unity, without constituent relations among themselves? The alternatives are clearly poles apart, but often confused. If a specific individual is one that exists as part of a relationship to an environment and to other individuals ('I', say, as specific to a 'you', a 'here' and a 'now'), a singular individual is one which like a creator-God transcends all such relations. The specific is indirectly relative to certain specified characteristics, whereas 'in-difference with respect to properties is what individuates and disseminates singularities'.[2] This distinction of singular and specific is, I think, essential to a broad evaluation of recent literary trends; it is especially so for obvious reasons, in the post-colonial domain. Much of what passes for specific in recent postcolonial writing and criticism should rather be interpreted as singular or singularising.

I

At issue here are our most elementary questions regarding individuation and relationality. What qualities must an individual have in order to remain distinct from other individuals? How does one individual relate to another? The four writers considered in this project, despite radically different backgrounds, styles and thematics, provide variations on what is an essentially comparable answer to these questions. They all suggest, more or less insistently and more or less consistently, that the only genuine individual is unique, one of a kind. It is this suggestion alone that justifies the comparative readings that make up this book. To the degree that the writers considered here write in or towards this singular mode, they actively seek to transcend the specific or relational. Even though their projects are often explicitly motivated by an interest *in* difference, the hybrid or the other, their singular conception of reality effectively absorbs or undermines the whole dimension of relations-with-others.

'Specific' and 'singular' are posited here as *general* logics of individuation. These logics are not themselves reducible to the postcolonial domain, nor indeed any given domain; rather, I posit them for heuristic purposes as the abstract invariants necessary for the comparison, across distinct contexts, of dissimilar variant situations.[3] The terms will frame this entire study: to explain them properly requires a preliminary step back from the pressing concerns and misleading familiarity of postcolonial criticism *per se*.

A singular conception of individuation recognises only one entity as fully individual (which does not exclude the potentially infinite multiplicity of *modes* of this individual). I will refer to such an individual as 'Creative' as distinct from the 'given' or 'created' (always capitalised, for the sake of clarity). *The singular creates the medium of its own substantial existence or expression.* The singularity of a Creator-god provides the concept with its exemplary form. By definition, there can only be one such Creator, and 'seen from the divine point of view', each creation is likewise singular, immediately accessible in its *haecceitas*: the individuality of a particular creature is not something to be deduced from the application of general categories and classifications (following Aristotle), but rather directly intuited as an expression or incarnation of the divine force (following Duns Scotus or Spinoza). Likewise, the big bang posited by most contemporary cosmologists is a singularity in the strict or technical sense: rather than an explosion occurring within an already unfolded field of time and space, it takes place as an 'inflation' creative of its own ongoing space of expansion.[1] A similar logic helps legitimate the expansion of the contemporary multinational market, the all-inclusive market of global capital. A 'specific' understanding of the market would have to follow Marx's lead, and analyse its emergence and procedures as abstractions of class *relations*, precisely – i.e. as a function of class struggle. But as presumed or glorified in the current orthodoxy of neo-classical economics, the market defines the sole dimension of what the French so accurately call today's *pensée unique*. Once the confrontational class-relational approach has been pushed aside (in the interests of 'modernisation' and 'efficiency') the market begins to look like a fundamentally *singular* institution – singular in the sense that it is neither specific to any particular place nor constrained by any logic outside the immanent criteria of its own operation. Abstracted from the relations of struggle that gave rise to it, the market seems to express only the univocal sphere of exchange value (the singular medium of its existence), abstracted from and unlimited by all other values. And when this abstraction is more or less complete, then the market begins to appear retrospectively singular as well: the emergence of market mechanisms need no longer be analysed in terms of conflict and struggle, but as the apparently natural and in any case inevitable development of a properly 'modern' economic rationality.

Other historical examples of singular logics might include the monarch of absolutist political theory, the sovereign of Rousseau or Robespierre, and the proletariat according to Stalin or Mao. Each becomes what it fundamentally *is* through its transcendence of relations with other sorts of social or political power.[5]

Perhaps the most complex and insightful philosophies of the metaphysically singular are to be found among the early Buddhist sutras and the various strands of neo-Platonism, from Plotinus and Proclus to al-Suhrawardi and Mulla Sadra. The most fully developed Western philosophies of the singular are provided by Spinoza and Hegel – the former already virtually immediate to itself, the latter forever imminent, a *becoming*-immediate accomplished through a relentless process of self-mediation.[6] After Spinoza and Hegel, perhaps the most powerful contemporary philosophy of the singular is the achievement of Gilles Deleuze. Deleuze preserves the fundamental tenet of a singular philosophy intact, pushing it beyond the transcendent confines of neo-Platonism: 'the One expresses in a single meaning all of the multiple. Being expresses in a single meaning all that differs'.[7] He explains how 'everything divides, but into itself'.[8] Thanks to his unrivalled insight into the nature and consequences of radical singularity, Deleuze's work will provide this study with one of its most constant points of theoretical reference (see below, section III [c]).

The singular, in each case, is constituent of itself, expressive of itself, immediate to itself. That the singular creates the medium of its existence means it is not specific to external criteria or frames of reference. The singular always obtains *as* singular in the absence or transcendence of the specific – or, same thing, in the orientation of the specific toward the singular, its singularisation.[9] Once fully de-specified, singular perception will be immediate to what it perceives, i.e. to its own self-expression. As Deleuze demonstrates (after Leibniz), every singular perception creates its own object.[10] Tautologically, singular immediacy is perceived to the degree that it is actively freed of mediation (social, psychological, figural), actively

3

dis-covered. Legitimate perception of the singular can only be literal. It is seen for what it is only when perceiver and perceived occupy the same level, only when the perceiver becomes a direct participant in its singularity. One of the things the writers discussed in this book have in common, though to variable degrees, is a commitment to what might be called the *literal imperative*. Since a singular reality is defined by its absolutely self-sufficient totality, there is no distinct place for the conscious interpretation or figuration *of* reality. In a certain sense, description of singular reality begins with the redundance of intentional consciousness as such.

Every singularity is hierarchical in its essence. As Deleuze's Nietzsche reminds us, within a singular conception of things 'hierarchy is the originary fact, the identity of difference and origin [...]; the origin is the difference in the origin, difference in the origin is hierarchy'.[11] There is no more asymmetrical relation than that, as Levinas never tires of telling us, between Creator and creature. Every singularity establishes a single scale of 'creative' intensity in which the most fundamental medium of difference is quantitative. Creatures relate, first and foremost, in terms of *how much* of the Creator they express. In Leibniz's exemplary terms, singular difference is determined by the divinely assigned degree of a monad's expressive clarity or power, measured by its proximity to pure Creative expression.

Singularity, as a result, should not be confused with universality. The singular is involved in its own genesis, it is self-constituent, an ongoing differentiation, whereas a universal principle is imposed in a specific situation through a particular intervention. A principle is universal if it is universalisable, i.e. if it holds as valid for all relations within that situation, but this holding is imposed from a position external to these relations. If in the last analysis the singular always harks back to a form of effectively divine or non-relational Creative power (a 'creationist' power, which creates its own medium of existence or expression), universals are posited so as to enable relational consistency. The singular *creates*, whereas the universal prescribes.

A *specific* rather than singular mode of individuation yields elements whose individuality can only be discerned through the relations they maintain with themselves, with their environment, and with other individuals. The condition of identity for such an individual is that it be constituted through and persist in relations with others. It is the unconditional status of relationality itself that allows us to anticipate and disarm an eventual deconstruction of the specific. When Bhabha, for instance, says that 'all cultural specificity is belated [and] different unto itself' (LC, 58) because constituted through what he calls 'enunciatory' differentiation, he evokes a register of dissociation and disruption that our specific orientation presumes in advance – and presumes as *banal*. Unlike Bhabha, we cannot say that the specific subject is different unto itself, or belated, or otherwise somehow dissociated from itself (deferred, delayed, split…) *because* constituted through relations of differentiation; rather, it is only specific, i.e. it only *is* what it is (and thus 'identical to itself') because it is constitutively relational in this way.[12] (I will have more to say about the specific in my first chapter and excursus IV.)

The singular and the specific divide most obviously, most naively, in their tolerance of positioned interests and 'worldliness' in the most general sense. According to a singular-immediate logic, in order to grasp the truth of the (created) *world* you have first to step outside it. Only those who can successfully transcend their worldly or specific place gain access to the truly Creative; they make of this transcendence the medium of a redemption from the world. Such transcendence involves in particular the refusal of any specific position or interest in relation to other positions, other selves, places, histories, and so on. The specific, on the other hand, implies a situation, a past, an intelligibility constrained by inherited conditions. The specific is the space of interests in relation to other interests, the space of the historical as such, forever ongoing, forever incomplete, the space where 'we make our own history but not in circumstances of our choosing'.[13] Within the world, the specific relates subject to subject and subject to other: the singular dissolves both in one beyond-subject.

II

Why these particular writers: Glissant, Johnson, Dib, Sarduy? Because within their respective domain, each provides perhaps the most powerful and most influential example of a singular conception of reality. Mohammed Dib is not only the most highly regarded of Algerian novelists, but with his fellow Maghrébins Abdelkebir Khatibi and Abdelwahab Meddeb, the most intensely haunted by the pursuit of an ineffable immediacy at the limits of recognition. Edouard Glissant is not only the major writer and theorist of the francophone Caribbean, but the most emphatic in his move from a specific nationalism to a singular plane of immanence, a singular 'totality-world' or 'chaosmos'. Severo Sarduy's work has been widely celebrated as the quintessential example of postmodern fiction in Cuba and as one of the most original contributions to a post-Boom Latin American aesthetic, if not indeed as the culmination of the Latin American novel; in strongly Deleuzian style, he writes a world of virtual becoming-other, of fundamental contingency and constant metamorphosis. And Charles Johnson's award-winning fiction has been received, alongside that of Toni Morrison, as a decisive step beyond the literature of conflict and complaint associated with a previous generation of African-American letters (from Richard Wright to

Amiri Baraka); his novels narrate the move towards Oedipal and racial reconciliation via an explicitly Buddhist redemption in a place beyond place,
towards a trans-individual coherence beyond distinction itself.

The eclectic thematic range of the authors studied here will be balanced, I hope, by the internal consistency of the singular immediate mode
itself. The irreducible *variety* of positions within, toward and away from
this mode, however, will be obvious in the trajectories traced by each particular author. One of the goals of this book as a whole is to investigate how
far this variety can extend before it becomes diversity in the proper sense
– a collection of distinctions more than variations of a single invariant. Of
the four writers studied, only Johnson has been consistent in his published
commitment to the singular immediate. Glissant and Dib both move from
an originally specific (counter-colonial) position to an eventually singular
or nearly singular (postcolonial) position: they both began with a commitment to recover or carve out a precisely situated subjective agency for a
dispossessed community, and they have both moved more recently to dissolve this subjectivity within a quasi-Deleuzian field of becoming-other or
becoming-imperceptible. But whereas Glissant tends to fill in these
becomings with the thematics of plenitude, proximity and hybridity, Dib
tends to subtract them from every association with the full and the near.
Glissant swirls relations together around a singular *tourbillon*, whereas Dib
evacuates them of substance and direction. So while Glissant joins Johnson
in the singular aesthetic of reconciliation, Dib brings his work only to the
austere limit of singularity: he *empties* the specific or relational, without
transcending them altogether. Glissant singularises; Dib de-specifies. By
contrast Sarduy moves, to some degree at least, in the opposite direction,
from an exuberantly singular to a tentatively specific position, so as to
explore, with his last novels, a fragile domain of irreducibly relational experience. I will develop these distinctions at some length: the goal is not to
reduce the peculiarity of each author's itinerary, but to provide a comparative framework both rigorous and flexible enough to assess this peculiarity as exactly as possible. It is precisely a matter of relating one author to
another, of providing a sort of echo chamber in which their voices, heavily
quoted in the chapters that follow, can begin to resonate with and against
each other.

III

What holds the parts of this project together, then, is the conceptual distinction of a singular as opposed to a specific mode of individuation. Needless to say, anything resembling a general history of the singular is far beyond
the limits of this study. In what's left of this introduction, I can provide only

a brief summary of those particular fragments of this history that most concern the writers involved: a version of Islamic mysticism (for Dib), versions of Buddhism (for Sarduy and Johnson), and a reading of Deleuze (for Glissant, and for much of the postcolonial field as a whole). It may also be worth including the singularity of the global market as a major environmental constraint for all four writers.[14]

Obvious thematic differences aside, these four logics have a number of essential things in common. First, each equates true reality with the expression of one principle, to the exclusion of all rival principles – the One God, the void [sunyata], vital energy or virtual differenciation, market forces. In the second place, all accept that this reality is not initially given but must be uncovered or liberated from inherited mediations. What is given is, respectively: sin, division, and exile from God; ignorance, dukkha, suffering, and relations of desire; ressentiment, representation, and the disfiguring mediation of vital energy; feudal anachronisms, the opacity of local customs, and stubborn nativism or particularism. In the third place, all insist that reality shall become what it is through the dissolution of the given – a surrender [Islam] to God; the transcendence of relations of desire and extinction [nirvana] of the self; the dissolution of the organism, of representation, of regulated desire-as-lack, of the territory; the violent elimination of local resistance to modernisation (enclosure, colonialism, proletarianisation). Fourth and final point: emerging as the consequence of this destruction, the singular comes to be in the absence of others, deprived of an ethical or political environment as such. The singular acts without criteria, or – it is the same thing – its criteria are wholly immanent to its action (its self-actualisation). God's designs are inscrutable; Buddha's sunyata is 'suchness' [tathagata] beyond distinction and discrimination; Deleuze's active force is essentially 'irresponsible' or 'beyond judgement'; the market cannot recognise any form of value other than that immanent to exchange itself. And if dissolution of the given is total, singular agency is free to act as pure self-actualisation, as literal or univocal self-expression, as self-explication in the Spinozist sense. The singular acts as univocal Creation, and is, in itself, a wholly virtual entity (i.e. an entity without given characteristics). The divine One occupies the neo-Platonic place of a 'Good' beyond being; the Buddha's void is empty of quality; Deleuze's philosophy is organised around the determining priority of the virtual over the actual; the market nowhere exists, but is everywhere effective.

As a rule, any fully singular conception of things is always equally singular on both ends of the spectrum, large and small. As Deleuze says, 'the smallest becomes the equal of the largest once it is not separated from what it can do';[15] in principle, 'the whole ought to belong to a single moment'.[16] Singular difference is intra- rather than inter-individual. To individuate any one 'small' unit as radically unique is simultaneously to refer it back, via some sort of immediate derivation, to an all-determining unity (as distinct from a closed totality). For instance, the radical particularity of Spinoza's modes, like that of Leibniz's monads, refers directly back to the univocity of their substance and Creator: modes exist as so many extended or explicated degrees of a purely implicated divine intensity. The singularity of any one commodity *qua* commodity, again, implies the singularity of the market mechanism that commodifies it.[17] A singular mode of individuation, in other words, always posits a single scale of reality, organised in terms of determined degrees of proximity to a principle that is itself effectively beyond being or pre-actual. All reality is here of the same essential nature or type, a single thought-matter or vital energy, a single creative point infinitely extended or a single material extension infinitely compressed. This ensures the identity of a thing's composition with its significance – a thing 'means' only what it *is* (what creates or composes it). Singular interpretations are always literal and immediate.

Before proceeding any further, it may be worth taking a slightly more detailed look at each of our three most pertinent examples in turn, along with a fourth whose relevance will become clear as we go along – the singular logic of an avant-garde *littérarité* in general. This will allow us not only to appreciate the direct intertextual value of these logics for the authors studied in this book, but also to isolate and confirm the most significant characteristics of a general concept of singularity. Believing with Balibar that all speculative thought, including 'what we traditionally consider as typically modern thought, is actually governed by very archaic schemes',[18] I have cast my conceptual net over a wide cultural-chronological sweep. The intertextual demands of more detailed chapters to come will more than justify, I hope, these essential references to ancient if not archetypical logics of creation and individuation.

(a) Mystical Islam: return to the One[19]

In the absence of a *church*, the notion of a discretely religious space makes little sense in classical Islam. Rather, Islam begins with the declaration of 'unity and unicity of God',[20] a unity beyond all conceivable boundary or distinction. The *Qur'anic* emphasis is clear: 'there is no divinity but Allah the Unique, the Invincible'.[21] The Islamic like the Christian God is the uncaused or unengendered (112:3), wholly beyond relation, beyond all possible 'association' (112:4; 2:115).

In itself, the divine One is wholly unknowable, a Creative Light so intense as to be absolutely blinding.[22] The whole multiplicity of creatures is invariably but unequally expressive of this one blinding light. As the great Sufi philosopher Ibn al-'Arabi puts it, in terms which anticipate Spinoza: 'the

Substance is One, although its modes are different [according to] certain degrees',[23] certain shades of opacity. The aim of any created being is to return, to the degree possible, back up to the pure Creative light from which it springs. This light is ontologically original but not *given* to the creature. What is given is material opacity, separation, veiled perception. Our 'visible world is not itself the Temple, it is the Temple's crypt', the place of an *exile* from the temple.[24] Opacity arises with the very movement of divine illumination, as the Creative light falls ever further away from the concentrated, blinding purity of its source. We are born at a distance from light, in what al-Suhrawardi calls our 'occidental' shadow or exile.[25] To accept and live *within* this distance is simply to confirm our initial, childlike ignorance of what we truly are. As Niffari writes, 'when you see yourself as existent, and do not see Me as the Cause of your existence, I veil My face and your own face appears to you'.[26] The ethical task can be summarised, then, as the transformation of our *initial* opacity into our *originally* Creative transparency or, in an parable that recurs throughout the Shi'ite and Sufi traditions, as the transformation of obscuring (self-conscious) veil into reflecting (self-effacing) mirror. 'The test of the Veil is the very meaning of Creation [...]. To pass the Test, the mystic must discover that his self-knowledge is nothing other than God's own self-perception. Then the veil becomes mirror...'.[27]

This is no purer expression of the logic of radical singularity than this. Since God's Creative unity is unlimited, so we ourselves are nothing other than the 'attributes by which we describe God; our existence is merely an objectification of His existence'.[28] Our task is simply – but there is no more difficult a task – to assume this objectification subjectively, i.e. to become free and active parts of the divine self-expression. All creatures *are* nothing other than expressions of God, yet most of these creatures remain trapped in an ignorant distance from God, cut off from the sole genuine source of insight and power. Redemption from such ignorance is achieved through a 'vision in which there is no longer any difference between the knower and the known'.[29] This means: a vision in which we see things from God's own point of view. The *Shadâdah*, the first and greatest pillar of Islam – the assertion that 'there is no God but God' – is a declaration whose force exceeds that of any merely specific speaker. Only God himself can proclaim the singular being of God. As Henry Corbin explains, 'God cannot be an object (an objective given). He can only be known through himself as absolute Subject, that is, as absolved from all unreal objectivity', as absolved from all specific or creaturely mediation.[30] The shift from creaturely ignorance to divine knowledge cannot, in other words, simply proceed through an improved knowledge of the creaturely as such. The redemptive shift requires a sharp break in the continuity of creation, a tearing away from the worldly to the divine. We can know God *qua* God – as opposed to a mere image or representation of God –only through God, and not through the creatural. Consequently, God himself must lead us from ignorance to knowledge, God himself must interrupt the normal order of creation, through direct 'inspiration'.[31] Islam is nothing other than an attempt to sustain the consequences of its original and utterly exceptional revelation.

Inspired and illuminated by God's word, the knowing subject ceases to be a subject in *relation* to an object. Rather, 'through the soul that knows, the real knows itself, becomes aware of itself'.[32] For al-Suhrawardi and Ibn al-'Arabi, as much as for Spinoza or Deleuze, the only true principle proofed against radical doubt is not '*I* think', but 'I am thought [by God]' – *cogitor* rather than *cogito*. Ultimately, it can only be God who thinks and acts, through us.[33] The true *subject* of Creative thought is singular by definition.

(b) Buddhism and the voiding of the given

Unlike Islam, Buddhism is not a monotheism, indeed it is not properly a theism at all. The fundamentally singular configuration of its classical sutras, however, is no less firmly oriented to an exceptional point beyond being and beyond distinction. Buddhism begins as a refusal of worldly coherence. The Buddha seeks deliverance from the realm of corruption, delusion and contrivance, through disciplined access to the insight that 'the One is none other than the All, the All none other than the One'.[34] All of the many variants of Buddhism maintain that 'reality – be it called "nature", self-nature, "original nature", "mind-nature", Buddha-nature, Dharma-nature or Suchness – is one [...]. In order to achieve final liberation, living beings must realise this unity of the real'.[35]

Such liberation must be realised, because what is initially given to us is the world of suffering (*dukkha*) and desire (*tanha*), the world of the distant or relational subject, the world of one-among-others.[36] The given fact is that 'this world is blinded, few only can see here'.[37] The whole effort of Buddhism is thus to eliminate the 'floating clouds of false thoughts' which obscure singular reality – 'to discard false views, this is the one great causal event'.[38] In Singh's nice phrase, 'every man is a hibernated God'.[39]

One attains truth to the degree that one becomes, so to speak, part of the *One*, rather than just one-among-others; the merely 'one' becomes-imperceptible in the One.[40] To know reality as One is at the same time to know the given (plurality) as simulacrum, illusion or fantasy. The essential means to such knowledge is the active dissolution of the self as such. The conventional notion of the self, of me as opposed to or related *to* you, is here the very form of a given ignorance. Every truth is without-self by definition. Insofar then as people 'indulge in I-making and mine-making, insofar as they take hold of things, they are defiled'.[41] Again, 'all defilements have the false theory of individuality for their root', which is to say that 'the defilements derive from discrimination' *as such*.[42] Since in true reality 'there is no individuation',[43] so 'not until the self we now call "I" has died past resurrecting will the Self appear which knows itself as One'.[44] *Nirvana* means nothing other than this: extinction of a merely specific or relational individuality. Buddhism is inspired at every step by the intuition of Unity without self, and what its teaching provides is first and foremost an elaborate mechanics for the voiding of self. In this, as in every absolutely singular case, the 'search after omniscience is, from a practical point of view, identical with the search after self-extinction'.[45]

More precisely, only self-extinction provides access to the quintessentially singular realm of *sunyata*, i.e. pure Creative emptiness as such, a creativity unlimited by creaturely actuality (or as Heidegger would say. pure Being beyond beings). As the canonical text puts it, 'in emptiness there is no form, nor feeling, nor perception, nor impulse, nor consciousness'.[46] Emptiness is the exhaustion of form. It consumes the given without trace. All discrimination and defilement are automatically 'stopped by emptiness'.[47] Emptiness is not the mere nothingness of the None, but the inconceivable Creative potentiality of the One as such. Consequently, the synonyms of emptiness include 'suchness [*tathagata*], the signless, the ultimate reality'.[48] Suchness is the singular grasped in the medium of its own immediacy: both Buddhist and Muslim know that the one Creative 'Mind can only be comprehended by mind directly and without a medium'.[49] And again, this Creative reality cannot be deduced or described from within given actuality as such, but only glimpsed as the truth of what lies beyond its horizon;[50] its singular virtuality can only be 'experienced' directly through the extinction or transcendence of all actuality.

(c) Deleuze and the univocity of Creation

It should come as no surprise that Deleuze and Guattari present the redemptive trajectory of their philosophy, the accession of thought to an 'immanent power of creation', as being broadly 'in agreement with a kind of Zen Buddhism'.[51] Deleuze's project begins with a critique of merely 'specific difference' (Aristotle, Hegel), so as to clear a space in which to think singular or Creative 'difference of difference as immediate element',[52] in which it is possible to recognise that 'every creation is singular'.[53] In Deleuze's somewhat idiosyncratic terminology, what is given is relational difference and identity, the 'shackles of mediation', subjective interiority, equivocity, signification, territoriality, desire-as-lack, transcendence, Oedipus, the 'long error' of representation, etc. What is real, by contrast, is a vitalist, self-differing force of Creativity in its purest form – an absolute intensity or virtuality in constant metamorphosis, a desire that is creative of its object, a perception that gives rise to what it perceives.

Deleuze accepts that 'there has only ever been one ontological proposition: Being is univocal. There has only ever been one ontology, that of Duns Scotus, which gave being a single voice'.[54] Being is one, *because* unrelated to and unlimited by the forms of being.[55] There is 'but one matter-energy',[56] and everything inheres within a single plane,

> a plane upon which everything is laid out, and which is like the intersection of all forms [...]. It is a fixed plane, upon which things are distinguished from one another only by speed and slowness A plane of immanence or *univocality opposed to analogy* [..], a single abstract Animal for all the assemblages that effectuate it.[57]

Within this real plane of immanence or consistency are dissolved all illusions of ontological equivocity, and with them all forms of figuration and interpretation. 'The plane of consistency is the abolition of all metaphor; all that consists is real [...]. The plane of consistency knows nothing of differences in level, orders of magnitude, or distances',[58] for 'there is only one kind of production, the production of the real'.[59] Deleuze's ontology thus opens out on to an immediate, unqualified empiricism, where 'empiricism in general is a kind of "physicalism"'. As a matter of fact, one must find a *fully* physical usage for principles whose nature is *only* physical',[60] i.e. purely mechanical principles geared to a single 'Mechanosphere'.[61]

All existent individuals, then, are simply the *immediately* produced, direct actualisations of one and the same Creative force, variously termed desire or desiring-production, life, *élan vital*, matter-energy, the virtual, or power – the force that governs the chaotic distribution of things across the plane of immanence. Within univocal being, there can be nothing *between* Creator and created. Desire, for instance, is not a relation between subject and object (a relation of 'lack'): rather, 'desire produces reality', desire *creates* its object in the most literal sense. 'Desire and its object are one and the same thing.'[62] Between the 'Creating' and the 'creature' there are only divergent paths of actualisation.

This is not to say, of course, that all creatures are the same. On the contrary, Deleuzian univocity is the condition of radically *singular* difference, i.e. difference free from the limits of constituent relations *between* the differed. Difference rests entirely in the 'Creating', so to speak. 'Equal, univocal being is immediately present in everything, without mediation or intermediary, even though things reside unequally in this equal being.'[63] Real differences, are solely a function of differences in creative intensity. Real differences are essentially quantitative. 'Quality is nothing other than contracted quantity';[64] 'quality is nothing but difference in quantity'.[65] In the succinct formula of Deleuze's *Cinéma 2*, 'irreducible difference allows resemblances to be graded'.[66] Or, following Leibniz: 'Everything is always the same thing, there is only one and same Basis; and: Everything is distinguished by degree, everything differs by manner [...]. These are the two principles of principles'.[67]

What is eliminated here is not difference, obviously, but specific or *relational* difference; 'what vanishes is merely all value that can be assigned to the terms of a relation [*un rapport*], for the gain of its inner reason, which precisely constitutes difference'.[68] The only significant 'relationship' between individuals must be measured in terms of the virtual which underlies them – a relation of purely quantitative difference along a single scale of proximity to the full Creative potential of intensity or Life.[69] In every case, the power of 'actualisation belongs to the virtual. The actualisation of the virtual is singularity, while the actual itself is [merely] constituted individuality'.[70] The multiple modes or singular actualisations of reality are no more related 'to' each other than are Leibniz's windowless monads.[71] The Creative 'movement goes, not from one actual term to another, nor from the general to the particular [through the specific], but from the virtual to its actualisation – through the intermediary of a determining individuation'.[72] Though any particular actual must actively learn 'what it can do' by experimenting in its relations with other actuals,[73] nevertheless, in the end the only genuinely creative relation between actual x and actual y is the immediate reference back to the virtual z which they both actualise to different degrees. To move from x to y is to jump from one degree or one fragment of the plane of immanence to another, via an immediate, instantaneous ellipse 'beyond distance' (i.e. via a shift in 'intensity' rather a change in 'extensity'). 'The virtuals communicate immediately above the actual that separates them'.[74] Consequently, 'the *relative* positions of the [actual terms in a given series] in relation to one another' depend only on their 'absolute' position in relation to 'the virtual paradoxical element' that distributes the whole series in the first place.[75]

As in the Islamic and Buddhist configurations, however, the immediately singular nature of Creative reality is obscured by its very actualisation in particular situations. Purely intense or 'implicated' difference 'is explicated in systems in which it tends to be cancelled',[76] just as 'life as movement alienates itself in the material form that it creates'.[77] 'Creatures', we might say, generally tend to forget their own creativity. The great purpose of Deleuze's work is thus the invention of various mechanisms whereby the given can be counter-actualised, 'real'-ised, deterritorialised or otherwise transfigured. One becomes real, naturally, by escaping the equivocal, the territorial, the relative, the mediate, the figural, the significant, the perceptible, and so on. Whereas the given is situated in a territory, within coordinated space, the Creatively real moves through space as a pure 'line of flight'. 'Lines of flight have no territory'.[78] 'Realisation' is thus experienced (by us) as a kind of *de-territorialisation*. To move from the given to real is once again to leap from created to Creator, from the confines of a particular organism to

> the *non-organic life of things* [...] which burns us [.. and] unleashes in our soul a *non-psychological life of the spirit*, which no longer belongs either to nature or to our organic individuality, which is the divine part in us, the spiritual relationship in which we are alone with God as light.[79]

All of the otherwise incompatible conceptual personae that populate Deleuze's work (Spinoza, Nietzsche, Masoch, Proust, Kafka, Beckett, Bacon, Artaud, the nomad, the schizo, the dice-thrower, etc.) pursue a similarly singularising itinerary.

Certain implications follow logically enough, and will echo through each of the chapters to come. First, all forms of discourse which relate a literal to a conventionally figurative meaning are to be replaced by an articulation of the literal pure and simple, as so many immediate verbalisations of virtual or Creative force. Ellipse rather than metaphor is the decisive figure of this discourse – the immediate, instantaneous leap from one proper-name of the real to another.[80] Second, all efforts to consolidate a stable territory must be re-directed along the (ultimately) vanishing lines of a global deterritorialisation. Third, social mediation that articulates a sense of self in relation to others must be overcome by a variety of techniques of de-personalisation, culminating in the celebration of a 'world without others'.[81] Deleuze deconstructs the subject in a much more emphatic sense than that generally pursued by Derrida and his followers. He literally *takes apart* the machinery of subjective mediation in the broadest sense, he breaks up that cluster of socio-cognitive faculties – the abilities to process information, coordinate movements, confront obstacles, react effectively to stimuli, and so on – which he groups under the name of the 'sensory-motor schema'. He ruins any merely creaturely coherence. He does this so as to accede the realm of pure Creativity as such, the realm of 'universal variation, which goes beyond the human limits of the sensory-motor schema towards a non-human world where movement equals matter, or else in the direction of a super-human world which speaks for a new spirit.'[82] There can no more succinct a description of the general effort pursued, in different ways and at different speeds, by the four writers studied in this book.

The *practical* question – or rather, the question that equates theory with practice –is thus always a variant of the question: 'how can we rid ourselves of ourselves and demolish ourselves?'[83] How can we 'attain once more the world before man, before our own dawn, the position where movement was [...] under the regime of universal variation [...], the luminous plane of immanence'?[84] This is the essential effort of any fully singular philosophy. Deleuze's enduring dream is to be thus present at the dawn of the world. Such is the link between imperceptibility, indiscernibility, and impersonality – the three virtues. To reduce oneself to an abstract line, a trait, in order to find one's zone of indiscernibility with other traits, and in this way enter the haecceity and impersonality of the creator One is then like grass…[85]

In the end, Deleuze's aim is to affirm 'Life' at a level of coherence which *excludes* that of the specific, living organism, a coherence affirmed through the dissolution of all organisms toward a single Body without Organs, one Brain immediate to the cosmos – one cosmos-Thought.[86] The power to overcome the organism will be the only genuine index of a creature's true power, the sign of its assigned degree of real Creativity.[87]

Deleuze's philosophy, in short, might best be approached as the reinvention (in apparently post-Darwinian terms) of a genuinely *contemporary* version of radical creationism.[88]

Arguably, Deleuze has written the most powerfully singular philosophy of recent times. His work demonstrates the consequences of the refusal of mediation in just about every context imaginable. His philosophy provides an unsurpassed frame of reference for a comparative investigation of singular individuation in contemporary literature. If others (for example, Badiou or Baudrillard) have written still 'purer', still less 'worldly' versions of a univocity beyond heterogeneity or an immanence beyond 'the production paradigm', Deleuze is remarkable for his commitment to writing the immediately other-worldly as productive of the world. For this reason he is truly, as Badiou himself admits, *'the* philosopher of our time'.[89]

(d) Singular *littérarité*

A further category of the singular and immediate will prove more or less directly relevant to all of the writers studied here – the singularity of a vanguard notion of literature or the 'literary field'.[90] Glissant, Johnson, Dib and Sarduy can all be situated more or less precisely within this field. As Bourdieu defines it, the literary field is essentially characterised by the affirmation of its productive *autonomy*. The literary field as such begins, with Flaubert and Baudelaire, when literature cuts its links with political and economic power, and establishes its own values in terms which transcend all such worldly interests. Literary value becomes a function of the transcendence of all merely specifiable value. Rather than a kind of privileged character among other characters, with Flaubert the author becomes 'a Spinozist God, immanent to and coextensive with his creation'.[91] In the hands of Flaubert and Baudelaire, and most emphatically after Mallarmé, literature becomes a fully sovereign expression, 'liberated from all servitude to any [socially] marked order of language'.[92] Such literature makes 'the distance from the praxis of life the content of [its] works'.[93] From Romanticism to Mallarmé, as Foucault summarises things,

> literature becomes progressively more differentiated from the discourse of ideas and encloses itself within a radical intransitivity [. ;] it becomes merely a manifestation of a language that has no other law than that of affirming [...] its own precipitous existence [. A]nd thus all its threads converge upon the finest of points – singular, instantaneous and yet absolutely universal – upon the simple act of writing.[94]

Foucault's colleague Roland Barthes confirms the radically singular notion of the literary text. 'The text is never a "dialogue"' nor a 'rivalry of idiolects'; rather, it establishes, in the midst of 'human relations', 'a sort of island, it manifests the asocial nature of pleasure' and the neutrality of *jouissance*. In a striking confirmation of the singular orientation of the avant-garde, Barthes adopts an image from Angelus Silesius. the text sees with an 'undifferentiated eye [...]; "the eye by which I see God is the same eye by which he sees me"'.[95]

It may be worth highlighting the essential moments of this in-differentiation, associated in the French field with Flaubert, Mallarmé and Blanchot, respectively.

If Balzac, say, narrates the specific, worldly relation of province to Paris, of character to character, or desire to object, as so many aspects of an effort to make sense of one's place in the world, then Flaubert, by contrast, narrates the experience of characters who are unable to read their society or find a place within it, and who remain, like the Frédéric of *L'Education sentimentale*, suspended in permanent indecision. Flaubert makes of this worldly failure to assume a place the very basis of his own placeless aesthetic, the principle of a radical *discours indirect libre* written from above or between the characters.[96] With Flaubert – like Sarduy, Johnson and the later Glissant – the author transcends the worldly relations that motivate characters in relation to other characters, so as to attain a pure, singular plane of composition perfectly isolated from the derivative planes of the composed. Flaubert holds that 'life is only tolerable on condition of not being in it':[97] an author worthy of the name should die to the world in order to claim, alongside Shakespeare, a 'superhuman impersonality'.[98] His writing is oriented around the transfiguration of reality from material opacity to a kind of formal or stylistic 'spirituality'. The result is what Flaubert calls beauty. Beauty varies with the independence of style from any material, contextual or otherwise 'external attachment'. Such is the logic of an art based very literally 'on nothing', i e. on nothing other than the 'internal strength of its style [...], style being all by itself an absolute way of seeing things.'[99]

With Mallarmé, the author then turns upon the instrument of this initial transcendence (literary language itself), and in a kind of self-reflexive 'purification' further singularises the singularising medium.[100] Poetry first silences the realm of worldly communication, so as to then silence itself in an ultimately ineffable 'Purity' or 'solitude'.[101] Mallarmé, more than any other modernist author, did the most to make such transcendence of experience the very principle of literature, and to confirm it for Blanchot, Barthes, Deleuze and others as the fundamental ambition of modernist writing in general.[102] Mallarmé equates in the most austerely sublime terms an ascetic de-personalisation with aesthetic revelation pure and simple.[103] At this extreme distance from the world, writing becomes simultaneously 'impersonal', 'independent' and 'absolute'.[104] Through Mallarmé's writing, as Georges Poulet puts it, 'each object is detached from the confusing plurality of the real world. Through abstraction, it simplifies itself, isolates itself, and reduces itself to its pure notion.'[105] All poetry *creates* its object in this way, after first 'breaking out of natural relation with things': 'the book replaces everything, for lack of everything'.[106] Mallarmé writes, in other words, towards a univocal, literal expression, towards the all-inclusive singularity of *Le Livre*, 'persuaded that in the end there can only be one'.[107] At the limit of this effort hovers the intuition of 'a state of the world in which everything would culminate [...] in a single conscious centre.'[108]

The essential features of this transcendent singularity have been re-invented or re-arranged by many of this century's avant-garde movements. *Littérarité* is a quintessentially singular term. To stick to the French situation, variants of a singular logic can be found at work in surrealism, in the more radical existentialist novels, in the anthropological speculations of the Collège de Sociologie, in the ascetic ambitions of Beckett, Sarraute and the *nouveau romanciers*, in *Tel Quel*'s inflated conception of textuality. The conversion of Saussure's initially heuristic isolation of the signifier into a full-blown theory of language as a self-constituent, essentially non-referential configuration is an exemplary case of the *singularisation* of the specific. Picking up where Mallarmé and Valéry left off, Maurice Blanchot's contribution to the paradigm stands out as particularly forceful. According to Blanchot, all literary discourse destroys and replaces its given object; through the voiding of the given, literary writing becomes fully creative of what it perceives. 'The word only has meaning if it gets rid of the object that it names', and poetry exists 'to detach us from being'.[109] Poetry is nothing other than the institution of silence as the sole adequate measure of the singular-immediate: 'literature aims to make of language an absolute, and to recognise in this absolute the equivalent of silence.'[110] To write is thus to undergo a radical detachment, to become *absolutely* alone,[111] impersonal, isolated within an im-mediate atemporality ('the time of the absence of time').[112] Like the Deleuze he inspires,

Blanchot tends to absorb all 'actual' writers as so many echoes of a singular 'murmure anonyme'.

The 'essential solitude' of the writer, then, is not that of an anguished isolation among others, but of a submersion within the aspecific or indifferent pure and simple, a space generally rendered in Blanchot's fiction as void, desert, snow, night or sea – spaces rediscovered, as we shall see, by the later novels of Mohammed Dib. Writing begins when the writer forgoes 'the power to say "I"'.[113] When I write, 'I am not there, there is nobody there, but the impersonal is there'.[114] What this impersonal affirmation finds, in anticipation of Deleuze's 'dawn of the world', is the immediate 'presence of things, before the world was, and their perseverance after the world has disappeared'.[115] Here, if 'nothing precedes writing', it is because writing composes itself directly out of this original nothingness, out of the singular reality which 'always precedes [being]' and which subsists in the 'exalting union of contraries'.[116] Considering the extension of these ideas in Bataille and Foucault, Susan Sontag notes the obvious analogy: 'as the activity of the mystic must end in a *via negativa*, a theology of God's absence, a craving for the cloud of unknowingness beyond knowledge and for the silence beyond speech, so art must tend toward anti-art, the elimination of the "subject" [...] and the pursuit of silence.'[117]

IV

Such are the singular configurations of reality that inform the projects studied in the chapters of this book. What these otherwise incompossible logics have in common should now be clear enough. The singular creates the medium of its own expression or expansion, and its operation is not subject to external criteria. Singularity is unlimited; it can be indifferently described as infinitely compressed (singular because punctual, without extension) or as infinitely extended (singular because all inclusive, without horizon). A singular mode of individuation must ultimately preclude the existence of others in the strict sense, i.e. it must preclude the existence of a plurality of individuals, as distinct from the multiplicity of modes of one univocal Individual.

Readers familiar with the dominant trends of postcolonial theory and criticism will recognise the polemic edge of this presentation. The things that usually qualify for inclusion in the postcolonial domain are almost automatically associated with the vague but insistent attributes of plurality, specificity, situation, relationality, engagement, embattlement and subversion. Most studies of postcolonial literature presume a field characterised by a multiplicity of finely situated subject positions, a wealth of positioned differences, a respect for otherness and plurality, relatively elaborate layers of figural complication, a certain amount of critical distance or irony, and a penchant for generalised dissensus balanced by a benevolent aura of communal solidarity or commitment. All of the items on this list certainly figure prominently in the received readings of the authors considered in this book. None of these things, however, should in my opinion be included among the *primary* and most distinctive qualities of their work. All of the writers considered here strive, to various degrees, to provide direct access to a reality that coheres in a world-without-others; to act in accordance with wholly immanent criteria; to assert the literal or Creative force of their perception; to privilege ellipse over metaphor; to work against or beyond the consolidation of character and territory; to eliminate any specifically ironic distance. Each writer has followed his own particular trajectory. But the general tendency of their work is the movement from specific to singular, and not the reverse.

This is not to argue, of course, that a refusal of the specific is typical of *all* the recent writing that has come out of the places under consideration here. My conclusion will suggest comparisons evocative of a specific alternative to the singular postcolonial mode. As opposed to Johnson, Toni Morrison's fiction assumes the burden of a past and a place – without allowing her characters to be *specified* by that burden. As opposed to Glissant and Dib, writers as far apart along the political spectrum as Mongo Beti, Assia Djebar and V.S. Naipaul presume and consolidate a degree of critical detachment, relate distinct perspectives, and work to compose scenarios that allow for the 'imposition' of judgement. And rather than write varied incantations of a Creative coherence that excludes our own, Deleuze's friend Foucault explores the many ways in which our experience is confined, classified, and specified. He writes, in short, to preserve the space of a forever undetermined, fully specific experience, at the 'limit' of all specification, pursued through the *evacuation* (rather than elimination) of relations.

Writers like Morrison and Djebar work within a firmly specific orientation. The relations they negotiate with others, with themselves, and with the limits of their experience, are constitutive of how they perceive and act in the world. This is enough to set them sharply apart from the prevailing postcolonial trend.

|

POSTCOLONIAL THEORY

Over the last twenty years or so, postcolonial theory has put together a distinctive and fairly elaborate package of critical priorities and expectations. Developing the terms put forward in my introduction, this first chapter will argue that, although these priorities are generally presented as *specific* or relational, they would most often be better understood as the expression of a fundamentally *singular* or non-relational orientation.

What to make then of the fact that one of the most powerful of postcolonial expectations links creative writing with nothing other than a peculiarly strong sense of context, place, history and situation? A large part of the reason for the recent spectacular growth of *general* interest in postcolonial studies can certainly be attributed to a growing dissatisfaction among cultural and literary critics with the available (i.e. mainly postmodern) theoretical means for dealing with appropriately 'specific' (i.e. non-Eurocentric) local contextualisation. Merely postmodern writing, the argument goes, tends toward a certain placelessness, a disembodied abstraction uncomfortably close to an ideological reflection of prevailing modes of production in the West. The initial promise of postmodern theory, in justifying our incredulity towards metanarratives, *seemed* to point toward a new era of many and divergent small narratives, the explosion of a 'multiplicity of images, interpretations and reconstructions' – a generalised 'disorientation which is at the same time also the liberation of difference, of local elements'.[1] The expected result was an 'irreversible pluralisation'.[2] From the supposed subversion of universals and the asserted contingency of identities, the postmodern was to derive a properly '*irreducible* pluralism',[3] a 'plurality without norms',[4] a 'boundless pluralism', a future in which 'cultures are being pluralised to the degree of total particularisation'.[5] Cornel West's enthusiastic description of the 'postmodern politics of cultural difference' hit all the key notes: it moved to trash the monolithic and homogeneous in the name of diversity, multiplicity and heterogeneity; to reject the abstract, general and universal in light of the concrete, specific and particular; and to historicise, contextualise and pluralise by highlighting the contingent, provisional, variable, tentative, shifting and changing.[6]

The postmodern version of fragmentation was supposed to lead, in other words, to a newly sensitive attention to context, understood as the conditions governing the 'construction of a plurality of subject positions', 'multiple, specific and heterogeneous ways of life', the rhythms of popular culture, the texture of the particular and the everyday, and so on.[7]

A number of critics were quick to realise that things cannot be quite so simple. As Nelly Richard suggests, if postmodern theory stresses 'specificity, plurality, heterogeneity and dissidence', still 'the fact is that no sooner are these differences posited and valued than they become subsumed into the metacategory of the "undifferentiated" which means that all singularities immediately become indistinguishable and interchangeable in a new, sophisticated economy of "sameness"'.[8] Today, no doubt, most critics who use (or attack) the notion of the postmodern are aware of the danger of a 'homogenising pluralism that obscures personal originality',[9] of that aspect of 'postmodernisation [that] is a process of cultural "de-differentiation"'.[10] Hence the multiplication of calls for a greater attention to context, to historical particularity and complexity – for 'an ever more complex understanding of difference and "marginality"',[11] of 'the indeterminacy and multiplicity of contexts',[12] in particular contexts conditioned by gender, ethnicity or culture.

However loosely defined, the vague criteria of the 'specific' seem to have emerged as the major critical imperative of in the wake of postmodern theory. If the heyday of fully postmodern readings – that is, readings explicitly allied to the postmodernity preached by Lyotard and Baudrillard – appears by now to have come and gone, it is because such readings have had real trouble meeting the challenge posed by this call to specification. Emphasis on pure contingency, incommensurability or fragmentation does not lend itself to anything but an *ad hoc* contextualisation.

Much of the recent interest in postcolonial issues and theories, then, can indeed be traced to an apparently more satisfying insistence on circumstances in which the explicitly situated character of theory and agency is unavoidable. Informed by 'plural and heterogeneous struggles' against homogeneity,[13] 'the category of postcolonialism must be read as a free-floating metaphor for cultural embattlement',[14] a clarion call in favour of truly *substantial* differences. Nothing is more orthodox in the postcolonial domain than an insistence on the multiple, particular, heterogeneous nature of contexts and subject-positions.[15] All postcolonial critics flaunt their 'constant awareness of the location of the individual and the circumstances of knowledge production'.[16] Ania Loomba dutifully reflects the general expectations of the field she surveys in her recent guide to *Colonialism/Postcolonialism* when she insists that all postcolonial positions must be seen as 'embedded in specific histories', as part of an 'empirical specificity'.[17] The charge of 'insufficient political specificity'[18] has become perhaps the most cutting accusation in the business, and it is perfectly standard postcolonial practice to argue that 'migrancy, hybridity, imbrication [...] remain particular and partial knowledges located in contingent constellations of the local and the extralocal, and cannot be emblematised as instances of a global other'.[19]

Such critical intentions are also, it must be admitted, among the most conventional and most cheaply earned of those currently in vogue. The call for specificity has become perhaps the most formulaic move in contemporary criticism, little more than a prelude to the ritual invocation of the ubiquitously *specifying* categories of gender, ethnicity, and community affiliation. Nevertheless, it is reasonable to assume that over the long term the fortunes of postcolonial theory will vary with the plausibility of its claim to be adequate to the specificity of its varied domain. What follows will demonstrate that this claim remains highly tenuous at best. As we shall see, it is no coincidence that several of the most distinctive and certainly the most widely read contributions to postcolonial theory are all more or less enthusiastically committed to an explicitly *deterritorialising* discourse in something close to the Deleuzian sense – a discourse so fragmented, so hybrid, as to deny its constituent elements any sustainable specificity at all.

I Postcolonial singularity

There should be no need, at this point, to document further the interest postcolonial criticism maintains in locating cultural performance and political agency in terms that emphasise their contingency, ambivalence and displacement.[20] For all its apparent suspicion of postmodern in-difference and placelessness, much of postcolonial theory can only be read as making a still more emphatic claim to the paradoxical place of *placelessness* itself. The merely postmodern multiplication of margins and migrations was too abstract, too presumptuous; the postcolonial emphasis on a similar agenda will be careful to situate this multiplication more precisely. What is at issue here, however, remains much the same: *who* (and *how*, *where*, under what circumstances) can make a plausible claim to that singular status which resists not merely specification but distinction in the most general sense? Which performances qualify as immanent to that radically hybrid space which transcends the merely relational (let alone binary) *between*?

Consider for instance James Clifford's seminal exploration of 'the predicament of culture'. Clifford's laudable goal is 'to displace any transcendent regime of [cultural] authenticity' or 'purity',[21] to demonstrate the always contingent, always contested criteria of cultural belonging. He is perfectly right to insist that our 'images of one another [...] are constituted in specific historical relations of dominance and dialogue' (23). But the 'poetics of displacement' he finds at work in the surreal ethnographic writings of Rimbaud, Segalen, Cendrars, Leiris, and Artaud (152) can easily slide into the virtual celebration of disruption for its own sake, a fascination with 'the modern experience of displacement: self and other [as] a sequence of encounters, detours, with the stable identity of each at issue' (157). Reacting against overly specified conceptions of culture associated with 'roots' and 'a stable, territorialised existence',[22] Clifford's work tends to idealise a certain u-topia of the *between* as such. To say that any positive, specified identity is 'constructed' (10) is one thing; to say that the very *dimension* of 'the individual is culturally constituted' (92), however, is to say something else altogether. Clifford tends to elide this difference. Like much postcolonial theory, his 'modern ethnography of conjunctures, constantly moving between cultures' (9) is a little too consistent for comfort with a quite particular set of cultural (and financial) privileges; the growth of 'rootlessness and mobility' does not *automatically* open on to 'a truly global space of cultural connections and dissolutions' (3–4). Iain Chambers' celebration of the growing 'multiplicity of cultural borders, historical temporalities and hybrid identities'[23] pushes a similar logic to new extremes. His postcolonial era is a time of 'perpetual movement of transmutation and transformation', closely aligned with 'the nomadic experience of language, wandering without a fixed home'.[24] Identity is 'always in mutation. [...] History gives way to histories, as the West gives way to the World'.[25]

There is no better example of this hybridising trend than the recent revival of *créolité* and *mestizaje* identity. Today's *créolité* extols a purely fluid difference beyond relations-with-others: through its constant self-transformation, it creates the dynamic medium of its own existence. As the authors of its most influential *Eloge* have argued, '*Créolité* is "the world diffracted but recomposed", a maelstrom of signifieds in a single signifier: a Totality.'[26] *Créolité* vibrates in the multiplicity of its modes, modes that express a single Creative substance. Like other singular configurations, this *créolité* acts in the absence of others and without external criteria: 'it involves a descent into oneself [*en soi-même*], but without the Other [...]. And here, we must admit, we are without points of reference, without certainties, without aesthetic criteria [...]; the intuition of our *créolité* must invent itself at every instant' (41). As its self-invention proceeds, *créolité* becomes its own absolute and exclusive point of reference.

Such a logic of self-constituent creation – however tinged with 'local colour' in its thematics – is typical of every singular configuration. It should come as no surprise to find this logic at play in the work of two of the most widely cited postcolonial theorists, Homi Bhabha and Gayatri Spivak.[27] However overrated their often repetitive and sometimes infuriating work might be, it retains an overwhelming influence over the postcolonial field as a whole. With Bhabha and Spivak, the singular orientation of postcolonial criticism appears in all its tortuously evasive clarity.

(a) Homi Bhabha

Few contemporary critics are likely to argue with Bhabha's critique of 'cultural continuism', the conception of 'culture as populist nostalgia' or 'patriotic instruction'.[28] What is more controversial is that Bhabha presents the *différance* he conceives as an alternative to such cultural specification in the fundamentally non-relational terms of *pure* 'incommensurability' or 'untranslatability' (LC, 207; 224). Bhabha's is an essentially singular category of difference.

Bhabha's incommensurability is not to be confused, he insists, with a 'naive and benevolent pluralism'.[29] Far from a matter of mere 'diversity',[30] cultural difference here implies 'the momentous, if momentary, extinction of the recognisable object of culture in the disturbed artifice of its signification, at the edge of experience' (LC, 126). As if to Deleuze's prescription, Bhabha wants to show cultural difference 'differing'.[31] 'The contour of difference is agonistic, shifting, splitting' (LC, 109). Rather than relate distinct and perhaps antagonistic perspectives to each other, Bhabha's difference is directly expressive of the Creative 'arbitrariness of the sign, the indeterminacy of writing, [and] the splitting of the subject of enunciation' (176) Bhabha's major concept, hybridity, is 'a difference "within"', a difference without binary terms.[32] He wants 'to see the cultural not as the source of conflict – different cultures – but as the effect of discriminatory practices – the production of cultural differentiation' (114). This differentiation is immanent to the singular logics of *différance*, displacement and supplementarity Bhabha borrows from Derrida to describe the process of cultural 'enunciation' or 'performance' in the broadest sense. Specific individuals are here always derivative, a result.

Bhabha's most insistent question – 'how does the deconstruction of the "sign", the emphasis on indeterminacy in cultural and political judgement, transform our sense of the "subject" of culture and the agent of historical change?' (LC, 174) – thus receives a relatively simple answer: the latter *incarnate* this indeterminacy pure and simple. They are Created by it. The whole effort of Bhabha's work is to move from what he calls the 'pedagogical' aspect of cultural identifications (fixed, exclusive, discriminatory) to the strictly enunciative or performative aspect of the articulation of identities (15), 'the disruptive temporality of enunciation' (37). Enunciation is intrinsically *différant*, and every 'subject of hybridisation is an enunciatory subject [...]. It is through the process of enunciation that the borders between objects or subjects or practices are being constituted.'[33] Again,

> All cultural statements are constructed in this contradictory and ambivalent space of enunciation [..]. Differences in culture and power are constituted through the social conditions of enunciation [..] The reason a cultural text or system of meaning cannot be sufficient unto itself is that the act of cultural enunciation – the place of utterance – is crossed by the *différance* of writing or *écriture*.[34]

Bhabha's goal is always to access, beyond given differences, the 'creative heterogeneity of the enunciatory "present"' (LC, 185), the 'postcolonial "enunciative" present' (251).

Bhabha has often been accused of imposing an 'idealist reduction of the social to the semiotic' and of exaggerating the heuristic value of the 'language metaphor'.[35] What is at issue in his work, however, is something more than the familiar poststructuralist inflation of linguistic categories. Rather than simply treat historical or social situations as linguistic or rhetorical ones, it would be more accurate to say that Bhabha equates Creative agency with the precise moment of this differing enunciation as such, the moment 'behind' or productive of language itself. The truly 'hybrid moment' lies 'outside the sentence' (LC, 181), it gives rise to it.

Enunciation as Bhabha conceives it is a pre-eminently singular operation. Postcolonial 'translations' do not 'simply revalue the contents of a cultural tradition' (LC, 241) but return them to the *différance* of their original enunciation, across the 'time-lag' Bhabha presumes as inherent to the signifying process.

> The emphasis on the disjunctive present of utterance [.] allows the articulation of subaltern agency to emerge as relocation and reinscription [...]. The process of reinscription and negotiation [...] happens in the temporal break initiated through the sign, deprived of subjectivity, in the realm of the intersubjective. Through this time-lag – the temporal break in representation – emerges the process of agency both as a historical development and as the narrative agency of historical discourse.[36]

What Bhabha calls 'postcolonial agency' emerges within this time-lag, i.e. from a perspective immediate to the internal mechanics of signification itself. From this perspective one grasps 'the whole performance [...] of modernity [...], revealing "everything that is involved in the act of staging *per se*"' (LC, 253–254, quoting Fanon). The postcolonial critic moves from the given or articulated to Creative articulation itself, from a derivative, signified stasis to the 'vicissitudes of the movement of the signifier' (24) in Derrida's sense. 'The alterity of the sign', Bhabha explains, 'in keeping with my account of the "supplementary question" of cultural signification, alienates the synchronicity of the imagined community [..., from which] emerges a *more instantaneous* and subaltern voice of the people, minority discourses that speak betwixt and between times and places'.[37] The critic helps bring the '"dead" symbols [of the national past] into the circulatory life of the "sign" of the present', i.e. the present of enunciation itself (254). Escaping from a situated position relative to other positions, the postcolonial slips between *every* possible position because it refers back, immediately, to that *one* logic that positions every possibility.

Everything turns, in other words, on this characterisation of articulation, enunciation or performance – what Bhabha, after Deleuze and Guattari, calls 'emergence-as-enunciation'[38] – as *inherently différant*, as differentiation itself. The colonial enterprise can then be figured as an *inevitably* unsuccessful effort to reduce enunciation to the relation of distinct (i.e. static) identities; the post-colonial enterprise appears, in turn, as the triumphant (and no less inevitable) dissolution of these distinctions through a return to the real process of enunciation, the restoration of its Creative *'différance* and enunciative modalities' (LC, 30). On this condition, certainly, 'the time of liberation is [...] a time of cultural uncertainty, and, most crucially, of significatory or representational undecidability' (35). But this liberation is now simply immediate to the (undecidable) nature of representation in itself. It's as if apartheid, say, was overthrown by the *différance* of its own enunciation or *écriture*. Politics and culture blur into a single discursive continuum, and all forms of domination would seem to be undone in advance by their own performance. 'In situations', Bhabha says, 'where cultural difference – race, sexuality, class location, generational or geographical specification – is the linchpin of a particular political edict or strategy, even the oppressor is being constituted through splitting [... and] actually, this allows the native or the subaltern or the colonised the strategy of attempting to disarticulate the voice of authority at that point of splitting.' The mere duality of hierarchical discrimination itself seems to effect a 'splitting [of] the language of authority'.[39] It would seem that lasting (if not catastrophic) oppression is thus effectively precluded as an enunciatory impossibility – a point Bhabha might have trouble explaining to, say, the Caribs, the Sioux, or the Palestinians.

What has been clear for some time is that for Bhabha matters of 'cultural politics' need not involve direct conflict or sustained popular mobilisation and empowerment.[40] The issues require hermeneutic finesse rather than blunt confrontation: 'I have always believed that "small differences" and slight alternatives and displacement are often the most significant elements in a process of subversion or transformation'.[41] The possibility of a militant decision, a decisive resolution for or against, be it theoretical or practical, is *written* away in advance. Instead, it is pre-eminently 'theory' itself that operates outside and beyond 'binary representations. It must work at the very point at which there is an infraction of discursive boundaries, or the boundedness of an event. The theoretical intervenes in the very moment of displacement that both demarcates and interrogates what it means to be inside and outside a discursive field'.[42] One and the same enunciatory logic is expressed in much the same way by 'theory' and the signifying 'practice' it advocates.

Bhabha's conception of the subject ensures its immanence within this same singular plane of consistency: 'the political subject – as indeed the subject of politics – is a discursive event' (LC, 23). It is individuated as *an* enunciation. Since what individuates enunciation is pure *différance*, it is difficult to see how this individuation does anything more than equate any particular individual with an instance of enunciation itself. More than any other writer in the field, Bhabha seems to have trouble remembering Brathwaite's simple point – that 'it is not language but people who make revolutions'.[43]

(b) Gayatri Chakravorty Spivak

Spivak 'follow[s] the good work of Homi Bhabha'[44] and runs, by and large, into comparable problems. Her approach is certainly the more nuanced of the two, the more attentive to all manner of 'heterogeneities'. But the fundamentally singular orientation of her work emerges clearly enough in her conceptions of criticism and subalternity, and more recently, of 'ethical impossibility' and 'globe-girdling' movements. Spivak's whole conception of 'literary criticism' is bound up with the peculiar project of 'disciplinarising the singular' (CPR, 375). The celebrity of Spivak's approach allows me, I hope, to take some short-cuts in the following presentation: I will dwell only on those aspects of her work that point the most suggestively toward this orientation. We might say that while Spivak, unlike Bhabha, stresses the diversity of types of enunciation or performance (and the consequent diversity of the methods – deconstructive, feminist and marxist – she employs) nevertheless her aim is not to engage with this diversity as such, but to describe *its* enunciation–differentiation, so to speak – its singular production *as* multiplicity.

The preliminary gesture is another sustained (and perfectly unobjectionable) critique of specified categories of subjective identity and territorial affiliation. Spivak grew up 'at a time when the people who were making the clamours for pure ethnicity and so on were on the extreme right in my own country',[45] and like all postcolonial theorists, she scrupulously emphasises the pitfalls of 'identitarian ethnicist claims of native or fundamental origin'.[46] Her writing always stresses 'work on the mechanics of the constitution of the Other' over and against 'invocations of the authenticity of the Other'.[47] In keeping with post-structuralist conventions, Spivak extends these mechanics to include the first term in the self/other binary, until she sees 'in the self perhaps only a (dis)figuring effect of a radical heterogeneity' (IOW, 16). It is a short step from here to the conclusion that '*the entire idea* of agency is structurally negotiable' (OTM, 12, my emphasis). The subject *is* nothing more than a subject-effect:

> A subject-effect can be briefly plotted as follows. that which seems to operate as a subject may be part of an immense discontinuous network ('text' in the general sense) of strands that may be termed politics, ideology, economics, history, sexuality, language, and so on [...]. Different knottings and configurations of these strands, determined by heterogeneous determinations which are themselves dependent upon myriad circumstances, produce the effect of an operating subject.[48]

So where *Subaltern Studies* once set out to write a history of the 'contribution made by the people on their own',[49] Spivak's enquiries famously turn away from the retrieval of a subaltern consciousness or subjectivity, toward an analysis of the production, inscription and manipulation of subject-positions (or subject-effects). Within the space Spivak qualifies as 'subaltern', it seems that 'the assumption and construction of a consciousness or subject' can only, 'in the long run, cohere with the work of *imperialist* subject-constitution'.[50] She objects to Foucault's prescription of 'localised resistance' (in hospitals, prisons, in the army, in the family...) for instance, not because it may dissipate and undermine collective action, but because it may 'accommodate unacknowledged privileging of the subject' (290): resistances of this kind are apparently not disseminated *enough*. Every actual 'identity [i]s a wound'.[51] Rather than work for the consolidation of *specific* 'identity and voice' Spivak thus pursues a 'self-separating project'.[52] Separation from oneself allows for a kind of ascetic return to the singular, Creative mobility of textual dissemination itself, an episodic intuition of that pre-specific, discontinuous *différance* that spawns the properly 'pathetic' illusions of subjective continuity precisely *as* its effects.

(1) A first way of approaching this singular discontinuity is suggested by Spivak's enduring interest in Marx's theory of value. One of the clearest of Spivak's several discussions of this question appears in her essay 'Foundations and Cultural Studies' (1993). In this essay, Spivak reminds us that Marx conceives of the abstract form of value as *inhaltlos und einfach*, 'contentless and simple'. Value is the empty medium presupposed by all sociality and exchange. A given mode of production, be it economic, social, cultural or psychological, is a particular way of coding this empty value

form. It is a certain way of *valuing*. What Spivak wants to preserve for critical practice, we might say, is a form of agency that coincides as directly as
possible with the singular indeterminacy of the pre-coded field as such, a
freedom subversive of all established relations of code.

Spivak builds here on the precedent established by Deleuze and Guattari, whose *Anti-Oedipus* extends Marx's concept of value to the whole
range of 'desiring-production' or 'coding' in the broadest possible sense.[53]
Paraphrasing their argument, she explains that what is peculiar about the
capitalist mode of production is its tendency to decode *all* values in the
direction of that most abstract, purely deterritorialised form of value –
money. This deterritorialisation is inherently anarchic and potentially liberating (commodification as such is indifferent to the distinction of centre
from periphery); its *unqualified* pursuit is thus supremely dangerous for the
continued operation of capitalist exploitation itself. The ongoing extraction
of surplus value and the endless accumulation of capital require a stable
division of labour and a firmly established sense of social order and hierarchy. In order to avert the danger of pure abstraction or absolute deterritorialisation (a purely anarchic or 'schizophrenic' mode of production),
capitalism therefore recodes certain components of the production process
as workers and consumers. Through mainly psychological and cultural
forms of investment, it directs the wild flows of desire into manageable
channels. It re-divides centre from margin. 'The codings of value in the cog-
nitive-political sphere, through the discursive system of marginality,
whether by way of psychoanalysis, culturalism or economism, are still part
of this crisis management' (160); what Spivak calls 'marginalities' are those
'reterritorialisations' capitalism itself invents in order to avoid the schizophrenic reality towards which its own deterritorialising movement tends.
The postcolonial critic concludes, like Deleuze and Guattari before her, that
she must avoid identifying with one of these defensive marginalities that
serve only to keep the system going. 'We cannot grasp value as such; it is a
possibility for grasping, without content. But if we position ourselves as
identities in terms of links in the chain of a value-coding, as if those links
were persons and things, and then ground our practice on that positioning,
we become part of the problem' (160).

The solution, then, would seem to be to work as closely as possible to
the pure contingency of the desiring flow itself, outside the economy of
identity. 'You take positions', Spivak advises, 'not in terms of the discovery
of historical grounds, but in terms of reversing, displacing and seizing the
apparatus of value-coding' (161). The space before 'ground' in which this
seizing might take place can only be, I would argue, an essentially singular
space. singular 'value as such' cannot be grasped because it is itself the
medium of the Creative movement that articulates values (in the plural).

The postcolonial critic purportedly operates at a level immediate to *this* articulation, i.e. at the level that produces subjective identification as its *effect*. (Hence a first and telling difference with more conventional Marxist positions: 'why', Spivak will ask, 'are Marxist intellectuals interested in holding things together, when "history", "culture", "real life" (big, difficult words) are forever on the move?' [CPR, 69]).

(ii) Another, more celebrated consequence of this articulation is Spivak's strained conjunction of critical discourse with subaltern silence. Critic and subaltern figure here as the two reciprocal, ultimately singular limits of subject-construction: on the one hand, the silenced immobility of a non-agent, and on the other, the forever restless, always excessive verbosity of a kind of meta-agent, the postcolonial critic herself.

In the first case, 'the subaltern cannot speak' because she falls entirely outside the framework of *all* conceivable representation or recognition.[34] To be sure, many of the frequent accusations levelled at Spivak for somehow stifling the subaltern are somewhat misplaced and undeserved.[35] That Spivak doesn't directly silence the subaltern in no way refutes the suggestion, however, that she does indeed *singularise* her. 'The disenfranchised woman, the figure I have called the "gendered subaltern"', is defined by 'her continuing heterogeneity, her continuing subalternisation and loneliness' (PCC, 103), as much as by the fact that '*we* strictly, historically, geopolitically cannot imagine' her (OTM, 139, my emphasis). The subaltern is defined in terms of absolute alterity: the word 'subaltern' is to be 'reserved for the sheer heterogeneity of decolonised space' (CPR, 310). As if to conform to the familiar strictures of negative theology, the subaltern is defined as inaccessible to relations of nomination, situation, and evaluation. She is inaccessible to conventional notions of mobilisation and solidarity. She occupies a super- or sub-nominal place, a unique 'space out of any serious touch with the logic of capitalism or socialism [...]. Please do not confuse it', Spivak implores her readers, 'with unorganised labour, women as such, the proletarian, the colonised, the object of ethnography, migrant labour, political refugees, etc. Nothing useful comes out of this confusion'.[36] The subaltern, in other words, is the theoretically *untouchable*, the altogether-beyond-relation: the attempt to 'relate' to the subaltern defines what Spivak will quite appropriately name an 'impossible ethical singularity' (more on this in a moment).

Subaltern and postcolonial critic only co-exist, then, in the non-relation of reciprocal inversion. The subaltern subsists entirely 'outside the lines of mobility' of modern society, whereas the postcolonial critic is 'always on the move' (PCC, 38). The critic seems to incarnate, in Spivak's own frequent and pointed allusions to her remarkable schedule of international conferences and interventions, a kind of pure intellectual mobility (a mobility doubled in the generally eclectic if not simply erratic organisation of her essays). The many stories Spivak tells of her displacement within the academy as within the world at large accumulate to paint a picture of someone always and 'everywhere [...] on the run'.[57]

The subaltern cannot speak, while the critic must never stop speaking, must never stop answering the question, 'from what space [am I] speaking?' (OTM, 54). Spivak is often accused of imposing western theory on Third World material: rather than dismiss such objections as impertinent, she often makes of them the very substance of her critical practice. 'My work lies in making clear my disciplinary predicament', as an incessant negotiation of 'institutional constraints' (PCC, 69, 34). Spivak knows that 'in disclosing complicities the critic-as-subject is herself complicit with the object of her critique' (IOW, 180), and the endless displacement of complicity demands an equally endless self-reflexive discussion of this complicity. Just as the subaltern is defined by all the labels that do not apply, so too Spivak identifies herself in mainly negative terms ('I'm not a deconstructionist', 'I'm not really a Marxist cultural critic', and so on), to the point that she herself becomes the elusive object of investigation.[58] The result is more than the usual postcolonial emphasis on ambivalence and ambiguity. Whereas militant political mobilisation has always depended upon the power and validity of essentially *anonymous* statements – statements that *anyone* could have made, articulating principles that compel agreement for their own sake – Spivak grabs every opportunity to foreground the complex subjective inflection and orientation of her own idiosyncratic discourse. Since, she admits, 'I never really know what my work is', so the effort to discover what it might be, compounded by the fact that 'I cannot write clearly',[59] seems to justify a quite extraordinary degree of introspective attention, self-description, and re-description.

Such introspection sits a little uncomfortably with the desperately urgent political issues her work so often evokes. Since true deconstructive practice 'is always different from itself, always defers itself' (IOW, 103), so the activist looking for *decisive* and *consistent* prescriptions can only recoil in frustration. Spivak anticipates this frustration, of course, and generally thinks it adequate compensation in its own right: 'my project is the careful project of un-learning our privilege as our loss [...]; all of us who can ask the question of specificity, all of us who can make public the question of feminist practice, in fact have been enabled by a long history to be in that position'.[60] Rather than work to include others within this privileged position, Spivak often labours to undo it from within. What is gained in so doing, presumably, is proximity to those excluded by 'the question of specificity'. The singular, wholly incommensurable (non)position of the subaltern is accessed through the equally singular theoretical articulation of incommensurability in itself. (A good example, perhaps, of what Spivak calls the mechanics of 'invagination', a variant on the fractal logic whereby 'what is a part also contains the whole' [CPR, 70, n.88].)

On the one hand, then, Spivak privileges 'non-narrativisable subaltern insurgenc[ies]', whose 'strength is that they're non-narrativisable' (PCC, 144). On the other hand, she privileges an apparently interminable narrative of the critic's own intra-institutional insurgency. The question arises as to what degree the efficacy of the latter depends on the assumed integrity of the former, i.e. its integrity *as* non-narrativisable or unpresentable. For it is because the subaltern cannot begin to answer the question, 'from which subject-position do I speak?', that the critic cannot interrupt her own response to that same question. It is because the postcolonial critic entertains *no relation with* the (unpresentable) subaltern object of inquiry that the critic's self-reflexive discourse 'about' the subaltern obtains effectively unlimited prescriptive power – unlimited, that is, by the burdens of transitive explanation or interpretation.[61]

Assuming that 'the emancipatory project is more likely to succeed if one thinks of other people as being different; ultimately, perhaps absolutely different' (PCC, 136), Spivak very logically concludes that the notion of explanation itself is suspect. 'Explaining, we exclude the possibility of the *radically* heterogeneous' (IOW, 104). Like the Lyotard of *Le Différend*, she seems to see the principal role of theory as a bearing-witness to an essential incommensurability beyond communication. Rather than *judge* different claims to political agency, Spivak aims her critique at the suspension of all such claims, through various demonstrations of catachresis. 'A concept-metaphor without an adequate referent is a catachresis': examples include 'nationhood, constitutionality, citizenship, democracy, even culturalism' (OTM, 60). According to Spivak, 'no *historically (or philosophically)* adequate claims can be produced in any space for the guiding words of political, military, economic, ideological emancipation and oppression [...]. This is what it means to say "the agenda of ontocultural commitments is negotiable"' (OTM, 63, my emphasis). In the apparent ease of this parenthetical shift from the 'historical' to the 'philosophical', the very possibility of emancipatory politics is eliminated at a stroke. Every universalising prescription – every assertion of egalitarian justice, every militant innovation 'in the name of all – is condemned in advance. (It is this same logic, presumably, that allows her to say, elsewhere, that 'we must [...] study the various cultural systems of Africa, Asia, Asia-Pacific and the Americas *as if* peopled by historical agents' [OTM, 278, my emphasis].)

(iii) Now it is certainly true that Spivak's most recent work indicates something of a shift in priorities. The argument that Spivak restricts or perhaps even eliminates 'the space in which the colonised can be written back into history' no longer holds up quite the way it did ten years ago.[62]

Among the recurring themes of Spivak's latest essays and interviews are the critique of 'Development' with a capital D ('an alibi for exploitation'),[63] the global division of labour, the manipulation of homeworking, the situation of indigenous women, the imposition of genetic engineering and population control, the pursuit of 'ecological justice', and a sense of 'sacred Nature'.[64] Her recent definition of 'transnationality' as an effect of 'the financialisation of the globe' and the cause of an 'increased migrancy of labour' has as much in common with Ahmad as it does with Bhabha.[65] Today, Spivak says, 'I'm trying to learn from real subalternity', informed by an awareness of what is involved in 'hard-core economic resistance'.[66] Most of Spivak's readers may also be glad to know that her 'words are becoming simpler'.[67] The pragmatic emphasis of these recent essays is such, indeed, that it is probably mistaken to search them for anything like a 'postcolonial theory' as such: they consist of little more than strings of broadly consensual ethico-political principles linked by a jumbling of anecdotal illustrations and allusions.

Nevertheless, the persistence of a singular orientation governing this otherwise eclectic body of work is suggested by Spivak's investment of the two 'impossible' poles of her new 'affirmative ethics', an orientation broadly in line with 'Derrida's work on the ethical, on justice and the gift' and Nancy's reinscription of 'the categorical imperative [a]s the mark of alterity in the ethical'.[68] At the microscopic end of the spectrum, she seeks 'an unascertainable ethical singularity that is not ever a sustainable condition'. At the other, properly cosmic extreme, she pursues 'the perhaps impossible vision of an ecologically just world'.[69]

In the first case, at the level of individual encounter, Spivak directs her readers to 'establish an ethical singularity with the woman in question [...]; the impossible project of ethical singularity, woman-on-woman, is the only way we teach, and learn'.[70] Very precisely, *an ethical position must entail universalisation of the singular* (OTM, 165, my emphasis). Her precise qualification of this effort should be taken literally: 'no amount of raised-consciousness fieldwork can even approach the painstaking labour to establish ethical singularity with the subaltern.'[71] She sets this unattainable goal as the only real test of any valid political intervention. 'Most political movements fail in the long run because of the absence of this engagement. In fact, it is impossible for all leaders (subaltern or otherwise) to engage every subaltern in this way, especially across the gender divide. This is why ethics is the experience of the impossible' (270). Once again, organised political mobilisation would seem to be doomed in advance.

At the other end of the scale, a similar condition constrains what Spivak calls 'an impossible global justice' (SR, 274). Why impossible? Because 'the non-Eurocentric feminist and ecological movements [...] are largely uninterested in state power […]; the non-Eurocentric, globe girdling movements or surges are not interested in state power on the model of some Eurocentric older New Social Movements.'[72] Deprived of an effective mechanism to implement their demands, these movements must rather cultivate an appreciation for the 'sacred' through a 'traffic with the incalculable'. They show us 'how to learn and construct a sense of sacred nature', how to 'open our minds to being haunted by the aboriginal'.[73]

There is very little, strictly speaking, *between* this singular 'incalculable' (of nature as a whole) and the equally incalculable 'responsibility' of an individual encounter with the subaltern. At both ends of the scale, impossibility emerges after the evacuation of any viable *relation* as such (among individuals, between nations). At both ends of the scale, reflection is oriented toward 'the singular and unverifiable margin' that both discloses and refracts the (non?)presence of the 'wholly other' (CPR, 175). On the one hand, Spivak prescribes a micro-politics condemned to fail in its pursuit of an unattainably absolute empathy with its beneficiary, a situation much closer to what Levinas calls the 'relation without relation' of an *absolute* ethical responsibility than to any sort of collective solidarity.[74] On the other hand, she calls for a macro-politics that deliberately denies itself the only available instrument with the power to implement and enforce the sort of environmental and social reforms she aims to promote, i.e. control of the nation-state. Any political engagement, in these circumstances, must indeed appear 'contradictory and aporetic'.[75] Combining the two strands of Spivak's recent work together, we are left with little more than the vague evocation of 'an impossible social justice glimpsed through remote and secret encounters with singular figures'.[76] There can be few better descriptions of the peculiarly postcolonial agenda.

In keeping with Bhabha and Spivak's example, and often bolstered by the additional inspiration of Deleuze and Guattari,[77] postcolonial studies now deserves to be recognised as the most ambitiously singular of all contemporary critical methodologies. in every postcolonial study worthy of the name, 'any carefully delineated border of periphery and metropole, colony and empire becomes blurred, de- territorialised, and unbounded'.[78] For instance, what Ashcroft calls the postcolonial 'poetics of transformation recognises the myth of parent and child, trunk and branch, stream and tributary by which the post-colonial is marginalised, and replaces it with a Deleuze and Guattari perception of the rhizomic nature of discursive power and resistance'.[79] The resulting 'excess of hybridity' ensures that 'being is firstly and above all else conveyed beyond all circumscribing restrictions'.[80]

Arjun Appadurai's much-cited article, 'Disjuncture and Difference in the Global Economy' [1990] provides a usefully compressed illustration of the general postcolonial perception of the world.[51] First and foremost, 'the new global cultural economy has to be seen as a complex, overlapping, disjunctive order' (328). The emphasis is on the heterogeneity and fluidity of the multiple landscapes and technologies in which we live. Particular attention goes to 'diaspora', 'mobility', 'deterritorialised communities and displaced populations' (336). In keeping with the Deleuzian diagnosis, 'the world we now live in seems rhizomatic – calling for theories of rootlessness, alienation and psychological distance' (325). Working to 'free us of the shackles of highly localised, boundary-oriented, holistic, primordialist images of cultural form and substance', Appadurai presents 'the configuration of cultural forms in today's world as fundamentally fractal, that is, as possessing no Euclidean boundaries, structures or regularities' (336–337). Any 'comparative work which relies on the clear separation of the entities to be compared' is to be avoided in favour of 'a human version of the theory that some scientists are calling "chaos" theory'. Only a singular theory of 'cultural "chaos"', it seems, is 'adequately global' (338). The final sections of the following chapter will provide ample corroboration of the point.

II Postcolonial specifications

The authority of Bhabha, Spivak and their supporters has not gone unchallenged, of course. Critics suspicious of the incursion of 'high theory' into the study of very concrete forms of oppression and resistance have responded with increasingly strident calls for still more 'context-specific' alternatives. Attacks on postcolonial theory, on the grounds that it 'downplays multiplicities of location and temporality'[52] are today becoming almost routine. Few critics want to be explicit associated with 'the fantasy of a powerless *utopia* of difference'.[53] Eschewing Derrida in favour of 'theories that emphasise the embeddedness of every utterance in its particular social contexts' – most significantly the theories of Mikhail Bakhtin, Michel Foucault and the later Wittgenstein – much of the most recent work in cultural and literary studies focuses almost obsessively on 'the means by which differentiation [itself] reproduces the experience of multiple but specific forms of social and political disempowerment'.[54] Bhabha's colonial discourse theory, in particular, has been much criticised for 'totalis[ing] a hegemonic global ideology, neither much tainted by its conditions of production nor transformed by the pragmatics of colonial encounters and struggles'.[55] Bhabha himself, in his more recent work, has foregrounded the universally obsessive question: 'how can we face the task of designating identities, specifying events, locating histories?'[56] In short, for many readers of postcolonial literature the need 'to grasp the specificity [...] of the location or the moment'[57] appears just as urgent – and just as uncertain – as ever.

35

It is a peculiar situation. By preserving on the lexical singularity of *the* postcolonial, while so often insisting that 'the heterogeneity [of the postcolonial] must regularly and arduously be affirmed',[88] postcolonial critics have devised an almost purely self-generating debate. The play of assertion and refutation between the heterogeneously postcolonial and the homogeneously postcolonial is eminently predictable. From these sterile premises we encourage only such bland 'conclusions' as this declaration of principle from Rajeswari Mohan: 'it is precisely the historical situatedness of post-colonial texts and their complex articulation within postmodern, nationalist and oppositional discourses that make them subversive – and interesting – in a multipronged fashion'.[89] How long interest and subversion of this kind is likely to last is hard to gauge. There is something profoundly paradoxical about what Laura Chrisman applauds as the growing 'materialist awareness of, and concern with (institutional, regional, professional, socio-economic), "locations" in which post-coloniality is produced and circulated'.[90] It is tempting to read such insistence on particularity, on 'the ways in which the meaning of the term [postcolonial] shifts across different locations'.[91] as little more than a compensatory strategy that reinforces the singular status of the postcolonial by conserving the symmetry of an internal tension: to the virtual Unity of *the* postcolonial corresponds the multiplicity of its actual expression.

An obvious alternative to bracket all these abstruse theoretical problems and simply stress the 'dense specificity' of the groups included in the formerly undifferentiated category of the 'Other'.[92] This is certainly one of the more popular critical choices being made in current research. But the equally obvious danger risked by these recent calls for specification is a retreat back to the kind of *specified* essentialism the postmodern and post-colonial projects set out to dethrone in the first place.[93] What guides the move to a postcolonial position proofed against a postmodern 'de-differentiation' usually seems to be nothing other than a still more emphatic insistence on the particular, communal, situated, embedded, embodied, and so on. Ella Shohat, for instance, objects to the postcolonial emphasis on hybridity because 'it comes dangerously close to dismissing all searches for communitarian origins.'[94] From a still less theory-friendly perspective, Bruce King calls for a postcolonial 'literary criticism with a precise awareness of social differentiation', equipped with the 'precise documentation that is needed to "place" a person or text in context'.[95] Again, Elleke Boehmer's recent emphasis on 'the otherness of the postcolonial text', its 'possibly untranslatable cultural specificity'.[96] leads to an almost unqualified affirmation of 'locally rooted and uniquely distinct perceptions' (248) for their own sake. According to Boehmer, 'it is crucial to remember [that] the postcolonial text emerges out of the grit and rank specificity of a local culture or cultures, history or histories' (244).

It is perhaps less of a substantial step than it might seem, from this bland contextual respect to the exuberantly nativist essentialism of Chinweizu and his collaborators, in their *Toward the Decolonisation of African Literature* (1983). Borrowing liberally from a biological register of virility and vitality and the mythical register of 'home' and 'blood', drawing on the 'absolute energy of the African oral poetry which is so firmly and deeply rooted in the African home soil', Chinweizu et al. affirm African literature as 'an autonomous entity separate and apart from all other literatures'.[97] A series of automatic prescriptions follows: a true African art must reflect and transcribe the immediate reality of African life (240), must be clearly accessible to a popular audience (243), must be consistent with 'tradition' (247–248, 264), and must be judged *pre-eminently* by its contributions to the society's thoughts and understanding' (303). Decolonisation along these lines is fully in line with Herder's cultural-nationalist prescription: 'the idea of every indigenous culture is confined to its own region'.[98] Even Ngugi wa Thiongo's more nuanced call for a 'decolonisation of the mind' – by reducing the gap between cultural representation and its immediate referent – nevertheless invites the deduction of similar conclusions. Ngugi's promotion of a firmly national theatre that represents the liberated community to itself with a minimum of aesthetic distance runs the unavoidable risk of a new and no doubt ultimately unsustainable conformity.[99]

Countless disavowals notwithstanding, the spectre of cultural authenticity haunts postcolonial criticism at every step. Even a critic as relentlessly suspicious of the authentic as Edward Said can nevertheless find it 'a very great problem' that 'Third World studies in the university are a very different thing from Soyinka or Salih in their own immediately post-colonial situation trying to write a narrative of their experience [...]; decolonising the mind is one thing for somebody who's been in prisons [..., and another for] somebody deciding, well, I'm going to specialise in decolonisation or the discourse of colonialism'.[100] Surely no-one will deny the narrow validity of the point. But Said of all people should know that some of its implications have no place in a genuinely *critical* context. What his comment illustrates is the inevitably awkward status of an academic discipline defined, in part, on highly sensitive and contested experiential territory. Of course it's possible to conceive of any such territory as the property of its actor-owners. Once an issue is specified as worthy of study *because* the property of a particular group, however, then critical inquiry is as good as over.

Honi Fern Haber's slight but representative book *Beyond Postmodern Politics* points very clearly to where this re-specifying trend usually leads. Searching for a 'genuine politics of difference' and a more substantial conception of pluralism, she defends a notion of the 'subject-in-community' against the postmodern tendency to deny both community and subject through the affirmation of an ultimately apolitical 'universal difference'. The possibility of presenting what has been unpresented or speaking in new voices is given with the extent to which we can come to *identify with alternative communities*'. Consequently, Haber advocates 'the creation of empowered identities, not just as women, but as black or Chicana women, as poor women, working women, lesbian or heterosexual women, educated or uneducated women'.[101] By this logic, it is not possible simply to speak, but only to *speak as*, i.e. only to speak as the suitably specified representative of a particular bundle of socio-cultural characteristics.

Nowhere are the general implications of this kind of approach spelt out more clearly than with Stanley Fish's long-standing insistence on the radical specification of 'interpretative communities'. Rejecting the possibility of a 'truth that exists independently of any temporal or local concern',[102] Fish presumes that all interpretations are essentially 'specifiable', determined by the institutions in which we are *'already* embedded'.[103] Such institutions create a 'structure whose categories *so fill our individual consciousness that they [are] rendered as one*, immediately investing phenomena with the significance they must have'.[104] From here it is another very small step to the admission that communication across divergent interests, communities or language games is effectively impossible.[105] Once again, we 'eliminate the subject object dichotomy' (336) only to commit ourselves to a new monism, the monism of an interpretative process wholly productive of both text, reader and meaning (16–17).

In postcolonial criticism proper, perhaps the most interesting example of the new investment in radical specification is provided by Asha Varadharajan's ambitious study, *Exotic Parodies* (1995).[106] Informed by Adorno's philosophy of the non-identical, Varadharajan pursues her mentor's 'desire to return thought to the palpable materiality of the body' and 'the object's resistance to the subject's identifications' (106, 140). The object as Adorno 'defines' it is what cannot be *grasped* by a subject; the non-identical object is 'all that is heterogeneous to concepts'.[107] Adorno's object is inherently resistant to its identification and manipulation by a subject. What is peculiar about Varadharajan's arrangement is that her 'colonised object (the particular)' is nothing other than what most other critics would call the anticolonial *subject*, i.e. 'peasant insurgence' and 'subaltern resistance'.[108] When Varadharajan talks about 'the resistant object' she means 'the racial, ethnic, and feminine object' (xi–xii). Her 'dialectic is no longer informed by the subject's desire; instead, it is animated by the opacity of the object' (74). This certainly ensures 'attention to the feminine and ethnic object's suffering' (xiv), but at the cost of investing this 'object' with the blank, thinglike impenetrability of an absolute alterity – a process uncomfortably reminiscent of what Césaire famously denounced as *'thingification'*.[109] In the

process, 'woman' not only 'ceases to be the agent of, occasion for, or catalyst to masculine self-knowledge'; her project also becomes, 'precisely,
incommensurable with his' (21). It is *as* this incommensurability that
Varadharajan's subalternity takes on an apparent political inflection. Radical specification can have no stricter formulation than this.

The attempt to equate the specific with the simply particular, parochial or
opaque cannot, in my opinion, provide a coherent theoretical approach to
questions of context and situation. It is not enough to harp on about 'the
danger that post-colonial theory may act as a globalising international force
to wipe out local differences and concerns'.[110] Few critics seem to appreciate the very real dangers of *over*-contextualisation. That everything exists
as specific to a situation does not mean that its significance and complexity
is reducible to a function of (or in) that situation; that every event has its
specific occasion does not mean that its significance is exhausted by that
occasion. (Excessive contextualisation, moreover, guarantees and justifies
the very ambivalence so characteristic of Bhabha's insufficiently context-
sensitive theory – the eclipse of decisive judgement in deference to a 'feel'
for complexity.)

Something more is needed, for at least two reasons. In the first place, it
should be obvious that the mere insistence on particularity (on the this-
ness of things) cannot resolve any *theoretical* question whatsoever. Hegel's
famous analysis of the insufficiency of sense certainty settled this matter
once and for all.[111] In a completely different context, critics of historicism
from Claude Lévi-Strauss to Paul Veyne and Hayden White have confirmed the endless divisibility of any particular historical moment or event,
and the consequent incoherence of a pure particularism. Any given event
can be both broken down into an innumerable succession of component
particularities and integrated into ever larger planes of intelligibility and
coherence (personal, temporal, semantic, biological, cosmological...): what
individuates an event is not the mere particularity of its components or
contexts, but the way these variables are *related* together to establish distinctions at different levels of analysis. Radical nominalism is no more sustainable a theory of the particular than Leibniz's hypothesis, in the face of
Zeno's ancient paradoxes, of an *actually* infinite division of things. Taken
together, the philosophies of Leibniz and Hegel confirm that the simple
notion of the 'particular' affords no stable position between the infinitely
small and the infinitely large.

In the second place, unless we are prepared to equate creative expression with the direct reflection of a specified community, culture or some
other underlying reality, we must find a way to account for the specific
without recourse to the criteria of the *authentic* (as measured by fidelity to

cultural origin or norm). Spivak and Said are absolutely right to refuse 'the tired nationalist claim that only a native can know the scene', for the same reason that Sartre rejected the 'criminal line of reasoning [by which] only the Southerner is competent to discuss slavery, because he alone knows the Negro'.[112] The specific must be scrupulously distinguished from the specified. The specified can only define the realm of the essence or essentialist, where the demarcation of an individual (subject, object or culture) follows from its accordance with recognised classifications. The specified, as the participle suggests, extends only to the realm of the passive or the objectified. Whether what is specified is identified as 'narrowly' nativist and particularist, or on the contrary, as humanist and universalist, makes little real difference here. In both cases, what counts is the compliance of actors with a presumed nature, and the consequent supervision of the relative authenticity of this compliance. This kind of position can only lead, however emancipatory its intent, to what Laclau calls 'self-apartheid'.[113] It should not be forgotten that South Africa's own apartheid legislation – the Bantu Education Act is perhaps the most notorious example – was explicitly built on the professed respect for specified *cultural* (rather than racial) differences.[114]

In politics as in science, we should find the courage to stand by the criteria of acultural and impersonal validity. As Badiou insists, '*I* am justified only to the degree that everyone is.'[115] As a matter of *principle*, 'when we abandon the universal, we have universal horror'.[116] So any particular political claim – say, calls for equal rights for women, or for African-Americans – is only a matter of *politics* (as distinct from socio-cultural 'negotiation') if and only if it is defensible within the logic of a strictly generic equality. 'It's absolutely indispensable', Badiou reminds us, 'to support [such claims] on other grounds than the existence of a community of African-Americans or women. The theme of equal rights is really progressive and really political, that is, emancipatory, only if it finds its arguments in a space open to everyone, a space of universality'.[117]

Whatever the political circumstances, the discourse of cultural authenticity or attachment, the *Volkgeist* elaborated by Herder and German Romanticism and later adopted by French counter-revolutionary thinkers and nationalist prophets can have no *intrinsically* progressive connotations. The celebration of a specified cultural or historical particularity provides no adequate ground for any emancipatory political claim *per se*. It is de Maistre's historical particularism that allows his reactionary conclusion that humanity in general does not exist, beyond 'the absolute and general reign of national dogmas, that is to say, useful prejudices'.[118] Likewise, the sort of 'we-intentions' invoked by Rorty and his fellow pragmatists to justify 'the way things get done around here' should never be confused with a reasoned, argued basis for judgements of value or justice. Mere appreciation of the fact that 'everyone is different and special in their own way'[119] belongs to such sophisticated institutions as Sesame Street and McDonald's Corporation as much as to postcolonial theory.

III The Marxist counter-attack

Only a few years ago, Michael Sprinker noted the 'indisputable [...] hegemony in current cultural theory dealing with imperialism of non- and anti-Marxist positions'.[120] Times have changed, and quickly. In the decade following the publication of Parry's 'Problems in Current Theories of Colonial Discourse' [1987], Marxist critics have assembled by far the most coherent and most powerful of the several assaults on postcolonial theory. The general argument is not complicated, and Dirlik makes it most succinctly: 'Postcolonialism coincides with the ideology of Global Capitalism'.[121]

The central postcolonial concepts of hybridity, flexibility and mobility, Lazarus notes, 'are of practical significance only to foreign elite and indigenous comprador classes: to the overwhelming masses of local people, they merely spell out exploitation in new letters'.[122] As its theory has unfolded, adds Dirlik, 'postcolonialism has turned into a repudiation of the possibility of radical challenges to the existing system of social and political relations'.[123] Postcolonial theory, in short, is dismissed for much the same reasons that Marxist critics from Jameson and Anderson to Eagleton and Norris have always opposed postmodern theory.[124]

The most forceful Marxist critic of postcolonial theory remains Aijaz Ahmad. He mounts a three-pronged critique of '(a) the theme of "hybridity", "ambivalence" and "contingency" (b) the theme of the collapse of the nation-state as a horizon of politics; and (c) the theme of globalised, postmodern electronic culture'.[125] He has little trouble in showing that 'dismissal of class and nation as so many "essentialisms" logically leads toward an ethic of non-attachment as the necessary condition of true understanding'.[126] This deracination of intellectual privilege, coupled with new institutional affiliations to replace earlier, more 'organic' connections, helps coordinate the academy with the prevailing international division of labour. The coordination is justified, Ahmad maintains, by the mainly French-inspired poststructuralist and 'textualist' theories that problematise issues of agency and interpretation, and thus undercut the militant articulation of political commitment.[127]

Following Ahmad's lead, what strikes the Filipino activist Epifanio San Juan as 'fatal' is the 'repudiation of foundations and objective validity that undermines any move to produce new forms of creative power and resistance against globalised inequalities and oppressions'.[128] San Juan grounds his critique of postcolonial theory and his affirmation of 'the revolutionary

41

power of native agency' (269) in compelling, detailed accounts of specific situations of exploitation and resistance (Guatemala [31–39], the Philippines [43–50], etc.).

It should be obvious by now, I hope, that I am largely sympathetic to the Marxist case. No postcolonial theorist, so far as I know, has yet composed – or perhaps even *tried* to compose – a convincing response to Ahmad and Parry's critique of hybridity and its cognates. As will become clear in the brief excursus that follows this chapter, I certainly accept most of what the Marxist critics have to say about the *objective* state of the world. As an analysis of global trends, Marxism today is if anything a more powerful explanatory system than ever before. The elementary presumption that colonialism must be understood as 'the progeny of a contradictory [and polarising] capitalist *system*'[129] should not even be controversial. The recent achievements of broadly Marx-sympathetic readings in the fields defined by imperialism and resistance writing speak for themselves.[130]

This doesn't mean, however, that there are no serious problems with the Marxist dismissal of postcolonial discourse. Six such problems stand out.

In the first place, the recurring opposition of history to textuality is overblown. Postcolonialism's materialist critics have always complained about its 'exorbitation of discourse and related incuriosity about enabling socio-economic and political institutions'.[131] Fair enough. Much of Bhabha's work, as we have seen, is flamboyantly guilty as charged. But when Parry objects that Bhabha and Spivak allow for 'no point outside discourse from which opposition can be engendered', she herself can provide no precise description of such a point, any more than she can engage *directly* with the deconstructive notions of textuality or *archi-écriture'* which inspire the postcolonial understanding of 'discourse'.[132] Thus begins an all too predictable debate, one guaranteed to drive the field into a theoretical cul-de-sac. Even in her most discourse-driven articles, Spivak can hardly be accused of ignoring the material and economic aspects of imperialism,[133] and she can always retort that social facts 'are never not discursively constituted' (IOW, 242). There is strictly nothing to be said, at the level of *general* theory, about how much importance critics (political or literary) should accord to rhetorical issues on the one hand and material issues on the other. The balance to be struck will always depend on the problem at hand. It would be as absurd to ignore the colonial context of Mongo Beti's early novels, say, as it would to attempt to *deduce* Spinoza's philosophy directly from the situation of exiled Jews in seventeenth-century Holland. The real theoretical alternative is not between 'matter' and 'discourse' but between singularising discourses on the one hand (which *include* some of the most radical materialisms, Spinoza and Deleuze among them) and specific discourses on the other, i.e. discourses that insist upon the constitutive role of relations between and across all components of a discourse (be they material, biological, rhetorical, social, technological...). Bakhtin and Voloshinov have already provided a perfectly workable Marxist theory of discourse, just as Spivak and Derrida can fairly claim to have developed a concept of textuality broad enough to include most of the things Marxist criticism calls extra-discursive. To argue that distinctly postcolonial discourse *singularises* its 'material', both discursive *and* social, is to say something rather more precise and perhaps more far-reaching than to accuse it of textualism.

A second problem follows on from the first: the tendency to lump quite distinct positions in a single basket called 'theory', to which the inflated charge of textualism is supposed to apply more or less indifferently. This tendency is particularly marked in Ahmad's book, where we find 'Derrida and Foucault, Lyotard and Baudrillard, Deleuze and Guattari' all affirming the 'death of the subject' and the 'the end of the social', and apparently advancing the claim that 'there is really nothing outside language, outside textuality, outside representation'.[134] Ahmad regrets that he has no space to defend his argument, but this is no excuse for making an indefensible argument. How can we read Deleuze and Guattari in terms of an end to the social, when they argue for the *immediately social* investment of even the most private desire?[135] Or as privileging representation, when they do nothing but denounce it? How can we read Foucault as in terms of a death of the subject, when he spent his life exploring ways to describe and escape the mechanisms of administrative specification and social constraint? Ahmad seems to equate Foucault's famous critique of the *constituent* subject (that 'Man' whose face is so memorably erased from the historical sand of *Les Mots et les choses*) with the subject *tout court* (the subject whose *limits*, whose radical indetermination Foucault never ceases to explore). Just because Foucault refuses to *specify* the subject (as mad, as criminal, as liberated, as resistant...) doesn't mean that his explorations of 'technologies of Power' are designed, as Ahmad quite maliciously suggests, to affirm the operation of power.[136] Again, like his Foucault, Ahmad's Derrida 'move[s] postmodernism in the direction of a self-reflexive celebration (one is free to choose any and all subject positions [...] because history has no subjects or collective projects in any case)', thereby allowing us to 'belong in all [cultures] by virtue of belonging properly in none' (130). But when has Derrida ever suggested or even implied that 'one is free to choose any and all subject positions'? What sort of space does Derrida's work really leave for *this* free-wheeling 'one'?[137] When Ahmad says, as if in retort, that it is time for theory to address 'the suppressed questions of institutional site and individual location' (7), he is simply repeating what Derrida had already been saying for fifteen years. As for the idea that 'there is really nothing outside language, outside textuality', this is a position that both Deleuze (always) and Foucault (at least from around 1969) explicitly and forcefully opposed; it is a position that holds only for a caricatural simplification of Lacan and Derrida, and it is quite emphatically inconsistent with Levinas (a major influence on both Derrida and Lyotard). The more mindless kinds of poststructuralism',[1] in short, are the only kinds Ahmad seems willing to engage with.

In the third place, by evaluating postcolonialism mainly in terms of essentially *objective* positions and by seeking to reveal 'the objective determination of the [postcolonial] theory itself by these material coordinates of its production, regardless of the individual agent's personal stance',[2] the Marxist critics of the postcolonial risk reversing the only truly critical movement any general theory of human action can prescribe: the movement from specified to specific. Parry's affirmation of 'liberation writing', for instance, comes dangerously close to instituting a new norm for what qualifies as worthy or legitimate writing on colonised terrain. Parry is clearly right to argue that the anti-colonial and anti-capitalist mobilisations of FRELIMO (in Mozambique) and the PAIGC (in Cape Verde) offer far more in the way of decisive political inspiration than can any affirmation of hybridity and indeterminacy. But when she asks, 'should not the writings of all anticolonial movements be understood as the products of temporal conditions, spatial locations and class interests?',[3] her question collapses the distinction between context and creativity (or between politics and literature) in a way that many artists, *as artists*, are justifiably reluctant to accept. Parry's conception of liberation writing sutures the literary and the political together in a *single* project whose long-term persistence, like that of her 'unified revolutionary Self standing in unmitigated opposition to the oppressor',[4] can only be problematic. More to the point, an emphasis on distinctly liberation or anti-colonial writing refutes only part of the postcolonial case, and the easy part at that. Parry is on firm ground with Fanon and Cabral, but rather less so, say, with Ahmadou Kourouma and Sony Labou Tansi, to say nothing of emphatically postcolonial writers like Rushdie or the later Glissant. The fact that works by these writers cannot easily be interpreted as 'products' of the sort Parry has in mind doesn't *by itself* invalidate the postcolonial agenda.

The Marxist critics of postcolonialism set out, of course, deliberately and systematically to blur the categories of politics and culture: any engagement with literature that does not then foreground its directly 'political' dimension is vulnerable to dismissal as complacent or reactionary. By contrast – again like Badiou, himself no stranger to the more militant forms of Marxism – I would argue that *what happens* or is created in literature must be considered as *a creative process in its own right*, without immediate, specifying reference to the context of its production or political affiliation. However complementary their effects may be in certain situations, as a matter of principle political commitment and literary production should be treated as thoroughly distinct processes. No didactic, Brecht-like coordination of literature and politics should be granted the power to direct or pre-determine the practice of 'legitimate' reading *in general*.[142] There is no universally valid yardstick by which we can measure the quality of literature written in embattled circumstances. Every encounter with a literary text is precisely that – an encounter – and should be treated as such.

Ahmad himself flirts with specification of a different kind. True to his theoretical roots, Ahmad grounds his critique of post-structuralism in an ultimate Historical unity of the kind that Sartre tried and failed to establish in the second volume of his *Critique de la raison dialectique*. Whereas a theory of the specific presumes only certain transcendental conditions of behaviour (as enabling, precisely, a plurality of histories), Ahmad defends 'the aspiration to formulate the premises of a universal history'.[143] His readings all lead back to 'the fundamental dialectic – between imperialism, decolonisation and the struggles for socialism – which in my view constitutes the contradictory unity of the world in our epoch'. Any reading which cannot be plausibly hitched to the third phase of the dialectical sequence is regressive by definition.[144] Ahmad's notion of class (and sometimes national) 'belonging' or 'attachment' is *automatically* specified as 'progressive' by the concrete Historical emancipation to which it contributes.[145] By thus deducing a critical position directly from Marxist prescription or class location, Ahmad preserves a notion of political engagement that is rather more internal to theory than the author of *In Theory* seems to believe. In practice, Ahmad's historical specifications seem to follow a logic little more elaborate than that of chronological coincidence (Northop Frye with McCarthy and Dulles, Bloom and De Man with Kennedy and the Vietnam war, Deleuze and Foucault with the end of socialist revolutionary struggle, etc.). Poststructural textualism, the product of an age dominated by Reagan and Thatcher, thus figures as the ideological culmination of a period of global reaction in the wake of the 'mass anti-imperialist movements of the 1960s' (*In Theory*, 5). The periodisation is at least debatable. Many Anglo-American readers will remember the 1980s as the decade inspired by Gramsci and de Beauvoir – the decade of Greenblatt, Lentricchia and Said, of Showalter and Irigaray, of Eagleton and Hall – in short, of a cultural studies informed by gender, race and social location, rather than rhetoric and close reading. In France, meanwhile, the real period of reaction would be far better described as *post*-poststructuralist; Ahmad forgets that the aggressively liberal *nouvelle philosophie* was formulated on the basis of a general renunciation of *la pensée soixante-huit*.[146]

45

Since Ahmad treats deconstruction, narratology, and 'New History of a Foucauldian kind' as variants of the same reactionary movement – i.e. as all more or less suspicious of Marxism (92–93) – his conclusions are not surprising. But this points to a fourth problem: Ahmad's insistence that only *one* theory can have any general legitimacy. A constant target of Ahmad's critique is 'eclecticism', what he calls a 'market-economy' approach to theory whereby one can swap and adopt various theoretical positions as so many articles of fashion and conspicuous consumption (70–71, 5). Ahmad presents 'Literature, Philosophy, radical Anthropology [and] Political Economy' (93) as if they were all competing for the *same* explanatory turf – as if more of the first implies less of the last. What he doesn't seem to realise is that a 'strict partisanship in the politics of theory' needn't imply an effectively command-economy approach, a sort of zero-sum model in which an interest in rhetoric implies the automatic devaluation of politics.[147] It is perfectly possible to endorse Marx's assessment of capitalist production, and insist on qualitatively irreducible spheres of engagement (Badiou) or the irreducibly equivocal nature of 'the' universal (Balibar), each aspect of which requires distinct theoretical tools.[148]

In the fifth place, since Ahmad is determined to see everything 'from the perspective of socialism as the emancipatory desire of our epoch' (92), it is disappointing that he spends so little time considering the reasons why this desire has been so widely deflected or *repressed*. It was precisely this question, after all, that inspired Deleuze and Guattari's first joint venture in the early 1970s.[149] Ahmad has almost nothing to say about the arguments within French Marxism during the 1950s–'1960s, i.e. the very arguments that contributed to the rise of the poststructuralist theory he deplores: the slow rejection of Stalinism, the partial embourgeoisement of the working class, the seeming dissolution of one all-encompassing History, etc. Elucidation of these arguments would help explain the trajectory of thinkers such as Baudrillard, Lyotard, Castoriadis, Sartre, and even Foucault or Camus, both one-time members of the Communist Party. Not all of the ugly consequences of state-based communism can be attributed to foreign aggression, and by the late 1970s (the last phase of the Cultural Revolution, the Vietnamese invasion of Cambodia, the Soviet invasion of Afghanistan…) it would have been strange indeed if many Marxists had not paused to reflect on the corruption of their ideal. To accuse a whole generation of mere complicity in anti-Marxism without tackling the substantial reasons for their ambivalence is to ignore decades of dedicated commitment as much as it is to dismiss, with the familiar arrogance of hindsight, an all too appropriately anguished uncertainty.

Finally, postcolonialism's materialist critics still seem unsure about how exactly they should develop Marx's own critique of imperialism. There is indeed much to be done before the unity of the global proletariat presumed in Ahmad's conception of History can become a revolutionary actuality. Marx himself, as Ahmad knows better than most, notoriously prescribed a violent but necessary detour through global imperialism as the only means of fulfilling the historical conditions for world revolution, i.e. as the only means of levelling the material differences between different national proletariats. (There should be no need to cite once more Marx's ambiguous words about the 'unconscious tool of history...'[150]). The argument that imperialism remains the necessarily evil means to the desirable end of global revolution has been since reformulated by Bill Warren's controversial book *Imperialism, Pioneer of Capitalism* (1980). Ahmad certainly offers a much more palatable understanding of uneven development than Warren, but he leaves open the question of how exactly national inequalities are to be ironed out, short of the strict condition set by Marx himself (i.e. the *unadulterated* triumph of global capitalism). And none of the Marxist critics of postcolonialism has yet provided a convincing account of how best to *preserve* what Lazarus calls 'the revolutionary transcendence of class society altogether'.[151] It is all very well to say that we must 'break the spell of "universal permanent capital"',[152] but no one has yet formulated a sustainable plan for the 'permanent revolution' that Lazarus and San Juan, after C.L.R. James, seem to posit as the necessary condition of liberation.[153] Indeed, the major theorist of global systemic change has recently concluded that in the wake of China's Cultural Revolution, '"revolution" – as the word was used in Marxist-Leninist movements – is no longer a viable concept. It has no meaning. At least no meaning now.'[154] The twentieth century has proved that the workers have no *intrinsically* revolutionary mandate.[155] However over-enthusiastic the recent dissociation of class from politics may be, even a thinker so vehemently opposed to the post-Marxist trend as Alain Badiou accepts that 'the age of revolutions is over', and that politics 'cannot be rendered immediately transitive to a scientific, objective study of how class functions in society'.[156]

To sum up: while I certainly concur with much of the recent Marxist assessment of the postcolonial trend, I don't entirely accept the suggested mechanics of cause and effect. Capital is only one of several historically significant singularities. To say that postcolonial discourse is just 'one more product of flexible, post-Fordist capitalism'[157] says very little about the work of, say, Mohammed Dib. Nor is it very helpful in explaining how so exuberantly 'commodified' a writer as Severo Sarduy might subvert any possible mode of *production* as such, let alone retreat, in his later novels, to a distinctly non-singular position. Only detailed analysis of the specific relational logics at work in these novels will allow us to tackle such questions with the degree of precision they deserve.

IV Towards a concept of the specific

Inasmuch as 'the main interest in life and work is to become someone else that you were not in the beginning'[15] – to become, that is, someone capable of making your *own* history – the first thing a concept of the specific must present is an alternative to a fully specified historical determination. We become specific, we become *subjects* as opposed to objects, we learn to *think* rather than merely recognise or represent, to the degree that we actively transcend the specified or objectified. To move from the specified to the specific, without yielding to the temptation of the singular: this is perhaps the only general goal that can be ascribed to a critical theory as such.

If the concept is to have any critical value, the specific must therefore be firmly distinguished from both the singular on the one hand and the specified on the other. As Ahmad points out, the prevailing

> tendency in cultural criticism is to waver constantly between the opposing polarities of cultural differentialism and cultural hybridity. We have, on the one hand, so extreme a rhetoric against Reason and Universality, and such finalist ideas of cultural difference that each culture is said to be so discrete and self-referential, so autonomous in its own authority, as to be unavailable for cognition or criticism from a space outside itself [.] At the other end of the spectrum, we have so vacuous a notion of cultural hybridity as to replace all historicity with mere contingency, to lose all sense of specificity in favour of the hyper-reality of an eternal and globalised present.[16]

Certainly, the *equally* specified approaches of nativism and humanism have so long presented their conflict as one of global significance that there has sometimes seemed to be no real alternative position available. Nevertheless there are clear signs that some such alternative is emerging today with new vigour, as a perspective in which self-reflexive, 'distanced' relations between irreducibly interested individuals are held to be constitutive of every situation. This kind of perspective links together, I think, the work of critics like Edward Said, Stuart Hall, Paul Gilroy, Judith Butler, Ernesto Laclau and Chantal Mouffe, to mention only a few of the more obvious names: all share in the effort to demolish notions of human behaviour as specified by an intrinsic essence (class, race, gender or nation), so as to privilege the relations that make different groups specific to each other and to the situation in which they come to exist.

A similar perspective may also finally make it possible to recognise, as Ahmad himself does not, that the decisive contribution of *la pensée 68* – of the generation of thinkers that included Lacan, Althusser, and Foucault – was not so much its *elimination* of the category of the subject as its radical *de-specification*. In no sense did these thinkers obliterate the subjective grounds of autonomy and innovation, understood as a freedom from the constraints of objective determination, social coordination or psychological normalisation: they simply pursued the critique of such determination and normalisation at a deeper level than ever before, at a level that *includes* every specified (every 'normal') understanding of the subject. In a sense, their work testifies to nothing other than the thoroughly *contemporary* redeployment of a quite ancient philosophical insight, and one whose general form would have been perfectly familiar to Plato, Spinoza or Kant – that the process of gaining freedom from determination, of learning how to think, or of becoming a subject in the true sense of the word (for these all amount to the same thing) is always the *result* of a difficult labour of emancipation and critique.

The same presumption underlines the reconceptualisation of the specific in the present study. What is referred to as *specific* here is always strictly distinct from *positively specified* or object-ified characteristics of any kind, be they racial, sexual, cultural, physical. The specific is always specific-to, in the constrained freedom opened by a distance from (rather than absence of) the object. We can say with Sartre, for instance, that consciousness is both free *and* intentional: it is always specific to an object (it is always conscious *of* something), but not specified by it. In the same way, every speaking *I* is specific to a *you*, without thereby being specified as a particular person with particular attributes. More generally, we are always specific *to* but not specified by our situation, at the apparent limit of that relation whereby the actions of any complex organism are specific to its environment, but not determined by it.

By definition then, the specific can only persist as a category of the *subject*, and if it is to be distinguished from the specified it must retain at least some of the characteristics implied by any viable notion of the subject: freedom from immediate determination, the ability to think and innovate, the ability to make a genuine decision and explore its consequences, etc. The specific comes to exist at a critical distance from the specified, for the same reason that every subject comes to exist by standing apart from the objectified. That the specific is subjective simply means that this 'standing apart' is a thoroughly active, altogether non-automatic process. The specific does not pre-exist its distance from the specified, it is itself the 'distancing' as such. The specific *is* a process of de-specification, just as every subject worthy of the name *is* the inventive process whereby it breaks free of objectivation. Although we all have (for reasons that as we shall see can reasonably be called transcendental) the potential to become subjects – i.e. to become free of determination, to begin thinking in our own right – still this process of *becoming* is irreducible. There is no subjective norm, no normal or normalisable state of subjective *being*. Properly speaking, every subject is a process of becoming-a-subject, in much the same way that genuinely spiritual truths are, substantially, nothing other than the process of their pursuit.

There is still no better example of the general logic of the specific defended here than Fanon's thoroughly 'subjectivist' understanding of the process of decolonisation. The actively decolonising subject is not endowed, in advance, with an innate freedom that need only be exposed through elimination of colonial constraints: the subject *qua* subject only comes into being *through* and as a result of the militant process of decolonisation as such.[160] *Despecification* – here the explosion of colonial constraints – *is itself the process of subjectivation.*

On the other hand, of course, despecification as such does not open the door to a *singular* subjectivity, i.e. to a properly self-constituent freedom à la Sartre. The specific subject is always specific precisely *to the relations* that it de-specifies. The subject is nothing other than the conversion of specified relationships into specific relations – the conversion of determination into *relational* indetermination – without appeal to a realm of *absolute* indetermination or pure Creativity. Far from a return to the singular Cartesian or phenomenological subject, specificity always presumes an irreducibly relational subject, a subject both with-others *and* against-others. The specific subject only is what it is – is only a discreet or 'self-identical' individual in any sense – *because* it is a relational process: an active, relational process of despecification.

This relationality implies the constitutive distinction and permanent co-implication of its terms: a subject *becomes* as distinct from, *as* co-implied with or against, the other. I only exist within a horizon peopled by others, and the de-specification of relationships (relationships of determination or automation) is at the same time the active *deciding* or inflection of relations with others, one way or another. The relational subject is inevitably partial, inevitably partisan, 'necessarily for one side or the other, in the thick of the battle...'[161] We might say that an individual becomes a subject to the degree that he or she is able to *take* (rather than inherit or adopt) *sides*, in the most active and deliberate sense. Despecification, subjectivation, and the taking of sides are aspects of one and the same process. This process is relational but, *pace* Levinas or Habermas, relationality itself is not inflected in a particular way. Specific relationality forces a *choice* of inflections. Inflection of a relation is contingent because the status of relationality is itself transcendental of all particular inflections; there is no attenuating the political responsibility of inflecting a relation in a certain way, for good or ill. This is why even the most dispossessed subjects are not determined or coordinated (or silenced, or justified...) by History or its equivalents.[162]

The specific subject, in other words, maintains a relation with others that is neither oriented toward fundamental consensus (Habermas), nor destined for dialectical absorption in a third and higher term (Hegel), nor reduced to the status of a contingent construct awaiting imminent deconstruction (Derrida, Bhabha, Spivak). The specific sustains itself *as ongoing relation*, i.e. as an ongoing *taking* of sides. It follows that when any particular identity ceases to be configured in a relation that is emancipatory *as a relation*, it can indeed become a prison. To consider with Finkielkraut only the most obvious case, we know that 'cultural identity was a means of resistance under colonial rule but became an instrument of repression after the Europeans left.'[163] Even if it is *specified* in the same way, nationalism is one thing when expressed by a hegemonic imperial power and another thing altogether when expressed by an embattled subordinate community. The critique of nationalism as a general concept is less important than an evaluation of its specific, positioned inflection – the kind of national unification it promotes (or imposes), the sort of position it occupies (or affirms) in the global division of labour, the sort of liberation it offers to its citizens (or neighbours), and so on.[164]

V Edward Said, between territory and deterritorialisation

In the post-colonial context, it is the name of Edward Said that is likely to be the most firmly associated with something like a theory of the specific in this neither-specified-nor-singular sense. Like most postcolonial critics, Said works in favour of 'fragmenting, dissociating, dislocating, and decentering the experiential terrain covered at present by universalising historicism', and explores a 'plurality of terrains [and] multiple experiences'.[165] But his configuration of this plurality, situated precisely at the frontier of the singular and the specific, is much the most productive in the field. He strives to see irreducibly 'discrepant' experiences – 'each with its particular agenda and pace of development' – precisely *as* interconnected and 'interacting with others' (CI, 36). He suggests a way of thinking through engagement and cultural criticism that is neither specified by any kind of essentialised identity on the one hand, nor emptied of political content by an ultimately *singular* conception of 'difference' or subversion on the other. He suggests a notion of partisan engagement that is fully specific to the situation concerned, but not immediately determined by the interests involved. He has tried to walk a fine line between Benda's reverence for the disinterested truth and Gramsci's notion of an affiliated 'organic intellectual' (PcD, 195–196; RI, 3–4); his long-standing commitment to the Palestinian cause detracts nothing from his equally firm suspicion, on principle, of nationalist and nativist theories of cultural difference. It would be hard to say if Said is better known for his insistence on the fundamentally worldly and power-driven interests of all cultural expression or for his unflinching adherence to the traditional virtues of a disinterested, broadly humanist criticism. And it would be a mistake not to see in this ambivalence one of the great opportunities or openings in contemporary criticism – a ground-breaking move toward a genuinely specific understanding of cultural relations.

However, it is the difficulty involved in distinguishing Said's specific engagement from an *eventually* or tendentially singular detachment that will hold my attention here, for it points to a cluster of problems which will recur throughout the remainder of this study. Said's critical principles and intentions are clear enough. But for all the suggestive promise of his approach, I will argue that Said has yet to devise a fully viable alternative to the singular orientation that conditions the postcolonial domain. His early work, *Orientalism* in particular, conforms at least in part to a notion of cultural relation as specifying rather than specific. His later work, on the other hand, in its increasing suspicion of 'territorial' allegiance and distrust of 'theoretical' mediation, eventually retreats to a *quasi*-singular conception of Critical authority – a kind of self-validating intuition or insight immediate to the 'living' experience it claims to convey. Over the last twenty years or so, Said's focus has thus shifted from the stringent critique of specifying prejudice to the celebration, inspired in part by Deleuze and Guattari's 'immensely rich book [*Mille plateaux*]', of a 'nomadic freedom' and critical deterritorialisation (CI, 402). Like most of his disciplinary colleagues, Said has come to accept that some 'notion of literature and indeed all culture as hybrid (in Homi Bhabha's complex sense of that word)' provides 'the essential idea for the revolutionary realities [of] today' (CI, 384). It is not entirely clear, in the wake of this acceptance, that his approach can prepare the ground for a fully sustainable, fully inter-mediate notion of critical relationality as such.

The following, relatively involved evaluation of Said's contribution to postcolonial theory thus falls naturally into three parts. (a) an appreciation of his effort to distinguish specified from specific; (b) a qualified critique of his understanding of relation and interrelation, and his consequent ambivalence concerning the role of the state and the status of national independence; and (c) an indication of the ultimately singular orientation of his critical ideal. (It should go without saying, I hope, that Said's literary-critical works cannot be read in isolation from his political writings without belittling the urgent importance of the latter and disregarding an essential principle of the former.)[166]

(a) **Anti-specifications**

As a critic of specified essentialism Said has few equals. He has always argued, in literary theory as much as in long and courageous political practice, against 'separatism of one sort or another'.[167] Since he presumes that 'every cultural form is radically, quintessentially hybrid', so any effort to distil 'a pure race, pure nation, or a pure collectivity' can only involve 'organised discrimination or persecution'.[168] Perhaps nothing is so consistent in Said's work as the critique of what he calls 'murderous essentialisations', the attempt 'to freeze the Other in a kind of basic objecthood' or specified identity.[169] This is why Said, somewhat against the grain of his discipline, sees 'the fetishisation and relentless celebration of "difference" and "otherness" [...] as an ominous trend' [170] On whatever pretext, 'to leave the historical world for the metaphysics of essences like négritude, Irishness, Islam, or Catholicism is to abandon history for essentialisations that have the power to turn human beings against each other' (CI, 276). In Said's own work, of course, the major offenders here are Orientalism and Zionism.[171] But the great national liberation movements of the 1950s and '1960s have not been immune to the same charge. 'Nationalist consciousness can very easily lead to frozen rigidity [...]. The dangers of chauvinism and xenophobia ("Africa for the Africans") are very real. It is best when Caliban sees his own history as an aspect of the history of all subjugated men and women ..' (CI, 258).

Consequently, Said conceives the irreducible ties between political power and aesthetic expression in terms of distanced, self-reflexive 'affiliation' rather than blind adherence or 'filiation'.[172] Unlike many public intellectuals, Said maintains that the only responsible form of criticism is one explicitly affiliated with a particular cause, or political movement; 'there has to be some identification' with a more or less *militant* political organisation.[173] But at the same time, he recognises that if there is a specific role for the intellectual, it is not to 'validate the culture and state of which he is a part', but to assert 'an independent critical consciousness, an oppositional critical consciousness'.[174] Genuine intellectuals must chose 'criticism' and a 'moral sense', the adherence to universal 'standards of truth about human misery and oppression' (RI, xi) above 'the service of power' (CvI, 164) or the security of 'cultural insiderism' (BV, 174–175).

At no point is Said more out of synch with the general postcolonial trend than in his firm dissociation of politics from culture. The *politics* of liberation must never be confused with the consolidation or affirmation of merely *cultural* identity. Under pressure, however, Said has not always been consistent in his adherence to this dissociation. On the one hand, he tends in general to associate everything 'cultural' with the quasi-biological sphere of filiation and blind or defensive group allegiance. He conceives of cultures as primarily 'defensive boundaries between polities',[175] and rarely as enabling or creative structures. He tends to identify, after (and against) Arnold, 'culture with the State', conceiving it as 'a system of values saturating downward [...] from the height of power and privilege' (WTC, 10, 9). It is then fairly easy to move straight on to the apparent conclusion, to twist one of Said's titles, that culture *is* imperialism.[176] In this sense, Said's position might be read as consistent with Badiou's: every truly political process of liberation proceeds through the evacuation or subtraction of specifically cultural issues.

On the other hand, when Said comes to justify the Palestinian demand for a sovereign state, he grounds this *particular* political demand in broadly cultural terms:

> The Palestinians have all the attributes of nationhood – a common history, language and set of traditions, a national culture, national institutions, a national representative [.]. Unmistakably and collectively, the Palestinian people has formulated its own sense of itself and of its future as intending the establishment of an independent Palestinian state on their historical national soil (BV, 290–291)

This logic can lead, it seems, to an argument that seems inconsistent with the whole critique of cultural consolidation – that the cultural and political spheres 'are not only connected but ultimately the same' (CI, 67). From here, it would seem easy to move on to the apparent conclusion that the only means toward genuine political liberation might seem to be a *culture* of detachment and criticism – that is, the sort of academic culture which presumes a pure intellectual freedom as the very medium of its existence, and whose relation to the specifying or top-down variety of culture is not clear.

(b) The ambivalence of affiliation

Partly as a result of this uncertain relation between politics and culture, the nature of a militant affiliation with a particular community or cause can only be as problematic as it is essential. As his friend Michael Sprinker suggests, Said's position has very little to do with the 'ossified anti-nationalism' so vigorously attacked in Ahmad's notorious critique;[177] for more than thirty years, Said has been much the most forceful and inspiring Western-based advocate of the Palestinian cause. The admirable consistency of this commitment cannot mask, however, an apparent inconsistency or ambivalence regarding the decisive questions of *territorial* sovereignty and an independent Palestinian state.

At least some of this ambivalence reflects the unavoidably constrained evolution of Palestinian responses to occupation and dispossession. For at least ten years after the decisive year of 1968, the general goal of the Palestinian Liberation Organisation (PLO) was clear:

> a democratic secular polity for Palestine, in which sectarian or national influences would play no part [.]. The vision of the democratic secular policy was not of one consisting of two separate and hostile communities, but of persons whose individual rights were primary and equal […]. It was fully

realised that this goal conflicted with Zionism and its embodiment in Israel. [... So] achievement of the first principle – establishment of a democratic secular polity in Palestine – could not be realised except by adherence to a second principle – the necessity for armed struggle by the Palestinian masses. Towards that end, the PLO undertook to mobilise and organise the Palestinians.[175]

Under the pressure created by adherence to this second principle, the plan was amended by 1977 to include 'an Independent Palestinian State under the control of the PLO', confirmed in 1981 with an appeal to UN to support 'the establishment of an independent Palestinian State specifically in the West Bank and Gaza' (BV, 256). The story of Said's defence of the Palestinian cause is the story of his ambivalence with respect to these two quite distinct conceptions of a Palestinian state – to the point that it is sometimes quite difficult to tell exactly which usage (communitarian or ecumenical) of the word 'Palestinian' he has in mind. In the main, he has endorsed a *national* Palestinian mobilisation in the occupied territories, if only as an essential means to the eventual secular, supra-national goal. He has written in favour of 'a genuinely unified Palestinian political self-consciousness minutely involved in contemporary history, minutely attuned to the community's slow progress toward self-determination' (QP, 141). He has cautiously endorsed, in the wake of the 1967 war, the emergence of new 'nationalist structures' in the occupied territories (ALS, 112). Most important among these, obviously, has been the PLO itself, an organisation which over the first decade of occupation came to resemble nothing so much as a surrogate Palestinian state (QP, 139–140).

It was not inconsistent of Said, then, to vote in favour of partition and independence at the decisive meeting of the Palestinian National Council in November 1988.[179] From that moment on, the PLO has been committed to the principle of 'self-determination for two peoples, not just for one'[180] – and obviously, 'self-determination is only possible when there is some clearly seen "self" to determine' (QP, 118). Said recognises that 'there is no such thing as partial independence or limited autonomy. You are either politically independent or you are not' (PcD, 29). He knows full well that reconciliation and dialogue are only possible between 'independent' and 'equal' partners.[181] His detailed discussions of the Palestinian situation testify, moreover, to the need of a strong national state on every page. Today's 'reality is a totally fractious, disintegrating community with no institutions at all left. There's no fighting force. There are no social institutions, no health institutions, no educational institutions [etc.].'[182] There is no control over Palestinian territory and land.[183] There is massive unemployment and general insecurity. Above all, perhaps, 'the fault that undermines our society is that its centre, its seat, its fixed point, is always elsewhere' (ALS, 120). The contrast with Israel is galling.

> whereas Israel can roll its tanks across borders, its airforce can bomb civil-
> ians at will [...], the Arabs for their part can only bleat out little squeaks of
> anger [...] Today the problem is Arab powerlessness [...]: we must all of us
> ask why it is that for the past five decades we have watched Israel violate our
> sovereignty, massacre our civilians, humiliate our soldiers and generals,
> colonise our land [184]

It is all the more curious, then, that so much of Said's work is dedicated
to a vigorous *refutation* of nationalist arguments for sovereignty. Only a
year before he spoke out in favour of independence, he declared his opposition to any division of territory: 'the whole idea of parcelling out pieces
for communities is just totally wrong'. More, 'the whole idea of a separate,
differential polity is a travesty of justice'.[185] And no sooner has Said urged
the creation of a strong Palestinian state than he recognises that 'Israelis
and Palestinians are too entwined in history, experience and actuality to
separate, even though each proclaims the need for separate statehood.'[186]
Separatist conceptions of belonging are ideas Said associates with people
who, like Michael Walzer, sacrifice genuine critical distance for 'the intimacy of shared ethnic and familial bond' (BV, 174–175).

Pursuing *this* line of the argument, Said thus tends to present national
'independence' and true collective liberation as mutually exclusive goals.
He attributes the disasters of newly independent postcolonial politics to
the perverse influence of the state and 'national security' issues.[187] Like
other enthusiasts of the new social movements, he now focuses on 'a real
alternative to the authority of the state [..., on] migrant workers, refugees,
urban squatters, students, popular insurrections, et cetera'.[188] He now
emphasises, after Fanon, 'the immense cultural shift from the terrain of
nationalist independence to the theoretical domain of liberation' (CI, 324).
What is involved in liberation is nothing less than 'the invent[ion] of new
souls', the

> reanimating and redirecting [of] an inert mass of silent natives into a new
> inclusive conception of history [.]. Liberation is neither a state nor is it a
> bureaucracy. It's an energy of the sort that, for example, you find when
> C.L.R. James takes Césaire and T.S Eliot and somehow makes them work
> together. That's what I'm really talking about.[189]

Such priorities put the PLO and other national liberation movements
in an almost impossible situation. On the one hand, Said now berates
the PLO for having narrowed its ambitions to those of one territorial
and sectarian interest among others – for having 'betrayed' the ideals of
universal liberation for 'short-range goals such as independence and the
establishment of a state'.[190] This Said would prefer to retain the (increasingly distant?) goal of generous civic cooperation with Israel in one truly

ecumenical, truly inclusive state. This Said continues to defend the idea that 'we can only develop ourselves in collaboration with the Israelis', in keeping with his general prescriptions regarding the hybrid, 'contrapuntal' nature of all identity.[191] Elsewhere, however, he condemns the post-Oslo PLO – and surely with good reason – for its betrayal of independence itself. He calls it 'the only liberation movement that I know of in the twentieth century that before independence, before the end of colonial occupation, turned itself into a collaborator with the occupying force', thereby becoming 'a sort of Vichy government for Palestinians'.[192] *This* Said seems to attack the PLO as *too* conciliatory, too cooperative. He bemoans the fact that after decades of Israeli 'psychological penetration', 'very few Palestinians have the capacity now to think independently. That is to say, there is this idea that we can only develop ourselves in collaboration with Israelis [...]. The will to resist is gone. That is the most important thing of all for me' (P&S, 150). In the end, Said's positions seem to culminate in a plainly double standard: 'I certainly believe in self-determination, so if people want to do that they should be able to do it: but I myself don't see any need to participate in it'.[193]

The parallel with Edouard Glissant's itinerary, as we shall see, is remarkably exact. Both men have for decades been among the most effective and articulate advocates for a losing cause. Although Said can in no sense be said to have given up on Palestine, the general tenor of his recent work has moved away from the more 'grounded' or territorial basis of his earlier polemics toward a dismissal of all divisive, exclusive claims to territory as such. He has certainly recognized the fact that 'the struggle over Palestine is grounded in the land itself',[194] and to this day, he understands that 'the task for the Palestinian people is still to assure its presence on the land'.[195] But over the years, it seems he has come to believe that only a 'contrapuntal and often nomadic' sense of identity 'is fully sensitive to the reality of historical experience'.[196] As distinct from nationalist mobilisation, Said now generally endorses as 'a much more useful and liberating instrument [...], a more unbuttoned, unfixed, and mobile mode of proceeding – that's why the Deleuzian idea of the nomadic is so interesting'.[197] Drawing on Deleuze's example, Said proposes as an eventual alternative to territorial nationalism the possibility of a 'counter-habitation: to live as migrants do in habitually uninhabited but nevertheless public spaces', to live in keeping with 'the spirit's nomadic wanderings' – this is a vision whose 'truth we can perceive on the political map of the contemporary world' (CI, 402).

Whether there is any real place on this new map for an independent Palestinian state is another question. In the meantime it would seem that in much of Said's recent work, many of the obviously negative features of Palestinian experience, including 'discontinuity', 'dispossession', and 'exile', have been effectively rehabilitated as *positive* aspects of a new 'travelling' order.[198] 'Unlike the potentate who must guard only one place and defend its frontiers, the traveller crosses over, traverses territory, and abandons fixed positions, all the time.'[199] It's as if Said wants to revalue as a general matter of theoretical *principle* the peculiar argument so often used by the Israelis to justify the practical expulsion of the previous inhabitants of their territory – the reduction of the Palestinians to the status of 'inconsequential nomads' indifferent to the land (BV, 3, 240). In lieu of an apparently unattainable national independence and security, Said seems to have settled for the ambiguous pleasure of 'crossing borders', the 'deprivations and exhilarations of migration' (CI, 373). Glissant and the other writers considered in this book have accepted, as we shall see, much the same sort of compensation.

(c) **Contrapuntal singularity and immediate criticism**

In what sense can this deterritorialising movement be called a shift from specific to singular? Surely, Said might respond, the 'hybrid' and the 'migrant' are nothing if not relational categories?

Consider Said's most distinctive contribution to the postcolonial lexicon: the notion of *counterpoint*. Said sees 'cultural identities not as essentialisations [...] but as contrapuntal ensembles, [... since] no identity can ever exist by itself and without an array of opposites, negatives, oppositions' (CI, 60). His use of the word goes back to his first publications.[200] Its origin is musical: 'in the counterpoint of Western classical music, various themes play off one another, with only a provisional privilege being given to any particular one; yet in the resulting polyphony there is concert and order, an organised interplay.'[201] Obvious relational connotations aside, what I think properly singular about this arrangement, in the first place, is the fact that this order emerges from only one perspective, the perspective of the *whole*. Counterpoint is 'the tying together of multiple voices in a kind of disciplined whole', as distinct from their 'simple reconciliation'.[202] Said opposes 'the contrapuntal lines of a global analysis' to the merely '*partial* analysis offered by the various national or systematically theoretical schools' (CI, 385, my emphasis). The global harmony emerges only at a distance from any particular theme. The person supplied with the sort of critical and aesthetic distance required to 'juxtapos[e] experiences with each other, letting them play off each other' (CI, 37), is clearly not in the same sort of position as the enthusiastic partisan of any one such experience. Where the militant partisan labours to blend various groups into an effectively united organisation, the contrapuntal critic 'submit[s] composite, hybrid identities to a negative dialectic which dissolves them into variously constructed components' (CI, 378). Counterpoint naturally lends itself to a contemplative rather than a militant stance; indeed, it eventually tends toward 'self-contemplation',[203] a *self*-variation little different, in the end, from the 'impossible union' of disparate allegiances.[204]

The underlying singularity of the contrapuntal configuration also emerges in the way Said invests it with the power directly to *orient* all particular themes toward this same global coordination. Contrapuntal criticism is not only a good strategy for dealing with cultural difference, it is also consistent with our hybrid *nature*. 'Our *truest reality*', Said believes, 'is expressed in the way we cross over from one place to another. We are migrants and perhaps hybrid in, but not of, any situation in which we find ourselves.'[205] From the form of counter-point, from the fact of historical inter-connection, Said seems to deduce something like the *automatic* rejection of a politics of 'blame' and antagonism (CI, 19). Once again, it is one thing to say that all identities exist in relation to others (this is the very definition of the specific); it is quite another thing to say that, *as a* result, all identities should conceive of themselves as fluid, contingent, or, that all should act in keeping with a method Said defines as 'collaborative or cooperative'.[206] This is a move that no theory of the specific should ever allow itself to make. 'Crossing-over' and 'staying-put' are both *equally* specific, equally relational – and 'collaboration', as the political history of the term bears out, is not always the preferable option. It is far from clear that progressive causes are always best served by 'an alternative both to a politics of blame and the even more destructive politics of confrontation and hostility' (CI, 19). Any decision between militant opposition or conciliatory tolerance should be purely a matter of *political* principle and strategic value; there can be no deriving the criteria of such value from the indifferent medium of the specific itself. In trying to deduce his conciliatory political principles directly from his contrapuntal conception of culture and identity, Said can only restrict the properly political realm of argument, decision and responsibility.

What has profited from this restriction, as several of Said's more cynical critics have pointed out, are the rather more nebulous values of humanity and individuality, along with the 'critical' sensitivity that expresses them with a minimum of 'theoretical' mediation.[207] Said has long understood that the 'irreducible subjective core [of] human experience [...] is not exhausted by totalising theories' (CI, 35). Few readers would argue the point. What many have had trouble accepting is the idea that the practice of *criticism* is somehow peculiarly sensitive to this core. Criticism, as Said conceives it, eschews the generalisations of theory so as to tap into 'the existential actualities of human life' and enable 'direct encounters with the human'.[208] Criticism is directly open to 'the hybridising intrusions of human history' (CI, 115). It is 'immediate' to the 'untidy' singularity of life itself. Criticism implies 'immediacy, basically.' It is 'relatively free of ideological pollution of one sort or another. Because it's just itself'.²⁰⁹ More, as if by singular prescription, 'criticism *creates* its subject matter' (WTC, 154, my italics): 'all of the major critics now writing [in 1983] make themselves over into critical instruments, as if from scratch' (WTC, 146). Criticism *is* that singular abstraction from established positions that makes itself open to a radical multiplicity of unpredictable possibilities (WTC, 247). It draws its force from its principled transcendence of cultural location. 'Its identity is its difference from other cultural activities and from systems of thought or of method', its refusal of all 'special interests' (WTC, 29). The critical intellectual, by extension, is *essentially* an 'outsider and exile', a 'migrant' by vocation.²¹⁰ Criticism, in other words, claims its power from its own autonomy, its own self-constituent authority, as if through an affirmation of the logic of Bourdieu's *champ littéraire*. What is Said's migrant, travelling critic if not – after Sartre's *pour soi*, Lacan's *phallus*, Derrida's *différance*, Deleuze's *aleatory point* – another version of that paradoxical power which is never in its place, that power which makes of its singular placelessness the sole 'foundation' of its own, infinitely varied expression?

Said's predominant interest, then, is not so much in the specific as such, as in an *almost* singular dis-interest. Liberation has become something like a singular project, isolated from relation at either end of the scale – a project unlimited, that is, by workable relations *with* others. Where he once saw himself as in 'the thick of a tremendous battle', Said is now generally more concerned with the private integrity of an individual's aesthetic or critical experience on the one hand and the disinterested 'production of the universal'²¹¹ on the other. In short, if the burning question of Said's earlier work on Palestine was: 'by what moral or political standard are we expected to lay aside our claims to our national existence, our land?' (QP, xxxv), then to a limited but nevertheless troubling degree, at least one aspect of his more recent theoretical work might be interpreted – though certainly against the grain of its explicit intent – as providing an outline of precisely such standards.

Obviously, the 'specificity' of any particular literary project has to be considered case by case. The broad theoretical interest of the writers studied in this book is that they illustrate, with an extraordinary subtlety and precision, the elusive yet fundamental frontier between the singular and the specific as general categories of individuation and relation. Glissant and Dib, for instance, both begin as embattled cultural nationalists, in almost perfect illustration of Said's most militant prescriptions. Their more mature work, however, soon veers into the giddy, vertiginous singularity more characteristic of Blanchot's 'essential solitude' or Deleuze's 'deterritorialisation' – the sort of writing more easily aligned with Bhabha and

Spivak than with Fanon or San Juan. At its limit, their work transcends the realm of the specific altogether, and with it the realm of relationship, of interest, and of engagement in the broadest sense. Just how this shift is diagnosed and received says a great deal, I think, about current critical expectations among the Western readers of these writers. It may be that Johnson's work is celebrated in comparable terms, by and large, precisely because he never wavers in his fidelity to a realm defined by just such transcendence – a properly u-topian realm of racial reconciliation achieved 'above' the constraints of any possible historical negotiation. The great interest of Sarduy's itinerary, by contrast – and the reason for the relative length accorded to my chapter on his work – is that, having written perhaps the most unambiguously singular novels of any Latin American author, his last works return, quite unexpectedly, to the frontier of a clearly specific (and minimally specified) domain, the domain of a dogged relation with disorientation and disease.

The importance of this return will only begin to emerge after a detailed demonstration of just how far postcolonial writing can go in the opposite direction. This demonstration quite properly begins with an analysis of one of the most prolific champions of postcolonial discourse, whose work is only beginning to get the general attention it deserves – Edouard Glissant.

A POSTCOLONIAL WORLD?

This is emphatically a book about literature and postcolonial theories of literature. But it is also part of an argument against the picture of the world advanced in most of these theories, as well as a defence of the view that any creative expression is irreducibly specific to (though not specified by) the situation of its articulation. Before moving on to consider the work of a writer who has made revealing and far-reaching claims about what he calls the *tout-monde* or 'whole-world', it is worth pausing briefly to remember a few elementary things about the world he purports to describe.

We know that postcolonial theory presents the world as 'a single place with systematic properties',[1] a 'single system' become 'increasingly centre-less, and featuring a multiplication of interacting parts that are increasingly fragmented and unstable'.[2] According to perhaps the most accomplished survey of postcolonial theory to date, today's '"centre" is just as heterogeneous and unstable, in terms of its class, gender and even (now) ethnic identities, as the "periphery"'; both positions are 'shifting' and are 'potentially almost infinitely complex'.[3] Everyone can recognise, certainly, the results of a growing 'inter-connection and inter-dependence' of diverse *cultures*.[4] There can be no doubting that, compared to earlier times, cultural production has been progressively uncoupled from its earlier territorial and social moorings, 'released from its traditional determinism in economic life, social class, gender, ethnicity, and region'.[5]

The presumption of an increasingly borderless world, however, is another matter altogether.[6] Global capitalism is no doubt the most aggressively singularising force the world has ever seen. But like any singularity, its operation is *hierarchical* through and through: it proceeds through the exploitation of differences and gaps, and its impact has proved every bit as polarising as Marx predicted. Segregation by poverty, insecurity and lack of opportunity – both internationally and intra-nationally – is probably more severe today than ever before. A recent global study of the current 'age of transition' confirms, contrary to postcolonial expectations, the 'systemic and ongoing peripheralisation, within the capitalist world-economy, of most of the world's peoples and production processes'.[7] The result has been an ever-growing inequality in 'world welfare' (236) and ever more 'austere living for the majority of the world's people' (118). Shifts in the ratio that measures the gap between the incomes of the richest and the poorest countries speak for themselves: estimated at roughly 3 to 1 in 1820, it rose to 35 to 1 in 1950, 44 to 1 in 1973, and 72 to 1 by 1992. In 1999, the total income of the 582 million people in all the so-called 'developing' countries ($146 billion) amounted to just over 10 per cent of the combined wealth of the world's 200 richest individuals ($1,135 billion). Life expectancy in impoverished countries like Sierra Leone has fallen to 38 years, exactly half of that in the richest nations.[8] Two-thirds of the sub-Saharan African population are now said to live in standards below those of the colonial period,[9] while every year some sixteen million of the world's children die from hunger and curable diseases.[10]

After the disappointment of revolutionary hopes in Chile, Iran, Nicaragua, Angola and Vietnam, in the wake of Soviet collapse and Cuban isolation, following the eclipse of any powerfully organised political alternative to capital, our age has surely been marked *above all else* by the emphatic confirmation of class differences at both the national and the international level. In a damning reflection of this situation, there is now no more significant a political issue in the wealthier nations than the ominously named 'immigrant question', a 'problem' which is nothing other than justification for the explicit reinforcement of borders.

Indeed, contrary to its conventional presentation, *contemporary* globalisation should be understood, in line with Ankie Hoogvelt's compelling analysis, as an increasingly 'implosive' process. As globalisation proceeds,

> ever larger segments of the world population, both inside the advanced countries but more numerous still inside the Third Word, are being expelled from the emerging 'thickening' network of human social and economic interaction. Rather than being an expansive process, the present process of globalisation appears to be an imploding or shrinking one.[11]

The result is that the economic relation of periphery to core has evolved from 'structural exploitation to structural *irrelevance*'.[12] Since 1982, when the debt crisis first began, the International Monetary Fund IMF and the World Bank have coordinated the economic re-orientation of the developing world in favour of an ever more efficient extraction of wealth for the benefit of first world creditors, share-holders and pension funds. Only five

years later, the *net* financial transfers from developing to developed countries already amounted to $250 billion (a sum four times larger, in real
terms, than the Marshall Aid provided by the United States to Europe after
World War Two).[13] As Hoogvelt points out, 'the scope and detail of the com-
bined IMF conditionality rules and the World Bank structural adjustment
contracts have amounted to a degree of economic intervention in the
debtor countries which matched, perhaps even exceeded the direct administration of bygone colonial governments' (167). For these 'adjustments' are
designed to undermine every aspect of life in the debtor nation that might
prove an obstacle to its conversion into the profitable plaything of international investment (including price regulations, minimum wage measures,
trade union rights, public spending, subsidies on food, the retention of
nationalised assets, etc.). In Africa as in so much of the world, the results
have been all too unambiguous. Over the 1980s, the terms of trade for
the principal sub-Saharan commodities collapsed while per capita incomes
fell by as much as a third; drastic reductions in the power of many states
to do anything more than purchase weapons and pay off bandit armies
has led to renewed civil wars, while any serious pretence at economic
development has largely been replaced by the cynical and aggressively
apolitical organisation of 'relief'.

In short, postcolonial theory emerged as the dominant paradigm for
understanding collective 'struggle' over the same years that witnessed the
massive and sustained asset-stripping of the third world. The properly
political value of this theory needs to be assessed in terms of the way it
responds to *this* situation.

More than anything else, this response undercuts the very possibility of
adopting a *specific* political position with respect to global trends. Instead,
like multinational companies before them, broadly postcolonial theories
generally look for ways to articulate the local and the global directly
together, as facets of one and the same singular configuration. 'The locali-
sation of globality'[14] and the 'universalisation of particularism'[15] figure as
symmetrical, inverted expressions of a single tendency. As Robertson
argues with particular force, globalisation is nothing other than 'the inter-
penetration of what are conventionally called the global and the local, or –
in a more abstract vein – the universal and the particular'.[16] What is becoming truly global, Robertson argues, is the universal compulsion – itself the
product of properly systemic pressures – to affirm local particularity and
uniqueness, through a kind of universal 'micromarketing' (29). Examples of
the consequent 'glocalisation' include global patterns of suburbanisation
and neighbourhood valorisation, global organisations to promote the values and identities of native peoples, the global tailoring of transnational
commodities to 'increasingly differentiated local markets' (28), and so on.

Even the 'critical localism' proposed by one of postcolonialism's most vigorous critics (Arif Dirlik) as a response to precisely this sort of 'guerrilla
capitalism', a response inspired by 'indigenous struggles' and based on
'local and particularistic' social movements, deliberately risks a dangerous
coordination with transnational capital.[17]

Once the local is *immediately* articulated with the global, there is little
space from which to prescribe the distanced imposition of political principle. Immediate articulation of the local with the global excludes the specific in advance (and with it, as we shall see, the 'universalisable'). What
exactly has happened to the once intermediary form, the collective, trans-
local form par excellence – the nation-state? The evolution of Glissant's
work provides, with unparalleled clarity and depth, an answer to this question which echoes the postcolonial trend as a whole.

2

EDOUARD GLISSANT:
FROM NATION TO RELATION[1]

Much of Glissant's work fits the postcolonial agenda to a T.[2] He offers a subtly argued critique of conventional categories of identity and difference, along with densely poetic, firmly grounded evocations of an unusually contested territory. It is this eminently desirable combination of a project both 'post-identitarian' *and* context-specific that best explains, I think, Edouard Glissant's remarkable rise to eminence in francophone studies.[3]

Certainly, the significance of this most emphatically Martinican writer is no longer controversial. His work is regularly compared with that of Edward Brathwaite, Wilson Harris, C.L.R. James, Alejo Carpentier, and Derek Walcott. 'If the next Nobel prize is given to a francophone writer', suggest Alain Baudot, 'it will very probably be given to Glissant'.[4] According to his two most important critics, Michael Dash and Celia Britton, 'Glissant is now the major writer and theorist from the French West Indies'.[5] His only serious rival for the title, Patrick Chamoiseau, is the first to affirm that Glissant is 'our great writer and our great thinker. Everything is there. [...]. *La Créolité* takes place through and with Glissant's thought.'[6] He has certainly written the most substantial francophone contribution toward an assertively *Caribbean* literature to date – an oeuvre including nine volumes of poetry, seven novels, and six books of theory and criticism.[7]

Glissant is famous for his belief that 'every way of speaking is a land [*une terre*]',' that 'every man is created to speak the truth of his land' (LZ, 105). Unsurprisingly, his work has generally been read as a kind of affirmative territorialisation, the empowerment of place consistent with the sophisticated recognition of other places. This territorial articulation seems to develop, moreover, in a sustained *relation* with the other: 'the world, in its exploded unity, requires [...] that each person strives toward the acknowledged opacity of the other' (DA, 13). For Glissant, 'to consent to opacity, i.e. the irreducible density of the other, is to accomplish truly, through the diverse [le divers], the human' (DA, 245; cf. 466). Glissant's work might thus appear to go in the most emphatic terms *against* the singular current described in this book, and toward the affirmation of specific relations-with and between.

However, Glissant's more recent writing makes this affirmation look a little more problematic. He stands today as perhaps the most thoroughly Deleuzian writer in the francophone world. His *Tout-monde* (1993) and *Poétique de la Relation* (1990) provide, in fiction and in theory, an extraordinary tribute to Deleuze's smoothly nomadological philosophy. We know that Deleuze's philosophy presents a radically *singular* picture of the cosmos. His absolute or singular conception of difference is expressly designed to exclude relational or specific conceptions of difference.⁹ In this chapter, I will argue that Glissant's enthusiasm for Deleuzian concepts of individuation is one symptom of a major shift in his priorities. Like that of Deleuze, Glissant's later work begins and ends with the assertion of a single and unlimited ontological Totality, an effectively deterritorialised plane of immanence. To be sure, most of this work is positively saturated with the *terminology* of relation and relativity. The distinction I want to make is to some degree more a matter of emphasis than an absolute break. Nevertheless, I will argue that Glissant's later concept of the *Tout-monde*, or whole-world, is not *fundamentally* relational in the specific sense used in the present study, so much as the medium and expression of a singular whirlwind of self-differentiation and constant or 'chaotic' metamorphosis. Like Deleuze, Glissant arrives at a theory of *la Relation* defined primarily by its transcendence of relations with or between specific individuals.

We must distinguish, then, between early and late moments in Glissant's engagement with the mechanics of individuation and specification. In a first moment, Glissant asserts a specificity defined only by its power to move beyond itself in its mediation of others. He asserts, in other words, a quasi-Hegelian specificity, defined as the coming-into-consciousness of a delegated part of the 'Totality' Glissant everywhere assumes. This moment is organised around the pursuit of a *national* specificity, which should never be confused with a popular or merely empirical specificity (the specificity of a particular way of doing things, what Glissant will call a particular *vécu*). His concept of the specific invariably requires a strict, qualitative distinction between *peuple* and nation, between folklore and knowledge (*connaissance*). Then, in a second moment, Glissant mostly abandons the nation in favour of a kind of self-asserting, self-constituting singular immediacy on the Deleuzian or Spinozist model – an 'already immediate' immediacy, so to speak. *This* is what he calls '*la Relation*'.

67

In short, Glissant first writes for the re-territorialisation of an independent Martinique – so as to celebrate an eventually global de-territorialisation. The long campaign against French *départementalisation* has subtly evolved into the affirmation of a rather more far-reaching incorporation, an incorporation into the univocity of a new world order based on nothing other than constant internal metamorphosis, dislocation and exchange. A matter of emphasis it may be, but the *shift* of emphasis is unmistakable, from an engagement with the constrained relation between and among others, toward inclusion in one all-embracing self-differentiation (which is never, of course, to be confused with mere uniformisation). The end result is compatible with the mechanics of a rigorously singular market of cultural production.

So we must further distinguish a consistent from an inconsistent aspect of Glissant's work. What is rigorously consistent in Glissant's work, early and late, is the end affirmed, the *Totality* that will ultimately subsume the local or the historical. For Glissant as for Deleuze – or Hegel, for that matter – the ultimate goal is *always* 'the search for totality'. 'Let us truly enter into the dialectic of totality' (PR, 30; cf. TTM, 192–193, 196–197). Always, 'poetic language must guarantee a vocation of unity that poetry will oppose to the dispersal of all things' (IP, 61), and 'everyone must earn, in their calm sharing and in the implant of their being, the right to be an actor of totality [*acteur du total*]' (IP, 161). These imperatives are constants. What changes dramatically, however, are the means asserted as appropriate to this end.

In the early moment, from *Soleil de la conscience* (1956) through *Le Discours antillais* (1981), Glissant insists upon the necessarily particular, grounded and conscious *means* toward the universal End. These means are summarised in the figure of a specifically *national* 'opacity' becoming conscious of itself: the nation affirms its specificity, so as to qualify for an eventually post-national expression of the *Tout*. Here, 'a national literature [...] must signify – and if it doesn't [...] it remains regionalist, that is folkloric and obsolete – the rapport of one people to another in the Diverse [*le Divers*], that which it brings to the totalisation'.[10] Glissant's early work remains compatible with what might be called the classically anti-colonial gesture, associated with Fanon and Césaire: the conversion of a passively colonised object into an actively anti-colonial subject. 'We should develop a poetics of the "subject", for the very reason that we have been too long "objectified"' (DA, 257; cf. 198). The preliminary task of the national subject is its own re-possession, the reversal of an inherited dispossession. Up to this point, Glissant's position is broadly consistent with Sartre's well-known conception of engagement: the close articulation of personal (authorial) commitment, literary representation, communal solidarity, and militant social intervention. The early Glissant, like the exemplary authors of Sartre's *Qu'est-ce que la littérature?*, writes an appeal to the *free* and deliberate awakening of his compatriots.[11] The shift from private authorial liberty to universal emancipation is only to be accomplished through a situated, communal intermediary. If Glissant's work is from the beginning oriented toward a 'universal reader', this orientation first takes shape through its *projection* in an inherited 'historical situation', a situation defined by the urgent needs and perspectives of a particular (communal or national) collectivity.[12] Were it not for their fundamental orientation toward an all-embracing Totality, Glissant's early conceptions of nation and relation would be broadly consistent with the notion of the specific defended in the present study.

In the second moment, however (starting from the early 1980s), the specific, national, 'mediative' moment is surpassed, and surpassed almost absolutely. In Glissant's later work, national mediation has become a positive liability in the articulation of a deterritorialised, 'rhizomatic' reality.[13] Now, 'the poet strives to enrhizomise his place in totality, to diffuse totality in his place' (TTM, 122), to articulate 'the infinite and unpredictable variances [*variances*] of the Chaos-world' (TTM, 114). The means appropriate to this second stage are, in characteristically Deleuzian fashion, *immediate* pure and simple. Glissant's poetics of Relation opens directly on to 'Excessiveness [*Démesure*] itself, unpredictable and incomplete' (TTM, 168), caught up in 'infinite change' (TTM, 84). Glissant's work becomes compatible with Deleuze's at the same time and for the same reason that it becomes incompatible with Fanon's or Sartre's. In the process he moves from a critique of dispossession toward its effective affirmation.

It is the shift in Glissant's writing from mediate to immediate, from specific to singular, that is characteristic of the dominant postcolonial trend. What follows is organised in terms of the moments defined by this shift. For the sake of analytical economy I will present Glissant's first theoretical works (*La Soleil de la Conscience*, *L'Intention poétique*, and *Le Discours antillais*) together in one group, so as to extract the essential features of his initial position. *La Poétique de la Relation* (1990) – broadly confirmed (and perhaps partially attenuated) by Glissant's more recent *Poétique du divers* (1996) and *Traité du tout-monde* (1997) – provides the theoretical basis for his later position. The novels, then, can for my purposes be read in terms of the movement from the one position to the other: *La Lézarde* (and *Le Quatrième Siècle*) as affirmative of the initial national programme, *Malemort* and *La Case du commandeur* as more or less despairing of it, and *Mahagony* and *Tout-monde* as broadly affirmative of the new, post-national or 'chaotic' alternative. It should go without saying, I hope, that this evolutionary schema, much at odds with the prevailing reception of Glissant, in no way suggests a sophistication let alone some kind of progress in his work. On the contrary. On balance, I think Glissant's work evolves emphatically toward its radical simplification. The shift from specific to singular always involves the refusal of worldly complexity, not the reverse.

I The critical consensus

The division of early and late proposed in these pages violates the first tenet of Glissant's many admiring readers: the fundamental consistency of his work. Of course, it is impossible to read Glissant and not be struck by the relentless recurrence of certain concepts motifs, themes and characters; his recent *Traité du tout-monde* (1997) amounts, indeed, to little more than a sustained exercise of self-pastiche, an almost wilfully redundant recycling of material from *Poétique de la Relation* and *Poétique du divers*. We might even say that the more open to the tout-monde Glissant gets, the more narrowly repetitive his work becomes, the more everything begins to sound the same – precisely *as* endlessly unpredictable, dynamic, disruptive, creative, and so on… But Glissant's major critics mistake repetition for consistency. Michael Dash, Glissant's most active and perhaps most perceptive commentator, reads his work as an 'uninterrupted internal debate'[14] and affirms a 'basic message which underlies Glissant's entire oeuvre' (45), 'consistent throughout his career' (55): 'Glissant's oeuvre does not evolve […], his major preoccupations are apparent from his earliest writing and return obsessively throughout the various phases of his work'.[15] Of particular interest for my purposes is the affirmation, in most recent criticism, of the continuity which obtains across Glissant's earlier theory and his later collection of essays, *La Poétique de la Relation* (1990). As one summary puts it, 'the principle of relation, the central concept of Glissant's thought, governs the constitution of his work'.[16]

According to Glissant's critics, what is most consistent about his work is precisely its *hostility* to 'Totality' (read Western 'universalism') – and in particular, of course, its hostility to Hegel.[17] It is generally agreed that 'all of Glissant's critical work provides one of the most powerful and most clairvoyant contemporary documents about the right to Difference'.[18] Recurrent keywords include fragmentation, disruption, interweaving, polyvocality. Glissant is applauded as a new and appropriately 'flexible' alternative to the Manichean essentialisms of Negritude.[19] Celia Britton's recent book tells us that Glissant's work is everywhere a struggle against 'the monolithic hegemony of 'sameness' […]; the plurality of discourses is crucial to Glissant's promotion of diversity against the domination of a single universalising truth.'[20] According to Dash, it is now 'overwhelmingly clear that Glissant's work represent[s] an epistemological break with earlier theories of universality and difference that have dominated Caribbean thought',[21] in favour of 'the specificity of lived experience':[22]

Glissant's vision […] demystifies the imperialistic myth of universal civilisation but also rejects the values of hegemonic systems […]. The pull of diversity is so powerful that it is false to establish any notion of poetic authority or of sameness, universality, or a grand supranational vision in order to contain it [.]. His vision of inexhaustible hybridity is an ideological breakthrough.[21]

Jacques André's Glissant, likewise, evokes only a 'evanescent land', 'adrift', one that 'evades all investigation'.[24] Sylvia Wynter's Glissant promotes an 'anti-Universal', the subversion of 'our present mode of being, of subjectivity, the Self'.[25] Again, Barbara Webb presents a Glissant opposed to 'all universalising theories of history and culture. Glissant rejects the "poetics of oneness" implicit in the archetype, emphasising instead the specificity and difference of West Indian cultural expression'.[26]

The actual specificity of this expression, according to the critical consensus, lies in the now familiar concepts of 'counter-poetics', 'forced-poetics', Creole subversion and other 'strategies of Diversion' or *Détour*. That virtually every critic of Glissant has pounced on these notions as proof of his deconstructive and anti-totalising orientation suggests, as we shall see, a certain amount of wishful thinking. Since Glissant's readers generally assume that as 'the function [of Creole] is not to communicate […] but to deconstruct, to subvert', so then Creole and the other *arts du Détour* provide forms of 'linguistic "*marronage*"' through which the 'language can outwit the [colonising] tongue installed within itself'.[27] Oral literature here 'counter[s] the effects of "occidental writing"'; it 'is not obsessed by the Universal'.[28] The folktale is duly celebrated as anti-writing, the 'exploration of lived reality',[29] as a 'disruptive counterpoetics, which undermines transcendental notions of literature and history'.[30] Much of the published commentary on Glissant involves little more than illustration of these subversions.[31]

I will argue, on the contrary, that Glissant is generally dismissive of *Détour*, folklore and Creole as little more than obstacles to be overcome in the constitution of a *national* consciousness; that the specificity he celebrates is never 'popular' or 'lived' but always filtered through a *written*, mastered relation to the particular; that when, eventually, he moves beyond a national consciousness, he turns against even this highly problematic notion of the specific as well.

II Origin and outcome: Glissant's *totalité*

Glissant begins with the assumption of ontological Totality, 'the concrete Unity of the earth', the unity of 'planetary thought'.[32] Always, 'the aim of poetry' is to express 'the revealing unity of the world' (SC, 34). Glissant was one of the first postcolonial theorists to realise that 'the unity of the Whole has for a consequence the nullity of dualisms' (IP, 106). Of course, 'unity is not uniformity' (IP, 61): genuine unity is to be distinguished from a false, neo-colonial universality.[33] But it is utterly mistaken to think that Glissant maintains a simple opposition between unity–totality on the one hand, and difference–diversity on the other. Glissant is adamant: our planet exists only in 'its real and dense totality' (IP, 152), and 'there remains no other depth to explore [...] outside totality' (IP, 16). The early Glissant is categorical on this point. 'The knowledge that [...] truth never sets out from a very concrete point of attachment, that it is measured in similar fashion for all those who seek it [...] – this is the most general, most widespread, most definitive thing I can affirm of Experience'.[34] In the modern situation, 'there are no more individuals, but one unique body turned toward its destiny [...]. Extraordinary opening of the world, and the consciousness, which crystallises, of this opening. Our most immediate power derives from this *lieu commun*' (SC, 59).

Glissant is hostile to Hegel's 'totalising Reason' (IP, 37), then, only to the degree that it is not totalising enough. Glissant 'know[s] that all truth lies in dialectical consummation' (SC, 16). Simply, 'Hegel is himself the prisoner, on occasion, of the parenthesis in which he imprisons the African' (IP, 37-38). Which is to say that Glissant writes an eminently Hegelian critique of Hegel, a Hegel negated and surpassed by a dialectic which includes him. The dialectic is complete only when the *whole* world has become immediate to itself in its concrete, all-inclusive totality (IP, 215–217). It is *because* the world is a totality that it encounters, at every moment, 'the discovery of the disparate, of the fundamental Other' (SC, 60). There is no room to retreat from the other, no '*hors-monde*' in which an isolated individual would *suffice*. Glissant always presumes 'an inclination to the Whole [*Tout*] which we want to be part of (since we discover ourselves in it)' (IP, 160).

Again like Hegel, Glissant goes on to argue that any particular 'individual is only 'total' in its relation to the other' (IP, 61). Why? Because both individual and other are themselves expressive fragments of a virtual totality which, though perfectly sufficient in itself, has yet to be 'actually' accomplished or 'totally expressed'. The virtual totality can be taken for granted 'every poetics engages in it, consciously or not' (IP, 152). The effective actualisation of the *Whole* through *all* its component parts, however, remains work in progress. If, 'outside totality (the realised, normalised relation of the Other to Me) the *Divers* dissolves' (IP, 101), by the same token, the (virtual) totality can only become actually or effectively total through the cultivation of all others. 'What is totality, once again, and through return, if not the relation of each matter to *all* the others?' (IP, 16; cf. 13, 208). In the compressed phrase of *L'Intention poétique*, 'the Other is in me, because I am me. In the same way, the I withers, whose Other is

absent (abstract)' (IP, 101). The constituent parts of the whole must themselves become whole, as parts, before the whole itself can *be* complete.

This conclusion directs Glissant's major effort through to the early 1980s.
'To everyone, the duty to be oneself, integral and integrated (but not assim-
ilated to the other) in totality' (IP, 148). Throughout this first stage of his
work, to come into consciousness of one's place in the *Totality* is to cultivate
one's positioned relation *with* the others that compose this totality. Glissant's project at this stage thus implies the distinction of three elements of
a single process: (1) the composition of a coming into consciousness, (2) the
assertion of a specific *location* of this coming into consciousness (as distinct
from the aspecific nature of the consciousness itself), and (3) the description
of the appropriate *vehicle* of this coming into consciousness, precisely as
that which empowers this location. This last element, the critical agent in
the dialectic, is what Glissant defines as *nation*. I will describe these three
components in turn.

In the first place, coming-into-consciousness is for the early Glissant
identical to *development* pure and simple. 'That which is lived is derisory
to the degree that thought has not corrected it' (SC, 35), and 'to be born to
the world is as much to come into the light of the sun as into the light of
consciousness – it is to be born to History (rather than submit to History)'
(IP, 147). In particular, the *writer* is consciousness incarnate (SC, 28).
Through literary writing, 'the cry of the world becomes word' (DA, 14). But
each *cri* remains – and this is the second point – the *cri* of a particular place.
Glissant's early notion of consciousness retains an emphatic (though not
confining) territorial aspect. He insists at length that 'all science of relation
is incomplete, that is not tied to a place in which
it opens out – and escapes' (IP, 66). Again: 'every being comes into consciousness of the world first through its own world: as universal as it is
particular; as generous and widespread as it has succeeded in becoming
alone [*devenir seul*], and vice-versa' (SC, 18).

The essential thing to understand at this point, however, is that the specificity of 'a land' or 'a world' is never anything more (nor less) than a delegated
moment of the totality. 'The work of art requires a totalising enrootedness
[*enracinement totalisant*]' (IP, 149). To be sure, all component parts of the
totality must be equally well-rooted, and at this point in Glissant's evolution,
'the poetics of relation presumes that each is proposed the density (the opacity) of the other. The more the other resists in his depth or fluidity (without
being limited to them), the more his reality becomes expressive, and the
relation fruitful' (IP, 23). But each can relate to others only because each relation is *already* a constituent element of the Totality that includes them
all; each 'one' can be known only as a contribution to the Whole. That is
why 'to name oneself is to write the world' (DA, 284), and vice versa (IP, 139).

For the same reason, 'the Whole is the requirement of the Diverse' (DA, 190–191). The specific is here that *through which the Whole realises itself.* 'The very concrete knowledge of peoples, their popular consciousness, leads to the knowledge of the universal. So proceeds Unity, nourishing humanity' (SC, 63). Glissant need never describe the relation from part *to* whole as such; the part is already expressive of the whole, from the beginning. Simply, parts can be *more or less* effectively expressive. Parts can be more or less silenced by other parts. Colonialism, of course, is the most dramatic of such silencings (DA, 191). 'The logic of totality: the weight of voices which slowly become our voices'.[35]

Glissant's early theory thus defends a poetics of specific *'accumulation'* toward the whole '[which] allows for the anchoring of the unique, particular, flashing principle of each community in the patience of its soon to be enlightened relation to the Other' (IP, 49). An expressive part of the whole must, at this stage of Glissant's work, remain attached to its point of view, lest it be swept away into a pure chaotic formlessness. We must be attuned to the global 'flux', 'but also remain attached to a certain piece of land, to everyday problems, to the strict moderation of our point of view. Otherwise, we are submerged in our delirium and the world evaporates in the smoke of the absolute disorder it has itself called forth. Art is indeed one of the domains of this fixation [*fixation*]' (SC, 70: with *Tout-monde* [1993], Glissant's poetics of the *tourbillon* will refute this formulation almost to the letter).

According to the early Glissant – coming now to the third point – the appropriate vehicle for a specific consciousness is the nation. The nation is a *terre* become *connaissance* (SC, 54). 'The decisive act, in the literary [as in the historical] realm, consists of building the nation' (IP, 185).

The nation is thus the pivotal concept in Glissant's early writings. 'What is a country', Glissant asks, 'if not the enrooted necessity of relation to the world? The nation is the expression, henceforth grouped and matured, of this relation' (IP, 72). A national 'necessity' follows directly from its status as part of that totality which itself exists necessarily. 'A national literature [...] must signify that which it brings to totalisation'.[36] The nation is that unit of consciousness that 'expresses itself "totally"'.[37] A nation is precisely the *totalisation* of a part of totality.[38] The nation is 'the voluntary effort towards its own self-consciousness which gives rise to the collectivity' (DA, 409), and inaugurates a genuinely total frame of reference. Remember that if 'every poetics is a search for reference', and if the only genuine 'reference is of totality', then genuine 'reference can exist only when those concerned are marked by it without exception' (IP, 191), without remainder. The nation is the vehicle of this collective marking.

Perhaps the most precise way of describing Glissant's nation is as a dialectical version of Leibniz's monad – the part which, very literally, comes to include the whole (which it expresses more or less 'clearly'). On the one hand, monadological or national points of view have no *substantial* existence beyond that of what they include or express.[39] (If we writers, then, 'cry out for those who have no voice, it is their word which sustains us there' [IP, 50].) But on the other hand, the totality has no *formal* existence outside the points of view (or specific consciousnesses) which express it, and here, anticipate it:

> that a consciousness precedes the state [..] which will assume it, such is one of the characteristic features of our situation [...]. Coming later (more 'constructed' and constrained) than the other peoples, we are not born from the slow work of aggregation but literally from the consciousness of our own necessity. Consciousness seems to precede the whole body, but it is being, each time imminent, which in the Gehenna of our history gave rise to the flowering of consciousness. A people, composite, scattered, but inevitable, a culture, innervated, diffuse, but particular and admissible, slowly explode in the unavowed consciousness of their being (IP, 193).

As Glissant put it in the early 1970s, 'obviously, the elitist consciousness precedes the popular consciousness, for this is one of the elements of the constituency of modern peoples [...]. It is [a] problem of going from a period when an elitist consciousness has set forth something in literature to another period when that something is taken up by the masses'.[40] Only then, in a second moment, 'must the author [...] be integrated with a common decision. The *we* becomes the place of the generative system, and the true subject'.[41] (It should be noted, however, that this second moment always appears as *indefinitely postponed*. As consciousness or form, the nation exists only as not yet attained: 'my nation in its duration, its depth, its science and its flavour, remains to be built, and with it my speech [*parole*]. The drama of the world. We are here a few individuals [...], we call for the future nation, and already we can breathe only through it'.[42])

Taken together, the two aspects of the nation, including and included, constitute a 'synthesis tending towards its own unity'; the work of the nation is 'the work of being arousing itself, and being born of its own will' (SC, 15; cf. IP, 202). The question of which comes first? – *conscience* or *peuple*, *pays* or *paysage* – is less important than the indissociable (if not circular) unity of the process:

> The work [of art] risks becoming pale and lifeless [.] if it doesn't receive approbation from its country [..]. In other words, the poem can precede and found the 'reason' of the land, but it cannot live at a distance from its substance and its flavour, which it signifies. In other words: the land must have throbbed at least once in its total freedom in order for the poem, which has signified the land, to install itself forever in its truth (IP, 150)

In the effort to 'assemble a common will, which will forge us [as one]' (IP, 185), Glissant composes himself into existence, *through* Martinique.

What this highly abstract conception of the nation accomplishes is the properly *constitutive* alignment with the writer's consciousness. 'When our people finally speaks our voice will be sure' (IP, 50), because what the people will say can only confirm what the writer has already said. What is effectively excluded from consideration here is the relation *between* the writer's language and the popular language, and this for the simple reason that, according to Glissant, the people do not speak a language. 'The Martinican has no language' (DA, 346, my emphasis). The people begin to speak as such only when the writer shapes their *cris* into genuine words. 'The collective consciousness "forms itself" [when it] is experienced as necessity, [when] it thus expresses itself "totally"' (DA, 397). In its reflexive totalisation, the nation is an 'unanimity' from the beginning (467). Very precisely, 'to represent oneself, to think oneself [*se penser*]: both are simply the very act of unity' (397). The nation is nothing other than this unification. Glissant invariably refers to the Martinican nation with the definitive article. To every nation, *one* consciousness.

III National redundance, dialectical *dépassement*

In keeping with a dialectical conception of things, the ultimate purpose of Glissant's situated means to totality is to accomplish their own redundance as such. Always, 'the Martinican reality can only be understood beginning from all of the possibilities, frustrated or no, of Relation, and of the moving-beyond we make of it [*du dépassement qu'on en réalise*].'[13] Most succinctly: 'interculturality [*le métissage*] as a proposition presumes its negation as a category' (DA, 251). Why? Because 'the intercultural community cannot deny the Other, nor history, nor the Nation, not the poetics of the One. It can only move beyond them [...]. In this way man runs towards an encounter with the world, and he gets rid, along the way, as if of a useless burden, of the weight of his being. But he must have himself in order to reject himself.'[14]

Nowhere is this mechanism of an auto-*dépassement* more obvious than with the logic of negritude (Césaire's version as much as Senghor's). 'Negritude [...] abolishes itself just as soon as being arrives at self-possession' (IP, 148). It is only a matter of when. 'Wherever Negroes [*des Nègres*] are oppressed, there is negritude. Each time that they take up a cutlass or a gun, negritude ends (for them).' Negritude has but one 'possible prolongation: the act by which it moves beyond itself [*se dépasse*]' (IP, 148). Glissant attacks negritude when, *under the appropriate conditions*, it refuses to overcome itself and so remains stuck in a particularism for its own sake.

A similar dialectical redundance awaits folklore, literature, the leader-writer, the nation, and ultimately, even specific relations-with-others themselves.

Folklore decorates the lowest zones of Glissant's scale of consciousness, and is therefore the first to be *dépassé*. Glissant addresses the point most directly in an essay about a national theatre: 'theatrical expression determines itself [*se fixe*] from the expression of a folkloric basis which thereby ceases to be lived so as to be represented, that is, thought [...]. This theatrical expression becomes that of the (total) community because it moves beyond the folkloric basis by assuming it.' In this sense, 'theatre is the act by which the collective consciousness sees itself, and consequently moves beyond itself'.[15]

Genuine *literature*, then, is what wills the nation into consciousness. Once the nation has been consolidated, literature has fulfilled its dialectical role. Every 'poetry has its source in a willing' [*vouloir*] (PR, 49), 'but the will, from being so sustained, eventually negates itself by realising itself. Willed literature destroys itself by accomplishing itself' (IP, 217). As Glissant conceives it, 'there is no art more linked than poetry to the apocalyptic course of human knowledge' (SC, 41), for 'the poem tends toward that indistinction [of language and things] which is not confusion but synthesis [...]. Hence the poem consumes itself in this future. In the very moment which it reaches what it says [*son dire*], it destroys itself' (IP, 89). Why? Again because poetry reveals 'the ever more realised approach [...] of totality' (IP, 63).

As for the *writer-leader*, Glissant asks, 'what help to you is knowledge, if you are not thereby, like your surroundings, overcome [*dépassé*]? Duration has value only to the degree that it is underlined in all, that it is We who live it' (IP, 217). The ultimate task of a philosophy of the *Tout* is 'the dissolution of the individual in the Whole' (PR, 61). While the writer remains, at this first stage, the *only* properly conscious member of the nation-to-be, his eventual aim is of course to establish that collective we in which his individual voice is justified, confirmed, *and dissolved*. 'Perhaps then we must put ourselves as if on the margins of ourselves' (MM, 167). A similar logic applies to the political realm - a logic ignored, Glissant maintains, by a Césaire become *established* 'father' of a dependent, pseudo-national community (MM, 74). The example of Toussaint L'Ouverture provides the inspiration here. Although the people become nation through Toussaint, the process is complete only with the sacrificial dissolution of their leader and 'medium' (MT, 7). As Glissant's Toussaint tells Dessalines, 'the country wants your sacrifice' (MT, 155). He knows that 'my country needs my absence' (126); 'I must go up into the woods for the sake of the general liberty' (20).

The same fate eventually awaits the *nation* itself. 'When the Nation enables itself, it also negates itself' (IP, 216), because 'the consciousness of the nation is consciousness of relation' (IP, 207) and 'relation lives [in] the overcoming [...] of the nation'.[16] For example, in order for Martinique to enter Relation, to become post-national, it had to lose its essential existence as Arawak nation (before going on to lose its existence as French, and then Martinican nations). Caribbean soil is 'dead to its essence (with those last Arawaks who leapt, the whole tribe without exception, into the Bay of the Trépassés) [...]. The land ceased to be essence, it became relation' (IP, 196–197). By generalising this process, Glissant like Hegel can look forward to one all-absorbing recuperation of specific histories. 'There where histories converge history ends',[17] and so the global "Epos will soon be of the One', *interplanetary* (205–206); 'the epic is in each one of us [...], the epic is born of us, because we must everywhere move-beyond [*dépasser*]'(IP, 207; cf. 18). Most concisely: the 'confluence [of Relation] abolishes trajectories (itineraries) even as it realises them at last [*la confluence abolit les trajets (les itinéraires) tout en les réalisant à la fin*].'[18] At that point, 'the desirable unity will cease to be linked to a national unanimity and will extend the opaque (the search for a common reference) to the planetary dimension' (IP, 204).

Ultimately, and even in his earlier work, Glissant suggests the eventual redundance of *specificity* as such, of relations with others. Already in *L'Intention poétique* he suggests the possibility of a *dépassement* beyond relationality itself. In nicely Deleuzian fashion, the precedent is established by Artaud and Michaux:

> When the poet travels in the infinite realms where there is no country, he opens a more deserving relation, in this space of an absolute elsewhere where everyone can strive to join it. (Artaud, Michaux. who have made so complete a tabula rasa of the old psychological notions in which Western poetics was confined; men who we can only encounter in the realm beyond relations, where every relation is already accomplished; [our] predecessors .). (IP, 22, my emphasis)

Glissant's famous defence of a 'right to opacity' (DA, 11), then, must be understood in *this* context – as a mechanism organised in the interest of its own eventual dissolution. 'There is a law which demands that we move apart, that we refuse to abolish ourselves in the other, only through this injunction to integrate ourselves in the totality, to rejoin it' (IP, 53). At a certain point in Glissant's more recent work, however, this distinction tends toward confusion. The specifically opaque will itself become the *means* to a more total becoming-transparent which surpasses and includes it. One way or another, the end is always an eventual 'unveiling' (IP, 185, 187–189), the slow revelation of 'the lived totality, in which opacity opens bit by bit, and the sharing is established' (IP, 90).

IV Against folklore, against Creole

What to do, then, with cultural specificities which stubbornly refuse to surpass and dissolve themselves? This is precisely the quality which, for Glissant, defines the folkloric *alternative* to the nation. The sequence of national self-constitution is always the same: first 'a being-folkloric then [the] theatrical overcoming of folklore'.[19] As a rule, 'a people which becomes politicised ceases to be folkloric [*se défolklorise*]' (DA, 398), or in the later terminology: 'to put in Relation – that is what is called to "defolklorise"' (PR, 215). Glissant's emphatically dismissive attitude to folklore and its related components (Creole, orality, the folk tale, *le Détour*, 'forced poetics', and so on) remains, in my view, one of the most fundamentally misunderstood aspects of his work. The misunderstanding stems directly from a reluctance to recognise the central role played in Glissant's theory by totality and the nation.

Folklore is condemned because, like negritude, it typically fails to eliminate itself in a 'higher' or more 'total' stage. In Martinique, 'the expression of [popular] beliefs never "comprehends" a total expression of the collectivity [...], the community presents itself, but does not think itself (does not represent itself): the folklore does not overcome itself' (DA, 404). The Plantation system itself is marked by much the same failure.[30] Glissant relies here upon a (somewhat simplistic) distinction between conscious and unconscious, *vécu* and *pensé*, knowledge and superstition. He believes that something which is 'represented, that is thought, [...] ceases thereby to be lived' (DA, 396). While the nation is consciousness incarnate, what Glissant calls folklore is unconscious, non-reflexive – stuck in mere immediacy in Hegel's 'primitive', sensory sense.[31] Folklore and its Creole vehicle, here dubbed '*délire verbal coutumier*' (DA, 242), constitute only 'a pathetic and uncontrollable response to an economic eradication. Customary verbal delirium is a substitute for a destroyed economic power',[32] rather than a genuinely political moving-beyond. By the same token 'the political conquest of these autonomous [social] relations [*liens*] nullifies the traumatic manifestation of the alienated relations which is customary verbal delirium' (DA, 369).

In other words, folklore for Glissant, just like Africa for Hegel, is not adequately historical or dialectical. In general, 'it is impossible to live folklore as will (it is always a non-concerted result), but we can ease, through willing, the passage from lived folklore to represented consciousness' (DA, 409). Folklore, that is, can only become legitimate when it ceases to be folklore, when it becomes *conscience* or *connaissance signifiante* – immediate to the whole (IP, 194). According to Glissant, the traditional forms of popular resistance in Martinique – the secret, initiatic role of Creole, shared participation in folk tales, religious syncretism, and so on – divert but do not engage the issue of dispossession.[33] Such diversionary tactics remain dependent, predicated on the continued presence of the oppressor. 'The discourse of popular belief in Martinique continues to invoke the ear of the Other [i.e. the coloniser]' (DA, 34); 'the expression of beliefs withers through the failure to find that echo of which we spoke – *le dépassement*' (403). Again, 'expressions of "popular beliefs" are a non-having which we must confirm, at the very moment in which, knowing them to be a non-having, *we will truly accomplish them by getting rid of them*' (400, my emphasis). At best, folklore provides raw material for the production of genuine (national) consciousness.

In Glissant's Martinique, then, the problem is that 'we cannot consciously overcome [...] that which is only the expression of an absence, of an imposed lack' (DA, 401). *Dépassement* must in this case be *forced*, artificially, from without. This is what Glissant means by the much misunderstood term, '*poétique forcée*' (DA, 236). '*Opération dérisoire*' (280), a forced poetics is characterised by 'impotence' and 'futility' (121). A forced poetics 'does not realise a "secularly" established collective knowledge [...]. Anti (or counter) poetics' (276), 'it marks an instinctive denial, which has not yet organised itself into a conscious collective refusal' (279). Stuck in their folkloric stasis, the Martinican people must be forced into national consciousness. For while national formation is '"harmonious" for those peoples constituted before the modern era – [for whom] the work of moving from lived to conscious is not "forced" [...] – there is nothing remotely similar here' (399). Conclusion: 'we must force the movement' (407).

Roughly speaking, then, the celebrated concepts of *Détour*, *errance*, and *poétique forcée*, far from constituting a radical alternative to negritude, have for Glissant more or less the *same* value as negritude – itself 'a sublimated aspect of Detour' (DA, 35) – and for the same reasons: they make possible the preliminary move toward a consciousness which will exceed and subsume them. They enable a future articulation. But in themselves, they stand as stages to be surpassed, rather than models to be emulated. They remain properly *primitive*, with all the loaded connotations of the word. Acts of 'detour [...] spare us the direct confrontation of our problem' (DA, 428). Detour *per se* merely encourages evasion of a national responsibility. The principal artists of Detour are guilty of evading the national problematic by projecting it elsewhere (Africa, Algeria).[34] Detour enables only an *ignorant* survival. 'The practice of Detour is the measure of this existence-without-knowledge. Hence one of the objectives of our discourse: to rejoin in depth that which we are, so that Detour can no longer maintain itself as an indispensable technique of existence' (DA, 36. n. 7). Detour and nation are thus almost mutually exclusive terms. 'There is no detour when the nation has been possible [...]. Detour is the ultimate recourse of a population whose domination by an Other has been hidden'.[35] In much the same way, *errance*, at this point in Glissant's work, mainly connotes a merely mindless wandering. 'The poetics of wandering [*errance*] is spun together in violence without cause. Violence which orients itself becomes a policy of settlement [*politique de l'enracinement*]' (IP, 189). *Errance* ends where nation begins. (In *Poétique de la Relation*, Glissant will invert these terms: 'Relational' *errance* will begin where the nation ends).

Hence Glissant's ambivalent attitude toward Creole, the linguistic incarnation of *Detour*.[36] The key to his position is his belief that '*the language of the people, Creole, is not the language of the collectivity*', that is, of the nation as such.[37] It is a remarkable declaration. According to Glissant, 'the national language is the language in which the nation *produces*' (DA, 357, my emphasis). But if French is only 'a language of consumption', nevertheless Creole is 'a language which does not serve to produce or create anything at all' (357). 'The Creole language is a language in which we no longer produce anything' (345; cf. 240). Unlike Haiti's national Creole, which 'has more quickly moved beyond Detour' (33), Martinican 'Creole has not managed to ponder itself [*se méditer*] – no more in popular wisdom than in elite decisions'.[38] Creole is thus that language 'which has fully assumed the derisory nature of its genesis. It is the *parvenu* of all pidgins' (32; cf. 237). This is why 'the Martinican has no language' in the proper sense; he is simply 'a passive interlocutor, who contributes nothing to the evolution of those languages which he essentially "consumes", without any power of intervention' (346). Creole consists only of 'the call of words which are not yet language', of 'these words consecrated in the pomp of initiations which provide only the material for the building of another language' (MM, 158). Creole, as Glissant describes it, is a language which has failed to grow up; it is 'one of the most extreme consequences of social irresponsibility' (DA, 242). 'Sugar cane, bananas, pineapples – these are the last phantoms of the Creole army. With them the language will disappear' (241).

V *La Lézarde* (1958): the promise of national consciousness

Glissant's first two novels are wholly engaged in his nationalist project, and illustrate its most optimistic phase.[39] In 1956 he writes. 'in the Antilles, where I come from, we can say that a people is positively in the process of constructing itself [...:] here is a synthesis of races, of customs, of knowledges, tending to its own unity' (SC, 15) This optimism continues to dominate *L'Intention poétique* (1969): if 'we are not yet acting' as a nation (IP, 224), nevertheless 'I see approaching over the land the inspired ones that we shall become' (IP, 218; cf. 12,43). *La Lézarde* describes the initial steps of these *inspirés*, the story of a group of young students working to build a sense of the Martinican nation in the immediate post-war era.

Three characters stand out, and will recur more or less insistently in all of Glissant's subsequent fiction (with the partial exception of *Malemort*): Mathieu, Mycéa, and Thaël. Mathieu and Thaël are complementary, the first highly self-reflexive, literary, more or less cerebral, a product of the plain and *bourg*, descendant of the plantation system; the second fundamentally impulsive, active, native to the *mornes* and hills of the great *marrons*. Mathieu and Thaël: the one becomes distinct, 'total', through the other. Thaël 'discovered in Mathieu the anonymous, torrid zone which everyone carries within himself, which he is unable to see' (LZ, 24/27), while 'Mathieu thinks that Thaël is like his nocturnal double, an alter ego: a Mathieu from the depths of the night' (117/91). As we shall see, in *Mahagony* and *Tout-monde*, Mathieu is in certain respects interchangeable with Glissant's own voice; Thaël is above all a tragically *driven* character. In *La Lézarde*, he is charged with the execution of the group's great militant act, the assassination of the *géreur* Garin; at the end of the novel, in a violent turn of fate, his beloved Valéry is killed by his own dogs when they fail to recognise her. As for Mycéa, she is for Glissant 'the secret and key to the mysteries of the country' (TM, 13), but only comes into her own in *La Case du commandeur* (1981); her rise to prominence in Glissant's fictional world is suggestive of the shift from the national to the post-national moments of his work, and will be considered in some detail later in this chapter.

La Lézarde describes both the varied, opaque elements of the nation awaiting integration into collective understanding, and the means through which they will achieve this integration (the anticipation of transparency). As in *Le Quatrième Siècle*, the elements here remain specific, and specifically arranged in dialectical pairs – *bourg* vs. *bois*, plain vs. *morne*, the French-dominated city as opposed to the 'legend-dominated' space of Alcide Lomé (LZ, 61/53), and so on. The river which gives the novel its title, as that which links these elements into a single, non-reductive coherence, is both its privileged milieu and ultimate hero.[6] Mathieu:

> we will make a song of enormous and unique beauty out of this chorus of ignorance and monotony. Yes, nothing is clear now. But soon we shall experience the deed [*l'acte*]! The river descends with a new precision, it is the Lézarde, it is every propitious river, it's water from the creeks where a people comes to splash about And then our delta will no longer be dirty! [...] And one day the Lézarde will arrive clear at its final destination, the sea. Like a self-confident people that steps out to lead the rest .. (LZ, 82–83/68tm)

Here, the collective experience is anchored in the productive, directing reality of the *land*. 'The land never ceases to give of itself' (56/49); 'the land speaks to everyone, like a pillow speaks to the ear lying on it. And *if a man says that he has seen this or that, no one can contradict him*, as long as it is part of the land, buried deep in its entrails' (105/82tm, my emphasis).

La Lézarde writes the transformation from *paysage* to *pays* as the rising dawn of a new day. And 'politics was the new arena in the battle for self-respect […], a passion for knowledge' (17/23); 'our people's history is still to be written […], and only thus will we know who we are' (81/67tm). The obscure will become known – 'we will go back to the very beginning. Mathieu is doing research […]' (186/143–144). Politics and history are to blend together in a single, empowering moment of initiation. Walking to find Thaël, Mathieu 'thinks about his present initiation. It is as if, in order to gain the full knowledge of this land, the full taste of each hidden corner, [etc…] he had to submit to this experience of the electoral campaign, alien to his taste, abstract to some extent' (117/90) – the time of the *conscience connaissante*.

Mathieu and Thaël's coming into manhood (here aged 21 and 18 respectively) doubles the popular 'coming into nationhood', and vice versa. 'Youthful passion must be curbed by foresight […] The land weighs heavily now. This burden must be carried'.[61] With Mathieu, Martinique begins to grow up. As Thaël realises,

the slow struggle through which his people, through so many illusions, were reaching out towards the exact quality of itself [… – Thaël] realised that in his heart this collective effort was beginning to grow, to take shape, the tense drama of reconciling love and anger, light and matter […]. This process of fulfilment which had divided a collective will into so many partial wills […], for each one knew, or symbolised or better embodied a part of the common heritage. (181/139–140)

Electoral triumph, then, when it comes, is more or less automatic, 'a crushing victory' (198/153). It is the irresistible manifestation of the *volonté générale*. 'Beyond all doubt, victory was assured' (190/146).

As opposed to the general movement that will infuse his later *Tout-monde*, Glissant's *La Lézarde* narrates the *territorialisation* of a space, its becoming-striated, organised, self-possessed. The national space is vectored, situated, politicised, divided into lines of movement between the high and low, coast and interior, legend (*le fromager, le flamboyant*) and clarity (*Lambrianne*).[62] By the midpoint of the novel, these vectors have been compressed to four cardinal movements, synchronised by their affiliation to the same point of reference, the same motivation, the same *root*:

> Four directions To the west, Mathieu, followed by Alphonse Tigamba. To the east, Thaël and Garin going down the river [...]. To the north, Valérie, drawn to the mountains [..] To the south, Margarita and Gilles question each other Four clear furrows in the surrounding confusion. And an inflexible will, a stubborn determination, an ability to fight [.] Four separate movements. But unleashed from a single subterranean source, like a wind fighting itself and turning against itself [...] Like a stubborn root. (136/104)

Cartographic rather than nomadic, the various movements of the characters weave together to form a single fabric, framed by that 'tangle of journeys, twisting across the country, linking past to future, and a man to the woman chosen in his heart, and the river to the sea! [...] All these roads take hold of the same impatience, order it to extinguish its flame until the moment of its culmination' (106/82–83tm). Within this space, the characters are driven by an irresistible force which seems to emanate from the vectors themselves – or rather from that seamless mix of landscape and narrative motivation which makes up the dialectical texture of the novel. 'Antilles, South America, they are a link to the earth [...], the vocation of an organic universal' (IP, 139). The land functions here as first cause, prime mover. The characters are driven forward to their 'encounter with destiny' like Thaël and Valérie who 'moved inexorably towards each other, with nothing able to keep them apart'.[63]

Within this vectored space, events are primarily organised by their simultaneity in the present tense, distributed only by space, by the *territory* itself. Virtually all chapters begin in the present. Events flow on side by side in their simultaneity, moving forward at more or less the same pace. After the dispersal from Lambrianne, the narrative progresses as a single movement drawn toward an inexorable conclusion, where the various episodes are arranged mostly according to coincidence across space. For example, as Longoué predicts Valérie's fate, we are told that 'at this same moment, Alphonse Tigamba saw that Mycéa looked happy and he went away' (79/65). The next chapter begins without a break from Thaël's perspective ('the afternoon was finally fading.. '). If there is of course no straight chronological line to the narrative, there is a dominant, meandering current, whose meanders detract nothing from the sea-bound rush of the water. When chapter eight opens – 'The Lézarde is slow and powerful at this point' (118/91) – it is the river's own movement which marks Thaël's progress and coordinates his position in relation to the others. At the same time that he crosses the river with Garin, 'now Mycéa [...] wanders off quite unaware' (102/79tm). Later, during 'the evening when Thaël and Garin saw the forest fire, a big political meeting was held in the marketplace of the town...' (131/101). Again, while Valérie murmurs 'lies, lies' to Mathieu, 'so Thaël and Garin pursue their destiny...' (111/86tm). And when Valérie, alone in the mountains, asks herself, 'Valérie, do you love him enough to do that?' it is Margarita, far to the south, who answers on the next page, 'No! I do not love him!' (138/106). Throughout the second part of the novel in particular, the narrative movement of the text itself is grafted on to the vectored landscape: up, during the approach ('up to the source of the river' [87/69] then down, winding down and around toward the symbolic place of purgation, the point where the river meets and mingles with the sea. Thaël's internal debate and the landscape's evolution along the river are so closely interconnected that it is effectively impossible to tell the two different subjects apart, Thaël-Garin and river. 'After this long search which led back to the source' where he will find Garin, Thaël feels drawn along 'as if the river compelled him to know its beginning, with its gentle spring whose flow gathers strength and makes fertile' (89/71tm). Gradually, it is the river which takes on the attributes of active subject, while Thaël becomes less sure of his mission right to the very moment of its virtually accidental accomplishment, an event engendered very precisely by the river's own energy.

This coherence of story and setting is confirmed by the narrator's place as both producer and product of the story.[61] His instructions: 'write a book filled with heat [...]. Write it like a river. Slow. Like the Lézarde. With rushing water, meanders [...], slowly gathering the earth from either bank' (224/175). The narrator is dispersed throughout the narrative only in order to multiply the points at which he himself can be over-determined in it. At once witness and participant: 'I, as a child (child of this story)' (31/33), 'I knew Mathieu and Thaël, and all their friends: and they were my brothers, they were my tutors in the uphill journey towards the world and the truth' (204/158tm). The story narrated in *La Lézarde* itself doubles as the coming-into-consciousness of its narrator. 'I will grow with this story' (31/33). The story as it took place created the person who tells it, on the Proustian model. diegetic outcome = narrative origin As the narrator says in his first direct interjection, 'I was both witness and object: the one who sees and must endure, who is called and who is shaped' (16/22). Container and contained, the narrator splits himself in a second person only to establish a perfectly transparent dialogue: 'I ask myself the question and immediately the answers come; they are there, indelibly written into the past [...] memory relentlessly unfolds the same actions and the same judgements passed on them... – I tell you what you did' (208–209/162tm).

Of course, in *La Lézarde*, the national dialectic is still incomplete. The nation remains, *as always* in Glissant, 'à bâtir'. The hills and the town stand separated along *la route coloniale*, 'guarded by the fearsome silk-cotton tree' (30/32), symbol of superstition (14/20–21). Colonial dependency and blind tradition remain vigorous (61/53). As Thaël urges, 'We must face this night! We are sons of the night, we must exhaust its secret fury!' (37/37tm). The national dialectic has yet to include the 'primordial' violence of the nocturnal hills. Thaël himself returns a stranger to his native land: 'he had lived close to the limitless sea, and henceforth an estranging force would come between him and the world of the mountains [...]. He had emerged from the world of obscure mystery and entered one which valued clarity and rational judgement' (247/191). He has been made 'distinct', separate. When he shouts the names of his dogs, his new 'calculated strength' (247/191tm) is unable to contain 'ferocious explosion of their strength, so long held in check' (249/192tm). Valéry is torn to pieces as a result. The mountains – realm of an absolute and brutal freedom, an unconquerable savagery – remain to be integrated into the national communion.

Nothing testifies more profoundly to the incomplete status of the national dialectic than the relationship of the heroes to the community in whose name they act. The heroes are both typical of *and* outside this community. As Luc tells the narrator, 'don't forget to say that it is not that we were right. It is the country [*pays*] which is right' (224/175tm). But if the *pays* has '*raison*' it is the heroes who have, as Lomé tells them, 'the most terrible gift of all, knowledge' (226/176). This knowledge sets them deliberately and explicitly apart from its object. 'Barefoot out of bravado' yet 'dandies' by night (17/23tm), the heroes always stand aside from the crowd. They listen to their representative 'with a kind of distracted passion, which separated them from the crowd's reaction [...], alone with their decision' (19/24tm). Even during the great day of national unity, the people 'would have loved to talk with Mathieu and Thaël, but the two men seemed to be isolated, confined in a world apart' (194/150). Through a kind of 'instinctive and youthful defiance' the heroes refuse to join 'the Peoples' Party' – which as we know with the narrator's authority, is 'the sole organisation which had the country's true interests at heart' – but they recognise it nevertheless to be 'the only real hope' for change (131–132/101). The mass mobilisation of the party marks the limit to the heroes' action:

> just as the deep waters of the river become tame [*s'humanisent*] close to the town, allowing the women to wash their clothes in it, so also the mysterious movement of those who are the leaven of the land, the patient, determined and unconscious striving of our young friends, pauses here and comes to fruition in the explosive clamour of the people. The people proclaimed their determination and its echo was not lost on these young people (132/102)

More, at the novel's end, along with Michel, Mathieu and Mycéa, the narrator sets off for France, the very agent of national dispossession, to become a 'proper' writer. Thaël, we later discover in *Tout-monde*, also departs to France, and then to Indochina and Algeria where he will serve on the side of the *French* expeditionary forces. How and where the movement will end remains a genuine question. 'Will you come back, Mathieu, you will come back? – I don't know. Who can tell?' (226/177).

Already, however, Glissant hints at his eventual solution to the problem of this relationship, of leader to *peuple*, consciousness to *pays* – its *dépassement* in the next level up. The river ends when it accomplishes its goal, when it flows into the sea. *The sea*: 'a broad expanse, a motionless surface, a measure of patience, where time stops and space is overwhelmed by its very magnitude [...]. Nothing moves but the sand [...]. Here, time patiently awaits you, nothing can prevent it taking you away. Where? To the boundless sea' (144/110–111). The sea is the perfect *espace lisse* in Deleuze's sense, a space where nothing moves, nothing *advances*, because everything is moving. Pure molecularity, such is 'the sea where all plans are undone' (146/113), 'which is outside everything, which limits, but which shapes and defines at the same time' (42/40tm). Glissant's work, we might say, flows with the dialectical energy of *Le Discours antillais* toward the singular and ultimately non-dialectical energy of *Poétique de la Relation*, just as *La Lézarde*, a vector for the people's arising, flows toward the Caribbean sea, space of the people's mingling. 'The river has done its part, now it is the turn of the sea. The Lézarde. The sea. An inevitable history' (145/112tm). At the last gathering of the heroes, 'they all call out to me. "Don't forget, don't forget. Remember us"'. As if words would become a river which comes down and spreads and then overflows' (LZ, 230/180), rushing toward the eventual declaration. 'There's the sea! The sea is there! [...] Trust in the sea!'[65]

VI *Malemort* (1975): the dialectic *en panne*[66]

By the time Glissant comes to publish his third, most innovative, most obscure and perhaps most accomplished novel, little of the optimism that propelled the forward-driving movement of his first two novels remains. By this stage, Glissant has to admit that 'there is perhaps no other community on earth as alienated as our own' (DA, 63). Far from continuing the push toward national consciousness, his Martinique has lapsed into the most abjectly passive form of neo-colonial dependency. A specifically Martinican reality is being erased 'day by day [...]. We can't stop disappearing [...] in the horrorless horror of a successful colonisation' (DA, 15). 'The irremediable' is close at hand, 'the point of no return' (DA, 176). Much of *Le Discours antillais* amounts to a diagnosis of this Martinican condition, dispossession in every sense of the word.[67] In some of Glissant's most effective pages, he demonstrates how departmentalisation (in 1946) has confirmed the collapse of a local economy geared, however unequally, to the satisfaction of local needs, and its replacement with the dependent provision of a 'regional spe-cialisation' within the French economy (DA, 29). The island now lives in a state of 'technical irresponsibility', cut off from any 'real mediation of its milieu' (DA, 103); there is no longer, 'in the proper sense, any Martinican economy'.⁴⁸ Deprived of the requisite national context, Martinican 'labour will henceforth be considered as an activity "in suspension", an activity that implies no possibility of a valorising *dépassement*' (DA, 42). In short, Mar-tinicans have become cultural consumers rather than producers, 'clients' rather than agents (DA, 72; cf. 465: it should be stressed that Glissant's critique of dispossession in *Le Discours antillais* still confirms the national project as the only available means toward an eventual repossession).

The fact of dispossession is as starkly evident in *Malemort* as it is in *Le Discours antillais*. 'It's the metropole your daddy your mammy your nurse' (MM, 188). The landscapes of *Malemort* are inhabited by 'the ghosts of abandoned scrap iron' and 'rotten sheet metal', by 'overcrowded parking lots, tower blocks [and] hotels crammed along the beach-tops' (MM, 205). *Malemort*'s Martinique is dominated by the image of the 'abandoned fac-tory' (177), the emblem of a once-productive economy become sterile and parasitic. The population has been worn down 'like a man who for four hundred years has tried to recover his image [from its watery reflection] but who in the yellow water of the ponds in the blue water of the swimming pools only disrupts with his foot the painted marionette he has become' (128). Rather than work towards self-consciousness, 'we [now] desire only recognition from above', from France (85; cf. 209).

In other words, *Malemort*'s Martinique lives (again in classically Hegelian fashion) the alienation of its essence, the projection of the nation outside itself. Glissant is now ready to admit that 'there is nothing (in con-testation or in opposition) that cannot here be recuperated by the system' (DA, 171), perhaps even including the most 'inalienable', the most irrecu-perable of things: national sovereignty itself. In *Malemort* even the question of 'cultural identity' has been co-opted, to become one of the 'constant preoccupation[s] of the [French] Government' (MM, 194). National con-sciousness has been replaced with the banality of 'the Empire the Union the Collective the Community the *Patrie*' (45), the '*Patrie* over-there', across the ocean (70). In this Martinique no less than in the Paris of Glissant's 1950s, 'everyone lives apart, if you can call it living. Apart from each other, destitute' (MM, 219; cf. SC, 62).

Even more than is usual in Glissant's later fiction, *Malemort* has no clearly demarcated plot in the usual sense of the word. The text is broken into fragmentary sections divided by setting, style and occasion, and con-tains Glissant's most assertively experimental prose writing. The very movement and organisation of the novel can be identified, up to a point, with the permanent 'deviation' and disorientation of that 'habitual verbal delirium [*délire verbal coutumier*]' analysed (and condemned) in *Le Discours antillais*.[6] *Malemort* is a book designed to frustrate and unnerve its readers. Set mainly in the present but reaching back occasionally across the last three centuries, the novel is conspicuously free of any forward-driving coordination. Characters drift between isolated encounters and dramatic spasms of violence, distracted by quixotic pursuits and broken by poverty and hopelessness. The three 'main' characters, Dlan, Médellus and Silacier, are less individuals in their own right than facets of a single illustration of the contemporary malaise; erratic and impulsive, they wander between odd jobs and welfare handouts, living on illusions of grandeur they are powerless to fulfil.

The dominant register of *Malemort* is the macabre. Typical scenes are set by 'this mechanical zombie slumped in a bend of the path', by 'the ghostly surrounding light' (MM, 67), by 'this parade of death that we might call [our] history' (132). The subject of the opening "He's dancing!" (15) is a corpse carried by a funeral procession. 'Burial [has] become a kind of national sport' (185). Like *La Case du commandeur*, the novel is punctuated with brutal, episodic violence – the recurring assassination(s) of Nainfol, 'shot dead in a corridor' (MM, 58; cf. 91; 216) and Beautemps (a.k.a. Maho, in *Mahagony*); the endless execution of *résistants* resurrected only to be killed once again, 'women children old men, they fell infinitely, they died infinitely' (118), and then 'corpses, they were raised to life as mummies...' (121; cf. 57, 127). Simultaneously 'dead and alive' (20), the unemployed *djobeurs* Dlan, Médellus and Silacier drift aimlessly from *dépannage* to *dépannage* in the midst of "this maelstrom without centre, without soul, henceforth without future' (29). For example, Médellus.

> he was standing in the idea of death, not his own, certainly – that is, certainly not the death of his body or the extinction of his breath – but the surrounding numbness, obliteration smiling in the paled greenness. Death wasn't like a broken line retied it was like a colour that slowly evaporates. (212)

Unlike the forward moving histories-in-action of the first novels, the parts of *Malemort* are linked together at apparent random, are introduced only by date, and remain divided by a heterogeneous collection of experimental styles (flow of consciousness, hallucination, dialogue, verse; one particularly striking chapter narrates, in a single unbroken sentence, the Vision of those who endlessly fall, shot, and stand back up... [115–133], an evocation of abortive, suppressed, pre-national uprisings from 1788 to 1974). The national reference now seems to be as sterile as the folklore it was to have replaced. 'We can find names for nothing, we have been worn down without our realising it, reduced not so much to a silence as to this threadless absence [*absence défilée*] in which we live and in which the mockeries of speech as much as our very muteness itself no longer means anything' (150). *Malemort* writes a time beyond dialectical recuperation, a 'time suspended in this repeating fusillade' (50), a time evaporated in 'the burning heat' of the sun (48):

> where to seek or find the time I mean the moment the slightest necessity (without at once being called a fool [...]) of asking ourselves why the mahogany and the ravines and the sad shade of the mango trees do not cause the slightest flutter in our hearts that might be called love or tenderness or passion or simply vision of the landscape or let's say of what is there in our surroundings. (60)

In *Malemort*, even the Lézarde river has all but dried up.[70] It is now 'the poisoned river' doomed to feed only 'what in derision they would later call [...] an industrial zone'.[71] Nor has the anonymous sea yet achieved its eventually redemptive potential. Here, to be 'condemned for ever to the sea' is simply another way of being 'a new zombie'.[72]

The *djobeurs* of *Malemort* refuse or are unable to work toward a mediate self-consciousness in relation with others. They refuse, in other words, to follow the river *to* the sea. They try instead to leap, immediately, into a coherence beyond our own,

> all of them trying, huddled on the same shore, to jump over in a single bound to the world which had eventually rejoined them (immobile enclosed), to touch it not with gestures acts or deeds not with a phrase a word but through the very effort in which they tired themselves out, through so many questions, by filling in both the white hole of time and the pale absence of speech: trying, trying But [.] the world doesn't understand you if your voice isn't heavy, if you don't call out your words. (MM, 69)

Deprived of the conscious (French) clarity of Mathieu, the *djobeurs* remain committed to Creole *diversion*. Their attempts at speech, their fragmented language don't allow them phrase and 'expose the problems' that need to be exposed (124).

In *Malemort*, the close association of *marronage* and initiation into awareness established in *Le Quatrième Siècle* no longer obtains. The country has forgotten 'the Negator, the primordial *Marron*' (MM, 189; cf. 67). Martinique has failed to make of *le Négateur* a creative, constitutive principle (it has failed, in other words, to make a properly Hegelian use of negation). 'The Negator, who in every language other than this absence and this lack [that is Creole] would no doubt have been called the Ancestor' now figures as no more than a 'vague knot in the stomach, a cry without root or leaf, a weeping without eyes, a death without return' (61). Rather than pursue an enlightened historical continuity 'we never stopped falling [...] into this hole of night' (163) in which all efforts of historical communion are consumed. Silacier, for example, is indeed 'the enemy of all authority' (32), but his revolt has no purpose. It does not surpass itself at a 'higher level'. 'Silacier was by nature ready to clear every public place with great sweeps of his cutlass' (67), but is incapable of anything more constructive (92). Beautemps, likewise, is not a proper *marron*; 'he was not a Negator, he was forced to be only a delinquent [and] an assassin' (54).

The national project, then, has broken down, never to recover. And in *Malemort* Glissant has not yet developed an affirmative conception of a post-national unity. The three main 'characters' of Malemort do indeed provide the structure of a diverging unity, but it remains negatively affected. 'Dlan Médellus Silacier, inseparable for the moment' (MM, 22); 'those three, they themselves us [*eux-mêmes nous*], they themselves mad' (23), our centre and the centre of this nothing from which we come' (23–24). All three are equally 'without future without theatre without culture without knowledge without career'.[73] They live as one unconscious jumble, without punctuation.

> Finding themselves in a crowd beside the sea, Dlan Médellus Silacier mixed together with so many others who also had crossed through the break [*franchi la casse*] without order or memory
> there adrift in themselves, mouths gaping for lack of words to explain their situation [74]

As they begin to take on distinct 'personalities' toward the novel's end, these present only variations on a shared futility. 'Cutlass in hand', Silacier cannot progress beyond the actions suggested by his name (191); Dlan 'finds the voice from On High' and retreats into religion (191); Médellus, 'endlessly dreaming the land', comes up with a utopian mockery of a national agenda (196–199) only to have it bulldozed away for 'the promotion of tourism' (205). As Glissant summarises things in a later novel, Silacier ends up 'in jail', Dlan becomes an 'Anabaptist', and Médellus finishes with his 'head in the clouds' (MH, 244).

VII *La Case du commandeur* (1981): despair and transition

In certain ways, *La Case du commandeur* picks up right where *Malemort* leaves off – in ignorance, dispossession and isolation. 'The absence of self [*moi*] encloses me in myself', cut off and un-related. The absence of history likewise disorients the present. 'past life, fallen trees, banished loves do not appear to us in the sculpted clarity of knowable things' (CC, 16). The *nous-narrateurs* are unable to situate or describe [..] the fold of the ground, name which river, identify which sand, nor indicate which hut (how could we, after so many terrors and so many seas, after sinking in so many night blue seas [...]), we are reliving, indistinctly, the pain and laughter in which we took shelter during our transfer [from Africa]. (CC, 16–17)

Now it seems that a national *nous* is to be forever out of reach – as if 'we were perhaps never to form, at the end of the day, this single body by which we were to begin to enter our stretch of land.' The narrative we is made up of 'exhausted mysel[ves]'. It is a we that rolls its several 'selves [*nos moi*] against each other without ever managing to to lay down foundations in this belt of islands' (CC, 16, 15).

The great question will eventually be – *the* question, in a sense, to be asked in *Poétique de la Relation* – can we make of this very failure, this dissemination of the *we*, the basis for a new becoming-adequate of the *Whole*? Can Glissant, in other words, make a viable shift from a (ruined) specificity to an effectively aspecific or singular orientation? To the degree he begins to answer this question here, with the character Mycéa and the riddle of '*qui est Odono?*', *La Case du commandeur* can be considered a transitional work. In what follows I will deal only with those aspects of the book that most explicitly anticipate the later novels discussed in the next section.

Through to the early 1980s, Glissant's answer to this general question still usually appears to be a fairly emphatic *no*. The narrative we of *Case du commandeur* is 'bursting with solitary "me's"' and 'sapped by shapeless knowledges' (CC, 19). 'We' evade responsibility. 'We don't want to know the answer. We want to astonish ourselves, or to dazzle ourselves with the question' (28). Mycéa's father Pythagore, for example, stumbles about in an ignorant *errance*. 'Pythagore had passed over to the realm of wandering dreams, dreams that do not locate their landscape, that were anchored in no soil. In other words he lost for ever the possibility [...] of distinguishing' between the irresponsible African dream and the concrete American reality (41–42). Although *La Case du commandeur*, like *Le Quatrième Siècle*, is structured as a genealogical excavation of the past, the search for origins now only fades away into an ever greater obscurity, into the 'hole [of] time gone past' (152). Looking 'forward' into the future, Melchior (born 1791) anticipates that the 'faraway-in-the-future [will be] given over to madness and forgetting' (127). The result, once again: *détour* and irresponsibility:

in trying not to be obsessed by the problem of origins [.] we were none the less inclined to mock, gently, any subject that might have threatened to bring us face to face – in our anguished depths – with such concerns. When anyone tries to work their way back up to this terrain, or even tries to describe the rocky paths that lead in that direction, we exclaim at once that the sun has gone to his head; we laugh [...], we cloak ourselves in scorn [–] so afraid are we of this hole in time gone past. (CC, 60–61, 152)

The community of this we is a community defined by the collective repression of any meaningful introspection. Clinging thought-lessly to the shreds of a role imposed from without, it is a community built on an extreme expression of 'bad faith' in the Sartrean sense.

Like *Malemort*, *La Case du commandeur* describes a morbid, dysfunctional society. The novel is organised, very loosely, around Mycéa's birth (1928) and her eventual release from an asylum (1978). Mycéa is a character hovering on (and sometime over) the brink of both madness and inspiration. The various dynasties that populate Glissant's fiction (the Longoués, the Béluses, the Celats, the Targins) flicker in and out of her awareness.[5] Much of the novel is broken up into episodes that relate, in a style reminiscent of García Márquez and the magical realism of *Cien años de soledad*, the (mainly tragic) lives of Mycéa's parents (Cinna Chimène and Pythagore) and ancestors. Successive chapters present (1) Mycéa's isolated childhood and the sudden separation of her mother and father, (2) her own mother's childhood and the misadventures of her grandparents Ephraïse and Ozonzo, (3) the story of her great-grandparents Adoline and Augustus in the days of slavery's abolition, and (4) the distant times of Liberté Longoué (b. 1833) and Anatolie Celat, the first of that name. Unlike *Le Quatrième Siècle*, this genealogical framework is not accompanied by a corresponding movement toward dynastic resolution and achievement. The abandoned overseer's hut that gives the book its title and one of its geographical and gravitational poles is a site of profoundly unresolved ambiguity, a legacy of the viciously cynical Euloge (the first slave made overseer of his fellows). Mycéa's uncertain insights are located between this relic of past collaboration and the psychiatric hospital that presents an equally ambiguous face of metropolitan power.

In *La Case du commandeur*, Glissant explicitly abandons the goal of a national continuity. 'The moment has come for us to know that we will not continue to descend melodically into the ravine, that having arrived at the edge of this hole of time we hurtle down all the faster by jumping from rock to rock [...]. *We jump from rock to rock in this time!*' (CC, 138). This is an unprecedented step in Glissant's fiction. With it, he moves from the continuity of the river to the fragmentation of the rock. What he had previously derided as mere 'pieces [pans] of history' (DA, 157) begin here, cautiously, tentatively, to acquire a more affirmative connotation. It is not an obviously compelling alternative. The rocks upon which the characters figuratively jump are made of a treacherously brittle substance. '*We are crushing into powder the rock of time. The powder of the rock in which we drift.* Time covered in tragic or grotesque beasts, our companions' (CC, 144–145). What sort of companions can live in this powdered time? 'Ants, for example […], the guardians of the end.' They appear when 'you are already at the limit of exhaustion. You have left the world in which people move forward and embraced the earth which frays and sinks away' (145).

This is not the most promising terrain for a new beginning. In the absence of a national continuity, relations with and between characters remain stuck in the mode of the *abrupt*. As Mathieu leaves Mycéa virtually without explanation (CC, 197) so, one day, 'Cinna Chimène disappeared, no-one ever knew why' (72). Later, she abandons her husband with equal indifference: very simply, 'Cinna Chimène left, one day', amazing all by the way 'she was able so totally to forget her former existence and move in with this man or that, depending on where her life took her' (43). Her return to the lowlands is as abrupt as her original departure. 'Off she went' (80). The death of her adoptive father Ozonzo is no less sudden, run down 'without apparent reason' by the mysterious mule discovered soon after the foundling Cinna Chimène (82–83). The overall impression is summarised by Mycéa's great, great-grandfather Liberté (b. 1833): 'our histories jump about in time, our different landscapes are muddled, our words jumble and fight against each, our heads are empty or over-full…' (126).

Considering the overall impact of *Malemort*, *Le Discours antillais* and *La Case du commandeur*, the critic Richard Burton concluded in 1984 that Glissant's 'vision […] is so extraordinarily pessimistic that one wonders quite how – if at all – Glissant's writing will develop in the future'.[76]

However, it would be a mistake to think of *La Case du commandeur* as a *wholly* pessimistic novel. For it is, above all, the novel of Mycéa, the novel which brings Mycéa to the centre of Glissant's fictional universe. Mycéa (a.k.a. Marie Celat), we come to learn, 'is so to speak the secret and the key to the mysteries of the country. She has known every sorrow and approached every truth, like someone Inspired' (TM, 13). Mycéa is 'she who enchants the poet, whom he names with every breath. But whom words cannot express'.[77] The point is not, in the first place, whether Mycéa represents a negative, pessimistic moment in Glissant's work (according to Burton), or another form of his consistent optimism (according to Dash),[78] but that she represents something *new*. With Mycéa, Glissant moves toward the vision of a singular reality without relation *to* the world. The affect of this reality (positive or negative) will be decided in terms completely different from those that governed the national project. Glissant's whole-world, his World beyond the world, is properly self-affecting. It is best read as incommensurable with the reality Glissant distinguishes, in his early work, as either conscious (national) *or* unconscious (folkloric). The new reality makes this very distinction impertinent.

With his fundamentally *singular* character Mycéa, Glissant begins to give a formally affirmative answer to the question posed at the beginning of this section – is it possible to make the failure of relations-with the basis for an alternative, post-national aesthetic? (For the moment, the issue is not whether it is a 'good' or compelling answer). Mycéa is the un-related, isolated character *par excellence*. She is unknowable, beyond relations with others (cf. MM, 212–213). She incarnates substance and expression together in a single articulation beyond 'representation'. For my purposes, she is the critical hinge in Glissant's fictional works. On the one hand, she is the product of a failed national enterprise, born of the breakdown of relations with others; on the other hand, she is prophet of a new order, the order which it falls to Mathieu, mainly, to spell out as '*Tout-monde*'.[9]

In her first aspect, Mycéa appears to live the dead-end of relation, *la relation avec l'autre consenti*, as Glissant had defended it throughout his early works. Her birth is celebrated, by her own father Pythagore, as a death (CC, 22). She is from the beginning a supremely solitary character – the *rock* in person. She is a 'thin, statufied child' (44; cf. 50). Sat down by her mother on a log of wood, the little Mycéa slowly becomes 'a piece of rock on this log' (78). Mycéa *resists* (erosion as much as comprehension). 'There was something in her that stiffened [...], and that gave her that indomitable aspect that Pythagore had feared even before he had confronted it' (49). Utterly misunderstood by her father (21), with no relation to speak of with her absent mother Cinna Chimène, Mycéa grows up alone. Her ancestor Adoline had set something of a precedent: solitary, withdrawn, Adoline is determined to harden herself against life, to 'dry out' life and survive its evaporation (108). Mycéa goes much further in the same direction. 'She had always kept herself out of the way [...]. Dry as a chilli plant' (45; cf. 186). The narrator eventually asks: 'was there a curse of solitude upon her head?' (199).

Mycéa is unable to maintain a 'relationship' in the ordinary sense of the term. Mathieu leaves her for slightly obscure reasons. Later, she lives within an indifferent flux of lovers. Men come and go, 'following after each other, resembling each other' (198). The father of her two sons literally disappears without a trace, and then 'Marie Celat let herself sink. She dropped through life in a single sweep. She found herself, one day, living in the company of a man; time rushed by, she had two children, boys. Later, she no longer remembered the way he looked, nor anything about him' (CC, 198–199, cf. TM, 349). Later still, she is no more able to 'relate' to her sons. Donou is an elusive dreamer quite literally at sea, whereas 'Patrice Celat [...] grew up in bottomless violence': his mother can only 'remain dumbfounded, excluded from everything by the surging savagery of her older son, paralysed by such excess [...]. Chloroformed, Marie Celat stopped reacting' (CC, 204). Nor does Mycéa keep many friends. 'She made fleeting friendships, soon riddled with stubborn revulsions' (CC, 214). She organises a kind of women's discussion group, only to have 'this group soon explode (there is no other word)' (208).

Like Deleuze's exemplary philosopher,[30] Mycéa lives in a realm beyond discussion:

> Marie Celat in particular couldn't bear to hear the word 'discuss' [..] Because what we see as ideas or expose in words becomes so foreign to what we accumulate inside like rocks Mycéa didn't rule over things with words [..] As she gradually submitted to the country, to her slow absorption in its pallid neutral life, she left behind the one [man, Mathieu,] whose voice expressed this life (CC. 189–190)

Isolated from others, Mycéa moves slowly toward an inarticulate empathy with the landscape and its trees, towards an ineffable communication with the imperceptible erosions of time. She has abandoned the early Glissant's pretension to ground the national consciousness in a reasoned, reflexive awareness of itself. Marie Celat is precisely that character who begins the semantic revaluation of the *sea*, the marine body for a new plane of immanence, 'a blue without measure', a blue of inspiration and insight beyond words. Eyes closed, 'seeing the depths of a sea [...], everything around her had taken on the colour of this blue [...]. Mathieu's words were blue-indistinct, simply filling up their space'. The field of vision is saturated in colour, rather than articulated in words. 'Marie Celat often swam in this field without limit, in such a way that she came to forget what we call time', attaining an 'unpredictable' grace, an always 'surprising' rhythm (195; cf. MH, 226–227).

The price she pays for such insight is high. Deprived of historical orientation, she 'screamed inside her head that nothing had any meaning'. She endures an absence or 'hole beyond which no one understood her thought, but where she nevertheless had looked', hearing 'only that wind that battered in her head' (CC, 191). In *La Case du commandeur*, Mycéa's regenerative potential remains tenuous at best. 'Exhaustion overcame Marie Celat [...]. Disorientation made her stumble in the streets, the books she started reading were lost under the bed, everything jumbled together with a kind of calm ferocity', as so many 'mechanical' components of a mainly traumatic existence (214).

Nevertheless, there can be no doubting the fundamental change in orientation here. The old national problematic has lost its credibility, and Mycéa clearly represents an incipient alternative, a still harrowing form of escape. Mycéa is self-sufficient, 'new and brutal', *'as if she had made herself* then polished herself' (CC, 171, my emphasis). She bypasses all national discussion – 'she laughed at our obsessive nicknaming of all things' (176) – in order to look further than others into the 'abyss' (171). 'Opaque by nature', 'she would become so light as to appear transparent' (173). she is that opacity which surrounds the *source* of light. She abandons the limits of a temporal-spatial coherence, in order to cultivate the power that comes from 'being lost in the night' (172). Against a univocal national coherence, 'she maintained [...] that there was no common domain, that the [only] passage was from one to one, from one rock in the river to another' (186).

Rather than a national coordination of specific and universal, Mycéa is at once wholly self-contained and wholly outward-looking. Emerging from her introspective silence, 'she harangue[s] the islands. Answer, Dominica. I summon you to conference...' (CC, 215). She skips the in-between. Unlimited by history, she returns to the *origin* in the mythical (almost metaphysical) sense. 'Marie Celat climbed back [in time] through the voice of Chérubin, back towards everything that she had not known but that resonated for her more clearly than the word of the first day [*la parole du premier jour*]' (233):

> Marie Celat sang in her head, and the sweetness of the song gradually penetrated the commander's hut [..] The music [had] come from so far away (not only in time but also in the cloth of space, woven from so many countries [.]) that it was impossible to hear it, except by stopping the body and starting off afresh on the primordial Path guarded by unnameable beasts. (CC, 234)

In this highly charged moment of epiphany, Mycéa perceives singular reality in the appropriately hallucinatory mode (i.e. as a perception which creates its own object). Her apparent madness is recognised as true insight ('you did not become mad, Chérubin was saying'). The passage continues: 'Marie Celat laughed softly in the thick atmosphere of the hut, feeling like an explosion in her body the growth of the light shining out into the depths of the night. Her head and her thought grew along the branches, she woke up without even realising she had been asleep...' (235). Rather than relate *to* the countryside [*le pays*], she here incorporates and expresses it. She 'becomes-*pays*' in something like the Deleuzian sense. For it 'seemed to us that this countryside (the uprooted trees, the forgotten names, the distorted voices, the extinguished rhythms) had in turn crouched down in her, made drowsy by this elusive emptiness which throbbed on every side, and that finally it rose up within her and drove her on anew' (224).

The singular profile of Mycéa is confirmed and developed in the later novels. Her *solitude*: 'Marie Celat is as alone as she was in the time of her youth' (TM, 368); 'no one spends time with Marie Celat [..]. It is the reason why she was chosen'.[51] Her *singularity*, beyond image or representation: as

Mathieu tells her, there is no picture [*image*] of you that resembles you, in any country of the world [...]. Marie Celat has no model' (TM, 348). Her *distance* from the specific: 'Mycéa [is] focused on her will not to seem alive or engaged in the disputes of the day: she desired only to float along in surroundings without reference'.[82] Strictly speaking, Mycéa finds the milieu of her quest within herself. As Mathieu tells her, 'you disappear into the country!' (TM, 359). 'Without leaving', she says, 'I go everywhere [...]. I am the rock...' (TM, 368); 'I retain everything' (CC, 238). Without moving, 'I [Mycéa] go to countries that cannot be counted [...]; it isn't that I want to fall into the night; the night falls in me' (TM, 361); '[I am] the only one to come from afar, like this wind! I map out the way for you [...] Here I am. Here is Celat! [*Mi Celat!*] [...] Now, leave me! I'm going alone' (TM, 359, 363–364).

In short, as the narrator insists, 'we have to accept once and for all that Marie Celat speaks a language that we cannot approach [...]. No one can summon her appearance [...], no one knows what she wants. She appears where she is not. Ho!' (TM, 358).

Most of all, Mycéa is the character whose particular story opens immediately out onto the universal story. Both stories are linked by the repetition of what Deleuze would call the 'paradoxical term', that absent, virtual term that organises a singular 'logic of sense'.[83] Here, this term is *Odono*, one name variously doubled and 'actualised' throughout the novel ('Odono Odono, Ozonzo, Donou...'), the recurrent sign of a single, quasi-mythical trauma. The name and legend of Odono echoes through the novel in almost rhizomatic fashion: 'it explodes in the branch in which night rises and is established, it descends to the light beneath the pond, it splinters in a spring at which dogs come to drink, it multiplies Odono in the hearts of those who walk without knowing, eat without thinking, drink without thirst' (166–167). The name 'Odono' is repeated with an insistence that matches the intensity of the legend's repression. To the recurrent question, 'who is Odono?', there is no straightforward answer. First and foremost, Odono is the name given to one of two ancestral blood brothers, whose mysterious betrayal is related in stories about the time before slavery Elucidation of this haunting myth of origins evades most of the characters in the novel. It turns out to be impossible to determine who was the betrayer and who the betrayed (166), and 'the beginning [of the story] fell away into a bottomless pit where no one was visible' (123). It is 'from this pit of the past', we learn, that 'break upon us the mass of memories' and omissions which 'we try to recompose [as] we don't know what history', a history 'cut up into pieces' (126). Odono is the name given, too, to another '*Négateur*' or *marron*, 'such that when we cried Odono, Odono, we couldn't know which of the two the name addressed.' For 'it was better', as Mycéa's forbear Liberté advises, 'to contemplate the past as in the depths of night, without being precise about names or times'.[84]

Odono's most recent incarnation is as Mycéa's younger son, who dies at the age of nineteen. Like his mother, this Odono (or Donou) is fascinated by the lure of a marine anonymity, an extinction of the self in 'the blue in which we dance and forget' (CC, 219). One day he dives down into the sea and doesn't come back up (223). His death completes what is for Mycéa a process of traumatic ascesis. In sequence, Mycéa loses her mother, her first lover (Thaël), then her current lover (Mathieu), before losing, one after the other, her two sons (Patrice and Odono). Such is the price to be paid for passage into a singular coherence (consistent with that undergone, as we shall see in the next chapter, by Johnson's characters Faith and Andrew).

Having lost everything she had to lose, Mycéa's lamentations become identical to the genealogical question which organises the novel in its entirety. Mycéa *is* that character in which the loss of personal interest and the restoration of the universal interest coincide. 'When she lay there thus, prostrate, asking everyone: "Have you seen Odono?" – some of us guessed that the person she was looking for was not her youngest-born, but the first of a line without descendants'.⁵⁵ When her son dies, 'she crie[s] out: Odono, where is Odono?' (217) – the same question her own tormented father asked at the moment of her birth (11, 17–18; 92, 96). With this repetition in difference, to adapt Deleuze's phrase, we intuit the 'sense' of an answer to the novel's inaugural question:

> How are we to guess that the word Odono (hardly a word. a sound) could have a sense [*sens*…]? How can we trace, over so many ocean swells, the trace of something, a howling pile of naked flesh called Odono? How can we locate [him], how can we find [him], where, by what calculation and with which instrument of measure? (CC, 17–18).

With these questions, this paradoxical repetition, this definitively post-Hegelian 'logic of sense', Glissant's fiction opens a new territory beyond territory, a coherence beyond the nation. There is no *actual* answer to the question 'where is Odono?', because Odono, beyond any binary distinctions, is a properly virtual term. It is that aleatory term that distributes its actualisation across an immanent field of remembrance and recovery. (I will come back to the Odono story below.) In *Case du commandeur*, this field remains only partially accessible. The veil begins to lift, however, in Glissant's subsequent fiction, which elaborates a new coherence, the singular coherence of the '*Tout-monde*'.

VIII *Mahagony* (1987), *Tout-monde* (1993): beyond national consciousness

In Glissant's last two novels, the transition from a historical–national perspective to an immanent–planetary perspective is taken more or less to completion. I stress the more or less. There is certainly no *sudden* break in Glissant's work, no sharply defined before and after. He continues, occasionally, to decry Martinique's economic dependency,[56] and in *Mahagony*, his Mathieu still emphasises the need for a kind of historical understanding (cf. MH, 14–15; 30). However, this understanding is no longer the dominant means of orientation in the world. In *Tout-monde*, 'our stories are [...] long respirations [*respirations*] without beginning or end [...], that have no concern with verification' (TM, 62). Here, to be 'broken up in the imperceptible' is to be 'consequently *visible at last to the blind eyes of everyone*' (TM, 164).

To the familiar themes of narrative fragmentation, an almost anthropomorphic presence of the landscape, and a somewhat aimless heroism, *Mahagony* adds a new emphasis on the artifice of representation and the writer as a direct semi-conscious product of his own fiction. Mathieu and Mycéa retain significant roles, alongside three mainly new characters, whose names are all derived from the title's tree: Maho, Gani, and Mani. One after the other, these three *marrons* escape their various forms of enslavement and strive, unsuccessfully, to consolidate an alternative existence. The solitary Gani incarnates a reckless, doomed *errance*. The overseer Maho, introduced briefly in *Malemort* as Beautemps, is an unwilling fugitive from (and eventual victim of) colonial violence, incarnated by the assassin Odibert. Mani is the quintessential rebel without a cause. Elusive, self-destructive and unreliable, he tends to slip away into a pure 'obscurity' and 'solitude'; eventually he disappears for good, through a quasi-mystical fusion with the same mahogany tree that sheltered Maho and inspired Gani (MH, 244). All three *marrons* are supported and nourished by the women of their community. They are unable, however, to lend this community the unity and direction it would need to break the cycle of oppression and evasion. Even in Mathieu's monologue which opens *Mahagony*, which emphasises the need for an awareness of the 'unicity of place' (MH, 20), this unity no longer seems *historical* in the earlier sense Glissant gave to the term. As regards the three *marrons* whose stories compose the framework of the novel – successively, Gani (dies 1831), Maho (dies 1943), and Mani (dies 1978) – Glissant's emphasis is now on the essential identity of the experience repeated, differently, in each consecutive context. *Marronage* is here both means and end, without any third dialectical term, just as 'Mani [is] the beginning and the end of this one mahogany [*mahogany*]'

(TM, 182 – 'Ma…ni'). This properly *literal* truth does not 'develop'. As Mathieu will affirm in the subsequent novel, Gani 'had all by himself invented the taste of resistance, for the pleasure of resistance, [and had] gone straight to the joy of resistance' with no intermediary step (TM, 181). With Gani and his successors, 'it was the same cry' in each case, 'the same figure of a same force diverted from its normal path' (MH, 21–22).

What is lost in this new identity is the distinction, central to Glissant's early work, between conscious, historically engaged action – the true *marronage* of the early *Négateurs* (model: Longoué), negation in the Hegelian sense – and unconscious, uninformed resistance, the pseudo *marronage* of vandalism and juvenile delinquency (model: Silacier). Here, as Eudoxie puts it, 'all winds are wind [*toutes* (sic) *vents c'est vent*]. All women are woman […]. All voices are voice' (MH, 50). As introduced in *Malemort*, Maho (a.k.a. Beautemps) 'was not a Negator, he was forced to be only a delinquent [and] an assassin' (MM, 54). Maho's violence now spills over into a kind of collective self-hatred.

> [Maho] looked too long at the wave on the horizon [.], it was only natural that he should begin despising himself Not only that He wanted others to despise him also, without respite. He went into houses at mealtimes, he sat down in the place reserved for the head of the household [.] The masters of the huts wept from having to suffer the humiliation He left without saying thanks. (MH, 187)

If *marronage* here continues to represent a kind of liberation, it is certainly not through contribution to the national community, but rather via an escape from it. Maho *géreur* [overseer] become *marron* celebrates a new kind of power: 'You can runs things as you like. You are master in the workshop of time and in the Plantation without end' (MH, 150). Free, he works to become ever 'more savage, more brutal, more pitiless' (153). Mani, again, was 'disorder' incarnate. 'He couldn't make the slightest gesture without breaking the air around him. Or else he didn't speak for days' (175, cf. 190). Mani lives 'the helplessness [*désarroi*] of youth that doesn't know what it wants' (203), 'it is ruin that he comes to find' (222). His is 'a *marronnage* of pure defiance, free of the anticipation of its preservation or victory. A passage on earth, to certify that it has moved without changing' (222). Like Mycéa's, his movement is one with its milieu: his 'night is restless, it takes refuge in itself' (223).

Gani, finally, 'want[s], as if carelessly, to escape to the hills [*maronner*] for the pure pleasure of it, without taking any of the [normal] precautions' (90). He does not run away, he just steps out of the loop binding bondsman and lord. *Marroné*, 'he had not hidden himself but simply moved over [*déplacé*] to patrol the rounds he had chosen'.⁵⁷ Strictly speaking, it is such smooth *déplacement* that is itself liberatory here. Gani pursues a nomadic liberation from place, in Deleuze's sense, rather than a reterritorialising resistance in Longoué's sense. 'Gani was everywhere present, like a cloud masked with sunlight' (MH, 89). He eludes dualism. 'I recognise [myself as] being the master or the slave both in the same way. I am transubstantiated' (89). More, 'I want to end, with me, all the races of men. What will live after me does not belong to humanity' (86). There is nothing like this in Glissant's earlier novels. Here, the exemplary act is one of self-constitution and self-elimination, as two sides of the same singular coin. Mani, for instance, 'was a specialist in disappearance' (200) and little else. Like Mycéa, Mani is a solitary, self-constituting creature. As he says to Ida, 'I do as Mani does. I have no need for examples' (198). He goes 'to the limit of his solitude [...]. Mani had gone alone into this desert', and 'it is there that he disappeared for ever'.⁴⁸ Like Mathieu, Mani points toward 'toward the first glimmering of a desert, purely virtual in its bounding spirituality [*tout virtuel d'une sautillante spiritualité*]' (30).

The nature of this virtual desert calls for more systematic attention. I consider here its main characteristics, in the following order: the refusal of co-implied binaries; the confusion of author and character; the collapse of frontiers; the affirmation of a single immanent matrix of the world. The last section of this chapter, on Glissant's *Poétique de la Relation*, will then provide a more formal theory to match this fictional transition.

There is to little to be gained from an attempt to summarise the systematically anti-systematic novel that is *Tout-monde*. It is one of the most stridently enthusiastic fictional incantations of a borderless world ever written. The familiar characters (Mathieu, Thaël, Mycéa) all reappear, alongside a massive and sundry collection of others (many drawn explicitly from Glissant's own personal experience). Mathieu's role as Glissant's *porte-parole* is consolidated and confirmed; Thaël tours the globe as a soldier of the French colonial armies; Mycéa has a less prominent role than in *Case*. There is no unity of place or plot. The novel's fundamental intertextuality (often between this and Glissant's own other works) is flaunted on every page. The division between fiction and theoretical reflection, already blurred in *Mahagony*, is now more or less entirely redundant. The characters swirl around the 'whirlwind' of the world (from Italy to Quebec to Paris to Algeria to Corsica to Guadeloupe...) in what reads as so many incidental illustrations of a general 'poetics of chaos'.⁴⁹ The basic principle of composition seems to be, quite simply. anything goes. Rather than pursue the scattered traces of plot and characterisation, we may do better to analyse this quintessentially singular composition at the relatively abstract level of analysis it seems to invite – the aspecific level on which it *works*. For this purpose, *Tout-monde* and

Mahagony can be treated together, as successive contributions to an emerging paradigm.

(a) Beyond *given* binaries

The first, essentially negative element of the new configuration is the definitive refusal of dualism or co-implication. Already, in *La Case du commandeur*, the genealogy of Odono is completely different from the genealogies of the Longoué, Béluse, Celat and Targin families which occupy Glissant up to and including much of *La Case du commandeur*. In his first two novels, the imminent national unity develops *through* the dualities that it does not dissolve – through the conflict of Longoué *marron* and Béluse *esclave* (in *Le Quatrième Siècle*), through Thaël and Garin, Thaël and Mathieu (in *La Lézarde*). In both these novels, forward-driven action takes place from hills to plain, or vice versa, and is mediated through the relationship of *conte* and *histoire*. Such dualisms map the space through which the heroes undergo their initiation into a national awareness. By contrast, in *La Case* and after, dualism as such seems to suggest impasse pure and simple.

The Odono story is certainly one of the most perplexing subplots in Glissant's fiction. *La Case*, the author of *Mahagony* explains, was written 'to explain that name' (MH, 173). As I read it, the Odono myth provides a genealogy of what I referred to in my introduction as our 'given' condition – the fact that we come into the world as separate from it, that our perception remains outside what we perceive, that our relations with others remain external, *competitive*, etc. What's given is a state resembling sin, a state of mediate duality (subject vs. object, self vs. other...), as opposed to an immediate, immanent monism. What dominates the irreducibly obscure story of 'Odono, Odono' is nothing other the very fact of dualism itself, abstracted from its terms. Odono, Odono – always repeated – are two primordial brothers, vaguely associated with Africa; one betrays the other, in a gesture associated just as vaguely with the Middle Passage. We know that the beginnings of the story are lost in a 'bottomless pit' of time, (CC, 123) and that it is impossible to determine which brother betrayed the other (125). Their concrete (specified) identities are impossible to establish. 'Which brother ran? Which brother was bound? No one knew, no one knows [*nul ne le sé*]...' (67). They are defined *only* by the conflict which turns one against the other; the question of which is which, Glissant explains, is not important, for 'the brother that betrayed will be sold in the very same boat' (91), and their struggle 'was nothing other than the mirror of a more ancient war or perhaps the forging of an irremediable fraternity' (125). More or less as in *Genesis*, the fracticidal motive is positioned desire itself, *my* as opposed to *your* desire. 'The sudden beast of envy and jealousy had bitten their flesh. Without apparent reason, for no known cause [...].

Odono sold Odono. A brother sold his brother…' (166; cf. 91) Ozonzo's version adds a new twist. It was, he says, 'the woman of the garden who divided the two brothers', just as it will be, he goes on, 'the garden of the woman that will bring them back together' (65). This mythical garden, we might say, is what turns into the 'Tout-monde'

Readers who demand clarity and narrative resolution, here as so often in Glissant's later work, are going to have to live with their frustration. The genealogical excavation of *this* conflict does not lead, as it did in *Le Quatrième Siècle*, to a greater awareness of the positioned specificity of its actors (Longoué vs. Béluse, Laroche vs. Senglis). It leads rather to the conclusion that it is the fact of conflict, the fact of the dualism, that must itself be overcome. The real answer to the Odono riddle is the monism of the 'Tout-monde' – 'let us dream together, since we cannot act with a single body' (TM, 165).

As a general rule, binary conflicts or dualisms in Glissant's later fiction figure as more or less inexplicable conflicts on the Odono model. As André rightly points out, 'the repeated struggles of Thaël against Mathieu, of Anne against Liberté, of Longoué against Béluse are lacking in *reasons*'.[90] Already in *Malemort*, Glissant presents a completely different picture of the relationship between unity and duality, univocity and multiplicity, to that which dominates his earlier work. Each time, the greater the sameness of the two contestants, the greater the conflict between them . To give some of many examples: 'the two bulls: Chinois and Soldat', that kill each other in a classic struggle for mastery (CC, 150–151; MM, 105); the verbal wars of Médellus and Lannec ('at their extremes, seeking the same postponed measure' [MM, 154]); Silacier and Néga ('the two madnesses balanced each other out, and exhausted themselves' [MM, 217]); the separation of Cinna Chimène and Pythagore ('they were the same nature dislocated in two irreconcilable bodies' [CC, 49]); the separation of Mycéa and Mathieu ('as before, distance and incomprehension brought them together in the same joy of not being understood' [CC, 206]). In *Malemort*, Glissant concludes merely that there is 'there is always a nigger [*nègre*] to enslave or massacre [another] nigger' (MM, 216; cf. 20). In *La Case*, even the founding dualism that conditions the whole initiatory quest of *La Quatrième Siècle* is reduced to a state of *malédiction* pure and simple; as Oriamé says to the first Longoué and Béluse, 'you are the seed of misery. Both of you, the one as much as the other!' (TM, 97; cf. CC, 224)

In *Tout-monde*, Glissant writes an apparently definitive effort to specify 'the obscure reason, the hidden source [of duality]' (TM, 428), a last attempt 'to go back along this wind of malediction and know why […] it has thus opposed us to ourselves' (428). Thus is framed the exemplary story of the emperor Askia's renunciation of Oriamé (430–433). The story 'explains' very little, however. Glissant summons the reader in suitably epic tones: 'know how he renounced Oriamé, because of this animal that ravages him inside' – but the *bête* in question is never named, never derived. It is rather, again, the very fact of two-ness that torments the emperor. Threatened by approaching colonial troops, 'what he fears isn't the line of [colonising] mercenaries who cut their way through the forest, no, it is the impossibility of being two [with Oriamé] in a single cry. The same impossibility which keeps one apart from the other, the people's chief and the gentle Oriamé' (430). The only 'reason' attributed to division is the fact of division itself, written like the very meeting of the lovers as the result of 'a chance [*hasard*] more implacable than every evil fate' (431). Askia's soldiers overthrow him in a *coup d'état*, for reasons which remain 'unfathomable'. Oriamé is captured. And so the kingdom falls, victim of 'this tragic malediction' (433). Glissant concludes that dualism is simply

> a fatality. How otherwise can you explain that there are always two (among us) who don't know why they oppose each other [..]. The first Béluse, the first Longoué, who filled this boat with a tireless grumbling. Mathieu Béluse Raphael Targin, both overflowing with a divinity that cannot gather its body together. Marie Celat Mathieu Béluse, who invented so many spells [*quimbois*] to invite misfortune upon themselves. Not to mention Laroche Senglis who never stopped killing himself. (TM, 427)

(b) The new coherence of the *Tout-monde*

Against dualism, Glissant now provides a radically reworked version of *la Totalité* become sufficient to itself, immediate to itself, one and the same as end and means. If *Mahagony* remains in part a transitional work, with *Tout-monde* Glissant has moved without reserve to a post-national coherence. The consequences are many. It is the only of Glissant's novels without unity of place and an at least relative unity of plot; it is the only novel to take place largely on foreign soil (opening in Italy, then moving at random through a mostly francophone world – France, Corsica, Indochina, Algeria, Quebec, as well as the United States). *Tout-monde*, unlike Glissant's carefully constructed previous novels, has no obvious organising principle at all, or rather, it makes of this lack of principle its own productive principle. 'The stiff elucidation of history is yielding to the pleasure of histories', as Glissant-narrator ('*celui qui commente*') will confess (MH, 229). The specific, organising dualisms of the early novels are nowhere to be found. Rather, Glissant recognises that 'we waste our time, which is already so short, in struggling [*rapailler*] amongst ourselves' (TM, 427).

> was it not time to reunite at last? To collect forms of knowledge from everywhere, all forms of knowledge, and bind them together? [ ] In our wanderings

[…], we had crossed, like the peoples of the world [… the] furious Ocean […]
And that is why, yes, we understand Chaos [*les Chaos*]. (TM, 407)

At this proximity to Chaos, rather than slowly work through historical dualisms we simply 'fall into the light of the world' (TM, 268), immediately, into a light beyond qualification or modalisation of any kind. The characters of *Tout-monde* perform a return to 'the source, *not yet diverted as mode*' (TM, 236, my emphasis). In *Mahagony* already, Mathieu 'had left the infinity of this minuscule country [Martinique] for the minuscule infinity that is our Earth in this universe', but returns to find the world virtually compressed in the monadological form of Martinique itself, an expressive fractal of the whole – 'the landscapes of the world are all inscribed in this one, suddenly' (MH, 24). The dominant temporality at work in the '*Tout-monde*' is a simultaneous coincidence effective beyond distance[91] (as opposed to the striated simultaneity of *La Lézarde*). The entire world is envisaged now as 'an enormous island in whose familiarity you can lose yourself and find yourself, without any elsewhere other than the infinity of stars under your feet' (MH, 215). Martinique is no longer a specific place of several or even many languages, but

> a country on earth where words are mixed together [..], all the languages of the world, known and unknown, more spread out than the unspeakable desert or more concentrated than a grain of *roucou*, and in the end a semblance of divinity speaks to you, which is the open mouth of what you call poetry. And so it follows on but without really following on, as what carries and what matters [*ce qui porte et importe*] is this over-flowing The parallels are wandering, the millimetres on the Map are infinite [92]

As Papa Longoué puts it, 'everyone now comes from far away, and those who are distant are all related, in the "*Tout-monde*"' (TM, 243).

The great philosophical inspiration behind this new global unity, of course, is the work of Deleuze and Guattari. Their book *Mille plateaux* figures explicitly in the text, as a work to which Glissant accords the status of precursor in a shared elaboration of 'the extension, the multiplication of the rhizome, that the philosophers of *Mille Plateaux* […] established later as a sort of prescient awareness of the *Tout-monde*'.[93] Like Deleuze and Guattari, Glissant confronts 'irremediable flux' as the first attribute of reality, a flux 'thought in a single movement' (TM, 52, 373). Like Deleuze, he now affirms a single immanence of the surface, infinitely extended. 'The only depth that matters to us is the palpable depth of surface [*l'étendue*]' (TM, 50). Like Deleuze, Glissant adopts some of the 'chaotic' terminology made fashionable by Prigogine and Stenghers, among others.[94] 'The earth's depth is its surface […]. The earth is a Chaos, Chaos has no high or low, and Chaos is beautiful' (54), both spontaneously and automatically'. Like Deleuze, Glissant adopts a neo-Spinozist 'expressive' vocabulary: 'when the Action expressed it, the flux flowed out one by one from each of the three springs [hope, faith, love] but converged in a single echo whose original trace could not, at that point, be detected' (TM, 373). The term 'rhizome', in particular, recurs throughout the novel, itself no small illustration of 'the spectacular growth of rhizome thought'.⁹⁵ In keeping with Deleuzian priorities, Glissant now abandons the pursuit of a territorial reconciliation of the dispossessed in favour of an unlimited play of free variation. 'Rather than tear yourself apart between these impossible alternatives (alienated being, liberated being, being this being that), summon forth landscapes, mix them together [...], imagine them, these landscapes, that blend into many...' (TM, 274).

Tout-monde develops, then, quite beyond the historical–national coherence celebrated in *La Lézarde* and *Le Quatrième Siècle*. 'There was perhaps a need in times gone by for the purity of chosen people in a chosen Territory', but this is no longer the case (TM, 510). Precisely those specific-universal formulas urgently invoked in *L'Intention poétique* are here singled out for special contempt.⁹⁶ The '*Tout-monde*' subverts all distinction between centre and periphery (TM, 38, 173; cf. PR, 41), just as it disperses all positioned names: 'these names of rocks, of flowers, of snakes, have also disappeared. We have deported names onto the Immense Waters' (TM, 426). The nation no longer enjoys a coherence of its own. One telling symptom: 'it is useless and impossible. today, to keep a travel diary. The world is moving too quickly. The notation is immediately rendered null and void' (TM, 445).

Rather, adequate notation here consists of becoming-immediate to the absolute speed of the world, i.e. the speed Glissant invokes, over and over, of the whirlwind [*tourbillon*]. 'This whirlwind invaded the infinity of mountains and seas and deserts, yes, simply from this minuscule [drop] of space and time, and it did so to affirm that there is no longer anything minuscule in space but everywhere an infinity that begins and that everywhere pursues itself' (TM, 81). Like Deleuze's aleatory point, the infinitely complex line of the *tourbillon* 'leads you and distributes you, in this tumult [*hélé*] of the world open[ing] above your heads and under your feet' (22). Its power is irresistible:

> don't try to escape, the *Tout-monde* catches you in its whirlwind, it names you in its surge, it associates your name – well, the name you think yours – with who knows how many others that you have never dreamed of [. ,], you are as if illuminated by your name, by yourself, you tumble down the whirlwind [until you] see the world from it doesn't matter which country's perspective [..., and this] coming and going is much more than universal, oh so much more (TM, 23; cf. TTM, 242)

Ultimately, again like Deleuze's aleatory point, the whirlwind equates absolute speed with absolute punctuality, absolute mobility with absolute fixity. 'A certain quality of whirlwind [can] find, in this way, a certain quality of fixity',[97] and 'this whirlwind acquired its meaning in only one region: that of an absolute immobility. It was the eye of the cyclone, it was the entire cyclone that floated thus in air and water, adjusting all things to a common measure' (TM, 150). In quintessentially singular fashion, this is 'a whirlwind of spaces and times that sharpened toward this fixed point' (153). And when 'the whirlwind touches its extreme point', it attains 'that absolute immobility that terrifies and makes sacred' (408). So then does this coherence beyond our own receive its conventionally 'awesome' affect.

The whirlwind is defined by its lack of limits, the lack of all distinction between here and there. 'It is the whole world that speaks to you through my voice of Panoply [*Panoplie*]' (TM, 24). From now on, the only legitimate frame of reference is the infinite as such. 'The *Tout-monde* is unfinishable, the far the farthest have neither meaning nor direction' (315; cf. 466), for 'there is no more an end to the world and soon there will be no centre' (38). The way is clear, then, for the creation of a fully circular logic, the logic taught by Papa Longoué's effective successor, Rocamarron (468). Rocamarron is the figure foretold by Longoué – he who unites all forms in one. As Mathieu knows, '"what is a woman a man an old body a child", it is you Rocamarron [...], you are all this at the same time'.[98] Rocamarron's Circle is a field of pure immanence – a field, by Deleuze's prescription, that is immanent only to itself.[99] As Rocamarron rebukes Mathieu, 'you still believe in the isolated thing, the race, the language, the terrain, the idea. You believe in unicity [whereas...] in the great Circle, everything is put into everything. He who has the strength to mix [*mélanger*] has the strength to find [...] the Vision', a Vision which leads 'towards the Great Mystery' (471, 473).

> this round [*rond*] of lands where there was no longer Here nor There Where everything was of a piece [...], countries, landscapes, ways of eating and singing [. .] I [Glissant] say to you, there is no longer a Here or There, and even those islets scattered around small islands are beginning to be brought together in the mesh without the slightest difference[100]

Within the circle, 'distance [is] abolished' (TM, 479). This singular plane immanence knows nothing of distances *between*, of properly *relative* distance. 'Everything was overturned into everything' (489), and 'all the lands are in land [*toutes les terres sont en terre*]' (236). As the archetypal Galibi hallucinated by the dying Papa Longoué puts it, 'the land [*la terre*] is not mine, nor yours, nor anyone else on earth's [...]; the land is for the land' (113). The land eludes merely specific transactions. Historical repossession is now an impertinent gesture (411). Recognising no limits of any kind, no conceptual impositions, the Circle is governed by a purely self-referential form of intuition. As Rocamarron says, 'you have no need of a guide [to] the knowledge of the great Circle, it is your divination that carries you onward' (470) and 'join[s] Here and There [in...] the Round of times and countries' (490).

Within the Tout-monde, then, Glissant celebrates a wholly new way of grasping the specificity of a place – which is precisely to *displace* it, to look for it in the pure 'between' of other places. 'The truth [...] of bodies and minds, of things and people, of trees and animals, is shared among the spaces and landscapes of the world' (TM, 82). We come to understand this sharing through nomadic travel. 'We learned to know the world. The *tout-monde*. We invented, then, immobile, or moving from country to country, something intangible to the skin, and which can truly be called, today, travel [*le voyage*]' (MH, 214). In characteristically Deleuzian fashion, 'travel' renders obsolete the distinction between movement and rest through a singular abstraction from place, a ongoing de-territorialisation. *Travel* joins means and end in itself ('this travelling, that grasps its end in itself'):[101]

> Travelling [.] is the preliminary to the relation in which the peoples shall henceforth be engaged [...]. Everyone can dream of travelling, without phantasm or pedantry. [Everyone can] dream the *tout-monde*, in these series of landscapes which, by their unity, contrasting or harmonious, constitute a country. (MH, 218, cf TM, 267)

Among Glissant's privileged roles in *Tout-monde*, then, is one rigorously excluded from the earlier *Le Discours antillais* – the role of the *tourist*, the 'mixer of spaces'.[102] 'Let travelling take its course [*laissez faire au voyage...*]. All the places of the world encounter each other' (TM, 29). His 'personal' travel diary (written in apparent defiance of the genre's imminent obsolescence) sweeps from Meso-American ruins to the great monuments of Ancient Egypt and is annotated by his own character, Mathieu.[103] The motivation (in the formalist sense) of several crucial passages of *Tout-monde* is likewise determined by a kind of tourist logic. For example: 'you are above the Sierra Maestra', and you stumble upon the Creole words of 'a Haitian from the last century', 'you climb up into the mists of the Pyrenees', and 'there goes a surreptitious fellow out from this white night, it is a Martinican migrant' (TM, 386), etc. Glissant's imagination wanders here from the 'the undefinable mornings of Mississippi' (165) to the frozen desert of Québec and the scorching desert of Algeria, via the Russia of Pushkin and Dostoyevski, in terms themselves reminiscent of tourist brochures:

> There was no longer any distance or distinction [..]. All that remained was to mix these lands together – as Longoué had suggested – to see which way this wind was blowing. For example, you navigate on the Nile in the country

of Egypt […] Or, it's the yellowy expanse of Atchafalaya near the Baton Rouge […] and this whole mixture propels you into the shoals of the Tracée in Martinique […]. Or else you will wander drowsily around the church at Saint-Germain-des-Prés in Paris […], and be thrown back to the time of the Banc des Sénateurs on the Savane in Fort-de-France.[114]

Perhaps the most curious example of Glissant's trans-world tourist variations is his derivation of Corsica from the Caribbean islands of Marie Galante and Dominique. He narrates it, as usual, in the third person, and in suitably oxymoronic concision. Trying to bring these two islands ('so different from each other') together in a kind of 'synthesis', the light that illuminates their landscapes divides to form an 'obscure' unity. The result: Corsica.

> The two lights, the one stretched and fleeting, the other densely opaque, conjugated their darkness [*conjuguèrent leur obscur*] in the heart of the poet. What does he see then, in the balancing of these landscapes, so near and yet so far? He sees the country of Corsica […]. The *Tout-monde*. You gather together enough earth and rock to continue drifting along, but sometimes you redistribute one place, someplace, much further away in another place. This is what happened when he wanted to reconcile in himself Marie-Galante and Dominique: he simply rediscovered Corsica. (TM, 277–278)

Glissant here achieves a perfect fusion of binaries without remainder and without relations between the two original elements. Most significantly, the 'seeing' of the third actual term, Corsica, is accomplished *without fulfilling that condition* that Glissant himself spells out when he was, as a tourist in his student days, actually *in* Corsica's 'unreal' landscape: 'we would have to wait for the country to show itself – in all the necessary convulsions of a nation – so as to be able eventually to *see* it' (TM, 249, my emphasis). At Glissant's new infinite distance from Corsica, this requirement no longer seems to matter. Rather, the seeing of Corsica is *immediately* deduced from the *Tout-monde*: 'the *Tout-monde* allows you to perceive how these countries, which you have deciphered, continue far-from-you…' (279), and turn up, suddenly, in an 'equivalence between such different landscapes, such distant languages' (442).

The landscape best suited to such free variation is, unsurprisingly, the desert. There are few references to desert-like landscapes in Glissant's work prior to Mathieu's annunciation in *Mahagony* of 'the first glimmering of a desert', in all its 'virtuality' (MH, 30). But in *Tout-monde*, the desert is that landscape which naturally becomes-other most immediately. As Thaël says of Algeria, 'it is a mountain, the desert, a mountain that has been made flat […]. It is the sea also, the desert, a sea that has been dried out […]. The desert resumes all the landscapes of the world, that is why [in the desert] your head whirls and you see the invisible' (317). Again, travelling in Québec, Thaël knew at last, with absolute certainty, that they had entered the immobile, that they were no longer moving forward, that the whirlwind had reached its peak, and that they would never leave this steppe, this tundra, this ocean, this desert, this jungle, this infinity. Raphaël Targin no longer thought of Quebec in any way but this. as a whirling infinity (TM, 404, cf. 464).

No more than the Corsicans derived from Marie Galante and Dominique, the inhabitants of these immobile landscapes are no longer required to 'express themselves' in order for the visitor to understand the common nature of their essence. (It is of course a cliché, that the desert of snow or sand is only indistinct to non-residents). Rather than work through a specificity established *sur place*, Glissant here has immediate access to a landscape in terms of its inherent intensity, its velocity measured from the Creative *tourbillon*. Now, 'we no longer make things on the spot [*sur place*], we fall, without precedent into the fragments of all the countries that are shattered around us, we spread [the idea] that coming-and-going are the same, you begin to perceive the Tout-monde' (415).

(c) **The new heroes of *l'errance***

The unity-totality which governs *Tout-monde* is no more empirically derived from specific differences than the *totalité* presupposed in Glissant's early theory. In the early theory, of course, the totality is expressed *through* specificities; here, it is more a matter of privileging those singularities which are themselves already 'total', all at once. The singular fragments that populate the *Tout-monde express* it, on the fractal or monadological model: the parts include or duplicate the whole. In other words, the privileged residents of the *Tout-monde* are those whose substantial being – displaced, migrant, in-between, hybrid – most immediately and sufficiently articulates the formal qualities of the singular *Tout*. *L'errance* is no longer a form of *détour*, a form always to be recuperated by a national consciousness. Rather, since ceaseless movement itself provides the sole basis for permanence and fixity – the permanence of constant change (TTM, 63–64) – so then 'wandering [*l'errance*] is precisely what enables us to stay put [*nous fixer...*]. The thought of *l'errance* frees the imaginary, it projects us out of this prison cave in which we have been trapped. We are [then] greater, greater with all the greatness of the world!' (TM, 124).

The new characters celebrated in *Tout-monde* are the masters of such wandering. They undertake that 'travelling that grasps its end it itself [...]. Neither being nor *errance* have a limit – and transformation is their permanence, ho!' (TM, 124). They are 'the salt of Diversity'. Migrants all, 'they have transcended limits and frontiers, they mix languages, they relocate languages, they traipse along, they fall into the madness of the world'. They are the deterritorialised par excellence, immanent only to the whole: 'they are repressed and excluded from the power of the Territory but listen, they are the land [*terre*] itself which never shall be territory [...], they are the prophets of Relation, they live this whirlwind...' (TM, 407). They are the *imperceptible* – they 'have moved beyond every perceptible dimension' (408). And their one imperative: 'Open to the world the field of your identity [...], this manner of space that supports you, but [do so] by invading yourself from everywhere, *when you no are no longer concerned with looking for reasons or confessing mistakes*'.[105]

The cast introduced in *Tout-monde* includes some new characters, as well as, mainly, old characters (Thaël in particular) presented from a new angle. Like Stepan 'executed' by the Nazis, like Mycéa bereft of her sons and lover, like Thaël bereft of Valéry, most of Glissant's privileged characters have now, in a sense, 'died to the world'.[106] They are the variously unhomed. For example: Anastasie ('I have neither location [location] nor lodging [....], I am open' [440]); Amina ('gypsy' and able to speak 'all the languages of the world', without 'settling herself in any privileged or dominant tongue' [40–41]); and most striking, Stepan Stepanovitch ('one of those wandering migrants from the Orient, that is Romania or Serbia or Hungary, could he tell which?' [337]). In his own words, 'Stepan can do everything, he knows! [...] Stepan's language very special! [...] Czech German Italian French! No, nobody no more! No more to know Stepan's language!' (371).

Glissant's new singular characters are at home in the midst of 'all these languages that crash against each other like the crests of tumultuous waves' (TM, 20). For instance, the author's guide in Egypt, 'Mahmoud, who is eleven years old, speaks more or less well four of the tourists' languages', and 'speaks in gasps and cries, having no need of a sustained syntax' (TM, 451). What need does the *Tout-monde* have of syntax, the imposition of 'external' order par excellence? Deterritorialised, words from across the *Tout-monde* flow together in a single immediate rush. Syntax is for nation-builders and other relics of the colonial past. On this condition and in this context, Creole takes on a wholly different value from that assigned by Glissant's earlier work. It now becomes a pure form of continuous variation, unstoppable and 'uncontainable', a 'continuous flux of creation' (388; cf. 51, 238).

In particular, among the new characters introduced in *Tout-monde* are a collection of what we might call 'miracle characters', anonymous *types* who illustrate Glissant's apparent belief that 'Martinicans are capable of anything at all' (TM, 413). Unlike the *marrons* of the early novels, these characters manipulate the status quo, rather than escape from it. Take for example the stories of 'the god of commerce and invention' (268), in a context where 'commerce is above all the pleasure of genius [*du génie*]' (270). Incarnating a street-smart *savoir-faire*, this 'god's' escapades range from the not so remarkable ability to ride the Paris bus system without paying a fare, to a rather more remarkable *calèche* ride, paid for by having the driver pull up at a chateau where *le Dieu* simply persuades the resident to buy the calèche, horse and all. The fortunes of the 'Caribbean pharmacist' are similarly blessed: taken prisoner by the Germans in 1940, he is immediately set free and given a military passport, 'written out in such a way that each time he had to present it, he was given a military salute by the men of the [German] army or police' (383). Why? Because his captor General Mülher once lived in Martinique (1934–38) and enjoys speaking Creole. Thanks to this happy chance, the pharmacist 'survives the Occupation', to reflect on 'this manner of proliferating [oneself] in vertiginous spaces then suddenly projecting [oneself] into an apparently definitive fixity. The *Tout-monde* whirls you around, so as to teach you immobility' (385). The moral of the story: 'you find a Martinican everywhere [...]. They scatter everywhere, like a powder, without imposing themselves anywhere [*sans insister nulle part*]' (385).

Among the abilities which ensure successful survival in the *Tout-monde*, then, is the ability to blend with its environment, to become-one with the whirlwind. Such is already the transfiguration of Mani, in *Mahagony*, who 'blends in with the mass of leaves' under the tree from which he takes his name, and 'becomes rock that endures, wood that resists...' (MH, 224). Stepan, likewise, has an uncanny ability to avoid detection, to escape in properly miraculous fashion a whole sequence of executions and 'certain deaths'. Those who give themselves over to the *Tout-monde* are, in a certain sense, re-born as shielded from conventional dangers. As Amina tells Mathieu, 'you are in the world as a whole, you see, nothing can happen to you, you are wholly in the world' (43). Simply, 'you're there, a piece of the world' (209).

Of all the characters narrated in *Tout-monde*, it is Thaël (a.k.a. Raphaël Targin) whose experience takes pride of place. 'Raphaël Targin, who had been at the tiny beginning of my story, turned out to be there for us at that moment when every story dilates in the air of the world, and is perhaps diluted in it' (MH, 242). If Mathieu remains the most articulate exponent of the *Tout-monde* – as Papa Longoué baptises him, he incarnates 'science and consciousness' (TM, 177) – Thaël, with Mycéa, is its most privileged actor and resident. 'In whirlwind matters, Raphaël Targin was the true and only master, that is, the one possessed [*le possédé*]' (TM, 374). Thaël moves at a speed closest to the absolute, 'the only one, among all the speeds of the world, that you can take into your head and your entire body...' (334). Where Mathieu writes and reflects, Thaël 'wrote nothing down, he would turn everything, life and countries, into words: immediate and mocking' (401). Just as Papa Longoué had brought them together in spirit (95), so

Thaël 'had contracted all the Beluses and all the Longoués together in his flesh and in his mind, had blended them within him along with those Targins, owners of lands and Residences [*Habitations*], and the Celats who rambled so' (94). Thaël fulfils all of the conditions required for a becoming-imperceptible. He has undergone the loss of a positioned interest, with the abrupt death of his beloved Valéry (Thaël 'had disappeared since that day of devastation that witnessed the death of Valerie and the sacrifice of his dogs', 'he had taken refuge in the *tout-monde*, so as to forget the source of *La Lézarde*' [MH, 238]). He has become-one with his surroundings: confronted with 'too much suffering' and having no 'remedy' to propose, 'I [Thaël] decided to become banal', unremarkable (MH, 241). Thaël is thus immediately 'affected by the world' (TM, 280), his character is the 'result of universal contagion' (MH, 241).

Of all Glissant's characters, Thaël is the most emphatically nomadic. "Oh me, I travel through the *Tout-monde* […], I'm free […], and so I zoom around everywhere, to see how things are organised' (TM, 328). What is perhaps most surprising about his *cours*, perhaps, is his main choice of vehicle: the French colonial army. Thaël leaves Martinique, where he at least helps to assassinate an agent of the colonial regime, only in order to serve with the French forces in Indochina and Algeria. It is not an obvious move, and the reader looks in vain for an explanation beyond the declaration: 'I look into the belly of the beast, that's why I'm in the army' (TM, 297). To be sure, he maintains that 'I've never loaded my rifle' (299). 'I fight', he says, 'to untangle things. There are so many people in the world who want to stop you from untying the knot. You have to journey everywhere' (302). Rather than take sides for *or* against colonialism, Thaël now professes an absolute scepticism. 'There is no reality in this business' (296). But as his friend Soussoul explains, when '[Thaël] goes to war' he does not avoid the conflict, he is 'always on patrol in the bush', forever looking out for his French comrades in arms (Soussoul and Santonin [289]), and so on. Even at the end of the Algerian campaign – where he learns to admire 'the Arabs' – he declares that 'he regrets nothing' (331, 335). More, in Algeria, Thaël notes with apparent surprise that certain 'Caribbeans, some students, have gone over to the Arabs' side'; he even mentions a certain 'Frank Fanon [sic]', with no further comment (325–326). When Thaël says, then, 'I fought against the world, and I lost' (61), there is a sense in which it is not clear whether it is Thaël or French colonialism that lost.

(d) The new authors of *la Totalité*

The univocal coherence of the *Tout-monde* requires a new kind of author to express it. In Glissant's earlier works, we know that the writer occupied a privileged position *among* other positions, distinct in the midst of a national dialectic on which his or her own authority depended. Here, Glissant works to make the authorial position immanent to the whole social field, dispersed across a variety of roles. The major effort of the author, in a sense, is to become-imperceptible, indistinct, one of the crowd of characters. Authorial responsibility is split, in particular, between Glissant 'himself' under various guises ('*le romancier*', '*le chroniqueur*', '*le poète*', '*le raconteur*', '*le déparleur*'[107]) and Mathieu, whose 'nominal' history is closely bound up with Glissant's own (TTM, 77–80). This evolution is generally affirmed by Glissant's commentators as a subversion of narrative authority, the fragmentation of voice, and so on. As I see it, however, it can only represent a newly ramified pretension to authority, a claim to an interpretative power now unlimited by positioned perspective. The result is the multiplication of a properly singular narrative voice.

Mahagony and *Tout-monde* employ opposite strategies to this end. In the first case, the authorial voice is distributed to a series of characters (literate or illiterate) who narrate and apparently write each section in turn, in the first person. In the second case, the first person narrator is eschewed even in those cases where it is Glissant 'himself' speaking, now become one historical character among others (in transit from Paris to Baton Rouge, on vacation with his friends Jean Paris and Maurice Roche, etc.). In both cases it is impossible, certainly, to locate a single privileged voice *among* others. But in both, what *is* clearly privileged is this very confusion of voices in the interests of a newly singular univocity.[108]

Such is certainly the effect of Glissant's own self-multiplication. Explicitly, his purpose is to limit his status to that of a participant, a wandering 'point of view'.[109] Explicitly, he reduces his role from channel of self-consciousness to mere transcriber, mere *déparleur* (rambling speaker) – 'the *déparleur* appreciated whirlwinds above all, he collected them' (TM, 401). Glissant is at pains to emphasise his passively humble status as 'irrelevant bystander', and nowhere more clearly than in the encounter between Mathieu and Rocamarron (470, 474). In practice, however, his new role allows him to do two somewhat incompatible things simultaneously. The first is to assert the authenticity of what is reported through personal attestation. Several stretches of *Tout-monde* (including student experiences, holidays, working-life in Paris) appear to be flatly autobiographical, or at least written as such, and borne out by the index of proper names at the back of the book (a list which includes Patrick Chamoiseau, Maurice Roche, Roger Giroux, Henri Pichette, and so on). In *Tout-monde* alone of all his novels, Glissant includes explicit *clins d'oeil* to his friends – for example, a trip to 'Toronto where Alain Baudot [...] undertakes the most extraordinary feats of archival editing and organisation possible' (TM, 464) – including most notably a massive 750-page annotated bibliography of

Edouard Glissant himself, who happened to receive an honorary doctorate from Baudot's university in 1989.

At the same time, the erasure of the authorial I earns that legitimacy conferred by an exact transcription of other voices – the legitimacy of a transparent or anonymous recording. When Glissant speaks in his 'own' voice at the end of *Mahagony*, 'he freely admits constructing it around the confidence[s] of he [Mathieu] who related it and who renounced the constraints of writing […], reserving himself for deeper explorations' (MH, 228). The important thing now is that 'word and writing mix' (TM, 155); here, 'what speaks [*ce qui parle*] is the endless echo of these voices [that] accompany written signs' (MH, 230). Most extravagantly, in *Tout-monde* Glissant invents a character, Anastasie, who travels from Martinique to visit the author in his own Paris office in order to confirm that 'you have written the very thing that I wanted [written]'.[110]

Indeed, in these later novels several of Glissant's characters themselves come to life in order to confirm the truth of what he writes. This is precisely what is achieved in the remarkable becoming-author of Mathieu Béluse, in both *Mahagony* and *Tout-monde*. From the beginning, Mathieu has been the intellectual of the group. He was the historian of *La Lézarde*. He is the most articulate of Glissant's characters, and author of what Glissant quotes as a *Traité du Tout-monde*. If Mycéa incarnates the *secret du pays*, 'Mathieu produced in ideas or in words that which Mycéa keep in the most untouchable part of herself.' Where Mycéa acts by 'letting off steam in great bursts of exaggerated life' (CC, 188), Mathieu is cautious and reflexive. Together, they form the dialectical couple of a consciousness no longer dependent on the negative (or mediate) role of the collective history.

Mahagony is largely dominated by the voice of Mathieu, who reflects on his own fictional status so as to escape 'from a chronicle in which […] the author had represented me without warning me or asking for my permission' (MH, 25). Mathieu becomes 'a man who has escaped from his bookish image (an image imposed by another but which wound up nonetheless by defining what I really was)' (MH, 29). What this awkward becoming-author accomplishes is the elimination of any residual gap *between* action and representation: 'since I was the thread [of the story], I could just as well become the narrator [*le révélateur*], no need of the *chroniqueur* [i.e. Glissant] for this work' (MH, 22). More, 'I experience – man, author and outlined parable all at the same time – the triple unity of this history that I had to relive' (MH, 31). Even the dialectic between character as self and author as other, between a self who acts but *as* represented, 'told by another' (25), is surpassed by a movement towards singular imperceptibility:

Thus, a character in a book, but freed from any preliminaries of writing, [.. I dreamt of] clarifying the shapeless original [story] and in this way make myself obsolete or even, really, redundant. Light cuts into time and in the agony of time I was to be liberated from my character (MH, 26)

The 'referent' of fiction becomes internal to it; the contained becomes container, in the self-reflexive writing of 'a real that doubled itself' in its own written discourse (MH, 32). Mathieu establishes this identity 'at the head of the work, that is at the foundation of the enterprise of which he was the creature and which he invested in his turn as it primary creator. I had been this creature, and I was become this creator…' (MH, 33). One of the abiding aspirations of every singular project is coming true for Glissant's Mathieu: to speak as a being-spoken, to think in a being-thought [*cogitor*], to exist in that circular derivation of creation in which the creature participates in its own creation.

The great consequence is the obsolescence of that historical problematic that had dominated Glissant's early fiction. The awkward relation *between* writer and people, fiction and history, is here replaced by their simple equation (*in* the fiction). Now, the effort 'to go back down the current of time, so enormously mixed with the avatars of my own existence' (MH, 32) is less the daunting dialectical project of Martinican self-constitution as such than of Mathieu's own fictional introspection. When 'he' writes: 'the character in a book that for a brief moment I am once again […] throws himself […] into the future of humanity – which we can induce then from the most subterranean part of its past [*son passé*]' (MH, 217) – it is not clear if the antecedent of *son passé* is humanity or Mathieu. At the same time, Mathieu ceases to be a discretely limited personality among others. 'Types of characters matter less to us than the wind sliding [*glissant*] under the acacias' (MH, 28), and 'I [Mathieu] was the yellow wind that climbs between the hills; I was the blue wind beating down the beaches […]; I was also the wind of froth that hurtles freely down to encounter other people and other countries [….]; one individual could never conceive this incommensurable dimension born of billions and billions of encounters, of chance events…' (MH, 23; cf. 251).

Ultimately, Mathieu and Glissant become indiscernible in the interests of a single, indivisible narrative authority. Native informant and ethnographer become one voice, 'such that the passage from the character that was Mathieu, to the separate man he had become, to the author himself […], has never stopped being disrupted. In the end neither the informant nor the author [can] recognise the one apart from the author; and the attentive reader [is] no more able to distinguish them, at least not without getting dizzy' (MH, 228–229). In short, 'Mathieu, the *déparleur*, the chronicler, the novelist, were four-in-one, if not more'.[111] In case things are not quite clear enough, Glissant adds some explicit instructions to the reader of *Tout-monde*. 'Notice then the multiplication that begins with Mathieu Béluse: Mathieu, the chronicler, the poet, the novelist, without countering he or she who is writing [this] at this very moment and who can taken neither for Mathieu, nor this chronicler, novelist or poetry; they proliferate, can we say that they are one-only divided in itself, or several who meet up as one?' (TM, 271). The truth is that it doesn't make much difference either way.

Glissant fragments, then, in order to become *more* rather than less total. Rather than one positioned voice among others, his 'larval selves' express the consensus embodied by a multiplicity of voices caught up in a single uni-vocity. For example, Thaël's 'anguish provoked by the mountains of Europe' is a feeling that 'he shared with the *déparleur*, the Mathieu [sic], the chronicler, the poet, the novelist, *a feeling we might qualify then as universal*' (TM, 403, my emphasis; Glissant does not ask if this universal anguish is shared by those who live *in* the mountains). Again, in the section of *Tout-monde* apparently culled from what Glissant presents as his own travel notes in Egypt, Glissant and Mathieu cooperate so as to 'double' the authority of the given text. Glissant adds the following note: 'In the novelist's [i.e. Glissant's] text, the passages here put in italics were underlined by Mathieu Béluse, *who no doubt recognised in them traces of himself. Let us follow them then with him. We might say that the novelist's words, sometimes, are the very same as those of* Mathieu Béluse' (TM, 445, note). The fact that this metanarrative assertion is itself italicised only adds to what Glissant would no doubt call its 'total' import.

IX Beyond specificity: *Poétique de la Relation* (1990) and after

In both the early and late stages of Glissant's work, his theoretical and fictional writing are closely interrelated. A brief review of the most significant of his recent essays amply confirms the trajectory suggested by his novels. *Poétique de la Relation* provides a detailed theory for the fully *immediate* expression of Totality, beyond the mediate-dialectical constitution of the nation. The concept of totality itself, along with certain other aspects of the new book, is of course consistent throughout Glissant's work. In my opinion, however, the substantial contrast between *La Poétique* and the earlier theory is profound and obvious, and implies a sweeping revaluation of categories only thinly masked by the persistence of familiar terms and figures.[112] The word 'Martinique' rarely appears in *La Poétique de la Relation*.[113] Glissant's *Relation* finally swaps a territorial for a planetary coherence. Here, 'the circulation and action of poetry are no longer the conjecture of a given people, but the becoming of planet earth' (PR, 44).

In Glissant's early work, 'to consent to opacity' was to recognise 'the irreducible density of the other' (DA, 245), and implied 'the thankless detailed inventory of the country' (DA, 265; cf. IP, 245). Glissant has since come to believe that 'for the first time, human cultures in the semi-totality are entirely and simultaneously in contact [...], and that for the first time, the world's peoples are totally conscious of the exchange' (TTM, 23). Now, the emphasis is on the fact that 'opacities can coexist, flow together, weaving materials which can be understood only from the texture of the weave and not from the nature of the composing elements' (PR, 204). With *La Poétique*, Glissant moves toward an immediate intuition of what he described in the exergue of *Le Sang rivé* as 'not works of art but the very material in which the work proceeds [...]. That which trembles, wavers and ceaselessly becomes – like a ravaged land – scattered.'[114]

Where the nation was 'the enrooted [*enracinée*] necessity of relation to the world' (IP, 72), *la Relation* is now defined by its refusal of *enracinement* (PR, 23–27). In the *Poétique*, nation is invariably considered as *contrary* to Relation. A Relative 'wandering [*errance*] emerges silently from the destructuring of national compacities, which only yesterday remained triumphant' (PR, 30). As wholly immanent to itself, as wholly smooth space, Glissant's new concept of Relation announces an age *beyond national itinerary* (PR, 41–42) – the age, in a sense, of places without or beyond nationhood. More, 'the trajectory, however bent, no longer matters',[115] for 'confluence [of Relation] abolishes trajectories (itineraries)' (171). Relation writes the last word in *dépassement*. The goal is now less national repossession than a movement toward a global 'economy of disorder', synchronised to 'this acceleration, this speed [which] races the Earth' (PR, 141). Against territorial reconciliation, Glissant now evokes as a 'nomadic' ideal that 'absent man who walks' and haunts the twelfth and final chapters of the *Poétique*, whose energy 'is without limits' (224). he 'exhausts no territory, he is rooted only in the sacredness of air and evaporation, in the pure refusal which changes nothing of the world' (PR, 224).

In short, if Glissant's early texts narrate the constitution of the nation, the later texts generally revel in its dissolution.[116] What is most remarkable, however, about this shift of emphasis is that the 'Martinican condition' analysed in such detail and with such urgency in *Le Discours antillais* – the *fact* of dispossession itself – has not changed. On the contrary. By Glissant's own description, 'banalisation' and dependency continue unabated. By 1987, Glissant's Martinique has become 'a museum. The Museum of the Colony [...]. We are proud to present to you a Colony in the pure state' (MH, 178). National status has become *dépassée*, but without fulfilling the conditions originally set for this redundance. Now it must be stressed that the early Glissant suggested very clear guidelines for a national self-dissolution: 'opaque speech and tragic unveiling' must be 'taken on board by each community' (IP, 204). Again, 'I can go beyond the

Nation – [only] if it is already accomplished in the fields of the One or if, new or imminent (plan-able) I conceive of it as a whole and carry it to the overcoming in which relation lives [*au dépassement où la relation vit*]' (IP, 216). These requirements are never met in Glissant's own theory. Rather than surpass a dialectic process *through* its resolution, as required in the early work, his later work simply changes criteria. It is precisely that problem which frustrated a national reconciliation in *Malemort* which now provides the opportunity for the newly global post-national reconciliation. In the process, Glissant's critique of dispossession risks conversion into an effective affirmation of dispossession (however 'positively' affected).

Against the dialectical historicism of *Le Discours antillais*, *Poétique de la Relation*, like the *Tout-monde* which it anticipates, is a profoundly Deleuzian text. Once again, all reality exists at the same level, and all binaries tend toward their own elimination within a single plane of immanence, of all-compatible singularities.[117] Reliance on Deleuze is explicit: 'Rhizome-thought will be the principle of what I call a poetics of Relation, according to which every identity spreads in a relation with the Other'.[118] Do not be fooled by the relational vocabulary: like Deleuze, Glissant has little time for the specific as such, for active differences-with and -between. Through this version of *Relation*, the singular replaces the specific.

There is of course no conceivable place for a national coming-into-consciousness within this new, quasi-Deleuzian universe; at the same time, those categories explicitly discounted within a mediate-national perspective (*créole*, *errance*, *détour*) are here rehabilitated as privileged agents of the immediate. The nation's loss is, as we would expect, Creole's gain. 'The Creole language' is now the 'most obvious symbol' of an 'unlimited interculturality [*métissage*]' – a language 'whose spirit is always to open itself out […] in the extraordinary explosion of cultures' (PR, 46; cf. 87). Creole is suddenly 'transfigured into word of the world' (88), without passing through the intermediary (national) term so crucial to *Le Discours antillais*. Similarly, *errance* is no longer a wandering 'outside history', but directly coincident with the productive movement of the world itself, an order beyond orientation – 'the urgency of conceiving the hidden order of the whole – so as to wander in it without getting lost' (145). *Errance* is now the very working towards totality, 'the search for totality' (30); 'the thought of *errance* is postulation of the sacred, which never gives itself and never erases itself' (33).

A particularly striking sign of the change at work here is the revaluation of Saint-John Perse, recognised as 'the most essential poet alive' (IP, 115) in *L'Intention poétique* but condemned as insufficiently specific in *Le Discours antillais*. Saint-John Perse (1887–1975) is generally recognised as the most significant of the (white) creole poets of the francophone Caribbean, and Glissant has on several occasions confronted what Chamoiseau and Confiant have called Perse's limited and ambiguous 'connivance with us [black] Antillians'.[119] In *Le Discours*, Perse appears as a poet of the Same, and it is *because* of his wandering, rootless origins that he fixes so obsessively on the Sameness, the anonymous universality ('a universal without particularity' of the West [DA4, 430–431])[etc.]. The Perse of *Le Discours* 'is not Caribbean [...]. Coloniser of the universe, Perse feels not the least bit guilty' (431, 432). With *Poétique de la Relation*, by contrast, Perse returns to favour as author of an 'erratic oeuvre', 'an oeuvre which invites totality',[120] which promotes of 'an aesthetic of the universe', 'an aesthetic of the chaos-world'.[121] His refusal of specificity is now a positive asset in the articulation of the *Whole*. 'By renouncing the effort to "comprehend" the history of the place in which he was born', Saint-John Perse 'projects, in an eternally given future, this Whole in which he founds himself' (PR, 50). The projection here depends upon the renunciation. 'Saint-John Perse's orality is not enclosed in the rustling of shadows, from which one discerns the surroundings [*l'entour*]' (51); this refusal of *l'entour* now opens out onto 'the always possible infinity. The round of the voice is multiplied in the world' (51), of 'the narration of the universe' (50). Again, 'Saint-John Perse does not bring together the torn memory of a place', but rather works toward 'a totalisation which we might call baroque' (52), 'a "naturalised" baroque, that is, one which lends itself to no reference' other than 'the materiality of the universe' itself (52, 54).

This Perse is typical of Glissant's newly post-territorial agenda. Radical dynamism has become the priority, on the assumption that 'movement is that which realises itself absolutely. Relation is movement'.[122] The 'universal' discourse is literally that discourse which conveys, all at once, the dynamic complexity of the universe. 'how do we know that he [the poet] speaks for everyone? [...]. We know it. It is because he piles cyclones upon the cold, the desert in the mountain larger than a whale, the wind which whistles [*pétaille*] near the rain which patters [*fifine*]'.[123] It is *given*, revealed, that 'force never dries up, for it is in itself turbulence' (PR, 173); 'poetic force' is, simply, 'the energy of the world, maintained alive in us' (173). As before, it is 'the knowledge of the Whole [...] which in the Whole liberates the knowledge of Relation' (20). At every moment, 'totality calls for us. Today every work of literature is inspired by it' (122). But now totality's call is more urgent in its insistence upon the dissolution of the specific. Against the generalised, linear One of the West, Glissant sides with the spiralled, 'Indian' philosophy of the whole (59), 'whose aim is the dissolution of the individual in the Whole' (PR, 59, 61; cf. TTM, 105–111). Very simply, 'everything is in everything, without forced confusion' (TTM, 23).

Here, Relation is a name for self-differentiating reality as such, it is not a 'relationship' *between* things. In what is perhaps the most important declaration of the book, Glissant explains that

> to the degree that our consciousness of Relation is total, that is immediate and turned immediately to the realisable totality of the world, *we no longer need, when we evoke a poetics of Relation, to add: relation between what and what?* That is why the French word 'Relation', which functions a bit like an intransitive verb, does not correspond for example to the English term 'relationship' (PR, 39–40).

Rather than elaborated through relationships-with and -between, Glissant's poetics now stem immediately from an expression of the totality itself, 'disseminated in this extension' (PR, 73). Relation is that which equates all forms of reality. Very precisely, Relation has no determinate '"content". Relation, because it is totalising, is intransitive' (TTM, 24). Relation abolishes all representation *of* Relation; ultimately, it even abolishes the very *idea* of Relation, to simply become-Relation. 'Only the idea of totality is an obstacle to totality' (PR, 206). It is not a question of claiming that being is Relation or Relation being – a proposition which would still, after all, actively *relate* – but rather to arrive at that perfect tautology, 'only Relation is relation' (184): 'then comes the time when Relation no longer announces itself through a series of trajectories, of itineraries [...], but, itself and in itself, explodes itself, like a weave inscribed in the sufficient totality of the world'.[124]

So it is not good enough to define Relation, as Celia Britton does, as 'a fluid and unsystematic system whose elements are engaged in a radically non-hierarchical free play of interrelatedness' – and thus to conclude, rather quickly, that 'Relation safeguards the Other's difference', that 'Relation is an anti-imperialist project'.[125] For this 'interrelatedness' – if the word applies at all – leaves the status of what it relates suspended in a kind of conceptual limbo. The essential thing to recognise is that Glissant's Relation is a properly *singular* concept. 'We call Relation the expression of this force, which is also its manner: that which makes itself of the world, and is expresses it' (174). The only 'task' of Relation is to complete itself. Relation is 'a totality [...] which by ceaseless poetic and practical force seeks to be perfect itself, to say itself, that is, simply to complete itself' (48). Inevitably, description of Relation is also Relation, and nothing else. 'Description does not prove, it simply adds to Relation' (188).

The same absolute, self-constituent force defines Glissant's 'naturalised baroque', one of the most important supporting concepts of the book. A naturalised baroque 'lends itself to no reference, to which it will be opposed [in general]. Its turning away is its only name or, if you like, its first nature' (PR, 52; cf. TTM, 115). The baroque collapses perception and perceived, knower and known, within a single field (PR, 92). As with the Relation it expresses, the enduring 'persistence of baroque naturalities and of the forms of the chaos-world [...] will not precede their work, the movement of taking hold [...] from which erupts, at the same time, their matter and their fullness of meaning' (116). Glissant's baroque is self-regulating, it is literally identical to nature, directly expressive of nature. In Glissant's 'today', 'the baroque completes its "self-naturalisation"'. Henceforth, that which it says in the world' follows from and is 'comprehended' in the very 'movement of the world' itself. At the same time, our scientific

> conceptions of Nature 'extend themselves', become relative [*se relativisent*] Such is the very foundation of the baroque propension [. .]. We can sum-marise as follows. there is a 'naturalisation' of the baroque, not only as art and as style, but as manner of living the unity–diversity of the world [. .], in order to extend it as uproarious [*chahuté*] mode of Relation [126]

Throughout the *Poétique* the only frame of reference worth the name is thus that frame *unlimited* by a particular reference – that 'baroque speech, inspired by all possible forms of speech' (PR, 89), or 'that Cry, in which we locate, nevertheless, the accent of every language in the world' (139). Glis-sant's 'baroque' is 'the result of all aesthetics, of all philosophies' (93). Such declarations are everywhere unqualified: 'the infinity of possible languages are today contained in embryo in *every* literature'; 'Relation, which is the newness of the world, precipitates in their speed *all* possible modes', and so on (37, 191, my emphases). Again, 'to create, in any given language, pre-sumes that we are inhabited by the impossible desire of all the languages of the world'.[127]

The 'specificity' occasionally celebrated in the *Poétique*, then, has little to do with relations-with and-between particularities as such. If 'it is the totality of really ensured particulars which alone guarantees the energy of the Diverse', a *particulier* here is that which 'each time, puts itself in Rela-tion in a wholly intransitive fashion, that is, with the finally realised totality of possible particulars' (PR, 44). Properly understood, particulars are more the various modes of a self-differing Relation than they are distinct indi-viduals related *to* each other. 'Relation, as we have insisted, does not play upon primary, separable or reducible elements' (186); it is instead produc-tive of singular particularities. 'We could not defend the notion that each particular culture constitutes a primary element among those put into play in Relation, as the latter defines the elements thus played at the same time that it moves them (changes them)' (183).

Glissant's field of Related singularities is governed by the same kind of pre-established harmony that rules a neo-Leibnizian universe – a totality of inter-folding equivalences, 'reconciling Homer and Plato, Hegel and the

African griot' (PR, 33). In the shift from *Le Discours antillais* to *La Poétique*, Glissant has moved from an emphasis on monadological self-constitution (via the nation) to the harmonious expression included and expressed by all monads (or singularities). An infinite variety of voices, all singing the same music. 'Each individual and each community form for themselves echo-worlds that they have imagined [...], to live or express confluences. Each individual makes this music, and each community as well. And the realised totality of individuals and communities also'.[125] As with Glissant's baroque predecessor, this harmony can *only* be pre-established. For Glissant as for Leibniz, Related singularities are necessarily *'confluant'*, necessarily compatible, for all express the same totality and nothing else. To conceive of *la Relation* is to conceive of 'the possibility for all to find themselves in it, at every moment, in solidarity and solitude' (145); *solidaire et solitaire* are here the rigorously synonymous qualities of one singularity–multiplicity.

In short, 'Relation is that which at the same time realises [baroque movement] and expresses it. It is the chaos-world which relates (itself) [*Elle est le chaos-monde qui (se) relate*]' (PR, 109). The final 'approximation' of Relation, then, is not its expression in a system but its liberation from *any* sort of representation, the liberation of the pure energy of its being – its liberation from all *specific* limits. 'In the end, having [...] approached Relation and accepted to anticipate the work, we must now de-individualise it as a system, enlarge it to the heap of its burgeoning energy and nothing more, finding ourselves in it with others' (211). The model form of mediation within this perfectly immediate world is neither representation, generalisation (across species) nor even reproduction, but *reincarnation* pure and simple. the literal embodiment of diversity, endlessly repeated. Against the linear orientations associated with Christ and Darwin, Glissant privileges the 'primordial circularity' associated with Buddha, in which 'the individual strives [...] toward dissolution in the Whole. His successive lives are cycles. [...]. At the end of a process, he reincarnates himself: he is the same and the other [...]. The coiled *bouddhique* is never a generalisation: it proceeds from no linearity' (63–64).

La Poétique de la Relation, then, marks both a break with and a 'completion' of Glissant's work. It completes the process of *dépassement* by breaking with the national dialectic. Glissant knows that 'the more *métissage* realises itself, the more the notion of *métissage* is erased' (PR, 106); Relation itself proceed 'by realising itself [*se réaliser*], that is, by accomplishing itself as common ground' (219). The equation of subject and world as a single process of Relation obliterates all 'in-between' space, the space of 'development' and conflict. That is, it obliterates precisely that movement narrated in *La Lézarde* and called for in *Le Discours antillais*. There can be no national repossession, for dispossession is now the condition (and opportunity) of Creative reality itself. Glissant's work shifts from the specific to the singular, from a cultivation of place (however problematic) to the cultivation of displacement (however 'liberating').

Just how exactly such displacement might work in the interests of the displaced themselves remains unclear. For as Glissant put it so clearly in *Le Discours antillais*, 'there is nothing here (in contestation or in opposition) which cannot be recuperated by the system' (DA, 171).

EXCURSUS II

ON THE NATION
AND ITS ALTERNATIVES

Glissant's creolisation is not fusion, its aim is not integration into a specified Unity'. No singular configuration implies uniformity. Nevertheless, what his creolisation effectively blocks, again like any singular configuration, is its own *interruption*. However 'unpredictable' its results, creolisation proceeds as a fundamentally continuous process. It may well penetrate every rigidly specified nationalism and undermine all exclusive authenticities. But it will also inhibit the articulation of a political sphere sharply distinct from its ongoing cultural contaminations. It will resist the conceptualisation of a political *cut* in the tangle of inter-cultural differences, the formulation of principles indifferent to the ramified cultural complexity of their enunciation.

Like most other postcolonial theorists, Glissant vigorously pursues the explicit fusion of the political and the cultural.[1] However open-ended the resulting community might be, the political process is here reduced, essentially, to one of several *expressions* or 'voicings' of that creolising community. To this extent, Glissant's work in particular and postcolonial theory in general can only obstruct what is arguably the great political task of our time: the articulation of fully inclusive, fully egalitarian political principles which, while *specific* to the particular situation of their declaration, are nevertheless *subtracted* from their cultural environment. We must strive to prescribe principles whose coherence does not rely upon *any* notion of community, any kind of *cultural* proximity, any cultural criteria of sharing or belonging.[2] All progressive politics must presume the cultural despecification of its participants as much as it resists the singular transcendence of a simply *sovereign* legitimation.

Pending the eventual emergence of genuinely global mobilisations (and genuinely global institutions capable of sustaining such mobilisations), the only really effective vehicle available for these articulations on a broad collective scale remains the *nation*, understood in a broadly Jacobin sense – the nation as made up of all those who, whatever their cultural origin or 'way of being', collectively *decide* to assert (or re-assert) the right of self-determination. For neo-Jacobin nationalists, there is 'no logical connection between the body of citizens of a territorial state and the identification of a "nation" on ethnic, linguistic or other grounds'. The French Revolution in particular was 'completely foreign to the principle or feeling of nationality; it was even hostile to it'.[3] The Revolutionary experience defines the nation as the vehicle of a collective liberty, a mechanism oriented toward the abstract common good or universal interest, as distinct from the consolidation of privilege or particularity. Such a definition is irreducible to any variation, however radical or ex-centric, of the concept of ethnicity or tribe.[4]

It is this *strictly political* conception of the nation, still very much alive in some of the great liberation movements of the mid twentieth century, that has since been pushed aside, as much by the postcolonial version of globalisation/creolisation as by the various forms of cultural or religious fundamentalism that have emerged in paranoid response. These apparently antithetical developments have in fact *too much in common*: they both presume the close articulation of politics and culture – the means of dissemination and intermingling for the one, and of definition or exclusion for the other. Postcolonial theory, we might say, has already conceded too much to its fundamentalist or chauvinist opponents by accepting to pursue the contest on the latter's chosen ground. An anti-nationalist conclusion then follows as a matter of course: *no* progressive conception of the nation can take root in such polluted soil.

Glissant's shift from nationalism to post-nationalism serves here to illustrate the postcolonial trend as a whole. One of the most widely shared postcolonial assumptions is that the days when 'one could give a certain amount of fidelity and attention to basic national identities [are] pretty much over' (Said).[5] The age of 'anti-colonial nationalism has passed', Buell tells us.[6] We need 'to think ourselves beyond the nation', says Appadurai, who sees the 'territorial state' as 'the last refuge of ethnic totalitarianism'.[7] Like many postcolonial critics, Bahri identifies the nation with the 'oppression of local culture'.[8] Any contemporary study of international politics, argues Sklair, should move away 'from the study of relations *between* nations to the study of "world society"' or better, to 'the global system based on transnational practices', classes, corporations and cultures.[9] *Cultures* above all. confronted with a political problem, postcolonial theory will tend to argue, as Radhakrishnan suggests, that

> whatever distances, differences and boundaries cannot be transcended or broken down politically can in fact be deconstructed through the universalist agency of Culture and Cultural Theory [...]. Culture is set up as a non-organic,

free-floating ambience that frees intellectuals and theorists from their solidarities to their regional mode of being. It is within this transcendent space that postcoloniality is actively cultivated as the cutting edge of cultural theory[10]

There is no clear space left for the nation between these regional ties and this free-floating transcendence. Caught between globalisation on the one hand and ethnic or regional particularisms on the other, the prevailing consensus is that the nation has become 'too small for the big problems of life and too big for the small problems of life'.[11] Post-national institutions with quasi-global jurisdiction threaten to undercut the traditional sovereignty of the state, while the apparently increased resistance of local loyalties to any sort of national integration has prompted one eminent sociologist to define our era, in a telling turn of phrase, as the 'time of the tribes'.[12] Spivak's position is typical of the more general chorus: she 'keep[s] repeating that [... the idea] that new social movements [are] interested in state power does not apply in the southern theatre' – a stance not unrelated, perhaps, to her belief that 'the nation-states are powerless in the developing world'.[13] Those campaigning for democracy in Burma and sovereignty in East Timor and Palestine, however, might not agree. Nor would those who fought in pursuit of national liberation under Arbenz, Allende, Castro and Mandela.

Before joining in the anti-nationalist chorus, it is worth remembering what Fanon meant when he equated the 'history of decolonisation' with the 'history of the nation'.[14] What identifies the nation according to Fanon is not some vague sense of cultural personality so much as a common sense of purpose and a solidarity born of radical commitment. Anti-colonial struggle affirms, to be sure, the indigenous values and priorities scorned by the colonial regime; it avoids, however, the lyrical mystification of tradition Fanon associates with negritude (258–262/212–215). National solidarity is the product of *deliberate* engagement, not shared cultural essence. 'The mobilisation of the masses, when it arises out of the war of liberation, introduces into each man's consciousness the ideas of a common cause, of a national destiny, and of a collective history'.[15] To fortify the newly independent nation, Fanon goes on, will necessarily involve the consolidation of this collective history. But this again is only the means toward a genuinely international empowerment. 'It is national liberation which leads the nation to play its part on the stage of history' (296/247), because only an independent actor can truly inter-act. The enabling condition of any dialogue worth the name is the *active* empowerment of its participants:

> The consciousness of self is not the closing of a door to communication [but...] its guarantee. National consciousness, which is not nationalism, is the only thing that will give us an international dimension [ ]. It is at the heart of national consciousness that international consciousness lives and grows.[16]

Confronted with an fundamentally violent antagonist, it is understandable that anti-colonial movements like Algeria's Front de libération nationale or South Africa's African National Congress had recourse, albeit only eventually and reluctantly, to violent counter-measures; in today's somewhat less flagrantly repressive circumstances, other strategies are no doubt more appropriate. But either way, it is precisely the deliberate, conscious mobilisation of the nation that provides the only substantial defence against a merely reactionary tribalism or particularism, just as subsequent engagement must move 'from national consciousness to political and social consciousness [...], in other words, into [universal] humanism'.[17] Fanon understood that the only alternative to a strictly political pursuit of universal values (justice, equality, liberty...) is the degradation of national liberation into the mere cultural nationalism that accompanies the rise of a new 'national middle class' (190/149).

Rather than engage directly with the *politics* of Fanon's national orientation, however, postcolonial theory has generally abandoned the concept of the nation for the sake of *cultural* hybridity and *cultural* mobility. It is an irreducibly culturalist definition of nation that sanctions the characteristically postcolonial definition of 'nation building [as] the hegemonic processes, structures and daily practices by which subordinated classes within a state consent to their domination'.[18] Similarly, it is because he tends to think of the nation as a cultural entity that Gilroy presents the Black Atlantic as a 'provisional attempt to figure a deterritorialised, multiplex and *anti-national* basis for the affinity or "identity of passions" between diverse black populations'.[19] By the same token, it is no less culturalist to define the nation as the very *opposite* of hegemonic or homogeneous, as a 'fluid and contradictory [...] multiplicity of diasporic identities'.[20]

This is clearly not the place to go back over the well-worn paths that separate firmly specified forms of 'ethnic' nationalism from quasi-singular versions of an abstract or 'constitutional' patriotism. The *specific* conception of the nation that this book defends, in passing, is one that grounds the validity of its self-determination purely in terms of the (oppressive, exploitative) relations it proposes to change. Very briefly, this conception presumes: that any *a priori* condemnation of political nationalism is unjustifiable;[21] that what determines the validity of any particular nationalist engagement is the nature of the *relation* involved (the nationalism that encourages imperialist aggression has *nothing* in common with the nationalism that resists it); that the only defensible criteria for inclusion in the nation must be indifferent to all *specified* differences; that the successful pursuit of national self-determination is the precondition for any meaningful internationalism.[22] The nation remains the essential intermediary between local concerns and universal aspirations, because it frames (or should frame) the most inclusive form of government that can plausibly remain *self*-government. In order to remain legitimate, national institutions must express principles that apply indifferently to *all* concerned, but for it to be effective this expression still needs to apply from within what Habermas calls the 'we-perspective of active self-determination'.[23] The political pursuit of self-determination does not justify the creation of a culturally homogeneous 'homeland' for a particular group of people, then, so much as the imposition of an arrangement whereby all of the people living in that space are able to participate as equals in the decisions which govern it. By the same token, independence becomes a politically valid objective not merely on account of a sense of cultural affinity *per se* – a sense not easily distinguished, in principle, from the supremely reactionary affirmations of a 'France for the French' or an 'Austria for the Austrians' – but when those who dominate the existing arrangement (as in Israel or colonial Algeria) refuse any alternative means to such equality.

To defend a specific or relational concept of the nation is to affirm the decisive and thus divisive power of national mobilisation for the sake of some fully inclusive value or cause, *as well as* the structural stability of a particular nation-state. Every national mobilisation is divisive because not all members of a community have an equal stake in the 'universal' interest (just as every specific campaign that pursues the interest of *all* workers is sure to be opposed by at least *some* employers). From within situations of injustice and inequality, there is no common project, no national 'address' indifferent to privilege, that is not immediately opposed by those who continue to defend the interests of privilege. And no such address can have lasting effects in the absence of state or state-like structures whose legitimacy is itself unspecified, i.e. indifferent to the particular qualities of those who administer them. Only popular prescription and mobilisation result in change, but only a state responsive to such prescription can make these changes stick.[24]

We already know that postcolonial theory, with its emphasis on the hybrid, blurred composition of cultural performances, downplays the possibility for inevitably divisive *political* action. The state is condemned for similar reasons. From the postcolonial perspective, the state serves only to obstruct the singular dynamics of cultural creolisation. This conclusion is reflected even in the recent evolution of Immanuel Wallerstein's staunchly materialist world system model. Up until the 'age of transition' inaugurated by the revolutions of 1968, Wallerstein tells us, 'national homogeneity within international heterogeneity [was] the formula of a world economy'.[25] Before those revolutions, the three great ideological alternatives of the one world system – Western social democracy, Marxist-Leninism, and the national liberation movements – were 'variants of a single strategy: the seizure of state power by a party claiming to incarnate the popular will, and using state power to develop the country.'[26] 1968, then, marks the 'fundamental break' in the modern history of the world system because it was a revolution *against* the state as such (rather than against a particular set of rulers). The subsequent development of the system, far from reversing this revolution, has confirmed its essential thrust, by severely reducing the 'structural possibilities' open to the state.[27] And as we have seen, the main response from the post-68 Left has been a 'new intellectual focus on culture as opposed to a focus on the "economy" or on "politics"'.[28]

If postcolonial theory provides the most striking illustration of this focus, it's remarkable that an equally culturalist logic also dominates one of the very few arguably 'post'-postcolonial alternatives yet to have emerged – Dirlik's affirmation of 'indigenous movements' as the paradigm for a new 'critical localism'. Critical localism is both post-national and 'post-revolutionary', and it foregrounds its avowedly culturalist orientation as an apparent alternative to 'bourgeois economism'.[29] Among other things, such 'indigenism' implies a society that grounds its laws in 'oral traditions' and favours 'matrilinearity versus patriarchy, extended versus nuclear families, and low versus high population densities', along with a world view informed by appreciation of 'the natural order's rhythms and cycles of life'.[30] Among the several things that Dirlik cannot easily explain, however, is how any version of such indigenism would be able, over the long term, to provide a genuine alternative to a reformed international state system. The same old problems of institutionalisation, representation, bureaucratisation, conflict resolution, etc., are bound to re-emerge. And in the absence of a strong state system, it is hard to see how these problems are likely to be solved before multinational capital has found any number of ways to play local regions off against each other or simply isolate, when necessary, truly resistant localities. Consider the fate of the Gaza strip...

To defend the retention of the state is not to argue, of course, that the nation-state is itself *politically* progressive. The forces that encourage the state to supervise and enforce what is quite properly known as the status quo are more than well known. All that matters is what the state is compelled to do. The mistake is to see it as intrinsically oppressive and reactionary (or for that matter, as intrinsically progressive). The state simply helps ensure that political action has a durable effect.

Three more fairly obvious things are worth remembering before we sign up to the prevailing post-national consensus. The first is that most groups of people who have yet to win national independence – in Palestine and Chechnya most dramatically – are curiously reluctant to go along with the cynical metropolitan evaluation of their goal. Having a state of one's own still seems to matter a great deal to those who don't have one. And as often as not, the cause of the eventual reversal or corruption of progressive state-sanctioned change in places such as Guatemala (1954), Chile (1970) and East Timor (1975) has been less the fault of the state *per se* than the violent intervention of another, more powerful state.

The second thing is that these already-powerful nations (Israel, China, the US, France, Britain, Australia, Japan…) show little sign of abandoning the very real sovereignty they retain. The American state, for instance, is perfectly aware of the role it plays in promoting 'competitive' industries at home and bolstering repressive regimes abroad, in places where the interests of American consumers require low wages and submissive wage-earners.[11] What international business has long pursued and now mainly achieved is clearly not so much an end to the state *per se* as 'a weak nation-state in relation to capital and a strong one in relation to labour'.[12]

The third thing to remember is that institutional alternatives to the national state remain hypothetical at best. As Wallerstein is the first to recognise, contemporary 'anti-systemic movements are in search of a new strategy, to replace the one they have used for 125 years – taking state power. But will they find an alternative strategy?'[11] Wallerstein has yet to answer his own question. So have most cultural critics. Post-national institutions on a global or continental scale are concerned with little more than the administration of the one thing that can be 'managed' at such a level of generalisation – international finance. At the other end of the scale, how experiments along the lines of Dirlik's indigenism would allow for progressive political change in mainly urban or multicultural countries remains somewhat obscure.

It is a mistake to believe, in the weary aftermath of structural adjustment and global liberalisation, that the age of incisive political invention is over. But if it is to have a lasting impact, then at least for the foreseeable future such invention will surely require the preservation, against *all* forms of culturalist *dépassement*, of that most ambiguous of modern political innovations: the democratic state.

3

CHARLES JOHNSON AND
THE TRANSCENDENCE OF PLACE

Charles Johnson's great achievement is to have sustained a radically singular perspective from within that most heavily 'specified' of all literary forms – the historical novel. Like the other writers considered in this book, Johnson believes that in order to describe the ultimate truth of the world, you have first to escape it. Like Dib and Glissant, his writing is conditioned by a shift from the specific and the mediate to the singular and immediate, and like them, he accomplishes this shift *through* an interest in the specific, in cultural difference or otherness. But unlike them, this move takes place *within* each of his published novels. It provides what could be called his master-plot. Again and again, Johnson's novels and stories narrate the emancipation of characters from the relations that fix their identity, their release from a sharply striated space into a neo-Deleuzian *smoothness*, a redemptive dissolution on the ultimate plane of consistency.[1] From within this plane, true perception is at one with its object. Genuine 'writing doesn't so much record an experience – or even imitate or represent it – as it creates that experience' (BR, 6). By the same token, the 'perceiving Subject' figures here as 'a palimpsest, interwoven with everything – literally everything – that can be thought or felt [... Not] a narrator who falteringly interprets the world, but a narrator who *is* that world' (OT, 152–153). What Johnson calls the 'dramatic scene' at the centre of a literary work is the scene that effects this shift from interpretation *of* the world to a becoming-world in the Deleuzian sense (as anonymous, immediate, immanent). His hero's conclusion: 'if nothing else, I had learned that the heart could survive anything by becoming everything' (OT, 159).

Johnson's work strives to equate the two principal meanings of the word 'original', through the coincidence of formal innovation and a properly primordial insight. The vehicle of this equation is a hero who learns to become what he or she most truly *is*, i.e. a fragment of Creative *indistinction*. Faith, Andrew and Rutherford, the protagonists of Johnson's three published novels, are all purged of the 'illusion of identity' so as to become expressive of the hybrid forces which compose them. They come to express their true substantial nature; as with any rigorously immanent philosophy, Johnson's work turns on *the confusion of substance and significance*. For Johnson as for Spinoza or Deleuze, any individual being can only truly express its own substance, literally and immediately. It is because both being and language are composed of the same 'stuff' that the expression of the one is perfectly immediate and adequate to the nature of the other. Like Deleuze, Johnson's heroes discover 'thought and things to be of the same species'.[2]

The philosophical orientation of Johnson's work is broadly Buddhist.[3] All of his novels proceed in keeping with the Buddhist effort to move from a positioned, worldly interest or desire (suffering, *dukkha*, illusion) through self-extinction (*nirvana*) to an other-worldly disinterest (Enlightenment). What situates Johnson's particular contribution to this effort is his response to various calls for 'racial uplift' associated with several of the major voices in the African-American tradition – Frederick Douglass, W.E.B. Du Bois, Booker T. Washington, Richard Wright and Amiri Baraka. Rather than consolidate any sort of identity (be it specified by ethnicity *or* specific to the relations it pursues with other identities), Johnson maintains that the African-American writer, like any other writer, must become fully disinterested, anonymous, 'ego-less' (BR, 123).

At the time of writing, in 2001, Johnson's oeuvre includes three novels, a collection of stories, and a book of essays (*Being and Race*, 1988) which contains his critique of 'ethnic' protest writing, and his celebration of a more experimental, more strictly literary alternative. After writing half a dozen of what he calls 'bad apprentice novels' inspired by Wright, Baldwin and the 'Black Aesthetic' (BR, 5), Johnson's first published novel (*Faith and the Good Thing*, 1974) established the pattern which recurs throughout his subsequent work: the renunciation of worldly order, the assertion of an other-worldly (magical, religious, aesthetic) order, and a narrative organised as quest or initiation into this alternative realm, guided by an appropriate series of mentors and punctuated by encounters with various exemplary characters. Faith, a young and newly orphaned girl, sets off a journey to find 'the Good thing' as commanded by her dying mother – a journey which begins with the mysterious advice of an already other-worldly creature, the Swamp Woman, then moves through her seduction into various kinds of material slavery, before ending with her traumatic purification from material things altogether.

Johnson's second and most acclaimed novel, *Ox-Herding Tale* (1982),[4] is set in the last years of the *ante bellum* South. It narrates the emancipation of the highly educated Andrew from, successively, the plantation version of slavery overseen by his father and controlled by his master, the sensual version of slavery maintained by a nymphomaniac called Flo, and the personal and familial versions of slavery dominated, as with Deleuze, by the figure of Oedipus. Andrew's father embodies a form of ethnic solidarity and 'uplift': Andrew first betrays his father (both symbolically and literally) by passing for white, and then, in the highly mystical culmination of the novel, absorbs and surpasses him through the body of his father's killer, Bannon (a.k.a. Soulcatcher).

Johnson's subsequent novel, *Middle Passage* (1991) charts a similar sequence: the hero, Rutherford Calhoun, a newly freed slave, and a thief by trade, stows away on a slave ship commanded by the psychotic Captain Falcon, incarnation of the imperialist dream in its purest form. By contrast, the ship's cargo – members of a fictional African tribe which recurs throughout Johnson's fiction, the Allmuseri – incarnate Johnson's own neo-Buddhist ideal. The 'Allmuseri had no words for I, you, mine, yours', and 'had, consequently, no experience of these things, either, only proper names that were variations on the Absolute' (OT, 97). *Middle Passage* describes the transformation of Rutherford and his shipmates through this confrontation with the Absolute, which ends with the total victory of Allmuseri principles.

The short story 'Menagerie, A Child's Fable' [1984] offers a nicely compressed illustration of the narrative sequence generally at issue in Johnson's fiction. The story demonstrates the consequences of a 'war of position' that erupts among the animals of a pet shop in the absence of its sovereign owner, Tilford, and the well-meaning but futile efforts of Tilford's under-appreciated watchdog Berkeley to negotiate a compromise among the warring interests. In the absence of their master's voice, the shop is

> an ear-shattering babble of tongues, squawks, trills, howls, mewling, bellows, hoots, blurting and belly growls because Tilford had collected everything from baby alligators to zebra-striped fish, an entire federation of cultures, with each animal having its own, distinct, inviolable nature (so they said), the rows and rows of counters screaming with a plurality of so many backgrounds, needs and viewpoints that Berkeley, his head splitting, could hardly hear his own voice above the din. (SA, 46)

Such is the state of *territorialised* nature, a state of incompatiblities, as opposed to the smoothly compatible multiplicity which defines the deterritorialised plane of consistency. Polyvocity as opposed to univocity. The result is a conflagration of truly Hobbesian proportions. The 'self-determination' proposed by Monkey and embraced by 'so many different creatures' produces instant chaos (48). The reptiles eat bird's eggs, Monkey eats fish, the mammals despise the cold-blooded creatures, and so on (50). In the end, Berkeley is shot by Monkey while the shop burns down. 'Flames licked along the floor. Fish floated belly up in a dark, unplugged fish tank. The females had torn Siamese to pieces. Speckled lizards were busy sucking baby canaries from their eggs...' (55). The story strongly suggests, moreover, that Berkeley's penchant for political negotiation, the pursuit of a balance between antagonistic yet related interests, is utterly inappropriate to the situation (52). What is required, it seems, is a *sovereign* more or less as Hobbes and Spinoza understand it – a power whose legitimacy is defined and produced by its transcendence of *all* positioned interest as such. Set against the real catastrophe, Berkeley dreams of just this kind of pure, absolute authority. In his dream, Tilford arrives and opens the door

> in a blast of wind and burst of preternatural brilliance that rayed the whole room, evaporated every shadow, and brought the squabbling, the conflict of interpretations, mutations, and internecine battles to a halt. No one dared move They stood frozen [.], the colourless light behind the owner so blinding it obliterated their outlines, blurred their precious differences, as if each were a rill of the same ancient light somehow imprisoned in form, with being-formed itself the most preposterous of conditions, outrageous, when you thought it through, because it occasioned suffering, meant separation from other forms, and the illusion of identity.. (SA, 56)

As in some of Dib's later novels, the 'illusion of identity' here dissolves in a light so bright, so clear, it blurs all shapes and shades into a single whiteness.

The reader might think that the root cause of the disaster is less the specificity of the animals as such than their *imprisonment* in the pet shop. At no point, however, does Johnson suggest that the 'unnatural' circumstances of this brutish state of nature are anything more than an allegory of the consequences of *self*-determination. Mere 'imprisonment in form', rather than social or commercial imprisonments, seems to provide the essential cause of the catastrophe. The only survivor is that animal whose shape is most literally a withdrawal from relations with others – Tortoise. 'Only he would survive the spreading fire, given his armour' (58). Tortoise is the one animal who refuses self-determination, who 'didn't want to be released'. He is the only animal to remain in his cage. 'Hunched inside his shell, hardly eating at all, Tortoise lived in the Shoppe, but you could hardly say he was part of it...' (49). Tortoise embodies the redemptive principle of renunciation, a role played by Reb in *Ox-Herding Tale* and Jackson and the Allmuseri in *Middle Passage*.

This chapter has seven sections of unequal length. Section one frames Johnson's renunciation of place in the wider context of current critical work in African-American literature, a field dominated by Houston Baker and Henry Louis Gates. I go on in section II to provide a summary reading of Johnson's first novel as a paradigm for his fiction in general. Section III outlines the elements of what Johnson calls his 'phenomenological method'; I will emphasise his refusal of relations *between* subjects. Section IV describes the plane of immanence exposed by this method, particularly in its Allmuseri version. Section V, the longest and most important section, considers Johnson's ways of reaching this plane, of becoming 'imperceptible' in something like the Deleuzian sense. Section VI, about the writing of immanence, deals with his major critical notion: 'drama'. The concluding section considers the various and prohibitive costs of Johnsonian singularisation.

It should be stressed that this analytic organisation of Johnson's fictional world is purely heuristic, and should not be confused with a dialectic or 'development' in the normal sense of the word. Johnson's writing does not narrate the movement from one place or condition from another so much as the shift away from such movement altogether, toward the paradoxical plenitude of what Buddhism calls *sunyata* and Deleuze 'absolute speed', the ultimate immobility of 'time in its pure state'. The singular alternative to movement is not another kind of movement, but immediacy itself. Strictly speaking, singularity does not and *cannot* 'develop'. It is either expressed or obscured.

I Critical contexts

Like the other literatures considered in this book, African-American literature has always been and continues to be highly conditioned by debates about its own specificity – what Baker and Gates call its 'blackness' – and its place within a larger, ambiguously 'inclusive' (American) specificity. Much of African-American literary history follows the development of various positions defended in these debates: integrative or segregative, conciliatory or assertive, traditional or experimental, universalist or particularist. My argument in this chapter is that Johnson works toward the immediate equation of an African-American specificity with a singular aspecificity, i.e. the equation of an African-American place with placelessness itself. 'Immediate' is once again the crucial word here, and is what would allow me to distinguish, for example, Johnson from Du Bois, Ellison or Morrison. These latter writers narrate a famously mediate or 'double' consciousness, a notion of the subject as relation between self and other, self and place – a relation particularly acute in a context both African *and*

American. By contrast, Johnson's is a subject which collapses the distinction of self and other into a single participation or fusion. Such a (quintessentially postcolonial) subject is *always* and *essentially* out of place, displaced, transcendent of place.

Although he is the first African-American since Ellison to win the National Book Award, Johnson's work has yet to receive the detailed treatment it certainly deserves. Pending more substantial studies, his work can be most usefully read in the context defined by two of the most influential contemporary readers of African-American literature – Houston A. Baker, Jr., and Henry Louis Gates, Jr. Baker and Gates have both made significant contributions to the development of postcolonial studies in the broadest sense; although neither one has yet written specifically on Charles Johnson, their work certainly sets the prevailing tone for his current reception, as it does for the reception of most contemporary African-American fiction. And in the curious compatibility of their major theories lies the key to Johnson's contemporary importance: it is hard to imagine a writer who, in certain respects at least, conforms better to the 'blues-vernacular' theory jointly proposed by Baker and Gates.[5]

Johnson, Baker and Gates all participate in what seems to be a paradigm shift in African-American letters, based largely on a rejection of the more dogmatic or essentialist aspects of the Black Arts movement once promoted by Amiri Baraka, Larry Neal and Stephen Henderson, among others.[6] With the early Houston Baker, 'blackness' is still the attribute of a particular community or national essence[7] and a measure of 'repudiation', the refusal of another (white) community.[8] The more vehement the repudiation, the blacker the text (hence the 'blackest' cannon: Baraka and Neal's *Black Fire*). With the later Baker, blackness is less an attribute than a particular mode of expression or performance, identified with New World expression in general – a function of what he calls the 'blues matrix'. Symmetrically, with the early Gates blackness is *a* trope, a trope among other tropes,[9] whereas with the later Gates it has become *the* trope, the trope of tropes, 'the metafigure itself'.[10] In the evolution of early Baker and early Gates to later Baker and later Gates, we move from *relational* concepts of blackness – the one related in struggle to whiteness, the other related to other rhetorical tropes – to an effectively non-relational one. We move from relational to singular terms. So if early Baker and early Gates have very little in common, the later Baker and Gates have a great deal in common. For both, blackness has taken on certain features of what seems to be characteristic of literariness itself. Johnson's work, I think, can be read as a contribution to *such* a conception of literature.

Baker's explicit aim has always been to articulate the *specifically* black aspect of African-American discourse – to isolate the features of what he calls a 'black vernacular', in keeping with the definition of vernacular as 'native or peculiar to a particular country or locality'.[11] Baker seeks to place this vernacular as precisely as possible through a thick description of its context and evolution.[12] But when Baker arrives at what he describes as the 'culmination' of his years of work on the place of black culture – a theory of the 'blues matrix' – he effectively identifies this place with *placelessness* pure and simple. The blues as Baker describes them mark a place of juncture, a place of 'transience', 'polymorphous and multidirectional', a 'place betwixt and between (ever *entre les deux*)': its 'inhabitants are always travellers – a multifarious assembly in transit'.[13] This blues-place is *fundamentally* nomadic and 'hybrid'.[14] 'Like signification itself, the blues are always nomadically wandering', in a celebration of America's 'boundless frontier energy'.[15] The blues are both a 'uniquely black 'already said''' *and* 'the fluid, mediating vernacular of the New World' as a whole (*Blues*, 25, 112). The 'blues seem implicitly to comprise the All of American culture' (13). Respectful of the 'sound lessons of poststructuralism', Baker's aim is to follow a 'nomadic traipsing over a boundless network of American rails' (1, 200). It is a familiar sequence:

> Fixity is a function of power Those who maintain place, who decide what takes place and dictate what has taken place, are powerbrokers of the traditional. The 'placeless', by contrast, are translators of the nontraditional. Rather than fixed [...] their language is fluid, nomadic, transitional. Their appropriate mark is a crossing sign of the junction. The crossing sign is the antithesis of a pace marker. It signifies, always, change, motion, transience, process [.] 'Do what you can', it demands, [...] on this placeless-place, this spotless-spot – to capture manifold intonations and implications of fluid experience [. .], to play, sing and decipher an endlessly proliferating significance of American literature, criticism and culture [16]

With Baker's blues, 'what emerges is not a filled subject, but an *anonymous* (nameless) voice issuing from the *black (w)hole*. The blues singer's signatory coda is always atopic, placeless [...]. The material thus slips into irreversible difference'.[17] African-American discourse, in short, speaks the immediate, virtual bedrock of America, its *original* script (in both senses of the word):

> The [blues] song is no stranger, can never be lost It is the 'changing same' matrix of America, an elusive juncture where thresholds and boundaries are helpless [...] The song names American land [...] As sign of vernacular dimensions in America, it insistently demands that if AMERICA is to be found(ed), it will be in the bedrock matrix of a blues-black song. Literary-critical and literary theoretical (indeed, 'expressive cultural investigative') discourse must come to fit blues terms with the AMERICA it inscribes. (*Blues*, 65)

In the process of this 'fitting', the relational field is narrowed to *one* intransitive becoming-black. 'What is possible is entry into the *singularity* at the black (w)hole's centre' (154, my emphasis).

Gates arrives at something comparable to Baker's eventual position from a very different starting point. From an early and exemplary place in the 'reconstructionist' camp, Gates has moved much closer to Baker's vernacular emphasis. Baker's *Blues* book and Gates' major work, *The Signifying Monkey*, have a clear and explicit symbiotic relationship.[18] Where in the early Gates, the agent of differing-disruption is the critical theorist, in the later Gates, it is the hybrid African-American culture itself. The privileged value – difference–disruption–hybridity – has not itself changed, of course. Rather, it has been singularised in a different way, attributed to a different sovereign space, a 'place' defined, once again, by its subversion or transcendence of place.

In a first moment, Gates like Baker emphasises the fact that 'value is specific, both culturally and temporally'.[19] Like Baker, he 'believe[s] it necessary to draw on the black tradition itself to define a theory of its nature and function'.[20] But rather more than Baker, Gates has always insisted that 'race is a text (an array of discursive practices), not an essence. It must be read with painstaking care and suspicion'.[21] In this sense, Gates appears to work as an *interpreter*, a mediator, a reader. Esu, the African prototype of the Signifying Monkey, and the central figure in Gates' hermeneutic paradigm seems at first glance to be nothing other than mediation incarnate, the very emblem of the specific as such.[22] Nevertheless, Gates' version of interpretation soon begins to look like an interpretation designed for its own *dépassement*. In Gates' theory, interpretation, the object of interpretation, the interpreter, the figures of interpretation, and the very evolution of interpretation, all become entities of the *same substance* or order. All of these things express 'indeterminacy', essentially. Against the closure of determinate (Western) signification, Gates' black Signifyin(g) celebrates and 'glorifies indeterminacy', it 'posits the notion of aesthetic play: the play of the tradition, the play on the tradition, the sheer play of indeterminacy itself' (FB, 260). Gates agrees with Hartman: 'indeterminacy functions as a bar separating understanding and truth.'[23] Esu/Legba 'is the indeterminacy of the interpretation of writing, and his traditional dwelling place at the crossroads, for the critic, is the crossroads of understanding and truth' (SM, 25). Indeterminacy, in short, is the truth that criticism seeks to understand.

Indeterminacy can be accounted for (by Gates), thanks to the immediate coincidence of writing and difference through what he calls figuration-in-itself, pure tropological displacement. It follows that the figure of figures – Signifyin(g) – will be the blackest (or most literary) of all discourse.[24] 'The literary discourse that is most consistently 'black', as read against our tradition's own theory of itself, is the most figurative' (SM, xxvii). By the same logic, 'it is Esu who retains dominance over the act of interpretation precisely because he signifies the *very divinity of the figurative*' (21, my emphasis). The various pieces of the interpretative schema – text, reading, reading of reading, history of reading, and so on – are all immanent aspects of a single divine 'figuration' or signification. 'Esu endlessly displaces meaning, deferring it by the play of signification. Esu is this element of displacement and deferral, *as well as its sign*' (42, my emphasis). Figuration, or 'formal signifying', the process of 'repetition and inversion', is both form and content, description and described. It provides Gates with his 'metaphor for literary history' (FB, 247), along with his metaphors for blackness, interpretation, and even writing itself. Less than mediation, then, Gates' Monkey performs, 'more properly, *antimediation*' (SM, 56). Antimediation does not interpret between binary terms, but creates the space of a pure in-between, an end to binaries altogether (a space where the 'specifically' black can become immediate to the universally figural).[25]

Gates' Esu, the union of interpreter and interpreted, thus emerges as a characteristically singular figure. '"Esu is One, infinitely multiplied"' (SM, 36). Esu/Legba is the 'principle of fluidity, of uncertainty' (28), 'Esu is the free play or element of undecidability' (42). Esu is 'genderless' (29), of an 'indeterminate if insatiable' sexuality, a variant of Deleuze and Guattari's desiring-machine. His world is 'dominated by multiplicity' (21). And as God of a *univocal* disparity, Esu attests to 'the unity of opposed forces' (6). Gates insists that 'this aspect of Esu cannot be emphasised too much':[26] Esu directs the virtual Event whose diverse actualisations remain ultimately *all-compatible*. 'Esu as the figure of indeterminacy extends directly from his lordship over the concept of plurality' (37).

At the root of all this lies the assumed sufficiency or singularity of the signifier in its purest form. For Gates as for so many contemporary theorists, the signifier's attribution of sense is unlimited by any kind of relationship *with* the signified. Esu's African-American equivalent, 'the Signifying Monkey, is often called the Signifier, he who wreaks havoc upon the Signified. One is signified upon by the signifier. He is indeed the "signifier as such", in Kristeva's phrase, "a presence that precedes the signification of object or emotion"'.[27] The Monkey's power, in this sense, is sovereign and unrestricted. 'As the Signifier, he *determines* the actions of the Signified.'[28] In other words, 'Signifyin(g)' is a rhetorical/aesthetic play *uncontaminated by merely semantic limitations*, associations and relations. Gates' Signifyin(g) effects a 'replacement of the semantic register by the rhetorical' (48). Signifyin(g) rhetoric floats free of all positioned meanings, preserved from 'the entrapment of usage'.[29] Truly black literature *is* essentially expressive or musical – that is, immediate to the indeterminate as such. At the most general level, then, 'improvisation *is* the play of black differences',[30] and the 'properly' black writer – Reed or Dunbar, for example – is precisely he who manages to erase his 'own' voice in the higher, anonymous expressivity of the speech-music itself.[31]

This preliminary reading of Baker and Gates suggests the two main reasons for Johnson's importance in the field of contemporary African-American literature – his affirmation of a placeless place, and his equation of writing with a rhetorical movement that itself creates the criteria for its own evaluation. The (relatively few) detailed studies of Johnson's work published thus far are generally consistent with Gates' approach in particular. Johnson's fiction tends to be read as an exemplary subversion of binary hierarchies.[32] Paul Gilroy includes Johnson's later two novels as contributions to the problematising of racial essence and traditional aesthetics within the hybrid space of a 'Black Atlantic'.[33] Forella Orowan sees *Ox-Herding Tale*'s Andrew as 'a man with no social place [...], who] can assume whatever identity is appropriate to the situation'.[34] Jonathan Little reads Andrew as 'a joyous and restless experiential composition [..., who] becomes the truly inclusive and comprehensive Self'.[35] For Steven Weisenburger as for Klaus Benesch, '*Ox-Herding Tale* translates the Zen enigma of in-betweeness to the ante-bellum South and to a beautifully voiced narrator named Andrew Hawkins, a mulatto who becomes a master of the in-between'.[36] Benesch in particular celebrates Johnson's 'cross-cultural fertilisation' of traditions; *Ox-Herding Tale*, Johnson's 'veritable masterpiece', is according to Benesch 'extremely effective in deconstructing the Western notion of the self as a given, prefabricated entity, a primordial essence that could be regained through a textual movement from uniformity to originality, from non-being to being'.[37] Benesch's Johnson is highly critical of the 'dangerous illusion of wholeness and absolute presence' (a 'time-honoured but fatal misconception of Western metaphysics') and instead affirms 'a form of self-assertion distinguished by its diversified perspective(s), a cross-cultural identity that thrives on its very complexity and heterogeneity' (170, 173). Benesch's Johnson, in short, is a perfect North American analogue to the received version of Edouard Glissant.

I will argue, by contrast, that Johnson promotes an effectively absolute version of presence beyond any merely relational limits, that he narrates the becoming-singular of a subject unrestricted by relations-with and-between. Whereas Johnson's critics tend to read his fiction as a liberation from 'the fixture of a Self',[38] as a 'subversive way of unpositioning oneself in the world',[39] I will argue that what is really at stake in this 'liberation' risks transforming the critique of *enforced* placement into the affirmation of displacement pure and simple.

II Johnson and the Good Thing

Johnson's first novel, *Faith and the Good Thing* (1974) can be read as a paradigm for the singular searching undertaken throughout his work. Faith, like the Reverend Brown of her childhood, wants 'to be absolutely sure' (FG, 77), and like her friend Barrett, she knows that 'as co-workers, we're questers for that which in all ages was the one thing denied man: absolute certainty' (93). As in all of Johnson's fiction, what is revealed here as 'certain', as *the* Good Thing, is precisely the process of singularisation itself – the process of becoming-unrelated, unqualified and unlimited, of attaining a Creative virtuality in an all-inclusive plane of immanence. The Good Thing is the One that, like Spinoza's Creative substance, transcends all merely numerical distinction.

As a child, Faith lives within the subjective limits of her will, within the ignorant, illusory world of 'winners and losers': she lives as situated being, as *relative* self, 'fighting with other children, always contesting her will against theirs' (FG, 70–71; cf. 52). Her adolescent quest then follows the itinerary of a redemptive escape from this relational self. Like *Ox-Herding Tale* (especially) and *Middle Passage*, the novel follows the fairly conventional stages of an initiation: loss of an original (parental) security; cryptic and unsettling advice; initial discouragement; a false triumph, leading to a second, more definitive failure, ending with an equally definitive triumph-renunciation. Her quest for the Good Thing is a quest for the realisation that the good is not *a* thing to be discovered, but *the* thing to become. What's 'good' is to become the nothing that the self *is*, as the condition for becoming something other than *a* self. The self must become as 'blank' as the pages of Barrett's *Doomsday Book*, 'the final vintage of a life devoted to incessant inquiry, the sum total of every truth I have come to know and believe' (87; 94). At the end of the novel, Faith's personal self is literally consumed in fire. She is stripped of body and baby and husband and lover, all traces of her past are destroyed (132–133), clearing the way for her to rejoin, finally, the Swamp Woman who incarnates the arcane plane of immanence.

Faith must thus *become nothing so as to become everything*. Becoming-nothing is the dominant movement of the novel. From the moment of her mother's death, 'the kitchen's former gloss of permanence was gone', its objects

> belonged, related to no one [..] Before her, out there, the wall stretched completely beyond all familiarity […] Things had only a tenuous connection. The unreality of life without Lavidia melted even the gloss of permanence she felt enveloped her own life. No longer was she Faith, only child of Todd and Lavidia Cross, no longer was she what she believed herself to be; only a

self-conscious pressure drifting about the empty, changing, charged-with-otherness kitchen . (FG, 5–6)

The novel goes on to narrate the search for a philosophy and a state of being adequate to and ultimately affirmative of this condition. It turns on acceptance of the absence of interiority as such – that 'there was nothing in here as the minister up front and Reverend Brown maintained. All was out there...' (78–79). The internal void is the inverse of the external plenitude.

Competing philosophies of the link between nothing and everything are paraded throughout the book, indeed *are* the book. Faith encounters these philosophies in sequence; the narrative is motivated largely by the shift from one to the other, as an ongoing approximation of the Creative truth. At the lowest end of the scale is the merely negative pessimism of Reverend Alexander Magnus: 'You are nothing! [...] You are damned for delighting in this world...' (FG, 9; 10–11). Then Big Todd, Faith's father, who advocates a resigned form of neo-Platonism. 'he told her that someday she would awaken from a life of everyday slumbers and realise all she considered familiar were just shadows' (18). Todd knows that 'everything that is is right, or it wouldn't be', that the 'secret' is to say '"Right" to everything' (8, 88). Next, Dr Lynch's cosmic immanence. 'life is composed of cells that come together, working in a harmony that destroys the strength each cell possessed as an independent entity [...] Life itself is the condition of death', and so 'that's the meaning of life – bigger and better means to detumescence [...]. We live to die – only to die' (37–39, my emphasis). Edging a little closer to Creative singularity, Faith's friend Barrett affirms the pure externality, the pure sufficiency of the real which 'must first, in every instance, be wholly removed from us and exist in some absolute, unsullied, perfect form. Yes, I know the principle originates in us – yes! – but it's better to say that it's realised through us' (91). Faith's lover Alpha, finally, expresses a more or less sufficient philosophy of the real as *self*-singularising. Alpha as artist 'tried to create himself anew' (157) in a becoming that fuses art, artist and artistry:

> A real artist is his own canvas [...;] someday, when I've got hit all together, there won't be a dime's worth of difference between what I'm creatin' and myself – you won't be able to separate me from my work by space, or by a difference in materials, because – and I know it sounds crazy – my life'll be the finished work. (159)

Alpha is unsituated and unsituatable. Consequently, it is impossible to have a *relationship* with him. 'I'm an experiment, y'see? Honey, I'm different – I can't settle down, or raise kids, or nothin' like that. I'm... an artist [...]. I'm outside things [...;] my life's not my own – hit's for art – the idea of perfection!'[40] What Alpha tells Faith about this One Good Thing ('the idea of perfection') only remains limited, then, by the *way* he tells her, i.e. as her lover, through a relationship.

The *best* philosophy of the Good Thing must come from a figure properly beyond relationality altogether – a figure who Faith *becomes*, in very much the Deleuzian sense. Such is the Swamp Woman, the incarnation of a purely anonymous creativity. She is a 'midwife for the things hiding like tumours beneath a man's personality' (FG, 17). Wholly singular, she is 'like God', 'the only substance of its kind in the world' (23). The Swamp Woman embodies her environment, she is a creature 'spawned', 'like the swamp' (19). And she inspires in Faith dreams of a *global* becoming-Swamp Woman, the novel's most radical becoming-singular:

> Around the shanty, the swamp bubbled, overflowed the borders of the bog [ ] The brew ran endlessly from her cauldron [...], it covered the world. Billions were covered with the brew And when they managed to smear it all off, they looked like her. the Swamp Woman [.] And all around the world people looked at each other, winked their clear yellow eyes evilly, and squealed in harmony 'Hee hee!' (FG, 48)

The Swamp Woman, finally, is witness to the primordial 'knowledge' of the Good Thing, and of how the Good Thing was lost. The Good Thing 'manifests itself in an infinity of forms'. It is lost through the desire to possess and *know* it, through the questions of 'the restless one, Kujichagulia [...] Who am I? What can I know [...] What am I?'[11] The Good Thing *is* only in the absence of these questions.

Faith's various mentors compete with a succession of false prophets, trapped in the delusions of selfish will and personal desire. Maxwell's is the most emphatically discredited. 'Society's composed of individuals, and every one of 'em's got an individual will. Society thrives on the clash of those wills...'[12] Maxwell's lampooned Nietzscheanism (116–117) is dismissed as sharply as the falsely comforting notion that the Good Thing is a function of the private self, a matter of the *heart*. The minister of the Church of Continual Light gets it half-right. He realises the truth must be immediate, that it cannot be 'far away', 'separate'. Truly, we must look for it 'so close we don't have to search all over the world no more!' (74). But by 'putting it' here, 'in your hearts', he runs the risk of situating the Good Thing in what Guattari calls the 'black hole' of subjective consciousness. The minister makes the mistake of one of Alpha's fellow prisoners, 'a damned fool! – [who] said all that mattered was my puttin' alla my feelings in hit, like kids do, and forgettin' form' (159). Looking inside herself, Faith has already learned that 'there's nothing there! [...] That's too easy... You all stopped looking in the world because it was too hard [...]. There's nothing inside, and there's nothing outside' (79). It is this identity of nothings, rather, that provides the means to redemption. It remains to affirm it.

The rest of the novel follows the path to this affirmation, defined by a sequence of partial, pre-figuring experiences of becoming-imperceptible, which take place at ever higher degrees of approximation to the 'truth'. The sequence can end only with death and transfiguration: death of the person is the price to pay for a global resurrection. Already as a child, Faith has experienced a 'complete freedom' beyond positioned perspective:

> she saw it clearly – all the possible number of things in space, all forms that had ever existed in time reflected back into time like a man's image trapped in a room of mirrors – she, herself, Faith Cross, fading back and forth on the continuum of time until she could no longer be certain of the images of herself [. .or] if in that crazy complex of images she existed at all. (FG, 12)

Such moments of insight replace illusion with truth as if the two are mutually and immediately exclusive. 'When it came, the world as it usually appeared... disappeared [...]. Only the present was immediate and everywhere, disclosed to her as miraculous...' (12). Her adolescent romance with Alpha effects a similar becoming-elemental, 'back to earth, deep within its strange fabric', anonymous and all-compatible. As a matter of course, 'no personalities existed in such a pure world of feeling, just flashes of human outlines in the quilt of creation where plants had their place, and animals – all coexisting, peacefully, lyrically, like notes in a lay' (13), in the pre-arranged harmony.

Despite differences in affect, the traumatic violation of self works to exactly the same effect. When Tippis rapes her, for example, Faith undergoes a kind of depersonalisation-by-fire: 'this was not happening to her, only to another, to a shadow of herself. To a thing apart, out there [... H]er mind – clear and as smooth as a sea stone beaten by waves and elements for a millennium – registered no sensation, held, in its broken glass frame, no reflections'.[43] Faith's prostitution, likewise, reveals the full despair of relations with others in almost Sartrean terms. 'What that other mind thought of her she was', she '*became* that and was nothing more' (69). In this way, she learns that '*You are nothing*' (69), the very knowledge that will be re-affected as the Good Thing itself. In a strictly formal sense, then, it is difficult to distinguish Faith's horrific experience as prostitute from her joyous, loving experience with Alpha. As her lover, 'Alpha projected the image of himself in her, as she did within him until they seemed to exist, not as two people, but one. Or stranger still, as nothing' (154).

Perhaps the most conventionally 'positive' form of creative singularisation in the novel is Faith's pregnancy, the apparent sufficiency of female fertility. The various male philosopher-questers Faith encounters remain trapped in the futile confines of the will to know, the place of interpretation *of* and relations-*with*. Pregnant, Faith knows that even Alpha,

> like all men, was a stranger to her, to the earth, and was driven by restlessness [.] It had stricken Lynch and Brown and Barrett alike, had laid its heavy hand on Big Todd – suffocating them with a sense of fragility and foolishness before the rhythm of the world. She knew that was it – life was music and they could not dance [...]. They could not be content as the humble caretakers of the garden of creation, could not create as she, or God, or a risible old witch woman could; they could not conjure beauty from the nothingness of all our lives. They were the dead living. Yet she had that connection with things, that capacity to dance if the universe said so, to sing if it demanded song. Unable to create, to conjure life from darkness, men railed against the world.. (167)

Pregnancy literally makes Faith's body consistent with the universe, a participant in the immanent process of creation. She embodies the uninterrupted flow of energy. 'The child, in an odd way, was the answer – it was all history focused on a single point – a trillion amoebae, plants and animals martyred by evolution to produce just this one child and no other, holding in microcosm all epochs, or so she believed; it pointed to every beast and tree and transformation of life, of that peculiar dance that had to be before it could be assembled by her...' (168). Pregnancy allows for an exemplary confusion of material composition and immaterial expression, of substance and significance.

Pregnancy allows her to move toward the immanent reality of things. But only loss of the baby can fully realise this reality, i.e. depersonalise it. Only then can Faith become midwife to *all* creation rather than mother to *a* child. Through the fire, Faith loses her *face* (one condition, very precisely, of Deleuzian anonymity[44]). Like the Swamp Woman, she becomes 'horrible!' (180; 19). She grasps and affirms the reality of 'freedom' through death, 'the boundary event through which all others were defined and delimited' (181). Death is the one event without limits. In her final resurrection, then, Faith comes to possess 'intuitive, immediate' truth (195), a version of Spinoza's third kind of knowledge. She learns the multiplicity-unity of the Good thing, that 'a man or woman or werewitch has a thousand'n one ways to look for what's good in life' (187), that the key is to become empty, unlimited inside, so as to be able to become everything, unlimited, outside.

At this ultimate point, Faith *becomes* the Good Thing, everything and nothing, the pure contingency of an unlimited, all-determining principle: 'the Good Thing's spontaneous; its absolutely nothin', but particularly it's everythin' [..]. Like God, the Good Thing's governed by what's called the Docta Ignorantia – that is, knowin' it always implies negativity, 'cause it's beyond, in the final analysis, everyday understanding' (FG, 193, 191–192)

III Phenomenological implications

With *Being and Race*, Johnson has provided an eclectic but broadly consistent theory for the interpretation of his work. He calls it a version of phenomenology. It is Husserl's call '"to the things themselves" [that] distinguishes phenomenology from previous disciplines of philosophy' (BR, ix). The general goal is to find a method of interpretation adequate to the abstract multiplicity of possible meanings, rather than one caught up in particular meanings. This goal is what distinguishes for Johnson artistic or true expression from 'ordinary' discourse. The former expresses the truth of multiplicity, the latter expresses only particular positions. The idea that art is in some sense 'everyday life given more form and colour', Johnson knows, is 'patently false'. Johnson's notion of art is firmly internal to the singular logic of what Bourdieu calls the 'literary field'. True art is freed here of any constitutive relation to the everyday world. Any art that tries to work through such a relation tends to get stuck in what Johnson calls 'ideology', a category which includes the Harlem Renaissance and negritude. Ideology 'closes off the free investigation of phenomena' (BR, 26), for such investigation must begin with the revelation of an ego-less or perspectiveless experience. 'The actor and writer – and all of us really – believe in the interchangeability of standpoints; we throw ourselves with a character toward his projects, divest ourselves of our own historically acquired peculiarities, and reconstruct his world.' True 'phenomenological description' serves, on the Heideggerian model, 'to fling the reader of fiction toward revelation and unsealed vision', immediate to the hidden 'essence of things' (BR, 43, 32–33).

There are two main character-types in Johnson's fiction: those who can access such revelation (more or less adequately), and those who can't. The *specified* characters who furnish the background of his texts – in *Middle Passage*, these include Isadora as bookish, plump, animal-loving, righteous, librarian-sister, Santos as indestructible thug, Zeringue as 'the very Ur-type of Gangster' (13), and Ngonyama as emblematic Allmuseri ('the Ur-tribe of humanity') – are generally confined to a well-defined narrative role. By contrast, those *singular* characters who occupy the narrative foreground are generally out of place, they are exceptional in the strongest sense of the word, as a result they have the opportunity to escape the limits of their particular perpsective and stake a claim to genuine 'phenomenological' insight. Ultimately, these singular characters are driven by versions of a sort of death-drive, a drive to overcome their merely personal coherence: in *Middle Passage*, they include Rutherford himself, Captain Falcon and Peter Cringle. All are super-educated polymorphs. Cringle has 'total recall of everything he'd read' (MPg, 25), and 'more than all the others, was out of place' due to his privileged background (MPg, 41). Falcon is fluent in 'seven African coastal dialects and could learn any new tongue in two weeks time' (30); he thinks 'simultaneously' in French, Latin and Greek (51). Rutherford himself has acquired an immense philosophical and religious learning through the efforts of his evangelical master, Chandler.

Where they differ is in their relative adherence to the illusions of self. Rutherford, like Andrew and Faith, eventually frees himself of this illusion. Cringle is limited by his inability to 'see himself, his own blighted history, in the slaves we intended to sell' (MPg, 66), but through his ultimate sacrifice, becomes-aspecific in the most literal sense (as digested by his comrades). Falcon remains ambiguously committed to the illusion of self to the end, but carries this very illusion to its singular limit. Falcon is a self without other: others have 'never been real to me. Only I'm real to me' (MPg, 95). Falcon, like the America he partly represents, 'felt expansive, eager to push back frontiers...' (50); 'he was, in a way, a specialist in survival. A *magister ludi* of the Hard Life', driven by 'a desire to achieve perfection'. He 'attributed his knack for survival in uncertain times to a series of exercises he'd developed [...] under the heading "*Self*-reliance"' (51, my emphasis). Falcon's 'belief that one must conquer death through some great deed or original discovery, his need to soar above contingency, accident...' (143), traps him within the limits of his own situated agency. For all his 'pseudo-genius', Falcon is unable to escape himself, to move beyond what Rutherford calls 'the disconnected manner of the autodidact', 'adrift from the laws and logic of the heart' (143).

All the same, Falcon is the only man on board who can apparently sustain the radically singular presence of the Allmuseri god: 'The Creature has a hundred ways to relieve men of their reason [...]. That's why no one goes near it but me' (102). And Falcon has a clear grasp of what is for Johnson the essential curse of humanity:

'*Man* is the problem [..], women as well, anythin' capable of *thought* [.] For a self to act, it must have somethin' to act *on* A nonself – some call this Nature – that resists, thwarts the will and *vetoes* the actor Well, suppose that nonself is another self? What then? As long as each sees a situation differently there will be slaughter and slavery' [ ] 'Conflict', says he, 'is what it means to be conscious. Dualism is a bloody structure of the mind Subject and object, perceiver and perceived, self and other [ ] are signs of a transcendental Fault, a deep crack in consciousness itself Mind was made for murder. Slavery: if you think this through, forcing yourself not to flinch, is the social correlate of a deeper, ontic wound.'[45]

Falcon, like Johnson's other 'individuated' characters, is a spokesman for the collapse of dualisms. But unlike the others, he achieves collapse *within* what Guattari called the black hole of subjective consciousness.[46] Falcon seeks self-annihilation, but precisely *through* the self: 'for all this obsession with survival, he had the air of a man who desperately wanted to die' (MPg, 52).

Falcon's mistake is an instance of what Johnson everywhere attacks as 'self-determination' (SA, 48), the effort to project a consistent image of yourself. An 'image of yoself' is the dead, enslaved part of a person. As *Ox-Herding Tale*'s Bannon puts it, 'you got to have something dead or static already inside you – an image of yoself – for a real slave catcher to latch onto' (OT, 174). This is why Johnson remains sceptical of the achievements of negritude and the Harlem renaissance, 'failures' rooted in 'the inherent difficulty in trying to control the image – meaning', of an experience. 'Image control has been the aim of black fiction – and perhaps its problem – from the very beginning' (BR, 17). According to Johnson, such control 'violates the truth-seeking telos of literature, which requires a complete disclosure, all the facts and let the chips fall where they may, saying in order to show more clearly a situation so that it can be responded to with courage' (BR, 108).

More controversially, Johnson argues against any self-determination or self-imaging undertaken *in relation* to other self-images. This is perhaps the most important contribution of phenomenology to Johnson's work – its engagement with the familiar problem of *several* private subjectivities, along the lines which lead to that mutual exclusion of self and other acknowledged in Sartre's *L'Etre et le néant*. As *Faith and the Good Thing*'s Arnold Tippis puts it, 'you, in society, are an object for others, hardly ever for yourself', and 'that's what the world is really all about – subject–object antagonism' (FG, 57–58). Like Schopenhauer, then, Johnson's goal will be to escape the world and the *privacy* of individual will. Those who like Falcon seek to affirm and even exaggerate this 'subject–object antagonism' live in a world of illusion and untruth. Arnold Tippis, George Hawkins, Isaac Maxwell, and Diamelo are other major proponents of the same approach. They preach worldly philosophies of conflict, competition, Will Power and success. They live the vanity of appearances and relations with. By contrast, those who, like the Swamp Woman, Jackson and Reb, refuse both this antagonism and this very relationality, those who seek to fold themselves within that plane of immanence which subsumes all subject–object distinction – they speak with the singular voice of truth. The 'evolution' of Johnson's central characters, roughly, confirms their inclusion within this second position.

The most concise way of describing Johnson's master-plot, then, is as the move to equate the two meanings of the word real-isation (the actuali-sation of a true 'reality', and the process of becoming *aware* of this reality) as aspects of a single revelation. Two of the stories collected in *The Sorcerer's Apprentice* provide particularly explicit dramatisations of this point.

The learned heroes of 'Aléthia' and 'Popper's Disease' both begin their narratives with an idea the story goes on to realise or bring to life. In the first, the professor learns that 'to say "Man clarifies Nature" is to say, oddly, that "Nature clarifies Nature", because man is a part of Nature, which suggests, stranger still, that man – if self-forgetful – is not an actor or agent at all' (SA, 104). In the second, the doctor ponders the possibility that 'the most intimate features of a man's personality, those special aspects he believed individual and subjective and unique – kinks and quirks – had their origin, like Oxydol and doorknobs, in the public sphere, probably in popular culture. In other words, what we took to be essential in man throughout history [i.e. his individuality] might be accidental. A startling thesis, I'd have to say' (130).

Both stories then go on to realise these realisations. The professor manages to 'forget himself' on the Nietzschean model, while the doctor is confronted with an alien culture that literally confirms his hypothesis. 'Aléthia' concludes with a drugged version of the plane of immanence, where 'the I was just a function, a flickerflash creation of this black chaos' and 'being sang being in a cycle that was endless' (SA, 110–111):

> I suddenly saw Wendy – not [. .] outside me as another subject in a contest of wills – but yet, as pure light, brilliance, fluid like the music, blending in a perfectly balanced world with the players Muslims petty thieves blacks Jews lumpenproles Daley-machine politicians West Indians loungers Africans the drug peddlers who, when it came to the crunch, were, in that plain, pure light, too, the Whole in drag... (SA, 111)

'Popper's Disease' dramatises the conclusion that the 'Plague' of living creatures 'is the Self and There is No Cure' (146). The *real* alternative is provided by the other-worldly 'Telecypher' of the alien ship, whose

> field dissolved the distinction between solid particle and the space surrounding them. (Don't get impatient, I'm coming to the point.) Continuous in time, everywhere in space, the field was the idea of polymorphy made fact, its particles mere concretions of energy, as if Being delighted in playing hide-and-seek with itself, dressing up, so to speak, as Everything, then sloughed off particularities when bored with the game. (SA, 144–145)

IV Allmuseri immanence[17]

Johnson's most detailed fictional evocation of a singular reality is his invented ethnography of the Allmuseri, 'the Ur-tribe of humanity'. The Allmuseri hover in the background of *Faith and the Good Thing* and *Ox-Herding Tale*, as ancestors for especially noble characters. They come to the fore-front of Johnson's fictional stage in *Middle Passage*, as the unwilling cargo of Falcon's slave-ship. Their subversion of the slave economy from within, so to speak, is at the same time the assertion of a singular univocity from without, from beyond the realm of merely positioned, specific resistance. Point by point, the Allmuseri way of life corresponds closely to a description of that Deleuzian plane of immanence briefly suggested in my Introduction (section III).

(i) *It is univocal.* 'The failure to experience the unity of Being everywhere was the Allmuseri vision of Hell' (MPg, 65). As 'a clan state they were as close-knit as cells in the body', and 'physically, they seemed a synthesis of several tribes [...], or – in the Hegelian equation – a clan distilled from the essence of everything that came earlier. Put another way, they might have been the Ur-tribe of humanity itself [...], a crowd spun from everything this vast [African] continent had created' (58, 61).

(ii) *It is impersonal.* 'No fingerprints' (MPg, 61). Like Deleuze, the Allmuseri refuse the depth of interiority. They 'did not use our sense of perspective but rather the flat, depthless technique of Egyptian art' (75). For the Allmuseri, 'even more important than [individual] freedom was the fact that no leaf fell, no word was uttered or deed executed that did not echo eternally throughout the universe' (140). The Allmuseri are defined by a radical refusal of the self, and of the relative difference that allows for the distinction of selves. Reb's ancestors 'hated personal pronouns', preferring to speak only through 'proper names that were variations on the Absolute' (OT, 97).

(iii) *It is immediate to itself.* The Allmuseri are exemplary empiricists in the Deleuzian sense. They 'are a people so incapable of abstraction no two instances of "hot" or "cold" were the same for them, this hot porridge today being so specific, unique and bound to the present that it had only a nominal resemblance to the hot porridge of yesterday' (61). The status of the 'specific' in Johnson is comparable to that of *haecceity* in Deleuze – it suggests a quasi-molecular singularity so differing, so free from merely relational orders of difference, that it expresses at the same time a cosmic universality.[48] Allmuseri language is the literal expression of reality itself: 'it was not so much like talking as the tones the savannah made at night' (MPg, 77). Their speech is remarkably similar to Deleuze's logic of sense, a logic that tries to render the *verbal event* as such (a *greening*, Deleuze would say, rather than the static predication of 'green' – a privilege of 'and' over 'is'[49]):

> Ngonyama told me the predication 'is' [...] had over the ages eroded into merely an article of faith for them Nouns or static substances hardly existed in their vocabulary at all. A 'bed' was called a 'resting', a 'robe' a 'warming' [...] When Ngonyama talked to his tribesmen it was as if the objects and others he referred to flowed together like water, taking different forms . [ ] Their written language [had to be grasped] in a single intuitive snap. (MPg, 77)

More, the Deleuzian-Leibnizian conception of a perception that creates what it perceives is confirmed by 'an old Allmuseri belief (hardly understood by one Westerner in a hundred) that each man outpictured his world from deep within his own heart [...], as if a man's soul was an alchemical cauldron where material events were fashioned from the raw stuff of feelings and ideas', themselves distilled from the substance of the universe (MPg, 164).

(iv) *It becomes-other.* The Allmuseri are less fixed essence than that form which is particularly open to *essential* change, primordial flux, a catalyst to all possible becomings. As Rutherford realises, they are 'process and Heraclitean change, like any men, not fixed but evolving and as vulnerable to metamorphosis as the body of the boy we'd thrown overboard' (MPg, 124). The Allmuseri *are* metamorphosis, and their ability to become-American is likewise the condition of Rutherford's becoming-Allmuseri. (As Deleuze insists, all becomings are double.) 'Just as Tommy's exposure to Africa had altered him, the slaves' life among the lowest strata of Yankee society [... was] subtly reshaping their souls [...] No longer Africans, yet not Americans either' (MPg, 125). The encounter with slavery, in this sense, helps actualise their virtual in-betweeness.

(v) *At its limit, it becomes-imperceptible.* Baleka's performance, for example, is rendered 'invisible' thanks to the subtle dynamics that absorb each individual in the collective chorus, 'blend[ing] them into an action so common the one and the many were as indistinguishable as ocean and wave' (MPg, 166). Ngonyama, too, is the embodiment of imperceptibility. 'He was so quiet sometimes he seemed to blend, then disappear into the background of shipboard life' (MPg, 75).

The ultimate expression of Allmuseri being is of course their god which Falcon has somehow managed to smuggle on board, in a crate. The Allmuseri 'say it sustains everything in the universe [...] creating and destroying the cosmos, then creating it again, cycle after cycle', perhaps sustaining 'alternate universes, parallel worlds and counterhistories...'. It has 'a thousand names', but no image, or rather, '*all things are its image*'. It is immediate to its creatures. In an almost explicitly Spinozist passage, Falcon explains the Allmuseri version of real distinction: their god is 'immaterial', and 'being unphysical means there can only be one of each kind of god or angel – one Throne, one Principality, one Archangel, 'cause there's only a formal (not a material) difference amongst 'em, so the one below is the *only creature of its kind* in the universe – is the universe, the Allmuseri say' (MPg, 101, my emphasis). Like Spinoza's substance, 'the Allmuseri god is everything, so the very knowing situation we mortals rely on – a separation between knower and known – never rises in its experience' (MPg, 101).

After Tommy O'Toole encounters the god, he loses his personal and linguistic coherence in favour of a hybridity so inclusive it exceeds the individual's capacity to survive. 'He was lost to us' (70), 'his words [...], a slabber of Bantu patois, Bushman, Cushitic and Sudanic tongues' (MPg, 68). Taken before the god, he fuses with it to form 'a single thing: singer, listener and song, light spilling into light, the boundaries of inside and out-side, here and there, today and tomorrow, obliterated as in the penetralia of the densest stars, or at the farthest hem of Heaven' (MPg, 69). When the post-god Tommy plays the flute it is 'less music, if you ask me, than the body's air alchemised into motion, or the song of hundred-year old trees from which the narrow flute was torn' (121).

A purely singular coherence always blurs the relationship of agent to environment. In Johnson's *Middle Passage* as in Glissant's *Poétique de la Relation*, this environment is of course primarily marine. The sea's true sig-nificance is grasped, unevenly, only by the privileged characters.[50] As Cringle puts it, "they skim along the surface, the others; they have no feel-ing for what the sea is [..., this] formless Naught, and I dislike it, Calhoun, being hemmed in by Nothing, this bottomless chaos breeding all manner of monstrosities...' (42). The Nothing of the Sea strips away identity and the self-bound will to life in a chaotic resolution of binaries. As Cringle knows, Falcon 'doesn't want to return [...] That's why he goes to sea' (62), for 'beneath the thrashing waves there was only bottomless death, the extinc-tion of personality' (162). In the gathering storm of 11 June, the sea seems 'without start or finish, a shifting cauldron of thalassic force, form superim-posed upon form, which grew neither bigger nor smaller, which endlessly spawned all creatures conceivable yet never consumed itself [..., a] theatre of transformations' (79). Johnson's sea, like Virilio's, is a quintessentially smooth space.

At sea, the *Republic* is a space beyond place, a space of dissolution and 'constant variation', 'it not being in the nature of any ship to remain the same on that thrashing Void called the Atlantic' (MPg, 36). No sooner does the ship begin to move than Rutherford's 'centre of gravity was instantly gone' (24). On board, Rutherford is 'deprived of such basic directions of left and right, up and down' (45). The ship itself 'was perpetually flying apart and re-forming during the voyage, falling to pieces beneath us [...]. Fal-con's crew spent most of their time literally rebuilding the *Republic* as we crawled along the waves. In a word, she was, from stem to stern, a process' (36). A change of command only confirms what seems to be the constant principle of the ship. After the Allmuseri take-over, the wind spins 'the crippled ship in a circle, without destination. We were dead in the water. Adrift. A creaking hulk of coppice oak tossing about on a sea the colour of slate' (130). The mutiny simply adds a further dimension to this experience, making Rutherford 'feel culturally dizzy, so displaced by this decentred interior and the Africans' takeover...' (142). In the days following Falcon's death, 'we were buffeted about by contrary winds, thrown off course frequently, so that often we flew in circles, retracing our path, or fell into a trance of sea and wind too frail to propel us, drifting aimlessly like men lost in the desert...' (152). And finally, during the last cataclysmic storm, 'it was impossible to tell where ship ended and sailor began [...], for in this chaosmos of roily water and fire, formless mist and men flying everywhere, the sea and all within it seemed a churning field that threw out forms indistinctly' (183). The sea here *realises* its nature, and overcomes the resistance of specific form.

V Becoming-impersonal

Almost all of Johnson's published fiction narrates a version of becoming-singular or imperceptible, an initiation into egolessness (BR, 123). Johnson quotes from *The Dhammapada*, the man who 'conquers himself is the greatest of heroes':[51] this is precisely the task facing Johnson's own heroes. As *Ox-Herding Tale*'s Vet puts it, 'the belief in personal identity, the notion that what we are is somehow distinct from other things', is a 'lie, [an] ancient stupidity [with] no foundation in scientific fact [...]. We do not have a sensation of solidity; we *are* the sensation, Andrew' (OT, 58). In order properly to *express* the sensation, we must become what we are. And according to a logic confirmed throughout this study, we *are* impersonal but are nevertheless *given* as personal. The person must become the impersonal being that it is.

The story 'Popper's Disease' is the closest Johnson comes to an explicit diagnosis of this *given* human condition – the imprisonment in self-consciousness – as a pathological condition, a constraint impossible to transcend but that demands to be transcended. Doctor Henry Popper stumbles upon a spacecraft which contains a quarantined, dying alien, along with a Telecypher sophisticated enough to figure out what has killed its pilot. Namely: '*It's the Self and There is no Cure*' (SA, 146, Johnson's emphasis – there is no cure, but *quarantine* indicates the nature of an appropriate palliative care. withdrawal from relation). The alien lists the symptoms of its condition – desires *for* things, an awareness of otherness, obstacles in the way of literal meanings, and so on. The alien suffers from 'the inability to determine *precisely* what things mean, and the peculiar sense that I am somehow dependent upon everything in my perceptual field' (SA, 138, my emphasis). It is driven by a desire for things 'which have a curious opacity, a marvellous beauty [...] yet threaten to [...] annihilate me completely because I am, in a word, deeply and inexorably *different* from them' (138). The terminal phase is indicated by the dying creature's last words: 'the idea has just occurred to me that all phenomena are products of my ego…' (142). The alien, in short, has failed to transcend subjective consciousness.

Exactly like the Buddhist adept or Sufi initiate, Johnson's heroes must die to the world in order to live in an other-worldly truth. So in the manner of much postmodern fiction, Johnson's narratives thus have a peculiarly posthumous feel: they are narratives enabled by the effective death of their heroes, or as Girard would have it, their *full*, ultimately mortal withdrawal from mimetic desire.[32] The narrated climax is not so much an event in the hero's life, followed by a denouement (itself followed, eventually, by death), so much as the hero's death itself, death in Girard's sense: death to self and position, death to desire-as-lack or desire as envious imitation. While this death is not the end of the narrative, it is the necessary price to be paid for 'enlightened' existence beyond the life of the organism altogether. Although narrated in the third person, this sequence of death-and-resurrection is explicit in *Faith and the Good Thing*. In *Ox-Herding Tale*, it is Andrew's private 'death', his becoming-Bannon (in a scene described below), that gives him the perspective from which the book that leads to that death is written. In *Middle Passage*, it is Rutherford's 'death' – 'then I fainted. Or died' (MPg, 171) – his absorption in the becoming-god and becoming-Riley, along with all the other mini-deaths suffered during the voyage, that determines him to write the log-book account that becomes the novel. Johnson's fiction provides a nice illustration of McHale's succinct point: 'postmodernist writing enables us to *rehearse* our own deaths'.[33]

All of Johnson's privileged characters share Rutherford's desire to consume the whole of life. 'I have always been drawn by nature to extremes […], I have never been able to do things halfway, and I hungered – literally hungered – for life in all its shades and hues' (MPg, 3). At the same time, this consumption requires consumption *of* the self within the whole. The professor of 'Aléthia', for example, is consumed in an orgy of drugs and music that allow him to become immediate to the full, burning virtuality of the reality, a becoming enabled by the paralysis of the self as such:

> Hours passed. Twice I tried to raise my arm, but could not budge. Neither could I look away Silently, I watched Helplessly, I accepted things to smoke, sniff and swallow [.] Slowly, a new prehension took hold of me, echoing like a voice in my ear. That man, the one in the Abo Po, lightly treading the measure, was me And this one dressed like Walt (or Joe) Frazier was me. If I existed at all, it was in the kaleidoscopic party, the pinwheel of colour, the I was just a function, a flickerflash creation of this black chaos […] Seer and seen were intertwined – if you took the long view – in perpetuity. (SA, 110–111)

Nowhere in Johnson's oeuvre is such self-ascesis more graphically written than in the story 'China' [1983], which narrates the singularisation of
the ageing mediocrity Rudolph through the envious, self-imprisoned eyes
of his wife, Evelyn. Rudolph begins the story as a hapless hypochondriac,
resigned to passivity. 'Liver, heart, and lungs – they'd worn down gradually
as his belly grew' (SA, 69). Impotence defines him (69). But he ends the
story a self-transcending martial artist, his body toned to perfection, his
sense of self, free of all self-image, dispersed across the entire fabric of the
universe. He 'himself, Rudolph Lee Jackson, [stands] at the centre of the
universe; for if the universe was infinite, any point where he stood would
be at its centre – it would shift and move with him' (SA, 87). In Zen *zazen*,
'at the bottom of the lake', his powers of meditation take 'into the vortices
of himself, into the Void – even the image of himself on the lake floor van-
ished' (87). Through the ascetic discipline of martial art, he consumes
himself without remainder.

> Gung-fu [...] asks me to give everything, body and soul, spirit and flesh. I've
> always felt [...that] everything I've ever done, it only demanded part of me,
> [...and] you never tried to touch all of me, to take everything [ ] Sometimes
> I get the feeling that the unused part – the unlived life – spoils, that you get
> cancer because it sits like fruit on the ground and rots. (SA, 76–77)

Eventually, Rudolph arrives at a stage marked by all the characteristic features of the Allmuseri plane immanence. (a) It is beyond others: he learns
how to '"close the Gap" between himself and an adversary, how to create
by his movements a negative space in which the other could be neutralised'
(80). (b) It is ontologically univocal, beyond relational judgement, beyond
the distinction between subject and object: 'Whatever is just is [...]. That's
all I know. Instead of worrying about whether it's good or bad, God or the
Devil, I just want to be quiet [...]: how can there be *two* things?' (SA, 90).
(c) It is impersonal: he comes to feel 'as if there were no interval between
himself and what he saw. His face was vacant, his eyes – like smoke. In this
afterglow, (he said) he saw without judging. *Without judgement there were
no distinctions*. Without distinctions there was no desire...'[51] This *sunyata*
is again an *original* state in the two senses of the word – a 'newly' mastered
actualisation of the primordial, as Rudolph explains the Sifu Chan use of
belts: 'Originally, all you got was a white belt. It symbolised innocence, vir-
ginity. As you worked, it got darker, dirtier, and turned brown. Then black
You were a master then. With even more work, the belt became frayed, the
threads come loose, you see, and the belt showed white again' (81).

Evelyn, by contrast, embodies the principle of *ressentiment* – of *relation*, pathetically affected. The prospect of death, 'the brutal fact of decay',
could 'only be blunted, it seemed to her, by decaying *with* someone, the

comfort every Negro couple felt, when, ageing, they knew enough to let things wind down...' (75). Sinking slowly into an obese inactivity – 'she'd seen the bottom of a few too many candy wrappers' (69) – her 'only comfort was knowing that, despite her infirmity, her Rudolph was in even worse health' (64). Rudolph's metamorphosis eliminates this comfort, and Evelyn dissolves into a pool of hysterical jelly. She 'whimpers' and 'sobs' (88), 'weeping uncontrollably' (94). 'She thought: he's doing this to hurt me. She wondered: what was it like to be powerful?' (84). And ultimately: 'Rudolph, I want you back the way you were: *sick*.'[55]

In 'China' the gendered nature of Johnson's metamorphoses is particularly transparent. Traditional notions of "penis envy" do not even begin to explain the distribution of roles, and the fact that the story is told through Evelyn's eyes only exaggerates the effect. The early Rudolph was plagued by 'the "Problem". 'His pecker shrank to no bigger than a pencil eraser each time he saw her undress...' (69). The later Rudolph's 'erections were outstanding – or upstanding – though lately he seemed to have no interest in sex' (84). Evelyn is obsessed with 'the vivid changes in his body', 'the grim firmness where before there was jolly fat, the disquieting steadiness of posture' (86). Rudolph's 'new flesh had the contours of the silhouetted figures on medical charts: the body as it must be in the mind of God' (84). Where before, Evelyn had sheltered in the knowledge that 'he would die before her' (70), at the story's end she realises in a trance that he 'would outlive her' (94). Watching him perform in a martial arts competition, she understands that

> this was not the man she'd slept with for twenty years Not her hypochondriac Rudolph [   ] She did not know him, perhaps had never known him, and now she never would, for the man on the floor, the man splashed in sweat, rising on the ball of his rear foot for a flying kick [...], would outlive her; he'd stand healthy and strong and think of her in a bubble, one hand on her headstone, and it was all right, she thought, weeping uncontrollably, it was all right that Rudolph would return home after visiting her wet grave, clean out her bedroom [..] and throw open her windows to let her sour, rotting smell escape, then move a younger woman's things [in. .]. And then Evelyn was on her feet, unsure why, but the crowd had stood suddenly to clap, and Evelyn clapped too, though for an instant she pounded her gloved hands together instinctively until her vision cleared, the momentary flash of retinal blindness giving way to a frame of her husband, the postman, twenty feet off the ground in a perfect flying kick that floored his opponent and made a Japanese judge who looked like Oddjob shout 'ippon' – one point – and the fighting in the farthest ring, in herself, perhaps in all the world, was over. (SA, 94-95)

It is hard to imagine a more complete triumph of impersonal virility over abject 'relation' as Johnson conceives it. Rudolph defeats not only his opponent but Evelyn and 'perhaps all the world'. Evelyn is led irresistibly, unconsciously, mechanically, to applaud the situation she has resisted for months. In one and the same passage she loses her idea of the future, her will, her emotional self-control, indeed her *own* ability to fight. She crumples before the manifestation of a properly singular if not sovereign power. As we shall see, a similarly though more discreetly gendered distribution of roles is at work in Johnson's second and third novels.

If in *Faith and the Good Thing* Faith's task is to realise (to understand) the immanent nature of the Good Thing, then in the later novels the process of singularisation involves less the first than the second sense of real-isation (its actualisation). Andrew and Rutherford are, from the outset, fully equipped with all the philosophical awareness Faith struggles so painfully to acquire. It is rather their material situation that must be altered, so as to come into line with the truth of indeterminacy. They must become what they *are*. In all three novels, the decisive mechanisms of the transformation include: loss or refusal of position; becoming-other; transcendence of Oedipus; renunciation of desire; renunciation of the body.

(a) The loss of position

Johnson's novels conform to some extent to what Baker has analysed as the prototypical model inherited from the slave narrative – the pursuit of freedom from an initially marginal, dispossessed position – a prototype he associates most decisively with Douglass' *Narrative* and Ellison's *Invisible Man* (along with *The Autobiography of an Ex-Colored Man, Native Son*, and the *Autobiography of Malcolm X*). In each of these narratives the hero must first escape his or her enforced place within the illegitimate (enslaving) society, so as eventually to win a legitimate place within a legitimate society. Douglass, like his literary descendants, must 'place himself (paradoxically) in an extra-legal position in order to obtain justice'.[56] In Johnson's novels, likewise, Faith becomes a prostitute, Andrew an impostor, while Rutherford himself goes so far as to sign up, unwittingly, as crew on a slave ship.

But Johnson takes this emancipatory sequence further that these predecessors could ever have imagined. Douglass and Ellison, within the limits imposed by time and circumstance, call the dominant modes of placement into question so as to clear the way for a new and more just affirmation of place. Johnson's characters, by contrast, make of their *lack* of place their redemptive opportunity. Faith is orphaned, her parent's home is burnt down, her possessions are stolen. Andrew is born literally between master and slave, educated by the one and destined for the other; he makes of this 'in-betweeness' the mechanism of survival. Rutherford is the most radically displaced of Johnson's heroes. A thief and a stowaway, Rutherford is a born trespasser.⁷ As McGaffin says, 'it's his nature to be in places he ain't supposed to be' (MPg, 91). The lone black crew member on a slaving ship, a philosopher among thugs, 'he's got nothing to lose [...], belongin' to nobody' (87-88). When he becomes a slave himself, Rutherford feels

> as if everything of value lay outside me Beyond [   ] I listened to everyone and took notes. I was open, like a hingeless door, to everything [..], for in myself I found nothing I could rightly call Rutherford Calhoun, only pieces and fragments of all the people who had touched me, all the places I had seen, all the homes I had broken into The 'I' that I was, was a mosaic of many countries, a patchwork of others and objects stretching backward to perhaps the beginning of time. What I felt, seeing this, was indebtedness [..], as though I was but a conduit or window through which my pillage and booty of 'experience' passed (MPg, 163)

It is this indebtedness that allows Rutherford to be the agent of redemption on the despairing ship: 'the injured were calmed [...] by the urgent belief they heard in my voice, and soon enough I came to desperately believe in it myself, for them I believed we would reach home...' (163).

Rutherford's story is the story of a man who is called upon to take a place or position, and defers his choice until that moment when the refusal to take position is itself identical with the taking of *every* position. It is the story of how he redeems and re-affects his initial failure to take his place alongside his brother Jackson – of how he converts his resentment into affirmation, how he is finally able to emulate Jackson's self-lessness, without remaining limited by his brother's formal subservience or his father's futility. Consequently, Rutherford is called to take a position alongside Isadora (16-17), Falcon ('I need someone to keep his eyes open and tell me of any signs of trouble') (57), Cringle ('are you with me...?') (63), Ngonyama (83), and McGaffin (87). Eventually pressured into compliance with the mutineers ('tis done' [92]), a few pages later he betrays them to Falcon without reserve. 'I withheld nothing [...] I outlined the mutineers' plan to deep-six him, citing each rebel by name...' (MPg, 96). When it comes to the crunch of taking sides, Rutherford

> suddenly could not breathe I felt caged. Wrong if I did as the first mate asked Wrong if I sided with Falcon I began hiccuping uncontrollably... (MPg, 125)

> 'I'm not on anybody's side!' [...] I don't know who's right or wrong on this ship anymore ' (137)

> In waters strange as these, where any allegiance looked misplaced, I could no longer find my loyalties All bonds, landside or on ships, between masters and mates, women and men, it struck me, were a lie forged briefly in the name of convenience .. (92)

But through this very paralysis of positioned action comes 'an inexplicable calm, *as if I were the sea now*, and the dam of my tears – the poisons built up since I left southern Illinois – burst, and I cried for all the sewage I carried in my spirit [...], and searching myself, I discovered I no longer cared if I lived or died'.[58] Rutherford's place is literally between or beyond any particular position.[59] He cannot be identified with *any* interest.

(b) Becoming-other

To become-other, once again, is not to relate *to* another but to create a new in-between space in which both self and other dissolve. It is impossible to become-other if either self or other remain tied to a self-image, 'something dead or static already inside you' (OT, 174). Rather, such an image or 'identity' is the condition of that imitation-*possession* of the other that Bannon employs in the hunting of his prey.

> You become a Negro by lettin' yoself see what he sees, feel what he feels, want what he wants. What does he want [?] Respectability, [...to go] unnoticed like people who have a right to be somewheres [...] His capture happens like a wish, somethin' he wants, a destiny that come from inside him, not outside.[60]

Slavery, in other words, is for Johnson not a condition so much as 'a way of seeing', an attachment to self-image. There are too many becomings-other in Johnson's work to give an adequate account of each. The most important are Andrew's becoming-Bannon/George, which I will consider in the next section, Faith's becoming-Swamp Woman, considered above, and Rutherford's becoming-Allmuseri, which I will consider here.

Rutherford becomes-Allmuseri enough for their adapted form of *capoeira* to become 'as natural to me as lifting my arm', allowing him eventually to overpower the indestructible Santos (193). In addition, 'I spoke in the slightly higher register of the slaves, had their accent, brisk tempo of talk', and 'when I wasn't watching myself, each figure floating past me possessed haecceitas but not quidditas, a uniqueness so radical I felt I could assume nothing about anyone or anything...' (194). This becoming is not limited to Rutherford alone. The middle passage narrated here unleashes a force of becoming-other that subsumes both slaver and slaved in a single apocalyptic con-fusion. 'The mills of the gods were still grinding, killing and remaking us all, and nothing I or anyone else did might stop the terrible forces and transformations our voyage had set free' (125). During the voyage, Rutherford learns to live in absolute, self-less presence to the one-all: 'every action had to be aimed at helping your fellow crewmen [...], if you hoped to see shore, you must devote yourself to the welfare of everyone' (186). Ego-loss, in every facet of Johnson's work, is the condition for a 'relation' with others that is less a relation *between* self and other than their equation in a single movement of ascesis.

> Looking back at the asceticism of the Middle Passage, I saw how the frame of mind I had adopted left me *unattached*, like the slaves who, not knowing what awaited them in the New World, put a high premium on living from moment to moment [. .] The voyage had irreversibly changed my seeing, made of me a cultural mongrel, and transformed the world into a fleeting shadow play I felt no need to possess or dominate, only appreciate in the ever extended present. Colours had been more vivid at sea, water *wetter*, ice *colder*… (187)

This asceticism is the required condition for the further becoming-Jackson – a variant on the same process, for 'Jackson might well have one of [the Allmuseri] priests' (109).

(c) Beyond Oedipus

Fathers are perhaps the most consistently problematic, most hapless characters in Johnson's novels.[61] The three main examples of the role – Big Todd (FG), George (OT) and Ryle (MPg) – are all either lynched or killed as renegade slaves. Such a fate here seems almost the *natural* outcome of a more or less partial commitment to self and self-image. George the most obviously: his racial paranoia reduces him to a 'warped and twisted profile of black (male) spirit, where every other bondsman – everything not oneself – was perceived as an enemy' (OT, 150). George makes the mistake of thinking that to 'be y'self' means to be loyal to the group that defines you. 'Whatever you do, Hawk, it pushes the race forward, or pulls us back' (21). Then Ryle: he blames his gambling, drinking and fighting on slavery – 'he'd say, "Looka what they done to us". You couldn't rightly blame a coloured man for acting like a child, could you…' (MPg, 169).

Faith's father Todd is more complicated. His quasi-singular impersonality remains *unmastered*. Like the Allmuseri, his is a world so immediate that 'he could call pots and pans by proper names he'd given them' (FG, 16). Todd knows that self-renunciation is the true path to survival, as he forces Willis to admit (72). Todd knows the secret of unqualified affirmation, and that 'everything had to do with ease – with the way water effortlessly wore away boulders, temples, and thrones' (88). But rather than work through appearances to the literal truth of things, Todd affirms the apparent as such, and strives to 'live as best as you could in the shadow of uncertainty' (15). Todd, like all Johnson's singular characters, 'ceased to be human simply' – he has learned 'to be, to taste, to hear and smell and see the infinity of worldly sensations'. But he 'enjoyed them through the odd, invisible bars of his imprisonment.' His escape from relation is imposed rather than seized, 'his world of pots and pans with proper names was not created by an act of freedom but by necessity – an escape it was'. Unable to master a relation with the white world, he remains 'servile and obsequious', 'never defiant, never confident save when he was alone' (64).

Reparation of the paternal failure is one of the major tasks facing Johnson's heroes. More exactly, they must escape their relation *with* their father, by absorbing him, by transcending the Oedipal situation altogether. Johnson's second and third novels in particular are firmly situated in an *anti-Oedipal* movement, in very much the Deleuzian sense. Andrew betrays his father by leaving the community and passing for white, whereas Rutherford had always 'hated [his father] because he had cut and run like hundreds of field hands before him' (MPg, 169). In both novels, it is less rivalry that is the problem – the son's need to articulate a *distinct* self relative to the father – so much as an excess of this distinction. Father and son stray too far apart, literally. Resolution of the conflict, then, does not take the form of a kind of negotiated recognition of specificity, father *and* son, but rather the collapse of specificity in the negation of distance. In both cases, resolution is achieved through a filial *absorption* of the father's death.

Rutherford's moment arrives through confrontation of the Allmuseri god in the form of 'my father, the fugitive Riley Calhoun' (MPg, 167). This is one of the most highly charged scenes in all of Johnson's work. Rutherford watches the moment of his father's death re-actualised by the god:

> A thousand soft undervoices jumped my jangling senses from his last, weakly syllabled wind to a mosaic of voices within voices, each one immanent in the other, none his but all strangely his, the result being that as [...] this deity from the dim beginnings of the black past folded my father back into the broader, shifting field – as waves vanish into water – his breathing blurred in a dissolution of sounds and I could only feel that identity was imagined; I had to listen harder to isolate him from the We that swelled each particle and pore of him, as if the (black) self was the greatest of all fictions; and then I could not find him at all He seemed everywhere, his presence, and that of countless others, in me as well as the chamber, which had subtly changed. Suddenly I knew the god's name Rutherford. And the feel of the ship beneath the wafer-thin soles of my boots was different. Not like any physical surface I knew, but rather as if every molecule of matter in her vibrated gently, almost imperceptibly (MPg, 171)

Many of the cardinal features of a becoming-imperceptible are written into this passage: an immanent univocity, the one-ness of the many-voiced; the identity of particle and wave; the imagined, ideological status of identity; the cosmic dimensions of the non-identical; the 'molecular' nature of matter...

Andrew's anti-Oedipal journey is in a sense the dominant motivation of *Ox-Herding Tale*. Andrew's quest is for a way to gain what 'I wanted more than anything else' – 'my father's approval' (OT, 21) – on his own terms. But by passing for white, Andrew contributes more decisively to his father's death, to the 'fifty-'leven pockets of death in him' (174), than Bannon himself, who merely executes what is already determined. '"You could pass", George says, 'if you wanted to. But if you did, it'd be like turning your back on me and everthin' I believes in'" (21). By betraying his father's deepest wish, Andrew makes a *positioned* reconciliation impossible. George eventually drowns in 'li'l pools of corruption that kept him so miserable [that] he begged [Bannon…] to blow out his lights' (174).

However, in the process of passing beyond his father, Andrew gains access to that knowledge which allows for 'unpositioned' reconciliation, reconciliation with Being itself (as opposed to beings). Andrew learns the answer to his last question about his father – 'what I must know is if he died feeling I despised him, or if he […] died hating me' (OT, 175) – in radically singular or immediate fashion, through the very body of George's *killer*, Bannon. Like Reb, Bannon is a wholly impersonal force of nature. 'Ah approves everthin'. Ah approves nothin'" (173). He is 'the death that defines everythin' befo' hit. Gives it form' (170), and conserves it. Grafted on to his body are the 'creatures Bannon had killed since childhood […], their metamorphosis having no purpose beyond the delight the universe took in diversity for its own sake, the proliferation of beauty, and yet all were conserved in this process of doubling, nothing was lost' (175). Through Bannon, Andrew comes to realise that 'all is conserved' in 'this field of energy where the profound mystery of the One and the Many gave me back my father again and again… I was my father's father, and he my child […]. If nothing else, I had learned that the heart could survive anything by becoming everything' (OT, 176, 159).

'The Sorcerer's Apprentice' provides a final variant on the confusion of fathers and sons. Allan's father plays a sketchy version of the Reb-Jackson role. He is a man of quiet presence and power who endures the loss of his hard-won fortune and the suicide of his wife with impassive silence. In order to penetrate his father's apparent indifference, Allan must surrender his desire to please, to make him proud. As an apprentice, 'each spell he showed proudly to his father', who remains silent and unreadable (SA, 152). It is only when he gives up on him-*self* that his father's control breaks, and the two 'impersonal' beings can fall into a chaste and manly embrace: 'Allan felt within his chest the first spring of resignation, a giving way of both the hunger to heal and the anxiety to avoid evil. Was this surrender the one thing the Sorcerer could not teach?' (SA, 168-169).

(d) Renunciation of desire

Once a month, the Allmuseri celebrate a Day of Renunciation, a day 'for giving up a deep-rooted, selfish desire; the Allmuseri made this day a celebration…' (MPg, 180). Like most Allmuseri attributes, such renunciation has clearly marked Buddhist connotations. We saw how it is performed by 'China's' Rudolph; in the novels, it is embodied by three exemplary mentor figures, Alpha of *Faith*, Reb of *Ox-Herding Tale*, and Jackson of *Middle Passage*. Alpha lives in neo-monastic withdrawal from the world, surrounded by the 'presence and warmth that glowed behind [his] voluntary retreat from the world' (FG, 149). Reb, like Bannon, has the supreme knowledge which separates the (selfless) living from the (self-bound) dead. Reb knows, for instance, that 'Flo Hatfield been dead, oh, for goin on fifteen years know… You kin tell. You kin feel it' (OT, 48). He is the character who, freed of all obligations, desires and possessions, most nearly approximates the intersubjective insight of his Allmuseri ancestors. And so Reb is the character who breaks the logic of enslavement as enforced by Bannon. Reb has 'no place inside him fo' me [Bannon] to settle. He wasn't *positioned* nowhere… Yo' friend didn't want nothin'. How the hell you gonna catch a Negro like that? He can't be caught, he's *already free*…' (173–174).

Rutherford's brother Jackson takes the refusal of self to the limit. 'Jackson often skipped meals secretly so I could have a little bit more' (MPg, 47). He was 'so gentle, so self-emptied' that birds 'would let him lie down upon them' and 'plants [would] explode into bloom from the blink of Jackson's eye' (112). Jackson was 'incapable of locking anything out of his heart' (113). He personifies William Law's principle, revered by Chandler: 'Love is infallible; it has no errors, for all errors are the want of love' (111). If Rutherford has 'all along been tellin' people he betrayed [me]' (108), this refers only to that betrayal of *self*-interest which is for Johnson the very principle of redemption. Due to inherit their master's estate, Jackson renounces personal private property:

> It don't seem right to ask for myself. I could ask for land, but how can any man, even you, sir, own something like those trees outside? Or take that pitcher there […] Nothing can stand by itself. Took a million years, I figure, for the copper and tin in that pitcher to come together as pewter. Took the sun, the seasons, the metalworker, his family and forebears. How can I say I own something like that […T]he property and profits of this farm should be divided equally among all your servants and hired hands, presently and formerly employed, for their labour helped create it [42]

A particularly important sign of achieved asceticism, in Johnson's work as in much of the mystical tradition he draws upon, is the renunciation of sexual desire. (Ordinary) sex doesn't mix well with the transcendence of self. Faith loves only the man who cannot be loved, Alpha. Trishanku's quest for Samsara is derailed by his obsession with Lila, just as Kujichagulia's is with

Imani (FG, 29) In *Ox-Herding Tale*, women terrify Andrew's mentor Ezekiel (OT, 29), whose obsession with the non-existent Althea leads to his death (suicide?). Flo incarnates the consequences of enslavement to pleasure (OT, 43). Peggy, finally, is more or less asexual ('plain as a pike') (OT, 124) and, after Andrew's initial enthusiasm for her 'vitality', is soon consigned to the anonymous role of Wife. Even Andrew's early desire for Minty is less romance than lust filtered through philosophy: 'what seemed physical shortcomings... seemed (to me) that afternoon to be purified features in a Whole... Was beauty truly in things? Was touch in me or in the things I touched?' (15, my emphasis). And by the novel's end, Minty pays a high symbolic price for having inspired such desires – diseased, ugly and unloved, she is *bought* by Andrew himself and becomes his servant.

The most condensed image of renunciation in Johnson's work is that of his male hero climbing into bed with a desirable (and desperate) seductress – only to refuse her. The image recurs. In 'China', we know that despite the newly ascetic Rudolph's 'outstanding' prowess, he 'seemed to have no interest in sex' (SA, 84): he converts his initial impotence to sexual indifference. In 'Aléthia', the 'timid Negro professor' winds up at the story's end with the super-sexy Wendy, yet remains chastely aloof. 'She pulled off her blouse, her skirt, her other boot [...] As she lay down, her cold feet flat against me, I lifted my arm to let her move closer, and at last let my mind sleep' (SA, 112). *Middle Passage* is more graphic. Rutherford begins the novel as a worldly man about town; he ends it in a neo-monastic asceticism. Isadora's main characteristic is to be desperately and defencelessly in love with the hero. Prepared at first to buy his hand in marriage (MPg, 17), she is later ready to seduce him by *any* means necessary. Rutherford only laughs at the spectacle. 'Her model, now that I think about it, was a temptress in a play we had seen a year ago, and as Isadora tried to imitate that actress' come-hither expression I could only answer by covering my lips to smother a sudden urge to laugh [...]. She was so sexually bold I began to squirm...' (206). Rutherford renounces temptation lavishly offered, in the interest of a chaste, impersonal *sufficiency*.

> Something was wrong [.. M]y memories of the Middle Passage kept coming back, [...] and in place of my longing for feverish love-making left only a vast stillness that felt remarkably full, a feeling that, just now, I wanted our futures blended, not our limbs, our histories perfectly twined for all time, not our flesh. Desire was too much of a wound, a rip of insufficiency and incompleteness that kept us, despite our proximity, constantly apart.. [. V]ery chaste [.] she lowered her head to my shoulder, as a sister might (MPg, 208–209)

(e) Renunciation of the flesh

The ultimate phase of renunciation, of course, is starkly marked by Christ's example. a wholly disinterested sacrifice of the body is the basis for a wholly inclusive redemption. Faith is stripped of baby, face and skin, becomes 'horrible!'. Andrew denies his parents and passes for white, before merging with Bannon's own patchworked skin. Rudolph tones his body so as to escape it 'at the bottom of the lake'. Tortoise, perhaps, has what is for Johnson the ideal body – a space of physical withdrawal pure and simple.

But nowhere is this withdrawal more graphically and enthusiastically described than in *Middle Passage*, where the disintegration of bodily coherence proceeds apace with the disintegration of the ship and of cultural identity in general. Confronted by the god, the revelation of truth, 'nausea plummeted from my [Rutherford's] belly straight down to my balls' (MPg, 168). Proximity to a singular and 'anorganic' anonymity produces *nausea* in the still-positioned self. *Middle Passage* celebrates this nausea with a more than Rabelaisian zeal. Obsession with the decay of the body begins from the moment Rutherford is first obliged to 'handle the dead':

> the underside of his body had the squishy, fluid-squirting feel of soft, over-ripe fruit. If you squeezed his calves, a cheeselike crasis oozed through the cracks and cuts made in his legs by the chains [...] I cannot say how sickened I felt. The sight and smell of him was a wild thing turned loose in my mind [...] His open eyes were unalive, mere kernels of muscle, though I still found myself poised vertiginously on their edge, falling through these dead holes deeper into the empty hulk he had become. (MPg, 123)

Johnson spares no details. When Falcon commits suicide, he 'blast[s] away half his head, painting the wall behind him pink with kernels of bloody scalp bid as peppercorns, a pâté of brains and blood'.[63] In the post-Falcon *Republic*, 'death climbed in through every portal. Falcon had left us a drifting laboratory of blood-chilling diseases [...] We dragged contaminated, pungled bodies to the rail...' (155). Amputation and 'dental extraction' are the principal forms of treatment.

> Every mother's son on board had lice and eczema, was continually scratching, covered with red blotches, complained of fever, constipation, fatigue and the bloody flux [... T]here were cases of distemper, a sort of maddening fever degenerating into a frenzy so violent that the victim ripped away his clothes, shredded his skin, or that of the man next to him, to hanging ribbons, then leaped into the sea. And these, I must add, were the milder cases aboard ship. Far more dreadful were the sufferers from Black Vomit [...who] went from apparent health to rot in a period of two days. (156–157)

Cringle, for example, comes down with typhus, scabies and scurvy. 'His legs were swollen. Two wisdom teeth were loose in his head, wobbling in gums going putrid', 'his skin rucked and sagging', 'his head was full of bald patches, the remaining tufts of brown hair being starched, bleached and brittle' (157). Across the middle passage, the body fragments and its fragmenting starts a kind of chain reaction. 'That bloody piece of him I held, dark and porous, with the first layers of liquefying tissue peeling back to reveal an orange underlayer [...] My stained hand [...] no longer felt like my own. Something in me said it would never be clean again...' (123). Rutherford 'had not known before that everything, within and without, could break down so thoroughly' (178, 180).

In this way, the *personal* coherence of the body yields to the indifferently vital coherence of matter, the unity of substance and the multiplicity of form. Falcon's neural damage, for example, is so extensive 'he could not control his bowels or the spastically dancing muscles of his face. Thus, smile followed morose expressions. These were replaced by petulance, surprise, delight, then grief, as if behind the tarp of his skin several men and women were struggling to break free' (MPg, 144). The body becomes one with the world it expresses, carved into the real as Ngonyama carves pork:

> It seemed, suddenly, as though the galley slipped in time and took on a trans-
> parent feel, as if everything round us were made of glass. Ngonyama began
> to carve. He slipped metal through meat as if it wasn't there or, leastways,
> wasn't solid [.], the blade guided by, I think, a knack that favoured the same
> touch I'd developed as a thief [..] He left no knife tracks. Not a trace [...] In
> every fibre of their [the Allmuseri's] lives you could sense this same quiet
> magic. (MPg, 76)

VI Writing on the plane of immanence

As we would expect, Johnson's notions of literature and drama are essen-
tially derived from the criteria of singularity itself. Writing provides his aesthetic counterpart to the singularising mechanisms described in the preceding section. To write is to key into an impersonal ascesis expressive of the One-All. To write is to lose oneself in a mastered form, like the martial arts student of *Being and Race* who 'feels as if the form performs him' (BR, 47). 'In an age of mediocre artists, as the Japanese say, it is easy to distinguish yourself' (OT, 130, my emphasis). Genuine art involves something quite different: the power to de-distinguish the self, to become-imperceptible, and thus free to become-other, to '*be* every character' (BR, 42). Johnson works more or less to Barthes' prescription. 'writing is that neutral, com-posite, oblique space where our subject slips away, the negative where all identity is lost, starting with the very identity of the body writing...'[64]

To adapt the terms proposed by Bourdieu, Johnson conforms to our con-
temporary 'rules of art' by making his character's experience (contingency, distance from one-self, the lack of a place) the very principle of his own aes-thetic.[65] To write – to become Andrew the narrator, as distinct from Andrew the character – is to be a Creator outside every created world. to be that

'opening through which the world is delivered' (OT, 153). *Ox-Herding Tale* begins from afar ('*long ago* my father and I were servants at Cripplegate... That *distant* place, the world of my childhood, is *ruin* now...' [OT, 3, my emphases]). Like *Tristam Shandy*, it begins not with the hero's birth but with a certain ironic detachment from the circumstances of his conception, and maintains this detachment right up to the revelations of the final pages. At the same time, it is the disciplined writing of his story that allows the hero-narrator to shape and manage the traumatic consequences of his progressive singularisation. For Rutherford, reeling from the shock of his self-transcending experience, 'only the hours I spent hunched over the skipper's logbook kept me steady [...], I returned to recording all I could remember, first as a means to free myself from the voices in my head', and later, driven by 'a different, stranger compulsion – a need to transcribe and thereby transfigure all we had experienced [... –] somehow through all this I found a way to make my peace with the written past by turning it into Word' (MPg, 190).

Genuine writing must further fit what Johnson calls the criteria of '*dramatic* narrative', where emphasis is placed, except in the most unusual of cases, on drama, the writer donning the hat of the playwright because certain information simply cannot be told, but must be shown' (BR, 71–72). A gift for *showing* is Johnson's principle yardstick of evaluation of other writer's work.[66] 'Dramatic scene', Johnson explains, is 'that special moment in fiction when the opposing aims of characters force them into a collision that changes them before our eyes, leading them toward self-discovery or a moment of recognition [...] that becomes in the best literary art the very core or heart of a novel, a story, or a play' (BR, 103). Drama here, as with the conflict between Andrew and Bannon, and Rutherford and Jackson, is that knot in the narrative required in order to achieve an eventual fusion of apparent opposites. In other words, drama results from a deferred reconciliation, where the narrative *is* nothing other than this deferral. Drama is a function of delayed 'immediation', we might say. Dramatisation centres on the 'difficult process of stripping bare a life so that we, as readers, can see how others and by implication ourselves might arrive at a certain place' (BR, 78). The drama of *Ox-Herding Tale*, for instance, is what allows Andrew to *become*, consciously, the impersonally placeless being that he *is* from the beginning. Owning 'nothing' – 'my knowledge, my clothes, my language, even, were shamefully second hand' – he decides that 'whatever my origin, I would be wholly responsible for the shape I gave myself in the future' (OT, 17). The outcome he attains makes him expressive of his original second-handedness, re-affected. He becomes that 'palimpsest, interwoven with everything', which is Johnson's prescriptive definition of the 'subject' (152).

The singular movement of drama bypasses interpretation as such. As Johnson describes it, drama creates aesthetic value through the *deferral* of its revelation-realisation, and nothing more. Johnson's fiction does not so much convey a knowledge of things as rehearse (or as Deleuze would say, *repeat*) the process required for an escape from knowledges *of*. Rutherford and Andrew's serenely retrospective narrative mode eliminates all suspense in advance. Rutherford, for example, describes just after his arrival on board the *Republic* 'the log in which I now write (but this months later after mutiny and death, the reporting on which I must put off for a while)' (MPg, 27). Drama lies in the timing of this reporting. Deferral of the Jackson story provides a good illustration. As early as page three Rutherford evokes 'the hour of my manumission, a day of such gloom and depression that I must put off its telling for a while', and refers without further explanation to 'my older brother Jackson's spineless behaviour in the face of freedom'. A few pages later, he reveals that after manumission 'Jackson stayed more deeply bound to our master than any of us dreamed. But I am not ready just yet to talk of Jackson Calhoun' (MPg, 8). Like Bannon, Jackson is generally evoked in terms of dread. Rutherford is ready to talk of Jackson only at the moment when he is effectively ready to *become*-Jackson, when his own experience of self-renunciation on board the *Republic* allows him to emulate his brother's selfless, exemplary concern.

In very much the same way, rather than narrate an undetermined sequence of events, most of the stories of *The Sorcerer's Apprentice* take effectively pre-determined situations to their logical conclusions.[67] Their drama turns on the 'happy' notion of [Heidegger's] *aléthia* – 'to call forth from concealedness' (SA, 104). 'Menagerie' narrates the apocalypse already implicit in specific difference. In 'Exchange Value', the theft of hoarded treasure from a woman killed by her own miserliness simply prompts the thieves to adopt and repeat her demented paranoia. 'Aléthia' itself equates theory and practice, i.e. a given theory ('man – if self-forgetful – is not an actor or agent at all' [SA, 104]) with a discovered practice: the Professor's drugged epiphany allows him to become a non-agent, coincident with nature. Again, the movement of 'Moving Pictures' is driven by the hero's growing awareness of the full futility of his initial situation.

The title story, above all, teaches the familiar lesson: become what you originally *are*, by learning to forget your (acquired or relational) *self*. Allan, the sorcerer's apprentice, initially bungles his education by imitating his teacher Rubin. He sets out to 'study everything – the words and timbre and tone of your voice as you conjure'.[68] In his first attempted solo cure, he 'mimed the Sorcerer so perfectly it seemed that Rubin, not Allan, worked magic in the room' (163). But the cure fails. Allan's one and only real success – the healing of Esther – occurs when, forgetting himself, he becomes adequate to the collective contingency of white magic.[69] 'The charm that cured Esther had whipped through him like wind through a weedpipe, or – more exactly, like music struggling to break free, liberate its volume and immensity from the confines of wood and brass. It made him feel unessential, anonymous, like a tool in which the spell sang itself, briefly borrowing his throat, then tossed him, Allan, aside, when the miracle ended' (156). As Rubin says, 'God took holt of you back there' (155). And he then goes on to make the discouraging prophecy: 'I don't see how you can do it that good again' (155): in other words, next time it must be a different 'you', another you, contingent, passing, impersonal. As Deleuze reminds us, only *pure* difference can truly repeat itself, precisely *as different*.[70]

The singularised subject is simply the vehicle or channel for a coherence that exceeds it. What the apprentice must learn is not a particular set of skills so much as a profound form of 'resignation' or passivity (SA, 168). Allan's initial mistake is to assume that because 'by themselves the tricks aren't good or evil', so 'if you plan to do good, then the results must be good.' He falls for the illusion of (good)will. He believes, 'even if you [Rubin] do not, that the secret of doing good is a good heart...' (150–151). Rubin tries to warn him: 'you can't be too faithful, or too eager, or the good becomes evil' (150). From a singular perspective, it is not so much that specific desires *are* good or evil as that *all* specific desire as such is the opportunity of evil. The essential thing is rather to move beyond desire altogether, to become open, empty, *'disponible'*. 'To conjure beauty [...], God, or creation, or the universe – it had several names – had to seize you, use you' (165). True 'white magic comes and goes', as Rubin says (151). The summoned devil Bazazath confirms the point: 'to love the good, the beautiful, is right, but to labour on and will the work when you are obviously beneath this service is to parody them, twist them beyond recognition, to lay hold of what was once beautiful and make it a monstrosity. It becomes black magic' (167).

VII The costs of singularisation

From a specific perspective, Johnson's vision is of course unacceptably expensive. It obtains only through a profoundly traumatic dislocation from history. Overwhelming loss is here the condition of personal divestment. After being robbed and raped, Faith loses her baby to a fire, her husband to his vanity, her lover to his artistic purity. Andrew and Rutherford undergo ordeals that take them to the edge of anonymity. Cringle is eaten by his comrades. Most dramatically, if the exemplary Reb 'wasn't positioned nowhere', if 'he's already free' (OT, 173–174), it is because his own positioned 'enslavement' – in the form of his wife and daughter – has been brutally destroyed in the distant past. 'His only strategy, the one option left, was *surrender* […]. The knots of his heart were broken […]. From that day on Reb took nothing on himself' (OT, 76, my emphasis). Reb's freedom from desire stems from a traumatised renunciation, it is perhaps less the product of an ascetic work upon himself than of the *social conditions* which force slaves, like Morrison's Paul D, to love 'only a little bit'. In somewhat the same way, Squibb, the most pathetically ineffectual member of the *Republic*'s crew, is so dramatically humiliated by his theft of a child's food that he has 'nothing more to lose. Being that far down he was no longer afraid to fall. In this new condition, the concepts of good and evil, sinner and saved, even of life and death, falsified the only question of significance aboard ship, which was this: What must he do next [… And] whatever was needful he did' (MPg, 175–176). Through his focused attention to pure Action, he becomes-Allmuseri.

> The result of Squibb's sea change was that his touch, as he worked the lancet, reminded me of Ngonyama's (or that of a thief), as if he could anticipate my pain […]. His breathing even resembled that of the Allmuseri [..]. I felt perfectly balanced crosscurrents of culture in him, each a pool of possibilities from which he was unconsciously drawing, moment by moment, to solve whatever problem was at hand. (MPg, 176)

Johnson's historical fiction is often included within a broader revision of the slave narrative and African-American fiction.[71] As histories or 'counter-histories', his novels work in the direction of what Jane Campbell calls the mythic 'transformation of history', an 'apocalyptic' revelation of a 'world beyond the world historical events would appear to spell out', a world of messianic potential and catastrophic revaluation.[72] As first-person novels, they belong to what Robert Stepto calls the moment of 'after-hibernation', a moment after Ellison's invisibility.[73] His books mark a definite departure from what Richard Yarborough called only a few years ago the 'striking scarcity of [African-American] novels and stories presented from the first-person'.[74]

But Johnson's assertive 'I' asserts only its own ephemeral passing, and his 'histories' are not to be found in or even near 'real' history.[75] Unlike Naipaul's semi-autobiographical first person, for example, his *I* is designed to refuse self-assertion. Johnson's traumatised selves enter a kind of ahistorical weightlessness or transparency. This condition deliberately undercuts any 'substantial' engagement with history and sets Johnson's fiction firmly apart from say, Toni Morrison's historical novels. In Johnson's fiction, as in Deleuze's vitalism, the Creatively virtual seems to actualise itself in created ('historical') forms that cancel or freeze its creativity.[76] In most of Johnson's work, the historical as such represents mere limitation. To be historical is to be 'limited in all your possibilities, enclosed within the small cage of what had passed before'. The alternative to a historical existence, 'the other way', is to 'be brand new each instant, remade…' *The* Good Thing, as that which exists beyond the realm of interpretative knowledge and situated agency, is 'above and beyond the wastepaper basket of the past' (FG, 59). Again, while the singular aspect of Big Todd lies in his ability to become-inhuman, to 'cease to be human' so as to be adequate to the 'infinity of worldly sensations', the 'pitiable side of Todd lay within the confines of history' (FG, 64). As historical being, Faith too is 'in bondage', 'encrusted with the filth of a past beyond her control' (FG, 109).

What power, then, do Johnson's heroes actually have to make their own history in something like Marx or Fanon's sense? The metaphysical audacity of Johnson's fiction sits uneasily alongside a certain degree of pragmatic caution. Once they have themselves attained placeless dimensions, Johnson's privileged characters generally go on to *accept* their ordained place in the world. The withdrawn Tortoise of 'Menagerie' is the only animal to survive the disaster, but also the only animal to remain in his cage. Rutherford eventually agrees to his 'arranged' marriage. As Rudolph and Todd both say, 'Everything that is is right, or it wouldn't be', 'whatever is just is. […] That's all I know' (FG, 8; SA, 90). Even enslavement is presented less as a historical condition with historical consequences than as a kind of meta-historical commitment to specificity itself. In some ways, to be enslaved is here less to lose one's initiative and capacity for action than it is to be committed to the very notions of individual initiative and action. Such is perhaps the most crucial and most problematic 'revision' of history in *Ox-Herding Tale*. At the end of the novel, it is the very ability to stand back, to *judge* and to distinguish, that has become central to the notion of slavery itself. 'I had never escaped' slavery, Andrew realises, 'it was a way of seeing, my inheritance from [my father] George Hawkins: *seeing distinctions*' (OT, 172). As for the solution to actual, material slavery, Johnson's approach is wonderfully simple: just pass for white. It is not obvious that this advice has the fully universal dimensions Johnson seems to claim. The *global* refusal of distinctions plays only too easily into the hands of a hegemonic order quite happy to manipulate 'multi-cultural diversity' in order to preserve its substantial hierarchies intact. Reb's advice to Andrew – 'if you got no power, you have to think like people who do so you kin make y'self over into what they want' (62) – is ambiguously liberating at best.

What most readings of Johnson neglect to point out are the specific terms of his unconditional 'surrender to Being'." What does it mean to write a *slave* narrative on the assumption that 'writing doesn't so much record an experience […] as it creates that experience' (BR, 6)? To be sure, Johnson aims to demonstrate a reality of becoming independent of the specified stasis of history. But much of what he narrates is determined, in fact, by an *absolute dependence upon history*. Douglass and Ellison's invisible men work *through* their histories; Bradley's *Chaneyville Incident* asserts 'a say' in one's place. By contrast, Johnson's heroes become *entirely* if not passively open to the full impact of events. Deleuze might say that they move from the specific position of the coordinated actor to the singular position of the pure spectator.[78] Andrew and Rutherford are *delivered* from slavery, without defence or appeal, by the supernatural oracle that determines their fate (Bannon and the god). When threatened, their survival is miraculous pure and simple. Rutherford is rescued from drowning by a passing ship. Andrew is at least metaphorically resurrected, and Faith is literally so.

In less benevolent circumstances, however, the collapse of relation leads only to self-destruction. The clearest example comes from perhaps the best of Johnson's stories, 'The Education of Mingo'. Like the novels, the story narrates a confusion of identities, but this time into what Guattari calls the black hole of *personal* identity – the guilty, slave-owning identity of Moses Green. The plot is simple: Moses decides to buy a slave, Mingo, and pattern the purchased mind on his own. Mingo becomes 'exactly the product of his own way of seeing', 'his own splitting image', 'his own emanation', to the point that any attempt to kill Mingo 'would be like killing Moses himself, destroying a part of his soul' (SA, 11, 7, 18). Mingo's subsequent murders actualise Moses' own virtual desires. As Mingo says, 'what Mingo know, Massa Green know'; 'Mingo lives through Massa Green, right?'[79] The pivotal concept in the story is this equation of being and having, the ways in which 'being and having were sorta the same thing' (SA, 8). And hence the 'moral' of the story: 'you couldn't rightly call a man responsible if, in some utterly alien place, he was without power, without privilege, without property – was, in fact, property – if he had no position, had nothing, or virtually next to nothing, and nothing was his product or judgement' (18).

This compelling condemnation of slavery is qualified, however, by the fact that Johnson's *unrelated* identities oscillate uncertainly between absolute fusion and absolute difference. On the one hand, Mingo *is* Moses, the two are as Moses dreams it, 'wired together like two ventriloquist's dummies, or opposite sides of the same coin' (16). On the other hand, 'Moses knew [that] *everything* about him and the African was as different as night and day, even what idealistic philosophers of his time called structures of intentional consciousness...' (6). After the murders, Moses is determined to have another go, to 'teach Mingo the difference between chicken hawks and strangers. But sure as day, he'd do it again. He couldn't change. What was *was*...' (19). The 'drama' of the story is driven, then, as in Johnson's novels, by the tension between two inconsistent notions of being – the one identical to having, the other incompatible with it. The story's strong critical message, however, presumes the effective identity of the two notions. This tension, in my view, is not resolved, and Johnson's refusal of relationality makes it unresolvable.

Like so much of Johnson's fiction, the 'drama' of the story resides in the elimination of mediate distortion, in the revelation of an essential truth beneath appearances. As Moses says, 'Mingo, you more me than I am myself. Me planed away to the bone [...]. All the wrong, all the good you do, now and tomorrow – it's me indirectly doing it but without the lies and excuses [...], with all the polite make-up and apologies removed' (22). But what this revealed truth *is* is held to be two different things simultaneously. Mingo is both absolutely identical to, and absolutely different from Moses, and neither alternative provides an inter-active sense of 'self'. The story reserves active redemptive power to one actor alone: Moses. Everything depends on Moses' *isolated* understanding of the situation, his affecting of the relationship as either paternal (in the beginning) or 'parricidal' (in the end).

It may be that a critique of slavery is no better served by the collapse of identities in a single immanent flux than it is by the strict, apartheid regulation of identities as absolute difference, absolute otherness.

EXCURSUS III

THE UNIVERSAL
AND THE TRANSCENDENTAL

In the wake of Dilthey and Cournot, the twentieth century has generally emphasised the *contextual variety* of knowledges and norms at the expense of universal constants or universalisable principles. The emphasis has been confirmed, variously, by the development of sociology, anthropology, and hermeneutics; by the linguistic turn and the insistence upon quasi-incommensurable 'language games'; by an emphasis on epistemic discontinuity and paradigm shifts; by the rise of communitarianism and (multi)culturalism; by the postmodern affirmation of local knowledges or *petits récits*.[1] The ground for the postcolonial aversion to universals has been well prepared. And true to form, postcolonial theorists duly provide 'universalising' condemnations of the universal. Spivak is categorical: 'there can be no universalist claims in the human sciences'.[2] Bhabha flaunts his refusal of any 'general theory', and tells us that 'the postcolonial perspective resists the attempt at holistic forms of social explanation'.[3] Griffiths says it is essential 'to resist incorporation into a new universalist paradigm',[4] while JanMohamed and Lloyd define their 'minority discourse' precisely as one which escapes inclusion in a 'universalistic' humanism.[5] Through our affirmation of the 'hyphen of hybridity', Chambers declares, 'the transcendental pretensions of reason, of the Western ratio that continually attempts to [...] render differences decidable, is decentred'.[6]

It would be very easy to pile up stacks of quotations along these lines. Suffice it to quote the perfectly representative ambitions of a recent special issue on *Postcolonialism*: 'the "local knowledges" constructed here make no claim to offer overriding conclusions or to theorise more than a specific and contingent instance'.[7] Postcolonial critics generally prefer 'malleable situational lessons' to hard matters of general principle.[8] We know that description of an allegedly 'borderless', increasingly 'chaotic' world actively encourages theories that 'focus on fuzziness and mélange, cut-and-mix, crisscross and crossover'.[9] The *distinctly postcolonial* concern is not so much with taking a universalisable position as it is with 'continually calculat[ing] the tensions between positions'.[10] And we know too that on this precise point, at least, many of the most frequently cited and most heavily anthologised *critiques* of postcolonial theory simply push a similarly anti-universalising logic one step further, striving to rethink 'the global situation as a multiplicity of powers and histories, which cannot be marshalled obediently under the flag of a single theoretical term',[11] or calling for 'more flexible relations among the various conceptual frameworks – a mobile set of grids, a diverse set of disciplinary as well as cultural-geopolitical lenses', as the basis for a still more tenuous affirmation of 'historical and geographical links'.[12] Resistance to universalising categories is one of the few things that unite the more theory-enthusiastic postcolonial critics like Bhabha and Spivak and the more theory-averse readers of postcolonial literature like King and Boehmer.

What are we to make of these denials? For we also know now that any *singular* configuration is essentially unlimited by its environment. We have seen that Glissant's work presumes a certain Totality and Johnson's an unbounded sphere of inclusion. As a general rule, all the major categories of postcolonial theory – border-crossing, hybridity, indeterminacy, ambivalence, etc. – refuse *every* boundary as a matter of *principle*. 'Postcolonial excess' is such that it necessarily saturates the entire field of its application, and in the end any such field can only be global in scope. On the other hand, we have seen that no singular category is merely 'universal' in the sense of something valid or constant within certain circumscribed parameters.[13] Rather, the singular is *self-universalising*, so to speak, in a much stronger sense: it creates these very parameters themselves. By creating the medium of its existence, a singularity effectively creates its own universe. No order of discourse is as universal as Bhabha's generic *enunciation*, for instance – not because certain regular features of its operation can be universally observed, but because it generates *all* particular enunciations as its effects. As Appiah very sensibly points out, it is characteristic of those (he is referring to Chinweizu, but we might include Bhabha as well) who 'pose as anti-universalists to use the term universalism as if it meant pseudouniversalism, and the fact is that their complaint is not with universalism at all. What they truly object to – and who would not – is Eurocentric hegemony posing as universalism'.[14] The performative contradiction involved in a principled condemnation of *all* universals is too obvious to warrant analysis.

More to the point, as critics of postmodernism from Habermas and Dews to Connor and Eagleton have long insisted, a political sphere deprived of any universal reference can only operate in line with a kind of law of the

jungle; if all political issues are to be decided by the strategic 'negotiation' of subject positions, then it stands to reason that eventually the most
powerful such positions will prevail. To deny the validity of universalisable
principles is to affirm, sooner or later, the equation of right with might. The
effort to dodge all universal imperatives must lead, as Connor notes,

> either to an irrationalist embrace of the agonistics of opposition [Lyotard] –
> to put it more simply, the adoption by default of the universal principle that
> might is right, or to the sunny complacency of pragmatism [Rorty], in which
> it is assumed that we can never ground our activities in ethical principles
> which have more force than just saying 'this is the sort of thing we do,
> because it suits us'. (In the end, in fact, the pragmatic option will always turn
> into the agonistic, since it will only work satisfactorily until somebody
> refuses to agree with you...)[15]

The Marxist critics of postcolonial theory, of course, are more comfort-
able with the language of universalism. Capitalism is by definition universal in its ambition and scope; so is socialism. Dirlik restates the familiar
retort to postmodern theory in a postcolonial context, noting the 'fundamental contradiction that faces contemporary radicalism. how to formulate
non-totalising solutions out of a situation where the forces of control and
oppression are quite totalistic in their reach and implications'.[16] 'Unless
capital itself is taken as the 'foundational' principle of contemporary life',
he says, emancipatory politics cannot engage with the real cause of
injustice (105). Lazarus and his collaborators follow suit, grounding their
'necessary universalism' in the observable, historical consequences of capitalism: 'the basis of our argument is the claim that the global purchase of
actually existing capitalism obliges us to develop concepts adequate to its
systematicity'.[17] According to Lazarus, the possibility of 'speaking in the
name of humanity at large' has only been enabled by the process that
brought Western and non-Western experiences together: 'imperialism',
and its aftermath.[18] (Earlier discourses with universalist pretensions – the
Buddhist sutras, the epistles of Saint Paul, the *Qur'an*, Spinoza's ethics –
are as usual passed over without mention).

These empirical, effectively 'falsifiable' concepts of totality endorsed by
postcolonialism's Marxist critics are characteristic of most universalistic
gestures in contemporary cultural theory (where they exist at all). The only
universalism generally acceptable today is a much chastened concept, one
reduced to the status of what Nancy Fraser calls 'large-scale empirical narratives', relating to things like long-term shifts in family organisation or
gender relations, i.e. to narratives that remain 'fallibilistic and non-founda-
tional'.[19] Wallerstein, for instance, urges the construction of 'a new universalism based on a foundation of countless groups', while Moore-Gilbert is

prepared to accept a category of the universal so long as it is seen to be 'constructed by the processes of history'.[20] What is remarkable about each such 'universal' is its insistent empirical contingency. These universals seem to be thrown together through an almost chance arrangement of materials or ephemeral conjunction of circumstances.

Can the term *universal* be properly applied to such categories? My own view is that they would be better named 'regularities' or 'tendencies'. If the universal is to mean anything at all, it surely *cannot be fallibilistic*. The patriarchal tendency, for example, however preponderant, is not a universal (there have been exceptions). Nor, strictly speaking, is capitalism, since as an empirical phenomenon its origins were limited in both time and place and its future development, however dominant it might seem now, is uncertain. It cannot be valid, in principle, to derive something like a philosophical anthropology or scheme of general values from *any* particular empirical formation.

Two other sorts of concepts make for more compelling candidates for qualification as universal. The first is a function of what specifies us as a particular species – a function of the 'universally specified', we might say; the second pretends to govern *how* we relate to each other. I propose to call the former *transcendental* of the specific (i.e. enabling of our specificity), and to reserve the adjective *universal*, or 'universalisable' (as here it will amount to the same thing) for the latter. In other words: (a) we are specified, by certain transcendental constants, to be relational beings; and (b) as relational beings, we are able to prescribe universalisable principles valid for all relations or at least, all relations of a certain kind. Given that we *are* relational creatures, 'universal' here will apply to the prescription of certain unconditional principles (as opposed to empirical regularities) that circumscribe *how* we are relational. Principles of justice and equality, for instance.

(a) Transcendental conditions

In the first case, I use the unfashionable adjective 'transcendental' to describe those banal facts that *specify* us as *Homo sapiens*: the fact that we are primates, breathe oxygen, use language to communicate, reproduce sexually, share certain genetic differences from other creatures, etc. *Relationality* and *value*, as general categories, are transcendental in something like the same sense: because a human life is unimaginable in their absence. (*Particular* relations and values, of course, are always specific to particular situations.) It should be obvious that the existence of such categories makes attempts, still common in cultural studies, to deny *any* sort of 'human nature' trivial and futile. We know that language, for instance, did not emerge in miraculous abstraction from the world of 'reference', as Lévi-Strauss and Lacan sometimes imply, so much as *evolve* at a certain specific distance from it. Even the 'now incontrovertible claim that selfhood is constructed and not received, a product and not an origin' is far from straightforward.[21] Our determination to say, without qualification, that *the* subject is an effect or that *every* aspect of identity is constructed, flies in the face of elementary principles established with considerable authority by cognitive science. Before we accept the facile consensus that 'identity is a product not an origin' we must have the modesty to admit that certain minimal conditions of identification as a dynamic process are indeed fundamental, i.e. genuine *species requirements*.

There is no space here to develop this point in the detail the history of philosophy allows. For our purposes here, it's enough to say that certain properly *basic* degrees of agency, subjectivity, relationality, sexuality, identification, and so on, must all be posited as transcendental processes in this strict sense. They are transcendental to any particular human experience because no such experience would be conceivable without them (including the effort to deny them their transcendental status). And they are purely formal, *contentless*, for the same reason: because fully transcendental to any experience, there is nothing 'in' them to fill, orient or determine that experience in a particular way. The experience must conform to their formal requirements, but how it does so is indeed invariably specific to the situation of that experience.

The nature of these transcendental requirements, in my view, is not properly a philosophical so much as a scientific problem. What consciousness *is*, for instance, as opposed to what we *do* or create as conscious beings, is a question more likely to be answered through empirical research in something resembling evolutionary psychology than by armchair reflection in either the continental or analytical philosophical traditions.[22] (Of course, in risking a reference to this most controversial branch of science, I don't mean to endorse reductionist arguments which claim that because the elementary capabilities of the mind [sensory perception, language capability, a problem-solving intelligence, etc.] presumably evolved as specialised adaptations under the pressure of natural selection, so therefore the same order of evolutionary explanation holds for properly *deliberate* or *historical* [and therefore political, technological, artistic...] change. Surely the main interest of studying history and culture lies in an appreciation of all that cannot be explained by more 'fundamental' orders of causal determination, other than innovation or improvisation themselves. Simply, I think that efforts to explain historical change or cultural innovation have nothing to gain by denying, as a matter of *principle*, an understanding of how the minds that accomplish these things have become capable of such accomplishments.)

The term 'transcendental', then, relates here more to our peculiar biological history than to philosophy. I assume that few readers are likely to deny that our collective genetic inheritance in some sense underlies our specifically cultural existence. The question is whether this inheritance imposes any constraints on cultural performances, or whether such performances are in each case *entirely free* (and thus entirely variable or particular) inventions. Have we inherited only an indeterminate 'capacity for culture', or are all cultures partly shaped by some of the same pressures or 'rules'? *On this precise point,* I would side with those who, like Robin Fox and Donald Brown, generalise from the application of Chomsky's basic insight: just as we don't simply inherit an indeterminate language capability, but rather a linguistic competence structured by certain 'deep' grammatical rules, so too our cultural competence carries with it some globally constituent constraints. It's not merely that the potential for culture lies in the unique biology of *homo sapiens*, any more than the general potential to learn, reason or speak, as Fox suggests, this very biology, beginning with our unusual brain development, is itself partly the result of our 'cultural' inventions. By using tools, acting collectively, developing ever more complex forms of communication, and so on, 'man took the cultural way before he was clearly distinguishable from the [other] animals, and in consequence found himself stuck with this mode of adaptation'. Subsequent selection pressures then favoured development of the cognitive skills at work in 'becoming cultural'. If Fox is right, then

> man is not simply the producer of institutions like the family, science, language, religion, warfare, kinship systems, and exogamy, he is the product of them. Hence it is scarcely surprising that man continually reproduces that which produced him. He was selected to do precisely this [...]. It is not only the capacity for culture, then, that lies in the brain; it is the *forms* of culture, the universal grammar of language *and* behaviour.[23]

In short, belief in true cultural *incommensurability* would seem to require disbelief in biological evolution.[24] Rigorous application of Spivak's assertion – that there can be no universalistic claims in the human sciences – would require precisely the kind of cut and dry demarcation between 'culture' and 'nature' that her own version of deconstruction has so often been deployed to undermine.

Consider again the exemplary case of linguistic variations. Even from perspectives *hostile* to Chomsky's general approach, there is considerable evidence to support 'the conclusion that all languages do indeed appear to share a common core, both in their lexical repertoire and in their grammar', and further, that this common core can be abstracted in such a way as to enable both a non-ethnocentric approach to the comparison of languages and an effectively meta-linguistic study of basic, universal patterns of cognition and emotion.[25] Wierzbicka and Goddard have made a compelling case, on strictly linguistic (rather than cognitive) grounds, that all languages do share some elementary lexical building blocks: certain basic substantives (in English. *I, you, someone, something, people, body*), determiners (*this, the same, other*), quantifiers (*one, two, some, many, all*), attributes (*good, bad, big, small*), actions (*do, happen, move*), logical concepts (*not, maybe, can, because, if*), indicators of space and time, comparatives and intensifiers, and so on. Wierzbicka suggests that 'all complex meanings, in all conceptual domains' and in all existing languages, can be crudely distinguished in terms of these sixty-odd basic conceptual elements. So while *particular* linguistic configurations of emotion (say, the distinctly *English* understandings of 'anger' or 'love') are certainly not universal,[26] *some* general configurations of feeling are. For instance, the cognitive scenario associated with the English word 'sadness' (combining the knowledge that 'something bad has happened' with an 'inability to do anything about it') is according to Wierzbicka 'readily translatable into any other language'.[27] Again, every language seems to have words describing the thoughts that 'something bad can happen to me' or that 'people can think something bad about me', i.e. words or phrases that overlap to some extent with the English words *afraid* and *ashamed*. All told, Wierzbicka proposes a dozen or so 'emotional universals' on the basis of comparative linguistics, including the ubiquity of links between certain facial gestures with positive or negative feelings, the ubiquity of words comparable with 'cry' and 'smile', the ubiquity of bodily based descriptions available for cognitively based feelings, and so on (275–276).

In short, while different cultures clearly apply immensely varied linguistic 'grids' to the understanding of emotion and provide equally varied 'scripts' that encourage their members to feel and express certain things in certain ways, nevertheless all these varied scripts draw to some extent from the same basic *language* of feeling. Without some such language, inter-cultural communication would be nothing short of miraculous. Note, however, that the existence of such a language in no way determines the composition of any particular script, let alone the course of any particular script-specific improvisation. Any recognition of a transcendental dimension runs counter to the general cultural-studies emphasis on contingency and 'negotiability', but it is essential to remember that this dimension is itself profound *dis-oriented*, i.e. it indicates no automatic path toward progress or reconciliation. (This is what distinguishes it from Habermas' quasi-transcendental' domain, say, itself oriented toward consensus and substantiated in language.)

(b) Universalisable principles[28]

We are specified to be relational, and this specification is transcendental to any particular relation (as to any particular 'we'). It is only with the second of the two classes of concepts mentioned above – the prescription of general criteria of relationality – that we are dealing with universals in the proper sense, i.e. concepts that apply universally, without exception, but *within* certain situational parameters, however inclusive or abstract these might be. Just as it is a mistake to confuse the specific with the specified, it is essential to avoid confusion of the transcendental and the universal. In particular, while evolutionary psychology *may* become well qualified to explain the genesis of our transcendental attributes, including certain so-called 'ethical' attributes like altruism and honesty, this new discipline can say nothing about the prescription of *specific* universalisable principles (which as Kant well knew, will never be justified in terms of vague and in any case 'pathological' inclinations towards cooperation, any more than they will be invalidated by appeals to our allegedly selfish or clannish nature). Access to the domain of the actively universalisable presumes the equally active, equally *subjective* passage through the conversion of the specified into the specific.

Universals can only apply to the frontier *between* the singular and the specific. On the one hand, principles of justice and equality, like other principles legitimated by reference to the universal interest, are not themselves relations but criteria prescribed as valid *for* all relations in the situation concerned. Though such principles relate only to specific situations (specific sets of relations) they are themselves *meta-specific*. Their legitimacy does not depend on the integrity of a particular determinate relation – say: the relation of employer to employee, of landlord to tenant, or of aristocrat to serf – but on normative criteria applied to relationality in general. (Particularism is nothing other than legitimation which proceeds directly from the specified content of certain privileged relations.) Hence one of the most telling differences between the singular and the universal: universal principles are not immanent to the expression of their (relational) medium, they cannot be immediately derived from the logic of relationality as such. Instead, they are imposed as if from without. They are decided, deliberated, as an external encouragement or constraint. Whereas singularity emerges directly as the expression of the singularising force (sovereignty, the market, the historical process…), universality persists as a fragile *assertion*, a projection from the specific: it holds only insofar as its proponents are able to make it stick.

So on the other hand, then, universal principles are clearly not transcendental, precisely because in every case this moment of *decision* is fundamental. Unlike singular attributes which become manifest through the 'explication' of singularity itself, universal principles must be imposed by subjects at a reflexive distance from the field of their application. Every universal principle is something *produced* in a particular situation at a particular time by particular subjects. The word universal is used here in an emphatically materialist sense: universals apply if and only if they are *made* to apply. Use of the adjective 'universal' is only appropriate if, *in practice*, it describes a principle that is actively universalisable.

(c) Universal productions: Badiou or Bourdieu?

Insofar as 'the key question' that has been raised by general debates about postcolonial theory is the status of 'a "new" universalism that accommodates cultural pluralism', it may be worth pausing here to mention two of the most fruitful contemporary efforts to re-conceptualise the universal.[29]

Much the most important contemporary contribution to a materialist understanding of the universal has, in my view, been made by Alain Badiou. Badiou is very explicitly a philosopher of *universal truths*, i.e. of principles that hold for all, or rather, principles *to which* all can 'hold true'. What is peculiar about Badiou's conception of truths is that he conceives them as invariably local and irreducibly subjective productions, the result of a particular decision taken in a particular situation and sustained (when they are sustained) by a particular form of fidelity to that decision. A universal truth always originates in one point, and expands through the elaboration of an unprecedented set of consequences. Every universal truth breaks with prevailing norms and expectations of the situation in which it takes place, by inventing its own and hitherto unjustifiable norms. What forces an exceptional decision of this sort is always some kind of 'event' whose implications and very existence are undecidable in the situation as it stands. A universal truth is thus composed through the exclusively subjective commitment of those who constitute themselves *as* subjects in the name of this event – for example, St Paul as the apostle who draws certain militant consequences from the (objectively undecidable, hitherto inconceivable) event of Christ's resurrection, or Robespierre and Saint-Just as the subjects of a revolution they declare to have closed the situation of the now *ancien* régime, or Berg and Webern as faithful to Schoenberg's unprecedented innovations in atonal music.[30] Such truths, deployed in a limited number of possible domains (politics, art, science, love), are universal and 'for all' precisely because empty of any objective criteria, i.e. because their innovation is 'founded' only upon that part of the situation which, from within the perspective characteristic of the situation's *status quo* or ruling class, appeared formless or void. And they persist only insofar as their subjects *hold true* to the punctual event from which they sprang and in the name of which they can act in the interests of all. Grounded in an incalculable event, unrecognisable from within the prevailing norms of the situation, the universal exists only as 'immanent exception'.[31] What passes for 'universal', then, 'is never given, it is underway, as a means of treating differences in the element of an (inter-minable) truth'.[32]

Badiou's philosophy provides some of the most promising available tools for the conceptualisation of universals, in the plural, as in each case *specific* to a situation, occasion, and (subjective) procedure. From the perspective of the present project, however, it falls short of a fully viable solution on three counts, each of which reflects Badiou's tendency to *singularise* his univer-sals. First, he has yet to explain how the exceptional 'truth procedures' relate to our general 'capacity for truth': in other words, he has yet to relate universals to what I've called their transcendental conditions of possibility. On this point, Badiou tends to take refuge in a kind of circular reasoning: we are able to invent exceptional truths, because we are endowed with an exceptional and somewhat mysterious capacity of 'thought', itself triggered in each case by its 'evental' occasion or provocation.[33] By emphasising the evental basis both of *a* truth *and* our very capacity for truth in general, Badiou sometimes seems to confuse the two – and this is to annul the difference between the universal and the transcendental. Second, and by extension of this first point, Badiou accepts as *truths* (distinct from knowl-edges) only those discourses which 'invent their rule of deliberation at the same time as they invent themselves', i.e. which create the medium of their expression *at the same time* as they are expressed.[34] Badiou's universals persist in the sovereignty of their self-proclamation, on the model of a math-ematical axiom.[35] Though every truth certainly proceeds *through* a specified tangle of local interests, institutions and constraints, the truth-affirming mechanism is itself fully 'subtracted' from this tangle. This leads to my third point: Badiou's subjects, like the truth they proclaim, are *fundamentally* non-relational. (Indeed, Badiou's peculiar set-theoretic ontology effectively denies being to relations as such.[36]) A truth coheres without any constituent relation to an other of any sort. Its procedure is devoid of external criteria: it is 'pure', 'unrelated', the very form of an ongoing 'un-linking' or *déliaison*.[37]

Pierre Bourdieu's less innovative but better known conception of 'cor-poratist' universals provides two components missing from or at least under-theorised in Badiou's account: a cumulative historical dimension (i.e. a degree of more-than-evental continuity), and an acknowledgement of the foundational rather than exclusively obstructive role played by insti-tutions and 'state structures' in the most general sense. Bourdieu begins with what he presumes to be a 'universal anthropological law, that there are benefits (symbolic and sometimes material) in subjecting oneself to the universal', i.e. in (apparently) subordinating your individual interest to common or general interest.[38] But any attempt to encourage the universal interest to dominate the practical administration of social life is vain, unless backed by the invention of institutions that directly reward deliberate subjection to the universal. Since 'political morality does not fall from heaven and it is not innate to human nature', so then only what Bourdieu calls a 'realpolitik of reason and morality can contribute favourably to the institution of a universe where all agents and their acts would be subject – notably through critique – to a kind of permanent test of universalisability which is practically instituted in the very logic of the field' in which these agents work.[39] Such a test, the measure of an agent's apparent devotion to the common good, becomes a political reality when the institutional organisation of the intellectual fields (science, journalism, law, education, politics…) both practically favours the public commitment to universal values and legitimates the ongoing critical effort to unmask hypocritical or mystifying instances of such commitment.

Bourdieu thus locates the historical development of universalising legitimation strategies in the concrete emergence of distinct fields of intellectual production – for example, a field of science as distinct from a field of religion or faith; a field of civil government, as distinct from dynastic rule, and so on. The more autonomous (i.e. the more independent of custom or privilege) such fields become in practice, the more a disinterested 'reason' becomes the sole legitimate arbiter of intra-field disputes. The *most* legitimate position will then be the one that best approximates the 'disinterested' or 'universal' interest of the field itself (say, the interest of science as such, or of government, or of education…). This allows Bourdieu to conceive of reason itself, the arbiter of disinterest or universality, as the historical product of these intra-field struggles for legitimacy – indeed, as the effectively unintentional *by-product* of an ongoing 'corporatism of the universal'.[40] And rather than issue empty ethical prescriptions, the proper role of a critical intellectual is thus summed up by the obligation 'to universalise the conditions of access to universality',[41] i.e. to free up access to those various fields in which *only* the most reasonable rather than the most privileged argument prevails.[42]

Bourdieu's account is better able than Badiou's to explain the 'normal' and cumulative (i.e. non-exceptional) aspect of universalisable principles, and it offers a firmly objective, socio-institutional *grounding* for the emergence of universalising legitimation strategies – an emergence which remains, to borrow Habermas' phrase, very much an 'incomplete project'. By the same token, of course, Bourdieu's approach downplays the discontinuous and radically subjective or militant *nature* of specific universalisable principles, which hold only if their advocates 'hold true' to their consequences. Both aspects are essential to any future conceptualisation of universals as precisely situated, materialist productions.

But so too is recognition of the transcendental conditions of universalisable principles. Bourdieu is no more able than Badiou to distinguish the historical dimension of the universal as product from the transcendental dimension enabling of historical production itself. In order fully to historicise the development of a universal reason Bourdieu parts company with Habermas at the very moment when the latter has recourse to a quasi-transcendental communicative competence. 'There is no need to invoke a "beyond history" [...]; we must, by taking historicist reduction to its logical conclusion, seek the origins of reason not in a human 'faculty', that is, a nature, but in the very history of these peculiar microcosms in which agents struggle, in the name of the universal, for the legitimate monopoly over the universal.'[11] But by making reason itself a fully historical category, Bourdieu risks confusing the evolution of the species with its history; his suspicion of any sort of 'transcendental illusion', his interpretation of reason as the *result* of social praxis, effectively deprives him of any means of understanding the cognitive conditions of such praxis. And without recognition of the transcendental, I don't think that productionist conceptions of the universal can make a fully convincing break with the anti-universalism of 'high' postmodern and postcolonial theory. They cannot, in other words, provide for a sustainable distinction between the universal (as meta-specific) and the singular (as that which creates the medium of its own existence).

Briefly, my suggestion is that any attempt to conceive of the universal *exclusively* as a historical project or result will eventually singularise it, i.e. present it as fundamentally self-conditioning or self-constituent. It is certainly true, however, that every merely transcendent invocation of supposedly universal norms, ideals or rights (i.e. every invocation of such values that is not mediated through a particular historical mobilisation in their assertion or defence) can only be an idealist abstraction, an abstraction whose purpose is generally to discourage or condemn precisely these mobilisations. Enabled by its transcendental conditions, grounded in the evolution of social and political institutions, the prescription of universalisable criteria is always a *project* in the most concrete – and most subjective – sense.

Neither Glissant nor Johnson, to say nothing of Bhabha or Spivak, has offered us a viable way of distinguishing the singular from the specific. With Mohammed Dib, however, we will at last begin to find some of the tools needed to make this distinction *work*.

MOHAMMED DIB AND THE 'ALAM AL-MITHAL: BETWEEN THE SINGULAR AND THE SPECIFIC

Like Glissant, Mohammed Dib begins his long writing career with an urgently specific programme but quickly moves on to explore some of the most vertiginously singular terrain in contemporary fiction. Considered by many to be the greatest living figure in Algerian literature,[1] Dib is celebrated as both 'the great writer of the Algerian Revolution'[2] *and* as the writer who has, in a sense, moved the Algerian literary agenda the farthest away from its early revolutionary priorities. Dib's first novels narrate the precisely situated coming into awareness of a young boy in Tlemcen, in the years just before the Algerian uprising. His most recent novels describe a complex process of depersonalisation, hallucination and becoming-imperceptible in the supremely ascetic conditions of the *desert*.

Dib's early writing evokes Fanon as much as Ousmane Sembène as allies in the campaign against colonial dispossession; his later writing, guided in part by the great mystics of Islam, sets out in pursuit of that secret Unity beyond relation or qualification, in search of what one compressed poem invokes as the 'sovereign language incompatible secret plunged in the universal flaying'.[3] At the limit of this pursuit lies an intuition of that singular 'Glory which is this emptiness come to pass in which everything sees and nothing comes to pass. Never attained, the place where time is extinguished [...], the place which does not take place, which has no place [...], you are, one [*unique*], the site of our expansion'.[4] If what Glissant found in Deleuze was an enthusiasm driven by the dynamic vitality of nature or the inventive machinations of culture, it's as if Dib develops his more austere, more subtractive aspect: his *inhuman* pursuit of 'sobriety', anonymity, and abstraction, his cold, almost lunar perception of a 'little time in its pure state...' Dib moves, in short, from Fanon's 'thankless inventory of the nation [*pays*]' to an almost unqualified *dépaysement* or deterritorialisation. His later work may well be the most dramatic, most innovative, most original francophone contribution to a properly 'generic' literature in Badiou's sense (i.e. a literature indifferent to the specifying qualities that govern the situation in which it was produced). It is also, per-haps, the most subtle, the most carefully composed, and the most resistant to simple categorisation.[5]

Nevertheless, the terms developed over the course of this book remain very useful, I think, for an elucidation of at least the *general* development of Dib's writing. Once again, Deleuze's work provides highly pertinent points of reference. So does the Islamic philosophy of *Ishraq*, as it develops in Iran from al-Suhrawardi (d. 587/1191) to Mulla Sadra (d. 1050/1641), and as elab-orated for contemporary French readers by Henry Corbin and Christian Jambet. Needless to say, recourse to these thinkers should not imply any-thing in the order of a direct influence, which Dib is the first to deny.[6] They provide only a flexible and sophisticated shorthand for a *comparative* evaluation, part of the shared framework through which the very different writers considered in these pages can be read in some sense together.

I begin this chapter with a brief review of the reception of Dib's work, paying particular attention to the readings proposed by Charles Bonn and Bachir Adjil, which demand comparison with my own. The bulk of what fol-lows obeys an essentially chronological order, divided into three moments: a first, relatively 'specified' beginning (c.1950 – c.1960), where the dominant tone is shaped by a critique of colonialism and the movement towards a col-lective militancy; a second, longer, minimally 'specific' moment (c. 1960–c. 1990), characterised by the disruption of specifiable categories, the dissolu-tion of historical continuity and the fragmentation of relations stretched to the very limits of madness and amnesia, a third moment, (c. 1990–1996) that verges on the intuition of an absolutely singular space and experience. This last is a moment balanced precariously on the *limits* of the ineffable, a moment of semi-mystical initiation into a coherence that exceeds our own.

The first moment is *specified*, in the sense that it presents a clearly denoted time and place and a clearly portrayed set of values. It insists on the specification of injustice, and the need for a properly territorial work of repossession. In the second moment, the faculty of judgement is con-founded by circumstances beyond reaction; the capacity for both collective and individual action is effectively paralysed. This is the moment of a relative deterritorialisation. It remains minimally *specific*, however, in that Dib's characters retain a more or less distinctly marked sense of them-selves in relation to place and to other selves. This sense is gradually worn down towards the third moment, which emerges imperceptibly at the subtractive limits of relationality. This is the moment of a *radical* deterrito-rialisation, evocative of a space in which '"one" is always in the middle'.[7]

Up to a point, however, and even in this third moment, Dib remains forever on the threshold of a fully absolute singularity. The main goal of what follows is a description of this *threshold* as such. It is a place that generally eludes, I think, the many – and mostly very useful – published readings of Dib's work.

I Models of development

The record of Dib's interviews with the literary press provides a helpful first description of the evolution of his work. In the 1950s, Dib insists that 'a work is of value only to the degree that it is rooted [in the place it describes], that it draws its sap from the country to which it belongs, that it introduces us into the world that is our own'.[8] Writing in the circumstances of severe cultural repression, national liberation takes precedence over all other considerations: 'it seems to us [writers] that a contract ties us to our people. We can fairly call ourselves public writers. We turn to the public first and foremost. We seek to grasp its structures and particular situations.'[9] The writer's task is to prepare the ground for an imminent revolution.[10] Hence the overwhelming importance of a direct testimony, as accurately transcribed as possible. For example, 'everything that is said about Omar [the main character of Dib's *La Grande Maison* (1952)] and of his environment was taken directly from reality. There is not a single detail – none, I can assure you – that was invented.'[11]

However, Dib was also one of the first Algerian writers to insist 'the independence [won] in 1962 constitutes a turning point [... From now on], a writer's first loyalty must be, above all, to his work'.[12] 'Just as Algeria herself is passing now from the stage of tutelage to the stage of maturity, so does the writer feel himself becoming a kind of adult who must take on responsibility for his problems.'[13] If Dib 'had been African when [he] had to be',[14] he very quickly realised that 'a writer who persevered exclusively in revolutionary literature would henceforth demonstrate only bad faith, a laziness of spirit, quite simply, a creative poverty. The Algerian writer has been delivered over to himself [*rendu à lui-même*].'[15] He is perhaps surprisingly categorical on this point. As he explains in 1964,

> For several reasons, my concern as a writer in my early novels was to blend my voice with the collective voice. Today, this great voice has fallen silent [. Before] we had to bear witness to a new country and to new realities. Insofar as these realities have since been made concrete, I have regained my attitude as a writer interested in problems of a psychological, novelistic or stylistic order [. .]. The time of engagement is over.[16]

For the older, post-revolutionary Dib, 'to write is to challenge oneself [*se mettre à l'épreuve*] and thus to challenge humanity, humanity in its entirety'.[17] The circumstances of this *épreuve* are deprived, now, of the stability of a common background or a public consensus around shared values and a shared engagement. The term evokes, as we will see, connotations of *épreuve* (trial) in the Sufi sense. In short, 'I moved from a realist, positive attitude, to a progressively relativistic attitude [...]; I have been seized by the aleatory character of all things'.[18]

This self-described development provides perhaps the most striking indication of a more general evolution in the reception of Algerian literature as a whole: from an early, nationalist engagement, to a more singular, more 'purely' literary enterprise, the exploration of a writing without reference. From politics to poetics, from 'simple' realism to a more technical, more complex, more 'creative' literature.[19] All of Dib's critics recognise a break of some kind between his mostly 'realist' first four novels and the more experimental if not 'surrealist' works which begin with *Qui se souvient de la mer* (1962). Dib's first readers appreciate, depending on their political stance, his trenchant critique of colonial injustice or his appeal to a broadly universal humanism. The early Algerian trilogy is received and celebrated as 'essentially realist[ic]'; 'Dib has painted the reality that we have known'.[20] As Jean Déjeux put it in one of his earliest pieces of literary criticism, 'Memmi, Dib, Mammeri touch us through a sort of attentive autopsy, a cautious inventory of injustice'.[21] Merad Ghani, writing in 1976, was still able to claim that 'the constant [theme] of Algerian literature is engagement [...,] the search for a self rooted in History and projected towards a better future' through a 'collective coming into consciousness'.[22]

Dib's *Danse du roi* (1968) coincides with a widely reflected shift toward a post-independence or post-revolutionary disillusionment;[23] Dib's critics generally regroup around a new consensus, 'that formal subversion compensates for subversion at the political level'.[24] Critical emphasis now goes to the experimental or *literary* dimensions of the work as such. In particular, from the moment of its appearance (1977), it has been customary to describe *Habel* (and Dib's subsequent novels) as an 'writing at/of the limits', 'the quest for an impossible language'.[25] As Charles Bonn put it in the early 1970s, Dib's work was evolving towards the 'radical intransitivity of literature' associated with Blanchot and Mallarmé.[26] With *Terrasses d'Orsol*, (1985) Jacqueline Arnaud concludes that 'Dib has arrived at a point of absolute exile',[27] a point close to that singular 'neutrality' celebrated by the later Barthes.[28]

Space does not permit a more inclusive review of the reception of Dib's work. My own argument, however, compels some engagement with the most powerful recent interpretation, associated above all with the insightful and prolific critic Charles Bonn, and developed in an impressively sophisticated study by Bachir Adjil. Broadly speaking, Bonn and Adjil present the least compromising version of the consensus which appears to hold for most of Dib's critics. Bonn presents the movement from Dib's early 'ideological' works to the later, more experimental novels mainly as a movement of *sophistication*, the movement by which Dib's writing qualifies as *littéraire* in something like Blanchot's sense. For Bonn's Dib, 'the only real question is that of the powers of language.'[29] On the one hand, his 'work endlessly pronounces the impotence of speech [*la parole*] confronted by the nothingness from which it stems' (9) in 'a language that endlessly confronts nothing other than its own impossibility' (122). On the other hand, it effects 'a *mise en spectacle* of languages' (18) in order to demonstrate their impotence, in order to stage 'the vanishing that is all writing' (20). According to Bonn, in Dib's later work (as in Mallarmé's later poetry) 'the place [*le lieu*] exists only in the very instance of its disappearance, it is only through its loss. Loss of the place that achieves the very nomination of the place through its desiring articulation'.[30] So here, in line with Blanchot's prescription, 'writing says nothing other than itself, endlessly'.[31] Bonn's reading pursues an *unqualified* elimination of the specific.[32] It's as if the void is alone productive of genuine meaning, as if 'the sole void contains all possible words'.[33]

Written in much the same vein, Adjil's choppy but sometimes brilliant book[34] cites Deleuze and Guattari's *Kafka*, works from the now fashionable concepts of 'minor literature' (16-18), 'deterritorialisation' (23) and 'becoming-animal' (144), and very rightly hints at the relevance of Ishraqi philosophy.[35] The whole of Adjil's enthusiastic use of these categories is again organised around a study of Dib's 'reflection on language' (9), in which 'speech is a total, limit experience' (62; cf. 65–66). This Dib articulates 'the empty space created by language itself [...], which creates its own space' and through which it 'rejoins its infinite origin, which is silence' (41, 49). Especially 'in the Nordic trilogy, the narrator's mystical ideal is inseparable from the experience of writing itself' (193). Adjil insists upon the wholly textual advent of a transformation achieved 'within the fictional world of writing'. And so 'we conclude with Paul Valéry (*Monsieur Teste*): the infinite, my dear friend, is no big deal – it's a matter of writing – the universe exists only on paper' (196).

As we will see, much of what Bonn and Adjil propose helps describe the 'subtractive' aspect of Dib's text. Their analysis is still more descriptive, however, of what many contemporary critics have looked for in recent literature generally, i.e. a confirmation of *literarity* itself, the radical autonomy of a writing without world (an autonomy not unrelated, no doubt, to their own disciplinary independence and validity). My own perspective, of course, blocks interpretation of the shift toward a singular or literal immediacy simply as a form of aesthetic sophistication. The real question is: does a description of Dib's refusal of specification grasp the full effect of his writing? I will argue that while the later Dib certainly evacuates the specified, he continues to write the minimally specific, more than the radically anonymous or purely littéraire. Less than immediate to the void or to a purely silent absence, I think Dib writes in relation to a hidden presence. His truth, I will argue, is secret rather than empty.

For Dib has always affirmed the importance of a 'a particular sensibility, born of the feeling of belonging to [...], let's dare the word, a civilisation without equivalent [...], my country, my particular country'.[36] As if to refute Bonn, one of Dib's most 'privileged' narrators insists that 'there is nothing I detest so much as this idea, "being without place" [être sans lieu]' (IM, 171). Dib could not be more emphatic about the constitutive importance of the relation that links writer to environment:

> In the beginning is the landscape – meaning the framework where being comes to life, then to consciousness
> In the end also
> And in the middle, too
> Before consciousness opens its eyes and sees the landscape, already its relationship with it is established [...]. No matter how far we distance ourselves from each other [my landscape and I], we never part, that is my only certainty in this life
> I behave, think, write, within this certainty[37]

Dib maintains – quite contrary to Adjil and Bonn's projection – that 'writing is a way of grasping the world'. And if 'this grasping is effected in a movement of withdrawal', nevertheless the creative effort takes place between distance and plenitude.[38] As if to Foucault's prescription, the specific task is here forever to 'create a space of liberty' through the limits set by inherited 'constraint' – and this 'always with your own references' (TL, 61). So to read any given text requires, as he explains in 1995,

> a code of reading, the key [to which] is supplied with our culture – the word culture being taken in the broadest sense to mean the formation of personality in a given society – in the form of a system of references. Only this latter enables us to open up the meaning of a work [.] A system of references is the grid which organises and orders expression and reading within and inside the coherence of a landscape common to both the producer and the receiver of the expression[39]

What is perhaps most remarkable about this otherwise anodyne argument, however, is that the example Dib gives is the desert as background to the Algerian experience, precisely as that space which eliminates the substantial or specified particularity of reference as such. He goes on: 'every desert resembles the desert as water resembles water. It is everywhere the place of a negation of History, just as, both through their message and the fact of their appearance [in History], the [revealed] religions are ahistorical.' The 'abyss of essence', place of a return to 'the original state', the desert effects the 'erasure' of the temporal at both 'ends': 'empire of the eternal, the desert is for the same reason the empire of the ephemeral' (5–6). Dib's 'grid of references', in other words, specifies its cultural place through a relation to a specific place.

Dib's work requires, I think, a reading which maintains this abstract but finely marked line between the specific and the singular or aspecific in its full and irreducible complexity. 'What' is experienced is indeed a movement toward radical depersonalisation, a becoming-imperceptible in almost the Deleuzian sense; but *how* it is experienced remains minimally specific, particular to *a* subject in a quite particular place. Dib insists, moreover, upon the importance of a narrative *relation* of and to this place (whose specifiable characteristics are stretched towards the imperceptible). It is this insistence that separates his work from the flatly void-driven nihilism he attributes to his friend Camus:

> Camus came into a world in ruins, a world flavoured with cinders and the sun, in which man is no longer even a survivor but already a shadow of Hiroshima man. And from beginning to end, his work refuses to offer even the slightest comfort to relieve this impression [...]. As far he's concerned, Camus has gone beyond Dostoyevsky's discovery that 'God is dead'. It is he himself who is dead, and all hope is forbidden. Such is the lesson in this work, a lesson that makes it great, and weak [10]

From the beginning, Dib makes a different literary choice than Camus – a difference which eludes Bonn's singular reading.

II Territory deferred

Dib's early work conforms perfectly to Fanon's description of literature's 'only truly pressing task, which is to move the community toward reflection and meditation' and so to transform 'the subjective certainty I have of my own value into objective, universally valid truth'.[11] In the 1950s, both writers agree that 'there shall be authentic disalienation only to the degree that things, in the most materialist sense of the word, will have been restored to their place'.[42] And like Fanon, Dib's first challenge is to confront a kind of naturalised inferiority complex, the conviction so many of his early characters express, that 'we are worth nothing' (IN, 38), that 'our life seems useless to us'.[13] No less than Fanon, Dib writes for 'a new soul' (IN, 88) and a 'new people' – 'we are, we ourselves, the witnesses of a new era' (IN, 48–49). No less than the early Glissant, Dib's vision of this new era is guided above all by the double conviction that (a) 'outside of your people you don't exist' (IN, 89) and that (b) deprived of its *land* the people cannot exist ('if you abandon your land, it will abandon you' [IN, 47]). Dib's early fiction is *territorial* first and foremost.

From the outset, then, it is essential to situate Dib's early work in the urgency of its context, in order to grasp how thoroughly it is oriented by the newly militant nationalism of the revolutionary movement. We must not forget that, after the defeat of Abd el Kader (1847) and the eventual 'pacification' of the country by the late 1870s, Algerian culture was subjected to a sustained repression with few parallels in the history of colonialism. *La souveraineté française* was established, from the beginning, on the wholesale conscription of the public realm, accomplished through the closure of Qur'anic schools, the break-up of inherited religious and social organisations, and other repressive measures contributing to the establishment of what Sahir Amin called a 'new feudalism'.[44] In the wake of the revolts of the mid-nineteenth century, many of the traditional institutions of popular expression and belief – the *marabouts* and brotherhoods [*confréries*] organised around local saints – were effectively disarmed if not co-opted by the colonial administration.[45] Through to the 1930s, as one historian puts it, 'the "indigenous people" were as if erased – the shadow, decor, or background of a stage occupied by the Europeans'.[46] Unsurprisingly, most of Dib's early readers drew attention to that immense weight of French contempt for the indigenous voice which Dib, with Feraoun and Mammeri, was among the first to articulate in print.[47]

So it should be stressed that Dib's early, 'rooted' writing was a highly appropriate response to what he called the 'emergency situation' in which he lived.[48] A number of subsequent studies have confirmed the description of French colonial policy precisely as a determined strategy of *déracinement*.[49] The brutal programme of *regroupement* begun during the war of independence simply extended an established pattern of systematic dispossession and 'pauperisation of the rural masses'.[50] As Bourdieu and Sayad pointed out soon after Dib's first novels appeared, much of the colonial enterprise turned on an effort to re-orient the landscape itself. 'Everything happens as if the coloniser rediscovered, instinctively, the ethnological law whereby the reorganisation of the habitat, the symbolic projection of the most fundamental structures of culture, entrains a generalised transformation of the cultural system.'[51]

The early Dib insists, consequently, that 'all the powers of creation of our writers and artists, offered in service to their oppressed brothers, will make of culture and the works they will produce, so many weapons of combat.' He goes on:

> To rescue from oblivion, to pull the national culture up from humiliation, to stand up with all one's strength against ideological oppression, to forge ahead and create new values – such are the tasks which today confront colonial intellectuals. But all this is only possible insofar as our artists and writers are able to find their place in the great and impetuous movement for national liberation [. .] Writers and artists must live this passionate struggle with all their heart, and devote their talents entirely to it.[52]

This early Dib writes with an urgency consonant with Sartre's famous declaration, that 'to speak is to act […]; in speaking, I unveil [in] the situation my very project to change it; I unveil it to myself and to others *so as to* change it'.[53] In *L'Algérie française*, this unveiling could have only one purpose, starkly summarised by the militant Mohammed-Chérif Sahli: 'a people ceases to be colonised when its ceases to be colonisable'.[54]

(a) *La Grande Maison* (1952)

Dib's first novel narrates a few months in the life of the ten-year-old boy Omar Dziri, set in the impoverished city of Tlemcen, 1939. The plot is loosely episodic, woven together from humdrum domestic events, arguments with siblings, quarrels between neighbours, first flirtations, life in the streets and at school. In the dilapidated block of flats that is the *grande maison* of Dar-Sbitar, shared by some 300 residents, Omar lives with his two sisters Aouïche and Mériem, his grandmother and his mother Aïni, widow of Ahmed Dziri, who died when Omar was very young.[55] Their life is dominated by a claustrophobic deprivation of every kind. The novel relates Omar's gradual coming into consciousness of his condition, a consciousness which remains on the threshold of imminent action. Like the other books of what is known as Dib's Algerian trilogy, *La Grande Maison* is a moment in an essentially pedagogical process, a learning to speak, to understand, and to act. 'Our misery is so great that we take it to be the natural condition of our people […]. We haven't yet learned to speak' (GM, 121).

A central episode of this first novel serves as a model of the development of the Algerian trilogy as a whole. One day the police come looking for the communist activist Hamid Saraj, the voice of inspiration and truth in Dib's first trilogy (GM, 42–45). Their arrival arouses the whole *quartier*. 'The tumult was incomprehensible', deafening (41), and very soon 'the police could feel that Dar-Sbitar had suddenly become [their] enemy' (45). At this point Hamid's sister Fatima is dragged out of her apartment. 'Her wailing rose, piercing, and all Dar-Sbitar vibrated, penetrated from one end to the other by the curses she hurled at them […]. All through the building there then rose a disturbing murmur' (48). This *rumeur* builds towards an eventual articulation – *but never quite reaches it*. Instead, Fatima's 'despair […] – monotonous, infinitely heavy – plodded along like an exhausted cart' (48). Her cries mix with the screams of Attyka, 'a poor mad woman', 'and the air beg[ins] to tremble' (50). The scene is punctuated, further, with verses of Ménoune's patriotic song which veers between sobs and affirmation, 'I who speak, Algeria, […] my voice will never cease to call to the plains and to the mountains…' (50). The song 'floats', becomes a 'cry of sorrow, […] and abruptly becomes a song again' (51). The sequence ends with exhortations of the old man Ben Sari, who knows that this (French) 'justice is made against us, because it is not a justice for everyone […]. I say this on behalf of all of us: let's have done with it!'[36] In Dib's first three novels, this pattern is repeated to exhaustion. Injustice provokes *plainte*, and complaint divides into various voices which announce but never reach an eventually militant 'harmony' (GM, 140).

The world of *La Grande Maison* is a world dominated by the lack of space, comfort, and food. Its inhabitants live 'on top of each other. Dar-Sbitar was crammed full like a hive' (GM, 72; cf. 99, 127, 154). Hunger stands out as the omnipresent, all-imposing fact of existence. From the novel's opening line – 'a scrap of what you're eating!' (7), 'Omar was terribly hungry, always […]. To stay alive [*subsister*], consequently, was for him his only preoccupation'.[37] Always, the immediate goal is to 'deceive hunger',[38] to feed it with the illusions of nutrition: watery soups, stale bread. Slowly but surely, the reality of colonial exploitation becomes clear. Omar's life comes to 'appear to him in all its hardship', and he begins to understand the ways in which his *grande maison* is itself a 'prison'.[39]

In these circumstances, daily existence is experienced as both cruelly monotonous and *abrupt*. Just as the novel jumps from one scene to another with little apparent motivation and a minimum of narrative accumulation, so Omar's major activity is one of constant flight. 'he ran to lose himself in the centre of the school' (GM, 7); 'he rushed outside' (12); 'he ran away [… and] fled into the street' (GM, 33); 'Omar ran off at top speed' (34); 'Omar ran away' (35); 'Omar spent his days wandering through the city' (IN, 146; cf. 165), and so on. Again and again, Omar is cut from his immediate surroundings: 'Omar had the sensation that all this came from another world' (GM, 114); 'It seemed to him that he had been lying here for centuries […], abandoned, solitary, rejected from life' (38); 'Omar felt he had been stripped away inside and shattered' (140); 'He suddenly seemed to be holding on to life in only an indistinct way. Everything became strange around him' (16).

What sets a limit to this *désarroi* is, first of all, Omar's unconquerable *youth*. 'Indomitable, pure, an implacable instinct, always alert, roused him against everything' (GM, 115). Omar will not be duped. 'He didn't believe the words of the grown-ups, he didn't acknowledge their reasons'.[40] This irreducible will to resist is the foundation for an imminent political mobilisation. Omar never stops asking, 'why are we poor? […]. No one revolts.

Why. It's incomprehensible' (GM, 117–118). Youthful endurance by itself, however, is not enough. 'Something obstinately prevented him from knowing a full and rewarding life. A veil separated him from this discovery' (116). Omar cannot escape his socially conditioned circumstances *alone*. He must learn the answer to his teacher Hassan's question: 'who among you knows the meaning of the word: *Patrie*?' (GM, 20). In *La Grande Maison* – as in Sembène's *Les Bouts de bois de Dieu*, Roumain's *Gouverneurs de la rosée* and Alexis' *Compère général soleil* – the path toward liberation is first indicated by a charismatic leader who best understands this question: the communist party militant, a role played here by Hamid Saraj.

Hamid is an exemplary character by every definition. He is indifferent to the deprivation that condemns Dar-Sbitar to a cycle of despair and petty recrimination (GM, 62-63). When Hamid speaks, he commands unmitigated attention. The gendered contrast is insistent. When the women of Dar Sbitar argue, 'they all spoke at the same time', in a senseless confusion (IN, 160). But when 'the men listen' to Hamid, then 'in the compact crowd, nobody moves' (GM, 119). 'Everything he says is right [*juste*].' Hamid tells his listeners their truth; they listen, and recognise themselves. 'A man who speaks like that is someone we can trust'.[61] Listening, 'a great calm came over [Omar]. He no longer knew when exactly he had begun listening. And he rediscovered or recognised in himself what was being said' (GM, 121). This speech occupies the centre of Dib's didactic work. Never again will such clear consensus be established in any of his novels. The intensity of the moment invites comparison with a religious conversion. But Hamid's exhortations are interrupted by his arrest, and partially diverted by the premature mobilisation prompted by the outbreak of World War Two. The war mobilises the crowd in favour of the wrong *patrie* (GM, 185).

La Grande Maison comes to an end amidst ambiguous and apocalyptic rumours (180). On the one hand, 'a new meaning of things and beings, forgotten until now and suddenly rediscovered, brought the people together. All this would have seemed ridiculous the day before. The Tlemceniens had given the word; they came out into the streets in a common accord', and no less suddenly, Omar 'was no longer a child. He became part of this great mute force affirming the will of the people against their own destruction' (GM, 184). But on the other hand, this rare instance of a *volonté générale* remains curiously underdetermined and abrupt. The generally omniscient narrator shifts into the interrogative mode:

> It was easy to imagine that they had something very important to say to each other. But everyone kept waiting to see who would speak first. Naturally, no one did. What did such an imposing crowd want to say? Why was it there? Did it want to protest against the war? But why, why then did it keep quiet? (GM, 184).

These questions go unanswered, and the novel ends when Omar returns home from the demonstrations. He announces, 'It's war [with Germany]! It's war! *He couldn't say anything else.*'[62] A genuine movement of the people for the people has yet to begin.

(b) *L'Incendie* (1954)

Such a movement begins with *L'Incendie*, which takes up almost immediately where *La Grande Maison* leaves off. *L'Incendie* provides at least three elements that were missing in the earlier work: time to ponder and reflect, a genuine space of *enracinement*, and a skeletal organisation for mass mobilisation. All three are specifically rural conditions: the first two-thirds or so of this novel take place in the country, during Omar's summer vacation. If Dar-Sbitar has become 'a terrible prison', the almost pastoral village of Bni Boublen offers the luxury of 'quiet times' (IN, 10, 12). These moments of tranquillity are mainly filled with measured political discussion, culminating in another climactic meeting with Hamid Saraj. After the great fire which gives the book its title and destroys what little possessions the peasants retain, the stage appears set for general political combustion in the country at large.

L'Incendie, then, is Dib's most militant work. Here, the organisation for a popular strike is already in place (IN, 125): 'everything had started with that agricultural workers' strike last February [i.e. 1939]', in protest against colonial enclosures and encroachments. 'Little by little the irritation was growing [...]. They had begun to speak of the weight of injustices' (31, 30). A decisive break with the past appears to have been made (34). Once again, however, the consequences of this break remain virtual, hanging in a kind of suspended animation. This most militant of Dib's novels is also, perhaps, the most discontinuous. Like *La Grande Maison*, the sequence of chapters is mostly episodic, almost cinematic – snatches of conversation, fragments of scenes, shifting from Omar's pastoral impressions to political debate, from Dar-Sbitar to Mama's domestic trials in Bni Boublen, from Hamid's semi-hallucinatory imprisonment to Omar's highly charged erotic encounters with the adolescent Zhor. There is little narrative basis here for a sustained *prise de conscience*. Omar himself is literally on vacation. Above all, the dominant metaphor of political awakening – *l'incendie* itself – is curiously at odds with the emphatically territorial basis of the awakening. The struggle is here a struggle for the land first and foremost. Land is here, as Khadda puts it, both 'the place and the stake [*le lieu et l'enjeu*] of the struggle'.[63] But the fire is both literally and figuratively a making-barren of this place. It is as if, in their fiery coming into awareness, the fellahs cut away the fuel and *ground* of their complaint.

The territorial register certainly dominates the novel. For Omar, the trip to Bni Boublen triggers initiation into 'the almost carnal, unconscious life of the land' (IN, 9). As guided by the grandfatherly Comandar, Omar's nascent awareness here finds the substantial, *patriotic* vehicle it requires: his understanding is grafted directly on to the landscape. Omar 'knew, now, the true alignment of things'.[64] Here, the *men* spring directly from the soil in an intimacy colonial repression is powerless to break (IN, 45, 47). As old Ba Dedouche says: 'everywhere, it is our country' (51); 'myself, I'm in the country [*pays*], he said, and I'm the only one to know it as a whole: the animals, the rocks, the people…' (58). And Comandar: 'my heart keeps me in contact with everything. It has visited every part of the country, every city, every village' (64). Such men 'really had the aspect, the colour, and even the smell of the land from which they came'.[65]

From the assertion 'all these lands are ours' follows the obvious conclusion: 'the [French] *colons* are thieves […], they make off with everything!'[66] The whole of Dib's properly didactic effort is to establish an *automatic* connection between dispossession and mobilisation (IN, 27, 30, 65, 67). As in *La Grande Maison*, the immediate shifter between physical dispossession and the articulation of complaint is *hunger* in the most literal sense. Dispossession has reached a level beyond interpretation or modalisation; the mouth that can no longer eat can only scream its outrage. Hunger reflects a systematic distribution of roles, and this system imposes upon the hungry an obsessive, forever present reflection on their condition – 'this reflection throbbed in them like the blood in their arteries' (IN, 32). Hunger has set a limit beyond qualification, a limit without reserve or *recul*, beyond which 'we feel this burning in the blood and the violence that accompanies it' (IN, 23). The desperate economies of both Dar-Sbitar and Bni Boublen are balanced on rigidly inflexible incomes, on the very margins of survival. Any further loss is translated *directly* into resentment.[67] With *L'Incendie*, as with the last writings of Mouloud Feraoun, the 'evolutionist' paradigm assumed by French colonialism has ceased to be even remotely plausible (a fact that their friend Camus never managed to grasp).[68] An especially important indicator of the trend is, as we would expect, the breakdown of that most critical 'evolutionary' institution. the colonial school.[69] Unlike many other early francophone novels, including Feraoun's *Fils du pauvre*, Kane's *Aventure ambigüe*, Zobel's *La Rue cases nègres*, and Laye's *Enfant noir*, Omar is unable to escape his circumstances through an education that would set him definitively apart from his original milieu (GM, 86–87, MaT, 57). Instead, the un-mediated impact of hunger ensures that the sequence from dispossession to mobilisation takes place on one and the same *physical and wholly physical* plane. 'It's overflowing, said Bensalem Adda. That's why we're speaking in this way. Everyone is speaking from the truest part of their hearts' (IN, 38). As an unnamed striker puts it, 'my children are dying of hunger. I say: yes to the strike. We've sunk to the limits of misery. What do we have to fear?'[70] At the same time, however – like the fire of *L'Incendie* – hunger may *consume* the energy of its host. For some, food alone matters. 'First, some bread. As much as possible. His dreams went no further than that.'[71] Hunger leads to awareness, but the articulation of awareness itself requires the suspension of hunger.[72]

What Dib must ensure, then, is the purity of the vehicle which allows for the immediate translation of hunger into action. The subject of hunger (those subjected to hunger) must be made, so to speak, of highly ductile material. Such purity is refined above all, in these early novels, by a sharply gendered discipline. Whereas women and children buckle under their bodies' need – Omar's sisters in particular (GM, 156–157), and the child in Omar himself (7, 50) – the men are made of sterner stuff. 'Our men are made from a mineral of the highest grade. The heart is intact and unalloyed [...]. Each man you see around you is a powder keg. Should a spark fall among them...' (IN, 33). Because the virile mineral does not yield under pressure, the current of protest flows through it undiluted. Dib insists on this point:

> Oh! Ba Dedouche! Aie! What a man! [.] Like everyone there, Ba Dedouche could hardly endure this fire burning in his chest. To do something... This desire lay deep in his thoughts, and unconsciously guided his actions [...]. In his every movement, there seemed to be a word of protest, a single word, alive and strong (IN, 57, 59)

> [Ben Youb] a man. A true man. [... N]o one here could deny that he been one all his life, that he still remained a man. Valiant and courageous, frankly spoken, with a righteous heart. He was dry, he was hard [.] Nothing prevented him from saying what he had to say; he couldn't keep silent the evil he observed. (IN, 46)

Every point of Omar's coming into *political* awareness is doubled by his becoming-a-man. Initially, of course, his childlike 'joy of existing' prevails; 'he gave himself over to carelessness, protected as he was by his childhood' (GM, 109). But as he learns about his situation, 'his childhood fell away from him' (IN, 167; cf. GM, 189). As Comandar says, 'whether you understand things or not, my lad, isn't what matters for the moment. Open your ears and remember what you hear. Later, when your reason has matured, will you make good use of your life?... Later, when you will be a man?' (IN, 13). This is the guiding question of the Algerian trilogy as a whole.

Hence the importance of the otherwise under-motivated sub-plot which puts Omar in *command* of Zhor's budding sexuality. The thirteen-year-old girl concentrates all the erotic energy of Dib's first novels (cf.

GM, 78–79). Immediately after the meeting with Hamid in *L'Incendie*, which secures 'the new soul' of his male audience, Omar has his first properly sexual encounter.[73] The rather laboured scene is worth describing in some detail. through the smoothly liquid body of Zhor, Omar becomes a purely ductile force of energy, a crystalline freedom racing away in unison with the land. Zhor herself, like the land she 'vibrates', is in full bloom. 'A few months previously, Zhor had been only a child. And now, all of a sudden, a vigorous life [*sève*] was bursting through her body on every side!' (IN, 173):

> she resurfaced sometimes from the depths she explored, it seemed, with her eyes closed. Around her, some unknown thing was growling in the heart of the mountains and valleys. It wasn't the wind, it was moving from the deep interior, hit the plains then rose up towards the heights of the country. The earth shook with it, everything trembled, the naked fields quivered, and to the limits of the horizon was heard ringing this torrent of captive forces that were one day going to flood the country (IN, 175–176).

Zhor sets the land – and Omar – aflame. Swimming and sunbathing, she lies immediate to the Algerian *current*: 'She slept with her eyes wide open, carried by a luminous and invincible current'; 'when the water finished flowing off her body that was as pure as the spring itself' (100), she lies herself out in a self-caressing isolation, stimulus to a most literal literary hunger:

> in her sleep, she moved her hand over her body, which was smooth, she felt that her skin was very soft A great calm flowed through her like *the current of an invincible river*. Gently a spring was born [.] Zhor had swallowed her saliva, but her mouth remained open until it was full again Now, the saliva flowed between her lips. She stretched out her arm and began languidly to caress her body…[74]

Zhor provides, in other words, the voyeur's fantasy *par excellence*: a subject both excited yet submissive, stimulated yet drowsy. Omar's encounter begins precisely from the voyeur's position, sneaking glimpses through the trees. The visual emphasis is maintained throughout, as Zhor offers herself without reserve in the most absolute passivity. '[Zhor] made no movement. She gave up her polished body to the light. He watched her for several minutes […]. Zhor, lying on her back, was moving no more than if she was asleep. Only her raised legs moved backwards and forwards from right to left, slightly open…' (IN, 98–99).

What's peculiar about this otherwise clichéd episode is that it is by *refusing* this temptation that Omar confirms his virility – his ductile and *self-sufficient* immediacy to the *courant*. Zhor is the occasion for Omar's becoming-a-man, but he does not contaminate his still literally unalloyed masculinity with the touch of woman. Instead, she triggers a curious series of displacements in Omar's mind, which send him scampering off into the distance in a kind of 'becoming-animal'. First, 'the image of a horse abruptly crossed his mind at the sight of Zhor's naked belly, a sumptuous horse, of a mysterious and somewhat baneful nature'. Then, he steals away from Zhor 'a small piece of white cloth that he discovered on her and which resembled a living animal; he felt its warmth'. Finally, no less abruptly, he spits and sprints away

> with wild resolution [… H]e fled along the path lit vividly by the sun, as if running on a tight rope. He moved away with ever increasing speed [.] The ball of material which he had stolen from Zhor fell during his flight without him seeing it and went rolling into a ditch *like an animal* that was neither tamed nor trained [ ] In the distance *Omar was nothing more than a grasshopper in red-gold dust* (IN, 98–100, my emphases)

Through Zhor, in short, Omar approaches the freely amorphous, ultimately transparent element of a landscape-in-flame. Like the other men of *L'Incendie*, he is now made of the pure, inflammatory material of a territory in arms (131–132).

The conditions for collective combustion are finally brought together with a meeting between the *fellahs* and Hamid. This scene occupies the dramatic centre of the novel (IN, 80-95). 'It was the first time that the fellahs discussed things in this way. An agreeable feeling rose up in them […]. They felt cleansed, scoured, lightened! […] It was a true fresh spirit that they felt at present' (94). The men become, essentially, transparent to each other, 'without the slightest awkwardness or timidity' (90). Hamid suggests a global alliance of the dispossessed, the emerging federation of the *indigènes*, the *enracinés* of every country (IN, 93). This sets the stage for the novel's eponymous fire, the literal spark of a nascent revolution. Lit by the treacherous Kara and the *colons*, in the end the fire 'consumes everything' (131). Regardless of the loss of their dwellings, the villagers now know that 'a fire had been set alight, and would never again be extinguished. It would continue to creep along in hiding, secret, subterranean' (131–132). The fire clears the way for the virile alliance *par excellence*, an alliance based on the supremely *specified* conditions of a shared experience, shared lands, and a common *blood*. Ba Dedouche knows that they will never find the perpetrators. But

> what is important [.] is that we know who the innocent are[1] [.] We know where the innocent are They are linked by prison, by injury, and also. . by blood. Our blood is being spilled, and will surely continue to be spilled, thus shall we be bound together [ ]. We cannot escape our blood. Not one of us will escape it. The whole country will be seized by its call [.] By the blood we share, let us remain united. This is what we must tell everyone (IN, 134)

With this conjunction of a literal and a figurative fire, the unity of the plane that stretches from a ravenous dispossession to a disciplined repossession attains its most emphatic, most *punctual* intensity. One limit-hunger flows immediately through the veins of a *peuple-sang*, transparent to its territory…

But the fire produces no immediate results. It consumes all of its material at once. 'Nothing happened; existence took up its usual course once more' (IN, 145). The fire that may one day grip the country may also be precisely the thing that burns it clean of a territorial specificity. In a passage that describes the late summer sun, Dib suggests the possible consequences:

> a furious conflagration followed its course, in triumph, from tree to tree, and each tree was a vibrating torch The old stones of the city, even they, were dressed in reddish lights Then, becoming absorbed in its own intensity, the fire fell back. Everything was purified in this incandescence, and from that moment, every feature of the land stood out through the luminous clarity of a softened atmosphere, their colours finally at rest. (IN, 146–147)

The question posed by Dib's later work, as by the philosophy of Ishraq which it so often evokes, will be precisely this. what remains of a strictly territorial coherence, in the aftermath of this *pureté incandescente*?

Belying the incendiary promise of its climax, Dib's second novel ends as it begins, with 'a desert-like country', in 'solitude' and 'boredom' (IN, 7, 15). 'What a desert! Nothing. Nobody. Silence and solitude […]. Muteness became one of the villagers' habits' (177). Hamid has been transferred to 'detention camp in the Sahara',[75] and the expected rural revolt has yet to materialise. Instead, the final chapters of *L'Incendie*, like Dib's subsequent two novels (*Le Métier à tisser* and *Un Eté africain*), are witness to an ever-increasing wealth of situations to which, in Deleuze's weighted phrase, 'one can no longer react'.[76] The onset of revolution does not inspire a *heroic* response from Dib. Rather, and in very much the Deleuzian sense, Dib's writing of the late 1950s rather narrates the literal breakdown of the 'sensory-motor system', the rise of a subjective paralysis – the ascetic condition of access to a coherence beyond transitive perception.[77]

In the first place, *Le Métier à tisser* (1957) is witness to a new kind of actor on the urban stage. Enter the rural dispossessed, a subaltern beggary beyond social mobilisation altogether, a 'crowded mass [of] men, women, old people, children', who slowly take possession of 'every neighbourhood […]. To the disrespectful treatment they received, to the insolence of the police, they opposed their indifference. An impulse whose strength no one understood was pushing them forwards. In this way, bizarrely deprived of life, they spread out far and wide…' (MaT, 12–13, cf. QSS, 67, 124–127). This new wave of beggars [*mendiants*] is quite distinct from the movement of *revendication* and mobilisation encouraged in *L'Incendie*: here the link between situation and reaction is broken beyond repair. The *mendiants* assert their presence and nothing more. They occupy a space of *irrecuperable* dispossession. They defy comprehension. 'At the time nobody understood what attracted them [...]. We understood nothing [...]. They came along, quite simply, and settled down wherever it suited them. Next, they surveyed all things with deadened eyes', utterly 'impassive' (MaT, 13; 80, 199). They exist as pure *spectators*, as a 'problem' beyond administered solution (17–18, 80–88).

In the second place, Omar's apprenticeship as a weaver puts him in daily contact with an industry unable to respond to its imminent obsolescence. As his friend Ocacha says, 'our business is worth nothing [...]. We need to learn something else, my little brother! Soon, whatever happens, everything will be made by machines' (MaT, 70). Ocacha is exemplary of a perfectly 'virile' character no longer able to sustain an effective defiance (122, 159). His only decisive action is precisely to abandon the struggle ('I'm going. Far!' [165]). At the other extreme, Omar's 'savage' and erratic acquaintance Hamedouch calls for immediate revolution *without* mobilisation, a revolution of terror alone.[?] There is no obvious middle ground between these equally ineffectual limits. On the whole, *Le Métier à tisser* describes a situation of paralysed dispossession that could have been transcribed directly from Fanon's clinical observations. Again and again, Dib's characters declare, like Abbas Sebagh, 'I am dissatisfied with myself, I can't manage to understand what's happening [...]. I no longer believe in anything, I no longer believe in what I'm doing' (MaT, 62). The strong voices of the workshop are silent by the novel's end. 'Once Ocacha had gone, Hamza disappeared mysteriously in his turn' (171).

A similar situation prevails in *Un Eté africain* (1959), considered from a completely different perspective. The actors belong, this time, to the urban bourgeoisie. The story relates nothing so much as a sustained breakdown of routine. The plot or rather the absence of plot is again episodic, mixing the first signs of war with snippets of everyday life. What prevails is a kind of generalised stupor, ranging from the frantic to the bemused.[?] Place – the living, occupied countryside of *L'Incendie* – has been converted into abandoned space, a space without specificity (what Deleuze will call 'any space whatever').[?] A characteristic image is that of the ageing Baba Allal stunned by the noise of passing military vehicles.

the old man remains standing without thought, feverish. The glare of the sun, the tumult, plays in his head [...] an invincible weakness nails him to the spot [ ] At the top of his longs, a public announcer proclaims no one knows what, something no one understands. Further away, a man with a red flushed face is beating his hands together and frenetically shaking his turbaned head

His face changes expression with every instant astonished, indignant, then enthusiastic, sombre (EA, 30)

As so often in this novel, the scene dissolves in a incoherent jumble of images, beyond the coordination of its central actor.

At the other end of the age spectrum, the young and unhappily betrothed Zakya slowly loses touch with her limited domestic reality, becoming a mere object among others, a surface of transient emotions set in a frozen background:

she looks at the garden which is completely dark, silent, from where the whispering of the water amidst the trees seems like a voice risen from another world.

–Bitterness and affection alternate in me like shadow and sun on a stormy day; they take turns in an imperceptible and irresistible succession I stare at the moving clouds above.

She looks up, and is lost in contemplation of the night sky.

–Soar, clouds…[51]

Zakya has no discernible place in the future prepared for her. As her mother says, 'marriage is something you don't want, a job is something you don't want; even your studies no longer seem to interest you […]. What are you going to do?' (EA, 98, 101). She is beyond relations with her parents (108). Isolated, despairing, she becomes another pure spectator, pure *spectre*, 'just like a ghost', wandering like 'a shadow' in a situation which defies comprehension. 'I don't know what's happening to me […]. Shadows, shadows, shadows…. I see only shadows, and there is no one who can listen to me' (190–191).

Above all, the main character in this novel and the next, Djamal Terraz,[52] is virtually defined by his inability to react or decide. From his first appearance in the novel, Djamal's characteristic condition is one of a 'semi-somnolence. He floats for a long time in this state, halfway between wakefulness and sleep. The rumbling sounds of the house blend with the murmuring of his thoughts' (EA, 62). Djamal is a character without internal equilibrium, liable always to 'fall into a morose astonishment. "Look at me! Either too enthusiastic, or too overwhelmed, with no [sense of] measure"' (65). Supported by his wife's income, Djamal moves 'mechanically' (79), knowing only that 'I don't know what to do […], I can find nothing' (80); 'I'm worth nothing' (81), 'miserable person that I am!'[53]

III Toward the limits of the specific

The difference between Dib's next novel (*Qui se souvient de la mer* [1962]) – without a doubt one of the most powerfully original works in francophone

literature – and his earlier, more conventional novels is profound and immediately striking. The constraints of an at least semi-realistic description are
here abandoned in favour of a surreal alchemy of the elements, where water,
air, fire and stone are the forces that inform a wholly plastic urban space.
The walls move, characters vanish, relations are mysterious, events esoteric.
The whole of the 'action' is now the extended development of a situation 'to
which one cannot react',[4] a development which concludes with the discovery of a fully rhizomatic plane of immanence in the subterranean city at war
with the city above ground (*la ville d'en haut*). At the same, the development
of the novel is for the first time organised by the rigorously *consistent* voice
of a first person narrator, and distracted by only one substantial side-plot –
memories from this narrator's childhood. The movement of the novel then,
is a *coherent* shift towards a more than worldly, a more than specified coherence. It carries us from the world of relative opacity and shadow *toward*
the absolute transparency of Light. We move from the worldly to the other-
worldly, from the lit to the en-lightening, from the personal to the impersonal. Similar movements, as we shall see, develop in different ways and
degrees, and to different outcomes, in all of Dib's subsequent work. We now
leave Fanon and the thematics of a territorial repossession firmly behind.

(a) *Qui se souvient de la mer* (1962)

Despite the many and obvious innovations of this most 'unprecedented' of
Dib's novels, it is of course a mistake to assume that *Qui se souvient*
emerges *ex nihilo* and without precedent in his earlier writing. On several
occasions in *Un Eté africain* Dib evokes an almost surreal atmosphere
beyond effective intervention (cf. EA, 163). Characters already have a curious tendency to disappear.[5] Situations beyond reaction, as we have seen,
arise as early as *L'Incendie*.[6] But with *Qui se souvient de la mer* such exceptional situations become the norm.[7] The novel follows the ramblings of an
unnamed narrator as he wanders through memories and relationships in a
city under siege from within and without. The story is punctuated with
'subterranean explosions, contortions of walls' (QSS, 146/93), and sudden
disappearances.[8] The narrator and his friends live precariously on the edge
of the void: 'our gestures, our looks, the movements of our thought, become
delicate, precarious things, in this veritable, this sultry threatening night,
that would take so little to be loosed upon us' (QSS, 68/40).

First and foremost, *Qui se souvient de la mer* confirms the definitive
demise of what Deleuze dubs the 'sensory motor schema'.[9] 'Something's
happening that we're incapable of dealing with' (QSS, 81/49); 'a great gash
has opened up in which everything, in the end, will be engulfed' (179/115).
The very 'beginning' of the story – 'these events, whose origins we had
nothing to do with' (78/47) – is beyond recuperation by those who must

endure it. 'An ancient and silent cataclysm having torn us from ourselves and the world, only a new cataclysm could restore us to it' (78/47). In the meantime, 'one is reduced to floating on the surface of things, a shadow stealing along, a shadow stealing along despite everything' (112/69tm). The narrator knows, in a crucial burst of awareness, that 'the shadow doesn't plan its effects; it's made in such a way that *it goes right to the heart of things*', and that 'the sun's origins are outlined in fugitive diagrams on our earth which they will come one day to seize in their grip. There'll be nothing left to do then but to get ourselves to the heights or discover the depths...' (65/38, 118/73, my emphasis). No space here for the uplifting speeches of a Hamid Saraj. From now on, in Dib's world 'fate is decided between words without weight or colour, gestures that no memory, no clay, no reflection ever captures. With us, outside us. I listened, one can always listen. *The other world, that too is ourselves, always ourselves*' (11/4). The other side – the side of a Light beyond opacity or reflection – is folded within our world of shadows and appearances. The task is, as Deleuze would say, is to tease open the folds, to find the point of return to a purely luminous intensity.

From the beginning, the narrator interprets his experience in light of a properly elemental organisation which will culminate, ultimately, in the saving 'remembrance' or apocalyptic advent of the sea.⁹⁰ In the absence of marine tranquillity and 'peace' (QSS, 115/71), 'we know now only the dry, mortal *waiting* of a world of stone' (114/71, my emphasis). Petrification is a constant risk (18–19/8–9, 25/13, 109/67–68, 168/108). Always, against the ephemeral rigidity of stone, the narrator evokes the 'the sea which, in its clemency, is alone still capable of making us see clearly into our own feelings' (52/29); 'only the sea justifies our aspirations; to it I am resolved to trust my fate, though the rock seize me in its grip' (172/111). For no matter how desperate things get *here*, 'somewhere else, the sea raised a single murmur of light toward man! [...] The wisdom of the sea always wins out in the end over man's little displays'.⁹¹ The *original* sufficiency of the sea, however, is not *given* to us as initially sufficient. The narrator's early attempts to commune are frustrated (QSS, 63–64/37). Through to the novel's end, the sea remains the object of prophecy, of an imminent arrival. 'It seems to say [...], 'I will come, I will come'. I wait for it and wonder whether the world will be beautiful enough to welcome it' (176/113).

In the interim, the narrator's lived experience proper is *overwhelmingly* puzzling. His is an experience that awaits its interpretative key. 'For me too the morning opens and the evening falls upon the void' (QSS, 17/8). The narrator has lost the ability to function as a 'normal' social being. As in the Beckett described by Deleuze and Badiou, Dib's characters are here reduced to their most rarefied functions – movements that go nowhere, discourses that say nothing, encounters that share no common experience.[92] As a rule, the narrator cannot relate to the people he meets, cannot grasp their meaning.[93] Cut off from his own past – 'between this past and my present life I was certain that no link remained, that all ties were broken' (52/29) – the narrator is no more able to sustain a genuine rapport with his wife Nafissa. Despite certain vaguely maternal connotations of comfort and reassurance associated with Nafissa (beginning with her name[94]), it is a mistake to see her as a more 'solid' or secure way out of the narrator's ongoing state of emergency. Rather, at every point, she eludes communication, disappearing more and more often as the novel moves toward the uncertain frontier of *l'en face*. Eventually, husband and wife are separated by 'an invisible wound' which threatens to 'absorb [...] all of creation'.[95]

Unable to *relate*, the narrator lives in a world where the organic links between actor and environment have been cut – in a world characterised, that is, by the disturbing *independence* of its environment. 'The flesh of this neighbourhood has grown limp, its blood and its thoughts, once so rich, are now only a disgusting grey mud' (QSS, 87/53–54). In particular, the life of the city is slowly squeezed to death by the rise of 'the new constructions [... that] wipe out whole neighbourhoods, which they seem to ingest one after another' (157/101tm). There can 'no longer [be] any question of going away. Go where? To do what?' (66/38). Established patterns of orientation collapse. Most of all,

> the walls shifted and took up positions around us, ignoring their former alignment, but not without observing what I can only call a general design, consisting of a deliberate attempt to envelope the inside as well as the outside [ ] A further consequence was that words stopped being words and changed into certain things resembling pebbles which we began to bump into everywhere in our efforts to sound the depths of the strata. (QSS, 9/18)

In a world in which objective reality fails to stay in its place, communication becomes a dream-like process in which the conscious speaker is the mere plaything of a Creative (unconscious and impersonal) agency beyond imagining. The normal relation between citizens and city – between 'subject' and 'object' – is reversed. It is the city-dwellers who become passive and inert, and the city that takes on an actively plastic mobility. 'The walls are driving the populace before them. [...] And where can we hide? While they vomit people out here they suck them in over there [..]. Pressed inward, our crowd is finally paralysed in the blind alley where it's been trapped' (QSS, 130/82). The narrator's lesson: 'to learn how to live without stirring in an increasingly confined space, a hole [...]: annihilation; that to which we are promised in the imminent future'. As 'the new constructions go right on growing [.], we know that it's possible to get rid of them, but on one condition: to dynamite the whole city, to dynamite ourselves' (132/83tm; cf. 67/39).

Such self-dissolution is the thing most urgently at stake here. For access to the esoteric legibility *d'en face* is a double process, both ascetic and – eventually – jubilant. 'Whatever happens, we expect no more news' (142/90). In this apocalyptic twilight, the environment takes on a 'particular beauty: that of abandoned cities, of cities dead but still moving through time, no longer vulnerable to attack' (143/90). Here is a space that leaves no role for the actor as such; it is only accessible, as Deleuze would say, to the *pure* spectator.'[6] This is another constant of the novel.

> I watch, no longer able to comprehend what's going on [.]. petrified, my skin crawling, I can do nothing but listen (QSS, 173, 43/112, 24)

> We remained where we were because no role had been assigned to us (22/11).

> Forgetting everything, I slipped into an irresistible drowsiness Never before had I known such detachment, I felt nothing, my suffering, appeased, became an elusive singing that stretched out in wonder 'I'm dead' These words rose like the murmur of running water such was my secret. (32–33/17–18)

Collapse of an *actively* subjective specificity enables the confusion of subject and object, as aspects of one, eventually common (in)coherence – a coherence won, as always, through the surrender of a personal coherence. The city is a form which can dissolve and re-materialise in different guise, like the narrator traumatised by a nearby explosion, eventually 'returned to my original shape but according to a different and unknown arrangement of material. I floated in air, slightly aching, light' (27/14tm). The more he escapes his personal position, the more the narrator becomes immanent to a properly elemental pull. Still in shock, 'I had, more and more, the physical feeling of being dragged by impatient hooks toward a blue-shaded crevice. I resisted as if made of stone although the flame rose up around me and in me…'[97] Later, a similar and decisive scene repeats the pattern:

> A distant explosion sounds [   ] We [Nafissa and I] have at the same instant the impression that the centre of the city is collapsing and, no doubt about it, that we are slipping a bit further underground. Then an utterly strange and unknown feeling invades me. Nafissa has disappeared, furtively withdrawn, leaving no trace. It's exactly what I'd been afraid would happen, what had to be avoided at any price, the irreparable [..]. Solitude restored, I find myself flung into a naked, black, boundless place All the walls are fallen, time no longer passes [..] At this moment I hear nearby a soft regular breathing, alternating with long periods of silence. The sea. It's rising. Its peace extends across the night, fills space (QSS, 85/51–52)

The movement of the novel as a whole is fully suggested in this single paragraph – from traumatic shock through absolute defamiliarisation and the loss of relations-with, toward the *'irrémédiable'* from which arises, ultimately, the promise of peace to come. On the condition, of course, that substantial worldly 'stuff' dissolves. 'How this world is getting picked bare[1] I too grow just a little emptier from one day to the next'. Objects lose their instrumental purpose and become transparent vehicles to the force *beyond* (86–87/52). As the novel develops, this kind of transformation becomes more and more pronounced. Subject and city flow into what Deleuze might call a singular cosmos-Brain, written as a sort of 'geology of insomnia, buckles, cracks, catastrophes [...]. I feel the corridors and underground passages that crisscross the inside of my head...'[9h]

Dib's narrator is accorded a few esoteric signs to help him along his singular path. Three stand out. The first takes place during his childhood, when the narrator is already sensitive to a luminous infinity, beyond the reaches of his claustrophobic home.'[91] Stifled by his parents, the boy is witness to a kind of *angelic* apparition, the sudden presence of another child, barefoot and sparkling. 'His arrival seemed a kind of leaping out at me [...]. The glow of the setting sun lit up his face [...], his look grew bright. It was only the light in his eyes of a last ray of sunlight passing across his face. By the time I had recovered, the sky had become a blue-black crater' (74/44). The narrator knows, too, that in order to see him again, 'I had to break the circle of brutality and pretence in which things were trying to trap me; yes, first break this circle [...], the world of things and of *others*' (75–76/45).

A second sign is hidden in the 'song [of] the beautiful star' which the narrator hears towards the beginning of the novel. 'Unforgotten, only the star breaks this calm which cannot find the heart' (QSS, 40/22), as it rouses 'in an ebb of water, of air, of fire/A single murmur of light' (39/21). The song runs through the full elemental progression from stone to sea, but its conclusion remains interrogative, enigmatic. 'the star turns to cinders that scorch the night and leave only our biological functions intact [...]. The bellowing of the star is such that the world seems plunged into a sort of coma' (40–41/22–23). The star drowns out all human voices, 'all overshadowed by that ceaseless and solemn voice of the star' (42/23).

A third sign, if that is the word, is wrapped up in the constant, mysteriously evocative presence of the birds Dib calls 'iriace' [*les iriaces*], 'these birds that are inaccessible to friendship but that, of their own accord, have become the companions of our population in its isolation from all else' (QSS, 106/65); 'their flight will forever cross the disaster that struck me' (127/79). Bringing only *'sarcasmes'* to those who seek 'friendship' (15/7, 128/80), at times the birds suggest a taking flight from the confines of worldly relations in general. It is 'a cloud of iriace' who take away the narrator's father's corpse (126/78). A few pages later, the narrator has a similar experience of his own: 'I stumble into the middle of a whirlwind of iriace, an unimaginable movement of flooding, ebbing, soaring, plunging, colliding, that carries me away and blinds me' (130/82). Above all, the iriace – like the other Ishraqi signs of the novel – call for interpretation [ta'wil]. In response, the narrator develops 'a new kind of science which I will call the theory of iriace behaviour', based on their number, direction, and time of passage, a way of reading 'the events which we may expect to take place' but whose 'meaning, clearly, belongs to a universe to which I have no access' (133–134/84).

Until, that is, the final sequence of the novel when, in El Hadj's boutique, the narrator finally comes face to face with the object of his apocalyptic desire:

> [..] with that roar the end of the world was unleashed. The sea! It returned in a swirling burst of laughter, the walls twisted into knots, slithering at top speed, and suddenly reared up, closing together over the city, raising a new night amid that night lit by a storm of spyrovirs. These quickly gave way to stars that disintegrated as soon as they appeared [.]. El Hadj shouted at me not to turn my head, whatever happened. He had no sooner finished telling me this than a star shone like a thousand suns on my back I was cold It sang. [..] I listened and drew from that singing the conviction that there was nothing left of El Hadj, that there was *nothing* behind me but an absolute, dark void [ ] And I had not seen – or heard – the barefoot youth arrive [.] – You'll understand later, he said (QSS, 183/117–118)

The return of the angelic figure – 'the barefoot youth', our first sign – marks the advent of a new order, and grants the (dying?) narrator access to the rhizomatic immanence of the under-ground [*sous-sol*]. This new space is described in the serenely present tense of the final chapter. The narrator has discovered that 'the underground city knows no limits [...], it sinks its roots [...] into the world, with which, by an infinite number of channels, of antennae, it enters into communication as the open-air city never did' (185/119). The *sous-sol* has a fully fractal coherence, the kind of coherence Dib will later lend to the *desert*.[100] The last paragraph records the spectacular fate of 'my former city'.

> Exploding one after the other, the new constructions all went up in smoke, down to the very last one, following which the walls fell apart and collapsed the city was dead, its remaining inhabitants standing in the middle of the ruins like desiccated trees, in the pose in which the cataclysm had surprised them, until the arrival of the sea, whose tumult had long been heard, and which quickly covered them beneath the endless rocking of the waves (187/120)

Worldly consumption is the price to be paid, tautologically, for an other-worldly redemption, for access to a singular place beyond constraint. The actor must die to this world to be reborn in that 'life [which] sings through the ages' (QSS, 182/117tm).

(b) Logics of engagement

For the reader of Dib's work as a whole, what demands explanation is this shift from the territorial to the deterritorialised. How to account for the new despecification of Dib's writing? We have seen that most of Dib's published readers celebrate this shift as more or less coincident with literary sophistication itself. His work is supposed, essentially, to have 'grown up'. The evolution from simple to complex, popular to hermetic, regional to universal, realist to post-realist, and so on – in short, from politics to poetry – coincides very nicely enough with the evolution of both the French and francophone *champs littéraires* themselves, their progressive *autonomisation*.[101]

My own view is that we should strive to describe Dib's development with as little reference as possible to the presumed norms of literary 'progress'. I say as little reference as possible because no doubt much of the explanation is indeed a matter of creative invention pure and simple, about which nothing *general* can be said. The virtue of considering Dib's development in the abstract terms of the specific and the singular on the one hand and the concretely *comparative* terms offered by certain Islamic references on the other, is that it permits a relatively precise description of what changes without necessarily imposing a normative evaluation. In the following paragraphs I will suggest, then, that Dib's work develops roughly from a position parallel to the engaged, nationalist specificity affirmed by Ben Badis and Algeria's 'Ulama movement of the 1930s and '40s, to a position roughly parallel, as we shall see, to the singular, esoteric hermeneutics developed by al-Suhrawardi and certain Sufi mystics close to his Ishraqi philosophy (whose most illustrious Tlemcenien representatives include Sidi Boumédienne and As-Sanoûsi). One model for such a shift is provided by the Emir Abd el Kader himself, the major focus of armed resistance in the nineteenth century, an important model for Fanon and the FLN[102] – *and* the author of one of the great modern compendia of mystical writings.[103] There can be no question, of course, of labelling Dib as an explicitly Islamic writer in the doctrinal sense, and still less of suggesting that his work merely translates Islam in fictional form. The relation is comparative rather than coincident. While the spiritual or mystical dimension of his work is fully explicit, Dib's own relation to Islam appears to be essentially similar to that of Ben Jelloun or Khatibi, i.e. more a matter of culture than religion *per se*.[104] The point is rather to try to make sense of the shift in the most appropriate terms, terms which respect, as much as possible, the particularity of Dib's *grille de références*.

What is especially helpful about the Islamic reference is the flexible continuity permitted, within a single doctrine, between the two poles marked by a nationalist engagement in the first case and a mystical experimentation in the second. The difference is perhaps more a matter of emphasis than of essence – an emphasis that varies with strategy and circumstance. If the 'progressive' aspect of Islam is generally a matter of reform in the properly conservative sense (a return to ancient values, to a discipline before corruption, a return forever *back* to the eternally sufficient revelation) the extent of the reform in question is a function of the corruption, degradation or *exile* to be overcome. Under colonial circumstances, the exile in question was obviously more political than metaphysical. In the postcolonial situation, as Dib conceives it, the confrontation with exile takes on, as it has from its earliest Shi'ite conception, immediately spiritual dimensions.

The first pole of our analogy can be dealt with fairly quickly. Most historians of contemporary Algeria agree that although 'less monolithic than certain Algerians in power themselves seem to think, Islam has been the only collective element to unite inhabitants across colonial or ethnological divisions. Moreover, religion has been the most important spiritual value to convey refusal and resistance to colonisation'.[105] The major vehicle of this refusal was *L'Association des 'Ulama Musulmans Algériens* formed by Ben Badis in Algiers in 1931 (and very strong in Dib's native Tlemcen), which quickly became, in Etienne's phrase, 'a true anticolonialist war machine', complete with its own network of schools and newspapers. Ben Badis' main message was simple· 'the Algerian nation has its own history, its own religious and linguistic unity'.[106] Under the slogan 'educate yourselves', the goal of the 'Ulama, as spelled out in their journal *Ech Chiheb* (1936), was to 'wake up our compatriots from their sleep, teach them to be on their guard, to lay claim to their part of the life of this world, to immerse themselves in the principles of their religion'.[107] According to the major historian of the movement, the most remarkable aspect of the reformist enterprise was its cultural particularism, its vehement refusal of an *Algérie française*, and its call for a moral renewal based on 'one [single] great idea, that of conceiving the destiny of Algeria as inseparable from Islam and Arabism [*l'arabisme*]'.[108] This is an Islam – particularly as integrated into the official ideology of post-war Algeria – firmly harnessed to the consolidation of territory and the supervision of identity.

Dib's own Islamic inspiration is oriented toward very different ends. Although his early work is consistent with the 'Ulama call for a political awakening, Dib draws from Islam only those themes that *undercut* any nationalist or communitarian project. Dib's Islam is not integrated with the assertion of a particular set of cultural values, but subverts the logic of particularity itself.

IV *Ta'wil*, *Ishraq* and the *'alam al-mithal*

Evocation of the Islamic mystical tradition known as Ishraq, a highly original re-working of Shi'ite and neoplatonist ideas begun by the immensely influential Iranian philosopher al-Suhrawardi (d. 587 AH/1191 AD),[109] has for good reason become standard critical practice in the reading of Dib's work.[110] By and large, however, the comparison remains allusive and thematic; few (if any) of Dib's critics actually cite al-Suhrawardi, or consider the full originality of the doctrine, especially by comparison with more familiar Sufi alternatives. Ishraq serves chiefly, in some of these analyses, to provide a dose of local colour to an otherwise 'straightforwardly' modernist literary enterprise. My aim here is to evoke, with as much care as space allows, the singular logic at work in al-Suhrawardi's thought, and to demonstrate that it does indeed provide a supremely useful point of reference to Dib's work (perhaps more as *logic* than as theme). Al-Suhrawardi provides a very precise way of comparing Dib's project with that of Johnson or Glissant, say, as well as a way of preserving it from the *purely* aspecific, intransitive literarity proposed by Bonn and Adjil. Like al-Suhrawardi, Dib remains, beyond the specified, on the *frontier* of singularity, the point where it is most indiscernible from the specific. This frontier is indeed a highly elusive, almost ephemeral place. But rather than the radical absence of place, it is perhaps the most precise conceptual description available of the sort of place so insistently claimed by Dib's later work.

As suggested briefly in section III(a) of my Introduction, Islamic philosophy 'exists only in reference to the religious fact'.[111] We know that Islam is above all a proclamation of 'the unity and unicity of God',[112] a unity beyond all conceivable boundary or distinction. Al-Suhrawardi's version of this unity conceives it as purely Creative Light, where all that *is* is Light and movement, and where what *is not* is an opaque resistance to light (corporal solidity or stasis). Like all visions of the Islamic deity, al-Suhrawardi's 'Light of Lights' is absolutely sovereign, 'subsistent through itself', 'subject to no condition [and...] no qualification'.[113] The pure One is itself wholly unknowable (*deus absconditus*), a Light so intense as to be what Ibn al-'Arabi calls absolute 'Blindness'.[114] The One is not an accessible whole but what, *wholly* inaccessible, gives rise to an unlimited multiplicity.

For al-Suhrawardi, then, an *immediate* access to the transcendent One – and this must never be forgotten, for by itself it serves to distinguish his position from Deleuze's uncompromising immanence – is impossible. The One is the blinding, inaccessible Light (or pure intensity) from which

215

emanates, in classically neoplatonic fashion, an infinite multiplicity of 'lightings',[115] each one invariably expressive of the One Light, but to variable degrees of intensity. Hence a strictly vertical arrangement, determined by proximity to God. Al-Suhrawardi like Avicenna before him develops a hierarchy of emanations, from the First Emanation or First Intelligence ('Aql, Noûs) to the Tenth Emanation (the celestial Adam), in a spectrum too complex for summary here.[116] The aim of any given being is to return, to the degree possible, back toward the One Light that is its source. Since 'to turn totally towards God is liberation', so 'everything which gets in the way of the Good, is Bad – everything which acts as a veil that blocks the spiritual path, is human impiety'.[117] As Dib himself will define it, 'evil is […] that in which everything is lost […], where the light of an object is no more than opacity, where this light is never kindled' (DD, 115). Our ethical task can be summarised, then, as the transformation of opacity into transparency, of object into prism, of veil into mirror.[118]

For Light is indeed original but it is not *given* as such to us: human beings do inherit an expressive covenant with God,[119] but as almost-forgotten. We begin with our backs to our oriental illumination, as exiles from the true and original light. The theme of an *occidental exile* is one that al-Suhrawardi develops in particular detail. Access to the true temple of Light from the darkness of our worldly 'crypt' thus requires two things. First, a new way of seeing the crypt *as crypt*. The world – 'this dark clump of mud that is our earth'[120] – must be seen for what it *is*, as non-being, veil, or arrest of movement.[121] Second, the seeing subject must pull away from the world, must work to grasp a spiritual and *only* spiritual existence. Sensual and spiritual perception are mutually exclusive.[122] When I join God, 'I separate myself from the world and join myself with the higher world'.[123] An inspired turning toward Light and the ascetic–traumatic process of moving through shadow necessarily begin as one and the same process.[124] A personal ascesis is basic to en-lightenment. As the Sufi poet Faridoddin 'Attar put it, 'your desire does not suffice, O you handful of earth, for from earth, you become pure spirit. Man, this product of semen in search of spirit, must suffer incurable torments. What supports this enterprise? Wandering [*l'errance*]. What heals this pain? Pain itself…'[125]

Ta'wil begins, then, in that *inspired* zone where the social and the historical end. Its pursuit, Jambet explains, involves turning 'against political relations [*liens*], so as to privilege the visionary assumption of the internal singularity of the spirit'.[126] Any (dialectical) effort to situate redemption in terms of some social or historical mediation is ruled out in advance, for 'it is only through his wrenching away from history that man rediscovers, by interpreting it, the origin of his being-historical – and frees himself of it'.[127] On this condition, the singular telos of mystical Islam as a whole – a return to Mohammed's state of *pure* inspiration – is within reach. The known and the knower, the cogito and the cogitor, are thereby united in a single spiritual immanence.[128] The creature becomes the purely transparent vehicle for the expression of its Creator. Freed of obstacles, Light reflects only upon light, in an 'invisible' illumination (invisible to any merely physical perception; this is visibility abstracted from *any* relation to an object).

To 'interpret' reality is thus nothing other than the effort 'to evade oneself'.[129] Ibn al-'Arabi is as clear on this point as Spinoza or Deleuze: 'that which there is in reality is the Creator-creature, creature in one dimension, creator in another, but the concrete whole is a single Whole'.[130] Nevertheless, as Hujwiri notes, there is an important 'difference between one who is burned by His Majesty in the fire of love, and one who is illuminated by this Beauty in the light of contemplation'.[131] The great question that confronts al-Suhrawardi, just as it was to confront Duns Scotus, Spinoza, Deleuze, and every broadly 'creationist' thinker (i.e. every thinker for whom the individuality of any particular being is the *direct* expression of some singularising force) is simply this: *what kind of individuality survives the 'extinction' of redemption?* Or in Deleuze's neo-Nietzschean (or anti-Schopenhauerian) terms: what kind of individuality survives the 'ontological test' of eternal return?[132]

The answer of certain radically ascetic Sufis, along with the more extreme Ismailis, is perfectly clear: none at all. While most Shi'ites maintain the co-implication of esoteric and exoteric as an ongoing process of symbolisation, for the Ismailis, 'the exoteric [as opposed to the esoteric] is a shell that must be broken once and for all.'[133] Divinity is pure intensity, we might say, and no form of extension can survive it. Likewise, the early Sufis seek fusion through 'extinction [*fana*'] of the created in the Uncreated, of the temporal in the Eternal'.[134] The Sufi *ittihâd* or 'becoming-one'[135] requires the stripping away of the corporal or lower soul, a project first developed by Kharraz (d. 286/899), Junayd (d. 297/909) and Tustari (d. 283/896).[136] As Baldick summarises things, an initial nearness to God leads finally to a 'forgetfulness of what one has been given by God and one's need of him. Then the mystic falls away and only God survives. All questions put to him receive the answer "God". If he is asked, "who are you?", he cannot reply "I". After this he reaches a point where he cannot even say "God".'[137]

Passing through the One, *this* path ends with a sort of 'None'. With the early Sufis Hasan Basrî (d. 110/728) and al-Hallâj (d. 309/922), there is no space for any kind of 'intermediate realm' between Creator and created.[138] Al-Hallâj insists that the goal for all creatures is an eventual *union* with or absorption within God. The mystic can hope to be restored to an immediate fusion with the Divine, but only through an experience of pure de-individualisation or de-differentiation. The essential process at work here, as Jambet summarises, is 'a universal and entire renunciation of the world' as the price to be paid for a *total* spiritual redemption. The 'cut between creature and Creator' must be preserved during the redemptive effort, so as to be all the more entirely overcome at its end. 'it is by making within oneself the void of self that we experience God as this very void'.[139] According to Hallâj and Hasan 'the One unites with himself in the void of the soul, and this union demands, therefore, that the love of the One pass through the condemnation of the Self'. The final revelation is then 'nothing other than the void itself, in which the mystic burns'.[140] To know the One is to become void, without remainder. *This* One, in short, can only become None (for us). Its intuition requires a kind of singularisation of the singular itself, an experience of pure de-differentiation

An interpretation of Dib's work clearly requires an alternative approach. It requires us to complicate the relatively consistent notion of singularity we have been able to deploy thus far (already at the cost, no doubt, of many simplifications). To be sure, as even a superficial reference to scholastic attempts at rationalising the logic of 'creationism' bears out, it is no simple matter to distinguish between the Creator on the one hand and the derivative field of creation on the other (itself not to be confused, as Heidegger would be quick to remind us, with the mere particularity of specified creatures, or beings). It may be impossible to draw a firm line between the radically in-different *limit* of singularity – what Deleuze might call its degree of absolute 'intensity', or pure 'implication' – and the infinitely differentiated field(s) of its varied explication or expression. Creation itself is pure differentiation–individuation. What 'gives rise to creation' must then in a certain sense be beyond differentiation itself (or else, it must be differentiation in its most concentrated, implicated or intensive form).

The familiar scholastic distinction of immanent and transcendent conceptions of creation still provides a useful way of classifying alternative approaches to our more general problem (neither of which, it should be stressed, yet opens on to a properly *specific* or relational – i.e. *post*-creationist or 'post-Darwinian' – orientation).

(a) We have seen that certain fully *immanent* conceptions of singularity, like those of Deleuze and Spinoza, seek to maintain the dynamic *continuity* between Creator and creation, in the interests of a generalised, unlimited and forever renewable creativity. A creature's only ethical imperative, from this perspective, is to strive to become a fluid or at least transparent vessel for the creative energy that gives rise to it (that it actualises), and thereby surpass itself, escape itself, become-other than itself. (At the *limit* of this process, Deleuze acknowledges, such a creature can only 'become-imperceptible', vector for a movement of 'infinite speed'.) This relation 'between' creature and Creator is essentially immediate. It does not pass through any inter-mediate realm of revelation, judgement or imagination. This is why the ethical subject, as conceived by Spinoza and Deleuze, is essentially subject *to* a pure determinism, an 'automaton' driven by the absolute sufficiency of divine causation.[141]

(b) The alternative approach (exemplified here by al-Suhrawardi) preserves the *transcendence* of the Creator, i.e. it conceives the Creator as radically inaccessible to the entire realm of creation. Al-Suhrawardi maintains 'the gap that separates for all eternity the *Deus absconditus* and the *Deus revelatus*'.[142] This irreducible *discontinuity* between Creator and creation opens the space for some kind of inter-mediate realm between the two, the space of some sort of modulation, inflection, or interpretation of Creative intensity (as distinct from its immediate explication, or actualisation). It is in this space, or gap, that al-Suhrawardi locates the intuition of what he calls 'Imaginal Forms', the exercise of a kind of pure imagination guided by a specifically *angelic* medium, as distinct from an immediately divine expression. Al-Suhrawardi's 'imaginal' realm (the *'alam al-mithal*, which Corbin translates as the *mundus imaginalis*) is not so much immediate to divine intensity as it is the space of an individuation on the frontier, so to speak, of that intensity. Absolute intensity or Light is itself beyond all individuation. The imaginal world is populated by discrete configurations of Light, i.e. by individual souls conceived as immaterial but distinct 'imaginings' of God.[143] *Our* access to the One Light, we might say, is always refracted through the prism of a particular soul. (As al-Suhrawardi teaches it, 'it is incumbent on you to read the *Qur'an* as if it had been revealed only for your *own* case'[144]). Ishraqi insight thus entails what Corbin calls the

> gradual initiation into knowledge of self as a knowledge which is neither the product of an abstraction, nor a re-presentation of the object through an intermediary form or species, but a Knowing which is identical to the soul itself, to *personal*, existential subjectivity, and which is essentially, as a result, life, light, and epiphany...[145]

Or as Dib will write: 'the whole memory of the world is in each human being',[146] but *as* filtered, each time, through a particular prism or 'grid' [*grille*]'. The (secret) whole *is* only as according *to* each. The later Dib is closer, we might say, to the earlier than the later Glissant.

The imaginal thus preserves a kind of *intermediary* individuality. Each imaginal form (each individual soul) exists as a distinct image between the highest realm of pure, perfectly transparent Intelligence (*Jabarût*) on the one hand, and the realm of an opaque, corporal stasis (*barzakh*, or shadow) – the world of sensory perception – on the other.[147] To perceive the imaginal requires a faculty that is itself between mere sensory perception and pure intelligence or reason. this faculty is none other than *imagination*. As al-Suhrawardi's commentator Qotboddîn Shirazî puts it, 'the imaginal world [...is] that world whose dimensions and extension fall only within the purview of imaginative perception. It is the world of autonomous imaginal Forms, that is to say, Forms un-mixed with a corruptible substrate, but suspended, like images suspended in a mirror.'[18] Much of Dib's later work, as we shall see, involves precisely this combination of imaginings and suspendings.

The spiritual task is then not so much a matter of striving toward immediate union with a pure Creative intensity beyond all extension or explication, as it is the ongoing effort, without ceasing to be 'oneself', to de-materialise or image-ine oneself (to perceive oneself as pure image without 'substrate'). This is where al-Suhrawardi differs from both Hallâj and Deleuze, as well as the Blanchot that inspires Bonn's reading of Dib. In contemporary terms, al-Suhrawardi is perhaps closer to Foucault's effort to *despecify* the subject (i.e. to purge the subject of everything that normalises and inhibits its relational interaction with other individuals) than he is to Deleuze's effort to follow those lines of flight that lead beyond the limits of the subject altogether. Of course, al-Suhrawardi's souls or images are no less insubstantial, no less *despecified*, than Deleuze's virtual degrees of intensity. The distinction at issue here is subtle, and should not be exaggerated. Simply, the imaginal forms preserve an irreducible *distance* from the pure Light that orients them, a distance that no amount of 'counter-actualisation' can cross. The imaginal forms retain a kind of minimal, subsistent particularity of their own – a 'transcendent' individuality, as Deleuze would no doubt call it. And it's because he accepts the fully transcendent status of the *absconditum* that al-Suhrawardi does not develop a precise mystical equivalent for Deleuze's various mechanisms of exposure to pure intensity, nothing resembling the mechanics of an individuation traced at infinite speed by an aleatory point or pure line of flight. Rather, al-Suhrawardi's world remains one of endless interpretation or *reflection* as such. The imaginal realm is made up of images and reflections in which, deprived of material opacity, everything *reflects*, and what is reflected are only other reflections. 'There are mirrors upon mirrors, without end [...]. All of creation, then, is interpretation.'[19] The imaginal forms reflect one another, they *are* nothing other than the reflection of other forms. And we might say that in a domain of pure light, such reflection is nothing other than relation in its most abstract or insubstantial form. Rather than transcend all relationality (thanks to the immediate sufficiency of a virtual determination), the imaginal forms exist in a kind of *purely relational* domain, one evacuated of substance and cut off from any direct access to a 'higher' or more virtual determining instance.

Entry into al-Suhrawardi's purely imaginal world is certainly a process of subtraction or extinction, the subtraction of all opacity. But – to pursue the comparison with Deleuze – this access does not proceed through re-configuration on a plane of consistency that coheres only at pre-individual degrees of intensity. Instead, it implies cultivation of a certain *way of seeing* (or imagining) through and beyond worldly opacity. Rather than pretend to see from God's point of view, Ishraqi perception has a properly *angelic* inspiration. The angel appears *between* the divine and the human intelligence. 'What is the Angel? It is what is accorded to us from the absolutely hidden Other', i.e. the One, or God.[150] Rather than a wholly other-worldly presence, al-Suhrawardi's Angel is a figure with *two* wings, one in shadow and one in light.[151] Access to the intermediary world ['*alam al-mithal*] is enabled by angelic visitation on the *border* of the two realms, and the form of this visitation is only *more or less* abstract, depending on the intensity of the revelation. To be sure, 'where the dazzling light is prolonged, it abolishes the form [of the visitation]; figures are removed, and the particular visitation is erased. And then we understand that what is being erased is yielding before a superior power'.[152] The definitive erasure of *all* particularity, however, remains a limit in the transcendental sense.

This is the limit that Dib's writing approaches (up to a point that the remainder of this chapter will attempt to determine) without ever *quite* reaching it.

What this fairly abstruse discussion makes available for a reading of Dib's work, and with it, for the development of the general theoretical project at issue in this study, is a description of the kind of limit specificity which eludes the more radically singular, more purely void-based reading proposed by Bonn and Adjil. It is this limit-specificity which will allow us to describe even Dib's most esoteric work as a *ta'wil* of the *secret* as such, the interpretation of a *hidden* presence, rather than an intuition of the void or the experience of absence.

But it must also be remembered that this limit-specificity does indeed subsist on the very edge of pure singularity and immediacy. The median status of this interworld makes it mediate or relational in only the most abstract and elusive sense. It is 'intermediary' in something close to the Deleuzian sense of a *pure* 'between' unrelated to its terms (a relation fully external to its terms).[153] Though intermediary, the '*alam al-mithal* remains the 'world of a tearing away from the world'.[154] In al-Suhrawardi's nice phrase, it is 'the country of the non-where'.[155] On the edge of the void, this imaginal specificity is supremely difficult to sustain, and is forever threatened by contamination from below or extinction from above. Any access to the imaginal requires a severely (though not absolutely) subtractive process of liberation from the corporal and the worldly. The pilgrim must literally go through hell in order to reach a Light in which he or she will be stripped of all worldly qualification (identity, place, memory…). The exuberant Creative confidence of Deleuze's philosophy or Glissant's later fiction is generally missing from Dib's more austere prose. 'Not to know that for which we search yet to continue searching it, this is to visit the outskirts of Hell…'[156]

If Dib admits in an early story that 'we still haven't learned how to leave ourselves',[157] his characters have, in a sense, never stopped moving toward 'this door where you must leave yourself in order to answer the call' (DSS, 202) – again, without ever quite managing to reach it. 'Because we have lived in darkness, we have wound up signing a pact with the monsters and larvae who take refuge in it. We must now break this pact and dare to look up at the day and stare directly at our sun of *Barbarie*' (DB, 206). As Kamal muses in *Dieu en barbarie*, a 'wall divides us in two, isolates in us the inside from the outside. The same veil will always cloak our errors and our truths, our false secrets and our true shadows […]. To rid ourselves of it, we must undo ourselves – and then remake ourselves' (DB, 190). In an effort to breach this wall, Rodwan of *La Danse du roi* strives to 'plunge into the sources of darkness and intercept these words at their true point of emission, not from a [human] face, but at their obscure origin, more forgotten than forgetting [itself]' (DSS, 52). Dib's hero must learn to will 'to happen to me that thing which *I* will stop feeling the more it happens'.[158] He must learn the measure of the affirmation at issue in Marthe's *Qur'anic* reference: 'I place my trust in the God of the dawn/against the wickedness of men/against the blackness of the dark'.[159] The exemplary characters Labâne and Hakim Madjar – in some ways the mystical successors of Hakim Saraj – live by just such principles. They know that the 'whole human adventure lies in the challenge [*le défi*] that exceeds it (MC, 101). Waiting for 'a column of fire to purify the world' (MC, 85), Labâne hears a 'Voice', saying. 'I am here, I in whom everyone can change. Only something must die somewhere first. Space will be broken, and after it, silence, to say who I am' (MC, 90; cf. 111).

Among the earlier novels, *Cours sur la rive sauvage* (1964) is especially emphatic in its Ishraqi orientation. Separated from his lover Radia on the day of their wedding, Iven Zohar (etymologically: 'son of Light') sets out to find her in a city become labyrinth of chaos and occasional illumination. Iven Zohar's search for Radia takes him to the edge – or perhaps over the edge – of madness and *sauvagerie*, at the same time that it develops his vision of a 'ville-nova', a 'ville-Radia' in which 'the light that seeped from each of the stones' pores was so unified and conferred so immaterial an aspect to all this architecture that there was nothing on which you could rest your gaze, no detail to focus on'.[160] He 'finds' Radia only to discover her changed (or renamed) into Hellé, a character beyond relation in the normal sense: 'you and I are only an/one image [*une image*…]. I [Iven] was in you

Iven Zohar'.[161] As Hellé says, 'we are made of that fire which brings life to every dwelling' (CR, 89). Thus *animé*, Iven Zohar sees himself as 'the man of wind into which I had been transformed, and the being of fire he [the man of wind] was as well [...]. Fervent yet soft, the fire that had taken my place purified itself in space. A thread of infinite length, taught. And me running along it...' (138). Blind to the world, Iven Zohar and Radia/Hellé become both subject and object of an other-worldly perception: 'I remained there, transformed into a dream object – as if I was myself the object of my dream' (CR, 106; cf. 134). Cogito has become *cogitor*, veil has become mirror.

If 'evil' is what stifles the Creative light in a specified opacity (DD, 115), the 'good' involves a partial making-transparent, the conversion of static matter into spiritual prism (partial, because it must not eliminate that minimal degree of opacity *a* prism's individuality requires). Perhaps the simplest illustration of this new logic in Dib's work is the parable of 'Lyyli belle and the pearl of happiness' told in *Neiges de marbre*, and remembered in *L'Infante maure*. In the story, Lyyli receives a beautiful pearl in a dream; it is lost when she wakes up. She looks everywhere, asks everyone, but there's 'no sign of the pearl anywhere' (NM, 88). Eventually, after much searching, she is told by Bonhomme Hibou where to find it. 'Right, um... In the middle of the highest red rose which is growing right here in your garden... Hoo! Very early in the morning when it opens up [...]. But you must be content only to look at it, not to touch it, Lyyli belle' (NM, 91). And so it happens. 'A miracle: like a drop of light, the pearl lies sparkling in the middle of the beautiful rose. Speechless with amazement, Lyyli doesn't take her eyes off it, stays rooted to the spot, looking at it and as she looks at it, her heart dissolves with happiness' (NM, 93). The pearl is 'located', in a sense, but as accessible only in a certain way, according to a certain discipline and reserve, a certain way of seeing. The drop of dew must not be touched or possessed: its role as prism depends on its distance from both the light it refracts and the hand that would gather it. On the owl's condition, Lyyli 'now know[s] where it is' and 'won't be afraid anymore that it might get lost'.[162]

V Towards extinction

Dib's critics have proposed a number of ways of making sense of his shift toward the mystical. For Sari as for Chikhi, it remains broadly consistent with the principle of a territorial *enracinement* asserted by the early Dib.[163] Khadda and Déjeux claim that Dib's mysticism is consistent with his humanism – it provides a more universal forum for an investigation of 'man'.[164] And we know that Bonn and Adjil argue, more persuasively, that it is consistent with his more purely *literary* post-independence writing, his experimentation with writing-in-itself: the mystical ascesis deterritorialises the person, the place, so as to 're-territorialise' within a language become autonomous, pure of subject, object and referent, a 'silent' language imme-diate to the void.[165] All of these critics, by and large – and Bonn most of all – concur as to the 'tragic' dimensions of Dib's version of *fana'* (extinction).[166]

In my view, if the humanist and engaged readings are mostly a matter of wishful thinking, the more or less *unqualified*, void-driven reading pro-posed by Bonn and Adjil, for all its theoretical sophistication, imposes a simplification which Dib himself has always refused. Dibian ascesis leads to and along the frontier of radical singularity but – for the most part at least – does not cross it. If we learn, in one of Dib's very earliest poems ('Vega', 1947), that 'a single Doric pillar/separates the void/and the poet',[167] we must not be too quick to get rid of this pillar. Dib himself insists on this – most emphatically, in the *prière d'insérer* appended to *Omneros* (1975), where the author relates how, in a commuter train bound to Versailles,

> I had a blinding vision of this *source* of light. It was enough for me to under-stand that we must resist its seductive power, even the idea of it – because whatever dissolves in it no longer feels its effects, and whoever is seized by it no longer exists. Discovering in this way that our hope perhaps lies precisely in our opacity. I looked searchingly at the human faces present in the carriage and was grateful that they were there.

Here, the poet refuses al-Hallâj's famous cry, *ana-al-Haqq!* ('I am Reality'), his dissolution within 'the source'. Rather, '[he] traces the limit' *between* source and derivation, between light and shadow, in the *relation* of eros that lends the collection its obsessive title.[168] The source itself remains inaccessible, secret.

(a) *Habel* (1977)

Along with *Le Désert sans détour*, *Habel* is the most experimental, the most difficult to summarise of Dib's novels. It is also one of the most easily aligned with an Ishraqi reading, angels and all. Perhaps the most succinct descrip-tion of the novel is Habel's answer to the question posed by his lover Sabine, 'what are you doing?' Reply: 'I'm trying to let my soul out of my body' (HB, 126). Habel is someone who will encounter 'the Angel covered with eyes that arrives only to separate the soul from the body', and who will yet remain 'still there, still alive' (151). Habel is a spirit, an imagining, in suspended sep-aration from its body. He is as Sabine says 'a guy who doesn't live in his body, who leaves it hanging around any old where' (82), a man gripped by 'the feel-ing of this solitude imprisoned in his body like a cold water, black, inacces-sible' (135). The sustained effort to escape a corporal opacity is, I think, the guiding principle of this supremely polyglossic and disjointed story.

Hero of the first of Dib's novels to be set outside Africa, Habel is a young North African exile in Paris, 'a man shorn of his history, his roots, a man without ties, a man given over entirely to destiny, a nameless man ready to reduce you to the same fate' (176). The narrative explores his relations with his lovers Sabine (worldly, sensual, and eventually inadequate) and Lily (other-worldly, mentally unstable, and eventually redemptive), and with an enigmatic transvestite writer called, depending on the circumstances, Le Vieux or La Dame de la Merci (proper name: Eric Merrain). Another first: this writerly character wields as we shall see a particular kind of authority in the enunciation of an other-worldly necessity, a discourse beyond the first person point of view. The plot of the novel, such as it is, is shaped mainly by Habel's obsessively repetitive return, night after night – not always in chronological sequence – to the street corner where, after a car skidded off the road, he nearly met his death. 'He heard the screeching of the tires tear the air [...]. A car, a black, demonic phaeton moving very fast, came toward him [...]. And a voice prophesied: now anything can happen!' (23). To return again and again to this moment when *anything is possible* is to 'expose my life, to risk death, telling myself, the same things in the same places' (44). Invariably, 'nothing happens, nothing takes place. But I am here, I wait.'[19]

Although completely different in tone, style and form from *Qui se souvient de la mer* as from Dib's other previous works, *Habel* maintains the continuity of his project in two obvious respects. In the first place, as in *Qui se souvient*, the real *cause* of what happens eludes narrative description. The beginning is beyond recovery. 'To be alone' is what Habel 'wants right away, with all his heart. Then to recover his own history, however forgotten it might be, to spell out its first words. And then to go still further back, as far back as possible' (HB, 44). But this excavation of the past reveals only (yet crucially) that.

> what had begun hadn't begun then, [Habel] cannot say when it was, but sometime before, a time that he knows nothing about, one of those times that you never know anything about [ ] Because that damned phaeton, or le Vieux, alias La Dame de la Merci, before, or Lily in an even earlier time, or Sabine later [...] – *everything has flowed down the same current [...], a current, a water that only comes, only goes through its life, so as to retreat and go backwards, arriving without arriving, crossing without crossing, and then beginning anew, [..], going back on itself*[20]

Because the original impetus to the narrated sequence is not itself narrated but rather envelops the narrative as a whole from an indiscernible position outside it, so *what* is narrated is both perfectly discontinuous in terms of the ordinary relations between characters and events ('inside the world', we might say), and perfectly continuous in terms of a general movement towards the other-worldly. This is the essential point to grasp here: however fragmentary the text, however enigmatic its fragments, the global movement towards a resolution beyond the textual and the personal is itself, I think, *supremely consistent*. Many, perhaps all of the most oddly jumbled pieces of the novel can be interpreted as contributions to this consistency, can find their place in this coherence which excludes our own.

In the second place, Habel, like the narrator of *Qui se souvient*, is more spectator than actor. He is another incarnation of what Deleuze calls the 'pure seer'.[171] Habel 'knows that everything that happens to him has not the slightest reason for happening to him [...]. No logic, nor order' (HB, 13). Unable to predict or anticipate things – unable to *reason* his way through the confusion of his experience – Habel's main 'activity' consists of a kind of waiting in its pure state. Habel is a waiting without object. 'We wait even when where there is nothing to wait for, when we're no longer waiting' (HB, 65). For as le Vieux says, in an important declaration.

> The moment comes when you find that you have overstepped the mark. Or the limit. You hesitate over what to call it, you no longer really know what it's about. And in fact you've seen nothing, known nothing, there was nothing. No inner conflict one way or the other, no sense of having transgressed while you were doing it. It is only afterwards, when you find yourself in surroundings that have been, so to speak, turned upside down, that you learn it as something both incontestable and without appeal (HB, 48–49)

The whole of *Habel* takes place on the other side of this limit, after this traumatic learning experience (after what Deleuze calls a 'clean break', a point of no return[172]). As le Vieux adds, 'you never come back, you never return from these incursions. There where you are, where you think you've arrived, everything is already burned, dry. You have to look for something else, elsewhere, despite whatever it might cost, and looking for it, you have to abandon all pride, all self-importance, the opinion one has of one's dignity, the opinion of others, this idea that the things which occupy us really matter'.[173] This other thing, this other place, can be attained at only the loss of the *here*, the *now*, and the *other*.

Hence the major difference between *Habel* and, say, *Qui se souvient*. If both novels work in favour of an exclusively 'spectral' logic – that is, a logic which paralyses the active subject so as to liberate the passive intuition of a reality beyond relation and prediction – *Habel* no longer maintains the coherence of *an* environment-subject moving toward global (and apocalyptic) change. In *Qui se souvient*, narrator and city are both immanent to the transformation that resolves their relationship. In *Habel*, change must come from fragmentation itself, through a more partial, more episodic process in a situation itself beyond *any* recuperation at all.

The first few pages of the novel set the tone. All that Habel is aware of is 'this solar cataclysm that pushes him toward stupor. And then, nothing. Vanishing, waiting, bedazzlement, torpor' (HB, 7). He lives in a 'world emptied of all substance' (7), in the 'silence of an empty world' (8). This *mutisme* is soon broken by three more-than-verbal interruptions. a quasi-biblical motif, by which (H)Abel's private dialogue with his brother claims allegorical value for an 'Aion' of exile and *errance*, an angelic apparition, which maintains the mute presence of death on the threshold of another way of seeing, another kind of *eye*; and the element of repetition itself, the 'illogical' logic of a death-drive beyond *analysis*, beyond motivation My discussion, inevitably, blurs these three elements together in a single procession.

To begin with, it should be stressed that the biblical theme is, up to point, a *faux ami*. Bewildered critics have often seized on this familiar archetype as a way of organising the novel. Certainly, throughout the novel, Habel maintains an ongoing monologue directed to his brother (simply, 'Frère'), 'the older and wiser of the two' (40), 'his only relative' (55), whose immemorial commandment is the closest thing to a first cause that the novel provides: 'Go [forth], discover cities, learn to know the nations' (55). But if this 'invitation' to exile is an act of symbolic murder, Dib's highly elliptical text suggests only that it is a crime beyond jurisdiction – a kind of '*tort*' in Lyotard's peculiar sense.[1] The brotherly relation remains forever unspecified. The Cain and Abel motif yields, rather, to a quite different way of thinking about original violence and death. The question of *Genesis* (4:9), 'am I my brother's keeper?' (HB, 60) – the words starkly written on an otherwise empty page – is answered in a sense by further declarations on similarly empty pages: 'Look at the Angel, Habel' (113), and 'the murder is in me' (149).

What might this mean? It means that death figures here less as the result of an initial fracticide, i.e. the result of an original and *attributable* fault, than as the subject of a *pure* revelation, a revelation beyond motivation of any kind. It is only this active subtraction of motives that makes sense of the story twice declared by 'the other voice', always italicised, that 'sweeps down on [Habel] and around him, like a tornado'. '*And God said. "You will be the guardian of death". I asked, "Lord, what is death?" God ordered the universe to break apart and uncover death, so that I could see it [. .] And God said, "this is death. I created it"*' (69). Nothing more. The whole of the telos and import of death is here compressed to the ascetic movement which links *s'écarter*, *découvrir*, *voir*, and *dire* – the movement, that is, of a stripping away of mediation, of a becoming-immediate (to death). To know death is to learn to see, in the absence of all material opacity, the unqualified or inarticulable as such.

Later in the novel, Habel has a vision of Azraïl, the many-eyed angel of death, 'a figure [that] has never begun. Quite obviously it has always changed within itself, always the same reality under its myriad eyes'.[175] Habel asks:

> 'Why are you appearing to me, Azraïl?'
> From above Habel is assailed by a voice that streams forth from every-where, from all the voices of the horizon, and it is like a thunderbolt, so mas-sive, so powerful and overwhelming that he can barely manage to remain conscious [...].
> 'I also, when God said: "You shall be the keeper of death", asked: 'Lord, what is death?'
> Then the same voice exclaims, unrelentingly.
> 'Death also, when the Lord gave me strength and I took it in my hand, asked "What am I?" Death also cried out to the heavens: "*Lord, why must I have a keeper?*"'
> Then the angel vanished above Paris, leaving it as no more than an abyss opened by a silent bomb (HB, 133, my emphasis)

This is indeed the great and truly profound question of the book. What is the relation between (limitless) death, and its living keeper or *guardian*? Concretely, this is the question which confronts Habel guardian of Lily, the question displaced from Cain guardian of Abel; abstractly, it is the question of a mystical theosophy which affirms both the absolute sufficiency of a Creator *and* the transient but irreducible passage of the created. In *guard-ing* death, the living moves toward that singular insight that is the sufficient reason of the living. The angel of death is nothing other than the angel of insight, the angel of a suprasensible, supra-personal sight. 'When he comes before his time, the Angel of Death grants you, they say, one of the many pairs of eyes that drape his body, and you then see what others cannot' (152). What happens in *Habel*, then, is what is required for Habel to learn to see with this other-worldly clarity, to become adequate to 'a night in some sense born of his own night and waiting for Habel to begin waiting, already looking for him' (72). Habel is slowly incorporated into a realm beyond situated choice, a realm of absolute necessity beyond 'reason' (close to an experience of what Deleuze analyses as a '*pure* choice', i.e. a choice without 'terms'[176]). The environment of this process is a Paris stripped of its ornamental façade, this 'city in which you are pursued, in which you stray, which closes around you and no more preserves a trace of your passage than the time that you have wasted along the way'.[177]

The accomplishment of Habel's choice beyond choices is enabled by two decisive encounters – with Le Vieux, on the mostly 'theoretical' plane, and with Lily, on the mostly affective plane. Le Vieux/La Dame – 'a woman that you won't encounter among the living' (41) – provides, essentially, access to that singular 'indirect discourse' in the peculiarly Deleuzian sense, 'that speaking [*parole*] that finds, that draws its obstination only from itself'.[175] If 'the world always speaks too much, and exhausts itself in words' (30), Habel seeks to allow 'the word [*la parole*] to speak itself, freed of all its chains and even of the name it carries, even the body, even the voice' (31). Le Vieux articulates precisely such a *parole*. Speaking in a 'voice without origin, without other origin than itself' (90), the Vieux suggests a plane of experience where 'there is no voice [*voix*] at all; there is no shame, no remorse'.[179] In particular, the Dame insists that 'when our world fashioned by human hands is shown to be such a failure, when the world willed by man is this abominable defilement, this failure, this misery [...]. We must perhaps then [...] begin to see things... in a different way... to seek something else, elsewhere Take a different path, a path...' (HB, 52). She doesn't finish these sentences. But she suggests that it is a way pure of contingency, pure of 'choice', the path of a self-asserting singularity. For '"when I am la Dame de la Merci, you see, my great friend, I cannot be anybody else. I hope you understand this". [This was] another explanation that went without saying and that left the unexplained things no less unexplained' (51). Which is to say (several times) that what is 'chosen' here is beyond any merely moral order:

> For a long time now that question [of morals], that old confrontation between good and bad, that old story, has no longer mattered – rather something else, nothing other than man and the path, that almost impersonal track that man finds himself alone able to pursue and fulfil, that open and desolate space, whatever you want to call it, vast like a catastrophe and at the same time as narrow as a razor blade, that we are, that we have always alone been capable of inhabiting, and of the impossibility of inhabiting it, of filling it [.] The real question [..] is to find out why we had necessarily to go that way, along this single [*unique*] road, without any possible choice (HB, 49 148–151)

Amor fati. Dib returns us here to the core of an ethical philosophy in a broadly Spinozist or Deleuzian sense. Ethical enlightenment is a function of becoming what one is or can be, so as to escape, in short, the realm of merely moral choice. And thereby to become immediate to a purely divine Light, to attain a reality beyond reaction, to move beyond interpretation in the conventional sense.[180]

With Lily, this is precisely what Habel begins to do: 'he will love [her] above this dead world' (168). From the beginning, he knows that 'every understanding [*entente*] rests on a prohibited space, an untouchable solitude, every existence rests exclusively on this' (15); later, he learns that 'there has probably never been a person so alone in the world as Lily' (121). His meeting with Lily is abrupt and unmotivated, a pure encounter (97).

He knows immediately that 'I will never abandon her, never [...]; you must become capable of accepting things that happen as they happen'. And this stoicism is very soon put to the test, with the first of a series of progressively estranging 'escapades' during which Lily disappears in the night: Habel finds her sleeping in the street with her eyes open, 'immobile, her green pupils dilated but empty of life and light' (103).

Despair follows, both shattering and numbing. If Lily is for Habel 'the greatest of seductions', so is 'death, he said to himself; death is also the supreme seduction. Lily is my death? Has she taken me alive, bound me, living, with her gaze?' (HB, 109–111). The trauma brings Habel, like Johnson's Reb, closer to an impersonal lucidity, a lucidity beyond pain. At one point, 'so strong an impression of abandonment seized him that *he saw himself finally as he [really] was*, a stranger face to face with a stranger, and still stranger still. He had finally come to this point, he had *the feeling of abandoning himself* (111, my emphasis). Such is the ascetic path toward a more than personal salvation. It is prefigured by Habel's discovery of an angelic Lily disguised as 'a street dancer', an 'angel dancing', 'an incomprehensible seraph [...]. From her flowed *that knowledge in which one touches oneself, manages to reach oneself, to surprise [and grasp] one's own secret without ceasing to be indestructibly tied to it*' (116, my emphasis). Lily's eventual madness, then, is a particularly brutal form of *fana'* (extinction). She has accomplished what Habel has only begun – the separation of body and mind, or the loss of a bodily opacity. 'A little opacity is necessary for everyone. But not for Lily' (129). Estranged from herself, she reveals the impersonal love she harbours hidden 'underneath' (161–162). Visiting Lily every week at her asylum, Habel finds someone 'already dead without being dead', (120), cut off from all worldly communication and value.[181] Lily lives in a space beyond relations with others, 'lost in a dream as incommunicable, as unsayable, as a prison; banished in a space in which language itself stops trying to make itself heard, in which even memories blur' (124).

Habel's final choice without terms, his choice without *raison*, is suggested as much in an extraordinary castration scene orchestrated by Le Vieux, as by his decision to commit *himself*, in a sense, to Lily's asylum. The self-mutilation ends with 'a cry that was less a cry of pain than of victory', screaming 'in the intoxication and the despair in which *one separates from oneself*, or would like to separate oneself, so as to fall back further away, somewhere else'.[182] The cut opens a wound in the worldly horizon. It opens the path of a 'line of flight' beyond the world. For Habel himself, this opening is located precisely in that quintessential space of worldly confinement (i.e. the confinement, within the world, of those in some sense already 'lost to the world'): the *maison de santé*. And so in the last pages of the novel, Habel decides to look for work in the asylum, at the risk, as Lily's doctor says, 'of losing your own reason'. Habel's only answer. 'I don't give a damn about my reason [...]. I want to stay close to Lily' (187). The closing lines turn, as so often in Dib's work, to the infinite expanse of the sky outside, 'this blue miracle, with a single silver cloud in its centre, kept reason [*gardait raison*] over everything, had the last word over everything' (188).

It should be stressed, finally, that for all its dizzying 'intransitivity', in some respects *Habel* still remains just within the furthest limits of the specific – limits which will be stretched still further in the works to come. For here, at least temporarily, 'I still have Lily. And I have Sabine. With them, with each of them, my life is guarded/kept [*gardée*], my life has denied its solitude, its ferocity' (32; cf. 7). Habel has risen to his brother's challenge, and survived. 'Your order', he tells his absent presence, 'was nothing but a way of making me lose myself' (93), but at some unknown point – 'it doesn't matter when [...], or where [...], my travels have wound up by finding their reason' (93). With Lily, Habel finds 'a woman, a reason to live. A reason, a warmth, a whiteness in which all answers converge and appear' (HB, 94; cf. 188). If these answers point *toward* a place beyond relation, their articulation here remains on the frontier of a specificity emptied of specification but not yet submerged in the absolute *éclat* of a singularity beyond rapport. Habel himself remains a relational being.

(b) *Les Terrasses d'Orsol* (1985), *Le Sommeil d'Eve* (1989)

Space allows only a very partial reading of these most polished and accomplished of Dib's novels, so I limit my analysis to one major element in each text: the impact of the mysterious abyss [*fosse*] in *Les Terrasses d'Orsol*, and Faina's becoming-wolf in *Le Sommeil d'Eve*. Both novels are narrated in the first person, both take place in insistently Nordic landscapes, and both turn, essentially, around madness. Basis for a comparison, certainly, but the shape and texture of each work is completely different, the one reserved but verging on shock, the other confidential but verging on psychosis.

Les Terrasses d'Orsol records, mostly in the first person, the mental breakdown of an envoy set to survey the economic prospects of a fictional northern city called Jarbher.[183] By the end of the novel, the narrator, Aëd, has forgotten his name and his past and lost the ability to distinguish real from possible or himself from his surroundings. Another variant, then, of traumatic depersonalisation as ascetic enlightenment – but one related almost wholly from *within*, within the deceptive control of what seems at first to be a most 'reasonable' narrative voice.

The novel begins, as if according to Deleuze's prescription, with an enigma. 'I ask myself, and keep asking myself, the question: what happened? What has happened, that might be told, that might be said? [...]. Never in my life have I had such a shock' (TO, 10). There are no immediate answers forthcoming. We begin, that is, on familiar territory – with a 'beginning before the beginning', and a situation beyond reaction. 'I tell myself: 'I need a…' At that very instant, I forget what I need, and I no longer know what I've said' (10, cf. 16). The first third of the novel reveals, partially, slowly, the apparent cause of this situation, 'this abomination' (11) that exhausts the isotope of horror. We know early on, with the anonymous authority of an italicised third person voice, that the narrator confronts here *something to which, once he has finally understood it, he will have to give himself over without reserve, and abandon everything, quit the terrain of his own truth [...and] endure that whose prey he has now become, and that haunts him, afflicts him, the truth that now possesses him, and dispossesses him'* (11). From the beginning, Dib carefully maintains the possibility of two readings of Aëd's experience – an 'objective' reading which reveals the viciously compromised if not diabolical foundations of Jarbher's grandeur and tranquillity (174–177), and a 'subjective' reading which reveals only Aëd's own growing derangement. Both readings are consistent with the enigmatic discomfort of the various characters whom Aëd tries to entice into explaining what he has seen. The reader must learn to accept that the narrator is *constitutively* 'divided between what he saw outside, this light, this malediction, and what he saw within, the same light, the same malediction' (15).

Just what Aëd has seen, in the narrow 'objective' sense, is revealed soon enough. He has discovered what we might call the *frontier* of the imaginal world. As so often in Dib, the ocean lies on the other side of this frontier: 'all of light is there, liquefied. An infinity of light that uncoils its heavy brilliant folds and never stops moving' (TO, 15–16). But between the narrator and the ocean, at the water's edge, there is an 'a sort of abyss of dizzying depth', an 'enormous excavation with sheer sides', surrounded by 'avalanches of light' (16). In this chasm he sees what might be called the *real* image of a merely human existence. But this unbearable image, as we would expect, is (given as) repressed.[14] At the bottom of the pit the narrator 'sees', in sequence, 'a dark herd of pachyderms' (16), 'a wave of reptiles on greenish rocks' – 'it's beyond my strength, I flee it once more' (17) – and then 'creatures resembling sea turtles, or better, giant crabs', or maybe a kind of 'spider' (28-29). During the fourth narrated visit to the abyss, he finds 'larvae confined in the entrails of the cursed pit' (42), then 'monstrous tarantulas' (43), before finally admitting what the reader has long suspected – that what he sees are human beings of a particularly 'spasmodic' and revolting sort (53).

The cause and purpose of the chasm is never explained. With Aëd perplexed by the unflinching silence of those Jarbhiens he confronts and questions, and 'stripped bare by the great, too great light that blinds me' (61; 70, 83), the remainder of the novel develops his progressive dissolution in the 'unbearable [*insoutenable*]'. The nature of his plight is most concisely explained in a sequence of questions without question-marks (the syntax of a properly hypothetical affirmation): 'has he not shared in this malediction of light, has it not reduced his flesh to cinders, has he not looked away, has he not turned his eyes away from it as from everything that comes of it'.[155] Eventually, our semi-delirious narrator learns how to answer, by the only means possible, his most essential question. 'is light something that we can look at/fix [*fixer*], I ask you, O my judges' (187). It is an answer drawn from 'a water than no human waste has soiled [...]. I discover it, finally, this resting, milky light [...]. It is bedazzlement' (110, 111). Thus bedazzled, Aëd grows 'incapable of distinguishing between what has happened and what has never happened.' 'He' (whoever 'he' has become) lives 'the dream of what has not happened' (181), a virtual reality on the 'other side' of things. 'I knock down each door at present, door after door, with inordinate, monstrous strength...' (184), says a speaker who wavers between first to third person, stumbling imperceptibly into anonymity until

> he will be nothing more than waiting, a waiting made of the void, a void made of waiting, a room of echoes where suddenly his voice, or another voice, will ring out, [ ] Letting everyone come [ ], he will forget everything even the very words, prey to the waiting, to emptiness He will do battle but alone, in a wasteland, in a desert.[156]

In the end there is only 'one voice that speaks and answers itself all alone'. But 'there has been, nevertheless, a call, or a reminder'.[157] Like *Habel, Les Terrasses* ends with a partial redemption-by-relation, in the figure of his lover Aëlle (214) and a vision of 'the place of return' (212). If he has forgotten his name and Aëlle's, he remembers the name of the film which has nagged at him throughout the novel – *For Ever*.

Le Sommeil d'Eve retains, likes *Les Terrasses*, a first person narrative voice – the mental diary kept by a woman (Faïna) on the verge of another kind of madness, and then, in its second half, a similar 'diary' kept by the man (Solh) who becomes, like Habel with Lily, her *keeper*. The novel tells the story of a discourse which becomes possessed by its own obsession – possessed, that is, by an ultimately inarticulate force beyond the human, a force embodied by the *wolf* and the northern landscape it inhabits.

Faïna has retreated home (to Finland) from France with her husband Oleg in order to give birth to her first born, leaving her real lover Solh behind. 'I love Solh. I love so much I could die' (SE, 26; cf. 38). Much of Faïna's diary is an effort to incant a *present* relationship with Solh across the distance and difference which keeps them apart. In the narrow sense, this effort fails. 'We find ourselves together, but where – nowhere. In a negative place' (16). Faïna is haunted by the possibility of an impending break with Solh (36, 42, 82). The novel as a whole, with the strict alternation of voices – first Faïna, *then* Solh – leaves little room for *dialogue* as such. At the same time, the insistence of the first person form throughout creates the illusion of one voice with two speakers.[18] With one exception, their actual conversations are recorded indirectly, and generally leave Faïna with 'the impression of being a stranger in this world – and useless too' (50, 59). Their one directly reported exchange (95-102) is a disaster.

Less than a rapport *with* Solh, then, Faïna is drawn through Solh *toward* a space beyond rapport – a space which here remains, still, only partly accessible. 'I am seeking something, without respite. But this thing [...] does not allow itself to be found [...]. *My project ties me to nobody*' (109, my emphasis). Rather, it calls her to a place of 'silence. Nobody, no trace of footsteps. A virgin snow' (17). Isolated in this immobility, Faïna struggles to cope with 'a total, absolute lack of confidence, that comes only from me [...]; it's incontestable. my own emptiness terrifies me' (22, 20). These circumstances literally put the *person* of Faïna to sleep, and allow the Wolf to awake, in an experience 'that I would not be able to name myself' (22). The sleep evoked by the title dominates the opening pages: 'I have an immense desire to sleep' (14), 'how tired I am', 'I am so very tired' (20, 21), 'I am more tired than ever' (48). And as the body grows ever more weary, 'I escape my body and evade my thought every time I feel acting in me this force – how can I describe it – this "impure" force' (23).

It takes some eighty pages for this force to reveal its true nature. A first clue is Faïna's appetite after her baby is delivered: 'I have only one thought in my mind: to eat blood. To eat it, because I recoil from drinking it' (29). At this point she notes for first time that 'you [Faïna] shall be called Wolf as well' (29), and sends Solh a post card reproduction called '*La Fiancée du Loup*, after a painting by Simberg'.[19] Her dreams become progressively more violent (83, 84, 85, 89, 92, 108), filled with scenes of her death or Solh's, choked, burnt, strangled. And then, abruptly, 'the indiscernible, the ungraspable, brushed against me' (87):

> Then it came, this morning. I howled and howled A she-wolf. The she-wolf who calls the wolf. Oleg shook me [   ] And night came. Again I couldn't resist it. Night when wolves howl I howled again. I called Solh-Wolf I called and called him I howled [20]

In the aftermath of this transformation, Faïna is drawn to this limits of the *rive sauvage*: 'time was elsewhere. As I was elsewhere, all the time [...]. And so here I am standing at the edge of the world, where the abyss begins, where you fall' (88). As in *Habel*, it is woman who goes over the edge, leaving man on the brink of insight (and despair). Far more than Lily, however,

Faïna is the true actor of this story, and it is more Solh who is the catalyst
of her transformation, not the reverse. It is only Faïna who truly acts, even
if what happens happens *to* her more than by her. At the limit, it is the
world that acts through her, and not the reverse. '*The forest in me folds
over, burning...*'[191] As Solh will later say, 'I cannot approach her, closed as
she is in her silence, her detachment [...]. She in the process of becoming
the world, in front of me [...]. Faïna has become only presence. An answer,
no. She is making herself into an object among the objects of this world and
mixes with them in the unsayable secret, the black tearing [*déchirure*] from
which rises no question and no answer.'[192]

VI And then?

Dib's most recent works continue and extend the project opened with *Qui
se souvient de la mer*. With this difference, perhaps: rather than move
towards the frontier of *l'indicible secret*, the aphasic limit of a worldly
coherence, Dib's main point of reference is now this frontier itself. There
is no sharp break here, nothing like the break between *Un Eté africain* and
Qui se souvient. But there is, I think, a subtle change in tone and ambition,
a more serenely audacious exploration of the imperceptible as such. *L'Infante maure* in particular affirms an experience which transforms the
'agent' of this experience – without remaining dependent on a semi-
redemptive relationship on the one hand (Habel, Aëlle, Solh...) nor falling
necessarily into madness (Lily, Aëd, Faïna) on the other.

Before describing these last novels individually, it may be worth considering very briefly some more general themes characteristic of Dib's later
work as a whole, which will allow us to assess its evolution a little more precisely. Three closely related elements stand out: the place of the secret, the
ta'wil of the pure name, and the persistence of narrative (even in the wake
of 'sensory motor dissolution'). All of these things, in a sense, constitute
aspects of the screen that protects even Dib's most despecified writing from
the unsayable pure and simple – the material aspects, so to speak, of that
imaginal realm which retains, just, a coherence of its own *between* worldly
opacity and the blinding singularity of the One beyond imagination.

(i) *Secret but not empty.* We saw that Faïna of *Le Sommeil d'Eve* moves
toward 'the unsayable secret, the black tearing from which rises no question
and no answer' (SE, 189). *L'indicible secret* is a good place from which to
approach Dib's most recent novels.[193] The theme goes back a long way – to
the secret *underground city* in *Qui se souvient*, Hellé's secret identity in
Cours, Lily's secret insight in *Habel*, the secret of the *fosse* in *Les Terrasses*,
the wolfish secret of *Le Sommeil d'Eve*. In Dib's later work, the relative
secrecy of *an* unknown privileged in relation *to* the known – i.e. secret in its

etymological sense – becomes almost absolute.[191] Now almost the *whole* of creation is secret, in a sense, a single process of veiling and unveiling. All is secret, all is veiled – so *all* knowledge is a process of unveiling. Lyyli Belle, the tree-climbing narrator of *L'Infante maure*, maintains 'a secret, from the top of my tree, for which I keep all the space that is its due' (IM, 113).

> I am melting in a bath of delight but also I feel myself being reborn. I am reborn, I take on new shape, and such a shape it is. a shape like I never hoped to have It is the secret. My secret. With a hovering smile, you realise that from this moment that you are one body with everything. You are a secret beaming in space, you are the sign that opens up the world and protects it (IM, 12)

Lyyli's 'guardianship of the world' begins with her faith in this secret, faith in the *indicible* as the quasi-transcendental *condition* of articulation in general.[195]

What separates Dib from Blanchot, in the end, is very precisely the difference between the void and the secret, between *le silence pur* and the hermeneutics of the hidden. The secret is inaccessible, but it is inaccessible *as* the frontier of relation. The secret is unspecified, but remains *minimally* specific, as the unknown-in-*relation*-to-the-known. To *know* the secret requires a becoming-secret on the part of the adept, a becoming-esoteric on the model of *ta'wil*. As the Sixth Shi'ite Imam (Ja'far Sâdiq) put it. 'our cause is a secret [*sirr*] in a secret, the secret of something that remains veiled, a secret that only another secret can teach; it is a secret of a secret that it is veiled by a secret'.[196] (The supreme example, of course, is death itself: in 'naming' death, we *know* nothing of what we say, we name only the space of a question, the space of a gap in knowledge.) In Deleuze's work, by contrast – and this is also one of the ways he is so different from Derrida, say – there is no place for the secret as such. The ontological domain is an essentially *empirical* one, once we accept the physical (though virtual) coherence of infinite speed. Ontology is then simply a matter of speeds and intensities, territories and trajectories. There *is* nothing transcendent (to thought), immanence is not immanent 'to' anything.[197] In Dib's work, however, as in al-Suhrawardi's theosophy, the ultimate ontological questions are forever veiled in secrecy, beyond the horizon of the only enlightenment we can manage: the liberation of imagination in the '*alam al-mithal* (imaginal world). In traditional monotheistic terms, secrecy shrouds what was lost through the advent of post-Edenic knowledge (after which we can only *know* God as secret, as hidden). Dib preserves this shroud, and with it the hermeneutic relation with the transcendent. Whatever access to the secret we can manage will never repeat the *literal* origin (DD, 38–39). Rather than return to a kind of immediate Adamic insight, Dib narrates a specific figural displacement *from* the literal-original (for the imaginal world *is* nothing other than pure interpretative displacement, or the reflection of reflection...). As one visionary voice will say,

> I am the promise and the test, together. [I am] that which presents itself in the form and aspect of a door, with all the innocence of a door, and through which you must go I am myself unaware of what waits or lies in wait beyond, if indeed there is anything at all. One thing, whatever happens, will remain unnamed, unnameable for ever [...]. But I guard it and allow to pass through those who must pass [...]. For the moment, I speak, I sing, I tell stories, my stories, your stories, I cry out things... (DD, 123)

(ii) *Named but not known*. The growing importance of the proper name in Dib's most recent work is consistent with this secret, inaccessible logic. The archetypal model is the gnosis of the divine name (in all three of the great monotheisms), the unknowable equation of word and thing, the sufficient but unsayable name of God. As Dib uses it, the name is precisely the interface *between* the specific and the singular. Aëd identifies 'the name [... as] the currency in which we can pay the ransom of exile [and win] our return'.[198] In the midst of his *dérangement*, he knows that 'in a short while, I will be the Other, the one who carries a real Name', a name the reader will never know (TO, 162). The most dramatic example is the substitution of *Louve* for *Faïna*. 'You know your real name at present, but shhh... This name must stay secret. It's only to be used within [these] four walls, between you and me. You take up your real nature, your she-wolf nature. You are called She-wolf. But shhh...' (SE, 68, 69). It is a rare moment of *franchise*. More typically, Dib's later characters follow the more strictly Ishraqi logic of the (anonymous) italicised voice of *Le Desert*:

> *My name? Oh, I'd rather not have to reveal it [   ] A name, this name, would you ask it of a shadow, in the west, when he who projects it is in the east [l'orient]? A shadow no less certain than this, it is not to it that you must ask the question Go asking after him over there, the holder of the name, into whose presence only the Angel can lead you, when he embraces the world, when everything will become one...* (DD, 13)

To know the name, in other words, is to engage with the Angel. It is to turn from the exoteric to the esoteric, from apparent to spiritual sense. For the true name can only name God, or the ungraspable subject of pure reflection as such (the anonymous 'I' that endlessly seeks to know myself, but that cannot 'itself' be *known*, that cannot be considered as an object, or self). It names introspective awareness in the most anonymous sense, at a point where 'private' intuition is indiscernible from transcendent inspiration. Derrida puts it very precisely, in a broadly comparable context. 'God is the name of the possibility I have of keeping a secret that is visible from the interior but not from the exterior [...], God is in me, he is the absolute "me" or "self"', who 'manifests his nonmanifestation when, in the structures of the living or the entity, there appears in the course of phylo- and ontogenetic history, the possibility of secrecy'. Such secrecy is the effect of 'a structure of conscience' organised around the hidden presence of an interior voice or 'witness that others cannot see' and that I 'myself' cannot know, a 'secret witnessing within me'.[199] Dib's most recent novels are nothing other than efforts to narrate such witnessing, in which one's 'incomparable name' (NM, 117) remains unknown, unknowable, even in its declaration. In *Neiges du marbre*, for example, Lyyl whispers to her father her 'incomprehensible'

> secret name. The only one apparently that she will recognise The one that she gives herself deep down. She has just named herself with this name, as if she had drawn back a curtain to reveal the sun shining inside her, and has done so only for me [...]. It is me and it is her. It is the trust that dares, fearing no betrayal [...]. And there it is. Another secret links us. I am becoming the tomb that keeps another secret.[200]

(iii) *Narrated but not related.* Declaration of the secret name is generally deferred. (Its advent – as in *Sommeil d'Eve* – marks the very limit of description as such.) This deferral of nomination conditions both the form and content of Dib's later narratives. On the threshold of anonymity, as Lyyli says, 'there is a always a moment that returns, a moment in which one is not yet lost, that repeats [...]. Oh, father, father... Such is our story, for both of us, and it will always be our story' (IM, 163). What Dib *narrates*, in his most recent work, is the repetition of precisely this story, the story of the moment just before loss of the worldly self.

In a statement that suggests a model of Dib's work as whole, Aëd realises, like Habel, that 'nothing has yet happened [*arrivé*], but events occur [*surviennent*] first, without relations between them, pure of intention, and then they establish such relations, discover an intention' (TO, 136). Likewise Lyyl's father in *Neiges de marbre*: 'I tell the story [...], and the words come in the order required, and not another, to formulate the story. And at a certain point, the story takes form from itself'.[201] Such (auto) organisation of linguistic experience in narrative form is an apparently mysterious yet *sufficient* fact. Like Deleuze, Dib proclaims his faith in a speech without speaker, an indirect discourse which speaks the cosmos as a whole – and that never stops speaking (TL, 99–100). '*If the narrator wanted to fall silent, his voice, the voice that says I, would nevertheless continue to speak all by itself*' (NM, 46). But unlike Deleuze's philosophy, Dibian discourse is organised as a story. It unfolds *between* a speaker and a listener, between a beginning and an end. Lyyli: 'this death, that happens when I drown myself in light [...], it ends up by making a story. But a story full of holes. No, it's me that is full of holes; not the story' (IM, 17). However 'holed', the cosmic story remains a story, a story told *from* the secret. It remains for us to bear it. To keep the secret.

In short, the alternative to a direct (singular) declaration of the name is the (specific) *narrative* of its deferred nomination. Dib has recently called attention to

> a question which I have never tackled without the cold sweat of anxiety: the question that has to do with the continuity of a narrative, with wonder or mischief, that constructs it and informs what, at the outset, is only a conglomerate, or a galaxy of mini-narratives. Where lies the secret of this alchemy, and how can it be discovered, and possessed [...]? We don't understand how continuity works, precisely because we are prisoners of it. [...W]e come out of a novel that we have been writing or reading in the same way that we come out of a dream: with this one question in mind, what is that makes meaning? Well, in my view, it can only be the mystery with which continuity always surrounds itself . [202]

Dib develops this mystery most explicitly in his recent collaborative effort with the photographer Philippe Bordas, *Tlemcen ou les lieux de l'écriture* (1994), through the evocation of childhood memories, customs of the city, the texture of place – nothing could be further from the utopic immediacy of *l'espace littéraire*.

It must still be stressed, however, that what is narrated here is indeed an irreversible movement toward (or back to) the secret, *toward* a literal, singular, or immediate nomination. Dib's narrative – unlike, for example, the quasi-Kantian faculty of narration asserted by Ricoeur – is a narrative that can, for any particular actor, only happen once. What is narrated eliminates, as it goes along, the possibility of its eventual re-presentation. Hakim Madjil's request is exemplary: 'let this thing happen to me, this thing that I will stop feeling the more it happens to me' (MC, 206). We move ever closer towards the moment when 'one has to face this light and learn what must be learned' (TO, 205), in the knowledge that what we learn we will not be able to *teach*. Dib's notion of narrative conforms to the Orphic model: this is narrative in which there can be no 'turning back'. At their narrative's end, Dib's heroes are no longer in a position to tell their story. The exception, as we shall see, is *L'Infante maure*. And precisely for this reason, this novel is not really a narrative at all; it is less a movement with beginning, middle and end than a collection of experiences which do nothing so much as repeat or suggest a naming of the secret in general.

(a) *Neiges de marbre* (1990) and *L'Infante maure* (1994)

Despite the years that separate their publication, these two novels can be treated together; *L'Infante maure* is perhaps the most explicitly consecutive of any of Dib's sequels. Both books can be fairly simply summarised as the day to day description, again in a Nordic environment and always in the first person, of the relationship between an (unnamed) father and his daughter Lyyl (Lyyli Belle in *L'Infante*), set against the more or less explicit failure of his relationship with his wife Roussia (unnamed in *L'Infante*).[203]

As in *Habel* and *Les Terrasses d'Orsol*, the themes of exile and cultural difference carry a certain *weight*. The (North African) father makes a point of emphasising the linguistic gap which separates him from his child (NM, 13, 22, 66, 88). He knows that 'I will soon have left this country. I must. I cannot prolong my stay with Roussia any further. My place is no longer here'. And as for Lyyl, 'I will no longer see her. Confiscated. She has already been confiscated'.[204] In *Neiges de marbre*, Lyyl lives the break-up of her parents, the end of their *rapport*.[205] The issue is all the more complicated by the fact that exile from Roussia is not the negation of a negation – a return home – but rather a return to another, earlier place of exile, the France of Paris and Reims. As Lyyli Belle will put it, 'Papa is a nomad [...], his country is a camp in the desert' (IM, 104; cf. 171).

But if Dib's later work as whole deals with exile with great subtlety and finesse, it would be wrong to attribute it more than a properly passing importance. Dib's version of exile is not, fundamentally, what is produced *by* displacement. His exile is not the effect of a *dépaysement* but an aspect of a more fundamental *cause*, the expression of a kind of *barzakh* (opacity). Lyyli Belle knows that 'we are everywhere born a foreigner [*étranger*]. But if you search for your places and find them, then the land/earth [*la terre*] becomes your land [...]. There is nothing I detest as much as this idea, to be without place' (IM, 171). The sort of place Lyyli has in mind, however, is a place of pure in-difference, or a place beyond belonging (the place of what Agamben might call the 'coming community'). Rather than return to some specified home, Lyyli seeks 'to return towards the country I left without wanting to leave' (IM, 61), back to a world in which

> no more than others, I will have no need to know if I am myself from here or elsewhere. No place will refuse to belong to me and nobody will live in a borrowed country. Let's go to the desert welcoming us, it will offer the nudity of its open hand. Recalled to its first state, the land [*la terre*] will accept the first person who comes along. (IM, 174)

The *lieu* claimed by Lyyli, in other words, is the place beyond particularity itself, a world in which exile is very literally an impossibility (because an inevitability).

Lyyli's claims thus revalue the ascetic process lived in the first place by her father, in the 'terrible absence of presence [...]. *I am brought back to the whiteness of moments in which nothing happens, to the whiteness of what every minute can become*' (NM, 173). *L'Infante maure* is, above all, the positive re-affection of this *same blancheur*. Where her father stumbles – 'you are walking in a landscape of snow, you can no longer find the path, there are no more paths' (NM, 214) – Lyyli glides in perfect security. Lyyl(i) is very exactly a character everywhere at home.[206] And she is, without a doubt, Dib's most developed experiment in this Ishraqi domain. From the beginning, she appears as 'an immortal' (NM, 14, 15), as 'Lyyl, miracle' (NM, 19). 'Lyyl is something new. She possesses no memory' (NM, 106). A typical sequence begins with that most Ishraqi of questions: 'where does the eye go when it goes further than the thing it sees, where does it lose itself? We don't know. What does the heart do, meanwhile. It leaves, but where, Lord, where?...' (IM, 133).

This is the question Lyyli never stops answering, through an initiation which begins with a re-appreciation of light itself. As her father says, 'you live here in another light, that doubles the light of the day. it is the light of silence. And this silence engenders the space around you' (NM, 133). Like her father, and more than her father, Lyyli hovers just 'before the vertigo of the new light' (IM, 53), clasping the moment of dawn as such, of a light before shadow (before 'direct' sunlight) or a light beyond shadow (nothing but sunlight). 'And I, where is my truth? In my light and in all the light sent by the sun, [it is] something naked and you are better dressed in its nudity than in your own clothes [...]. There is only the sun. It fills everything all by itself. Well, as long as no word comes to ruin this beautiful silence! [...]. Happiness is this minute that does not pass. A thing that is, simply' (IM, 68, 175). Much of Lyyli's energy is consumed by the absolutely concentrated contemplation of this *chose*, this utterly generic *thing*. This is contemplation in something like Deleuze's sense. an elemental contraction, a folding of light that envelopes perceiver and perceived, a perception that creates, in a swirling of intensity, its hallucinatory object and its nomadic subject.[207] Lyyli knows that 'something else moves and we don't know what it is. Something else comes, to enter into everything, traverse everything [...]. We don't know. Hush, *it's the shadow of light*, rushing, crossing, entering' (IM, 38, my emphasis). Here we reach the heart of Dib's *revelation*:

> Somewhere, there is a thing. I don't know what, it is simply lost It is a lost thing which is always there. It gives joy [ ] Very early in the morning, it is this thing which beckons the light in the leaves The sun knows that it is hidden there And there where the thing is, the sun seeks it out When it speaks as it is doing now. I can hear what can't be heard If this sun continues like this, I will end up drowning. I am swimming [..] Everything is swimming I am all black with the sun (NM, 37–38)

> The magic thing is approaching You can't hear it, can't see it, you feel it. A thing that changes as it is approaches It comes alone A light Only your

heart can make it out. [It is] the thing before things, the thing on the other side of things I can't see it, but I can feel that it's there. Perhaps I'll see it if I wait and don't move [..]. It is on the verge of appearing [...]. I spend my time looking for it. I will recognise it and [...] it will be strong, very strong, so strong that it will crush my heart It will be beautiful, it will be awful because it is beautiful And if it were something ugly in its awfulness? It will be an angry angel I will say words to it that have never been said [...], I'll say things like. all-powerful God or Lord. Words like that. They don't mean anything, obviously.[208]

In these and similar passages, Lyyli explores *l'essence de la manifestation* with a rigour that invites comparison with the ideal phenomenology explored in a strictly parallel sense by al-Suhrawardi, Corbin or Michel Henry.[209] (A rigour only superficially disguised by the naive, childlike language of its presentation.) The *appearing of apparition itself* – of phenomenality – is not itself a phenomenon, but an auto-revelation, an 'auto-affection' of the transcendent. As Henry puts it, *I* am less the active subject of a *'je m'affecte'* than the transparent vehicle or object of an ideal *'je suis auto-affecté'*.[210] The appearing of apparition, in each case, is the process by which the absolute reflects upon itself or expresses itself to itself ('through' that which we appears, or perceives). This process cannot be *known* directly by its merely relative, merely human support – the 'thing' is *there*, but *lost* for us. It is *secret*. Lyyli can become immediate *to* Light (*je suis toute noire de soleil*) but she cannot (quite) become pure Light itself.[211]

Armed with her supreme sensitivity to the esoteric, able to 'perceive' the invisible reality which *makes* apparent, Lyyli undertakes a survey of the imaginal domain remarkably similar to that risked by al-Suhrawardi and his followers in the *oriental* tradition. It is a survey guided by the Image as such, the autonomy of a reflection without object, a Light without shadow – a Light refracted through the most transparent of prisms. Lyyli's is a journey mixing oneiric clairvoyance ('let us make our way along forgotten paths, those of the dream that we seek to remember' [IM, 69]) with a microscopic attention to surroundings considered *strictly* as extensions of oneself. 'I am the sister and the brother of all trees, flowers, shadows, lights [...], even stones' (IM, 69), of trees in particular (IM, 37–39). Lyyli-tree lives a world of 'watery landscapes [...], water that is transparent, unfathomable, light [...]. You can disappear [in it], everything could disappear in the abyss of an unperishable joy' (IM, 11; cf. 15, 74). She lives in a perfectly 'smooth' world (*lisse*, in the Deleuzian sense). Lyyli's 'country has no mountains' (41), since a mountain is something that 'nothing can break; mountain is hard, thick, opaque' (IM, 71). Instead, the geography of her world is dominated by the rhizomatic intermingling of myriad lakes, 'of silence become water, light' (71).

At the horizon of this world, 'beyond the mountains [...], there is the desert' (IM, 71). The movement that propels most of the second half of *L'Infante maure* is the integration of desert, the smoothness of sand, within Lyyli's own smoothly Nordic space, composed of trees, water and snow. The elemental opposites of sand and snow are revealed to be perfectly symmetrical in the rigorous logic of an (almost) absolute deterritorialisation. For in the desert 'everything can happen. [It is a] vacant expanse, entirely open' (DD, 41). The desert is governed by its unqualified identity to itself (IM, 71) – 'the desert which [...] plays only at chasing itself, at finding itself then losing itself so as to gather itself together further away and so to overflow, still immobile, after a last fall, beyond the horizon' (IM, 173). Above all, 'in a desert, you are always in the middle, Papa says. Me, I'm planted precisely in the middle, in this middle that is everywhere...' (IM, 147). The point is confirmed at some length with Lyyli's vision of her Bedouin grandfather, *gardien* of the desert, a sequence in which Lyyli makes full use of her quasi-ishraqi way of seeing (IM, 147–160).

It is this kind of *Creative* seeing, creative in a quasi-mystical sense, that underlies what Dib presents in these novels as a virtual writer's testament: the closest thing his fiction provides to a description of its own procedure. 'What [Lyyl] is in the middle of discovering is that words can speak themselves, carry on their own language, be brought to play...' (NM, 23). Like her father, Lyyli pushes this insight to its full conclusion. As always, the articulation of self-speaking *parole* requires 'the strength to silence *yourself* [*se* taire]' (NM, 28). For 'if it [*la chose*] wants to speak, it will be able to speak all by itself, and find its words' unaided (IM, 111). The writer is that quiet, almost transparent surface which vibrates with the sound (or light, or fire) of creation, 'this space that I know at present, in which very quickly you find yourself at the limits of silence [...], all wrapped up in an irrevocable transparency' (IM, 163, my emphasis). Both Lyyli and her grandfather are 'guardians' to their space, just as the writer, it seems, is guardian to space in general. 'As for me I am not that sort of fire that goes to sleep from time to time. Me, all the time, it's the same: I burn [...] Me: I am everywhere the same sensitive point'.[212]

Less than an engagement in or inventory of the world, then, the writer's task appears to be the *keeping* of the secret, the secret whose very secrecy exists only in the deferral of its declaration. Lyyli Belle 'knows precisely what is hidden behind things'. But 'there remains the thing whose limits remain forever out of reach. The immense thing that resists every grasp' (165). As her grandfather commands: '"Bear witness. Bear witness to what your eyes perhaps have not seen [...]". And now I have but one goal in life. to bear witness, whereas before I just looked at things without thinking...'[213]

(b) *Le Désert sans détour* (1992)

We return to the limits of the absolute with this the most esoteric of all Dib's novels, the most evocative in both content and form of *ta'wil* [esoteric interpretation] in al-Suhrawardi's sense. Here 'the unsayable is as if represented, something is happening that should not be seen' (DD, 135). Visions abound – of Eden, of monstrous tentacled creatures, of the Devil, and always, of the sun itself, the sun become absolute in a desert 'beyond return', a journey without end. Strictly speaking, 'there is only the desert. There is nothing to see [...]. Already we no longer have a history' (DD, 12–13). Little, then, can be said of a plot in the ordinary sense. The novel begins with traces of war (11), traces that persist in the (anonymous) italicised voice of a captive in the desert; this voice relates a series of visions culminating in an apparently definitive absorption within the Angelic absolute. Meanwhile, we are witness to the peculiar quest of two displaced characters (Hagg-Bar and Siklist – perhaps only imagined figments of the italicised voice? [55]), reminiscent in some obvious but trivial ways of Beckett's *En attendant Godot*. An unexplained order has been given, and 'in the order received, in its constraint, there is, unexpressed, a promise.'[211] It takes them some time to realise that desert is itself the promise and the promised. 'The desert has this particularity, that, in whichever direction you go, and however far you go, you stay where you are, you stay in the middle of the desert' (DD, 60). Which is to say, also, that 'the desert has this other particularity that walking in it you walk toward yourself' (60) – but as a self in a largely disembodied, depersonalised sense, a self, as always in Dib's later fiction, beyond *reaction* (29). The desert landscape unfolds like that singularly 'luminous whirlwind' which dominates it, which 'towers up yet spreads also in all directions. Without hesitating, it seems to inhale these same directions, to dissolve them, seeking only to scatter them again in an empty brightness, in an emaciated whiteness in which wanders the ghost of a voice; then, enigmatically, pulls itself together again...' (17). Not only is the desert thereby beyond orientation in the geographical sense (because fully oriented in the metaphysical sense) – but, and for the same reason, it sustains no merely *sensory* faculty of orientation. 'Sight itself gets lost in it' (33). The desert is very exactly a situation in which 'there is no way of leaving' (33), where the task is to become adequate to a state 'beyond the beyond'. The desert is a situation without limits or intermediaries. The desert is a situation in which 'you have to consider things differently. The thing directly. Yes. The thing itself' (34), illuminated by this blazing 'inferno that feeds itself and waits for them [Hagg-Bar and Siklist] to come and be consumed within it' (82–83; cf. 95).

Their mistake is to go not far enough in this direction (DD, 55–56).
Hagg-Bar is determined to find positive 'traces of abandoned campsites,
the signs of a mysterious writing' he hopes to decipher with 'the
umbrella!… the instrument for reading them!' (85). The absurdity of a will
to *decipher* the desert is neatly suggested by the usefulness of an umbrella
in a place where it never rains. Hagg-Bar, committed to his pathetic belief
that a 'chancellor [*chancelier*]' will come to lend an instrumental purpose
to their quest (57, 60–62, 81), dies in an eventual delirium. In the end, 'he
cannot perceive [… his] shadow', and sees only, through burning eyes,

> a land that recoils in terror, a salty land where no one lives, the sphinx whose
> blind eyes see in front and behind.
> But
> Hagg-Bar doesn't know it.
> And at that precise moment, the effect of light, the effect of heat, both
> at their height, – the sphinx begins to sing […]. – I am the consciousness
> [*conscience*] of the desert (DD. 114; cf. 124–125)

It falls to the anonymous, italicised voice – the voice that seems 'to know' –
to suggest what is at stake in this transformation (13). Of all Dib's 'characters', this voice is the closest, in thematic terms, to the voice of an explicitly
oriental illumination (i.e. an illumination closest to its solar source). The italicised voice – a voice without body, a voice imprisoned but not specified[215]
– is a voice haunted by an Angelic presence, it has crossed to the 'other side'
and come back to bear witness, come back as guardian of the desert's dream.
'*We are the dream of the desert*' (69), '*we all come from the arch of [the
desert's] dream*' (107), for '*our dream never leaves its dream*' (41). There is
no other place to go. The italicised voice declares the presence of Allah – of
the indivisible, the One 'without associate' – in the absence of objects.

> [It] could rightly be called infinite in the way that it seems to create its self
> from itself and without respite or rest, perfects itself, modifies itself, grows
> right up to the sky […] Until the point, the deepest point in me, where tomb-
> like, I hear my quiet voice. '*Imân, islâm, ihsân*' Say 'intelligence with things,
> with everything, freedom of speech' And again. 'Speak, *kun*! That which
> establishes us as beings of truth and as present to truth [..]
>
> I can only see this flame, it tires the eyes, it alone is true. I in my turn
> can only be true as coming from it, encircled by it [.] One and unique, the
> light cleanses the earth, bleaches it white It wouldn't be light if it did any-
> thing else [216]

We approach here the limits of singular insight in all its blinding purity.
What alone keeps it at a distance, even as it incants its advent, is the
medium of language. Language is at once the vehicle of a confrontation
with the *indicible* that lies beyond, and that which must be surpassed in

order to reveal this unsayable as such. The anonymous italicised voice 'speaks' this impossible task, in a discourse held beyond 'aphasia' (53). For in the

> *silence of silence, the void will have made its home in you and here you are like everyone else open to every wind, having as substance and shelter only this void that knows only this void [and that will] dissolve you in the blazing of the day But however burned you are by its touch, you put out the flames in yourself, and it's then that you come back to life, back to the world. Angel, pass then across my body, consume me, consume me. . (DD, 107–108)*

The sequence is now familiar: to be consumed here is to *return* every-where, to cease to be lit is to light, and the only real mistake is always to hold on to body and world, to remain stuck in the confines of a doomed opacity. The Angel arrives in due course to confirm the point, 'archangel of the desert with your names known and unknown [...], before the open door set against the desert', 'more luminous than the day'. Source of space, the Angel is not itself *in* space; source of language, the Angel is that silence that calls the desert itself to speak (117). '*It is enough, Archangel, that you pro-ject a shadow, and that it be me, this shadow [...]. At the extreme, at the black limit of forgetting, dark, I will become memory of the desert and bird come to fly over it*'.[217]

At this extreme distance from the world, there is little left to say. From his *grande maison* to this *désert sans détour*, Dib has perhaps taken his singu-larising journey to its narratable limits. At its end it may be too late to remember that only the journey counts.

RETURN TO THE SPECIFIC

Mohammed Dib has obliged us to refine our understanding of the tension between singular and specific. This tension increases, as we shall see, in the last works of Severo Sarduy. Before going on to consider his work it may be helpful to clarify briefly what is at stake in the concept of the specific that has been present throughout this book but never yet formulated with any precision. To do so with the sort of thoroughness it demands is clearly beyond the limits of this study; what follows is at best the preface to a more complete investigation.

We have established (in chapter 1:IV) that if it is to be firmly distinguished from the objectively specified, then use of the word 'specific' should be reserved to the *actively* or *subjectively* relational. Definition of the term along these lines clearly opens a field of enquiry as vast as that of the comparative analysis of its singular alternative. Something like a proper genealogy of the specific might include, among other things: discussion of a sequence of relational metaphysical configurations ranging from Aristotle's conception of specific difference to Hegel's concept of negation; an assessment of the relational dimension at work in Marx's notion of class, Darwin's notion of species, and Freud's notion of identification; an acknowledgement of phenomenology's contribution to the characterisation of consciousness as relational (or 'of something'); the development, after Sartre, of a general theory of *situation*, i.e. a theory of subjectivation undertaken as a *project* specific to a particular situation; the critical evaluation of a whole series of models of interpretation, interaction, communication and competition from Bakhtin to Bourdieu and Habermas to Honneth; the testing of these models against the altogether more *decisive* conceptions of subjectivation developed in different ways by Fanon, Laclau, Žižek and Badiou. Above all, perhaps, and against the Deleuzian interpretation of his work, it would have to demonstrate the fundamentally and consistently specific orientation of Foucault's work, from his early essay on Binswanger to his last books on ancient sexuality. Needless to say, there is nothing 'specifically' postcolonial or anticolonial about the specific *per se*, and as with the excursus on the universal, the appropriate frame of reference here must itself be as aspecific as possible (it is only the limits of my education that oblige the location of *these* references in mainly contemporary European thought).

(a) We know that the specific must be distinguished from the specified on the one hand and the merely particular on the other. By contrast with the objectifying passivity of the specified and the fleeting inconsistency of the particular, the specific introduces an irreducibly dynamic subjective element, the element of *how* over *what*. The specific presumes a fundamentally *militant* conception of the subject, understood as a decisive and divisive process of despecification. The subject does not pre-exist this process of specification, it is pursuit of the process that brings it into being in the first place (or rather, the subject *is* nothing other than this pursuit). A political class, for instance, is specific to its rivals in struggle before it is specified by its sociological attributes and position: a specific understanding of class, which can alone give rise to a properly political or militant understanding of the term, must be conceived solely in terms of its dynamic relations with and against other classes, other positions in the struggle for political and economic power, rather than identified in terms of occupations and characteristics, let alone habits or 'tastes'. Building on Foucault's lead, we might say that power in the broadest sense is nothing other than the cluster of mechanisms that serve, in the ultimate interests of a particular class configuration, to *specify* its subjects, i.e. to convert its subjects into (classifiable, manageable, governable) objects: to specify or normalise an individual is to confine that individual to its 'appropriate' and predictable place. (The shift from feudal to modern forms of power, Foucault has shown, is not itself a shift from the specified to the specific, but a switch in the tactics of specification.)

To move from the specified to the specific, in the circumstances we have inherited, is not limited to a merely theoretical shift in consciousness. It involves the active dismantling of specifying mechanisms on every level (sociological, cultural, psychological, political, artistic…). As Bourdieu says, we only have a chance of achieving 'real communication' when we systematically investigate and 'master the various kinds of historical unconscious separating us, meaning the specific histories of intellectual universes which have produced our categories of perception and thought'.[1] The unconsciously specified or specifying must be made consciously and *practically* specific. Habitual relationships must be converted into deliberate relations.

A version of such making-specific, or despecification, or deliberation, is at issue for instance in processes of aesthetic defamiliarisation (which foreground, relative to the ordinary or familiar, the isolated and extra-ordinary experience of perception as such, without immediate reference to the specification of what is seen), in existentialist configurations of decision or choice (which emphasise relations of existence before demonstrations of essence), and in psychoanalytic treatment (which refers the development of character or neurosis less to matters of innate disposition than to distinct histories or relations of desire).

Every making-specific is thus an irreducibly subjective process, and the subject is nothing other than a *practice* of de-specification. The subject *qua* subject can only exist at a distance from the specified or objectified – or as Sartre would say: at a distance from the temptations of bad faith [*mauvaise foi*]. This distance is its only 'definition'. If every modern conception of the subject must still compare itself with Kant's, it is because Kant was the first to abstract the pure *form* of despecification – the emancipation from all 'pathological' heteronomy – as the sole *content* of free subjectivity.[2] There can be no deriving concrete, specifiable answers to the general question 'what should I do?' The actions of a free subject cannot be determined through reference to a positive collective conception of the Good (civic virtue, public order, general prosperity...), any more than to personal ambitions or inclinations. Strictly speaking, subjects only acts *as subjects* – i.e. as free from determination – when they themselves prescribe the norms that bind them, with the force of their own deliberate commitment.[3]

(b) It is an illusion however, to believe, as some partisans of the Kantian and existentialist traditions do, that this freedom truly *isolates* the subject. Once the subject is simply *cut off* from all specification it can only become – as it does with Kant himself, and to a degree with Sartre, Žižek and Badiou as well – a rigorously singular category. A specific conception of the subject, by contrast, will identify it with the process of despecification itself, i.e. with the process that converts essentially static (habitual, coercive, unconscious...) relationships into dynamic and deliberate relations. The process of subjectivation, or despecification, is sustained by an assumption of the active *work* of relating to others and through others, to oneself. The specific subject is necessarily, and at every stage of its existence, a subject-with-others. The subject's intersubjective orientation is part of its *nature* in the strictest sense. In Marx's words, 'the human being is in the most literal sense a political animal [...], an animal that can individuate itself only in the midst of society'.[4] Being-with [*Mitsein*] is indeed, as the early Heidegger suggested, an effectively transcendental dimension of experience.[5] Specific individuals *are* what they are only in their relations to other individuals. Relationality thus implies both the original and irreducible distinction of its terms (distinct from the very *beginning* of their relation), as well as their equally original co-implication: the self is only distinct from the other *as* co-implied with the other. This is why there can be no question of deconstructing relationality as such. the related terms only have the degree of self-identity that they have *because* they are differed and deferred through the medium of the relation itself. Relational terms are constitutively ex-centric, and it is this very ex-centricity that endows them with the potential to sustain a consistent self-identity – which means: to maintain a consistent practice of relating to others, a consequential practice of deliberation. In short, only relational beings can maintain an active fidelity to the universalisable implications of a 'specific' decision.

(c) The specific can be distinguished from the singular in two other ways. First, whereas the singular *Creates* the situation in which it operates, the specific is always specific-*to* (though not specified by) a situation external to its operation. I take for granted the principle presumed by any activist or interventionist conception of thought: any element can be individuated only with reference to a precise situation. Or more exactly – only with reference to the relationships that serve to produce an apparently stable and coherent situation, be it historical, political, social, personal, psychological... . We know that even at the very general level of the species, an organism's present existence is nothing other than the ultimately fortuitous result of its selective adaptation to that environment; in evolutionary terms, 'what a body can do', to adapt Spinoza's phrase, is the cumulative result of competitive interaction with the opportunities provided by this environment. Relations with other species are in the most literal sense constitutive of any particular species, including the human species.

Second, where a singular configuration presumes the immediate articulation of both limits of its exclusive scale of existence – the infinitely large with the infinitely small, the infinitely far with the infinitely near – every specific understanding of individuation interrupts this articulation by distinguishing relatively autonomous *levels* of analysis. Discernment of these levels identifies the various planes of description and action that make up any particular situation. For instance, in biology, the levels of organelle, cell, organ, organism, group of organisms, species, and ecosystem; in linguistics, the levels of the *mérisme*, phoneme, morpheme, word, and sentence; in history, the levels of geographical evolution (or *la longue durée*), economic and social change, shifts in collective *mentalité*, breaks in the pattern of cultural inheritance, and political events: each level has its own distinctive coherence and 'speed', each is subject to forces and pressures of a distinctive kind.[6] For the subjects that belong to such situations, discernment of such levels is itself part of the situation's de-specification, undertaken at a critical distance from the apparently continuous configuration of the whole.

Only some such discernment can prepare the way for an intervention suitable to each particular level. Only the rigorous discernment of economic, social, cultural and political spheres, for example, will allow for effective intervention in any one sphere – and this no matter how significant or complex the relations it might entertain with other spheres. As both Said and Badiou suggest, in very different ways, any particular subjective engagement must begin in the present of a particular situation and can initially change only *that* situation. That you must use the specified language of a particular community does not mean you cannot use that language to question its accumulated conventions and clichés (Said); that we always exist, objectively, within some sort of status quo (or 'state of the situation') does not mean that, as *subjects*, we are unable occasionally to subtract ourselves from this state and act in keeping with a universal truth, i.e. a principle that holds for all those belonging to this situation, including those excluded by its state (Badiou).[7]

A specific understanding of individuation thus assumes that the world of experience is made up of components that, however complex their inter-componental relations might be, are as discrete or 'modular' as those which populate the world of chemical elements or biological species. Every specific intervention takes place in the medium of such discretion. For the particular *speaking* beings that we are, it is of course language itself, language as the field of actively intersubjective discourse, that provides the paradigm of such a medium. Our every word, Voloshinov reminds us, is 'the product of the reciprocal relationship between speaker and listener',[8] and any discreetly individual identity, to use Taylor's borrowed phrase, is 'fundamentally dialogical [...]. my own identity crucially depends on my dialogical relations with others'.[9] Every concrete use of the abstract pronoun 'I' is specific to a particular locutionary situation, and it is as specific to this situation that it counts as *one*, as *a* first person, the inexhaustible complexity of a particular speaking subject. This is how the operative level of the I at least *allows for* the isolation of a specific and decisive enunciatory *present*, one enabled by its mutual co-implication with a you (whether explicit or implicit). Such co-implication, however, should under no circumstances be mistaken for the confusion of self and other. Rather, the specific always implies a form of autonomy in something like Castoriadis' sense:

> Autonomy, as I understand it in the field of the individual, is not a watertight frontier against everything else, a well out of which spring absolutely spontaneously, absolutely original contents Autonomy is an ongoing process, whereby you always have contents which are given, borrowed [.] It is in this world that we have to have a workable and effective concept of autonomy Autonomy does not mean I am totally separated from everything external [. .but that in] relation to my own contents, which are 99 per cent borrowed

[.] from outside, I have a reflective, critical, deliberative activity, and I can to a significant degree say yes and no.[10]

Relationality, in short, is not itself dialectical (even though many relations are clearly inflected in a dialectical way). Relation is the unchanging medium and transcendental condition of our existence. Once despecified, particular relations are capable of virtually any manner of investment or determination, but relationality itself does not develop, does not tend toward consensus (Habermas) or dissensus (Lyotard). Relation does not progress toward the realisation of its own autonomy (Bourdieu) any more than it flaunts its own impossibility (Spivak). Relation is not a category or construct liable to deconstruction (Derrida, Agamben). Relation does not orient the creature in the 'non-relation' of an infinite responsibility to its transcendent Creator (Levinas).[11] Relation is not made up of anything more primitive than itself, and has no substance other than the individuals it relates. Relation does not distribute its 'terms' in a singular dissemination, but provides the medium in which these terms persist and change.

So my argument against Glissant's 'Relational' *créolisation* and its various postcolonial equivalents in no sense depends on a denial of the actual reality and growth of inter-cultural relations as such. My resistance concerns their allegedly exemplary status and their apparently political implications. The definition of the specific defended in this book *presupposes* both inter- *and* intra-cultural relationality as the transcendental condition of every possible identity. Identities are *banally* relational, so to speak. Simply, there is nothing *in* this condition as such that orients the expression of these differences toward an anarchic dissemination any more than toward a disciplined coordination. There can be no automatic derivation of a politics of creolisation and hybridity. The question of whether to organise our differences in terms that privilege heterogeneity or homogeneity is in every case to be answered by a political decision. It is not something to be deduced from a more primitive meditation on Being, difference, community, or humanity. By contrast, one of the singular characteristics of postcolonial approaches is their general claim to orient the expression of differences in line with a general theory of expression itself (expression as differentiation, enunciation as hybridisation, articulation as creolisation, and so on), so as to prepare the way for the conclusion that certain political strategies – national empowerment or militant collective action, for instance – are *inherently* oppressive, Eurocentric, neo-colonial…

There is nothing especially unusual, of course, about a close association of the specific and the relational. Foucault has stressed 'the strictly relational character of power relationships',[12] and Laclau has demonstrated 'the radical relationalism of social identities'.[13] There should be no need to refer here to Bourdieu's well-known conception of 'relational reality' or Habermas' still better known conception of inter-subjective validation. What distinguishes a properly *specific* conception of relationality, I think, is (a) its transcendental (ahistorical, non-contextual) condition of possibility, (b) its constitutively *subjective* basis, its equation of the process of subjectivation with the always laborious process of despecification; (c) its insistence on the partial but nonnegotiable, non-derivative autonomy of the individuals related, and (d) its refusal of any transcendent telos of relation, be it consensus, hybridity, responsibility or dissemination. There can be no automatic deduction of the 'good' inflection from a theoretical study of the nature of relation itself. The only irreducible criteria for such inflection are those which acknowledge the conditions of possibility of relation itself, beginning with the partial, irreducibly *interested* autonomy of those related.

This is why the only two general tasks of a philosophy of the specific are everywhere (i) to despecify, i.e. to denaturalise apparently natural specifications, and (ii) to demystify the pretensions of a singular disinterest. As our most steadfastly 'specific intellectual' once put it, 'the real political task in a society such as ours is to criticise the workings of institutions which appear to be both neutral and independent; to criticise and attack them in such a manner that the political violence which has always exercised itself obscurely through them will be unmasked, so that one can fight against them'.[14] Beyond that, there is no evading the irreducibly deliberate responsibility of deciding a relation one way or another. While the singular presumes that the only valid criteria for Creation are immanent to creation itself, the specific recognises that the essential criteria for action are always external to the particular action itself – and thus a matter of conflict, deliberation, and decision.

Only some such inventively deliberate process of despecification, in my opinion, can offer a viable way of avoiding what Césaire once called the 'two paths to doom: by segregation, by walling yourself in the particular; or by dilution, by thinning off into the emptiness of the "universal".'[15] The specific cannot be reduced to a specified particularity, any more than its practice can be subsumed within the abstract generality of its transcendental condition. The specific recognises 'the peculiarity of 'our place in the world'' yet understands that 'our paths towards the future […] aren't ready-traced on any map; they remain to be discovered, and the job of discovering them is our and no one else's affair'.[16]

Few writers demonstrate the point in more flamboyant fashion than that most brilliantly innovative of contemporary novelists, Severo Sarduy.

SEVERO SARDUY:
SUNYATA AND BEYOND

Sarduy's work provides a fitting climax to this project for two reasons. On the one hand, his major novels break new ground in the singular composition of a fully *Creative* literary world. On the other hand, his later writing works at a distance from any straightforwardly singular configuration, and begins to explore a subtly situated realm of the specific as such.

It is certainly the first aspect that is likely to make the most powerful impression. In most of his mature fiction, Sarduy writes a sovereign exercise in *travesty*, a radical disruption of all given norms (psychological, sexual, ethical, cultural...). Sarduy would have agreed with Baudrillard, that the only 'absolute space is that of simulation'. Such a space unfolds along the lines of flight initiated by its own metamorphoses. It creates, in the absence of all prescriptive criteria, a field of pure 'otherness without others' – a field in which, 'each individual being condensed in a hyper-potential point, *others* virtually no longer exist'.[1] Sarduy writes the *ne plus ultra* of a thoroughly *nomadic* desire. He creates a world where, very literally, 'desire produces reality', in which 'desire and its object are one and the same thing'.[2] Again like Deleuze and Glissant, Sarduy explores a univocal regime of 'constant variation', a singular plane of immanence in which 'everything is real' and everything coheres on the same level, the same exclusive (or all-inclusive) scale of intensity. The plane's infinite extension corresponds rigorously to its infinitely compressed, all-generating point of origin: the (Buddhist) 'void [*sunyata*]' which is both pole and matrix of the scale. Within Sarduy's plane of consistency, forms circulate at speeds which correspond to their power to become-other and eventually, to become-imperceptible, immediate to the void.

With his last novels, however, Sarduy moves tentatively but unmistakably into a specific field of relations with others – a field of a minimally situated (dis)orientation. In other words, although Sarduy's creative itinerary begins as a familiar development from particular to singular, it ends in territory hitherto excluded from the confines of this book. His earliest works had already moved, in an accelerated version of the shift already at work with Glissant and Dib, from a militant investigation of *home – lo cubano* as a certain specified condition, a particular way of *being* in the world – to a highly specific investigation of Cuba as a particular way of *speaking*, a discourse that obtains only in the polyvalent, intertextual relations it enjoys with other discourses. And in his very last works, after repeated experiments in radical deterritorialisation, he steps back from the singular vortex of transformations to sketch a perhaps still more remarkable vision of the specific as such – a field that is positioned but not fixed in place, personal but not psychological, oriented but not determined. It is precisely the question of a *specific* orientation – in relation to a place, to others, to oneself – that supplants or at least complements, in these last works, the problem of a cosmic or singular disorientation.

Despite significant thematic continuities, then, the mechanics of individuation and differentiation in Sarduy's work develops considerably, and this development can be divided into five or six distinct moments.

(a) Sarduy's earliest articles (1959–1960), written in defence of the Revolution, support a 'national culture' in more or less Glissant's sense, i.e. the nation as self-conscious superimposition of distinct traditions and identities: 'folklore' becomes, through its militant nationalist composition, *thought*. Sarduy's first novel *Gestos* (1963) maintains this national context, but as cut off from its capacity for militant action. In Deleuzian terms, *Gestos* narrates the progressive paralysis of the sensory-motor schema, the conversion of actors into spectators, the supremacy of an aesthetic composition over composed actions and reactions. The unnamed heroine, a (black) laundry-woman and cabaret singer pressed into revolutionary terrorism on behalf of her (white) lover, retains a locatable position of sorts, but one 'stupefied' in various ways by circumstances beyond her control. *Gestos* presents a specified world, in crisis.

(b) *De donde son los cantantes* (1967) then presents, in a second moment, a national context composed through the superimposition of different ways of escaping or trading positions – different speeds on the plane of consistency, different powers of transformation and articulation. The aim here is to present a Cuban reality in the very language itself, as opposed to a representation *of* Cuba. *De donde* presents a language-world at the limits of the specific, now beyond crisis because beyond norm. This is a world of *pure* parody. The novel is made up of three loosely connected narratives, corresponding to the three principal ethnographic 'layers' of Cuban culture (in sequence, Chinese, African, Spanish): in the first story, a lecherous General pursues the cipher 'Lotus Flower', character or actress of the Changhai vaudeville theatre in Havana; in the second, Dolores Rondón, Afro-Cuban courtesan from Camagüey, lives her rise and fall according to the peculiar metric demands of the eulogy engraved upon her tombstone, the third episode travels across the centuries through the evolution of the Spanish language itself, a mock-epic journey that eventually processes a rotting wooden effigy of Christ across Cuba.

(c) *Cobra* (1972) and *Maitreya* (1978) – probably Sarduy's best-known works – provide the substance of our third moment. These are fully deterritorialised texts. If they refer to things Cuban it is only as means to a radically singular realm. Both novels defy any attempt at a conventional plot summary; in both novels, as González Echevarría points out, 'there is no effort whatsoever at mimesis, no illusion of creating a fictional world that is a reflection of everyday reality'.[1] Cobra is variously a doll-puppet, a transvestite actress or prostitute working in the Lyrical Theatre of Dolls, set in an unspecified place, her quest for smaller feet (or a sex change) leads her and her double Pup to Morocco and a Doctor Ktazob who performs the castration, and from there into a double 'Initiation', guided by a gang of leather jacketed thugs and/or Tantric Buddhist monks. The novel ends with an 'Indian Journal', set in the India/Cuba confused by Columbus' initial mistake. In *Maitreya*, Sarduy's most openly (and most parodically) Buddhist novel, a first part witnesses reincarnation of the Master in a small boy spirited away by the scheming Leng sisters; a second part follows the career of the twin Tremendas, obese divas on a journey beyond transgression In both novels, desire is one with the movement of metamorphosis and displacement.[1]

(d) Sarduy's last novels, however, return to *some* notion of position, or at least some relation to the loss of position *Colibri* (1984) is a pivotal work (our fourth moment): it retains much of the parodic verve of *Cobra*, but channelled now through the elusive consistency of a central character, a central obsessive object of desire. It narrates the pursuit of the blond, nimble Colibri by the 'hunters' of La Casona, a seedy gay bar set in a Latin American delta, on the edge of the jungle. The composition remains artificial above all, but the metamorphosis at issue here is one regulated by the consistency of what might be called the *relations* of desire – between the blond, nimble Colibri and his Japanese rival, between Colibri and the obese Regente of La Casona whom he eventually comes to replace, and between these dominant 'leaders' and their submissive 'followers'. We might say that *Colibri* writes a re-territorialisation of deterritorialised desire as such (through specifically homosexual relations; through relations between young and old; through relations between beginning and end; through relations to the 'murmur of the earth').

(e) *Cocuyo* (1990) strikes an altogether new chord in Sarduy's fiction, opening a fifth and final moment. it is a work informed by a specifically childish fear and nostalgia for security, a work haunted by a disorientation that can no longer be affirmed simply as cosmic metamorphosis. It narrates the picaresque misadventures of the young Cocuyo, from his early famili-cidal revenge through his confinement in an orphanage whose real purpose – slavery and prostitution – he slowly discovers. *Pájaros de la playa* (1993), finally, is a work organised by confrontation with terminal illness; set in an island hospice, it presents various perspectives on living and dying, remembrance and the refusal of remembrance, different ways of coping with disease, different forms of 'treatment'.

To summarise, we might say that Sarduy's work moves from an initial assertion of a specified national culture to a minimally specific parody of a national culture through to a singular Creative cosmology, before pushing on to engage, finally, in a specific engagement with those limits of the per-sonal that are disorientation and death.

To make sense of Sarduy's work requires recourse less to the conven-tional tools of literary criticism than to a bundle of concepts inspired by philosophy, religion, and cosmology: if Sarduy's work flaunts its supreme *littérarité*, it does so in a most self-consciously *epistemological* sense. Above all else, literature is here a way of perceiving the true nature of real-ity beyond the trivial delusions of habit, with a rigour approaching that of an experimental science. Sarduy notes in 1987 that if the 'new carnavali-sation' of the 'neobaroque' has become an established fact of contempo-rary Latin American literature – a literature of fragmentation, innovation, inversion – 'this neobaroque lacks an epistemology of its own, and more, it lacks a reading that would be attentive to the *substrato*', to what pro-duces it *as* fragmentation, dissemination, and so on (NI, 35). Sarduy's many interviews, critical essays, and theoretical investigations provide a wealth of material for the elaboration of just such an epistemology. As in previous chapters, Deleuze and other contemporary thinkers (Barthes, Lacan, Baudrillard…) retain an immediate comparative relevance here, in keeping with Sarduy's own prescription, 'that it is not possible to think or establish a coherent critical system […] without establishing a dialogue […] with the great constructions [*andamiajes*] of contemporary thought'.[5] And all of Sarduy's work (at least up to our fifth moment), critical or cre-ative, is expressive of much the same epistemology, the same immediacy of void and plane, whose guiding rule is the assumption that 'what disap-pears in the symbolic order reappears in the real to hallucinate us' (MY, 91/207). Writing in all its forms is an actualisation of the Creatively real, rather than the mere manipulation of appearances (or rather, it serves to incorporate the latter within the former).[6] Writing is less a strictly aes-thetic or artistic endeavour than an exercise in *Creative thought* in the Deleuzian sense.

What is at stake here exceeds merely monographic limits. Perhaps more than the work of any other Latin American writer, Sarduy's fiction is invoked to illustrate patterns and suggest shifts across the field in general. Juan Goytisolo finds in Sarduy that 'example of extreme rigour, both literary and moral, which allows us to measure the work and "development" [*carrera*] of the writers of our time; [he is our] point of reference'.[7] For *Tel Quel* critic Philippe Sollers, Sarduy's work is 'representa[tive] of the enormous possibilities of Latin American writing, offering us an absolutely free play of signifiers, narrative, cultural, aesthetic'.[8] As a rule, 'Sarduy is generally thought of as the epitome of the neo-baroque writer of Latin America',[9] 'without parallels in what is called neo-baroque Latin American narrative'.[10] According to Sarduy's friend and most insightful reader, Roberto González Echevarría, his '*Cobra* seeks to incarnate nothing less than the subconscious of hispanoamerican narrative' as a whole,[11] while for his translator the same novel 'represents, in many ways, the culmination of the New Latin American Novel'.[12]

Again more than any other contemporary writer, Sarduy is at the centre of Latin American debates about modernism and post-modernism, 'Boom' and 'post-Boom'.[13] As is well-known, the Boom writers of the late 1950s and 1960s – Carlos Fuentes, Mario Vargas Llosa, Julio Cortázar, Gabriel García Márquez, Alejo Carpentier and others – employed modernist, experimental techniques to disrupt the conventions of characterisation and narration that governed the regionalist telluric novels of the Latin American tradition (exemplified by Gallego's *Doña Barbara* [1929] and Rivera's *La Voragine* [1924]).[14] But according to Sarduy, such 'writing remains in the service of an experience other than itself', be it external reality or inner subjective privacy ('*le vécu, quel mot!*') – magical realism itself being merely the 'bastard solution' that mixes the two.[15] Sarduy objects strongly to the Boom novelists' alleged 'lack of rigorous thinking about writing [...], the critical "impressionism" they indulge in. Everything they do is subjective, idealistic, without method or seriousness'.[16] Sarduy's own writing, then, is characterised both by a kind of literary autonomy and by a rigorous 'method' explicating this autonomy.[17] However playful, inventive and transgressive Sarduy's writing, it is this *rigour* that will most concern us here. Sarduy insists that,

> of thought's three transgressions as discussed by Bataille (thought itself, eroticism, and death), I believe that only one, the first, continues to exist with its original force [...]. The one thing the bourgeoisie will not tolerate, what really drives it crazy, is the idea that *thought can think about thought*, that *language can talk about language*, that an author *does not write about something but writes something*, as Joyce said (ES, 238/12-13)

The issues raised by Sarduy's work are thoroughly consistent with those considered throughout this book. As González Echevarría notes, 'Sarduy has served as intellectual bridge between the French literary theoreticians and the Latin American intellectual community'.[18] One of the more promising young writers of the immediate Revolutionary aftermath, Sarduy left Cuba in 1960 on a scholarship to Paris and eventually decided to remain there. In France Sarduy became the companion of François Wahl and a close friend of Roland Barthes and Philippe Sollers. His writing invites comparisons with certain aspects of the work of Artaud, Bataille, and Blanchot. He makes a major contribution to what Lyotard described as that 'strange aesthetics in which what supports the aesthetic feeling is no longer the free synthesis of forms by the [Kantian] imagination [...], but the failure to synthesise' – a literature of the *purely* incommensurable, a *différend* without mediation.[19] Like Glissant, Sarduy's early work works toward a recuperation of an explicitly 'national' culture, the liberation from inherited 'repression'.[20] Like Johnson, Sarduy affirms a version of Buddhism and accords supreme value to the renunciation of position or 'attachment'. Like Dib, Sarduy acknowledges an interest in gnostic, esoteric theosophy. Very much as an 'Occidental exile' in the Ishraqi sense, he believes with Jambet that 'the day is near when we will read al-Suhrawardi as we read Hegel'.[21]

Most of all, before Deleuze and Guattari came to describe their 'desiring machines', Sarduy knew that 'the poet, freed from all romantic residue, continues the work of machines' (ES, 311/85). Sarduy's fiction is extraordinarily compatible with Deleuzian 'mechanics' in the properly cosmological sense.[22] Alongside Goytisolo he works toward 'deterritorialisation',[23] and with *Cobra* he elaborates a kind of 'nomadisme sexuel'.[24] Sarduy's novels, like those of Deleuze and Guattari's *Kafka*, evoke rhizomatic spaces, 'places that are not at all juxtaposed, that send the characters to the four corners of the earth'.[25] Citing the *Logique du sens*, Sarduy supports Deleuze's 'subversion of Platonism' through the proliferation of 'copies-icons or simulacra-phantasms' (SI, 59/96). Again like Deleuze and Guattari, he works for 'the destruction of the individual as metropole – the conscience or "soul" – with its colonies: voice, sex, etc. Dissolution of the I [*del yo*]'.[26] Echoing Deleuze's 'world without others', he writes so as to let go 'of the weight of one's self, of the punctual watchfulness of the Other in the omnipresent shape of the Law'.[27]

Sarduy's point of departure is the conclusion reached by years of avant-garde speculation, from Sartre's *Transcendance de l'ego* to Deleuze's *Nietzsche et la philosophie* and Lacan's *Ecrits*: 'the self, the ego or personality, the individual or what have you, is not one, monolithic, something solid, visible, certain, but a bundle [*haz*], a series, constantly changing', and 'illusion consists of solidifying this series of instants, of making of it a personality, an entity'.[28] Sarduy's baroque tableaux 'do not admit in [their] dense, charged network the possibility of a generative I, of a central individual referent which would express itself – the baroque functions in the void [al vacío] – which would orient or contain the overflow of signs' (BO, 175). Instead, Sarduy's most famous works – De donde, Cobra, Maitreya – strive for the liberation of desire, of pure expenditure-in-itself, from its *subjection* in an 'economy of work', broadly understood. His fiction breaks with both poles of transcendence analysed in *Anti-Oedipus*: the impersonal over-coding of desire accomplished by the State, and the personal normalising of desire accomplished through the adoption of a (post-Oedipal) identity. Liberation from both is achieved through dissolution of *family* in the widest sense: the refusal of genealogical continuity, the confusion of sexual distinctions, the contingency of all identifying marks. In these novels, Sarduy writes a deterritorialisation at both the personal and the planetary level. Like a Tantric mantra, like Artaud's 'Alchemical Theatre', Sarduy's *Cobra* presents 'an inhuman world'. Through tumultuous conflicts and metamorphoses, it 'ultimately evokes in the spirit an absolute and abstract purity, beyond which there can be nothing, and which can be conceived as a unique sound, a defining note, caught on the wing, the organic part of an indescribable vibration'.[29]

The great question that arises, of course, is how to make sense of this other, 'indescribable' coherence. Most of Sarduy's published readers emphasise the *essentially* fragmented nature of his fiction, and present it as generally 'contradictory, irreducible to a rational, coherent synthesis',[30] a feast of 'exaggeration and multiplicity', of the 'polyvalence of signs underscoring the multiplicity of sense',[31] the product of 'conflicting interpretations' themselves generated through a 'perceptual disharmony between appearance and reality'.[32] Sarduy's work is generally presented as supremely polyphonic or dialogical, a carnivalesque dispersion of narrative authority and ontological univocity across an unlimited range of incompossible voices and registers. As Montero puts it, 'in the polyphonic text, there is no hierarchy of narrative voices; all contribute to the plurality of discourse'.[33]

Now we know, with Sarduy's friend Barthes, 'that a text is not made up of line of words offering a single, in some sense theological meaning (which would be the "message" of the Author-God), but is a space of multiple dimensions, in which mix and struggle varied writings, none of which are original'.[34] As González Echevarría observes, 'it seems that the major change in recent Spanish American literature is the gradual abandonment of the theme of cultural identity' and its replacement 'by local narratives'.[35] The whole question is then, what sort of relations govern this local variety? What sort of locality? What sort of narratives? Is it a matter of specific or singular difference, of relational plurality or non-relational multiplicity? Is it a matter of difference *between* others, or rather of a self-generating, self-differing difference that obtains precisely in the absence of such relations, in a world effectively without others? As we have seen throughout this study, this is a distinction that postcolonial literary criticism finds very difficult to make.

It is generally agreed that 'Sarduy destroys the mimetic function of literature through which the novel considered itself transparent to external "history"'.[36] The assumed consequence is a complication of opacity or mediation, an accumulation of incompatibilities, a relentlessly *equivocal* proliferation of meanings. González Echevarría, for example, reads Sarduy's work as striving for the 'recuperation' of 'local, contingent' histories that 'resist global interpretation', as writing in 'the defence of [threatened traditional] religions and cultures, the preservation of a type of symbolic activity on the margins of the totalising claims of the West'.[37] Sarduy's commentators usually assume that the fragmentation in question is indeed polyphonic in more or less the Bakhtinian sense – i.e. that it is achieved through the *inter-action* of distinct, specific voices and perspectives.[38] But many of these same commentators follow Sarduy's own insistence that his text eliminates all reference to an external world and eschews all merely 'cultural' indicators. Sarduy's commentators generally present *both* a writer of 'polyphonic' differences and one through whom 'all opposites are annulled'.[39]

The reception of Sarduy's writing has yet to find a fully viable way of relating both these aspects of his work. Two broad approaches prevail. The first emphasises the specified, Cuban aspects of his writing, and underlines the generally parodic intertextual relations maintained with major figures in the Cuban, Latin American, and Spanish traditions. According to this reading, Sarduy's work, like that of Haroldo de Campos, 'resembles the exaltation and unfolding of a region of diction, of a speech space as vast and baroque as the map of his country'.[40] This Sarduy is read in terms of vernacular allusions, 'encyclopaedic' references, and cross-cultural relations.[41] By contrast, the second (and more compelling) approach stresses the radical autonomy of Sarduy's text, its affirmation of an *espace littéraire* in more or less the Blanchotian sense: intransitive, self-referential, hermetic, austere. Sarduy certainly affirms the 'autonomy of the aesthetic process' (ES, 256/32), a strict literarity (266/41) whose contemporary elaboration is still mainly associated with the work of his friend Roland Barthes. More than any other major critic, Barthes has encouraged the prevailing reception of Sarduy as writer of *textes de jouissance*,[42] as aligned with Mallarmé in the effort to produce a 'free signifier' (i.e. one freed of any 'message'[43]). Barthes quite appropriately finds in Sarduy an assertion of the *souveraineté du langage*. In often quoted words, he says that this sovereign expression deploys only but supremely 'the great theme particular to the signifier, the only predicate of essence that it can in all truthfulness endure, and which is metamorphosis [...], demonstrating [...] that there is nothing to see behind language'.[44] Most of Sarduy's critics follow suit, striving to evacuate his work of all but purely 'literary' devices.[45]

The limits of both interpretations are obvious enough. For Sarduy has always maintained that 'I am Cuban from head to toe!',[46] and any reading of Sarduy must acknowledge the Cuban specificity of his work. This specificity must be assessed, however, *along with* the explicitly 'deterritorialising' aspect of his work. Sarduy himself hopes that if his work 'transgresses, surpasses, the novel of the Boom', it will be because 'my books are not specifically "Latin American". I don't believe that literature or art should be informed by an ideology predicated upon an ethno-geography'.[47] As we would expect, Sarduy has a horror of 'indigenism – this affliction!'[48] If he plays with reference, it is less to work for the recuperation or consolidation of place than to advance, through the disruption of reference, 'toward distopia: the no-place, wandering, the attribute – and not the ambience – of he who is without a land'.[49] At the same time, the ascribed autonomy of his texts is belied in a trivial sense by the fact that he draws happily enough from perfectly 'real' sources,[50] indeed that he draws much of his inspiration from *science*.[51] More importantly, Sarduy insists that *littérarité* as such is never more than the means to a more profound end. 'What has been cele-brated in my work, very kindly, to the point that I have been called a 'millionaire of language', is what matters least to me. Namely, the baroque, the brilliance [*el brillo*], the humour, the fascination, the verbal elegance, the multiplication of adjectives: all of this seems to me to be the exterior of the work, the screen which hides the work [...;] this is not (the) writing [*eso no es la escritura*]'.[52] The real task of the critic is to consider not only 'the impermanence and emptiness of everything',[53] but how and in what sense *the void is form* [*el vacío es la forma*]. Form is the void'.[54] This equation is conceivable only in a realm which – like the Buddhism that inspires him or the Deleuzian *Logic of Sense* that runs parallel to him – *identifies* language and reference, rather than separates them. Sarduy's writing claims a prop-erly *singular* Creativity beyond the dichotomy of language and reference altogether, elaborated within one univocal desiring-production, in pursuit of an immediate actualisation of sense in line with the Deleuzian example.

The full measure of this sovereignty eludes, I think, even the most pow-erful effort to bridge the two main critical approaches: González Echevar-ría's *La Ruta de Severo Sarduy*. González Echevarría rejects a reading of Sarduy's fiction informed mainly by Sarduy's 'own theoretical principles' (iv), and stresses instead its 'cultural, historical and linguistic referents' (v), to illustrate the point that 'Sarduy faithfully reflects – with near micro-scopic attention and documentation – the themes and social and ideologi-cal realities of his time'.[55] González Echevarría reads Sarduy as 'an act of recuperation' (*Ruta*, 3), an effort 'to recuperate Cuba through literature'.[56] Even Sarduy's most recent texts are supposed to provide 'a rigorous analysis of the American tradition', an attempt to answer the question, 'what does it mean to be a hispanoamerican writer?' (211). Assuming that 'figural interpretation' is at the centre of Sarduy's text (176), González Echevarría's general approach is *allegorical*, of the type '*x quiere decir y...*'[57] In the terms of his seminal readings of Latin American fiction as a whole, Sarduy remains a problematic but firmly territorialised writer, a writer of what González Echevarría calls 'archival fictions'.[58] 'Archival fictions [...] delve into the structure of mediation, as the constitutive structure of Latin American narrative.'[59] As González Echevarría insists, the archive presents 'not a quiet dialogue of texts – pluralistic utopia [...] – but a clash of texts, an imbalance of texts', i.e. relations of competition and imitation *between* texts' (9–10). A similar assumption underlies his influential presentation of Sarduy's novels as post-Boom fictions – a condition characterised by the affirmation of 'local narratives', the 'absence of metadiscourse',[60] and the consequent 'elimination of ironic reflexivity'.[61] Here a fully specific plurality prevails, just as 'the Archive questions authority by holding warring discourses in promiscuous and mutually contaminating contiguity, a contiguity that often erases the difference separating them' (*Myth*, 153; cf. 182).

This possibility of a contiguity without difference is precisely the question at issue in this chapter, as throughout this entire study. The intelligence and utility of González Echevarría's readings is beyond debate. But I will argue that the aspect of Sarduy he presents as equivocal, territorial and pluralist (in *De donde* through *Maitreya*) is better conceived as *univocal, deterritorialised*, and *singular*. Where González Echevarría investigates 'mediations' and 'figurative interpretation', I see confirmation of a literal immediacy on the Deleuzian model. Where González Echevarría celebrates polyphonic pluralism, I read univocal multiplicity. Where González Echevarría explores the constrained negotiation with a particular (Latin-American) situation, I see affirmation of an inventive power Creative of all situations. And far, then, from subverting traditional narrative authority, Sarduy's most experimental works affirm something like that literary *sovereignty* claimed, in their different ways, by Johnson, Glissant and Dib. We must take the full measure of Sarduy's asserted 'autonomy of writing', achieved very precisely through 'the continuous erasure of spatial points of reference', the assertion of a 'coexistence in one instant [...]; it is this synchronisation of the action [...] that most of all sends us back to the exclusive dimensions of the written'.[62]

These dimensions are, to use the terms developed in my Introduction, *real* but not *given*. Literature *is* autonomous, but is given as trapped, as mediated in a world of significant exchange and predictable relations-with-others.

263

'Language is unlimited', but it is given as limited: 'the imagination, I would say, is like a bird that, disposing of the whole sky [*todo el aire*], limits its flight to a few gardens, to a single forest'.[63] The whole effort of Sarduy's work is to gain access to *todo el aire*, to the 'place that has no limits, that space of conversion, of transformations and disguises: the space of language' (ES, 261/35). So I will argue that the relations which govern Sarduy's 'plurality' – relations *between* fragments, so to speak – must be understood in terms of the dialectic between given and real which dominates Sarduy's thinking about literature and existence itself. This dialectic is governed in turn by a certain conjugation, inspired by Buddhist philosophy, of the void and the infinite. First and foremost, it invokes a voiding of all specified forms, the dissolution of all positioned identities. It then calls forth, immediately, a self-differing infinity of contingent mutations, like so many transient actualisations of a compressed, intensive virtuality, very much in the Deleuzian sense. As Sarduy reads them, Antonio Saura's neo-baroque portraits pursue a similar itinerary, aiming 'not to individualise, to personalise the model, but on the contrary, to dissolve it in the anonymity of a few features common to the [human] species' – secure in the knowledge that these features will indeed 'come together [..., at the] zero degree of the face', in that singular, pre-individual face common to all humanity.[64]

The fragments that make up the world of *Cobra* and *Maitreya*, then, are less the stuff of relational differences than very literally *interchangeable* actualisations of a single virtual voice, elements of a single univocal expression traced at infinite speed. The extraordinary intertextual dimensions of Sarduy's work should be understood above all as a celebration of this still more fundamental *univocity*. They meet the requirements of an unlimited *combinatoire*. The writing that survives the 'voiding' – Sarduy's version of the Eternal Return – is by definition open to a mechanics of splicing, citation, and appropriation in which everything exists on one and the same level, configurations of one and the same stuff. As González Echevarría points out in *Ruta*, 'it is obvious that when he writes about Saura, Marta Kuhn-Weber or Botero, Sarduy is talking obliquely, or through the echo, about himself' (218). The truth of literature applies equally to all inhabitants of its sphere. Everything can be converted, everything connects.

This major moment in Sarduy's work is governed by a principle of fundamental *reversibility*, loosely derived from Einstein's elaboration of space-time. Within general relativity, space and time become 'reversible the one in the other', aspects of 'one and the same undifferentiated energy: as if the whole universe was nothing but a controlled system of mutations and metamorphoses'.[65] The characters of *De donde son los cantantes* or *Cobra* live a fundamentally inexhaustible existence, a flow of events *without consequence*: Dolores Rondón's story is told in reverse, beginning with her death,

Cobra comes back from the dead as if nothing had happened; Maitreya, of course, is reincarnated, while Colibri eventually replaces the Regente who pursues him. For Sarduy as for Baudrillard, 'what is fascinating is always what belies this so solid-seeming order of temporal irreversibility'.[66] Hence the precise imperative: 'ex-terminate every term…'.[67]

I will argue that Sarduy does indeed move beyond this dialectic (beyond reversibility), but not in order to return to some specified notion of a more fully 'Latin American' writing. Rather, he moves on because the elimination of relations through the void can no longer satisfy a writer whose own relation to ex-termination and disorientation appears to go through a dramatic shift. Living resources, so to speak, suddenly appear limited rather than unlimited. The celebration of infinite *dépense* ceases to be a properly sustainable option. The later Sarduy seeks to consolidate a minimally positioned relation *to* disorientation, to the voiding of forms, without returning to a substantially specified identity or tradition. Through confrontation with disorientation and disease, time adopts a more linear, accumulative weight. *Cocuyo* is organised as *Bildungsroman* and detective story, a double coming-into-awareness; in *Pájaros de la playa*, illness and old age force a 'preparation to not be', while *Siempreviva*'s attempted reversal of time is a sham that only confirms the heavy precedence of those past events (the death of the architect, the flight of Isidro) that condition her present choice.

I Territorial beginnings

The point of departure for Sarduy's movement through the singular to the specific is itself, like that of Dib and Glissant, firmly specified. Sarduy's earliest writings are mainly contributions to an emerging national culture in post-Batista Cuba.[68] In the ten months following the January revolution of 1959, Sarduy – then 22 years old – published eighteen short pieces in the new daily, *Revolución*, seven of them in its literary page, 'Nueva generación' and another five in the literary supplement *Lunes de Révolución*. The fictional contributions – three brief stories – provide punchy, ironic variations on what were already conventional revolutionary themes. 'El torturador', for example, stresses the grotesque sadism of the Batista regime, through a lampoon of the last words of 'the best torturer of the [Republican] regime' (the fictional executioner of at least forty insurgents and the inventor of machines that pop eyes out of sockets and nails from fingers…) as he is led, unknowing, to the revolutionary firing squad.[69]

In most of the critical pieces, likewise, Sarduy emphasises the political dimensions of art, its relation to 'the spirit of our nationality',[70] its power 'to influence […] apparent reality, decisively, and transform it'.[71] An art worthy of the name is to be 'explored within Cuban reality'.[72] Some kind of '*preocupación social*' is an emphasis in many of these articles[73] and most are directed toward 'the success of a national art in our country'.[74] Poetry figures here as '*une forma viva de la Revolución*',[75] while with Rolando Ferer the young Sarduy works to make 'our national theatre as lofty [*alto*] and powerful as the Revolution itself'.[76] Above all, painting is 'the art that most defines us'.[77] Sarduy's privileged values are here strongly autochthonous. He insists that Cuban painting should produced only by Cubans , that 'we should go towards it alone, as our work evolves in an absolute faith in ourselves, never importing elements' from elsewhere.[78] As a rule, the goal is to 'participate vigorously in history, [as] called to this opportune moment by the strong voices of the people [*las fuertes voces del pueblo*]',[79] to show that 'our people is indeed interested in the national theme'.[80] In one piece he goes so far as to say that 'if Cuba had had a figure like Diego Rivera it would not have had a dictatorship'.[81]

Sarduy's early cultural nationalism should not be mistaken, of course, for a commitment to some kind of crude socialist realism. He has no time for more 'badly painted portraits of bearded men'.[82] Like the early Glissant, the Sarduy of 1959 refuses recourse to folklore.[83] He recognises that a directly militant or 'objective' art is 'useless':

> It is too late. Popular Painting, Objective Art, had to be done before [..]. Yes, we want a national art but we can produce a national [style of] painting without filling canvases with peasants and palm trees, we can produce a national theatre without *gallegos y negritos*, we can produce a national poetry that does not sing to tourists and soldiers .[84]

Ultimately, however, the early Sarduy is less opposed to '*an arte de panfletos*' than to 'an excessively gratuitous art, whose only merit lies in its technical wonders'.[85] What matters most at this point is how 'poetry forms tangible reality and begins to take on the category of fact [*hecho*]'.[86]

II *Gestos* (1963): toward paralysis of the 'sensory-motor schema'

Sarduy shapes his first novel around the 'inquiry, almost of an inquisitorial order, around what we Cubans *are* [*qué somos los cubanos*]. Around what is Cubaness [*la cubanidad*]', a question whose 'clear impulse was, obviously, the fact of the Revolution'.[87] But now the answer is deprived, or almost deprived, of the instrument that lends a relative coherence to earlier answers (telluric or Boom) of the question. This instrument corresponds to the mechanism of what Deleuze very broadly calls the 'sensory-motor schema': the integrity of character, the ability to react and act, to intervene effectively in a situation, and so on. In *Gestos* such sensory-motor connection has almost been replaced by other, less 'personal' principles of coherence: the coherence of composing frames, a kind of verbal painting; the meandering of blind movements through virtually deserted space; a collective stupor, a crowd's drifting into inertia. In *Gestos*, we witness the conversion of (Revolutionary) actors into (post-revolutionary) spectators, what Deleuze will call 'pure seers', occupants of 'any space whatever'.[88]

The plot is straightforward by comparison with Sarduy's later novels. It is set in Havana during the last moments of the Batista regime, in a city marked by terrorism and the rhythm of shuffling crowds, mixed with a mainly Afro-Cuban music that alone retains a clearly distinct voice. The heroine, an anonymous mulatta who sings in a club by night and works in a laundry by day, forever complaining of headaches and stress, is eventually charged by her shadowy lover with the task of planting a bomb in the city's main electrical plant. After the explosion the narrative cuts to the heroine's performance of what appears to be *Antigone*, followed by scenes from a corrupt political campaign which ends amid the uncertainty of Castro's imminent arrival in the city.

If *Gestos* was published at much the same time as the first generation of Revolutionary novels in Cuba, it has little in common with these mainly linear narratives driving from oppression and bad faith toward *engagement* and the redeeming triumph of 1959.[89] *Gestos* presents a world of rumours and suspicion, the fragile, anxious moment of the *last* – the last days of decadence – more than the euphoria of the first steps toward a new beginning. The permanent present tense of the novel ensures a lack of depth, the isolation of fragmented action without connection to a past or future. Above all, the novel moves to equate the supremely militant action – terrorism – with theatre. Our heroine *acts* in both senses; more, she acts as if spectator of her own role, itself scripted, as we shall see, according to mainly aesthetic demands.[90]

The novel opens with a distinctly *nouveau romanesque* vision of the *mass* as such, the crowd manipulated and pushed, as people 'go from one side to the other, from one side of the street to the other. The circulation never stops [...]. They go, always rushing, they come from work, they go, they go, they still go, they come even if they have no work...' (GS, 7). This is a recurrent theme (52–54). In much of the novel, the two major characters often 'speak in the third person, attributing to others what they think themselves, what happened, what they just heard. They say what others say, think what others think, answer only when others ask them' (47). Sarduy explains that as the Revolution was a 'movement that negates the subject [...], the self in favour of the collective', so his goal with *Gestos* was to render 'this always moving collectivity as *tropisms* (for that is what is signified by these movements at the limit of the nameable, movements of the subject as much as of the collective)'.[91] (Sarduy adapts from Nathalie

267

Sarraute the literary use of 'tropisms' to name the microscopic description of pre-individual and effectively pre-verbal responses provoked by almost imperceptible perceptions or interactions.[92]) In *Gestos*, what this negation or collectivisation achieves is the conversion of subjects into objects. In the absence of 'subjects', the crowd accumulates ('they never stop coming' [120–121]), swells, flows, and above all, *flees*: 'they flee without knowing from what' (67). By the novel's end, with Castro's troops on the verge of triumphant entry into the city (the very moment of civic unification in more conventional Revolutionary novels) this 'tumultuous crowd' disintegrates into an almost irrecuperable disorder. 'They have run away, they have dispersed, they have thrown themselves against each other, they have rushed away in every direction' (135).

In this absence of a collective orientation, the heroine and her elusive lover wander in a present of their own making, a sequence of '*nows*'. 'Now they are talking, alone' (GS, 23). 'Now they walk down an alley between two buildings' (25). 'Now she climbs the deserted staircase, crosses the corridors' (56). And so on. The heroine's *now* is deprived of all psychological depth, at the mercy of a slightly frantic style of constant crisis management, forever burdened by 'the general oppression of others, of things' (34) and cursed by a permanent and acute 'headache'.[93] Characters provide only a minimum of perceptive synthesis. Impressions are recorded in staccato succession. For instance, the arrival of the police: 'A car. The headlights which turn and pass over your eyes. Blinding. The brakes. The slippery pavement. The voice. The white roof…' (64). The components of description tend to accumulate in tersely noted fragments,[94] and space does not cohere in alignment with a conventionally positioned perspective. The opening urban scene sets the tone: 'the gaze is unable to integrate into a whole the upper part [of the house] and the luminous signs, the window full of souvenirs and the red sign of the bus stop. You'd think it was a montage, the superimposition of two engravings' of different times, representing the same place (9).

In other words, the *seat* of coherence, so to speak, is here reserved less for a character, or for a collective civic integration, or for the plot, or indeed any sense of oriented development, than it is immediate to the very pulse of time itself, the rhythm that links repetition with acceleration and deceleration, an almost musical orchestration of crescendos and decrescendos. The novel as a whole follows the pattern set by the orchestra which rehearses in chapter four:

> They set about tuning their instruments, running the scale, from top to bottom and bottom to top, pausing sometimes on a note which they repeat over and over [. .]. Then, from the chaos of instruments, noises, conversations, the melody is set by a flute, then repeated by the piano, which repeats it until

picked up three violins, soon joined by the singers who repeat the previous notes, and weight them with a confused text, banal, almost an onomatopoeia [...] And so on to the point of satiation, of nausea· the same theme, the same notes, the same words are taken up by one of the singers, or by the whole trio, or in a duet of singers and piano, of the violins and the flute, to the exhaustion of all the possible combinations. (GS, 41–43)

Gestos presents descriptive fragments largely beyond synthetic or sensory-motor recuperation. It presents 'noise, outside. The road rises and falls, flees and comes back, in waves. Curve. Stairs, houses, bombs, gardens, roots, rivers, hands which say goodbye, rifles, chateaux which turn and burn, grenades. Everything in disorder. Grows distant, comes closer, rises, turns' (39). People come and go, 'voices trail off, diluted among the noise' (53). Just like the orchestra he often describes, Sarduy repeats these movements of rise and fall, fade-in/fade-out, to saturation, until it is repetition itself that becomes the very substance of description. 'A scratched record repeats, indefinitely, the same piano cords, the same phrase' (55); 'In the street one hears confident footsteps, which come closer, move away, come back, forever repeating the same trajectory' (57); 'The two hands join, sway, separate, join, sway [...]. The hands join, sway, separate, join. The hands' (79). Such reiteration evokes the mildly hallucinatory quality that prevails on the *edge* of sleep, a semi-conscious awareness of speech and movement reduced to their purely sensory qualities (volume, pitch, rhythm). Or rather, less than a fully dreamlike atmosphere, it evokes precisely that border between sleep and action, the failing effort to remain awake (35–36).

But it would be a mistake to over-emphasise the paralysis of the sensory-motor link in this first novel. Definitive collapse is reserved for later works. However fragmentary the novel as a whole, its second half is mostly taken up with the story – almost a thriller – of our singer's successful terrorist operation. As her contact says, 'the moment is not for headaches and sculpted nails' but for action (GS, 74), and the action is duly narrated as more suspenseful than parodic. It is a sequence quite unlike anything else in Sarduy's work, beginning with detailed preparations and moving through near disaster with the police to her successful penetration of the plant. Once inside, presentation of the scene evolves *with* (rather than beyond or against) her own moving perception (GS, 100). As she moves through the installation, it is as if the installation itself moves. 'Cubes give rise to cylinders [...]. The door *comes closer* [..]. *According to the rhythm of her walk*, through the sequence of black lines, the machines move, spheres pile up...' (GS, 100–102, my emphasis). Framed in relation to traversable space, perception here retains *some* link to that sensory-motor coordination that *is* the heroine, even if it is organised more in the interests of the framing itself

269

Moreover, what sets *Gestos* clearly off from Sarduy's later fiction is the fact that if characters (both collective and individual) have lost a certain measure of ordered coherence, this order is retained, as if at their expense, at the level of the narration itself. The narrative voice here generally remains, through its occasionally experimental variations,[95] calmly, even flatly assertive, neutral, and detached. Music, for example, remains more an object of description, as opposed to the very medium of description. On occasion Sarduy adopts an almost ethnographic tone: '[Afro-Cuban] music is arbitrary and the words without rhyme or scansion are freely improvised [...]. Sometimes two or three voices unite for a chorus, or else different soloists sing different melodies [...]. Often, the verses flow without pause...' (GS, 11). The integrity of the description itself is not put into question by this 'arbitrary' rhythm. Again, if *Gestos* is punctuated with explosions, the text does not itself explode. If anything, it mirrors the numb, stupefied curiosity of the onlookers:

> [S]hards of glass fall [...], the accumulation of dust extinguishes the patches of light. In the stairways of the building, people run, move in groups, among the cries, the voices, the crying of children, to the vestibule, to the street. People leave in tumult. Then a great silence swallows everything [..] The bomb stuns them still as if the explosion hung in the air, latent.. (GS, 45–46)

> The windows blow out broken into tiny splinters, the glass vibrates, rises in the air, like so many birds [..]. The steel groans, cracks, breaks on the roof and takes off like grapeshot. A cloud of glass, birds, and iron falls to the street Further on, the worm-eaten wood of the barrier explodes in uneven fragments, red and white. The rusty lawn disappears under the accumulation of unsoldered cables, shards of blue marble, dented boxes, tiles. On the greasy water of the river, the debris of the insulation floats and accumulates on the banks, among the rushes.
> On the pavement, black dust [...]. People freeze, rigid. (104–105)

In short, *Gestos* maintains an ambiguous relation to the coherence of character and place, while suggesting a transfer of authority from what Deleuze calls 'composed' to 'composing forces' – from the agency of positioned actors, to the autonomy of artistic composition as such.[96]

III Organisation by frame

It is in its explicit, studied attention to the organisation of scenes as so many *tableaux* that *Gestos* most anticipates Sarduy's later work. As Sarduy likes to confess, 'thanks to a deformation or deficiency that has always been with me, I have no sense of direction and cannot orient myself. But a painting – even if the perspective is distorted – lends me this ability'.[97] It is precisely the artificial, imposed coherence of a tableau that compensates for Sarduy's lack of a natural or 'innate' sense of orientation.[98] Sarduy insists that 'what I see always passes through painting'.[99] More, for Sarduy 'painting and writing are the same thing and I don't know which I'm going to do when I sit down at the table':[100] '[I] write with colours, [...I] paint not with oil and canvas, but syntax and paper – the blank [*blanco*] of the support is the same'.[101]

Sarduy himself presents *Gestos* as 'an effort to reconstitute a reality – the Cuban reality – from plastic [*plásticas*] perceptions. The electric plant I describe, for example, is a Vasarely and then a Soto; the walls are Dubuffet. These gestures [*gestos*] are not, as has been said, the movements of people who speak [...], but gesticular painting'.[102] The novel is laced with visual arrangings, 'panorama[s]' (GS, 27), down to the prevalence of constructions like '*algunas vueltas más descubren dos patios...*', '*van apareciendo*', '*se ve[n]*', '*dejan ver*', '*parece*'.[103] A whole staging of the gaze: 'From this same window [...] you could see the musicians perfectly. You can hear them very distinctly' (GS, 41); 'We see him [...]. We hear [...] the first words of his speech. We see him gesture, take off his hat. We hear [...]. We see [...]' (127). *What* is thus seen is generally arranged as an independent composition, in different styles (impressionist, Cubist, monochromatic) – so independent, in fact, that when we come to a passage describing a rain of 'plastic bodies' bouncing down a spiral metal staircase, it takes a moment to realise that Sarduy is indeed describing children's dolls rather than people – props in a theatrical earthquake (GS, 71; cf. 97). The coherence of a scene is determined by the principles of its composition, rather than limited by the individuality of the objects composed. For example, the white and blue of the police van blends with the white and blue of police uniforms in broad strokes of colour, blurring the distinction between the two (50). Again, when a man approaches a stoplight changing red–orange–green, the colours spill over on to his red socks and green trousers: even as he moves into the centre of the representation – the apparent subject of the scene – it is the colours themselves that determine the distinction of shapes or roles.[104]

A similar painterly attention to composition characterises much of Sarduy's subsequent fiction. In later novels, the further dissolution of character enables the autonomy of the composition as such, as frame and subject merge in the description of one painting-flow. For example, in *De donde*, the fresco in which appear 'Little Torture Face, the two Fat Ladies, Chong and Si-Yuen, all with shaven skulls, naked to the navel and barefoot, on top of clouds...' (DS, 130/47) is itself part of the scenery: the navel of one of the Fat Ladies in the fresco is the lock on the actual room's door (DS, 131/49). In *Cobra* in particular, much of the text reads like transcription of images set in an especially eclectic gallery of styles, each stamped with a signature aesthetic. *Cobra's* Pup is drawn through a series of metamorphoses presented as a '*Petit Ensemble Caravaggesque*', through successive associations with Rembrandt's *Night Watch*, Velázquez's *Las Meninas*, Carreño's *Vestida*, and Pieter de Hooch's *Interior*.[105] A rainy street appears à la Brueghel: 'behind the rain people pass, outlines blurred; beneath the striped halo of street lights, blue rectangle, the store windows frame fruit baskets full of apples, pastry bowls dripping honey, kitchen boys with starched white caps, iron ovens where, stuffed with almonds, surrounded by laurel wreaths, whole animals revolve' (CB, 128/71). Several critics have explored Sarduy's signalled interest in the CoBrA painters implied by the novel's polysemic title, who provide the author with 'the plastic equivalent of a certain kind of deformation, the distortion of verbal linearity'.[106] The more strictly textual equivalent of such distortion, in much of Sarduy's fiction, is provided by a certain ritualised, highly *artificial* notion of theatre or theatrical staging. Sarduy compares his baroque to 'a theatre in which the characters would be texts',[107] and as we shall see, theatrical themes figure in most of his novels and dominate much of *De donde*, *Cobra* and *Colibri* in particular.[108]

The decisive moment is achieved when painterly composition takes over all initiative, so to speak, from the painted character who becomes a mere posture in the profusely detailed canvas. Action blurs into tableau, until the action is less a reaction to or alteration of the situation than simply another contribution to its composition. On one occasion, Cobra dreams that she is

> among reefs dashed by waves. Stuck to the stones, rags, locks of hair, candles and votive offerings; cylinders crowned with livid turbans. around the lime marabout tombs arose She made an offering of saffron and flowers and burned camphor in circles, among chalk and snail marks she plucked a pigeon. over the turbans she spilled ointments, she polished the cylinders with a thick milk which, among the rocks. splattered copper-toned crab shells (CB, 111/62)

Surrounded by Santería symbols, Cobra figures here as artist of her own representation, marking, anointing, polishing the scene itself. In *Cobra*, even a chase scene, the 'action' sequence *par excellence*, succumbs to the stasis of the frame: pursued by the police, when Tiger stamps his foot 'flowers sprout everywhere': 'sandalwoods and white lilies bud on the enemy motorcycles; gardenias on the handlebars [..]. The foliage covers the cops, remains of petrified pursuers [..]. The vice squad, in its frozeness, is already a snapshot, a photostat copy of the primitive squad, a wax museum, a gathering of cardboard demons. the abandoned props of a cheap circus…' (CB, 146/82). Beyond the parody of flower-power, action is transformed into spectacle, the animal into vegetable, through a kind of organic petrification that spells the utter dissolution of the sensory-motor schema. The body becomes thread of the single cosmic weave, painted into the canvas of one all-embracing Tantric aesthetic: 'corpses fell./Scorpions nested in the ears./Crows covered the frozen feet. Mushrooms sprouted on the orbs. Snakes came into their anuses' (CB, 224/126). The body does not *act*: 'the body is a support [*un chassis*...], the body is a page',[109] canvas or 'ground' for the proliferation of detail, an accumulation that exceeds reaction.

From *Gestos* to *Cobra*, Sarduy moves from what Deleuze describes as (a) the priority of montage in the older, classical cinema – the 'composition of movement-images as constituting an indirect image of time', achieved via the coordination of 'differentiated parts, relative dimensions and convergent actions', accomplished precisely through 'the *intermediary* of montage' – to (b) the perfect fusion of montage and image in 'the direct time-image', the intuition of pure time without *any* sort of intermediary or mediation, 'free from any linkage' (be it psychological, neurological or technological).[110] Sarduy's relation to graphic art evolves in keeping with the general movement of his work as a whole. In an early moment, painting plays a properly mediate role – it 'serves me as intermediary [*intermediario*] with reality [...]. Plastic perceptions allow us, I would say, to decipher reality'.[111] But it soon becomes wholly self-sufficient or immediate, an art through which 'the object and its inner sound have been freed to such an extent that we have become their object' (ES, 316/90).

Eventually, the lavishly baroque aspect of Sarduy's painterly descriptions yield, in accordance with the general movement of his work, to a monochromatic sobriety, the visual equivalent of silence. Rothko's paintings in particular evoke, as one of Sarduy's sonnets suggests, 'nothing more than silence; the feeling/of being in his present',[112] and it is no surprise that for Sarduy 'Rothko is a genuine god [...]. His paintings are life'.[113] At the limit such life prevails, like Deleuze's vital force, in the absence of the merely *living*, just as 'the monochromatic is the limit of painting and, in the space of a baroque of subtraction [*barroco de la substracción*], its final crown/corona [*corona*]'.[114] The monochromatic is immediate to life as such, un-mediated by particular organisms (particular modulations of life). It is extracted through 'the successive ascesis of effects and media/means [*medios*]' (53), until it opens directly on to 'the *fulguration* of the void, the absence of colour' (54). The more elements or dimensions (textures, gestures, forms, colours) thus 'subtracted', Sarduy explains, the more 'concentrated' and *intense* are those that remain. 'The last of them, the unique colour, has received the density and impact of all of those eliminated' (54). At the pole of the scale, of course, lies '*el blanco*' – the blank whiteness of the Tibetan Kundalini Shakti, which 'signifies access to a point of superior

273

contract between cosmic energy and the physical body of the practicant',
an experience 'beyond colour', the 'sarva-anandamaya' or *pleno-de-Ale-
gría*, a state 'overflowing with joy, in which the adept participates in union.
It suggests a point of light beyond all colours – and by definition, beyond
all words – such that it is represented as something uncoloured.'[115]

IV Sarduy's neo-baroque

Sarduy's many discussions of the baroque are the obvious place to begin an
analysis of his aesthetic. As Guerrero observes, the baroque has become a
highly fashionable term in contemporary Latin American studies, applied
variously to Ernesto Sábato, Alejo Carpentier, Lezama Lima, Reinaldo
Arenas, Fernando del Paso, Guillermo Cabrera Infante, and associated
more or less loosely with Neruda, Paz, and Retamar, among others.[116]
According to the most comprehensive survey, the Latin American neo-
baroque explores 'a shattered world expressed through waste and ellipse,
poles which group together so many other baroque resources: reiteration,
intertextuality, semantic games, hyperbole, theatre, parody, deformation,
oneiric atmosphere'.[117] More than any other contemporary author, perhaps,
Sarduy is responsible for the prevalence of this particular usage.

Sarduy's use of the term begins with a rejection of the specifically
grounded or territorialised notion of the baroque promoted by Eugenio
d'Ors and Carpentier. According to Carpentier's famous definition, the
American baroque is a faithful expression of *natural* American reality. 'Our
art has always been baroque', because America is a continent of extremes,
of 'hurricanes and cyclones';[118] 'everything that refers to an American
cosmogony [...] is within the baroque'.[119] As you might expect, Sarduy
objects to any notion of the baroque as 'a return to nature – to a preferably
disordered nature', and to any notion of art 'animated by the nostalgia for a
paradise lost' or by the marvels' of the New World's 'incredible vegetation'.
Rather, for Sarduy, the baroque is 'the apotheosis of artifice, as irony and
derision of nature; writing is a practice of *"artificialisation"*', and 'my world
is the world of neon, you might say, of pure artifice'.[120]

In an important article, Sarduy breaks this process of artificialisation
down into three aspects. (a) 'Substitution' ensures constant displacement
along a metonymic chain of signifiers more or less according to Lacanian
prescription, and thus the violation of any natural or inherent relation
between signifier and signified. (b) The 'proliferation' of signifiers keeps
the play of desiring substitution in constant motion while (c) 'condensation'
ensures 'permutation, mirroring, fusion, mixing between the elements
[...] of the signifying chain' – a veritable process of becoming-other.[121]
With Glauber Rocha, for example, 'it is not simply a matter of a variation of

structurally analogous sequences – as occurs in Robbe-Grillet's cinema – but the creation of a tension between very different, very distant sequences that an indicator obliges us to "connect" in such a way that they lose their autonomy' (174).

Precisely because Sarduy's baroque tends to dissolve specific frontiers and to burrow rhizome-like *through* distinctions rather than maintain them, the question of its own historical particularity is difficult to assess. On the one hand, he presents it as an exceptionally privileged aesthetic, closest, in some sense, to the reality of the purely aesthetic as such. This presentation tends to downplay both its chronological and geographic limitations, to include things as diverse as Lezama Lima's fiction, Kepler's cosmology, Spanish American cathedrals, and 'the temple of Kajuraho, that enormous Indian pyramid of copulating figures'.[122] On the other hand, however, Sarduy presents the baroque as an 'epistemic break [*corte*]' very much in Foucault's sense.[123] Throughout his work, Sarduy affirms the notion of a coherent 'episteme' peculiar to an age, inclusive of its science as much as of its 'fiction, music, painting, cosmology, and architecture' (NI, 9). Like Foucault, Sarduy is looking for 'the epistemology underlying all the mechanisms of the baroque', the 'episteme which the baroque makes explicit and puts into practice'.[124] This particular episteme includes: Kepler's description of elliptical planetary orbits; Harvey's discovery that 'the circulation of the blood traces a kind of ellipse around the heart'; the redistribution of space in a 'baroque city [which] presents itself as an open weave, without reference to a privileged signifier to orient it and confer its meaning upon it' (BO, 181); a similar reorganisation of the physical space of the (Catholic) Church, now 'decentralised', almost rhizomatic ('a building without specific entrances and exits'[125]). Perhaps the closest comparable paradigm is Deleuze's revaluation of the Leibnizian baroque as a perception creative of its object, which 'entails neither falling into nor emerging from illusion but rather realising something in illusion itself'.[126] Deleuze's baroque yields not 'a variation of truth according to the subject but the condition in which the truth of variation appears *to* the subject. This is the very idea of Baroque perspective', as it is of modern Relativity, a 'perspectivism as a truth of relativity (and not a relativity of the true)'.[127]

Sarduy's baroque retains the moral, polemic aspect of its historical predecessor[128] – but turned now, after Nietzsche, *against* the basis of conventional morality. The 'revolutionary' quality of the baroque lies in its refusal of conservation, of communication, of responsibility. Sarduy's baroque affirms a morality of 'squandering, of waste',[129] the very opposite of that piety-inducing *lack* which Deleuze and Guattari find at the heart of the Oedipal system. Building on Bataille's example, Sarduy's own notion of *dépense* has both an economic, an erotic, and a cosmic function. A baroque economy puts an end to work as such, 'the moral of *homo faber*, of being-for-work',[130] and replaces it with 'game, loss, waste, ecstasy' (BO, 210):

> To be baroque, today, I think, means to threaten, judge and parody the bourgeois economy, based on the stingy – or as one says, 'rational' – administration of goods, at the very centre and foundation of this administration and everything it supports: language, the space of signs, the symbolic cement of society and the guarantee of its functioning, of its communication [.]. In the baroque, language, contrary to its domestic use, is not the function of information but of pleasure, it is an attack on moral and 'natural' good sense on which is based the whole ideology of consumption and accumulation.[131]

A baroque eroticism, consequently – as opposed to sexual reproduction – 'carries with it no "information"'.[132] Like Baudrillard, Sarduy is opposed to all notions of sexual economy, sex as *production*, i.e. a process envisaged as 'an individual enterprise based on a form of natural energy'.[133] Sarduy's impersonal, artifice-driven 'eroticism [is] a purely ludic activity, which parodies reproduction in a transgression of the useful and 'natural' dialogue of bodies' (BO, 210) in a language beyond thrift. The baroque accomplishes the textual equivalent of free love, 'the uninhibited coupling of words',[134] because 'like baroque rhetoric, eroticism implies a total rupture with denotation' (BO, 210–211). Sarduy agrees with Barthes: 'figuration [is] the erotic body's mode of apparition in the profile of the text'.[135] The erotic is the figurative in itself, the figure which relates to no 'proper' meaning. As we shall see, Sarduy rejects the figurative *relation* of metaphor in favour of the self-contained velocity of the ellipse.

The erotic body is 'cosmic', finally, because like the body without organs of *Anti-Oedipus*, it is immediate to its 'partial objects' without the intermediary interference of organic constraint.[136] With Veruschka's body art for instance, the body itself is 'like a blank page'[137] – the place, then, of an *unlimited* inscription (unlimited by earlier, 'organic' inscriptions). The erotic body is both subject and object, producer and product of the same desiring-production. The body is itself 'book' or text, spoken by a single indirect discourse without subject.[138] Eros escapes conscious or semantic censure: 'eroticism renders the antipodes identical, because its true meaning escapes reason' (ES, 234/9).

Sarduy's next novel writes the decisive step toward this truth.

V *De donde son los cantantes* (1967): at the limits of *lo cubano*

De donde is Sarduy's first fully 'baroque' novel and anticipates much of the theory he was to develop in the early 1970s. But it does so through a particularly contorted 'answer to the same problem as before, the problem of *cubanidad*', i.e. an effort to determine the 'ontological possibilities, the possibilities of *being* [de *ser*] of my country'.[139] *De donde* is written very much within the relation, the measured *distance*, of exile and home. (Remember that Sarduy had left Cuba in 1960, and as the regime changed over the 1960s, decided to stay in Paris.) 'In distancing myself from Cuba I understood what Cuba was'.[140] According to Sarduy, 'Cubans are incapable of addressing the theme of the nation head-on [*frontalmente*]. The theme is always addressed indirectly'.[141] *De donde* is not a deterritorialised but a deterritorialising text, an exercise in radical defamiliarisation. The constituent link between language and territory has been broken, but the language used remains – once reworked – the language of *that* territory. As Barthes says of another of Sarduy's books (*Escrito*), 'this book comes not from Cuba but from the language of Cuba'.[142]

The Cubaness of *De donde* is apparent in the many *cubanismos* documented by Sanchez-Boudy. in the allusions to popular songs,[143] to Afro-Cuban religion and mythology, and above all, perhaps, through recourse to that characteristically Cuban form of humour, *choteo*. 'The choteo', Sarduy explains, 'is generalised parody', basis for '*una risa total*'. Sarduy sees choteo as 'a kind of *koan*, a kind of zen exercise' – that is, as a suspension of the normal laws of meaning and inference, a violation of worldly expectations that forces the reader to look for another, other-worldly coherence, a coherence beyond the dichotomy of model and copy or original and fake. 'Through the choteo, *everything* becomes mask, simulacrum, make-up, fake'.[144] It effects a 'systematic' if 'indecent descent from the empyrean to the dungheap',[145] abolishing the hierarchy of low and high, vulgar and sublime, profane and sacred.

But precisely because choteo, like the koan, tends toward an *absolute* subversion, so with *De donde* Sarduy takes the specifically Cuban to the frontier of a singularity which exceeds its territory; the novel performs a kind of singularisation of the Cuban, its 'becoming-other' than itself. In the midst of *lo cubano*, we find kirsch factories, a subway, snow, and 'subtle indications of a flora and fauna that are not Cuban. The process ends with the total assimilation with the exterior [*lo exterior*] that is the snowstorm'.[146] This subversion of territorial integrity is as relentless and exhaustive as Auxilio and Socorro's obsessive search for the elusive Mortal of 'The Entry of Christ into Havana' (DC, 189/106).

De donde aims, then. to give a 'total' representation of Cuba, but as a *virtual* totality, the impossible sum of its possibilities. It sets out to achieve 'the rescue of realities that were lost, among infinite possible realities, when History selected its reality [...]. The poet's role is to discover those potentialities, make them visible, reflect them in the concavity of language and even use them to displace the truth of written History [...]. Writing is seizing the possible and its exclusions' (ES, 298/71-72); it is writing against the ontological repression of history itself. In this way, *De donde* contributes to that 'catharsis which is being effected [in Cuba], that of all the repressed censures during the centuries beginning with the Inquisition'.[147] And to give such a virtual 'total image of the country' is at the same time, 'paradoxically, to deny its unity'; the virtual totality is extracted from the fragments of its *given*, merely apparent unity.[148] Sarduy agrees with his sometime mentor Lezama Lima, that 'Cuba is not a synthesis, a syncretic culture, but a superposition. A Cuban novel must make explicit all the strata in that superposition', all the 'tales' of its history – Spanish, African, Chinese – 'and achieve Cuban reality through the meeting of those tales, through their coexistence in the book's volume'.[149] Whereas syncretism, however heterogeneous its ingredients, flattens approximations in the elaboration of a new norm – a new 'breed', so to speak – superposition accumulates contiguous approximations as so many actualisations and counter-actualisations of the same virtual *event*. The result, as González Echevarría notes in *Ruta*, is 'probably the most furiously experimental text in Latin American literature of the time' (98).

In a brief note appended to the novel, Sarduy explains that its three 'fables share in common three characters – or themes: Mortal, the blond Spaniard whose Castillian is spotless and who possesses the always uncertain attributes of power, and Auxilio and Socorro [Help and Mercy], also called the Flower Girls' (DC, 235/154). A kind of preface, entitled 'Curriculum Cubense', introduces the characters. Both Auxilio and Socorro want 'to disappear, to be someone else: therefore the constant transformation, the wealth of cosmetics, artifices' (DC, 237/156). The first story, 'By the River of Rose Ashes', takes place under the sign of China, and narrates Mortal's amorous pursuit of a supposed soprano called Lotus Flower, of the 'Chinatown Opera House'. Mortal is here a 'lecherous old general' usually referred to as 'G', while Auxilio and Socorro are 'chorus girls at the Opera and two-bit whores' (DC, 235/154). The second (African) story tells the story of the mulatta Dolores Rondón, her rise and fall synchronised with the political career of the local councillor, senator and ex-senator Mortal Perez; the sequence is organised not chronologically but according to the verbal order imposed by the ten-line poem she has engraved on her tombstone. In the third (Castillian) story, 'The Entry of Christ in Havana', Sarduy says,

> Mortal is an absent young lover who is going to become a metaphor of Christ. Auxilio and Socorro search for him; the desire for Mortal that ails them will turn into a thirst for eternal life. Here the two women will illustrate the two main currents of Hispanic culture – Faith and Experience in the tapestry – opposites which polarise the continuous turns of the texts [...], if Socorro quixotises, Auxilio is a Sancho Panza collection of proverbs. With a wooden Christ and Bruno

– the Prince and his guest, Hiccups, in the tapestry – both will go on a pilgrimage through Cuba. The corruption of that wood corresponds to the corruption of time, and context. growing anachronisms, other landscapes superimposed on the Cuban, the reiteration and unreality of snow.[150]

Compared to *Gestos*, *De donde* operates at a wholly different speed, a wholly different vector of literary transgression. The drug of choice, so to speak, moves from aspirin to cocaine (DC, 236/155). And whereas 'transvestites' in *Gestos* were introduced either for 'the folkloric note' or as preamble to the main act,[151] transvestism here becomes the very substance of writing. Sarduy agrees with Baudrillard: 'we are all transsexuals'.[152]

There is space to consider in more detail only the first story, 'By the River of Rose Ashes'. Here 'everything is looking, contemplation, evanescent reality'.[153] The narrative presents 'a series of appearances, of illusions [...], it is a matter of heterotopias, of places which become detached and are transformed, of *espacios décrochés* [sic].'[154] Lotus Flower herself is a pure cipher – perhaps only figment of the General's imagination, perhaps character in a mock Chinese opera, perhaps actress and/or whore. General has an apparently simple demand: 'All I want to know is where she is, who she is.' But the Sisters are adamant: 'We can't just say it any old way. She's a secret, she's an appearance, she's...' (DC, 134/52). As a performer,

> Lotus Flower leaps up and, like the fish that jumping out of water becomes a hummingbird, she flies among lianas Now she's the white mask striped by shadows of sugar canes, now the flight of a dove, the streak of a rabbit. Try and see her. You can't [...], she is mimicry.[155]

After performing, Lotus 'will unmask herself. She will cease to be Empress Ming; she will be a piece of paint-smeared hide' (DC, 115/31). But 'if Lotus Flower is actually is a paint-smeared fraud, Auxilio and Socorro [really] are gifted with (and abuse) the power of metamorphosis' (235/154). 'Chorus girls of the Shanghai District Opera, [...they] are keepers of the secret of the seventy-eight metamorphoses' (DC, 112/28): 'they are fluorescent, they are acetylene, they are drums that hypnotise birds, they are helicopters, they are chairs at the bottom of an aquarium, they are obese eunuchs [etc.]' (DC, 119/35). They are initiates into the mysteries of becomings in a broadly Deleuzian sense, virtualities able to take on an effectively unlimited range of actualisations. They demonstrate the full range (and more) of what a body can do. They incarnate 'continuous variation'. Without warning,

> in the twinkling of an eye the cry 'Metamorphosis' was heard in G flat, and the Two [sisters] immediately appear mounted on racing Vespas, at full speed, and armed with Thompson machine guns, two-tongued knives, javelins, flame-throwers, pum-pum guns, hand grenades and tear-gas bombs [.]. What is even more surprising is that each One is supplied with three

heads and seven arms The tetradecapodous and hexacephalous aluminium
artefact is a sight to see!
  My dear, what a getup! What a Sivaic band! [.] Auxilio pulls a hair out
of [an 'albino stream'], knots it twice and blows upon it, and at the sound of
'Metamorphosis!' it turns into a snake that wriggles in the air like a butterfly
in someone's mouth, breaks against the ground and becomes a chameleon,
toad, giant shrimps So she populates the square with animals: monkey
actors, red antelopes on sun clocks, frightened cranes, camels laden with
hydraulic organs [etc] (DC, 117-118/33–34)

The result is a systematic distortion of scale, the intermingling of parallel
but incompossible universes. The General wears 'himself out in all the
Possibles', (DC, 122/39), as the text shifts without clear transition from theatre to brothel, from rehearsal to performance, from reality to dream ('was it
all a dream?' [DC, 122/47]), even from theatre to Mass (DC, 132/50). The theatrical description itself moves imperceptibly between the 'reality' portrayed
on stage and the artifice of its portrayal. Auxilio and Socorro 'come out butterflies and turn into toads', become hummingbirds, while their Director
'glides in outer space', through imitation velvet curtains and cardboard walls.
The flight of the Divine Ones, 'chlorophyll striped', is described as 'suspended by plastic wires the colour of the background curtain'; 'Lotus Flower
[…] crosse[s] northern auroras of stage time' (DC, 113/29). The drugged
Director's dreams merge with his stage directions. Dialogue among the
('real') characters is presented as theatrical script. The whole sequence, in
short, is staged, a staged sequence 'about' staging itself.
  Conventional logical distinctions cease to obtain. One of the more
characteristic features of Sarduy's prose is to use several options or simi-
les in a single sentence, drawn from often incompatible registers. For
example, in 'The Entry of Christ', we learn that 'Mortal left for Córdoba,
he left for Medina, he stayed, all at once, because he is everywhere' (DC,
178/94). Again, in 'Curriculum Cubense', Auxilio shows customers at a
Self-Service restaurant a picture of her 'in a guayabera shirt and cap,
drinking coffee in front of a cardboard tower, or a Mardi Gras float, or a
mausoleum lettered in Arabic'.[136] The staging itself is all, and permutations
of perception are in themselves the principle motivation of the text (cf.
DC, 117/33).
  In *De donde*, however – as distinct from *Cobra* or *Maitreya* – these
permutations remain at least partially limited by the constituent relation of
perception itself, the relation between author and reader, between 'reality'
and 'representation'. The deterritorialisation of Cuba that is *De donde* is
achieved *through* the disruption of relations which continue to function,
or rather, malfunction (and not simply in the absence of these relations). As
in most of Sarduy's work, the authorial position *per se* presents itself as

undecided among the infinite range of possibilities as any other character (cf. 114/30). The author remains commentator, complicit with the reader–voyeur. As the Sisters loot the General's apartment, for example, the narrator protests: 'Oh this is too much. Look at that. Auxilio is dragging a red marble bathtub mounted on four bronze paws toward the street...' (DC, 135/53). Again, considering four entangled bodies – the General, Auxilio, the 'oriental in white rice powder makeup', and the 'big-titted black girl, very double breasted' – the narrator has to rush to keep up, so to speak. 'Already they're breaking loose, already they're looking at each other. How cute!' (DC, 103/22). Like a harried sports announcer, the narrator–commentator is always a step behind the events reported, and always slightly in the dark as to what will happen next. For example: 'whether she was dressed to receive ambassadors from the provinces in the Garden of Ming; or wearing black slacks and a linen guayabera, as usual [etc.], we'll never know' (DC, 108/24). Elsewhere, with drums rolling and the General marching, we wonder: 'does he hear the bagpipes of a march? Does he receive voices of command?' (DC, 123/40). These kind of questions make a direct appeal to the reader to impose some degree of order upon the text, and the novel is punctuated with friendly assurances that true textual chaos will be kept at bay (see esp. DC, 133/51–52). Confusing it may be, but the confusion of 'By the River of Rose Ashes' remains, at least in part, the confusion *of* the specific roles attributed to spectator, author, actor, and character.[157]

VI Empty foundations

These specific roles, in Sarduy's next two novels, are undermined to such a degree that it makes little sense to refer to them at all. The form of expression that prevails in these Sarduy's most celebrated works no longer relates in any substantial way to the play of relations *between* speakers, between speakers and spoken. Rather, the texts cohere, essentially and paradoxically, in that absence of all relations that is the *void*. Like Baudrillard, Sarduy writes on the assumption that literally 'nothing remains for us to base anything on';[158] at the origin of all things there is simply 'a uniform light/without colour or support [*suporte*]' (NI, 47). Already in *De donde*, 'everything is perceived as pure effect, as emptiness [*vacuidad*], as pure system of metamorphoses, of metaphors'.[159] Through to *Maitreya*, the void-based orientation of Sarduy's work becomes ever more emphatic.

It should be stressed from the beginning that Sarduy's explicitly Buddhist notion of the void is not mere negativity or absolute emptiness, but rather the *evacuation of actuality*. The void is that wholly virtual, *actually* inaccessible yet all-determining singularity–multiplicity analogous in some ways to al-Suhrawardi's pure Light or Deleuze's infinite speed. The void is beyond thought or representation, forever empty of actuality yet incomprehensibly full of intensity. It is the seat of pure *Creative* energy, the purely implicated source of all explicated expression. According to Sarduy, very much in the Buddhist tradition, perceived 'REALITY is not the real [*LA REALITE n'est pas le réel*], but the effect of a phantasm which has as its function the filling, with its apparent fullness, of an irreparable void'.[160] We must engage with this assertion in all its complexity.

God's death is old news: the only rigorous consequence is the originality of the void. In the beginning was the void, and nothing more. Unbounded by any substance or actuality external to itself, Sarduy's void or zero is rather the sufficient foundation *for* the infinite derivation of actualities (or numbers). 'It is the Void, or the initial zero, which in its mimesis and simulation of form projects a one from which the entire series of numbers and things will begin, the initial explosion [...] of pure non-presence that, transvestised in pure energy, engenders the visible world with its simulacrum'.[161] The only adequate *expression* of this Creative principle is the one offered by the material universe itself – the explicated consequence, so to speak, of that exploded singularity that was the Big Bang, the original, founding void of space itself. Today's universe is 'in violent expansion, without limits, without any possible form: a mad race of galaxies to nowhere' (BO [Fr. ed.], 15); its expansion is *without limits* because its foundation leaves no trace other than its explication in space itself. There is nothing, no-space, outside the echo of the Bang itself. 'Time, space and material are nothing more, say, than metaphors for one and the same "reality"',[162] whose extension is itself nothing more than the explication of an originally pure intensity. As a critic of literature or art, Sarduy looks then for those works of art 'in which are reflected the diverse models of the origin. Where are the multiple echo chambers of this forever inaudible explosion? Where are the shadows projected by this ray of black light whose intensity is the same in all points of space?' (BO [Fr. ed.], 19).

First impressions aside, *these* are the questions that best orient a reading of even Sarduy's most 'excessive' texts. Baroque word-play – like colour with Rothko or movement with Nureyev – provides merely 'external material [of] the least importance', compared with the real effort: 'to *say* the void [*decir la vacuidad*]'.[163] Articulation of the void is Sarduy's only ultimate goal. The exuberant play of 'actual' simulation provides nothing more than means to this properly meta-physical end. 'Beyond the pleasure of what it stages, like predictable, familiar fiestas, simulation enunciates the void and death' (SI, 84). The difficult question concerns the relation between this enunciation (simulation) and what is enunciated (the void). The one must become immediate to the other, through the dissolution of *given* regimes of significance, interpretation and communication. 'Real' literature must displace the regime of signs and equivocation, in order to clear a space for an asignificant but fully self-sufficient univocity. For like every singularity, the void is radically self-sufficient. 'The void, as Buddhists know very well, suffices to signify itself'.[164] Only to the degree that he recuperates a language immediate to the void can Sarduy be said to affirm a neo-Deleuzian 'autonomy' of language, a reality that 'materially writes', a 'writing flush with the Real'.[165] A becoming-real of writing must 'abandon, obliterate, or at least displace, transform, "shake" the foundation of meaning', itself the ultimate 'guarantee of the functioning of a civilisation based [...] on the correspondence without residue or ambiguity between the two terms of the sign'.[166] The obliteration (more than the evacuation) of meaning as such is generally part of the price to be paid for access to a fully Creative reality, i.e. one unlimited by the constraints of significance.

Hence the essentially redemptive aspect of Sarduy's work, his refusal, for all his hedonism, of a worldly condition not so different from that condemned, say, by St Paul: a world of (commercial) exchange and (merely *common*) sense.

> There is a kind of writing which serves as epistemic support of the bourgeoisie, as of any established system. The economy is nothing more than one of the visible figures [*cifras*] of this central code. By undermining writing, by transgressing the laws, we erode the whole edifice of common sense.[167]

Through the 'subtraction' of this interested mediation of the real, 'emptied out toward pure legibility', the exemplary work of art 'repels all complicity, all will to read, exhibiting a total simplicity, an absence of meaning [*sentido*] which is the guarantee of its estrangement', its pure exteriority or immediacy.[168] In the absence of the mediate, the original work of art approaches the *original* void in the immediacy of the instant. The same effect is produced, at either end of the chronological scale, by the prehistoric megaliths of Carnac and a painting by Antonio Seguí, both described in Sarduy's *Cristo de la Rue Jacob*: 'the place of the inscribed refers, as if this were the essential thing, to the place of things neutral, to the void' (RJ, 66/83). In each case, Sarduy looks for contributions to Deleuze's dream of an aesthetic timed to coincide with the 'dawn of man'.[169] For instance, the exemplary experience of Henri Le Saux:

> He wanted to dissolve into totality, into a proliferation of all colours and all things, or into that thought in which all things have the same dimension [ ] Then [..] dissolution into everything manifest, into everything endowed with appearance. was no longer enough for him. He wanted to stop being; he sought annihilation, sought to suppress even the idea of an 'I', to reach a silence so absolute that there would be no one capable of verifying his existence (RJ, 39/49)

In (or toward) this eventual absence of mediation, the coincidence of void and excess becomes, tautologically, immediate. 'In art' – that is, in the absence of commercial mediation – 'proliferation and disappearance have the same sense [*sentido*]. The extreme baroque, the total saturation of the work, the horror of the void [...], leads to the same result as radical austerity, rigorous economy [...–] this "reduction of media" [*medios*]'.[170] Both are achieved through the elimination of what is *between* – i.e. what Deleuze calls the sensory-motor schema, and Sarduy the 'author', or the mediating subject. 'The rococo, superabundance, lack of restraint, *gaspillage*, produce the same effect as total austerity. I mean that a chapel by Churriguera, a façade by Aleijadinho [...] are as lacking in "author" as a sculpture by Bob Morris, by Larry Bell, by Smith.'[171] Just as Deleuze distinguishes two approaches to a wholly literal or 'imperceptible' writing – the ascetic *épuisement* of Beckett, or the unlimited proliferation of Joyce[172] – so Sarduy concludes that the effort to 'enunciate the void [*decir la vacuidad*]' can have only 'two solutions'. Either the direct presentation of '*la tela en blanco*', a restriction of writing to 'the production of a hai-kú, that is, to writing a single word on a page, thereby convoking the whiteness/blankness [*el blanco*] directly'.[173] Or, through 'saturation, proliferation', the chaotic profusion of signs, which eliminates the possibility of any one central author. The first option is typical of Puig's *Boquitas pintadas*, as of Sarduy's own play, *La Playa*, which deploys a language stripped of its vehicular function as 'medium of transmission and support for received ideas'. The second option is illustrated by Spanish baroque cathedrals or Maurice Roche's *Compacte*, the creation of 'a hypergraphic substance'.[174] Either way, the singular *literal imperative* is sustained.

VII The Buddhist path

As Sarduy explains, 'the void I try to define proceeds from Tibetan Buddhism, according to which enlightenment would be the perception – instantaneous and shattering – of reality in its entirety as a metaphor of an initial emptiness [...]. For Buddhism, everything is like a *fluoresencia del vacio*. A transparent void, without limits or centre'.[175] Sarduy has always emphasised the importance of this intuition:

> The supreme experience for whoever is interested in the teachings of the Buddha and for whoever has lived, as I have, in the great monasteries of the Himalayas, is the convocation of emptiness. The centre of Buddhism is emptiness. And I had the supreme experience of my life in the ancient grottoes of Ajanta, near Bombay, where a group of exiled Tibetan monks came together to worship a huge ritual image of Buddha located in those caves In that moment, perhaps the only important moment of my life, I was able to grasp the instantaneous perception of emptiness [*vacuidad*] [176]

Indeed, Buddhism is so clearly the single most important theoretical and intertextual register in Sarduy's work that it is intriguing to speculate why it has received so little critical attention. This omission must be remedied here, in the compressed detail that space allows.

The essential point is simple enough: to know the *real* as void of actuality is at the same time to know *given* actuality as simulacrum, illusion or fantasy. Siddharta Gautama, the 'historical' Buddha, advised his followers: 'Regard this phantom world/as a star at dawn, a bubble in a stream,/a flash of lightning in a summer cloud,/a flickering lamp – a phantom – and a dream'.[177] Sarduy takes this advice fully to heart:

> In the East, at the heart of its great theogonies – Buddhism, Taoism – we find not a full presence, god, man, logos, but a generative emptiness whose metaphor and simulation is visible reality [...] Born from and functions of that nothing which is most present when imitations of the model are most intense, camouflage most successful, analogies and usurpations most precise – this is how the phenomena enumerated here must be read, for, seen from original emptiness, they themselves are no more than the theatricality and maximum saturation of all other phenomena.[178]

The normal or given world is a tissue of illusions, a world in which insight sleeps. But while we generally stumble about in our given slumber, the Buddha is *awake*, and sees the world for what it is. To rise from the sleep of the world is to become what we really are, an expression of the one univocal Mind that sustains the universe.[179] Enlightened, we see that 'the One is none other than the All, the All none other than the One'.[180] The Buddhist One, though void of all actuality, enfolds an infinite intensity that invites comparison with Deleuze's univocal cosmology.

Since I touched on some of the main concepts of Buddhism in outline in my introduction (III:b), in this section I will briefly review only those two particular forms of Buddhism most relevant to Sarduy's texts: Zen and Tantra. Both claim the honour of being 'the most extreme form of Buddhism', in almost antithetical ways. Tantra celebrates the physical, sensual holism of the cosmic Buddha-body, an absolute totality both material and spiritual, while Zen advocates a wholly cerebral pursuit of truth deprived even of the concept of truth, without notions of soul or salvation, deprived of scripture, ritual or vow.

(1) *Zen: no-mind and koan.* 'Zen is the way of direct enlightenment', without means or mediation, 'a leap from second-hand to direct experience'.[181] Like all Buddhisms, Zen is an introspective method for dissolving the limits of the self and ultimately, the limits of all distinction or discrimination as such.

Three features distinguish the Zen approach. In the first place, Zen is unusually determined in its commitment to *no-mind* [*wu-nien*], i.e. to the active paralysis of conscious intellect. 'The whole technique of Zen is to jolt people out of their intellectual ruts and their conventional morality'; it begins with an effort 'to clear aside all definitions, intellectual concepts and speculation'.[182] As Suzuki notes, 'psychological impasse is the necessary antecedent of *satori* [enlightenment]'.[183]

In the second place, Zen insists upon the *sudden*, immediate nature of enlightenment, its literal irruption *ex nihilo*.[184] 'Zen realisation is characterised by abruptness or immediacy, for this is the nature of *Prajña* [transcendental wisdom] itself [...]. Prajña acts intuitively, and what it perceives is perceived at once, without any mediation or deliberation'.[185] Zen refuses all 'interference' or 'obstruction'; 'it is an immediate awareness of things', grasped by a 'mind of no-hesitation, no-interruption, no-mediacy'.[186] The Zen version of enlightenment (*satori*) is described as a kind of instantaneous flash or explosion, 'a sort of mental catastrophe'.[187] Adepts recall that in satori, 'my one thought covered eternity' (Koho), that 'there was a sense of utmost transparency' (Hakuin),[188] that all others 'were myself [..., that] no individual existed'.[189] Enlightenment is dis-locating by definition, without place or home.

Third, Zen provides a highly refined means to this total concentration, through the art of the *koan*.[190] Beyond rational solution, a koan is a 'kind of spoof on the human intellect'.[191] It is a brief paradoxical utterance that confounds and eventually exhausts the conscious mind. Like Deleuze's irreducible 'Problems' or 'Questions', a koan 'silences all empirical responses which purport to suppress it, in order to "force" the one response which always continues and maintains it'.[192] Every koan presents a doubly impersonal aspect. On the one hand, the term koan connotes something public, something held in *common* (along the lines of a legal controversy, or public work of art). 'A koan does not represent the private opinion of a single man, but rather the highest principle, received alike by us and by the hundreds and thousands of bodhisattvas', it acts 'like a great fire that consumes all who come near it'.[193] On the other hand, the koan *isolates* its subject beyond all relation, transitive or introspective. Koan study is 'positive concentration on a single object of thought, which is called a state of oneness (*ekagra*). It is also known as a state of *daigi* or "fixation"', through which the absolute can be 'realised directly within oneself'.[194] The instructions for use are invariably of the type, 'fix your attention exclusively on the koan, as if you were oppressed under the obligation of a very heavy debt...'[195] Through the koan, 'the entirety of one's consciousness and psychic life is filled with one thought': when it becomes *fully* singular, it breaks open in the flash of limitless satori.[196]

A koan usually takes the form of a question with no logical answer. For instance: 'if you meet a man of Tao on the way, greet him neither with words nor with silence; now tell me, how will you greet him?'[197] The solution, by definition inexpressible in words or silence, opens the way to an encounter beyond dualism, beyond the notion of 'encounter' altogether, an absolute *realisation* of Oneness. Or again, to take one of the most familiar examples: what is the sound of one hand clapping? Hakuin explains that 'if concepts and discriminations are not mixed within it [...] and if you proceed without interruption in the study of this koan, then [...] one grasps the pure supernatural sound of hearing any sound anywhere' and accedes to 'the pure supernatural power of going anywhere or doing anything'.[198] In short, 'all koans are the utterances of satori with no intellectual mediations; hence their uncouthness and incomprehensibility'.[199] They are pronounced in words, but as if from an enlightened perspective itself beyond words. To 'solve' the koan is not to eliminate the paradox, to unravel it, but rather to maintain it in its most extravagant intensity, at the point where words collapse. 'Once one has penetrated completely into one of the Koans, it is sufficient. The great Enlightenment is once and for all'.[200]

(ii) *Tantra and the cosmic body-without-organs.* Tantra, the dominant current of Tibetan Buddhism, emerged around the eighth century CE from a complex syncretism of 'aboriginal nature-worship of India and Hindu mysticism, served, as it were, through the terminology of the Mahayana'.[201] Unlike other forms of Buddhism, Tantra reserves a redemptive use for our *given* 'delusions' – desires, senses, relations... – as part of the multiform pursuit of true real-isation.[202] Most notoriously, Tantric ritual accords an important place to sexual union, as *ex-stasis*, the literal, bodily pursuit of 'ecstatic, egoless, beatific bliss in the realisation of transcendent identity'.[203] Through the disciplined cultivation of desire, 'you are able to melt the elements within your body, resulting in the experience of a non-conceptual state'.[204] Tantra 'stresses the doctrine that Ultimate Being was ever present in all things living', that 'everything is Buddha without exception', as part of the universal 'Buddha-body'.[205] Rather like Artaud's Alchemical Theatre – or Sarduy's *Cobra* – Tantra strives 'by *conjunctions unimaginably strange to our waking minds* to resolve or even annihilate every conflict produced by the antagonism of matter and mind, idea and form, concrete and abstract, and to dissolve all appearances into one unique expression'.[206]

Like all forms of Buddhism, Tantra is primarily clinical or therapeutic, a 'practical method for realising the truth';[207] perceives actuality as void; assumes that perfect Wisdom 'is naturally translucent, completely unproduced and without any basis';[208] refuses any *ultimate* distinction between Samsara and Nirvana. 'Central to tantra's teachings is the concept that Reality is unity, an indivisible whole [...]. The individual has the potential to realise and equate himself with Cosmic Consciousness: to intuit this reality is the purpose of tantra'.[209] Like Zen, 'the mysticism of Tantra denotes a state of consciousness which is characterised by a complete cessation of sensation, ideas, concepts, and subject–object relationship';[210] like Zen, Tantra urges its disciple to 'renounce the vanity of discussion […] and be not moved from singleness';[211] again like Zen, through Tantric practice, 'experience and realisation burst forth spontaneously'.[212] As Sarduy himself puts it, in 'ancient Tibet […], everything dissolves, is annulled, silenced'.[213] But where Zen clears the mind of all objects, Tantra clears objects, so to speak, of all mind. The goal is to reach a state in which 'the sense objects themselves provide you with awareness'.[214] Such awareness will be utterly 'uncensored'. Unlike other forms of Buddhism, Tantra encourages what one critic calls 'the rather dangerous view that all things are legitimate to those who fully know the truth'.[215] Both Zen and Tantra are flamboyantly amoral and aim at a coherence beyond karmic responsibility, 'beyond good and evil' – the one through the mind, the other through the body.[216]

Tantra thus takes 'Body as its object'.[217] It is 'the last and most extreme expression of Buddhist "corporisation" […]. For Tantra, the body is the real double of the universe which, in turn, is a manifestation of the adamantine and incorruptible body of Buddha'.[218] The Buddha 'has the miraculous power of transforming his one body and making it pervade the entire universe'.[219] We must recognise ourselves as aspects of this singular body, through a transcendence of our merely *given* body. (Or as Deleuze would say: in order to be reunited with the vital anorganic life that burns within us, we must first annul the organs and dissolve the organism[220]) If Tantra, like Sarduy's fiction, is emphatically 'pleasure-oriented', nevertheless to be an adept you must first 'reduce yourself to numbness. This is absolutely necessary. Having done that, then you regain your perception'.[221] Real *jouissance* obtains only in the transmutation of merely given pleasure. On this strict condition, supreme enlightenment is to be attained 'by the enjoyment of all desires, to which one devotes oneself just as one pleases'.[222] The moment of absolute indulgence is to be followed by the 'highest bliss', a state beyond indulgence, where 'there is neither self nor other', where 'the faculties of sense subside […]. O friend, such is the Body Innate'.[223] At the limit of this initiation, the Tantric adept literally *embodies* that awareness whereby 'the individual being and universal being are one'.[224]

It would be possible to make sense of a great deal of Sarduy's fiction in terms borrowed from Zen and Tantric practice. There are clear, often detailed allusions to Tantric ritual in *Cobra* and *Maitreya*.[225] Tantric liberation 'consists in the abolition or fusion of contraries. masculine and feminine. subject and object, the phenomenal world and the transcendental world';[226] its 'poetic language' is characterised, as Paz observes, by 'reversibility: each word can be converted into its contrary'.[227] It is no accident that 'in *Cobra*, the opposition of the sexes could only be further ended in one site where, by definition, all oppositions are abolished: Buddhism'.[228] Like Sarduy's prose, Tantra suggests a cosmology compatible with general Relativity and the Big Bang;[229] like Sarduy, it maintains that the real is written immediately upon the body;[230] amoral, it likewise insists that 'no code of social ethics can hold the body prisoner'[231] and duly affirms a radical, transgressive *dépense*.[232]

Furthermore, much of *De donde* and *Cobra* reads like a series of run-on koans, inciting, exciting, and eventually frustrating the mind. Sarduy agrees with Deleuze: 'paradox is the force of the unconscious', 'paradox breaks up the common exercise of the faculties and places [...] thought before the unthinkable which it alone is nevertheless capable of thinking'.[233] Paradox is 'the passion of philosophy' precisely because it puts an end to what Husserl called intentionality – the *aboutness* of thought, of 'second-hand life'. As Sarduy points out, 'an enigma has no solution. The only answer is another enigma' (RJ, 66/82–83). All the great cosmological questions that dominate Sarduy's theoretical and critical writings – what is the origin of time, of the universe, of space? – are koans *par excellence* (NI, 30). We know that Sarduy considers his *choteo* to be a 'koan exercise'.[234] And in his essay on the 'Koan' (SI, 119–122), Sarduy notes that a koan-art (the painting of Tàpies) destroys the apparent solidity of conventional perspective, that it attains 'the no-colour [of] unified grey', that it creates 'a sudden void, the brutal exemption from meaning' through which 'the question and the questioner are returned to the emptiness, the same silence' (SI, 121). The koan explodes conscious interpretation. One Chinese character in *De donde* gives an example: 'The being of the birds is not the tone of the trills but feathers falling at each change. White, they are other birds in the snow, the signature of the first; red, fish that becomes butterfly when attacked'.[235]

More generally, echoes of Buddhist *sunyata* [emptiness] abound in *Cobra* and *Maitreya*. Fully in character, one Buddhist ecstatic in *Maitreya* proclaims that 'apart from thought, there is nothing [...], absolutely nothing: neither subject, merit nor fault'.[236] The dying master of the same novel knows that the perception of 'even a white, immaterial light was only the beguiling projection of the lowest part of his brain, as meticulously false, as lacking in reality as whatever it is that serves as a screen to life' (MY, 22/159; cf. PP, 221). Less obviously but perhaps most importantly, the redemptive logic of Buddhism – the effort to *real-ise* a *dharma* (doctrine) or koan *given* in ordinary speech but generated directly from real singularity itself – illuminates the major effort of Sarduy's work on language. We might say that his first move is to take given, ordinary language to the limit of its performance, to the edge of utility and communication; that he then, in the consequent absence of meaning, seeks out the virtual as wholly compressed, as

pure immediate metamorphosis in itself; and that finally he acts as the verbal 'channel' for this intensity, the vehicle for a new proliferation of words
unbounded by merely semantic or logical constraints. Amidst the ruins of
el pensamiento común, Sarduy writes a verbal explosion into being, rigorously *ex nihilo*. His 'Indian Journal' puts it well: 'your destructive dance has
extinguished the Earth. Now, panting, you contemplate the devastated
space [...]. From your navel the lotus flower will emerge, and from her, the
creator' (CB, 253/143–144). As with a koan, the actual words or images are
the 'same' at either end of the process, but if properly real-ised, they reveal
the truth of the virtual itself (as void, as pure metamorphosis). *Writing is
itself this redemptive process, the shift from given to real, creature to Creator*. Writing is what restores the creativity of language.

A novel like *Cobra*, in short, might be described as an assemblage of
koans and mantras, sifted through a baroque *Tel Quel* filter. *Cobra* and
Maitreya can be called properly *sacred* texts to the degree that they evoke,
like Carlos Fuentes' *Zona sagrada*, 'that space which is sacred because the
distance between sacred and profane has been abolished' (ES, 248/23). For
'what is the sacred? It is the moment in which the opposition between
sacred and profane is annulled'.[237] The sacred *is* that becoming-one
(becoming-indistinct, imperceptible) of its initial (given) distinction, its
subtraction from its initial relation *to* the profane. The real, the sacred, is
that which will have existed in the absence of distinction or obstruction. As
Sarduy puts it, 'a man who is in the sacred is totally present to himself, as
much conceptually as physically [...], in such a way that there is nothing
which blocks his thought, nothing which escapes representation [...]; he
lives in a space as free as that of dreams. And at the same time, as lucid,
as vigilant as the day...'.[238] Once immediate to the void, there can be no
possible limits to a free articulation. Nothing can then inhibit the free
explosion-expression into space. The *return* of the Big Bang will have gone
off unhindered.

VIII *Cobra* (1972)

Cobra opens in the cavernous Lyrical Theatre of the Dolls, a Bunraku
inspired puppet workshop become alchemical factory, pure 'heterotopia –
tavern, ritual theatre and/or doll factory, lyrical bawdy house' (CB,
12–13/4). Cobra begins as doll or puppet (or girl), with 'glass hair' (12/3),
one among the ruling Madam's many 'mutants', a mass of makeup, facial
creams and costume jewellery. 'Cobra was the Madam's greatest accomplishment' (50/25; cf. 14/5), flawed only in the excssive size of her feet.
These unfortunate appendages are subsequently 'treated' through various
orthopaedic tortures and conjurings, in search of 'the elixir of reduction,

the juice that shrinks' (30/14). Somewhere along the way, Cobra finds Pup, a 'mouldy, wrinkled' doll become 'an articulated and quite human toy' through the so-called 'phenomenon of i.p.s. (indefinitely proceeding sequences, of course) which this is not the place to analyse' (51/26). Pup is white dwarf become puppet, 'the transvestite with the very small radius who had reached the end of her evolution'.[239] She is also 'the unsuccessful and derisive double of the transvestite': 'Cobra = Pup^2' (90/49, 53/27).

This unholy trinity, Madam–Cobra–Pup, aspects of one and the same will to reduction, set off via Madrid, Guadeloupe and Toledo in search of one Doctor Ktazob, who 'in crafty Tangerian abortion houses uproots the superfluous with an incision and sculpts in its place lewd slits'.[240] They find him in Tangiers, in a Polynesian brothel with 'nude waiters and floor level tables topped with kif pipes that never went out, narguiles of opium and overflowing bottles of mescaline, harmaline, LSD 6, bufotenin, muscarine and bulbocapnin' (CB, 96/54). The eventual surgery is described with more than Sadistic zeal and padded out with 'lacquered psychosomatic aphorisms' and no small number of 'Doctor K's analgesic theories'. While Pup 'twists and turns' like a dervish in the closet, object of a lampooned Lacanian transference, 'among tarnished hypnotic pendulums, stained pincers and surgical knives piled in Romeo y Julieta cigar boxes, with a musical background of Qur'anic strains, [Ktazob] rambled on about ethesia [...], spontaneous narcosis, the visions of interregnum and the episteme of the Cut' (107–108/60).

Part two begins with the newly altered Cobra's night out in what appears to be something like Amsterdam's red-light district. 'He' soon comes upon four 'black jackets'[241] – initially named Tiger, Tundra, Totem, and Scorpion – whose pose simultaneously as 'western delinquents or oriental monks'.[242] Much of the remainder of the novel involves a complex initiation into this double collective, part Tantric ritual, part sadistic orgy. Initiation requires passage 'through submission [...] to the point of nausea' (CB, 138/77) and eventually death. Cobra is apparently dead by page 185/104, his head 'perforated' and 'crushed' (188/106), but a 'COBRA' reappears in the next chapter, 'climbing a column' (201/114). The first-person Cobra of the second part of the novel, after his 'Initiation' into the leather gang, is rebaptised 'Cobra' as part of a symbolic becoming-snake, 'so that he will poison. So that he will strangle. So that [...] his breath will hypnotise and his eyes will shine in the night, monstrous, golden' (154/87). The gang members become cocaine refiners and addicts, 'traders of white' (199–200/113), and slip further and further into drugged hallucinations, forever richer in Tantric imagery. Once COBRA learns that 'the time has come for you to seek the Path/Your breathing is about to cease', the novel abandons narrative orientation altogether: 'your instructor has set you face to face to the Clear Light;/and now you are about to experience it:/heaven empty things,/clear intelligence,/ transparent void/without circumference or centre…' (185/104).

Of the many aspects of *Cobra* that literally grab attention, none is more gripping than the graphic transformation of organic bodies into bodies-without-organs – bodies, that is, without centred, purposeful order. The reader encounters bodies clogged with 'hydrosulphuric demons and vermin which corroded [their] ganglia and spleen' (CB, 89/49), bodies jumbled 'among sacks one on top of the other, in a steam of rotten grapes, of milk, of excrement and vomit, playing, rolled inside burrows of hay, fornicating' (242/137). More than anything else, over the course of the novel, Cobra learns to 'see that I am not me, that one's body is not one's own, that the things that make us and the forces which put them together are passing fancies' (141/79) – mainly sadistic fancies. The four *blousons noirs* are 'impervious to pain, to human presence' (170/95). They are sado-masochistic heroes, venerated like Gods with mocking panegyrics, streaked with 'blood and cum'. Such is the body as plaything, according to Ktazob the Alterer:

> Take an open-winged bat. nail him to a plank Have fun making him smoke
> He chokes. Shrieks. Give him a light. Take a rabbit. bleed him through the
> eyes Take a little man who smiles, tied to a beam. Cram him with cocaine.
> One by one, bloodlessly – brief cuts in the tendons of his joints – separate
> him into pieces, one by one, up to one hundred [etc].[213]

Cobra's staging of an inhuman, anorganic body corresponds nicely to the prescriptions of Artaud's theatre of cruelty, in which violent physical images crush and hypnotise the sensibility of the spectator, through pressure 'acting directly on the organism', making it 'burn like fire, as immediate as fire itself'.[214]

The body in *Cobra* is a collection of pieces without organic shape. It does not add up to a whole, but disperses like the semantic dissemination of Borges' 'Chinese encyclopaedia'. Cobra. 'she is invaded by reddish spots like enlarged freckles […], small Philippine fluvial fish and pus. She curls around the red columns of a temple of the Asiatic tropics, the ankles of an ascetic, motionless on one foot, the knees and elbows of a corpse abandoned to the vultures in a tower, the neck of a Ceylonese streetwalker smeared with rice powder, the wrists of a dancing god' (120/68). This bundle of partial objects is held together only by the skin, or rather, by *makeup* applied to the skin. After her castration/sex-change, Cobra's appearance is reduced almost entirely to a cosmetic mask: 'her makeup is violent, her mouth painted with branches. Her orbs are black and aluminium-plated [etc.]. Up to her neck she is a woman: above, her body becomes a kind of heraldic animal with a baroque snout…'[215]

Cobra's first 'conversion' is described as 'the butchery' (CB, 103/57); the second conversion, her initiation, leads directly to his/her (apparent) death. The corpse becomes the object of extraordinarily involved ritual attention, somewhere between the carnivalesque macabre and a Tantric celebration of a more than human life. As 'yellow sap' secretes from the orifices, Scorpion traces the 'curriculum mortis':

> black grass grows in COBRA's intestines [...]. At this moment he is contemplating the fifty-eight divinities, irritated hoarders of Knowledge, inserted in concentric hoops of fire. Wrathful and blood-sucking flames surround him. Four dishevelled black demons make faces at him while they devour small bodies in large chunks. Surrounding these large-fanged monsters, beasts with pelicans and frog heads, drooling blood and ganglia, scream upon a dark rainbow (CB, 195/110–111)

The boys then slash Cobra's 'wrists with a scalpel [...], from the wound gushed a black paste which they collected in a small case [...]. They cut his skin into strips which they nailed to the rocks. They crushed his bones. They mixed this dust with barley flour. They scattered it to the winds' (197–198/111–112). So begins a more than a grotesque banquet that leaves comparisons with Rabelais far behind. It is a banquet crowned, according to Tantric prescription, with 'the five ambrosias: COBRA's blood/TIGER's urine/TUNDRA's excrement/SCORPION's saliva/TOTEM's semen'.[216]

Rather than a sensory-motor body, in other words, Sarduy writes a body that is slowly usurped by the accumulation of words that describe it, by the litany of hallucinatory detail. Two major consequences follow. The first secures the equation of body = text. Through the initiation, 'they read you [Cobra], they enumerated your parts, named your viscera' (CB, 197/111); 'your skin is a map' (213/120). As Cobra's Madam puts it, 'the body, before reaching its lasting state [...], is a book in which the divine judgement is written' (87–88/48). As Levine suggests, the obvious comparison is with Frankenstein, a Frankenstein who stitches together bits of text rather than flesh.[217] Just as the body flaunts its sexuality and mortality, so Cobra's text flaunts its flamboyant intertextuality. Sarduy includes a list of credits for the Lyrical Theatre of Dolls in an auto-pastiche: decor by Roland Barthes ('Leçon d'écriture'); Cobra's costume by Flaubert (Queen of Sheba, in the Tentation de Saint Antoine); makeup by Giancarlo Marmori (Storia de Vous), 'the Dwarf, Mabel and la Raba are the three women of Manuel Puig's Boquitas pintadas'.[218] Scattered through the text, we find allusions to 'Lezamesque secretions' (76/42); 'Churrigueresque faith' (86/47), a 'Lezamesque purple' (34/16), a 'Churrigueresque cage', 'Calderonian' cats, a 'Faiyumesque' mouth (56/30). The Madam struggles to control her 'Benvenistean' urges; 'her favourite advice, be Brechtian'.[219] More spectacularly, 'out of a chewing gum machine, Don Luis de Góngora emerges...' (180/102), while William Burroughs composes 'in hieroglyphs, the exhaustive biography of Ktazob' (96/53). More, *Cobra* like *Maitreya* is laced with self-quotation,[250] in addition to references to Sarduy's other works. The Madam refers to *Escrito sobre un cuerpo* by name (88/48), while Tundra quotes from *De donde* (205/116; cf. DC, 98/17) and the trio Madam–Cobra–Pup run into *De donde*'s Auxilio and Socorro whom they find 'more than simply textual' (91/50; cf. 68/37).

As a second consequence, in the absence of a 'centred' bodily mediation (the sensory-motor schema), description takes on a crushingly immediate, literally crippling quality. There is nothing here between sensation and its registration. As Deleuze says of Francis Bacon's painting: liberated from any intermediary representation, it is free to 'act directly upon the nervous system'[251]. Verbal transformations veer between a maximum proximity or over-determination – as when, before castrating Cobra, Ktazob 'hoist[s] an overwhelming cigar whose tip he amputated with his sharpened cigar cutter' (CB, 111/62) – and a maximum distance or estrangement, as when Pup (on the same page), stewed for nine days in ice and 'passive substances', emerges a 'spherical all-day lollipop for big-headed carnival mannequins' (110/62). No sensory-motor schema intervenes to organise passing sensations into coherent, recognisable shapes. *All* perception here retains a properly hallucinatory intensity.

Cobra operates at maximum sensory over-load, without repose. There are no periods of rest or recuperation, there is no time to catch up. Especially apparent in *Cobra* is a certain carnivalesque practice of enumeration, which buries its subject under the accumulation of simultaneous but incompossible alternatives (109/61, 127/71). For instance, the Madam

> went / barefoot, dragging incensories,
> / smeared with crosses of black oil,
> / in a Carmelite cassock, a yellow rope at her waist,
> / wrapped in damasks and white cloths, with a wide-brimmed hat and a staff,
> / naked and wounded, beneath a dunce cap. (CB, 22/10)

It is the reader's choice, or all of the above. Elsewhere, 'in the drawing projected on the wall two men were fighting. Or not' (CB, 138/77). Again, Cobrita, newly 'diminished': is (a) 'exactly like a crowned and rickety albino girl, crossing a company of musketeers on their nightwatch, pulled along by a servant and carrying a dead chicken tied to her waist'; (b) is a 'Burmese leopard catching pheasants'; (c) 'a two-legged Tomar window, [which] accumulates to an extreme anchors and cords, corals and crosses, armillary spheres and Portuguese Gothic bracelets – imploring a rainfall of Fly' (47–49/24–25).

Rather than describe an object, such koan-like sequences claim, in the voiding of all actual objectivity, a Creative coherence of their own.

IX *Maitreya* (1978)[252]

Maitreya is the most emphatically other-worldly of Sarduy's novels, the most koan-driven of them all. Sarduy calls the novel his '*koantestación*'; it is 'a detective novel whose sought-for object is God, Divinity, and it is the same novel that I live, constantly'. It is a novel driven by repetition or doubling – a doubling in time (reincarnation) in part one, and a doubling in space (twinning) in part two. The story has its 'genesis' in the effort 'to parody and to invert *Cobra*'. It begins where the earlier novel leaves off, in a monastery, and then inverts the earlier movement from West to East by dragging its hero across Asia to Cuba, Miami and the United States.[253] *Maitreya* begins with the death of a 'master' (MY, 20/157) who predicts his rebirth: 'we emerge from noncreation, and we return to it in the twinkling of an eye' (21/158). His last words quote the *Heart Sutra*: 'The void is the form. The form is the void... That ought to keep you busy for years' (22/159). Funeral proceedings are dispersed by Chinese gunshots (25/161), but soon after the reincarnated Maitreya (i.e. future Buddha) is found for what is declared to be the last time, in the guise of a small boy living with the two old Leng sisters, who steal the sought-after child across the sea to Colombo. There the child-master wanders through the 'sleeping city' (46/174), though 'little is known of what he said' (43/171). It's not long before the young divine begins 'to take his mission lightly and was drinking double martinis in the kitchen' (55/180); he eventually slips away with the Lengs' niece, Illuminated, to Matanzas (Cuba), where overcome by indifference for worldly things and refusing answers to all questions, he stops his breathing and dies (70/190).

Part two opens in modern Cuba with the birth of identical twins. The children become miraculous healers. They lose their powers at puberty (91/206), and become sopranos known as the 'Ladies Divine and Tremendous' (93/208 – Lady Tremendous 'followed, or rather duplicated, by Lady Divine' [109/217]); their performances range from Chinese opera to 'the enraptured roars of frenzied fat divas from the repertoire of Richard Wagner' (125–126/228). They are joined by Louis Leng, a Chinese cook lifted from Lezama's novel *Paradiso*.[254] Accompanied by the ubiquitous dwarf, the three wind up in Miami and become members of 'the up-and-coming sex sect "F.F.A.": Fist Fuckers of America' (110/218), whose 'goal is total chaos' (113/220). The successful singer(s) are soon threatened by the mysterious, gleefully satanic Gloomy Gals, who with the help of 'diabolical artefacts' are able to turn 'structured Mozartian arpeggios' into 'discordant cackles, convulsive hiccups and scratchy creakings' (141/240). In response, Lady Tremendous takes 'realer than real measures' (143/241) and generates a new decoy, a new double, *plus vraie que nature*': 'from an inflated doll on the verge of bursting, she had achieved a reproduction, indistinguishable from the original, of Lady Tremendous'.[255]

Rid of the Gloomy Gals and displaced to Oman, Lady T is free to pursue 'the apotheosis of the fist' (MY, 154/249), a ritual dominated by 'prescribed infamies' and plenty of vaseline, administered by the dwarf: 'the pygmy's knotting little fingers wait for [the initiate], erect and bundled in rubber, like sickly asparagus in green cellophane' (159/252). The FFA soon runs into trouble with the local regime, and the dwarf is pursued by thugs from the Caliphate before finding Lady Tremendous with her stud-chauffeur at the Grand Hôtel de France (169/260). There, 'they indulged in rites until they were bored or stupefied. To prove the impermanence and the emptiness of everything' (187/273). The chauffeur eventually loses his mind and Lady T disappears, 'never [to be] heard from again' (184/271).

As according to Zen prescription, this most 'religious' of Sarduy's novels is also, and for the same reason, the most opaque, the most resistant to theological *interpretation* as such. As the infant Buddha says: 'I will give neither questions nor answers, then, nor any exercise; only indications, suggestions of staging, as if I were nailing in a banana tree little leather figures' (MY, 32/165). Lost in 'total indifference' (66/187), surrounded by initiates, he 'refused to elucidate [...] the origin and end of the universe, the reality of reincarnation, the existence of an individual soul, etc.' (68/189). He says only that 'whatever is, cannot be recaptured by the intellect or by the senses [...]. I didn't squander knowledge: I marked its empty nomadic place'.[256] These enigmatic *suggestions of staging* – theatrical, rhetorical, aesthetic, metaphysical – provide the only acceptable scaffolding of a meditation without support, founded solely upon the void. The child-master:

> Without further incentive than nocturnal contemplation he scrutinised the changing landscape, reduced it to words, to pure shadows, to overlapping circles of different blues [ ] he was meditating without any support whatsoever.
> And then neither with nor without support
> He perceived the thick promontories as one more attribute of the void, as arbitrary in their form and devoid of consistency as the mist that blanched them. (MY, 52/178)

Thus freed from the interpretative relation of intentional consciousness ('aboutness'), the text gives free reign to a vision-revelation beyond perspectival constraints. Action becomes pure spectacle, movements blurred together as part of a moving tableau, the composition of situations beyond reaction. For example, Lady T, skating through what might be Miami:

> The pavement and background moved as if pulled by giant rollers but not her [..]. Drunks. Drugged blacks. [..] The steam from the sewers enveloped her in a pillar of gas· she skated downtown diffuse, formless, a soft saffron seraph. She was slowing down as if the hot puffs of smoke and the streets she crossed resisted her with fine veils (MY, 136/237).

The movement is displaced from subject to environment, converted into passing impressions, random sounds, while contours blend and soften in a post-impressionist confusion (steam, diffuse, formless, smoke, veils). Composed, the environment – the streets she crosses – *resists* the subject. The description writes a space which excludes the merely 'mobile' subject, a space become composition on its own strictly asubjective terms.

As in *De donde*, such tableaux break down the distinction between 'artistic' and 'real' settings (cf. MY, 88/204). One example is worth quoting almost in full – Louis Leng's 'marine' encounter with two naked Chinese girls, propelled by his jade-ringed phallic 'mast'. The girls wrap him in a bedspread which registers the topographic transcription of a movement literally converted into surface canvas:

> Placed over the besmeared macho, the net of black trigraphs covered the projections of that topography of brief valleys. a Meru raised in the middle like the main support of a circus canvas. The fabric indicated, upon falling, the first forms, the plateaus […], the slightest inflections were underline. the jade ring with its dragons An oily stain extended in concentric circles outward from the mast, whose throbs shook the tent with brief seismic seizures [. .]
> 'Make waves', he quietly ordered them.
> The big yellow gals, still at the head and feet of the River, grabbed the tips of the bedspread with their fingertips, excessively cautious – were they performing a senseless rite, repeating until it was a simulacrum? [.]; finally it was a raging typhoon sea, waves as high as lake houses and abysses that swept sargasso over the sand
> At each low tide the cloth perched on the merlon: the fiction of the rough trigraphs hardened and dilated the burnished cupola [.]. Lady Tremendous was all eyes, or rather, deposited her gaze, as if surrendering it to the paintbrush, upon the descending cloth […]. She followed the undulations of the Tao, flabbergasted by that torturous up-and-down [.].
> 'Grab it with your mouth, without touching it', Leng ordered her
> [.] She wanted to catch it but caught nothing [..] Exhausted she tried here, then there The capillary hulk jingled and jangled
> She was about to collapse when the column sank into her mouth (MY, 120–122/226–227)

The final objective is achieved, as Zen dictates, only through the exhaustion of individual will. The text-tableau replaces the 'object' of its description, through the sheer accumulation of detail and *métaphores filées*. The scene recalls the becoming-land of the sea and becoming-sea of the land, in Elstir's paintings. But with Sarduy, rather more than Proust, it is the most frenzied of *action*-sequences that are the most emphatically converted into spectacle, that attract the most intense voyeurism.

Less than organising principle of the tableau, the body in *Maitreya* provides raw material for the composition which alone 'acts'. The body is something to be *worked*, and never more so than when it has no life of its own. The elaborate 'posthumous preparations' of the master's corpse, for instance, echo themes introduced by Cobra's initiation.[257] But once deprived of theatrical-cosmetic support, unsustained by spectators' eyes, the body sinks back into the flaccid formlessness from whence it came. Lady Tremendous, post-performance: 'her face was falling: crumbling cellulitic terraces, fatty wrinkled love handles from forehead to double chin, no longer sustained by the taut bandages under her wig' (MY, 130/232). She later 'spreads all over the place. They put her on a circular sofa to jell, supported by cushions' (145/243). As the mould alone gives form, so between 'Lady Delirium and [the] rubber bosom buddy' she spawns to distract the Gloomy Gals, it is quickly impossible to tell who is 'the nominal mammoth' (134/235). The unsupported body here sprawls, shapeless, into pure topography, so much space to be traversed or penetrated. This will begin to change with *Colibri*.

X Sarduy's singular univocity

The Buddhist dialectic of void and plenitude allows us to set out the fundamental dimensions of *Cobra* and *Maitreya* more precisely, in terms of one coherent aesthetic with several components. These components are rigorously compatible with the Deleuzian paradigm developed in my introduction: a purely immanent conception of the universe, in which everything exists or inheres on the same plane, as aspects of one matter-energy or intensity, a wholly literal conception of expression (including 'metaphorical' expression); a wholly immediate conception of action or transformation.

Before describing these components, we would do well to return briefly to the alternative, 'equivocal' reading – the reading that assumes that Sarduy's writing 'corresponds to no univocal code',[258] that 'univocity is replaced by doubling [*el doble*] at every level'.[259] In particular, there is among Sarduy's critics a general assumption that his work relies upon a 'underlying Derridian and Lacanian metaphysics'.[260] What drives these readings is precisely the position *attacked* in Deleuze and Guattari's *Anti-Oedipus*:

adherence to desire-as-lack, an emphasis on the *absent* object of desire, the deferral of signification, castration, the primacy of writing over speech, and so on. In González Echevarría's reading, for example, the 'subconscious is made up of [the] symptoms/signifiers that keep at bay the object of desire',[261] while Sarduy's 'Oriental is writing [and] writing arises from the opposition to voice, which is the uncontaminated origin' (*Ruta*, 158), an origin banished by Sarduy's *écriture*.[262]

In my view, Sarduy's major works (*Cobra, Maitreya*) do not take an equivocal, 'mediated' situation and make it more so. Rather, he *converts the equivocal into the univocal*. He converts a (deferred) significance into a (Creative) expression. Hence for example his very non-Derridian, quasi-mantric affirmation of sound and voice that ultimately eclipses the merely grammatological dimension.[263] Less than Derrida's deferral of presence, Sarduy affirms a vigorously *immediate* notion of "concreteness", meant to be a particular state of condensation of verbal material, or saturation or intensity, of the presence of the signifier to itself: desire of the text which in its corporeity can either meet itself or coincide with the baroque effect'.[264] As opposed to Lacan and Derrida, we know that Deleuze's elliptical logic of sense rejects all notions of absence, lack and deferral (none of which should be confused with *sunyata*), along with the whole dimension of interpretation as such. And like Deleuze, Sarduy proposes a verbal system in which '*enunciado*' and '*apariencia*' are aspects of one and the same expression. 'We think that we are dealing with two separate things: they are, in reality, one and the same [*una sola*]' (NI, 15), twice actualised. Again like Deleuze, Sarduy affirms a modernity which prefers 'rhizomatic ramification to the root', the 'multiple to the defined' (NI, 24). Less than Lacan's desiring subject, driven by lack from one signifier to another, it is Deleuze's fully affirmative, fully expressive subject or aleatory point that provides the most useful parallel to Sarduy's work in contemporary French thought. A world of partial objects, yes, but precisely one in which 'nothing is lacking'.[265] If in Botero's exemplary neo-baroque painting, for instance, 'everything is in the accessory, in the ornament, in splendour, it is because everything is in desire satisfied [*le désir comblé*], in the tactile, erotic *jouissance* of the materials'.[266] Sarduy's fiction is *anti-Oedipal* in precisely the Deleuzian sense: in the absence of the family,[267] it incants the liberation of an *unchannelled* sexuality.

Eroticism in Sarduy is not transgressive – it does not presuppose an economy of lack – but is rather the immediate expression of an essentially Creative universe on something like the Tantric model, a world swollen with semen, a world of 'a thousand tiny sexes'.[268] In all of Sarduy's work, the distinction between 'normal' and 'erotic' experience or description is dissolved without trace. His writing presumes a single erotic norm (or anti-norm), a single desiring-production. Sexual sequences are described with the same precision as any other tableau, through the same work of composition, far from any merely pornographic identification or experience. For example, as the *Maitreya*'s Iranian chauffeur wanders over Lady T's 'spreading gluteals', we follow the scene with an almost medical attention: 'the Iranian, spitting into his hand, his fingers joined in a cone, sank it as far as the phalanxes, into the tunnel that dilated as he passed. It didn't slide in smoothly, like an oiled embolus, but rather forcing rings, unrhythmically, with abrupt pushes. The dilated hoop, pink elastic, squeezed the protuberance of little bones like a ligament soaked in reddish ointments [etc.]' (MY, 178/266). Far from writing a generalised castration, Sarduy writes a global defence *against* castration (against the separation of subject and object), precisely because 'everything that is not textual is castratable' (SI, 88/121). With Veruschka's supremely textual dress art, for instance, 'the entire body is in a state of erection, subjected to absolute visibility or, on the contrary, plunged into a night of ink, devoured by the surface that backs it' (SI, 88/121). Either way, there is no protrusion, no 'member' to be amputated; all is of a piece, a single Eros-texture, beyond a merely 'organic' vulnerability.

If Sarduy indeed claims a 'merely' *literary* autonomy, it is one whose only parallel is the expanding universe itself. Both are actualisations of the same univocal energy or force.

(i) *One matter energy.* Like Spinoza, like Deleuze, Sarduy assumes the 'homogeneity of matter', the extension of 'an undefined universe without regions' (BO, 168–169), a space without territories. At its most sacred limit, 'on the banks of the Ganges, what thinks is space itself'.[269] Extension is itself the explication of a pure (virtual, absent) intensity. After Deleuze, Sarduy dispels what he calls 'the illusion of a metric universe' (BO [Fr. ed.], 23). For 'everything – mass, light... – is nothing but the visible aspect of one and the same value, undefinable in itself, of which transformation is the only index'.[270] At every step, Sarduy affirms a baroque reading in which 'all that counts is the energy of conversion' (SI, 66/100). With Sollers' *Paradis*, for example, Sarduy reads 'the syllable not as parcel of signification [...] but as a mantra: unity whose repetition creates a *modèle vibratoire* [japa]. Each syllable is a deposit of energy, an undulating nucleus ready to be integrated within the expanding universe...'.[271] The major aesthetic consequence is the impossibility of a transitive relationship between language and this plastic universe. Language can only be included as *part* of this univocal matter-energy, as 'simply one more piece of the whole'.[272] It can only provide a literal *image* (in Lezama's sense) or actualisation of the universe, rather than a representation of it. *Cobra* provides a nice example: 'Totem paints on his chest, over his heart, a heart'.[273] The contemporary cosmology Sarduy affirms is not a matter of describing the actual – the presently visible, as it was for Kepler – but of establishing an expressive connection with the invisible, virtual origin of the actual (i.e. of counter-actualising). 'It is not a matter of saving appearances, but rather – and cosmology is by definition the scene of this drama – of finding *a link with the origin*, a valid deduction from this zero point' that is the Bang (NI, 38), the wholly virtual outside of space-time. If we accept the Big Bang theory, Sarduy argues, 'then I think poetry or literature can/should do or be nothing but an image of the universe'.[274] Sarduy's major works thus aim at a

> poetic big bang that defines a space and time inherent in the unfolding of signs, interchangeable as 'versions' of a single energy, and unthinkable before the explosion. Matter – the letter – is born in the incandescence and dies in the final cooling down of the universe, but meanwhile [..] it is combined in infinite 'unbirths' or 'birthdeaths', semantic rainbow that glitters on the whiteness, reverberates, dazzles and goes out, in order to be re-formed after that new nothingness [275]

Time itself is nothing other than the medium of this equation of the infinitely compressed with the infinitely extended – the extension of its singular point, so to speak.

(ii) *One plane of immanence*. Since univocity ensures that 'a real metadiscourse is impossible',[276] Sarduy writes a discourse which inheres entirely on one level. As with Puig and Roche 'the page is a polished surface, flat, without breaks',[277] such that through a baroque disruption of perspective, 'everything is, through the fact of derision, set on a single plane, without depth. And this is what interests me'.[278] *Cobra*'s 'Indian Journal', for instance, evokes a space in which 'there is neither down nor up: the world has been concentrated into this serene rectangle' (CB, 229/129). Sarduy's enduring aim is to sustain a 'dialogue with the largest possible number of textures possible, in the space of one and the same level'.[279] What is not to be counted among this largest possible number, of course, is the notion of an external reality *mediated* by the text. If realism 'assumes a reality outside the text, outside the literalness of writing',[280] we know that in a truly creative work like Roche's *Compact*, 'nothing evokes a referent outside the book itself' (ES, 264/39). The writer's perspective can only exist within the same dimension as its range of objects.

Within this one and only dimension, however, the writerly perspective as such (i.e. the Creative position immediate to the void) remains purely virtual, 'unattainable by definition' (ES, 234/9). All we *have* are writings. Just the Creator *qua* Creator is not to be found 'in' creation, so too the writer's position is excluded from (written) actuality. This is precisely the situation Sarduy tries to describe with his many allusions to 'the object that fascinates me most, that I think of most' – Velázquez's *Las Meninas*.[281] The *given* painting (the painting called *Las Meninas*) has a double status. On the one hand, it is the spectator's point of departure, the material substance of our interpretation; on the other hand, it is presumably the *product* of the process portrayed in the painting (the painting in the painting). Unlike Foucault's famous reading, Sarduy assumes that the *real* subject of the painting is not the royal couple and/or the spectator, but the maids themselves. This would mean that the painting is simply about itself, rather than part of a complex play of displaced references and reflections. 'Velázquez, in *Las Meninas*, and in a tautology typical of the baroque, is painting *Las Meninas*. It is a question of an ultimate avatar of the ellipse. Here, it is representation itself that finds itself doubled in an inversion in the work, elided, like an illegible surface.'[282] The painter paints himself painting the picture we see, but what we *actually* see nevertheless reveals only the blank back of the 'real' (*virtual*) painting within the painting. The real surface of creation remains invisible, or virtual. In short, within our given situation, the painter–writer can certainly represent the movement toward the Creative (toward a virtuality immediate to the void), but only as back to front, as illegible; only from the inaccessible other side would it become visible as such, from the side accessed by an absolute break with this our given, *actual* side.

The most radical attempts to access this other side would strive to reduce the gap between actual and virtual to zero, to work like Deleuze's schizophrenic as immediate 'to the burning, living centre of matter [...], to an intense point identical with the production of the real'.[283] This is precisely Sarduy's agenda. 'not at the limit, but beyond all limits, it is a question of erasing, abolishing, assuring the disappearance of the body/support through total identification with the surface that backs it, with the ground where it lights, becomes fixed'.[284] Hence the notion of art as tattoo,[285] as something *escrito sobre un cuerpo*, immediate to the body become undifferentiated support (body without organs). The tattoo is flush to the skin, yet still 'added', artificial. It is a covered nakedness, so to speak. Its application requires a removal of *given* clothing, an initial stripping, so as to accomplish the eventual 'apotheosis of contiguity – clothing as body' (ES, 254/29). Veruschka's camouflages provide the best example: 'the separation between support – body/canvas, body/page – and representation – a dress painted on a body – has been reduced to zero, making the coincidence total: there is no interstice, no void to "distance" the phantasmal adherence between stretcher and illusion' (SI, 86/119).

(iii) '*Literal metaphors*'. If, like Baudrillard or Deleuze, you believe that '*everything* is metamorphosis', then it follows that 'the body of metamorphosis knows neither metaphor nor the operation of meaning'.[286] Hence the strongly and explicitly *literal* emphasis of Sarduy's literary theory. While most of his commentator's emphasise the equivocal, the polyvalent, the disruptive, figural, metaphorical character of his fiction, Sarduy himself believes that 'we are beginning to explore a plane of literalness previously off limits' (ES, 247/22). Sarduy has no time for 'symbolic' or hermeneutic readings. Like Kandinsky (but so unlike Derrida), Sarduy is convinced that 'every object has an inner sound independent of its external meaning', a sound that can resonate, in an 'art of the object', once this 'external' or 'everyday meaning is suppressed' (ES, 312/86). Like a Tantric mantra, such art would reproduce sound without interference. Since 'there are not two levels, one of which, deciphered, would produce the other, but multiple textures that coexist in one and the same surface, [p]erhaps one could formulate a whole theory of a non-symbolic reading...'[287] Just as he applauds 'Góngora's literalness' and Elizondo's 'discovery of the real base hidden behind all signals' (ES, 285/58; 245/20), so too does Sarduy affirm Puig's *Boquitas pintadas*, in which '(stereo)typical situations [*situations-types*] proceed [...] from this unique narrative, this chain of *variantes* whose readability is immediate – the minimum degree of decoding'.[288]

If Sarduy further insists, then, that 'everything is metaphor', that 'every word is already a metaphor, i.e. a mask',[289] we should not be fooled. When he uses the word 'metaphor', it is generally as 'metaphor in the literal sense of the term: displacement, moving out [...], expulsion towards the periphery'.[290] He goes on: 'as everything is metaphor, [so] everything is metonymy, that is, the basis of metaphor',[291] a movement of constant slippage or sliding, the rhetorical basis for a universal variation. In other words, Sarduy writes the *literalisation of an original metaphor*, rather than a figuration of a supposedly literal or denotative origin. Everything is metaphor, as even 'science doesn't use a literal, denotative, dry language, but a language of figures, imagined, weaved of metaphors' – white dwarves, red giants, red shift, light fatigue, black holes, and so on. And what a novel like *Cobra* does is 'take the metaphors of scientific discourse [...] and make them literal. Of each scientific metaphor it makes a character, that is, it creates an absurd universe parallel to the supposedly real universe'.[292] Pup appears fully in astronomical character as white dwarf; red giants appear as great fat transvestites covered in henna. By contrast, merely figurative 'metaphors force everything around them to remain in denotative purity'.[293] Sarduy's goal is to sweep up both figured exception and norm in a single expression, a single depravation of ordinary demonstrative language (ES, 271-272/45–46).

Genuine metaphors, then, *consume* their object – they become their other in the Deleuzian sense. 'Metaphor as conjuring. If the ritual formulation of the *like* is exact [...], the second term devours the object, seizes its body' (ES, 279/53). For example, 'in Lezama the seizing of reality, the voracious capture of the image, works by duplication, by mirage. A virtual double that will gradually besiege and surround the original, undermining it with imitation, with parody, until it is supplanted'.[294] As Rousset suggests, the Baroque effort is directed – like Tantra – towards 'making of metaphor a reality'.[295] At the outcome of this process, the figurative relation *per se* will no longer obtain. Sarduy promotes, in short, a notion of metaphor comparable to that exceptional sense affirmed by Deleuze's Proust – metaphor as the immediate complication of virtual essence, an essence beyond a constituent relation *with* the actual.[296]

(iv) *An elliptical anonymity*. In *Cobra* we told what any singular logic would lead us to expect: that 'writing is the art of ellipsis'.[297] The 'relation' that governs the literal immediacy of a single textual plane can only be an elliptical non-relation, both as elision of a referent (as voiding of the given) and as invitation to an unrestricted and entirely contingent contiguity. 'The two versions of a same *figure*' (BO, 179; cf. NI, 36) – ellipse in both the geometrical and rhetorical senses – govern both the baroque movement of the celestial bodies and the elements of a linguistic constant variation, so many 'facts without links, dissociated, expenditure without exchange [...], a purely artificial liaison of encounter' (BO, 224). The general goal is to overturn 'literature for the sake of a new practice of the sentence, disconnected and free. A practice whose only pattern would be the indication of a gaping absence, of the hole opened in the *zeal* of simulation'.[298] Ellipse is the refusal of relation, just as Caravagism, 'the zenithal point of the baroque', establishes 'contrast without mediation between zone of shadow and zone of light. Suppression of all transition between one term and another, by an abrupt juxtaposition of contraries' – and thus the basis for a knowledge 'taught through [...] designations without verbal links, through antithetical relations between subject and predicate'.[299]

(v) *Becoming-imperceptible*. Sarduy's work offers a wide variety of ways to see the universe 'from the point of view of nobody'.[300] Nobody is without territory, 'without a land'.[301] Nobody is without internal identity or consistency. Above all, nobody is without others, without relations Sarduy's '*I* is no longer a monolith but a crossroads, a series of ephemeral, unconnected elements'.[302] The wholly 'unconnected' cannot *relate*. Just as Deleuze's becoming-other implies not relations-with others but the dissolution of such relations, so too does Sarduy's (male) transvestite not relate 'to' woman so much as replace her. Becomings are intransitive.

> The transvestite does not imitate woman. For him, at the limit, there is no woman; he knows – and paradoxically he may be the only who knows this – that she is just appearance [...]. The transvestite does not copy; he simulates, since there is no norm to invite and magnetise his transformation, to determine his metaphor instead, it is the non-existence of the worshipped

being that constitutes the space, the region, or the support of his simulation. (SI, 55/93)

The only end of becoming is becoming itself – or, same thing, the imperceptibility of *what* it becomes. Pure becoming is Creation abstracted from 'what' is created. As if to Deleuzian prescription, the transvestite simulates a *virtual* or

> ideal woman, the essence, which is to say, the model and the copy have struck up a relationship of impossible coincidence and *nothing is conceivable as long as their is an effort to make one of the terms be an image of the other* [...]. In order for everything to signify it is necessary to accept that I am not inhabited by duality but by an intensity of simulation that constitutes its own end. outside of whatever it imitates: what is simulated? Simulation. (ES, 54–55/2)

Sarduy details two apparently contradictory approaches to this end of an absolute becoming-imperceptible (Deleuze's 'cosmic formula' of becomings).[303] On the one hand, and most obviously, he describes a becoming-mobile. This is the *imperceptible-as-blur*. We know that for Sarduy as for Klossowski reader of Sade, 'only motion is real: living creatures represent no more than changing phases' (ES, 230/6) – just as, from a Deleuze–Bergsonian perspective, every distinct species is merely an interruption of or pause in the vital movement of Creative evolution itself. The Indian costume maker of *Cobra*, for instance, begins as a fighter in the court of a Maharajah, near Kashmir. He then becomes a wrestling teacher in Benares, revives a tea concession in Ceylon, works as a spice importer in Colombo and a boxer in Smyrna; he bottles coke without a licence, smuggles ivory in COpenhagen, BRussels and Amsterdam, before meeting the Madam in a steam bath in the suburbs of Marseilles. Madam and Cobrita of the same novel become 'dwarfs', then 'two gauntlets, two autogenous mills, two Burmese leopards' (CB, 48/24). The agile contingency of identities is such that when Pup, transformed, goes into the bathroom and finds that 'behind an oval mirror, a Mongol peasant woman, opening her eyes, looked out at her', it takes a minute to realise that she is looking at her 'own' reflection (CB, 74/41).

On the other hand, however, and just as insistently, Sarduy describes a becoming-immobile. This is the *imperceptible-as-camouflaged*. Within a perfectly smooth space, as Baudrillard explains, all forms of movement 'are concentrated in a single fixed point, in an immobility which is no longer that of non-movement, but of a potential ubiquity, an absolute mobility which annuls its own space by dint of traversing it ceaselessly and effortlessly'.[304] Such is the movement described by Caillois' account of animal mimesis, a movement toward 'disappearance, an artificial loss of individuality', towards 'immobility and inertia'.[305] Such is the outcome of the transvestite's para-doxical 'representation of invisibility'.[306] Such too is the movement of Lezama Lima's exemplary writing. 'Lezama fixes [...]. When Lezama wants something, he pronounces it. He immobilises it phonetically, traps it among vowels and consonants, dissects it, freezes it in motion' (ES, 279–280/53). Again: 'immobility is one of Lezama's obsessions: the symbol of his work could be a scarab trapped in a paperweight: life caught at a specific moment and fixed there forever'.[307]

Once again, the apparent contradiction disappears through the singular dialectic of given and real. The more one believes that 'only motion is real', the more one is haunted, 'dominated, lacerated, by the phantom of fixity' (ES, 230–231/6). Our merely *given* (limited, or relative) mobility must become immobile, paralysed, so as to liberate the non-organic, aspecific, inhuman mobility of the Creative cosmos. Every becoming presumes or achieves the death of the given, positioned element or identity, just as 'in human *travestissement*, it is not a matter of superimposing one sex on another [...] but rather of imposing the fixity of death on a sex'[308] – and at this price, liberating a kind of 'pure sexuality' beyond dualism, beyond sexual distinction itself. Sarduy insists, after Caillois, that what drives animal mimetism is not a merely defensive 'biological necessity', but rather an 'excessive drive which operates like a lethal supplement', a hypertelic exuberance in futile self-expenditure, 'representing nothing more than an unbridled desire for waste' (SI, 58/95). At the unbearable limit of a personal or positioned immobility, the immobilised is swept away by the absolute mobility of the expanding universe itself.[309]

XI *Colibri* (1984) and the renewal of situation

Colibri provides the first indications of what will become a very different conception of the person in Sarduy's later work – a minimally specific, almost self-consistent individual, a body that flees invasion, eludes capture; a body that *acts and reacts*. Sarduy presents his fifth novel as 'a total *return* to *lo cubano*, or at least to South America'.[310] It narrates this return, certainly, within many of the parameters that govern his earlier fiction. But *Colibri* marks a clear shift of formal emphasis too. Not only does it maintain (relative) unities of time and place, but the focus is here on *relations* of possession and evasion, friendship and domination, between caricatural but clearly recognisable positions. It is this, perhaps more than a return to the Cuban *specified*, that suggests an eventual movement toward a properly specific mode of individuation. From this point on, only extraordinary *individuals*, 'only heroes and immortals have the right to hallucination' (COL, 28).

The mistake would be to posit something like a *break* in Sarduy's work. There is rather a shift from the singular *toward* the specific, a shift which exaggerates certain aspects of his earlier writing. As early as 1966, Sarduy had said that 'what gives unity [to the work…] are the characters which are forever the same and forever distinct',[311] in the particularity of a rapport between the mobile and the immobile. They retain, precisely, a kind of virtual 'unity' (variously actualised). Sarduy's characters have that serial coherence that obtains in the elaboration of multiple names along a clearly identified isotope. *Maitreya's* Lady Tremendosa, for example, is variously called Lady T, Fatso, Colossal, Roly-Poly, Monumental Miss, Bacon Fat, Mucha-Mass, the Obese One, Lady Delirium, even 'the conceited pachydermic goddess'.[312] Less than variations upon a central proper name, figurations of the truth, the proliferation of names develops a series without centre, a system without a subject. 'In appearing to name, the Baroque whistles what it denotes, it annuls it: its meaning is an insistence upon its play.'[313] The impersonal names – 'the Flower Girls, the Ever Present, the Siamese Twins, the Divine Ones, the Thirsty Ones, the Majas […] the Fates' (DC, 235/154), all so many substitutions for Auxilio and Socorro – sustain each other in the absence of a stable referent or proper name.[314]

Sarduy certainly works, like Deleuze and Guattari, for 'the destruction of the individual as metropole […] with its colonies: voice, sex, etc.'.[315] What survives this destruction is a certain *style*, a certain tone of voice or manner of expression. Sarduy explains that in the composition of a novel, it is the characters

> who first impose themselves, but each one entirely independently [..]. As for what happens to the characters, I discover this next, bit by bit, but not by chance or by force, it's as if they unfold what they are, as if they unveiled what was already inscribed in them, unknown to me, when they appeared Simply, these characters are not organised around a psychology. They are all, each in their own style, a way of showing or hiding themselves, of withdrawing or searching. It is this style that comes across in the 'events' [of the plot]. And if descriptions and arrangements matter so much to me, it's because they too prolong the style of the character […]. A novel is nothing other than variations around a character who is himself *not an entity but a tone given to his manner of existing.*[316]

Sarduy's characters, in other words, have a unity on something like the monadological model; a perspective which includes the whole world, but inflected in such a way as to express it *partially*. This partiality remains singular, rather than specific, to the degree that there is no relation between it and the world it expresses; it is rather that the world itself *is* a certain way of being perceived, according to the various partialities (a world according to Flor, to Auxilio, to Lady T, and so on).

But this partiality shifts from a singular to a specific form of coherence once the relation, however tenuous, *between* character and world begins to persist as such. And whereas in *De donde* or *Cobra*, particular positions are generally so many paths to the dissolution of position, Colibri's own position, and those of his antagonists, are mobile but at least relatively self-perpetuating. Here it is position as such that provides the medium of experience. Colibri himself will eventually take over the position of his pursuer, but the abstract distinction of positions – pursuers and pursued, dominating and dominated – will remain.

The situation (the site) affirmed by *Colibri*, likewise, is less that American heartland developed by the telluric tradition or explored in Carpentier's *Pasos perdidos*[317] than a newly *disciplined* simulation–deterritorialisation of this particular site. On the model of Goytisolo's *Makbara*, *Colibri* here begins with a 'taking position [*toma de posición*], in the literal sense of the term, that is, the adoption of a place, a site, from which the story will be told'.[318] The site itself is indeed quintessentially Latin American, a mix of jungle and delta. But it is a Latin America *staged* from elsewhere, from an outside. Less a 'recuperated nature – the real nature of the Amazonian jungle', *Colibri* presents a 'studio nature, seeming more real than the real nature. I wonder if in *Colibri* there is not a trap of simulation, of the simulacrum [...]. It may be that this nature is nothing other than a higher modality of *travestisme'*.[319] Control of the 'set' is the explicit object of staged struggles between the narrator ('Sarduy' himself) and 'gangsters' bent on turning the narrative to their own ends. Swiss alpine landscapes abruptly interrupt the lush vegetation and scatter the traces of a pre-Columbian past. Sarduy's narrator retains only a very partial control over events. As in the earlier novels, many descriptions foreground their apparent uncertainty, in the interrogative mode, and the narrator makes frequent appeals to the reader's help in piecing the puzzle of what happens together.[320]

Compared to *Maitreya* and *Cobra*, there is no doubt that *Colibri* marks a retreat of sorts from the *void* as exclusive textual foundation. The differences – comparable precisely through the familiar thematics of the cabaret, the carnivalesque, the cosmetic, the bluff, the artificial – are obvious enough in the mainly linear development of the story. *Colibri* is 'a novel about rivalry among men, a homosexual novel in the literal sense of the word, *un roman de rustres et de richards*, very South American'.[321] It orbits around a sleazy gay club simply called La Casona, that treats its sluggish customers to 'simulated fights' (COL, 169) between suitably nubile youths, a cross between the dozens and gladiatorial combat, part dance, part duel. The Casona is run by La Regente, an ageing Madame or transvestite, with the help of the Little Giant [*Gigantito*] and the ever ubiquitous Dwarf.

Colibri (literally: hummingbird) appears on the scene, without preamble, as the victor of a particularly savoury tussle with a burly Japanese karate master [*el Japonesote*]. His subsequent disappearance provokes a full-scale pursuit by the Regente's lusty 'hunters', which organises the rest of the novel.

After losing his pursuers in the jungle, Colibri finds temporary safety in the workshop of an old couple who decorate, of all things, tamed fleas – a kind of miniaturising 'body art' reproducing cosmetic features '*plus vrai que nature*, as the expression goes' (COL, 60–61). After a dramatic showdown Colibri is captured by the Little Giant, drugged and dumped in an apparently urban version of the Casona, become massage parlour/brothel. He soon escapes again (82) and while his pursuers tangle with each other, strolls into an unexpected mountain decor where he meets a solitary shepherd and eludes capture for another few pages. Taken prisoner a second time and tortured in some 'ignominious pages imposed on me by [the] gangsters' (129) who harass the hapless narrator, Colibri is this time saved by Little Giant and sped back into the jungle, triggering a series of small simultaneous explosions. Moving with superhuman fluidity, Colibri is seen, 'as if called by urgent need, or snatched up by the void', passing through walls (139). When Colibri meets up with the hunters for a last encounter, he is finally welcomed as the saviour who will take power and destroy the old order – 'long live him who flies without moving' (158). Become a 'true leader [*jefe*]' (164), he soon wields properly autocratic power. Ruling with the stern 'aplomb and pose of a *tirano en ciernos*' (167), he intervenes precisely to monitor desire, breaking up the couplings of the hunters and Moorish whores found *en route* back to the Casona, and leaving his new followers possessed by 'an evil without name [...]. In the end they became afraid of one another, and no longer dared to touch each other' (168). Back at the Casona, he flushes out the old patrons with fire and establishes a new ascetic rule, forbidding 'alcohol and drugs' along with everything that 'corrupts and weakens' (177). He ends the novel very much like the Regente who first pursued him, aged and sagging, losing his hair. His last lines, however, call for dancing and new life.[122] The cycle, no doubt, will begin again.

What drives *Colibri*, from start to finish, is what might be called a force of desiring-projection: still close to a univocal desiring production, but channelled now through relation to a particular object, through an at least partially specific investment. We are now as much caught up in the empty Lacanian orbit of an elusive *objet a* as transfigured by the pure intensity of Deleuze's schizo-flux. As always, however, this desiring force is Creative or projective rather than negative or frustrated. The Regente's obsession is more than 'merely the quest for new strength, but something far deeper, and which was impossible for her to express, awake [*en la lenguaje de la vigilia*]' (42). On one level, then, Colibri is simply a more 'substantial' version of Flor, the elusive object of desire *par excellence*, the clichéd homo-erotic fantasy: young, 'albino-blond', with long flowing hair, dressed in a 'leather slip', and so on (13–14). He is agility and grace personified, a 'weightless acrobat' (103). But on another level, Colibri has a kind of self-possession denied Flor, and indeed denied most of Sarduy's earlier characters. Not psychological depth or self-conscious 'maturity', of course, but an almost elemental integrity, an irreducible will to resist capture. Colibri's masterful becomings-other are generally turned to his own personal advantage, rather than toward a pure becoming-imperceptible as such. Pursued, Colibri 'seemed to float [...]. He was a falcon, the sleepless sentinel keeping watch, born by the four winds...' (COL, 48). For Sarduy – and it is the supreme compliment – 'Colibri is like [the dancer] Nureyev: he who can write with his body'.[323] The Regente's lust pulls Colibri in a verbal war of possession, laced with spells and incantations designed 'to capture the fugitive, asphyxiated in this verbal net' (67). But Colibri knows that 'no one will ever lay a hand on me, not even a god', for he is 'the master of red ink and black ink', covered with 'ferocious glyphs: [...] teeth, claws, beaks, hooves, concentric bulging eyes, inflated testicles, bloody sex organs hanging out of a gaping mouth' (68). If 'God is simulation' (75), and if 'the kingdom of heaven belongs to those who feign' (74), then it is Colibri, in the image of Christ, who is God's elect.[324]

Colibri's relation to the earth is, in turn, quite different from that 'denied' to Auxilio or Cobra. In *Colibri*, perhaps for the first time in Sarduy's work, 'we hear [...] the murmur of the earth' (146); 'the force that flowed through the boy, at the rhythm marked by the beating of his blood [...], came from the source *par excellence*: with him, *Eldorado* returned' (27). Lavish evocation of 'swampy vegetation' (42) and the 'the brouhaha of the jungle' (45) serves as a backdrop to our hero's ability to read the landscape and use it to his own advantage. While his hunters get literally 'bogged down' (42-43), Colibri has 'free access to the tenacious euphoria of leaves-that-know [*las hojas que saben*], and whose force regenerates more quickly the more it is spent' (28). The land is alive (45), and Colibri is its privileged inhabitant. He follows his path through the jungle 'without effort, as one moves through the memorised turns of a familiar or elementary maze' (144).

Colibri's irreducible agility contrasts with the lumbering 'whales' and sleepy 'dreamless crows' (COL, 114) who make up the Casona's clientele. The 'whales' are undifferentiated. While Colibri flits about unhindered, fully mobile, the Regente is 'petrified' by the sight of him, her 'dancers immobilised in a spasm, blocked in the middle of their orthopaedic swayings' (171). While Colibri hovers with perfect poise, his admirers, confused by the prospect of 'harpoons', are somnolent in a 'submarine forest of jelly-fish', in which 'a translucent, clinging film seemed to stick to the fish-tank of drowsy whales, like so many figures of melted wax' (39). The rhythm of life in the Casona obeys a kind of drug-induced pattern of moments of intense hyperawareness separated by long stretches of suspended anima-tion, further punctuated by black-outs like 'the cataleptic interregnum' that sets in after Colibri's initial disappearance. The party thrown in anticipa-tion of Colibri's capture, for instance, generates wild excess followed by a return to torpor; as 'the party lost its momentum, faces faded, gestures grew exhausted, overwhelmed by a sudden lassitude'.[125] Colibri is set *apart*, in other words, through sustained differentiation from the mass of those who would dominate him (and who will eventually be dominated by him).

The narrative itself, finally, is specific in relation to its own staging, and this in a slightly different sense than the purely theatrical artifice of *De donde* or *Cobra*. The artifice of narration is here both more systematic and more coherent, more *deliberate*. On the one hand, Sarduy plays with the apparent severity of fictional necessity, explaining various events in terms of a 'rigorous respect of the script'.[126] On the other hand, he violates this necessity in the most flamboyant terms, through inclusion of a mysterious band of counter-narrators, 'gangsters' set on ruining the integrity of the composition – 'kleptomaniacs of the story, the putative authors of some of the preceding chapters' (144; cf. 97). While 'Sarduy' accuses the 'gangsters' of 'mixing the background and inserting their landscapes into those of my story, thereby pulverising its precious unity of place' (99), his hero pro-ceeds through 'the mute incoherence of the landscape', puzzled by 'the unreality of his physical effort, the false presence of things' (109), but unable to guess the cause. As for 'himself', Sarduy provides his readers with a full 'scenario', complete with location on 'a colonial patio in the Cuban provinces' (98), irascible father, 'triple chin' and 'my third beer of the morning'.[127] By the time his 'normal' voice takes over (beginning with the lines: 'In reality he had…'), the reader has to ask, along with the other narrators: 'in which reality, sweetheart?' (100). As in Sarduy's earlier nov-els, the narrative maintains multiple possibilities in an impossibly pregnant present: if '*el Japonesete*' was apparently shot dead by the Regente's toy revolver, for instance, the narrator later reveals that such was simply the story 'she had told them [the plot thieves], stealing in turn the plot of these adventures […]. In truth, the rubbery karate man had escaped, lightly per-forated of course, but alive and kicking' (144). The Regente herself appears 'now as an eighty-year-old hussy, or a white Russian with wrinkles of the same colour' (81), while the folds of her flesh evoke, successively or alter-natively, 'the ceiling of a grotto, a series of larval strata, or the replastered roof of a funereal chapel in the Neapolitan rococo style' (19). A few pages later, looking at her from the back of the room, 'it is impossible to say with certainty whether we're dealing with a hill under frost, a reef crowned with polar birds, the extension of a fallacious wintry fresco, a pile of ermine, or quite simply a cloud' (32). The reader's choice.

Certainly, then, *Colibri* retains much of the comic, irreverent verve and exuberant artifice of Sarduy's earlier novels. The metaphors remain impossibly far-fetched, the play of desire is still as creative and deranged, the coherence of territory more insistent but still fluid. If *Colibri*'s own position is more finely marked, it remains a shifting position loosely set against the pure mobility of desire. When one character declares that (s)he has had enough of 'these crude simulacra that you all use and abuse, yes all, without exception, including the stubborn narrator of these pages', she could be referring to either *De donde, Cobra, Maitreya* or *Colibri*. 'Enough of appearances, of *bluffs*, empty scenes, twisted mannerisms!' (COL, 86). In Sarduy's next novel, however, the stakes involved in such complaint are to be of a very different order.

XII *Cocuyo* (1990) and disorientation

If as Sarduy confesses *Colibri* was begun in 'anxiety', 'with neither a good grasp of the characters [...] and without a hint of a plot' (RJ, 13/10), his next novel, in a sense, is *about* this very anxiety, about someone who cannot decipher the people and places that surround him. The most linear of his novels, it relates the picaresque childhood and adolescence of a boy unable to get his bearings in the world. *Cocuyo*, Sarduy admits, is the first of his novels to be closely associated with his own experience, and is much the most anguished. 'Cocuyo, the character, is entirely autobiographical, since he's me'.[328] *Cocuyo* is the novel most inflected by a nostalgia for home. As Sarduy told Macé in 1991,

> at a certain moment you ask yourself who you are, you ask about the nature of your 'profound' being, to the degree that being – if there is such a thing – can be profound. And when all is said and done, there's been a major break in my life, and I've returned to Cuba, first through texts, and then, I think, 'physically', even if I haven't actually gone back there [..] All of a sudden there's a call from something that is you, which is Camagüey, which is there. It's a slightly Heideggerian question, this place where the earth exists for you, as your concern, and so, it was the beginning of a return.[329]

Until we have access to Sarduy's letters and unpublished manuscripts, it is difficult to date this questioning, this *territorialising 'cassure'*, very precisely. With the deaths of his friends Roland Barthes (1980) Jacques Lacan (1981), and Michel Foucault (1984), Sarduy was newly isolated in an intellectual climate become more suspicious of 'high theory' and literary experimentation.[330] His book of personal addresses, he notes in 1987, had become a 'Tibetan book of the dead'.[331] Perhaps too the imminent crumbling of the Iron Curtain led him to rethink his relation to Cuba. For the moment we can only say that for whatever reason, *Cocuyo* is both Sarduy's most personal novel, and the most preoccupied by that 'slightly Heideggerian question', the question of a fundamentally 'territorial' orientation. Sarduy has always insisted that 'I have no sense of chronology nor of space', that 'I don't understand the sequence of events [...], I don't believe in the idea of continuity'.[332] With *Cocuyo*, this lack of understanding becomes more troubling than liberating, and Sarduy's later work as a whole is consolidated around notions of *therapy* or *clinique*. Just as 'tantrism practices a cromotherapy' through the mandala's distribution of colours, so 'my writing is likewise therapeutic: I write to cure myself of something. Of exile, in [*Colibrí's*] case...'[333] – perhaps of homelessness in *Cocuyo*, and of disease itself in *Pájaros*.

Cocuyo (literally: firefly) is a Chinese-Cuban boy, haunted throughout the novel by fears of abandonment and parental betrayal. The story begins with comic though excruciating humiliation on a chamber pot; the mocking laughter of his aunts sets a pattern for the future (CY, 14; 134; 148). In order to escape his 'fear of being watched' Cocuyo resorts to the extreme measure of poisoning his entire family, and feigns his own coma in order to escape the subsequent medical examination, conducted by two rival specialists, Caimán and Isidro. Our hero escapes from the hospital-leprosaurium in supremely picaresque style, to be helped by an 'elderly and tidy Negress' (CY, 55) on to a home (*el patronato*) run by an imperious matron generally called the 'Most Good' or 'All Good'. Cocuyo grows up isolated and insecure in these new surroundings, falls for the young Ada (CY, 63–64), dabbles in alcohol, runs errands for notaries and lawyers, and slowly comes to understand that the *patronato* deals in prostitution if not slavery, in alliance with the corrupt Caimán and Isidro. Much of *Cocuyo* is structured as a kind of detective story, driven by the question: 'what was the truth, what role was the Too Good playing?' (79). Soon after Cocuyo witnesses the sale of the adolescent Ada into prostitution (111–113) he discovers the 'malevolent, diabolical' tower worked by former residents of the *patronato* (126), a place where 'they sell virgins to the highest bidder' (170).

The remainder of the novel has Cocuyo wander through an urban purgatory, finding disturbing signs of his past and still more disturbing signs of the present, in the form of labyrinths, riddles and deception. He comes to understand that 'for years, he had been manipulated, used, the easy victim of petty chiefs, of their venomous games, of their meticulous work [*trabajo*] of simulation' (CY, 168). The novel ends with Cocuyo's encounter with a drugged Ada dancing naked in Caimán and Isidro's club (The Pavillion of the Pure Orchid), set in 'pestilent swamps' (188). Beaten almost senseless by the club's bouncers, Cocuyo 'felt imprisoned and alone [...;] everyone had betrayed him [...]. But deep down, he told himself, he was grateful to them: they had showed him the true face of man, his fundamental duplicity, his need, as peremptory as that of hunger or thirst, for ruse and meanness' (207–208). The novel ends with his determination to return 'to exterminate them all. And himself with them, and so to sweep the universe clean of all this manure' (209).

Although *Cocuyo* maintains many of the familiar elements of Sarduy's earlier fiction – a penchant for becomings-animal, a playful narrative style, a proliferation of namings, a more-than-realist intensity of description, and so on – what is most striking about the novel is its virtually systematic *revaluation* of the categories of transgression so heartily affirmed in *De donde*, *Cobra* or *Maitreya*. The implications of sensory-motor paralysis, of disorientation, of sexuality, and even of narrative incoherence, are all thrown into question here. Broadly speaking, despite the occasionally playful or ironic quality of this quasi-autobiographical tale, *Cocuyo* suggests something of a crisis in Sarduy's commitment to radical singularity, a moment of profound doubt and uncertainty.

In the first place, the breakdown of sensory-motor coordination is as emphatic here as it is in *De donde*, but it is now experienced as loss rather than liberation. Cocuyo lives his life as 'indecipherable'; 'his story was a frayed tapestry, without apparent design, seen in a dream' (CY, 155), like the purgatorial brothel tapestried with 'scenes that Cocuyo couldn't decipher [...], collages of sundry animals, grotesque claws that defied understanding and parodied reason' (159–160). Cocuyo has indeed been transformed into pure seer or spectator – but through a crippling anxiety. He has become someone who 'waits for something, even though he know with a certainty that no one would come' (104). The novel is punctuated with less deliberate blanks: Cocuyo faints when Ada is taken from the *patronato* (115), and blacks out when she is paraded for sale, to wake up, dazed, in a tavern of the port (167). Such traumatic moments provoke a recurrent *paralysis of voice* – the very seat, as we shall see, of personal identity in Sarduy's last novels: 'As if in a dream, he tried to scream. He expelled the air from the back of his throat, from his chest, his belly. With all his strength. Nothing' (CY, 51); 'Not a word would come out' (99); 'He wanted to call for help; but he knew the effort was useless: this kind of failure had become familiar; he opened his mouth and nothing came out' (191).

The paralysis of voice not only suggests a crisis of expression in the most general sense, but reflects a more general revaluation of orientation and relation. The mute Cocuyo cannot intervene effectively in circumstances that exceed reaction. Trapped in quicksand near the Pavillion, his external silence is matched by internal estrangement: 'his body was something alien, which he couldn't feel and didn't want to feel, a crude, poorly articulated object [...]. His body soon became an undifferentiated thing, mixing with the mud [...]; he had become inert matter' (191-192). Such mimetic becoming now appears to be an exclusively negative experience. If it fulfils Cocuyo's original wish – spied fumbling on his chamber-pot, 'he would have liked to disappear forever in the bottom of the jar' (14) – it is driven by self-loathing, impotence and frustration, rather than the effort to transcend these merely personal experiences. Again, if his leap to freedom from the leprosaurium reflects 'the urgent necessity [...] of being an other, which explains his ability to double himself' (50), this necessity now stems from 'his disgust for himself', his conviction of absolute and irrevocable *guilt*. Leaping, he feels his body to be 'so dirty and contemptible that he sees in it only a charcoal mass, a filthy rag, a useless weight'.[334] The desire 'to become another' now derives from his desire 'to de-exist', merely (53–54).

Above all, wandering through the dark streets of the city, Cocuyo realises, 'in a manner as definitive and certain as death, that he was missing that thing which for others was so natural a part of life that they were not even aware of it. the sense of orientation [...]. He grasped, dimly, as if receiving an inarticulate but dreadful warning, that he would be forever lost, disoriented, without an internal compass to guide him, as if the whole world was for him a laborious labyrinth...' (CY, 146–147; cf. 61). Plunged in a 'total obscurity', Cocuyo 'didn't know how to decode the reality which surrounded him. And this opacity was lethal...' (107). More, he realises 'that never would he be able to count on someone else to guide him, that his deficiency appeared to others as a vice' (148). He lives this absence of relation as traumatic rather than transformative. From his first strugglings with 'the fear of being watched' (14), the friendless, solitary Cocuyo is unable to 'connect' in the most literal sense. On his wanderings outside the *patronato*, 'he spoke to nobody, went into no tavern [...] If he drank a beer, he drank it alone' (CY, 94), living an uninterrupted 'exile without return'.[335]

Unlike Auxilio or Cobra, Cocuyo cannot convert this exile into an otherworldly inheritance. Hallucination is now tinged with the fear of manipulation, as when he wakes up, hung over, after Caimán and Isidro's mysterious visit: 'had he dreamed the whole scene? [...] Was it all just delirium [...]? Or rather, once again, had they tried to take advantage of him, make fun of him, manipulate his fragility the more relentlessly, enjoying it. But to what end?'[336] Disorientating perception is now just that, rather than re-orientating. For example, watching a procession of monks, 'Cocuyo saw images pass by without order or sequence, accelerated in the way that we see things, so they say, in the seconds which precede the moment of death, exaggerated, torn, twisted, changing form and colour, the one

becoming the other, monstrous, drawn out, helical, gilded...' (149). Meanwhile, outside, 'the mauvish blue shadows of things seemed to turn rapidly
around him, as if the moon, become mad, cut across the sky in a single
swipe. Or perhaps it was his own body that had changed, inhabited by
someone else' (153). The self is here usurped rather than transformed.
Seduced in the sinister brothel, Cocuyo hears his lost, beloved sister as if
calling from 'the coast: "Cocuyo, Cocuyo!" But he paid her no heed.
Besides, the voice was unreal, distant, or perhaps imitated by someone
else' (135). There is no way to tell.

Sexual experience itself lacks much of its formerly tantric property. Ada's
sale is trumped up as a deceitful 'becoming-woman'; her ears are pierced in
a ritual penetration ('Ada's cry was that of an animal struck by an arrow' [113])
that has nothing to do with liberation. The trappings of sex are now the literal emblems of slavery.[337] Sex is described as that almost archetypal relation
between shame and liberation – between the remembered humiliation and
awkwardness of the child Cocuyo's toilet traumas (134), and the promise of
passionate abandon. While 'all that mattered was to let himself go, to let himself be carried away without resistance by the swell' (135), Cocuyo cannot
manage more than a stifled movement. 'He felt oppressed, as if all the
branches of his bronchial tree were blocked, and the air remained stuck
in each of these disjunctions, unable to chose a way out, until he lost his
clarity, sooty and lethal'.[338] His eventual orgasm is less explosion than wound
– 'he felt like he was losing all his blood' – incurred in the midst of a
chattering indifference (137). In *Cocuyo* we find the first symptoms of
desire-as-lack, rather than a purely affirmative desiring-production.[339]

We also find a new concern for 'defenceless deformity' (CY, 26), along
with a kind of anticipated nostalgia for 'the future in which, before being
devoured by the present, things exist in an ideal state, incorruptible' (107).
Far from celebrating the superhuman masochism of *Cobra's blousons
noirs*, Sarduy here puts a new emphasis on the 'fragility of the body' (71),
the vulnerability of a *child* as such, as opposed to a dwarf-spawn doll.[340]
Through an abandoned and broken-hearted Cocuyo, Sarduy asks a question without precedent in his oeuvre: 'My God, how is it possible that so
limited and fragile a body manages to endure such suffering?' (163). With
Cocuyo, in short, Sarduy addresses for the first time the relation between
innocence and *evil*. There could be no place for malevolence in a novel like
Cobra, of course. But here we encounter a genuinely malicious practice of
slavery – not only Ada's enslavement, but the apparently anachronistic
slave markets of nineteenth-century Havana (180-181). We also encounter,
for the first time, a *merely vicious* sadism, in the form of a Caimán with
'face fixed in an infanticidal smile' (97) and a natural world more predatory
than prolific (18, 155). The novel is laced with disgust for the human

species in general, presented as 'an irrecuperable dejection, rubbish' (179). Cocuyo concludes, simply, that 'man is the shit of the universe' (205). If the pathos of the novel is sometimes exaggerated, sometimes ironic, the overall effect is less carnivalesque than heart-felt in the proper sense, an indictment of treachery and malice (208).

The consequent change in narrative style is no less significant. The narrative of Cocuyo's systematic disorientation is itself the most clearly oriented, the most coherent in the conventional sense, of all Sarduy's stories. The *Bildungsroman* aspect of the story, Cocuyo's slow coming-into-awareness of 'the lie', lends a strongly linear momentum to the novel. Cocuyo is soon sceptical both of 'the goodness of the *Bondadosa* [i.e. the Señora] and of what happened, in general, apparently or in reality' (CY, 77). Slowly 'he perceived – but in an immaterial, indemonstrable way – the dark emanation of the facts, something like a scrambled echo, a tenuous shadow: that which remains, impalpable, in a room after a crime has been committed, and which no one can put their finger on, but which some people experience as unbearably obvious' (85). Detective of his own sanity, 'he was looking for a clue. Or rather: for the proof that he was, yes, healthy in mind' (86). And this search duly reveals an order every bit as coherent as that hidden within the traditional detective novel. 'The causes appeared interwoven, tied to their consequences by indestructible links, like animals which devour and then vomit each other, toward eventual extinction' (87).

Compared with *De donde* or *Cobra*, or even *Colibri*, *Cocuyo* cannot fail to strike the reader by its often over-determined narrative coherence. On balance, everything comes together with minimum recourse to *Cobra*'s 'art of digression' (CB, 16/6). For example, the first chapter introduces, in succession: Cocuyo's shy fear of mockery, the severity of his aunts, the availability of rat poison, and the traumatic storm, before concluding, in a couple of tight, almost minimalist sentences, with the denouement: a humiliated Cocuyo, frightened by the storm, serves his family tea laced with rat-poison. The final sentence echoes the chapter's title – 'so that no one knows I'm afraid' (CY, 27). Further examples of narrative integrity abound: a girl expelled from the orphanage on suspicion of sorcery turns up later as a 'witch' working for the brothel; Caimán and Isidro, introduced as vaguely malevolent doctors, turn out to be at the centre of the conspiracy; Cocuyo's apparently unmotivated prediction, on the eve of the storm, of the arrival of bats (21), is confirmed by Caimán's discussion of the 'nocturnal sucking of certain bats' (46) as a possible but unlikely cause for the familial coma, and so on.[341]

Not only does Sarduy's narrator take new trouble to guide his readers,[342] but in *Cocuyo* writing is itself a response to disorientation, a countermeasure. To write is here to find a way through the apparent obscurity of things, to see what is 'really going on'. Dizzied by a 'monstrous' play of 'reflections', the passing shapes of a monastic procession seen both 'through' and 'upon' the glass of a window pane, Cocuyo struggles to make an inventory of what he sees: 'in the foreground [...], spread fingers, ringed [...] behind, like the fragile and ephemeral fragments of a mosaic seen under water, points and stripes [...]: the clock... the smell of Ada... [...] the taste of creme de vie...' He concludes:

> it must be this, what is called writing: *to be able to distinguish things from their reflections* [. .] 'If I wrote', he said to himself, 'I could make things appear and disappear in their thickness [*en su espesura*], and not as they appear on the glass, confused with their reflections, in disorder.' (CY, 149–150, my emphasis)

Living among stacks of legal documents, the pre-literate Cocuyo is immediately fascinated by print and reading (68). Later, he copies legal writings, as if 'to conjure a phobia'[343] – the phobia, perhaps, of displacement and disorientation, conjured away with this minimal imposition of order and relation, a literary figuration of 'home'.

In a note appended to *Cocuyo*, Sarduy invites interpretation of the 'advice' provided by recourse to the Bible: 'And warned in a dream not to return to Herod, they went home another way'.[344] The storm which evokes the Inquisition and the massacre of the innocents (18–19) appears here to be blowing against the flame of extinction [*Nirvana*] which burns so brightly in *Cobra* and *Maitreya*. Beginning with *Cocuyo*, Sarduy is looking to go home by another way – not via the mass 'annihilation' of worldly or specific categories, but through them. Not via a writing conceived as immanent to a pure non-attachment or placelessness, but through a writing conceived as the figuration of relations without specifying substance, relations qua relations (of trust or deception, domination or obedience, love or enmity...). In his last novel, the testament that is *Pájaros de la playa*, this writing takes up the most difficult relation of them all: the relation *between* life and death.

XIII From death to dying

The relation of life and death is of course hardly a new theme in Sarduy's work. Death is a constant companion of his earlier novels, 'always beside us, industrious, infinitesimal' (CB, 245/139), an integral part of the one vital flow, an 'unceasing reconversion' (ES, 230/6). But in the earlier works death retains a mainly carnivalesque aspect.[345] The author of *Cobra* would agree with Baudrillard: death is not an end (the 'dead' Cobra returns) but rather 'a form in which the determinacy of the subject and of [economic] value is lost'.[346] *De donde* begins with the cheerful call to 'Drop dead! [...], fuck yourself. Turn to dust, to ashes' (DC, 91/11). Its rotting wooden Christ remains philosophical: 'Why all this moaning? – He said – Kicking the bucket is great fun. Life only begins after death'.[347] Dolores of the same novel 'enters death in a major key, as she once entered life [...]. "Let there be rum at my wake"' (DC, 148/63). As a general rule, in these earlier novels, 'death – the pause that refreshes – is *part* of life' (CB, 230/130), and in most of Sarduy's work, as in Marmori's *Storia de Vous*, 'there is not a single sign, explicit or otherwise, of resistance to suffering' (ES, 239/14).

Throughout Sarduy's fiction, there is certainly much talk of the '*la ardua voluptuosidad de sufrir*',[348] of the intimate relation of pleasure and pain. 'Submission' to such pain is not properly related *to* a sufferer, however, but provides further means to escape this relation. We have seen how *Cobra's blousons noirs* are 'impervious to pain'; their sadistic rituals turn real agony on its head, until 'blood can become ketchup, and semen, yoghurt'.[349] The pain of Cobra's own transformation is transferred onto Pup's staged immolation, presented as a mainly astronomical sequence. For most of Sarduy's work, the body is a puppet, stage prop or cartoon image, to be broken and remade at will. This happy fragility is of course consistent with Sarduy's main project – an effort to present the *yo*, the self, as a series of 'totally ephemeral' and 'unconnected elements'. This 'Buddhist notion of the subject [...] has no existence [*entidad*], no being [*ser*]' in the conventional sense.[350] The major presumption at work in Sarduy's writing up to this point is that of the *inexhaustible* resources of an impersonal or non-organic life, based on the incomprehensible fullness or virtual intensity that is the void [*sunyata*]. His baroque is first and foremost 'superabundance, overflowing cornucopia'.[351] Like Deleuze's philosophy, most of Sarduy's novels assume an ever-receding vital frontier, a capacity for infinite expansion and renewal. The baroque morality of waste and expenditure presumes the transcendence of a properly economic sphere. Waste in this context is a rigorously inconsequential experience; nothing is ever *lost*. As Auxilio quips, 'Reality is a simple matter of birth and death, so why worry ourselves sick?' (DC, 194/112). What changes in *Pájaros*, very simply, is that now we *are* sick. Worry results.

It is hard to pinpoint exactly how this change comes about. It is not just a matter, certainly, of drawing a direct consequence of Sarduy's own illness.[352] That an awareness of Aids informs the writing of *Pájaros* is obvious enough, but the shift in Sarduy's writing begins some years before he began composing this last novel. Writing in 1987, Sarduy notes in a chilling passage that 'Aids is a stalking. It feels as if someone, at any moment, under any pretext at all, could knock on the door and carry you off forever, as if an undetermined danger hovered in the air and could solidify, jell in the space of an instant. Who will be next? For how long will you escape?' (RJ, 27–28/34). The disease violates, in other words, the once smooth space of metamorphosis, it congeals the vital flow, surrounds it with a limiting *horizon*. The age of limitless expenditure is suddenly undermined by the pressures of conservation.

If *Pájaros* (1993) is the first novel to address the personal process of dying rather than the anonymous void of death,[353] still the ways in which Sarduy here approaches the question develop the long-term shift away from radical singularity that began with *Colibrí* (1984). We have seen how *Cocuyo* revalues Sarduy's life-long experience of disorientation. In parts of *El Cristo* too the pre-eminent gestures of Sarduy's previous literary practice – substitution, erasure and repetition – are refused in favour of that most sentimental of *relations*: personal attachment to a friend in the face of death (RJ, 84/103). For one reason or another, Sarduy is drawn to redefine his notion of the individual as more specific than singular. The *dying* individual is one who relates *to* death, rather than mutate in keeping with an impersonal becoming-death or becoming-imperceptible.

Like *Escrito sobre un cuerpo*, *El Cristo* engages in a reading of the body – but unlike the earlier book, it is now 'the reading of *my* body' (RJ, 13/9, my emphasis). As before, the skin is the 'deepest' layer of the body (cf. RJ, 8/vii). The body remains surface, but it is now a surface striated, marked, specified – a surface upon which experience accumulates. In the first 'epiphany' narrated here, the child Sarduy moves from being 'literally almost the same person' as his mother to knowing 'that I was the owner of a different skin'. The knowledge is won through pain, the stab of a massive thorn into his skull. Under the surgeon's blade, Sarduy knows that 'the pain was mine'; his body's 'boundaries had been burned in blood, its edges blazed'.[354] This is a properly post-sadistic notion of pain, it is an *individualising* pain. The experience distinguishes. Throughout *El Cristo*, Sarduy searches for 'the fleeting suppression of loneliness, the foolish interruption of one's isolation' (RJ, 17/18).

A new sobriety prevails in this text. Describing a 'party, our party: fusion, relatives bound fast in a space beyond all prohibition' – the dominant tone is that of a 'sadness from before time'. It is 'a mortuary fiesta: our baroque is funereal [...]. The characters are bound fast, as in a Laocoön, but each one is trapped in loneliness' (RJ, 62/75). Sarduy engages directly here with his own 'phobia, my lack of close ties: the phantom that haunts every exile' (83/101). He reflects now on 'over a quarter of a century of texts wrought by melancholy and exile' (99/124). *El Cristo* is informed by a new sense of unease. Confronted with catastrophe in the 'real world', the intransitive quality of writing now appears in a rather different light:

> Writing is useless. It does nothing to rescue those who are swept away by a sea of lava [...]. Writing, and the rest. A lesson in the ephemeral for anyone who looks helplessly at those bodies covered with mud, shielded, asphyxiated

by a scab that slowly hardens [...]. In the face of these passing images, a healthy divertissement is the diligent threading of words, aligning them precisely and rhythmically: absurd hobby of the idle, benign vice of the unemployed.

Blink your eyes, string a phrase together, and an entire city has been buried, every sleeping citizen petrified [...]. Writing presumes a lack of awareness, or slight irresponsibility, on the part of the one who forgets or evades while, caught in the magma, the precipitous shroud solidifying around her, a little girl asks her mother to pray.[355]

For perhaps the first time, Sarduy turns to conventional irony, even outrage. The next sequence in the collection, 'Soldiers', describes how Soviet troops 'razed an [Afghan] hovel and machine-gunned its seventeen inhabitants [...], three grenades in the windows and incinerated the whole family. The smell of scorched bodies, burning blood, excrement and urine was so strong that the soldiers, after that brave assault, fainted or doubled over with spasms of vomit. But they continued to liberate their sister country. (They're given heroin and opium, so that it will all seem like a game)' (RJ, 77/95–96). 'Just gaming' is no longer an option; drugs do more than deterritorialise; the body is more than a toy.

Of course, the political stakes of a novel such as *Cobra* are every bit as high as those raised in *Cocuyo* or *Pájaros*. Sarduy was always a supremely *serious* writer, a militant believer in the transformative power of art. The point is simply that the terms of engagement have changed. The ideal is now more Bodhissatva's than Buddha's. Sarduy's last texts work through positions, through territories, through relations, through experiences, rather than transcend them. Consider for example the revaluation of voice. If Sarduy has always maintained the privilege of a kind of vocal presence – 'the voice: [...] a vessel of protection against violence' (MY, 17/155) – this presence begins as fully impersonal, as Blanchot's *murmure anonyme* or Deleuze's indirect discourse. For the earlier Sarduy, exactly as for Deleuze, 'the voice – the voices, from recitative modulation to operatic tessitura, from correct pronunciation to stammering – has no owner, no centred subject to phony it up, no psychological producer of signs; it has been freed, decolonised'. Instead, Sarduy's writing follows the 'discourse murmur' as if following a 'maze, a hidden passageway',[356] a rhizomatic sequence. In his radio play *Las Matadoras de hormigas*, for example, 'what one character says could be said, in the last instance, by another. The voice is not the indicator of a psychology or a personality'.[357]

For the later Sarduy, however, although the voice never becomes a psychological or specified aspect of personality, it does become at least *relative to* a person. Voice becomes precisely the relation between the personal and the cosmic, between individual inflection and the 'murmur of the earth'.

Voice now evokes the specific if not the specified nature of a particular thing. For example, a drunken Cocuyo sees objects as if 'they were full not of texture or colour, but of themselves, of their voice or the muffled echo of their being' (CY, 82). The cosmologist of *Pájaros* writes that 'the voice is the truth of the body [...]. The voice perishes before the person, and survives the person. Not its physical texture, which degrades, breaks, and falls, but its mental image, close to speech, which rises up, as if pulled by the zenith of an invisible sun' (PP, 160). Voice is now associated with the most durable, most essential aspect of a thing or person – the most lasting or memorable aspect. However 'alien', voice remains forever *recognisable*. One of the murmuring noises of Cocuyo's childhood, for instance, is 'that of children whose throats were cut by the Inquisition, who returned with their interminable complaint, their voices torn but recognisable. For only the voice remains intact after death.'[358]

XIV *Pájaros de la playa* (1993)[359]

In 1984, Sarduy happily compares his neo-baroque to the process of '*cancerización* – the anarchic proliferation of cells without model, without paradigm to regulate this proliferation, without subject, I would say'.[360] His last novel presents a very different picture of pathology, from a totally different *point of view* – the point of view, precisely, of the *subject* of pathology (the person subjected). *Pájaros* is about memory, ageing, dying and disease – about 'preparing not to be [*no ser*]' (PP, 133). The encounter with disease provokes a newly urgent sense of isolation, a more searching form of introspection. In one sense, there is no more Buddhist a theme than this call for a disciplined approach to extinction.[361] In another sense, however, the struggle to deal with these issues takes Sarduy far from the fundamental logic, if not the thematics, of his earlier work. There is certainly no nostalgia for a substantial self-identity, a specified sense of self. But there is new interest in a particular relationship *to* the loss of this specification. Between the singularity of extinction and a re-specification of the self, *Pájaros* charts an unusual exploration of the specific as such.

The novel takes place mainly within the walls of a hospice for those stricken with a terminal disease, more or less explicitly identified as Aids.[362] Its inmates, 'the old ones', are 'young people prematurely ravaged by a lack of strength, abruptly struck by the evil [*el mal*]' (PP, 20). The hospice is set in an isolated island, ringed with beaches. The novel begins with a description of joggers on the beach, muscled, powerful, making daily tribute to 'health' (11). Meanwhile, members of a nudist colony perform exercises, raising their arms like the title's 'birds of the beach pictured at the moment of their first flight, trying their fragile wings' (12). But the colony, once 'as mobile as multitudinous', is now 'reduced to nothing: aged, and anaemic' (13). This opening sequence establishes a prevailing tone of lethargy and fatigue (13, 19). The narrator calls it 'an anaemic, fetid, closed-in world, in which every character follows an irreversible decline towards *caquexia* and the final disincarnation'.[363] The hospice inmates spend their time discussing the virtues of various healing strategies, and search for ways to endure the steps of their daily existence. Doctors Caimán and Isidro, adapted from *Cocuyo*,[364] present a choice of therapies soon decided in favour of Caimán's holistic herbalism, but treatment serves mainly as distraction. There is clearly no chance of a genuine cure.

Only two characters are fleshed out in any detail: the cosmologist, and Siempreviva. Together they personify, up to a point, the two poles of Sarduy's aesthetic, his 'two paths' to insight: sobriety or excess, *el blanco* or the explosion of colour.[365] On the one hand, the unnamed cosmologist – whose journal provides the only direct, first-person discourse of the novel, and whose voice comes to dominate the second half of the book – is the only character to say 'I', but he remains effectively anonymous, without past or place. The cosmologist is pure voice. He speaks with all the authority Sarduy lends this most privileged branch of science, 'the true poetry of our time'.[366] He has 'seen the stars and knows what happens in their centre [...], I know what form has the universe and where it comes from' (102). He writes in preparation for 'an abandoning of oneself. To free the way to cease being' (129). He eventually withdraws alone to a quasi-monastic 'cell in order to write a journal of the extinction of the cosmos and its metaphor: disease' (120); 'I write here, in this absence of time and place, so that this negation may be said, so that everyone may feel in themselves this immobile privation of being' (130). Such words could have been taken straight from the *Prajñaparamita* sutras.[367]

The cosmologist, in other words, writes an ascetic becoming-imperceptible, an approach to singularity through subtraction rather than proliferation. His illness eliminates the world of *accessories* in the broadest sense. 'Now there are no more spectators. Nobody who watches, who names or who judges another, anymore than there is a different state, object, or being to affront. Everything is established or dissolved in the same thirst for unity' (PP, 112). As the Zen tradition says: 'loosing and dropping off body and mind, see before you your true nature'.[368] The cosmologist writes on the edge of existence, poised on the brink of non-being, transparent to the 'central void' (PP, 221): 'Hurtling down/toward non-being/where nothing manifests/Divinity/nor any range of colour./[...]. To strive not to be./To blend with that [*fusionar con eso*]' (222–223). Like the earlier Sarduy, the cosmologist concludes that 'behind appearances – those of people and those of things – there is nothing' (164). But the emphasis

here is on an ascetic subtraction *from* appearances, rather than their proliferation. The introspection required forces him back on this most personal of forms, the journal. It is an introspection directed toward its
imminent redundancy, but it is written as a confrontation *with* this immi-
nence, rather than a celebration of its accomplished immanence. Illness
condenses but does not eliminate the particular attributes of the stricken
self: the 'sick man would like [...] to reduce his days to two or three essential syllables which would be like the few characters engraved on the inside
of a wedding ring, the invisible mark of a passage on Earth, the guarantee
of his particularity [*su singularidad*]' (131). The sufferer turns to cleansers
more than cosmetics: 'To reject clothing./To rub your hands with alco-
hol/[...]. So that from your pores/is expelled/the smell of death' (221–222).

Siempreviva, on the other hand, presents a desiring vitality consistent
with her name, powerful enough to reverse, temporarily, the process of
ageing itself. While her story is related in the third person, she is the only
character equipped with a past and a place. She arrives with a 'whole
panoply of cosmetics' (PP, 31) and huge chests of clothes which she parades
like a 'fashion show' (34). With Siempreviva, 'the accessory – what was with
everyone else the forgettable detail – was essential [...]: the fashion show
as the meaning of life' (198). Like Sarduy himself, she lives 'a notion of time
as pliable as that of a paper house' (33). It is Siempreviva who sparks the
most recognisably 'Sarduyesque' sequences of the novel. Rivals for her
attention, Caimán and Isidro become-animals through their rivalry, cay-
man and horse, each with their particular anatomical advantages.[369] Siempreviva has a vision which evokes the whole menagerie of Sarduy's work:
she sees the Horse

> surrounded by a circle of animals which were devouring each other. A green-
> ish and voracious caiman was strangling itself by swallowing a cobra which
> rippled in the hands of an Indian god, the same cobra was swallowing
> a weightless hummingbird [*colibri*] suspended in the air above a piece of a
> sugar, the bird, in its turn, attracted by the phosphorescence, gulped down
> a firefly [*cocuyo*] in a single mouthful. The Horse occupied the centre of
> this chain of swallowing animal-emblems. a circle of bulging eyes, of claws,
> feathers and scales.[370]

Arriving at the hospice discouraged and worn out, Siempreviva is soon
revitalised by Isidro's 'equine corpulence' (40). Rather than retreat into the
cosmologist's solitude, she draws new energy from this supremely metaphysical relationship: 'loving bodies are never the real bodies, but others
invoked and projected by the lovers' imaginations', says Siempreviva (44)
and after meeting 'the Horse', she 'had only one idea in her mind [...],
an obsession, more like: she wanted to grow young again' (46). Where the

cosmologist turns to the purifying emptiness of outer space, Siempreviva turns her ear to the healing 'murmur of the earth'.[371] She wakes up one morning with 'desires to live' (115) and abandons her cosmetics, pronounced 'ruinous, artificially coloured and toxic', in order to 'return to a bright life, in harmony with the air and the light' (100). Almost immediately, her skin turns smooth, and she begins to grow younger. Credit is given to Caimán's 'green medicine' (117), 'a real phytotherapeutic triumph' (178).

The novel is further punctuated with flashbacks to Siempreviva's youth (in which she retains her given name, Sonia).[372] Here we find vintage Sarduy sequences of carnival and excess – parties, orchestras, vomitings, albinos, and so on (141–146). It is with this same Sonia that Sarduy evokes, as if following Deleuzian instructions, 'that devout silence, that incredulous meditation, half astonished, half sepulchral, which seals every true discovery of a work of art, however fleeting it may be, and which plunges the discoverer into an inexplicable absence, a non-being close to idiocy, to aphasia or to beatitude' (PP, 85–86). The atmosphere evoked in these passages has all the ephemeral intensity of a dream or mirage. Sonia herself appears 'absent, as if her true being was elsewhere' (147), and the general tone is suggested by the fragile delicacy of images in frost, spread over a nocturnal volcano's rocks – purely 'artificial form, without solidity nor substance; a decor without thickness nor foundation [...], on the edge of collapse or of disappearance' (148).

Siempreviva's story plays the ambiguity of simulation through to the end. Cosmetics-queen or new-age homoeopath, her frantic explorations of the 'vital surface' never escape an ultimate futility. Caimán's apparent success, 'celebrated with repeated gulps of parsley juice' (118), is achieved through a 'green botanical terrorism' soon revealed to be a 'total phytotechnical imposture' (100), narrated with wry detachment if not ridicule, and refused by the cosmologist who knows better. While Siempreviva grows younger in body, her mind 'deteriorates' (179); her apparent senility recalls the pampered Sonia with her blue Bugatti. Her simulated energy is exposed, in the end, as a sham. After a time, 'old age returned, incurable; even more deceitful than disease' (212). If her costumes impress, still 'a costume shines for an instant and will then be, the next instant, useless, shapeless, even ridiculous. A cast-off: like the body which we deliver to death. Clothes, like butterflies, dazzle and then fall. La mode, c'est la mort' (199). Siempreviva's path leads her to death and extinction as surely as does simulation itself.[373] It is, as Sarduy has been telling us all along, another means to the Buddhist-cosmologist's end.

The stories of Sonia and the cosmologist converge, up to a point, in the voice of her lover the architect, 'the precursor' (172), who forty years before the cosmologist strives to hear 'the echo of the Big Bang' in the 'murmur of the Earth' (87–88). He builds a house based on a perception of 'nature as a single living being [...], beneath the reefs', where he 'listen[s] to the murmur of the tides by day and, at night, deep in its strata, the almost imperceptible murmur of the earth as it turns, or that of the origin, the echo of the original explosion' (93). But the cosmologist knows, as the architect learns, that is impossible to *settle down* within this echo. As the Buddhist scriptures insist, 'in no dwelling place have sages/ever apprehended [Perfect Wisdom]';[374] Buddha's wisdom exists only in 'a homeless state'.[375] The architect's project is soon flushed out by a cyclone, and then crushed to oblivion by the collapse of the extinct volcano, which fell like 'a star destroyed by its own compacity' (212).

Siempreviva ends the novel similarly unhomed: the only way to live within the 'single living being' is to keep moving, or to attain an immobility beyond place. The novel ends suspended on a deliberately inconclusive note. Caimán and Isidro suddenly disappear and Siempreviva sets off in pursuit, through a landscape now littered with fast-food chains. Her story stops mid-route, with the discovery of the architect's ruined house, leaving her torn between the lure of travel or a return to the hospice, between youth and age – 'tangles and denouements [*enlaces y desenlaces*] that I will return to relate' (213). The cosmologist gets the last word, with the inclusion of Buddhist-inspired poems from his Journal.

Taken *together*, the cosmologist's journal and Siempreviva's story point, I think, to a new approach to identity and relation in Sarduy's work, made up of materials drawn from his earlier preoccupations. The two voices present mainly parallel universes, without apparent interconnection. Where they coincide directly is with a certain attitude to *fatigue*. The cosmologist: 'To identify completely with something: with fatigue. Let there be no boundaries, let there be nothing between it and me. We absorb each other in this morbid unity, like two mutually devouring amoebas, as insatiable as we are sickly' (PP, 112). And Siempreviva: her tiredness 'is that of another world. As if it had no limits. Something that becomes our very body, the air we breathe [...]. There comes a time when between fatigue and oneself there is no longer a difference. It is, or we are, the same thing'.[376] The immanence of a single becoming-imperceptible? Partly. But within this new immanence, however, fatigue remains a restriction *upon* what the body can do, rather than its liberation into unlimited becoming. Fatigue limits the self, defines its range. For it is as healthy that 'we manage to forget life, or to consider it something transparent, indestructible [...]. So it goes until suddenly, one day, we realise that the gift, the gratuity that we have enjoyed, is about to be taken away from us: a realisation signalled by failing energy, the inevitable loss of weight...' (155). The blood and sperm celebrated in *Cobra*, now poisoned, 'nourish all that is morbid' (PP, 74). The morbid circumscribes life – or rather, co-implied with death, organic life takes on a specific *rarity* of its own. To be ill is 'to see one's body from the outside, like the object of an experiment, while the evil achieves its patient work' (196; cf. 156).

This separation of the body defines it not as a free-floating singularity, but as isolated-in-relation to others. Disease eliminates radical autonomy. 'To be sick means to be connected to different machines' (PP, 109), just as it means to be tied to the *past.* According to the cosmologist, 'ill is the person who goes back over his past. He knows – he suspects, dimly – that no future awaits him, not even that miserable future which consists of watching things happen, being silent witness to their inextricable succession. He abandons himself then, meticulous, to the ordering of what has gone by' (131). What is difficult now is precisely what was so perfectly easy (indeed almost automatic) before: digression. 'That's the hard thing: to think of something else. To move on to something different' (135).

The smoothly reversible temporality of Sarduy's earlier fiction does not survive this encounter with disease. Terminal illness orients the present toward an inevitable end. In an earlier novel like *De donde son los cantantes*, as Montero notes, the authorial '"I" fades it and out [...], signalling its role as "shifter", as empty sign. Far from alluding to a human plenitude, it signals the linguistic dependence of such plenitude, and drains it of the metaphor of vitality, leaving the pronoun as a shell, now literally floating, adrift, only temporarily filled by the reader'.[177] This situation, again, has changed with disease (a line of distinction that no amount of sympathy can cross). However contagious its biological basis, the experience of disease is not itself transferable. Ill, the patient works within the horizon of real but limited goals, defined by an *economy* of limited expenditure. 'The great project of the day: "We'll go as far as the lime trees"' (23). The next day's 'objective':

> to create the image of themselves dressed, freshly washed, shaved, healthy and perfumed, writing, reading, alert and joyful in the morning sun. They tried to attain this image... First: lower the right leg until it touches the ground. Then, get up a little bit, using the left hand Watch out for the vertebra. Hold on to the edge of the bed with the right hand. Sitting. Grab a sock. Put it on. A first step toward the ideal image... (PP, 27)

When a young person is struck with terminal illness, Sarduy writes, they tend to react in one of two ways: 'some revolt against everything, even against themselves', while others close themselves away in a 'mutism without appeal' (74). But one thing, 'nevertheless, unites the closed and screeching: the obsession of [their body-]weight, the panic of seeing themselves disembodied alive' (74). The inmates struggle to *retain* weight. They strive to remain substantial, or at least to seem so. They rig the scales, have recourse to muscle building formulas or a chalky powder developed for anorexics (with the same result: diarrhoea [76]). The stricken are possessed by the 'inexplicable and urgent necessity to do something, to make something with their hands or with their corroded intellect [...], to sign reality with their seal' (153).

Pájaros does not write the eventual evaluation of disease as a primarily negative experience, as a limitation imposed upon an intrinsically healthy singularity: it is not a rewriting of *Cobra*, taken sick. *Pájaros* is in no sense a despairing text. It is not really a text *about* disease so much as it is an affirmation of life made through a confrontation *with* disease. If *Pájaros* must in some sense be read as Sarduy's 'last will and testament', we should not identify his voice with either that of the cosmologist or of Siempreviva, but with a revision of that peculiar combination of the two pursued, in a sense, through all his work. Sarduy's project has always worked through the dialectic of void and plenitude, subtraction and excess. The austere asceticism of the one, and the 'irresponsible' vitality of the other, have always represented alternate paths to a common goal. But if in *Cobra* and *Maitreya* this dialectic works toward the *equation* of the two positions in the singular immanence of an ongoing Creation, in *Pájaros* the two voices stand side by side, each distinct yet incomplete, in a dialogue without consensus, without dissolution, without imminent resolution in a third or higher term. The relation remains inconclusive, to be unravelled – which is to say that it remains precisely a relation, a being-with.

Ultimately, what both the cosmologist and Siempreviva share is the attitude of that Mexican street sweeper described in *El Cristo* (§20) – the refusal to submit to a coherence that exceeds their own, the refusal to submerge a personal confrontation within this other coherence. As another patient puts it, 'there remains to me one final freedom: the freedom to rise up against the divine disorder, against the simulacrum of a universal harmony. Men and birds are struck down in the face of God's indifference' (PP, 25). At the antipodes of *Cobra*, say, *Pájaros*, after *Cocuyo*, presents a human difference in relation to a simulated indifference – a specific difference in relation to the singularity that would transcend it.

CONCLUSION

I have used the terms singular and specific in this book to name mutually exclusive approaches to the analysis of differentiation and individuation. Neither category should be confused with the merely particular as such. We have seen that every singular configuration emerges through the dissolution of relationality, as the expression of a non-relational, self-creative or self-constituent force; the only *limit* of such a configuration is marked by the impossible intuition of a purely implicated, purely intensive point of unrestricted Creativity. The persistence of a specific configuration, by contrast, presumes the constraint of relationality as the transcendental condition of its distance from every merely specified determination; the limit of the specific is marked by the *evacuation* (rather than obliteration) of relations, by the effort to explore the empty form of relationality as such. The specific is a function of subjective perspective, and characterises the medium of any divisively universalisable engagement or decision; singularisation points toward a coherence in which the general distinction of subject and object no longer applies.

My main argument in these pages has been that the only precise and useful meaning of the label 'postcolonial' is one that makes explicit its singularising implications. In the limited space of this conclusion it may be worth pointing very briefly, from within the literary territory usually claimed by more conventionally inclusive understandings of the postcolonial, to a few of the more obviously specific alternatives to the singular projects analysed in the preceding chapters, before ending with a somewhat old-fashioned defence of the specificity of literary studies as such.

I have suggested that the specific is distinct from the specified on the one hand and the singular on the other. The specified is the realm of the objective as such, the sort of particularity accessible to direct, positive characterisation. Singularisation, we know, is the effort to equate subject and object in a term Creative or transcendent of both. The specific, then, maintains the relation between subject and object (and between subjects) *as a relation* in the strict sense. The specific arises only within the subjective domain, but this domain is itself specific to the specified objectivity of its situation.[1] Every subjective relation is specific in this sense, but the condition of relation is itself transcendental of all specificity and indifferent to any attempt at singularisation (it is impossible to 'become-transcendental'). Relation is not itself ethical or oriented toward some inherent social good. The universal criteria by which relations are to be valued or inflected remains a matter of inter-subjective *decision*. The criteria of this decision cannot be simply immanent to its actualisation but must rather be prescribed and imposed across the field of relation as a whole.

By way of a general theoretical illustration, we might consider Michel Foucault's work as a specific counterpart to Deleuze's emphatically singular project. As if in defiance of Deleuze's own influential reading of his philosophy (1986), Foucault moves away from an impossibly literal or immediate experience of a singular 'outside [*dehors*]' (madness, death, language-in-itself), toward the composition of specific histories of how our experience has been *specified* and confined. Foucault's early fascination with the limits of experience is less a form of suicidal mysticism than an interest in the ultimate limits to specification as such (and ultimately, in the purely abstract Limit *to which* every radical freedom, though minimally specified, remains forever specific). Deleuze seeks to write a philosophy without limits, through immediate intuition of the unlimited, or *purely* Creative; Foucault writes a philosophy of the limit as such, working at the limits of classification, at the edge of the void that lies beyond every order of recognition or normalisation. Where Deleuze tries to articulate a field of pure or immediate difference, a deterritorialising difference whose (virtual) relations are external to their (actual) terms, Foucault explores the necessarily historical *territory* in which people are 'made subject', so as to ask the eventual question: 'what is or is no longer indispensable for the constitution of ourselves as autonomous subjects?'[2] His eventual understanding of philosophy as ethical self-fashioning, the on-going *relation* of self to self and self to other, would thus be less the betrayal of an earlier anti-humanist intransigence than the culmination of a fully specific programme – the isolation of subjective experience from *all* specified conformity. Foucault's enduring goal is to alter 'one's way of seeing, to modify the horizon of what one knows',[3] so as to be forever 'other than what we are'.[4] Although Foucault uses different terminology, what he calls 'the critical ontology of ourselves' amounts to nothing other than a general effort to move from the specified to the specific, without recourse to a singular authority or plenitude:

The critical ontology of ourselves has to be considered not, certainly, as a theory, a doctrine, not even as a permanent body of knowledge that is accumulating; it has to be considered as an attitude, an ethos, a philosophical life in which the critique of what we are is at one and the same time the historical analysis of the limits that are imposed on us and an experiment [*épreuve*] with the possibility of going beyond them.[5]

What is consistent throughout Foucault's work, then, is a militant refusal of the specified, of specification (however rational, progressive or 'humane') as an acceptable way of approaching human experience. The specific is not something to be attained at some future point of theoretical sophistication, or pending some further restriction of perspective. The specific must not be confused with the merely particular, nor swept away in a singular conflagration. Specificity is the irreducible medium of our *present* existence, the sole dimension of our here and now.

There is no shortage of properly specific projects in contemporary literature, of course. I limit myself here to superficial consideration of three of the more familiar candidates, chosen to contrast with the more singular schemes of Johnson, Glissant and Dib.

The most obvious novelist to pick as rival to Johnson's redemptive vision is Toni Morrison.[6] Both writers favour a more or less 'typically' postmodern complication of the historical novel. Both problematise questions of testimony, of bearing witness, and of *telling* the truth. Both turn to the supernatural in an effort to express otherwise inexpressible events. But where, for Johnson, the supernatural provides a kind of release from our falsely *related* nature, for Morrison the supernatural is a way of over-naturalising, of reinforcing the natural and ways of dealing with the natural. For Morrison, the supernatural – the ghostly, the mythical, the telepathic – generally exposes the natural itself in super-concentrated form. And where for Johnson, history is essentially a limit wrapped around the singular reality of becomings-other, the historical is for Morrison the very medium of fiction. Johnson's characters speak themselves out of history, while Morrison's speak themselves *into* history. Confronted with a history that was and could be only selectively narrated by the actors themselves, Morrison sees her task as 'how to rip that veil drawn over proceedings too terrible to be related', to 'find and expose truth about the interior life of people who didn't write it'.[7] While the singular represents, in a sense, both end and means for Johnson (his notion of 'drama'), qualification of Morrison's work as specific is merely a preliminary acknowledgement of its irreducible *complexity*. For Johnson, the final telos of a becoming-immanent is a sort of disembodiment, a movement towards the imperceptible; Morrison's fiction, by contrast, asserts again and again that 'you can't just fly off and leave a body' (*Song of Solomon*). The ghosts return, the bones must be collected, the dead must be carried, the memories tended; the leap into flight must first be grounded, like Milkman's, upon an informed sense of people and place, upon the recovery of names and the reconstitution of stories. Morrison sustains the depth of particularity, the poetry of place and memory *as* the literary, where the literary exists in strained relation to the lived and the 'ordinary'. With Johnson, by contrast, the literary and the lived cohere on entirely different planes, and particularities are something that '"Being" sloughs off when bored with the game'.[8] Unlike Johnson, Morrison narrates the story of characters who seek and manage to *impose* themselves – tentatively, marginally, even invisibly – by *composing* their story.[9]

A comparable effort governs much of V.S. Naipaul's controversial fiction. (There is surely no writer less beloved of postcolonial theorists than this self-proclaimed advocate of elitism and 'high culture'.) Where Glissant's concern is with the integration of Martinique into a global totality that eventually demands its radical deterritorialisation, Naipaul's concern begins with 'truth to a particular experience'[10] – the pursuit of a 'house for Mr. Biswas' or 'a cottage in Wiltshire', a place of relative security from which one can *evaluate the world* (fairly or unfairly).[11] Whereas the nomadic Martinicans of Glissant's *Tout-monde* 'scatter everywhere, like a powder, without insisting anywhere [*sans insister nulle part*]' (TM, 385), Naipaul's characters and autobiographical personae search precisely for a place to *insist*. Naipaul's work is not less 'political' than Glissant's; it is neither more parochial nor more universal in scope. It is simply specific rather than singular, inflected through the experience of a positioned narrator or character and maintained as a network of (more or less dysfunctional) relationships. Nowhere *at home*, Naipaul puts himself and his characters in a *position* of judgement, as alternately judge and judged. However much one may disagree with his particular verdicts, their form allows, even encourages, disagreement.[12] Glissant's *Tout-monde*, by contrast, effectively absorbs the possibility of relational difference: in both form and content, it implies a univocity beyond mere integration.

Finally, whereas Dib's mature novels narrate the deterritorialisation of character, its withdrawal from relation, Assia Djebar's fiction explores what is involved in the positioning of a perspective (French and Algerian, innovative and traditional, female and male, inside and outside, house-bound and mobile…). These perspectives are not described as static, self-sufficient windows upon the world, but as rivals within a field of interested, competitive alternatives – the field excavated by a kind of militant curiosity. A novel like *L'Amour, la fantasia* pits one gaze against another in a series of staged confrontations skipping between 1830 and the recent past, in a historical setting both constitutive of and reconstituted by its historian–narrator.[13] The written word – testimony, historical reconstruction, propaganda, war memoir, love letter – serves not to 'bare [*dénuder*]' (72) an expressive soul so much as to give voice to the silenced and lend *weight* to the ephemeral; it allows for the excavation and reinterpretation of a sometimes literally buried history (68, 89-93), its liberation from all *enfermement* (sexual, patriarchal, ideological...).

To accept a specific configuration is to drop the notion of an intrinsic orientation or automatic prescription – say, an inherently ethical responsibility for others, an inherently revolutionary History, an inherently subversive (or elitist) direction in postmodern literature, an *essentially* progressive (or reactionary) agenda for cultural studies. In no obvious sense do the writers I have somewhat randomly singled out for attention as specific (Foucault, Djebar, Naipaul, Morrison) produce a *directly* progressive political effect. What they do provide is a way of making sense of a position, of choosing between positions. All we can say is that only a specific configuration provides for *decision* as such, as opposed to a specified automation on the one hand or a singular inherence on the other. The movement from specified to specific, guarded against absorption into the singular, is the only philosophical movement whose empty, contentess course has a kind of global validity (that is, a validity indifferent to particular values). There is nothing *in* experience, no ultimate value or pre-ontological ethical orientation, that will save us in the last resort. The question of how any given relation is to be valued will always remain a matter of active *valuing*, with all the properly subjective responsibility that implies.

I stress this point again, in closing, because it seems to me the only acceptable way of re-affirming *today* the rare opportunity of literary studies as such. Any literary work, however mimetic its intent, involves some degree of despecification, some degree of imaginative transcendence, some distance taken from convention-bound routine. The privilege of literary study is the privilege of that detachment which allows us as readers to step back from representation, suspend its natural flow, and pay an 'artificial' attention to *how it works*. Like any specific process, this paying-attention is value neutral. It would be presumptuous indeed to invest it with any sort of directly political let alone moral virtue. The academy as such is certainly no model zone of engagement (even if some of its members may well engage effectively in *other* zones). But it remains as urgent today as ever to make the most of the chance offered by even a limited experience of that elementary suspension of the specified which engagement with genuinely imaginative work always invites. The argument has often been made before but deserves to be made again, for each time it is a genuine re-discovery.

however it is circumscribed, the realm of the aesthetic invariably solicits the exercise of a *thought-ful* freedom. Between the immediately singularising pressures of contemporary commodification and the reactively specifying pressures of 'ethnic' or 'traditionalist' responses to such commodification, what goes by the name of artistic or creative writing will continue to open a fragile space of relational detachment and imaginative engagement.

Both postcolonial theorists and their more stringent Marxist critics too often deny or downplay these opportunities. Suspicion of the 'soft' or 'creative' dimensions of literature seems today to be a special point of theoretical pride among many professional readers. Sprinker, for instance, shares Ahmad's conviction that 'the scarcely viable notion that literature is an autonomous entity above or outside of the material determinations of political and social history will have to be given a decent, but more or less summary, burial'.[14] Dirlik censures postcolonial theory because it presents itself as a 'liberating discourse that divorces itself from the material conditions of life'.[15] Parry objects to the tendency whereby 'the analysis of the internal structures of texts, enunciations, and signifying systems has become detached from a concurrent examination of social and experiential circumstances'.[16] Appadurai follows suit when he writes that 'there is a disturbing tendency in the Western academy today to divorce [...] the study of literary discourse from the mundane discourses of bureaucracies, armies, private corporations'.[17]

One can only presume that this tendency is more disturbing for bureaucrats, soldiers and CEOs than it is for literary scholars themselves. To apply such logic without qualification to the mature work of writers like Dib or Sarduy is simply to deny their projects of all validity in advance. If literature did not offer *some* degree of creative disengagement from material circumstances and still more from bureaucratic discourse it would have been buried long before its materialist critics began arranging the funeral. The more forceful Marxist critics sometimes seem to forget that the postcolonial criticism they attack is primarily *literary* criticism, i.e. a practice of reading designed first and foremost to account for certain particular literary phenomena. It is not enough, then, simply to condemn the theory for its inadequate attention to other disciplines like 'political economy'.[18] To argue that 'literary criticism must become social theory and social criticism'[19] is surely to condemn the field, in the end, to the supervision of ultimately specified social interests and cultural identities.

However objectionable it may be, postcolonial theory merits evaluation as an interpretation of *literature* as such. Less than its undeniable but hardly surprising inflation of literary values over socio-materialist ones, what is perhaps more peculiar about postcolonial criticism as a genre is just how *little* it has to say about its own 'home' discipline, about literature proper. Having long since absorbed the boundary-blurring lessons of deconstruction, many postcolonial literary critics seem embarrassed by what remains of their disciplinary affiliation. Most postcolonial readings are brief, often insubstantial, sometimes simply anecdotal. Only rarely do such readings engage with a text 'on its own terms', as a more or less free-standing field in which what Badiou would call specifically literary 'events' (innovations, inventions, violations, inaugurations...) come to pass.[20]

It would be absurd, of course, to retreat to the indefensible position that art has *nothing* to do with society or culture. We have seen that there is indeed no more singular a theory than that which conceives literature as *radically* autonomous and self-constituent, as free from all but purely imma-nent criteria. Those who – like King, Boehmer and Griffiths, for instance – over-react against the theorisation of postcolonial literature risk making the opposite mistake: the bland veneration of 'creative writing' as its own (and only) standard of value, so as to preserve it from the neo-imperialist aggression of imported theories. This strikes me as a contradictory and unnecessary gesture. If we are prepared to acknowledge literature's partial transcendence of material circumstances, why not recognise that it has a similar resilience in the face of theoretical appropriation? As Paulo Freire puts it with incomparable concision (and in an obviously *social* context), 'true generosity consists in fighting to destroy the causes which nourish false charity'.[21] Though it's all too obvious that in many circumstances writers still need political protection, their work should have no need of *critical* protec-tion. The criteria governing theoretical speculation must never be specified in advance, in terms of generic conformity or cultural authenticity. A theory's value depends solely on what it allows its *every* user to do.

All that can be said, in theory, is that we should not defer our normative aesthetic and political choices to theory. It is worth defending literature as one of the few fields that actively discourages this deference.

NOTES

PREFACE

1 Where a reference contains two page numbers separated by a forward slash, the first number refers to the original edition and the second to the translation listed in the bibliography; 'tm' stands for 'translation modified'. When no note accompanies a quotation, the reference is included in the next note.

2 The recent *Companion to Postcolonial Studies* (eds. Schwarz and Ray, 2000), for instance, in addition to theoretical reviews of imperialism, colonialism, hybridity, postmodernism, multiculturalism, transnationalism, feminism, queer theory, and English studies, includes more empirically focused surveys of topics ranging from patriotic literature in South Asia, Arabic literature in the 'middle east', the handover of Hong Kong, 'Japan and East Asia' and 'failed narratives of the nation in late colonial Java', to studies of 'settler colonies', 'Ireland after history', orality in the Caribbean, and 'Africa. varied colonial legacies' For all their disciplinary hubris, however, postcolonial studies are ageing fast. Much current output in the field amounts to little more than academic souvenirs – anthologies, surveys and reader's guides – and it didn't take long for books and articles with the title 'Beyond Postcolonial Theory' to appear (see for instance. San Juan Jr., *Beyond Postcolonial Theory* [1998], Schulze-Engler, 'Beyond Post-Colonialism', in Collier, ed., *Us/Them* [1992])

3 Spivak, 'Asked to Talk About Myself' [1992], 10. And Bhabha. 'I have attempted no general theory' (Bhabha, *The Location of Culture*, 170)

4 Seshadri-Crooks, 'At the Margins of Postcolonial Studies', 67; cf Slemon, 'Postcolonialism and its Discontents', 7

5 Parry, 'The Postcolonial', 3.

6 Shohat, 'Notes on the "Post-Colonial"', 323–326, cf. Ahmad, 'Postcolonialism. What's in a Name?', 28

7 Trivedi, 'Postcolonial or Transcolonial', 271.

8 Cf. Chrisman, 'Inventing Post-Colonial Theory', 210, Shohat, 'Notes', 321, 330, McClintock, 'Angel of Progress', 293–294.

9 Said, *Culture and Imperialism*, 275

10 Césaire, *Discours sur le colonialisme*, 18/21.

11 Fanon, *Damnés de la terre*, 81/51 Parry's seminal article of 1987, 'Problems in Current Theories of Colonial Discourse', remains the most forceful expression of this distinction

12 Nederveen Pieterse and Parekh, *Decolonization of Imagination*, 10–11.

13 Sara Suleri's confident assertion is typical of the consensus· today 'no self-respect-ing cultural critic would be caught dead with a binarism' (Suleri, 'Multiculturalism and its Discontents', 17).

14 See for instance Spivak, *Critique of Postcolonial Reason*, 37, 39 The themes addressed by the essays collected in a special issue of the *PMLA* on 'Colonialism and the Postcolonial Condition' illustrate the more general trend: every essay, the issue editor announces, engages in 'crossing borders [and] challenging boundaries', and each defies 'any single binary construction of oppression', be it east/west, fem-inine/masculine, homosexual/heterosexual, coloniser/colonised, power/resistance, or capitalist/precapitalist (Hutcheon, 'Complexities Abounding', *PMLA* 110 1 (Jan-uary 1995), 12).

15 Césaire, *Discours sur le colonialisme*, 19/21.

16 See in particular Ashcroft et al., *The Empire Writes Back*, 180, 185.

17 Cf. Ahmad, *In Theory*, 192; Lazarus, 'Doubting the New World Order', 94–95; Nor-ris, *What's Wrong with Postmodernism*, 3–4; Eagleton, *Literary Theory*, 205. Robert Young suggests 'the emergence of postcolonial theory could be viewed as marking the moment in which the Third World moved from an affiliation with the Second World to the First' (Young, 'Ideologies of the Postcolonial', 6).

18 Nederveen Pieterse, 'Globalisation as Hybridisation', 64. Even the author of a book *On The Dictatorship of the Proletariat* (1976) has written, more recently, in protest against the 'dualistic model' of society that opposes 'rulers to ruled', the dominant to the dominated, and calls for an end to 'the traditional structure of politics that is essentially structured by the opposition of classes, camps, or ideologies ("friends and foes")' (Balibar, 'Has the 'World' Changed?', in Callari, ed., *Marxism in the Post-modern Age* [1995], 411).

19 If not as 'postcolonial', how then should the bulk of literature from formerly colonised countries be classified? My own view is that the conventional mix of chronological, geographical, generic, and thematic labels is generally adequate. One alternative I would most emphatically reject is any term that divides the world into more or less explicitly *incommensurable* sub-worlds (three worlds theory, indigenous worlds, 'other' worlds...). There is and can only be *one world*, only one human species, only one realm of specificity – whose diversity resists a singular coordination as much as it eludes stasis in a specified particularity

20 Gandhi, *Postcolonial Theory*, 11.

21 Parry, 'Liberation Movements', 50

22 Bhabha, 'Culture's in between', 212.

23 Bhabha, 'Postcolonial Criticism,' 439, cf. Bhabha, 'Minority Maneuvers', 433.

24 Mbembe, 'Prosaics of Servitude', 132.

25 Mbembe, 'The Banality of Power', 3, cf Mbembe, 'Prosaics of Servitude', 127.

26 IPD, 106

27 Harris, *Tradition, The Writer, and Society*, 30, *Womb of Space*, 86, 65.

28 Harris, *Womb of Space*, 18, 107, 48, 61, 63, *Tradition*, 34.

29 Dance, Interview with Harris, *New World Adams*, 82, 86.

30 Harris, *Womb of Space*, xvi, 5 The decisive images of Harris' *Carnival Trilogy*, for instance, are meant to crystallise 'the continuity of insoluble wholeness', like 'por-tent[s] of a healed humanity across all terrifying barriers' (Harris, *Carnival Trilogy*, ix).

31 I take for granted here the widely endorsed assumption that, in certain essential respects, African-American literature qualifies for inclusion in the postcolonial domain. See for instance MacLeod, 'Black American Literature and the Postcolo-nial Debate', 53–55; Childs and Williams, *Post-Colonial Theory*, 78–81; Bhabha,

'Postcolonial Criticism' [1992], 438; Spivak, 'Subaltern Talk' [1993], SR, 294–295, Parry, 'The Postcolonial' [1997], 4, Rajan and Mohanram, 'Locating Postcoloniality', *Postcolonial Discourse*, 11, Christopher Wise, 'The Dialectics of Negritude. Or, the (Post-)Colonial Subject in Contemporary African-American Literature', in Rajan and Mohanram, *Post Colonial Discourse*, 34

32 This is the move often recommended in Said's most recent work, and adopted as a matter of principle in a couple of recent books (including Boehmer's *Colonial and Postcolonial Literature* and King's *New National and Post-Colonial Literatures*). King and Griffiths are quite right to point to 'a gross neglect of the contribution made by the literary texts of the post-colonial world themselves to the theorisation of the issues of post-colonialism' (Griffiths, 'The Post-Colonial Project', in King, *New National and Post-Colonial Literatures*, 173). I see no need, however, to present the issue in terms of an either-or: *either* literature *or* theory.

33 Miyoshi, 'A Borderless World?', 742

34 Badiou, *L'Ethique*, 25, cf. Badiou, *Saint Paul et la fondation de l'universalisme*, 117. 'The acknowledgement of difference, hybridity, multiplicity', as Eagleton was quick to realise, 'is a drastically impoverished kind of political ethic in contrast to the affirmation of human solidarity and reciprocity' (Eagleton, 'Postcolonialism and 'Postcolonialism'', 26).

35 Badiou is again a helpful point of reference here. See his *Petit Manuel d'inesthétique*, 15–22; *Le Siècle*, 121–122.

INTRODUCTION Singular or specific?

1 Levinas, 'Enigma and Phenomenon', *Basic Philosophical Writings*, 77
2 Agamben, *The Coming Community*, 19.
3 I adopt this variant–invariant terminology from Veyne, *L'Inventaire des différences* (1976)
4 A singularity is 'a state of infinite curvature of spacetime. In a singularity, all places and times are the same. Hence the big bang did not take place in a pre-existing space; all space was embroiled in the big bang' (Ferris, *The Whole Shebang. A State-of-the-Universe(s) Report*, 17).
5 I use the verb 'to be' in this sentence to describe the logic used to *justify* such singular configurations, and not to describe their true nature or objective being (and this applies, in my view, to the true nature of the universe as much as it does to that of the more obviously 'ideological' conceptions of God, sovereignty, or the market)
6 As Laclau recognises, 'there is no real alternative between Spinoza and Hegel' (Laclau, *Emancipation(s)*, 21) – it is question of *speed* alone.
7 Deleuze and Guattari, *Mille plateaux*, 311/254, cf. Deleuze, *Bergsonisme*, 20/29.
8 Deleuze and Guattari, *Anti-Oedipe*, 91/76
9 Examples might include the alignment of particular wills in Spinoza's 'reasonable' polity and Rousseau's *volonté générale*, or the fusion of particular interests in the univocity of one class interest (or rather, of one post-class, proletarian dis-interest).
10 'Every perception is hallucinatory because perception has no object' (Deleuze, *Le Pli*, 125/93), Deleuze promotes with Godard and Robbe-Grillet a description which '*replaces* its own object', which 'erases or *destroys* its reality' (Deleuze, *Cinéma 2*, 18/7, cf. 34/22, 68–69/44–45)
11 Deleuze, *Nietzsche et la philosophie*, 8–9/8
12 Stanley Cavell makes a similar point, with reference to Derrida's deconstruction of

the iterable sign (Cavell, *A Pitch of Philosophy*, 71ff.); Stephen Mulhall recently renewed this argument in dialogue with Derrida himself, in a forum entitled 'Derrida's Arguments' (Queen Mary and Westfield College, University of London, 10 March 2000).

13 Paraphrasing Marx, *The Eighteenth Brumaire of Louis Napoleon*, in Marx and Engels, *Selected Works*, 247. 'Everything is historical, but there are only partial histories' (Veyne, *Comment on écrit l'histoire*, 41).

14 Whatever else it is, the singular is not the preserve of certain Western modern or postmodern thinkers. The widespread belief that 'the privilege of standing above cultural particularism, of aspiring to the universalist power that speaks for humanity [...], is a privilege invented by a totalising Western liberalism' (Clifford, *Predicament*, 263) testifies to our ignorance of Islam and Buddhism, to mention only them The assumption that all non-Western discourse works only within modestly limited, effectively 'tribal' perspectives, has absolutely no justification.

15 Deleuze, *Différence et répétition*, 55/37tm Likewise, each singular 'event is the smallest time, smaller than the minimum of continuous thinkable time [..], but it is also the longest time, longer than the maximum of continuous thinkable time' (Deleuze, *Logique du sens*, 80/63); Creative 'auto-affection' always implies the 'conversion of far and near' (*Cinéma 2*, 111/83)

16 Deleuze, *Nietzsche et la philosophie*, 81/72.

17 Again, a singularity in the technical sense of contemporary physics implies an environment of *unqualified* (as opposed to relative) chaos, the singularity, according to Marx's criteria, of a genuine political revolution (as opposed to local reform or 'opportunism') refers back immediately to the singularity of the proletariat and the world historical process. Classical Buddhist scripture provides especially insistent illustration of the point. Buddha is unlimited at both ends of the scale, as indivisible point 'without self', and as inclusive of the entire universe Conceived in its singularity, 'the infinitely Far-away is not only near, but it is infinitely near' (*The Heart Sutra*, 83), and once restored to their Creative virtuality, 'the indescribable infinite Lands/all assemble in a hair's tip' (*Hwa Yen Sutra*, in Chang, *The Buddhist Teaching of Totality*, 5). Enlightened, 'my one thought covered eternity' (Koho, in Suzuki, *Essays in Zen Buddhism*, i, 253–257).

18 Balibar, 'Has the "World" Changed?', 407

19 Well-known doctrinal differences aside, I accept Corbin and Jambet's argument that there is enough consensus across the major forms of esoteric Islam (Shi'ite, Ismaili, Sufi, and Ishraqi), at least regarding the issues that concern us here, to justify description of *an* Islamic gnosis. See Corbin, *Philosophie iranienne*, 45; Corbin, *Histoire*, 55–56, 152–153, 264–269.

20 Vitray-Meyerovitch, 'La Poétique de l'Islam', 206

21 *Qur'an*, 38 65, cf. 112·1–2, 18:110; 21.108; 41.5.

22 Ibn al-'Arabi, quoted in Corbin, *L'Imagination créatrice*, 330; cf al-Suhrawardi, *Sagesse orientale*, §129–130

23 Ibn al-'Arabi, in Nicholson, *Studies*, 152

24 Corbin, *Temple et contemplation*, 293.

25 al-Suhrawardi, 'Le Récit de l'exil occidental', in *L'Archange empourpré*, 274.

26 Nicholson, *The Mystics of Islam*, 85.

27 Corbin, *Histoire*, 394

28 The phenomenal world 'exists as the self-revelation or other self of the Absolute' (Ibn al-'Arabi, in Nicholson, *Studies*, 83).

29 Vitray-Meyerovitch, 'La Poétique de l'Islam', 216, cf Corbin, *Histoire*, 26

30 Corbin, *Histoire*, 357· 'I created perception in you only so as to become there the object of my own perception' (Ibn al-'Arabi', in Corbin, *L'Homme de lumière*, 41)

31 Corbin, *Histoire*, 78–79.

32 Jambet, *Logique*, 38.

33 Jambet, *Logique*, 118, 224–225.

34 Poem by Seng Ts'an, in Conze, *Buddhist Scriptures*, 174–175.

35 Dumoulin, *Zen Buddhism*, 139.

36 *Tanha* consists of all 'those inclinations which tend to continue or increase separateness, the separate existence of the subject of desire [...]. Life being one, all that tends to separate one aspect from another must cause suffering to the unit which even unconsciously works against the Law Our duty to our fellows is to understand them as extensions, other aspects, of ourselves – fellow facets of the same Reality' (Humphreys, *Buddhism*, 91).

37 *Dhammapada*, verse 174.

38 Hui-nêng, *Platform Sutra*, 139, 166.

39 Singh, *Tantra*, 178

40 Of course, ontological univocity in no way implies ontological uniformity. The way is One, but 'there are a thousand different paths' ('Wu-men's verse', *Gateless Barrier*, 4), there is only one Buddha-reality, but 'millions of Buddhas', 'countless Buddhas' (*Lotus Sutra*, 50–51), all of which 'express' the same truth, differently (*Milindapanha*, 285, in Conze, *Buddhist Texts*, 110).

41 Conze, *Buddhist Texts*, 153; cf. *The Perfection of Wisdom in 8,000 Lines*, 151.

42 Conze, *Buddhist Texts*, 167–168.

43 Seng-Ts'an, in Conze, *Buddhist Scriptures*, 173, cf. *Dhammapada*, v. 279; *Diamond Sutra*, 62–63.

44 Humphreys, *Buddhism*, 20.

45 Conze, *Buddhism*, 138. 'The true mind is the Unconscious [*wu-nien*]' (Suzuki, *Essays in Zen Buddhism*, iii, 27), in a sense not unlike that of Deleuze and Guattari.

46 *Heart Sutra*, 89.

47 Chang, *The Buddhist Teaching of Totality*, 21.

48 Maitreyanatha, in Conze, *Buddhist Texts*, 170.

49 Suzuki, *The Zen Doctrine of No-Mind*, 15

50 *The Perfection of Wisdom in 8,000 Lines*, 85.

51 The full passage reads: conventional 'logic can only show [.] this sphere of the virtual, this Thought-nature, without ever being able to grasp it in propositions or relate it to a reference. Then logic is silent, and it is only interesting when it is silent. Paradigm for paradigm, it is then in agreement with a kind of Zen Buddhism' (Deleuze and Guattari, *Qu'est-ce que la philosophie?*, 133/140) For more detailed readings of Deleuze along these singularising lines, see my 'Deleuze and the Redemption from Interest' (1997) and 'Deleuze and the "World Without Others"' (1997). Badiou has likewise emphasised some of the singular consequences of Deleuze's univocity in his landmark book on *Deleuze. la clameur de l'être* (1997, translated 1999).

52 Deleuze, *Différence et répétition*, 95/69. This pure differing element is necessarily 'not known' (Deleuze, *Foucault*, 80–81/74)

53 Deleuze and Guattari, *Qu'est-ce que la philosophie?*, 12/7tm.

54 Deleuze, *Différence et répétition*, 52/35. 'Everything I've written is vitalistic, at least I hope it is' (Deleuze, *Pourparlers*, 196/143).

55 Deleuze, *Spinoza et le problème de l'expression*, 59–60/69–70

56 Deleuze, *Le Pli*, 11/7

57 Deleuze and Guattari, *Mille plateaux*, 311–312/254–255, my emphasis. 'The plane divides into a multiplicity of planes [...], but all the planes make up only one, following the path that leads to the virtual' (Deleuze, 'L'Actuel et le virtuel', *Dialogues*, 180).

58 Deleuze and Guattari, *Mille plateaux*, 89/69. 'Immanence is immanent only to itself and consequently captures everything, absorbs All-One, and leaves nothing remaining to which it could be immanent...' (Deleuze and Guattari, *Qu'est-ce que la philosophie?*, 47/45).

59 Deleuze and Guattari, *Anti-Oedipe*, 40/32

60 Deleuze, *Empirisme et subjectivité*, 136/119.

61 Deleuze and Guattari, *Mille plateaux*, 641/514.

62 Deleuze and Guattari, *Anti-Oedipe*, 37/30, 34/26.

63 Deleuze, *Différence et répétition*, 55/37.

64 Deleuze, *Bergsonisme*, 73/74.

65 Deleuze, *Nietzsche et la philosophie*, 50/44.

66 Deleuze, *Cinéma 2*, 234/180.

67 Deleuze, referring to Leibniz, in *Le Pli*, 78/58. To stick to the most significant example, 'individuation is, in Spinoza, neither qualitative nor extrinsic, but quantitative and intrinsic, intensive', '*purely quantitative*', according to 'the degree of [a thing's] power' (Deleuze, *Spinoza et le problème de l'expression*, 180/197; 166/183, cf Deleuze, *Différence et répétition*, 105/77). Every 'mode has a singular essence, which is a degree of power or intensive part, *pars aeterna*' (Deleuze, *Spinoza. philosophie pratique*, 109/76).

68 'Difference no longer exists *between* the polygon and the circle, but in the pure variability of the sides of the polygon' (Deleuze, *Le Pli*, 88/65, my emphasis).

69 Deleuze, *Bergsonisme*, 99–100/97; *Le Pli*, 135–136/103.

70 Deleuze, 'L'Actuel et le virtuel', *Dialogues*, 181.

71 Leibniz's monads express the entire world, but have 'no windows', and no relations with each other (Leibniz, *Monadology*, *Philosophical Works*, §7). Since 'the world does not exist outside of the monads that express it, the latter are not in contact and have no horizontal relations among them, no intraworldly connections, but only an indirect harmonic contact to the extent they share the same expression' (Deleuze, *Le Pli*, 110/81).

72 Deleuze, *Différence et répétition*, 324/251tm

73 As Deleuze often insists, we creatures *are* nothing but creatings, but all creatures 'are born in conditions such that they are cut off in advance from their essence or their degree of power, cut off from that of which they are capable, from their power of action We can know by reasoning that the power of action is the sole expression of our essence, the sole affirmation of our power of being affected. But this knowledge remains abstract We do not know what this power is, nor how we may acquire or discover it. And we will certainly never know this, if we do not concretely try to become active' (*Spinoza et le problème de l'expression*, 206–207/226). This effort clearly involves an exploration of how we might 'enter into composition with other affects, with the affects of another body' (*Mille plateaux*, 314/257). But however important this relational process might seem, it is an *ultimately* disposable one. relations with other creatures are not properly constitutive of creativity, they simply provide the means whereby any particular creature may discover the most effective means of becoming a more active and more adequate channel for the singular Creative force that flows through it, that expresses itself through it.

74 'L'Actuel et le virtuel', *Dialogues*, 185.

75 Deleuze, *Logique du sens*, 99/81. Each singular 'event is adequate to the Aion in its entirety [..], all form one and the same single event, event of the Aion in which they have an eternal truth' (80–81/64).

76 Deleuze, *Différence et répétition*, 293/228. our limited minds can 'know intensity only as already developed within an extensity' (288/223).

77 Deleuze, *Bergsonisme*, 108/104.

78 Deleuze, *Dialogues*, 62/50.

79 Deleuze, *Cinéma 1*, 80/57.

80 The effort to 'kill metaphor' (Deleuze and Guattari, *Kafka*, 127/70) is one of the more striking and consistent aspects of Deleuze's work. In any art worthy of the name, 'what disappears is all metaphor or figure [...]. One must speak and show literally, or else not show and speak at all' (Deleuze, *Cinéma 2*, 238/183). It is always essential to proceed 'literally, without metaphor, [and so] to bring forth the thing in itself' (Deleuze, *Cinéma 2*, 32/21tm, cf. 226/173)

81 Deleuze, *Logique du sens*, 350/301.

82 Deleuze, *Cinéma 2*, 57–58 /40 'As soon as it stops being related to an interval as sensory-motor centre, movement finds its absolute quality again' (57/40)

83 Deleuze, *Cinéma 1*, 97/66.

84 Deleuze, *Cinéma 1*, 100/68 'To get beyond the human condition, such is the meaning of philosophy' (*Foucault*, 139–140/124–125tm).

85 Deleuze and Guattari, *Mille plateaux*, 343–344/280, cf Deleuze, *Cinéma 1*, 171/122.

86 Deleuze and Guattari, *Qu'est-ce que la philosophie?*, 196–199/208–211.

87 The obvious problem that then arises is how to explain the individuation of these self-singularising beings in a wholly deterritorialised space, without recourse to some kind of intrinsic and determining – i.e. ultimately specified – essence or Idea, more or less on the Platonic model.

88 Hence the working title of my own book on Deleuze: *Creationism in Philosophy: Deleuze* (in preparation).

89 Badiou, 'Séminaire sur Saint Paul et la fondation de l'universel', Collège International de la Philosophie, Paris, 8 November 1995 (Badiou himself is perhaps the only serious rival for the title).

90 Bourdieu, 'La Conquête de l'autonomie', *Les Règles de l'art*, 75–164/47–112. Peter Burger's history of vanguard modernism traces a similar 'break with society', the 'detachment of art from the praxis of life' (Burger, *Theory of the Avant-Garde*, 33, 24). Literary *post*modernism can then be interpreted as another step 'towards radical aesthetic autonomy' (Bertens, *Idea of the Postmodern*, 4).

91 Bourdieu, *Règles de l'art*, 164/112 Flaubert's penchant for Spinoza is well-known.

92 Barthes, *Le Degré zéro de l'écriture* [1953], *Oeuvres complètes*, i, 179.

93 Bürger, *Theory of the Avant-Garde*, 49

94 Foucault, *Les Mots et les choses*, 313/300

95 Barthes, *Le Plaisir du texte*, *Oeuvres complètes*, ii, 1502.

96 Because undisturbed by its object, 'poetry is as precise a thing as geometry' (Flaubert, *Correspondance*, ii, 392)

97 Flaubert, *Correspondance*, ii, 255.

98 Flaubert, *Correspondance*, ii, 62.

99 Flaubert, *Correspondance*, ii, 31

100 See Badiou, *Théorie du sujet*, 90–98.

101 Cf Burger, *Theory of the Avant-Garde*, 24, 33–34, 49; Hassan, *The Dismemberment of Orpheus*, 48–78

102   Cf. Barthes, *Essais critiques* [1954], *Oeuvres complètes*, I, 1198, 1245.
103   See in particular Mallarmé to Cazalis, 14 May 1867, *Correspondance*, I, 240–242.
104   Blanchot, 'Le mythe de Mallarmé', *La Part du feu*, 48.
105   Poulet, *Métamorphoses du Cercle*, 447.
106   Mallarmé, quoted in Guilmette, *Deleuze et la modernité*, 70.
107   Mallarmé, *Oeuvres complètes*, 663.
108   Mallarmé, quoted in Giroux, *Désir de synthèse*, 37; cf Mallarmé, *Igitur*, *Oeuvres complètes*, 435
109   Blanchot, *La Part du feu*, 37, 47
110   Blanchot, *La Part du Feu*, 68, cf Benjamin, 'The Task of the Translator', *Illuminations*, 80.
111   Blanchot, *L'Espace littéraire*, 21.
112   Blanchot, *L'Espace littéraire*, 25–26, cf 186.
113   Blanchot, *L'Espace littéraire*, 19.
114   Blanchot, *L'Espace littéraire*, 27
115   Blanchot, *Part du feu*, 317
116   Blanchot, *L'Entretien infini*, 631, 593; cf Blanchot, *Après-coup*, 97–98. Foucault posed the obvious question 'In granting a primordial status to writing, do we not, in effect, simply reinscribe in transcendental terms the theological affirmation of the sacred origin or a critical belief in its creative nature?' (Foucault, 'Qu'est-ce qu'un auteur?' [1969], *Dits et écrits*, I, 795)
117   Sontag, 'The Aesthetics of Silence', *Styles of Radical Will*, 4–5.

CHAPTER 1   Postcolonial theory

1   Vattimo, *The Transparent Society*, 7–8
2   Vattimo, *The Transparent Society*, 68.
3   White, *Political Theory and Postmodernism*, 11, my emphasis
4   Bürger, *Theory of the Avant-Garde*, 122, cf. 87.
5   Agnes Heller, 'Existentialism, Alienation, Postmodernism', Milner, *Postmodern Conditions*, 11
6   West, 'The New Cultural Politics of Difference' [1990], *Keeping Faith*, 3.
7   Henry Giroux, 'Postmodernism as Border Pedagogy', Natoli and Hutcheon, *A Postmodern Reader*, 464–465, 479, cf Appiah, 'Is the Post- in Postmodernism the Post- in Postcolonialism?', CPT, 58.
8   Nelly Richard, 'Postmodernism and Periphery' [1987], in Docherty, *Postmodernism. A Reader*, 468.
9   Russell, *Poets, Prophets and Revolutionaries*, 239, cf. Hal Foster, *Recodings*, 6, 177–178.
10   Lash, *Sociology of Postmodernism*, ix, cf Norris, *The Truth About Postmodernism*, 24–26.
11   Lionnet, 'Preface', *Postcolonial Representations*, ix.
12   Benhabib, *Situating the Self*, 3, cf. Best and Kellner, *Postmodern Theory*, 260, 263–273
13   Dipesh Chakrabarty, 'Postcoloniality and the Artifice of History', CPT, 241.
14   Suleri, 'Woman Skin Deep', 338.
15   See for instance Mongia, 'Introduction', CPT [1996], 3, and Shohat, 'Notes on the "Post-Colonial"' [1992], CPT, 321.
16   Williams and Chrisman, 'Introduction', *Colonial Discourse*, 12.
17   Loomba, *Colonialism/Postcolonialism*, 15, 258, cf. 17, 83. See also Walder, *Post-*

Colonial Literatures, 69–70, Chrisman, 'Inventing Post-Colonial Theory', 211; Loomba and Kaul, 'Introduction. Location, Culture, Post-Coloniality', 4–5, Hutcheon, 'Complexities Abounding', 10; Bahri, 'Once More with Feeling', 53–55

18 Spivak, 'Translator's Afterword to Mashaweta Devi, *Imaginary Maps*' [1994], SR, 277.
19 Prakash, 'Introduction', *After Colonialism*, 12
20 Among innumerable examples, see Mongia, 'Introduction', CPT, 7, Boehmer, *Colonial and Postcolonial Literature*, 232–233
21 Clifford, *Predicament*, 10–11
22 Clifford, *Predicament*, 338. Clifford's more recent book (*Routes*, 1997), for all its emphasis on 'travelling theory', on *routes* over *roots*, is at pains to distinguish between a purely utopic postmodernity, and a more 'responsible' conception of *relative* mobility and situated negotiation.
23 Iain Chambers, 'Signs of Silence, Lines of Listening', PCQ, 50.
24 Chambers, *Migrancy*, 3–4.
25 Chambers, *Migrancy*, 5. Chambers goes so far as to cite the middle passage as an illustration of this shift 'to be forced to cross the Atlantic as a slave in chains [   ] is to acquire the habit of living between worlds, [...]o come from elsewhere, from "there" and not "here", and hence to be simultaneously "inside" and "outside"' (6)
26 Bernabé et al , *Eloge de la créolité*, 26–27; cf. 48. See also Benítez-Rojo, *The Repeating Island*, 18–19, 26, de Alva, 'The Postcolonization of the (Latin) American Experience', 243, 253, Spillers, *Comparative American Identities*, 5.
27 By general agreement, 'Said, Bhabha and Spivak constitute the Holy-Trinity' of postcolonial criticism (Young, *Colonial Desire*, 163).
28 Bhabha, in Bayley, 'Imaginings'.
29 Bhabha, 'Unpacking my library ... Again' [1996], 203.
30 Bhabha, LC, 60, 124, 154–155 Glissant will add. creolisation is not mere 'synthesis' (TTM, 16)
31 Deleuze. 'every object, every thing must see its own identity swallowed up in difference [...]. Difference must be shown *differing*' (*Différence et répétition*, 79/56).
32 LC, 13, 14 Bhabha is only interested in a 'form of cultural value that does not depend on binary divisions' ('Unpacking my library', 207).
33 Bhabha, 'Interview with Olson and Worsham', 19.
34 LC, 37, 242, 'Commitment to Theory', 128.
35 Callinicos, 'Wonders Taken for Signs', 111; Parry, 'Problems', 40–42, Parry, 'Signs of our Times', 5, 12; JanMohamed, 'The Economy of Manichean Allegory', 60. Parry and Lazarus have been especially forceful in countering Bhabha's reading of Fanon as a 'premature poststructuralist' and his consequent dilution of 'Fanon's specifications of relentless conflict' (Parry, 'Problems', 31; cf. Lazarus, 'Disavowing Decolonisation', 86–90, Lazarus, 'Transnationalism and the Alleged Death of the Nation-State', 40–45).
36 Bhabha, 'In a Spirit of Calm Violence', 329
37 LC, 158, my emphasis; cf. Bhabha, 'Freedom's Basis in the Indeterminate', 57.
38 Bhabha, 'Minority Maneuvers', 441.
39 Bhabha, 'The Translator Translated' [1995], 82
40 Cf. JanMohamed, 'The Economy of Manichean Allegory', 60.
41 Bhabha, 'The Translator Translated', 82
42 Bhabha, 'The Translator Translated', 83.
43 Brathwaite, *History of the Voice*, 13.
44 Spivak, 'What Is It For?', 73.
45 Spivak, 'Spivak on the Politics of the Subaltern', 87.

46 Spivak, 'Poststructuralism, Marginality, Postcoloniality, and Value', 204, cf 'Diasporas Old and New', 252.
47 Spivak, 'Can the Subaltern Speak?', 294.
48 IOW, 204. Spivak's belief that 'identity is, in the larger sense, a text – a socio-semiotic labyrinth shading off into indefinite margins not fully accessible to the "individual"' (Spivak, 'Foundations and Cultural Studies', 162) is a good example of what might be called the 'substantialist' fallacy This is the mistaken belief that because something is *made up* of a certain 'stuff' (here, textual interweaving), it must therefore act and *behave* in keeping with the nature of this stuff (here, as elusive, ambivalent, fragmented, deferred, indecisive, and so on).
49 Guha, 'On some aspects of the historiography of Colonial India', 3.
50 Spivak, 'Can the Subaltern Speak?', 295.
51 Spivak, 'Acting Bits/Identity Talk', 770; cf. 803.
52 Spivak, 'Bonding in Difference', SR, 21. Spivak's recognition that the illusion of an autonomous subject, a subject capable of decision and choice, appears to be 'among the conditions of the production of doing, knowing, being' (OTM, 10) prompts only a superficial revision of her system. The solution, famously, is 'strategically to take shelter in essentialism', while keeping the necessarily contingent identity terms 'under erasure' (IOW, 202). The effect is to set up a new machinery of self-supervision under which it is still more difficult to imagine taking decisive action.
53 Spivak, 'Foundations and Cultural Studies', 159, referring to Marx, 'Preface to the First Edition', *Capital*, vol. i, 90.
54 Spivak, 'Can the Subaltern Speak?', 308, cf. PCC, 158.
55 See among many others San Juan, *Beyond Postcolonial Theory*, 85 In subsequent interviews, Spivak has explained the difference between talking and speaking. that the subaltern cannot speak, she says, means simply that they are 'not able to be heard' in any meaningful way ('Subaltern Talk', SR, 292). She gives as 'a spectacular example of the subaltern not being able to "speak"' an instance when British colonial police failed to grasp the utility and importance of ancient, pre-colonial irrigation canals in Bangladesh – to their own eventual cost (290–291). If this is what Spivak meant by 'unable to speak', then the originality and force of her initial argument has been drastically reduced. In any case, she certainly encouraged confusion when in her original piece she described the subaltern as not simply 'unheard' but 'mute' (Spivak, 'Can the Subaltern Speak?', 295).
56 Spivak, 'Supplementing Marxism', 115. Spivak argues that 'the habitat of the subproletariat or the subaltern' is 'outside of organised labour', outside 'the classed social circuit', beyond any 'established agency of traffic with the culture of imperialism', and excluded, finally, from 'the new [postcolonial] nation' (OTM, 78, 139).
57 PCC, 37: 'I think it's important for people not to feel rooted in one place [...]. I have never taught anywhere where I would feel the special burden [...] of citizenship.' 'This whole business of speaking [. .] as a citizen' (PCC, 75) is something Spivak quite happily admits she has never had to endure.
58 See Moore-Gilbert, *Postcolonial Theory*, 78–80.
59 Spivak, 'Neocolonialism and the Secret Agent of Knowledge', 229; Spivak, 'Interview with Leon De Kock' [1992], 40. Nowhere is this self-indulgent quality more obvious than in the perversely named *Critique of Postcolonial Reason*, where the decision to work 'through the discontinuity of odd connections' (CPR, 65) rather than through frontal oppositions is reflected in the structure of the text itself, tacked together as it is from separately published, largely episodic texts, and punctuated with occasional musings about what the author *would* have written had she

chosen to follow this or that alternative 'invagination' (see for instance p. 70) In much of this rambling book, apparently aimed mainly at other 'globe-trotting post-colonials ready for entanglements in new global complicities' (363), Spivak's under-standable ambivalence about her status as being one of the world's most privileged 'interlocutors' (if that is the best word) of the ultra-exploited comes across as being almost of more importance than an incisive analysis of this exploitation itself

60 PCC, 9, cf Spivak, 'Can the Subaltern Speak?', 295

61 See in particular OTM, 137.

62 Parry, 'Problems in Current Theories of Colonial Discourse', 39.

63 Spivak and Plotke, 'A Dialogue on Democracy', 5, cf Spivak, 'Supplementing Marxism', 114.

64 'Translator's Afterword to Mashaweta Devi, *Imaginary Maps*', SR, 274–275, cf CPR, 27 n.32. For an enthusiastic overview, see Morton, 'Postcolonialism and Spectrality', 606ff.

65 Spivak, 'Setting to Work', 166; Spivak, 'Diasporas Old and New', 245

66 'Setting to Work', 165, Spivak and Plotke, 'A Dialogue on Democracy', 11.

67 Spivak, 'An Interview with Danius and Jonsson', 33.

68 CPR, 175, 123 Derrida's own ethical perspective is itself a fundamentally singular one. Following on from Levinas, Derrida says that I am responsible to the other, I am called to obey the call of the other (more, of *every* other) precisely *because* the other (every other) is indeed *other*, absolutely other. '*Tout autre est tout autre*' (Der-rida, *Donner la mort*, 68/68, 76–77/78). This formula ensures the explicitly redemp-tive confusion of 'each' or 'every' other with the 'altogether other', or *God*, the 'secretively' singular figure par excellence (83–84/87)

69 Spivak, 'Love, Cruelty and Cultural Talks in the Hot Peace', 10–11.

70 Spivak, 'In the New World Order', 92; Spivak, 'What Is It For?', 79 'The Call to the Ethical in general [...] is differed/deferred in its differential contaminations', and so the task of 'the assimilated-colonial-ethnic-minority (ACEM)', here, is to 'assume the differantially contaminated other as the subject of an ethics that remains unthinkable' (OTM, 175–177).

71 'Translator's Preface to Mashaweta Devi, *Imaginary Maps*', SR, 269.

72 Spivak, 'In the New World Order', 91; Spivak, 'Supplementing Marxism', 115, cf. CPR, 381

73 Spivak, 'Supplementing Marxism', 115, cf Spivak, 'Response to Jean-Luc Nancy', 43

74 Levinas, *Totalité et infini*, 79/80. Even more than Derrida's, Levinas' conception of ethics can in many ways serve as the paradigm of a singular conception of non-relation. Since 'the I *qua* I is absolutely unique', and since 'the Other has nothing in common with me', so 'the Other remains absolute and absolves itself from the relation which it enters into' (Levinas, *Basic Philosophical Writings*, 16, 28). My responsibility for this Other is consequently absolute, immediate, without appeal and without criteria, a form of 'unconditional obedience' (19) To be responsible in this sense is to be the creature of a Creator beyond relation, a Creator whose infinite Reality lies beyond and prior to the realm of finitude and ontology (or 'creation') itself.

75 Spivak, 'Diasporas Old and New', 258, cf CPR, 246, 399

76 'Translator's Afterword to Mashaweta Devi, *Imaginary Maps*', SR, 274. In her *Cri-tique of Postcolonial Reason* (CPR), Spivak's general ethical imperative mainly takes the form of a discontinuous, episodic engagement with 'the (im)possible perspec-tive of the "native informant"' (CPR, 49), a perspective foreclosed, she argues, by the Marxist tradition (68) as much as by the ethnographic discourse in which it

serves only to provide 'objective' information for the active (Western) subject of knowledge

77 Among the recent projects that draw on Deleuzian concepts are JanMohamed, 'Negating the Negation', in Jan Mohamed and Lloyd, *Nature and Context*, 103; Lawrence Grossberg, 'The Space of Culture, The Power of Space', PCQ, 178, Young, *Torn Halves*, 8. Bhabha has recently explored 'the *anxiety* of minority enunciation' in Deleuze and Guattari's sense – a 'becoming-minoritarian' as 'a movement *within* the "in-between"' (Bhabha, 'Minority Maneuvers', 439–444). See also Gandhi, *Postcolonial Theory*, 43, 53.

78 Moharan and Rajan, 'Introduction', in *English Postcoloniality*, 8; cf. Prakash, 'Introduction', *After Colonialism*, 10 Moore-Gilbert appears confident that this tendency to 'multiply the margins' is itself proof against any critical complicity in an homogenising process of globalisation (*Postcolonial Theory*, 11, 189).

79 Ashcroft, 'English Studies and Postcolonial Transformation', 125.

80 Bill Ashcroft, 'Excess. Postcolonialism and the Verandahs of Meaning', in Tiffin and Lawson, *De-Scribing Empire*, 33.

81 Arjun Appadurai, 'Disjuncture and Difference in the Global Economy', in Williams and Chrisman, *Colonial Discourse and Post-Colonial Theory*, 328

82 Shohat, 'Notes', 325.

83 Stuart Hall, 'When Was the 'Post-Colonial'', PCQ, 249; cf Miller, *Theories of Africans*, 24, 50.

84 Annie Coombes, 'The Recalcitrant Object', in Barker, *Colonial Discourse/Postcolonial Theory*, 91.

85 Thomas, *Colonialism's Culture*, 60.

86 Bhabha, 'Minority Maneuvers', 433.

87 Frankenberg and Mani, 'Crosscurrents, Crosstalk', CPT, 362; cf Miller, *Theories*, 64–66.

88 Ray, 'Shifting Subjects Shifting Ground', 199.

89 Mohan, 'Dodging the Crossfire', 276.

90 Thieme, 'Introduction', *Arnold Anthology of Postcolonial Literatures*, 40.

91 Loomba, *Colonialism/Postcolonialism*, 19.

92 Krishnaswamy, 'Mythologies of Migrancy', 129

93 As Nicholas Thomas points out in another context, the *incommensurability* privileged in the work of critics such as JanMohamed and Bhabha risks repeating 'what is itself a familiar cry of colonial representation the unintelligible, indescribable, inscrutable and unknown character of other places and peoples' (Thomas, *Colonialism's Culture*, 52)

94 Shohat, 'Notes', 330.

95 King, 'Introduction', *New National and Post-Colonial Literatures*, 19, 21.

96 Boehmer *Colonial and Postcolonial Literature*, 245.

97 Chinweizu et al , *Toward the Decolonisation of African Literature*, vol. i, 4.

98 Herder, *Outlines of a Philosophy of the History of Man*, cited in Pagden, 'The Effacement of Difference', 142

99 See Ngugi, *Decolonizing the Mind*, 41–45, 56–62.

100 Said, 'Criticism, Culture and Performance', 39.

101 Haber, *Beyond Postmodern Politics*, 121–122, my emphasis

102 Fish, 'Consequences', 93

103 Fish, *Is There a Text in this Class?*, 14–16, 331

104 Fish, *Is There a Text in this Class?*, 333, my emphasis An interpretative community defines its members and 'fills their consciousness' (Fish, *Professional Correctness*,

14). This strongly communitarian orientation is characteristic of a whole current of post-Wittgensteinian culturalist theory. Clifford Geertz, for example, conceives 'the community as the shop in which thoughts are constructed and deconstructed.' That 'thinking is to be understood "ethnographically"' means 'describing the world in which it makes whatever sense it makes' (Geertz, *Local Knowledge*, 153, 152) – to the detriment, no doubt, of approaches that cultivate the invention of apparent 'non-sense', i.e. *new* and disruptive forms of sense.

105 See Fish, 'Being Interdisciplinary Is so Very Hard to Do', 107; cf Fairlamb, *Critical Conditions*, 25, 43

106 Varadharajan, *Exotic Parodies*.

107 Adorno, *Negative Dialectics*, 161–162; 4.

108 Varadharajan, *Exotic Parodies*, 130, 140, 139.

109 Césaire, *Discours sur le colonialisme*, 19/21, cf Fanon, *Damnés*, 67/37.

110 Gareth Griffiths, 'The Post-Colonial Project', in King ed., *New Literatures*, 168.

111 Hegel, 'Sense Certainty', *The Phenomenology of Mind*, 58–66.

112 Spivak, *In Other Worlds*, 135; Said, *Culture and Imperialism*, 35–36, Sartre, 'Preface', Memmi, *The Colonizer and the Colonized*, xxi

113 Laclau, *Emancipation(s)*, 32.

114 Cf. Kuper, *South Africa and the Anthropologists*.

115 Badiou, *Saint Paul*, 103

116 Badiou, *Théorie du sujet*, 197

117 Badiou, 'Being by Numbers', 123; cf. Badiou, *Conditions*, 245, 250.

118 de Maistre, 'Des Origines de la souveraineté', quoted in Finkielkraut, *Défaite*, 109/79.

119 'Let's Be Friends', *Sesame Street Live* at the Madison Square Garden, 7–23 February 1997, sponsored by McDonald's Corporation (February 1997).

120 Sprinker, 'The National Question' [1993], 24.

121 Dirlik, *After the Revolution*, 97, cf. Dirlik, *The Postcolonial Aura*, viii, Miyoshi, 'A Borderless World?', 751, San Juan, *Beyond Postcolonial Theory*, 9–10.

122 Lazarus, 'Doubting the New World Order', 99.

123 Dirlik, *The Postcolonial Aura*, ix; cf. Dirlik, *After the Revolution*, 91–100.

124 'Postcolonial thought is the last refuge of the postmodernist' (Callinicos, 'Wonders Taken for Signs', 98).

125 Ahmad, 'The Politics of Literary Postcoloniality', 284.

126 Ahmad, *In Theory*, 36; cf. 129.

127 Ahmad, *In Theory*, 38, 3.

128 San Juan, *Beyond Postcolonial Theory*, 8.

129 Parry, 'Liberation Movements', 49.

130 Lazarus provides a useful list of such readings in his *Nationalism and Cultural Practice*, 15 n.34.

131 Parry, 'Problems', 43, Ahmad, *In Theory*, 6. 'The rise of postcolonial textualism is symptomatic of the attenuation of Third World resistance in the eighties' (San Juan, *Beyond Postcolonial Theory*, 265).

132 Parry, 'Problems', 43, see also Parry, 'The Postcolonial', 12, Dirlik, *The Postcolonial Aura*, 166 and passim; Chrisman, 'Inventing Post-Colonial Theory', 208–209

133 See for example Spivak, 'Can the Subaltern Speak?', 287–288.

134 Ahmad, *In Theory*, 60, 56. Lazarus likewise lumps a very loose (if not simply undefined) collection of figures under the label of '"post-"theory' (Lazarus, *Nationalism and Cultural Practice*, 10–11).

135 'There is only desire and the social, and nothing else' (Deleuze and Guattari, *L'Anti-Oedipe*, 36/29)

136 Ahmad attributes to Foucault 'a bleak sense of human entrapment in Discourses of Power' (In Theory, 130– 131; cf. 3, 14). This calls for immediate refutation. It is simply wrong to suggest that Foucault is complicit with the power he identifies fundamentally as specification pure and simple (the specification of individuals as mad, deviant, perverse, criminal, gay, straight, etc.). Foucault's deliberate and often militant resistance to such specification in all its forms is consistent throughout his career. Moreover, to recognise the fact that power to some degree 'produces' the field in which it is effective (for example, the domain of public health) is in no way to surrender to its domination. It requires wilful misreading not to notice the barely suppressed outrage that informs so much of La Volonté de savoir – simply recall the quintessentially Foucauldian treatment of the pathetic incident of Charles Jouy of Lapcourt (Foucault, Volonté, 43–44/31–32). Wittingly or not, Ahmad's argument simply duplicates the most vehemently conservative dismissals of Foucault's work.

137 Since he defends this remarkable reading with a quotation from Rushdie rather than Derrida himself, it is hard to know what particular text Ahmad has in mind here certainly not the ones that emphasise the quasi-transcendental dimension of logocentric assumptions, the situated character of every particular reading, the laborious working-through of every apparently 'proper' notion of belonging

138 Ahmad, In Theory, 64 Ahmad's presentation of Lyotard as the merely 'bourgeois' prophet of 'the age of the enjoyment of goods and services' (In Theory, 71) is especially unfair to the long-standing member of Socialisme ou barbarie and quite an absurd description of the author of Le Différend.

139 Ahmad, In Theory, 6.

140 Parry, 'Liberation Movements', 46, 50

141 Parry, 'Problems', 30 (referring to Fanon), cf 38, 42–43

142 See Badiou, 'Art et philosophie', Petit Manuel d'inesthétique, 15–18.

143 Ahmad, In Theory, 242

144 Ahmad, In Theory, 9, cf 11, 38, 50–51.

145 Cf Hall, 'When Was the Post-Colonial?', PCQ, 243–244

146 See in particular Badiou, L'Éthique, 8–9.

147 Ahmad, In Theory. Ahmad's argument implies, for instance, that Frye and Bloom have no theoretical value simply because they work on literary Romanticism rather than on 'the configuration of the class forces and sociopolitical practices' (11) at work in a particular historical formation.

148 See Balibar, 'Ambiguous Universality', 48–49 Badiou distinguishes sharply between four possible modes of 'subjectivation' or 'truth', of which politics is only one the others are art, science, and love. See Badiou, Manifeste pour la philosophie, 60–69, Conditions, 79

149 Deleuze and Guattari, 'Anti-Oedipe, 36–37/29–30.

150 Marx and Engels, The First Indian War of Independence, 16–17 Ahmad himself provides a much-needed corrective to prevailing misinterpretations with his 'Marx on India' (Ahmad, In Theory, 221–242). See also Ahmad's response to Warren, 'Imperialism and Progress' (1983).

151 Lazarus et al., 'The Necessity of Universalism', 125.

152 Meszaros, Beyond Capital, 2, cf. San Juan, Beyond Postcolonial Theory, 240

153 San Juan, Beyond Postcolonial Theory, 39. Fanon's call for an effectively 'endless' mobilisation of the masses arising directly 'out of the war of liberation' has proved impossible to sustain after victory in that same war (Fanon, Dannés, 126–127/93–94).

154 Wallerstein, 'Revolution as Strategy' [1995], 229. Touraine concurs. 'the era of revolutions is over' (Touraine, 'The Idea of Revolution' [1990], 140).

155 Balibar is only one of a whole generation of western Marxists – and hardly the most enthusiastic at that – to note the contemporary 'degeneration of class struggle [....,] "historical" class struggle has come to an end', leaving the field to a 'multiplicity of different struggles' (Balibar, 'Has the "World" Changed?', 410).

156 Badiou, *Théorie axiomatique du sujet*, 26.11 97; Badiou, 'Politics and Philosophy', 114.

157 San Juan, *Beyond Postcolonial Theory*, 8.

158 Foucault, *Dits et écrits*, IV, 777, trans. as 'Truth, Power, Self', *Technologies of the Self*, 9 'What is the point of striving after knowledge if it ensures only the acquisition of things known [*connaissances*] and not, in a certain way and to the greatest extent possible, the disorientation [*égarement*] of he who knows?' (Foucault, *L'Usage des plaisirs*, 14/8tm).

159 Ahmad, 'Politics of Literary Postcoloniality', 289, cf. *In Theory*, 65.

160 See Fanon, *Damnés*, 67

161 Foucault, 'Cours de 14 janvier, 1976', *Dits et écrits*, iii, 127.

162 'I am not the prisoner of History I don't have to find the meaning of my destiny in it [. .]. The density of History determines none of my actions' (Fanon, *Peau noire, masques blancs*, 186–187/229–231tm).

163 Finkielkraut, *Défaite de la pensée*, 95/68.

164 The point is made well by Ahmad, *In Theory*, 11, 16, 291–292, cf Lazarus, 'National Consciousness', 216–220

165 Said, 'Orientalism Reconsidered', 102–105

166 Childs and Williams argue for a similarly comprehensive sweep (*Post-Colonial Theory*, 97).

167 Said, 'Interview with Buttigieg and Bove', 8.

168 CI, 68, xxix, Said, 'An Ideology of Difference', PD, 81.

169 ME, 51–52; cf. OR, 108, 322.

170 Said, 'Representing the Colonized', 213.

171 As Said's account has made well known, orientalism proceeds through a massive, cumulative effort to submerge the lived diversity of virtually everything east of Europe under a blanket 'schematisation' (OR, 68). Orientalism depends upon and confirms 'the presumed representativeness of everything Oriental' (OR, 231). And Zionism, according to Said's critique, makes a comparable specification by religion and race the organising principle of an *essentially* Jewish State – as opposed to an ecumenical Palestinian state open to all the inhabitants of present-day Israel and its occupied territories (PD, 80; QP, 84–88). 'Zionist apartheid' specifies citizenship by religion, claims an 'inherent right' to its primordially promised land, promotes a cultural policy of 'Judaisation', and can only be maintained through a policy of essentially aggressive military settlement (QP, 103) The corresponding tendency in the contemporary Arab world 'to ground one's identity in some distant, pure, and primitive first state, whether it's Islam or a tribe or a border [.. is] something very new' (PD, 310).

172 WTC, 16–17, 34–35, 175, CI, 12–13

173 Said, 'The Intellectuals and the War', PD, 317; cf. Said, 'Opponents, Audiences, Constituencies and Community', 158.

174 OR, 326. 'What Fanon and Césaire required of their own partisans', for instance, 'even during the heat of struggle, was to abandon fixed ideas of settled identity and culturally authorised definition' ('Representing the Colonized', 225).

175 Said, 'Representing the Colonized', 225.

176 Orientalism, in this sense, is just an extreme case of cultural representation in general – the process whereby a living, shapeless reality is transformed into the

ordered 'stuff of texts' (OR, 86; cf 273–274). With Said, representation itself bears
an aggressive connotation (cf. Ahmad, *In Theory*, 194, Young, *White Mythologies*,
130–131). As several critics have pointed out, *Orientalism* pushes the argument that
representation equals misrepresentation to such an extreme that it often seems that
orientalist discourse not only radically distorts its object(s) but 'creates' it altogether
(OR, 40, 87, 121; see especially Clifford, *Predicament*, 260; Pathak et al , 'The Prisonhouse of Orientalism', 215, Moore-Gilbert, *Postcolonial Theory*, 49–50). *Orientalism* is not merely a book about cultural misrepresentation and prejudice. Its fame
and originality rest on the argument that, in effect, the relation between occident
and orient was a *wholly specifying* relation, a purely 'one-way exchange' (OR, 160).

177 Sprinker, 'The National Question', 16; Ahmad, 'Orientalism and After', *In Theory*,
159–219.

178 BV, 254–255, cf. Said, 'The Palestinian Experience' [1968–1969], PD, 22; QP, 220,
P&S, 91, 166

179 'I was one of the pioneers of the idea [..] of accepting a two-state solution' (Said,
'Introduction' [1994], PD, xxv). Said emerged from the meeting 'very pleased' (PD,
xx). His (obviously intermittent) support for a 'binational solution' goes back at least
to 1975 (PD, 327; cf. QP, 175). More recently, however, he has confessed that 'at the
psychological level, I was never able to let go of the bitterness resulting from the
loss of the PLO's old goal, that is the establishment of secular democracy in Palestine. From this angle, perhaps, I [.] cannot but admit that I might have been wrong
in the way I voted [in 1988]' (PcD, 188).

180 Said, 'Palestine Agenda' [1988], PD, 148.

181 PcD, xxii, 22, 35–37.

182 P&S, 147, cf ALS, 11, 160

183 'In a very literal way the Palestinian predicament since 1948 is that to be a Palestinian at all has been to live in a utopia, a nonplace, of some sort' (QP, 124).

184 Said, 'A Powerless People', 15; cf. Said, 'Fury of the Dispossessed', 23; PcD, xxi, 5

185 Interview with Salusinszky [1987], 128–130. 'I'm totally against separatism' ('Interview with *Radical Philosophy*' [1992], 77). See also 'Media, Margins and Modernity', 180.

186 Said, 'Fury of the Dispossessed', 23.

187 CI, xiii, 319–320, Said, 'Identity, authority, and freedom', 7.

188 CI, 395 At the same time, Said recognises the 'striking fact that no successful liberation movement in the post-World War II twentieth century was successful without the Soviet Union We [the Palestinians] are without the Soviet Union' (P&S, 53)
What is just as striking is that the implications of this fact get so little attention in
Said's own writing about liberation.

189 CI, 325, Said, 'Interview with Buttigieg and Bove,', 114

190 P&S, 166, Said, '1992 Preface', QP, xv.

191 Said, 'Israel–Palestine. a third way' [1998], 6–7.

192 P&S, 151; Said, 'Cry Palestine', 27; cf PD, xxxiv, 414–415 A frequent point of comparison is provided by Mandela and the ANC, who always refused to compromise
on their essential demands (PcD, 62, 140–141).

193 Said, Interview with Salusinszky, 129

194 Said, 'Epilogue', QP, 244. 'Since the beginning, the struggle over Palestine has been
a battle over territorial sovereignty' ('Epilogue', PD, 416); 'at bottom what I am
really writing about [.] is the contest over territory' (Said, 'Interview with
Buttigieg and Bove', 3).

195 Said, '1992 Preface', QP, xxxv

196 CI, xxix. As McGowan observes, Said 'strongly implies throughout his work that any movement from a position of exile into a community constitutes a kind of tragic fall into blindness and away from ethical purity' (McGowan, *Postmodernism and its Critics*, 171, n.40).

197 Said, 'Interview with Wicke and Sprinker' [1989], 241. It would be wrong to exaggerate the shift in Said's position – it is more a matter of relative emphasis He has long supported Deleuze's notion that 'knowledge, insofar as it is intelligible, is apprehensible in terms of nomadic centres, provisional structures that are never permanent, always straying from one set of information to another' (Said, *Beginnings* [1976], 376). Ahmad exaggerates the allegedly 'dramatic' switch in Said's work from an early 'straightforward Third-Worldist cultural nationalism' to a 'strident [rejection of] nationalism, national boundaries, nations as such' (*In Theory*, 200–201).

198 'Palestine is exile, dispossession' (ALS, 30), 'Palestinian life is scattered, discontinuous' (ALS, 20) Seen from an appropriately contrapuntal perspective, however, these features can look like the positively enviable signs of a new 'universality' (P&S, 61) Like the Martinican proponents of *créolité*, Said stresses the 'fantastic conjuncture' of cultures that intersect in Palestine, which allows it to 'wriggle free of one confining label or another' (P&S, 26; cf. ALS, 6, 150, PD, 310).

199 'Identity, authority, and freedom' [1991], 17. Said quotes Hugo of St Victor. 'the strong person has extended his love to all places, the perfect man has extinguished his'" (CI, 406–407, cf WTC, 14, OR, 259).

200 Said, *Joseph Conrad*, 196 Said's earliest article on Palestine contrasts the 'Jewish rhythm-of-life' asserted by Zionism with 'a more inclusive one, the Palestinian, which had and would allow Christian, Muslim and Jew to live in counterpoint with each other' ('The Palestinian Experience' [1968–1969], PD, 22). Later, he writes that Palestinian experiences 'form a counterpoint (if not a cacophony) of multiple, almost desperate dramas' (ALS, 159).

201 CI, 59. It was the 'variation-structure works, like the *Goldberg Variations*, for example, or Bach's *Canonic Variations* [.] that I found tremendously useful in writing *Culture and Imperialism*' (Said, 'Interview with Buttigieg and Bove', 2).

202 Said, 'Criticism, Culture and Performance', 26.

203 ME, 103 Said's most detailed musical exposition of contrapuntal technique presents it not so much as the intertwining of disparate themes, as the consideration of 'one musical line in conjunction with several others *that derive from* and relate to it [...], through imitation, repetition, or ornamentation' (ME, 102, my emphasis).

204 See for example CI, 339–340.

205 ALS, 164, my emphasis.

206 Said, 'Media, Margins and Modernity', 182.

207 Said, 'Interview with *Radical Philosophy*' [1992], 73; cf. Clifford, *Predicament*, 255 ff, Young, *White Mythologies*, 138–139. Particularly striking are Said's references to what Wordsworth called 'the still sad music of humanity' (WTC, 74, Said, *Beginnings*, 261) and Yeats the 'uncontrollable mystery on the bestial floor' (ME, 51, OR, 230, 110).

208 WTC, 5, cf. 242; OR, 93.

209 Said, 'Interview with Buttigieg and Bove', 25. Increasingly, Said legitimates his position through recourse to 'characterisations that are fundamentally private' and 'unprovable' (ME, 94) – for instance, through 'a kind of private experience of pleasure in reading' those 'autonomous literary texts' that make up 'what I consider in a kind of dumb way "great art"' (Wicke and Sprinker, 'Interview with Said', 250, 246–247).

There are limits, however, to how far Said is willing to go in this direction. He draws a line, for instance, with the 'paralysed' mastery and purely formal autonomy of music associated with Schoenberg and his followers, because it has 'withdrawn completely from the social dialectic that produced it in the first place' (Said, 'From Silence to Sound and Back Again', 9–10). Like the later Dib, Said seems to want to preserve a relation *between* silence and sound, rather than absorb one in the other.

210 RI, 39; 44–45. Adorno, for instance: 'paradoxical, ironic, mercilessly critical, Adorno was the quintessential intellectual, hating all systems [...]; for him life was at its most false in the aggregate' (RI, 41).

211 Said, 'Interview with Buttigieg and Bove', 19.

EXCURSUS I A postcolonial world?

1 Robertson and Lechner, 'Modernisation, Globalisation, and the Problem of Culture', 103.

2 Buell, *National Culture and the New Global System*, 10; cf. Featherstone, 'Global and Local Cultures' and 'Localism, Globalism, and Cultural Identity', in his *Undoing Culture*, 86–125.

3 Moore-Gilbert, *Postcolonial Theory*, 194.

4 Catherine Hall, 'Histories, Empires and the Post-Colonial Moment', PCQ, 66.

5 Featherstone, *Undoing Culture*, 2.

6 See in particular Miyoshi's incisive analysis, 'A Borderless World?', 726–751.

7 Wallerstein and Hopkins, *The Age of Transition*, 4. As a rule, where multinational 'penetration is high [...], personal income distribution is more unequal' (Volker Bornshier, quoted in Miyoshi, 'A Borderless World?', 742, n.42).

8 United Nations, *Human Development Report 2000*, in *The Guardian*, 29 June 2000, p. 14

9 Ahmad, 'Politics of Literary Postcoloniality', 286

10 United Nations statistics, quoted in Mandel, 'The Relevance of Marxist Theory' [1995], 440.

11 Hoogvelt, *Globalisation*, xiv, 84.

12 Hoogvelt, *Globalisation*, 66–67, 84.

13 Hoogvelt, *Globalisation*, 166

14 Featherstone, *Undoing Culture*, 92.

15 Robertson, *Globalisation*, 130.

16 Robertson, 'Glocalisation', 30.

17 Dirlik, *The Postcolonial Aura*, 16–19, 92–93, 98–99.

CHAPTER 2 Edouard Glissant

1 Except where noted all translations are my own; in order to evoke Glissant's often peculiar syntax, I have remained as close as possible to the original French. I am grateful to Michael Dash and Celia Britton for their help with a couple of the more translation-resistant of Glissant's phrasings.

2 Celia Britton's recent book makes an especially forceful case for connecting Glissant's work with that of Bhabha, Spivak, Gates and Said – albeit for a different purpose than mine (Britton, *Glissant*, 4, 16–18, 53–57, 86–94, 112–119, and *passim*.). All the while emphasising his opacity, his subversion of all integrative discourses, all criteria of 'sameness', and so on, Britton's book amounts to the most concerted effort yet

published to *integrate* Glissant with one of the most broadly *consensual* discourses in contemporary literature – postcolonial theory.

3 Mackey, like Gikandi and Parry, finds in Glissant an exemplary attention to the specific particularity of a discourse (Mackey, *Discrepant Engagement*, 10, 12–13, 16, 261; Gikandi, *Writing in Limbo*, 10, Parry, 'Resistance Theory', 86).

4 Baudot, *Bibliographie annotée d'Edouard Glissant*, 558, n. 1.

5 Dash, *Glissant*, 3, Britton, *Glissant*, 5. Cf. Cailler, *Conquérants de la nuit nue*, 175.

6 Chamoiseau, in Pied, 'Eloge de la créolité', 7–8; cf. Bernabé et al., *Eloge de la créolité*, 33.

7 For reasons of space I restrict my discussion to the theory and all but one of the novels.

8 *Un champ d'îles*, PC, 65, cf. IP, 209, SC, 60

9 Deleuze, *Différence et répétition*, 45–52/30–35, 318–326/247–255.

10 DA, 193 The utter incompatibility of Glissant and Deleuze in *this* respect is suggested by how impossible it is to imagine Deleuze linking the validity of his project to his particular or personal opacity as constituent member of the *French* nation.

11 Sartre, *Qu'est-ce que la littérature?*, 60–61.

12 Sartre, *Qu'est-ce que la littérature?*, 87, 90–91.

13 Deleuze and Guattari claim that 'multiplicities are rhizomatic' (*Mille plateaux*, 14/8), meaning that they exist as part of a singular, self-dividing force Unlike their conceptual opposites, trees, rhizomes multiply in one and same plane, without distinguishing up from down or centre from periphery.

14 Dash, *Glissant*, 20

15 Dash, *Glissant*, 27; cf. Britton, *Glissant*, 11ff.; André, *Caraïbales*, 112–113.

16 'Glissant', in J.-L. Joubert, ed., *Littérature francophone*, 302. Among many examples, see the reviews collected in Baudot, *Bibliographie*, 592–596.

17 Cf Cailler, *Conquérants*, 54, 176; André, *Caraïbales*, 111–112.

18 Pontes, 'Edouard Glissant', 79, 69.

19 Whereas most of Glissant's readers present him as incompatible with Césaire's 'heroics of self-formulation' and 'Senghor's totalising subject' (Dash, 'Writing the Body', 609; cf. Dash, *Glissant*, 17, 31; Radford, *Glissant*, 16, Bernabé et al , *Eloge de la créolité*, 21), I will argue that only Glissant's later work represents a genuine alternative to negritude – and then precisely because it moves *away* from the specific and the particular and toward a newly 'totalising' version of the subject.

20 Britton, *Glissant*, 179, 168

21 Dash, *Glissant*, 21; cf. Melas, 'Versions of Incommensurability', 279, Gallagher, 'La Poétique de la diversité', 33

22 Dash, *Glissant*, 165, cf Ormerod, *Introduction to the French Caribbean Novel*, 39, Cailler, *Conquérants*, 123

23 Dash, *Glissant*, 32–33; 148 In particular, Dash says, Glissant works for 'subversion of the individual as free agent [.] Glissant's oeuvre in general and *Caribbean Discourse* in particular are [thus] predicated on a dislocation or deconstruction of the notion of individual agency in a post-Cartesian, post-Sartrean sense [..] Glissant is a natural deconstructionist who celebrates latency, opacity, infinite metamorphosis' (Dash, 'Introduction' (1989), xii, cf. Dash, 'Writing the Body', 609).

24 André, *Caraïbales*, 113.

25 Wynter, 'Beyond the Word of Man', 638–641, 645.

26 Webb, *Myth and History*, 6, cf. 152, 161n.28.

27 Praeger, 'Edouard Glissant', 43.

28 Praeger, 'Edouard Glissant', 42–43, 45.

29 Roget, 'Land and Myth in the Writings of Edouard Glissant', 628.
30 Webb, *Myth and History*, 7; cf. Dash, *Glissant*, 150; Cailler, *Conquérants*, 173, Cailler, 'Creolization vs Francophonie', 59; Durix, *Mimesis, Genres, and Post-Colonial Discourse*, 163–164.
31 Britton's book provides the most emphatic and most compelling example. Like almost every other critic, Britton does her best to harness the admittedly 'ambiguous' virtues of Creole to an unambiguously resistant project of 'subversion' (Britton, *Glissant*, 25–27), emphasising 'paradox', 'indeterminacy', 'lack', 'constraint', 'compromise', 'ruse', and so on, to connote resistance and empowerment (30–31; cf. 137–140). If this strategy seems convincing, it is mainly because well-established habits encourage us to recognise these connotations in advance
32 IP, 13, 27; cf. DA, 284; PR, 177–178.
33 DA, 12; cf. 159; IP, 27–29
34 SC, 60. Glissant's privileged Poets, 'at the edge of the total world, express the One which aspires to the Universe' (IP, 91)
35 IP, 160; 52–53, cf. 101.
36 DA, 193, my emphasis, cf IP, 52.
37 DA, 397. Cf. Cailler, *Conquérants*, 35, 179
38 Following a similar logic, *Monsieur Toussaint* is written so as to 'totalise a historical fact' (MT, 'Avertissement de 1986', 9). The nation here serves as guarantee against what is for Glissant the supreme evil: the separation of an expressive part from the Totality it expresses The 'individual closed within his or her abyssal liberty' (IP, 41) is the product of the Western effort to 'to isolate man [*l'homme*], to bring him back ceaselessly to his "role" as individual, to confine him to himself' (IP, 59). The distinctively *French* problem is thus a lack than an excess of national community (SC, 62, IP, 71). Glissant is hostile to negritude, and the racial separatism espoused by Malcolm X, for the same reason. it isolates the subject, eliminates his relation with the *Totalité* (IP, 181).
39 See Leibniz, *Monadology, Philosophical Works* §6, §57 Any monad 'represents' the Totality of creation or the 'whole universe', Leibniz explains, but in all non-divine monads, 'this representation of the details of the whole universe is confused, and can only be distinct with respect to a small part of things, namely those which are either closest or largest in relation to each monad [...]. It is not in the object of their knowledge, but in its modification, that monads are bounded. They all reach confusedly to infinity, to everything, but they are limited and differentiated by their level of distinct perception' (§60). We might say that Glissant's goal, in Leibnizian terms, is to 'modify' and enlarge the level of Martinique's 'distinct perception' with respect to what is 'closest' to it, so that it might become more able to perceive the true nature of what is most universal (or furthest away).
40 Clark, 'IME Revisited', 604
41 DA, 258, cf 153, 285, n 5.
42 IP, 50. In 1969, Glissant is looking forward to that 'national problematic which sooner or later will rise up [in Martinique]' (IP, 134), he is still looking in 1981 (DA, 464; cf. MM, 231)
43 DA, 465, my emphasis. *Dépasser* connotes 'to move beyond' as much as it does 'to overcome' or 'supersede'
44 IP, 219; SC, 41. Such is the accomplishment, in particular, of Papa Longoué, who appears in most of Glissant's novels. the Longoué line ends with the heirless Papa, but as duly *dépassé*, that is, universalised 'Exhausted, the Longoués rest in everyone' (QS, 287; cf. TM, 94–96).
45 'Théâtre, conscience du peuple' [1971], DA, 396.

46 IP, 215. 'Intention is thus perfected in Relation' (IP, 217).

47 IP, 215. 'Before overcoming itself, History strives to achieve the harmony of all the Histories. Such is the wish for today's pressing time' (IP, 49)

48 PR, 171. 'Cultures in evolution infer Relation, the overcoming [*dépassement*] which founds their unity-diversity' (PR, 13).

49 'Théâtre, conscience du peuple', DA, 396. If the nation is that social unit which expresses its condition as a specific part of the Totality, colonised Martinique is a mere *peuple*, a merely *empirical* particularity, unconscious, heterogeneous, which lives only the 'turmoil of this consciousness whose necessity it anticipates, but that is incapable of "making emerge" or "making pass into the everyday"' (DA, 130–131).

50 'The Plantation system collapsed abruptly or progressively, without engendering its own *dépassements*' (PR, 77).

51 Here, 'l'*immédiaté*' signifies simply the mechanical or 'direct repercussion of pressures' (DA, 436).

52 DA, 485; cf. MM, 192, 201.

53 The folktale provides an instructive example. It is the model '*art du Détour*' (DA, 152), just as 'the Creole language is the first geography of Detour' (33). In itself, the folktale is *merely* 'transparent'. 'The Caribbean folktale delimits an un-possessed landscape. it is anti-History' (152). The 'empty *shrillness [acuité]* of the landscape in the creole folktale' evokes nothing but 'a plane of successive places, which we traverse [...]. This is because the landscape is not destined to be inhabited: place of passage, it is not yet a country' (DA, 243; 150–151, cf. IP, 141).

54 For example, Marcus Garvey, Fanon, Césaire and the negritude writers – 'these forms of Detour are then so many camouflaged or sublimated forms of a Return to Africa' (DA, 35)

55 DA, 32. They are not *wholly* exclusive, because detour may of course (like Negritude) lead *to* the nation – it may surpass itself, as in Haiti (33).

56 Creole is a language of 'lisping, lagging behind, idiocy. Camouflage. It is a *mise-en-scène* of Detour The Creole language constituted itself around such a ruse' (DA, 278–279).

57 DA, 281, my emphasis, cf PR, 103.

58 DA, 281; cf. 237, 396–397.

59 For reasons of space, I omit discussion of what may be Glissant's best known novel, *Le Quatrième siècle* (QS, 1964), which for my purposes is broadly consistent with the logic described in *La Lézarde* (LZ).

60 Cf. Cailler, *Conquérants*, 130.

61 LZ, 115–117/89–91. By the novel's end, 'youth [is] finished It is time to live' (224).

62 Cf. Anderson, *Imagined Communities*, 90, 127.

63 LZ, 73/61tm. Alphonse is pushed uncontrollably along by his love for Mycéa, Valérie goes north because 'drawn to the mountains', 'drawn in spite of herself to Thaël's world' (136–137/105–105). Meanwhile, 'nothing can stop Thael and Garin [..], they move forward, heavy, unswerving, two concentrations of destiny' (137/105, 145/112). Thaël, moving south with Valérie, is 'driven by some strange necessity' (180/139tm) – and so on.

64 In *La Case du Commandeur* Mathieu encourages us to identify this narrator with Glissant himself.

65 QS, 93; cf. SC, 43; MT, 65; LZ, 42/40tm.

66 *Malemort* is the most obviously experimental and most obviously 'creolised' of Glissant's novels, my translations, consequently, may sound especially forced and

artificial.

67 See in particular 'La dépossession', DA, 58–67.

68 DA, 60; cf. 123; MM, 72.

69 DA, 485, cf. Dash, *Glissant*, 116.

70 MM, 123; cf. IP, 220, CC, 191, TM, 346.

71 MM, 61. The dying up of the river is dated 1960 (MM, 190).

72 MM, 221, cf. MH, 162–164. Even in *La Lézarde*, the only character actually consumed in the sea is the vile Garin, in *Malemort*, it is Odibert killer of Beautemps – 'Odibert, the zombie in all of us' (MM, 192), 'Odibert who always wanted to kill in himself the image his neighbour there inspired' (183) – who like Garin is 'condemned to attempt without respite a crossing of the sea' (51).

73 MM, 189 'Dlan Silacier Médellus (us, part of them)' (148, cf 190)

74 MM, 68 (quoted as in text).

75 As Dash observes, 'the entire novel, conceivably, takes place in the overseer's cabin during Mycéa's vigil after her escape from the psychiatric hospital' (Dash, *Glissant*, 134).

76 Burton, 'Comment peut-on être Martiniquais?', 311–312.

77 *Pays rêvé, pays réel*, 104, in PC, 350.

78 Dash, *Glissant*, 124–125, 140.

79 In the first two novels, Mycéa had a rather different profile. In *La Lézarde*, she 'seemed to live only on political passion' (LZ, 24/28tm). In the immediate post-*Lézarde* era, we are told that she is 'already a wife, preoccupied with the well-being of her husband' (QS, 272–273)

80 'Every philosopher runs away when he or she hears someone say, "let's discuss this" [...]. Philosophy has a horror of discussions', and 'debate is unbearable to it' (Deleuze and Guattari, *Qu'est-ce que la philosophie?*, 32/28-29)

81 TM, 347, cf. MH, 170.

82 TM, 342. Both Mathieu and Mycéa 'thus abandon what, around them, is still living. Closed, they evade the outside world. You would have said – they said it themselves – that they have nothing in common with those making noises around them...' (368).

83 Deleuze's synonyms for this 'paradoxical term' include the 'aleatory point', the dark precursor, and the 'nonsense term' All are equipped with the Creative power of a 'divine, solitary game' (Deleuze, *Différence et répétition*, 361/282). The 'virtual paradoxical element' is what distributes every actual series as its effects (Deleuze, *Logique du sens*, 99/81).

84 CC, 125 In Ozonzo's version of the story, in Africa 'all the people were Odono' (81).

85 CC, 224 Already as a child, Mycéa figures as an opportunity to *know* Odono, to educate the ancestor, so to speak: '"Odono, Odono. Come, come, please. I'll teach you your abc's"' (CC, 51–52). The young Mycéa has only one question for Papa Longoué. 'who was that Odono of her childhood, whom she still vaguely remembers'? (175: Longoué doesn't know)

86 Cf. MH, 140, TM, 52, 164, 222.

87 MH, 90. He dies with 'a bitter, negligent scream, like a crying child' (92).

88 MH, 205. Mani is eclipsed only by Marny's still more violent 'carnage' (MH, 198), still more glorious 'évasion' (199), and still more tragic death (205).

89 In keeping with her enthusiastically postcolonial orientation, Britton provides a more sympathetic gloss. with *Tout-monde*, her Glissant 'open[s] up the possibility of a free, equal, collective participation in the construction of discourse [..]. Conflict is dissolved in the deliberately open-ended, ramified, heterogeneous, and

dispersed (non-)structure of the text, [..in] a "chaotic", liberated multiplicity of free-floating idioms' (Britton, *Glissant*, 7–8; 180)

90 André, *Caraïbales*, 153.

91 'All these countries in the distance, where everything is happening in the same way, at the same time at the same moment' (TM, 205, cf 136, 229, MH, 245).

92 TM, 236. 'The languages of the world mix here [in the Antilles] and speak with a single multiplied voice' (275).

93 TM, 55–56 (the novel is dedicated to the memory of Félix Guattari) The ancient tree of *Mahagony* sets the new rhizomatic process in motion, so to speak, when at that novel's end, adding to the many sprawlings of branches and roots', Mathieu imagines it 'multiplied in so many trees in so many countries of the world' (MH, 252).

94 Prigogine and Stenghers, *La nouvelle alliance* (1979).

95 'Banyan trees, rhizomes, fig trees. The same disordering of chaos, in forms both identical and dissimilar' (TM, 56; cf. 58, 438–439). Massala provides Glissant's most detailed example of a rhizomatic logic. 'the continuous without Here nor There, without periphery nor Centre, massala has its own essence, but at the same time, it dissolves in its possible combinations [.] Food is a rhizome' (478).

96 For example, the notion 'that we are never more universal than when we recognise our particularity' is now quoted as 'a tranquil stupidity of the universal' (TM, 434–435; compare with SC, 70 and IP, 49).

97 TM, 388; cf. MH, 222, 224, 230

98 TM, 472 The formula echoes Deleuze. we are 'simultaneously childhood, adolescence, old age and maturity' (*Cinéma 2*, 130/99).

99 Deleuze and Guattari, *Qu'est-ce que la philosophie?*, 47/45.

100 TM, 477, 479, cf 486.

101 Mathieu, *Traité*, TM, 124

102 Mathieu, likewise, is he who 'puts all this in circulation. .' (TM, 186). By the end of the novel, Mathieu has lived 'mixtures to infinity', and knows that 'what's divine is the surface as much as the upheavals of depth...' (TM, 510) Glissant uses *exactly* the same words to describe the universality of Henry Corbin ('Avant-dire: Dialogue d'Artémise et de Marie-Anne sur le poème d'Henry Corbin', *Clairières du temps*, 7, reprinted in Baudot, *Bibliographie*, 198).

103 'Glissant' the travel-writer (in the text) concludes· 'the important thing is that they [the tourists] were brought together above all horizons, and that the [different] spaces were exploded' (TM, 502).

104 TM, 234; cf. 165; MH, 220

105 Mathieu, *Traité*, TM, 158, 159, my emphasis.

106 In one of the most cogent chapters of *Tout-monde*, 'Les quatre morts de Papa Longoué', death is described as the effective condition of access to the 'Tout-monde'

107 See esp. TM, 340, 461, 516–517

108 In Britton's reading, by contrast, the proliferation of these 'narrative relays' generates a complex 'web of intersubjective connections' that undermine any pretence of narrative coherence and authorial control, or 'monolingualism' (Britton, *Glissant*, 168–171).

109 For example, *Mahagony* refers to a discussion between Longoué, Thaél, and Glissant himself (MH, 94).

110 TM, 195. The merging of fiction and 'theory' is further encouraged by the inclusion of '*Le traité du Tout-Monde* de Mathieu Béluse' – another opportunity for a review of Glissant's previous fiction – in Glissant's book of the same name (TTM, 43–71).

'I'm discovering', Mathieu-Glissant observes, 'just how much what we call real life is mixed up with the virtuality of a story, or a novel' (56).

111 TM, 345. 'He, he, was it the *déparleur*, the novelist, the Mathieu, the chronicler, the poet [...], nobody could have said, in this half-light' (TM, 408).

112 Glissant's exemplary figures – Perse, Faulkner, Segalen, and so on – remain the same. The names assigned to the central concepts – *opacité, errance, relation*, even, briefly, *accumulation* (PR, 45) – remain the same. Glissant himself certainly insists that *La Poétique* is the 'recomposed echo, or the re-saying in spiral' of *L'Intention poétique* and *Le Discours antillais* (PR, 28, cf TTM, 20).

113 Martinique is mentioned as Fanon's home (PR, 31), in passing on page 79, and again on pages 159–160 with reference to a 'politics of ecology'

114 *Le Sang rivé*, PC, 9.

115 PR, 45. 'The old space of the trajectory, the spirituality of the itinerary [...] cede the terrain to the realised *compacité* of the world. We must enter into the equivalences of Relation' (43).

116 I admit that *after* the *Poétique*, Glissant slightly softens his singular stance In *Traité du tout-monde*, Glissant takes more care to distinguish Relation from the uniformity of the 'absolute', puts more of an emphasis on a reflexive distance from the literal surging of the Chaos-world (TTM, 161), and finds some space to renew calls for Martinican independence (precisely so as to allow it to 'become excessive, that is, to align it with the Excess [*Démesure*] of the world' (231–232) Nevertheless, the *essentially* singular (rhizomatic, chaotic, self-differentiating, intransitive) dimension of Relation remains consistent in Glissant's work of the 1990s

117 For Deleuze and Guattari, drawing on Spinoza's concept of substance, a 'plane of immanence' is plane of '*univocality as opposed to analogy*', a plane in which everything exists 'on the same level' and in the same way (*Mille plateaux*, 311–312/254–255).

118 PR, 23, cf TTM, 21–22, 195–196. In *La Poétique*, if 'Rhizome' is the only direct reference to Deleuze and Guattari that Glissant provides, the text is at least consistent with Deleuze on the following points the critique of generality and identity (PR, 64, 151–152), of 'territory' (158), and of Oedipus (71); affirmation of the crowd or swarm ('we know ourselves as a crowd' [21]), of the baroque as proliferation (51, 91–94), of '*l'étendue*' or surface as opposed to 'filiation' or depth (59, 65), of 'experimental thought' (148), of continuous 'variation' (156), of linguistic 'deterritorialisation' (17). Perhaps most striking is the typically Deleuzian affirmation of *quantity* over quality. For example· 'being in the world is nothing without the *quantified* totality of all the ways of being-in-society' (93), 'the Diverse, the *quantifiable* totality of all possible differences, is the motor of universal energy' (42), 'baroque naturality [. .] will follow, as it goes along, the measurable *quantity* of its dizzying variances' (116); 'baroque art [.] exalts *quantity* infinitely reconsidered' (92); 'chaos has no language, it invokes one by *quantifiable myriades*' (139, my emphases), and so on

119 Chamoiseau and Confiant, *Lettres créoles*, 160.

120 PR, 31, cf TM, 55, 460

121 PR, 108 Glissant's interest in chaos and fractals invites comparison with the perspective adopted by Antonio Benítez-Rojo in his influential study of Caribbean writing, *The Repeating Island* (see for instance pages 3–4).

122 PR, 185–186; cf. TM, 48, 403, *Pays rêvé*, PC, 30–31; 71.

123 Glissant, 'Avant-dire', in Corbin, *Clairières du temps* (1992), 7, in Baudot, *Bibliographie*, 198.

124 PR, 41–42; repeated 211. Relation, in other words, is an *autonomous* composition, just as 'painting which creates its own space also creates its own autonomous speech', or as 'the painter who creates his space generates Relation' (Glissant, 'Stèles', text du catalogue Sylvie Sémavoine [Bois-Colombes: Galérie Charlemagne, 1992], reprinted in Baudot, *Bibliographie*, 202). Lam's paintings, for instance, 'hurl themselves in every direction and come to end, that is realise themselves in the surprise of the enormous worldly relation [*relation mondiale*]' (Glissant, 'Lam, l'envol et la réunion', CARE 10 (April, 1983), 15).

125 Britton, *Glissant*, 11, 12, 18.

126 PR, 93–94. More, '*the baroque is the privileged speech of these [Creole] cultures, even if it is henceforth the speech of all*' (105, my emphasis).

127 PR, 122. 'we write in the presence of all the world's languages' (TTM, 85, cf 26).

128 PR, 108. It's true that Glissant is occasionally troubled by the risk of uniformity, as a possible consequence of singularity – hence the importance in *La Poétique* of certain effectively *specified* concepts (*l'opacité, le Divers, le multilingue*) which regulate the idea of Totality and prevent it from collapsing inward towards the universal sameness it evokes. For example. 'the thought of the opaque saves me from univocal paths and irreversible choices' (206): 'we will therefore call opacity that which protects the Diverse' (75). This definition should be taken as literally as possible – Glissant will now call *opacité* that which his theory requires for protection against its own tendency to collapse *all* distinctions into a single 'écho-monde', an undifferentiated chaos.

EXCURSUS II On the nation and its alternatives

1 See in particular TTM, 247ff

2 On the broader philosophical questions at stake here, see Badiou, *Peut-on penser la politique?* (1984), and *Abrégé de métapolitique* (1998). The main criticism that Badiou levels at Deleuze – that his conception of ontology, however convoluted its mechanics and disjunctive its expression, presumes a fundamentally organic continuity which precludes the possibility of a radical break with being-as-being (i.e. the sort of break Badiou calls an *event*) – could be applied *tel quel* to much of the later work of Glissant. Like Deleuze, Glissant privileges the logic of the baroque *fold* over that of the classical *cut* (cf Badiou, 'Gilles Deleuze. Le Pli', 171–173, Badiou, *Deleuze*, 114–116/74–76, 135–137/90–92).

3 Hobsbawm, *Nations and Nationalism*, 19, quoting Maurice Block, cf. Kedourie, *Nationalism*, 14–15; Brubaker, *Citizenship and Nationhood*, 35–49.

4 Among many recent contributions to a broadly Jacobin understanding of nation, see in particular Dominique Schnapper, *La Communauté des citoyens* (1994). The nation, as Schnapper presents it, *is* nothing other than the deliberate transcendence of 'particularisms of all kinds', via the expressly 'artificial' mechanisms of citizenship (24, cf 104–108). See also Viroli, 'Patriotism without Nationalism', *For the Love of Country*, 184–185, David Miller, 'Nationality and Cultural Pluralism', *On Nationality*, 150–154.

5 Said, 'Criticism, Culture, and Performance', 40.

6 Buell, *National Culture*, 233.

7 Appadurai, 'Patriotism and its Futures', 411–412.

8 Bahri, 'Once More with Feeling', 57

9 Sklair, *Sociology of the Global System*, 3, 6, my emphasis. Sklair's version of this system, like that of Wallerstein and Friedman, retains more of a political edge than most postcolonial forms of anti-nationalism.

10 Radhakrishnan, 'Postcoloniality and the Boundaries of Identity', 751.

11 Daniel Bell, quoted in Giddens, *Consequences of Modernity*, 65, cf. Hobsbawm, *Nations and Nationalism*, 191; Featherstone, *Undoing Culture*, 90.

12 Michel Maffesoli, *Le Temps des tribus* (1988).

13 Spivak and Plotke, 'A Dialogue on Democracy', 9, Spivak, 'Attention: Postcolonialism!', 169, cf. Spivak, 'In the New World Order' [1994], 90.

14 Fanon, *Damnés*, 82/51.

15 Fanon, *Damnés*, 126/93. Everything, as Césaire had argued some years earlier, 'boils down to one postulate. the right to take the initiative' (Césaire, *Letter to Maurice Thorez*, 11)

16 Fanon, *Damnés*, 295–296/247–248 Cf Lazarus, 'National Consciousness', 216.

17 Fanon, *Damnés*, 247/203–204; cf. San Juan, *Beyond Postcolonial Theory*, 250. As Lenin recognised long ago, the effort to unite the international working class is perfectly consistent with an unequivocal recognition of 'the full right of all nations to self-determination', just as it is inconsistent with 'reactionary' appeals to 'cultural and national autonomy' (Lenin, 'Socialist Revolution and the Right of Nations to Self-Determination', *Selected Works*, 158–168).

18 Basch et al., *Nations Unbound*, 36, cf. Rushdie, *Imaginary Homelands*, 124 Postcolonial writers are not the only ones, of course, to think this way. Since Gellner believes that the link between 'state and culture [...] is what nationalism is about', he sees (and attacks) the ongoing supervision of 'standardised, homogeneous, centrally sustained high cultures' as one of the chief political functions of the state. 'It is nationalism which engenders nations' (Gellner, *Nations and Nationalism*, 38, 55). Likewise, it is because he presents the nation and the nation-state as an effect of *cultural* nationalism that Hobsbawm applauds the recent 'decline of the old nation-state as an operational entity', both 'politically' and 'culturally'. Like Gellner, Hobsbawm directs his critique at mainly 'homogeneous nation-states', i.e. at 'ethno-linguistic territorial [..] units' (Hobsbawm, *Nations and Nationalism*, 191, 187, 66) But since Hobsbawm himself admits that today 'not much more than a dozen states out of some 180 can plausibly claim that their citizens coincide in any real sense with a single ethnic or linguistic group' (186), then it need not follow that the nation-state has outlived its *political* utility

19 Gilroy, 'Route Work', PCQ, 18, my emphasis; cf Gilroy *Black Atlantic*, 18–19, 33, *Small Acts*, 67–70, 192–194. Gilroy himself argues strongly against 'the fatal junction of the concept of nationality with the concept of culture' (*Black Atlantic*, 2).

20 Mishra, 'Postcolonial differend', 7 Eagleton notes that the rise of postcolonial theory is one of several symptoms of the '"rampant culturalism' which has recently swept across Western cultural theory, over-emphasising the cultural dimensions of human life in understandable overreaction to a previous biologism, humanism or economism' (Eagleton, *Literary Theory*, 205).

21 Cf Lazarus, *Nationalism and Cultural Practice*, 74–77. The main effect of a *principled* condemnation of nationalism is to reinforce what Lazarus is right to denounce as the indefensible distinction between 'legitimate' First World or long-established nationalisms ('modernising, unifying, democratising') and the suspect 'persistence' or 'resurgence' of 'still unfolding nationalisms', associated with 'atavism, anarchy, irrationality and power-mongering' (Lazarus, 'Transnationalism', 29). To apply as universal absolutes the polite criteria of those 'civilised' nations whose own (generally violent) national liberation lies in the now distant past is simply to endorse the *status quo* for its own sake

22 As one of the main critics of contemporary nationalism himself acknowledges, most anticolonial nationalisms, by urging the transcendence of 'tribalism' for the sake of a more universal interest, already acted as a kind of 'internationalism' (Hobsbawm, *Nations and Nationalism*, 185)

23 Habermas, 'Citizenship and National Identity: Some Reflections on the Future of Europe, in Beiner, *Theorising Citizenship*, 263 I draw here on Cécile Laborde's suggestive paper, 'From Constitutional to Civic Patriotism', forthcoming in *The British Journal of Political Science*.

24 Cf. Miyoshi, 'Sites of Resistance in the Global Economy', 55, Lazarus, 'Disavowing Decolonisation', 69–71, 85–86

25 Wallerstein, *Modern World System*, 353.

26 Wallerstein, *Geopolitics and Geoculture*, 96

27 Wallerstein and Hopkins, *The Age of Transition*, 11, 237

28 Wallerstein, *Geopolitics and Geoculture*, 12.

29 Dirlik, *Postcolonial Aura*, 27, cf 222. Dirlik defends 'the radicalism of cultural activity against efforts to subsume the question of culture within other, seemingly more radical activities' (23).

30 Dirlik, *Postcolonial Aura*, 223, quoting Jamies, 'Native American Identity and Survival' (1994)

31 Cf Chomsky, *World Orders, Old and New*, 100–109.

32 Ahmad, 'Politics', 285.

33 Wallerstein, 'Post-America and the Collapse of the Communisms', 99; cf. Wallerstein, *Geopolitics and Geoculture*, 77–78.

CHAPTER 3 Charles Johnson

1 As in earlier chapters, I use Deleuzian terminology only because it provides a particularly economical description of what Johnson's writing *does* To my knowledge, Johnson has never mentioned Deleuze in print, and there are no obvious signs of a direct connection between the two.

2 'Popper's Disease', SA, 146. 'Thinking and being are [.] one and the same' (Deleuze and Guattari, *Qu'est-ce que la philosophie?*, 41/38, cf. 46/44)

3 As Johnson told *Contemporary Authors*, 'I have been a practicing Buddhist since about 1980' (May, *Contemporary Authors*, vol. 116, p. 235). Buddhist motifs are scattered throughout his work, from the parable of the 'Ox-herding Tale' which provides the title of his second novel, to the archetypal stories of Kujichagulia and Imani in *Faith and the Good Thing* (FG).

4 The title refers to a well-known Zen sequence The ten symbolic 'Ox-herding pictures' provide pictorial form to a version of Wu-tsu's koan· enlightenment is 'like a buffalo that passes through a latticed window. Its head, horns and four legs all pass through Why can't its tail pass through as well?' (*Gateless Barrier*, 231). The pictures present a herdsman with an ox, a figure of essential Nature, progressively 'sought, glimpsed, captured, tamed and ultimately forgotten'. In the tenth picture, the ox has become invisible, and has with the 'herdsman become Pu-tai entering the marketplace with bliss-bestowing hands' (*Gateless Barrier*, commentary, 232) The tail – the least part of the ox – lingers as that non-remainder which 'remains' of a process without remainder, as Dogen puts it, 'no trace of realisation remains and this no-trace is continued endlessly' (Dogen, in *Gateless Barrier*, 232; cf. Kapleau, *Three Pillars of Zen*, 301–311, Suzuki, *Essays in Zen Buddhism*, i, 363–378).

5 Cf. Crouch, 'Charles Johnson. Free at Last!', 30, 32.

6 With Stephen Henderson, for example, 'Black poetry' and its 'ethnic roots' are 'ultimately understood only by Black people themselves', and black criticism is a matter of isolating the ways in which 'Black poetry is most distinctively and effectively Black' (Henderson, 'The Forms of Things Unknown', *Understanding the New Black Poetry*, 7–8, 30).

7 'The boundaries of our nation are marked by the colour of our skin, Harold Cruse tells us [in *Black Fire*], and we are willing to accept his assessment' (Baker, *Long Black Song*, 17).

8 Baker, *Long Black Song*, chapter one.

9 Gates, *Figures in Black*, 40.

10 Gates, *The Signifying Monkey*, 53.

11 Baker, *Blues*, xii.

12 Baker, *The Journey Back*, xii, 163, cf *Long Black Song*, 142–143.

13 Baker, *Blues*, 7.

14 Baker, *Black Studies*, 89. In this later book, Baker declares rap to be the new world-music, and looks forward to 'a telecommunal, popular space in which a global audience interacts with performative artists' (94, cf. 99–100).

15 Baker, *Blues*, 8, 11. How other American nomads feel about this 'frontier energy' is not a question Baker chooses to address here

16 Baker, *Blues*, 202 Baker is not always consistent about this In more recent work, the 'centre' of African-American life has become 'the Woman's PLACE', and the blues, accordingly, are 'in their classic manifestation, a black woman's PLACE' (*Workings of the Spirit*, 132) Here, 'space and place merge in the event of the mother She is a sustaining place-time' (200). In a more recent book, he invokes 'the spaces of the voodoo priestess, who, in a very real sense, is never at an "intersection" but always at the perceptual and imaginative beginnings and endings of all roads that lead everywhere' (*Black Studies*, 71).

17 Baker, *Blues*, 5, my emphasis. It is remarkable that there is almost no trace of musical analysis in a book that makes such unqualified claims about a musical form, reading Baker, you would have no idea that traditional blues is based among other things upon a generally repetitive, eminently linear chord progression

18 See Gates, 'Literary Theory and the Black Tradition', *Figures in Black*, 48; Gates, *The Signifying Monkey*, x. As Baker himself puts it, 'from a dramatic and somewhat mystifying castigator of black critical thinking about the vernacular, [Gates] has become a convert to such thinking' (*Blues*, 111)

19 Gates, *Figures in Black*, xx.

20 Gates, *The Signifying Monkey*, xxiv, cf. Gates, *Loose Canons*, 65–66, 83.

21 Gates, 'Talking Black', *Loose Canons*, 79.

22 'Above all else, Esu is the Black Interpreter' (Gates, *Figures in Black*, 238).

23 Hartman, *Criticism in the Wilderness*, 272, in Gates, *Figures in Black*, 270 and *The Signifying Monkey*, 24.

24 'Signifyin(g) is the black trope of tropes', 'the figure of the figure' (Gates, *The Signifying Monkey*, 51, 77, cf *Figures in Black*, 243).

25 Cf. Gates, *The Signifying Monkey*, 238, Gates, *Figures in Black*, 177

26 'The most fundamental absolute of the Yoruba is that there exist, simultaneously, three stages of existence. the past, the present, and the unborn. Esu represents these stages, and makes their simultaneous existence possible, "without any contradiction"' (Gates, *The Signifying Monkey*, 37)

27 Gates, 'The Blackness of Blackness', *Figures in Black*, 238

28 Gates, *Figures in Black*, 241, my emphasis

29 Gates, 'Dis and Dat: Dialect and Descent', *Figures in Black*, 179

30 Kimberly Benston, quoted as epigraph by Gates, *The Signifying Monkey*, vii; my emphasis.

31 Gates, 'Dis and Dat. Dialect and Descent', *Figures in Black*, 179. Gates reads Walker's *The Color Purple* in very similar terms (*The Signifying Monkey*, 131; 239–258).

32 Benesch, *The Threat of History*, 183–184.

33 Gilroy, *The Black Atlantic*, 218, 221.

34 Orowan, review of *Ox-Herding Tale*, in *Literature, Fiction and the Arts Review* (30, June 1983), reprinted in May, *Contemporary Authors*, vol 116, p. 23.

35 Little, 'Charles Johnson's Revolutionary *Ox-Herding Tale*', 143, 146

36 Weisenburger, 'In-Between', 153, Benesch, *The Threat of History*, 186.

37 Benesch, 'Charles Johnson', 170.

38 Weisenburger, 'In-Between', 155.

39 Rushdy, 'The Phenomenology of the Allmuseri', 391.

40 FG, 165–166. Faith learns eventually to accept this as 'just' (182).

41 FG, 28. Imani (the Swamp Woman herself) – 'I am an I' – does not trouble herself with such questions.

42 FG, 99. This phenomenological either–or is repeated by Arnold Tippis (57–58, 83) and the discredited minister of The Church of Continual Light (74).

43 FG, 62–63. "'I am Faith Cross.. " "I am Faith. " "I am..." "I. .?'" (62).

44 Deleuze and Guattari, *Mille plateaux*, 144–145/115, 232–233/190–191.

45 MPg, 97–98. Listening, Rutherford looks for 'a defense against Falcon's dark counsel and arguments that broke my head. To my everlasting shame, I knew of none…' (98)

46 Deleuze and Guattari, *Mille plateaux*, 166/133.

47 Although *Middle Passage* (MPg) gives the most extended treatment of the Allmuseri, Mingo and Rubin are early examples from *The Sorcerer's Apprentice* (SA), and *Ox-Herding Tale*'s (OT) Reb is a direct descendant.

48 Haecceity is a privileged term in Johnson's fiction, as it is in Deleuze's philosophy. Cf. BR, 49; MPg, 194; FG, 93.

49 Deleuze, *Logique du sens*, 33/21.

50 Already in New Orleans, from the pier 'you could believe, like the ancient philosopher Thales, that the analog for life was water, the formless, omnific sea' (MPg, 4)

51 The passage appears as the epithet to the story 'China' (SA, 61).

52 Girard, *Mensonge romantique et vérité romanesque*, 321–323

53 McHale, *Postmodern Fiction*, 232

54 SA, 85, my emphasis; cf. OT, 172

55 SA, 89. In *Faith and the Good Thing*, Lavidia plays the same role, as the clinging-possessive mother who thwarts her daughter's romance (FG, 15)

56 Baker, *Singers of Daybreak*, 10

57 The very practice of theft, Rutherford explains, effects a transcendence of self, 'the breath coming deep from the belly, easily, as if the room itself were breathing, limbs light like hollow reeds, free of tension, all parts of me flowing as a single piece…' (MPg, 46)

58 MPg, 126–127, my emphasis In fact, Rutherford is only 'saved' from position because other, more 'specific' (more militant) actors pre-empt his indecision (128–129).

59 The one exception is his alliance with the young Allmuseri girl, Baleka The two become 'inseparable' (MPg, 79). Less than a relation *with* Baleka, however,

Rutherford becomes-Baleka. 'If she bruises herself, I feel bruised Night and day I pray all will go well for her, even after I am gone...' (195).

60 OT, 115; cf. MPg, 104

61 Cringle and Falcon illustrate the opposite extremes of Oedipus unresolved. Both are and remain driven to compensate for a father too dominant on the one hand and too pliant on the other. Falcon strives to 'outperform' his father and lavish gifts upon his mother Cringle's life is the story of a man crushed by his father (MPg, 159) – 'you can never make a man like *my* father accept you on your own terms', he 'hasn't left you any room to *do* anything except join his legion of admirers' (160)

62 MPg, 117. From the perspective of Rutherford the rebel, the nonconformist, Jackson 'was (to me) the possible-me that lived my life's alternate options, the me I fled', he was 'me if I gave in' (112). If Jackson's renunciation is flawed, it is because he remains 'ashamed of Riley Calhoun', their father (113). He is unable fully to affirm himself in the process of over-coming himself. His overcoming remains consistent with the subservient fidelity to Chandler in which Jackson's 'shamed self' lives As Rutherford sees it, he remains compromised by the 'selfless' desire to be a model 'gentleman of colour' (114) Jackson, in short, has yet to undergo his own version of the middle passage.

63 MPg, 151, see in particular 173–174

64 Barthes, 'La Mort de l'auteur' [1968], *Oeuvres complètes*, ii, 491

65 Bourdieu, *Les Règles de l'art* (1992)

66 For example, because they 'tell' rather than show, Johnson is highly critical of Alice Walker (BR, 107) and Octavia Butler (BR, 117).

67 The exceptions – 'China', 'Popper's Disease' – turn indeed upon a revelation which transforms a given situation. But *what* is revealed is revealed precisely as a discovery, a stripping away of what has concealed the truth of ascesis, the diagnosis of the 'Self' as the human plague. In 'China', Rudolph loses the fat which literally conceals the body from its nature, from how it exists 'in the mind of God'. And in the second story, what Popper learns restores him, in a sense, to the wisdom of his ancestors 'My ancestors – or so I've read – had a hundred concepts for the African community, but none for the individual...' (SA, 134)

68 'The Sorcerer's Apprentice', SA, 151

69 Rubin describes the spells as 'a web of history and culture, like the king-sized quilts you saw as curiosities at country fairs, sewn by every woman in Abbeville, each having finished only a section, a single flower perhaps, so no man, strictly speaking, could own a mystic spell' (SA, 154)

70 Deleuze, *Différence et répétition*, *passim*

71 *Ox-Herding Tale*, for example, is regularly grouped with Margaret Walker's *Jubilee* (1966), Ernest Gaines' *The Autobiography of Miss Jane Pittman* (1971), Ishmael Reed's *Flight to Canada* (1976), Alex Haley's *Roots* (1976), David Bradley's The *Chaneyville Incident* (1978), Barbara Chase-Riboud's *Sally Hemmings* (1979), Octavia Butler's *Kindred* (1979), and Toni Morrison's *Beloved* (1988). Similar lists are proposed by Benesch, *The Threat of History*, 204–206, Richard Yarborough, 'The First-Person in African-American Fiction', in Baker and Redmond, *African-American Literary Study*, 110–111, Crouch, 'Free at Last!', 30. Johnson himself considers several of these novels in his discussion of the 'Novel of Memory' (BR, 74–82)

72 Campbell, *Mythic Black Fiction*, xiv, 155–157

73 Stepto, 'After Modernism, After Hibernation', 470–486.

74 Yarborough, 'The First-Person in African-American Fiction', in Baker and Redmond, *African-American Literary Study*, 110–111

75 The question of 'referential truth' as such is of little concern to Johnson In *Faith and the Good Thing*, Johnson provides his own criteria of viable history telling. 'before you ask if anythin's true, first ask y'self if it's good, and if it's beautiful! [.]. You've got to believe in it. Don't be interrupting to ask if the tale is true' (FG, 30, 196).

76 Cf. Deleuze, *Différence et répétition*, 293/228, Deleuze, *Bergsonisme*, 108/104, Deleuze, *Spinoza et le problème de l'expression*, 195–196/214–215.

77 With more space it would be easy, though perhaps unnecessary, to show that the costs of becoming immanent are not evenly shared across genders. Johnson has two rather different roles for women characters Some embody the principle of relation and *ressentiment* (Evelyn, Lydia, Flo), as a clinging, parasitic softness. The more positively affected women are *passively* coincident with themselves – they suffice, but as merely *self*-sufficient (see in particular OT, 30, 55–56, 172) For all their apparent plenitude, they have only a minimal ability to become-other. For Johnson the literary critic, women writers are less 'experimental', less interested in matters of 'drama' and 'form' than men (BR, 118); for Johnson the novelist, women and feminine space in general provides the background for active male heroes, and little more. To take only the most obvious example, 'the *Republic* was, above all else, a ship of men', 'without the civilising presence of women' (MPg, 41; to be sure, Johnson lampoons the absurd virility of the crew). Women serve only to spur the men to travel and adventure (MPg, 49), and their own becoming is generally limited to a becoming-*thin* Isadora, for instance, is and remains, like *Ox-Herding Tal*'s Peggy, 'innocent', a 'still, uncorrupted centre', and this despite a tragically violent youth (MPg, 18) But wheras she begins the novel as 'the sort of lonely, intelligent woman who found comfort in food' (6), by its end she has acquired a 'heart-stabbing' beauty. 'Added to that, she had lost about fifty pounds' (192); 'so much slimmer', she has gained a 'figure of faint-inducing grace' (207).

78 Deleuze, *Cinéma 2*, 59/41 and passim.

79 SA, 15. As the narrator remarks. 'how strange that owner and owned magically dissolved into each other like two crossing shafts of light' (19).

EXCURSUS III The universal and the transcendental

1 See the useful discussion in Saint-Sernin's survey, *La Raison au XXe siècle* [1995].

2 Spivak, 'Foundations and Cultural Studies', 153

3 Bhabha, *The Location of Culture*, 170, 173. Bhabha accepts only 'truths that are partial, limited and unstable' ('In a Spirit of Calm Violence', 330).

4 Gareth Griffiths, 'The Post-Colonial Project', in King ed., *New Literatures*, 174.

5 JanMohamed and Lloyd, 'Introduction', *Nature and Context of Minority Discourse*, 1

6 Chambers, 'Signs of Silence, Lines of Listening', PCQ, 49–50

7 McCallum, 'Introductory Notes' to Slemon, 'Postcolonialism and its Discontents', 20.

8 Spivak, 'Echo', SR, 178. The strange idea that only *Europe* ever devised universal concepts betrays an especially stubborn form of Eurocentrism

9 Nederveen Pieterse, 'Globalisation as Hybridisation', 55.

10 Bhabha, 'Interview with Olson and Worsham', 20

11 McClintock, 'Angel of Progress', 303.

12 Shohat, 'Notes on the 'Post-Colonial', 332

13 See above, page 4.

14 Appiah, *In My Father's House*, 58

15 Connor, *Postmodernist Culture*, 243–244.

16 Dirlik, *After the Revolution*, 77

17 Lazarus et al., 'The Necessity of Universalism', 85; cf. Lazarus, *Nationalism and Cultural Practice*, 16–17. Lazarus is critical of Giddens and Gilroy for the same reason: they retain a geographic bias (Western or Atlantic) in their understanding of modernity, rather than assert a fully *global* – i.e capital-driven – one (Lazarus, *Nationalism and Cultural Practice*, 23–24, 61–62).

18 Lazarus, *Nationalism and Cultural Practice*, 8. Ahmad likewise posits universality as the *result* of 'the global operation of a single mode of production' (*In Theory*, 103).

19 Nancy Fraser, 'False Antitheses', in Benhabib et al., *Feminist Contentions*, 62, cf. West, *Prophetic Reflections*, 70.

20 Wallerstein, 'Revolution as Strategy', 231, Moore-Gilbert, *Postcolonial Theory*, 193.

21 'Introduction', in Ansell-Pearson et al., *Cultural Readings of Imperialism*, 19.

22 Landmarks in the field include Barkow et al., *The Adapted Mind*, Plotkin, *Evolution in Mind*; Steven Pinker, *How the Mind Works*, Corballis and Lea, *The Descent of Mind*.

23 Fox, *The Search for Society*, 30. Drawing on the work of Chomsky and Fox, Donald Brown makes a case for the universal or quasi universal distribution of certain basic features of human experience and behaviour (for example incest avoidance, certain emotions and facial expressions, certain linguistic universals, an emphasis on status, and so on), and concludes that evolutionary psychology is the key to their interpretation (Brown, *Human Universals*, 42 ff.). Kwasi Wiredu arrives at a broadly similar conclusion 'from an African perspective': if many 'alleged universals' have clearly been nothing more than 'home grown particulars' imposed upon other particulars, nevertheless 'the possibility of cultural universals is predicated on our common biological identity', itself the basis for 'what I take to be the three supreme laws of thought and conduct, namely, the principles of non-contradiction, induction, and the categorical imperative' (Wiredu, *Cultural Universals and Particulars*, 2; cf. 41).

24 See for instance Spiro, 'Cultural Relativism and the Future of Anthropology', 266–269.

25 Wierzbicka, *Emotions Across Languages* (1999), 36; see also Wierzbicka and Goddard, *Semantic and Lexical Universals* (1994), Comrie, *Language Universals* (1981).

26 Many languages apparently lack words that link, as the English word 'love' does, empathy and joy. Again, 'anger' as understood as English is not 'universal', since the closest equivalents in some languages (for instance the word *song*, in Ifaluk) do not include the aspect of hostile reaction to the cause of anger. *song* would be better translated as 'reproach' or 'admonition'. Rather more than Pinker, then, Wierzbicka can claim to avoid the tacit generalisation of particular linguistic configurations (Wierzbicka, *Emotions Across Languages*, 273–274, 293; cf. Pinker, *The Language Instinct*, 82, Pinker, *How the Mind Works*, 404 and *passim*).

27 Wierzbicka, *Emotions Across Languages*, 39.

28 My account of the universal here owes much to the philosophy of Alain Badiou, see section (c) below.

29 Nederveen Pieterse and Parekh, *Decolonization of Imagination*, 15. With more space, this discussion would also profit from a comparison between the competing notions of universality advanced by Butler, Laclau and Žižek in their jointly authored *Contingency, Hegemony, Universality* (2000).

30 Cf. Badiou, *Théorie du sujet*, 143, Badiou, *L'Etre et l'événement*, 201–202; 235–237; Badiou, 'Huit thèses sur l'universel', lecture at the Collège International de philosophie (Paris), 4 November 1998.

31 '*N'est universel que ce qui est en exception immanente*' (Badiou, *Saint Paul ou la fondation de l'universalisme*, 119). That truth is always subjective, then, in no means that it is somehow less rigorous or more whimsical than any more objective

conception of truth. On the contrary, 'he who is a militant of truth identifies him-self, like everyone else, on the [sole] basis of the universal. *The production of the Same is itself internal to the law of the Same*' (117). Badiou's every subject is 'generic', always anybody at all (6); 'subjective', here, means 'impersonal' and 'universal', never 'idiosyncratic'.

32 Badiou, letter to the author, 11 June 1996
33 Badiou, *Abrégé de métapolitique*, 111; cf. 'Politics and Philosophy', 128. For lack of a better alternative, I translate Badiou's term *événementiel* as 'evental'.
34 Badiou, 'Politics and Philosophy', 122.
35 Badiou, *Conditions*, 240.
36 In a move too complicated to summarise here, Badiou equates ontology (the dis-course of being-*qua*-being) with modern *set* theory, i e. that part of mathematics which accounts for the derivation and nature, or 'being', of mathematical entities and operations. One of the axiomatic assumptions of set theory ensures that a set is defined 'extensionally', i.e. simply as the collection of its elements (x, y, z...). As a result, relations between these elements (x as related to y) are literally of no onto-logical consequence Set theory ensures that a 'relation' is itself nothing other than a set (see Badiou, *L'Etre et l'événement*, appendix 2).
37 Badiou, 'D'un sujet enfin sans objet', 21.
38 Bourdieu, *Raisons pratiques*, 236/142
39 Bourdieu, *Raisons pratiques*, 239/144, cf. Bourdieu, *Méditations pascaliennes*, 96.
40 Bourdieu, *Les Règles de l'art*, 461–472/339–348.
41 Bourdieu, *Raisons pratiques*, 229/137.
42 Bourdieu, *Raisons pratiques*, 231/139.
43 Bourdieu, *Raisons pratiques*, 231/139 'transhistorical universals of communication do not exist, but socially established forms of communication favouring the pro-duction of universals do exist' (Bourdieu, 'Universal Corporatism', 661; cf. Bour-dieu, *Les Règles de l'art*, 471–472/348) The polemic disguises the similarity of Bourdieu's recent conclusions to Habermas' own *earliest* work, in particular his *Structural Transformation of the Public Sphere* [1962].

CHAPTER 4 Mohammed Dib

1 As applauded in the Algerian weekly *El Moudjahid*, Dib is the author '[who] lit the torch of Algerian literature' (*El Moudjahid*, 7 January 1980, in Chikhi, *Probléma-tique de l'écriture*, 15 n 2). For Déjeux, perhaps the most widely read critic of Maghrebine literature, 'Dib remains the most important of the Algerian writers' (Déjeux, *La Littérature maghrébine d'expression française*, 27).
2 Sari, 'Dib et la Révolution Algérienne', *Kalim* no. 6, 170. Khatibi agrees that 'it was above all Dib and Kateb Yacine who managed to develop the theme of the revolu-tion into viable novel form' (Khatibi, *Le Roman maghrébin*, 94).
3 Dib, *Formulaires*, 75.
4 Dib, *L'Aube Ismael* [1996], 31–33, cf TL, 99–100.
5 Unfortunately, space precludes consideration of several of Dib's works altogether – his poetry and stories, along with what are *arguably* the least innovative of his nov-els (*La Danse du roi* (DSR), *Dieu en Barbarie* (DB), and *Le Maître de chasse* (MC)) Their exclusion inevitably distorts my argument to some degree.
6 Conversation with the author, 7 May 1996, in Paris.
7 Deleuze and Guattari, *Mille plateaux*, 31/21, 37/25, Deleuze, *Cinéma 1*, 11/3.
8 Dib, Interview with *Témoignage chrétien*, 7 February 1958: most quotations in the

following section are taken from the folder of press clippings held in the library of the Université de Paris XIII.

9 *Témoignage chrétien*, 7 February 1958.

10 Interview with *L'Afrique action*, 13 March 1961.

11 Interview with *L'Effort Algérien*, 19 December 1952. Déjeux confirms that Dib's *L'Incendie* (IN) is likewise based very closely on actual events transposed to different settings (Déjeux, 'A l'origine de *L'Incendie* de Mohammed Dib', 3–8).

12 Interview with *L'Afrique littéraire et artistique*, 18 (August, 1971), 14

13 Interview with *Les Lettres françaises*, 7 February 1963.

14 Interview with *Le Figaro littéraire*, 4–10 July 1964.

15 Interview with *Combat*, February 1963.

16 Interview with *Le Figaro littéraire*, 4–10 July 1964.

17 Dib [1985], in Fogel and Rondeau, *Pourquoi écrivez vous*, 15.

18 Dib, Interview with *Celfan Review*, 24–25.

19 Khatibi, *Le Roman maghrébin*, 59, 94–99, 115–116; Bonn, *Le Roman algérien*, 312

20 Belhadj, *Thème de la dépossession*, 83, 93.

21 Déjeux, 'Regards sur la littérature maghrébine d'expression française', 84; cf. Cadi, 'Mohammed Dib. un romancier qui dérange', *Kalim* 6, 39–41.

22 Merad, *La Littérature algérienne*, 105–106, cf. Khatibi, *Le Roman maghrébin*, 7, 11.

23 A shift expressed at much the same time in Boudjedra's *La Répudiation* (1969) and Bourboune's *La Muezzin* (1968) as in, elsewhere, Ouologuem's *Le Devoir de violence* (1968) and Kourouma's *Les Soleils des indépendances* (1969).

24 Khadda, *L'oeuvre romanesque*, 326; cf. Chikhi, *Problématique de l'écriture*, 153, 244–245; Sari, 'Dib et la Révolution Algérienne', 137–138, 169–170; Madelain, *L'Errance et l'itinéraire*, 12.

25 Arnaud, *Littérature maghrébine*, ı, 246; Déjeux, *La Littérature maghrébine d'expression française*, 28

26 Bonn, *La Littérature algérienne*, 16, 18.

27 Arnaud, *Littérature maghrébine*, i, 247

28 Cf. Barthes, *Le Plaisir du texte*, in *Oeuvres complètes*, ii, 1502.

29 Bonn, *Lecture présente*, 7–8, cf. 168, 205, 239.

30 Bonn, *Le Roman algérien*, 326, cf. Bonn, *Lecture présente*, 161.

31 Bonn, *Lecture présente*, 21. 'The body of this writing, can it be anything other than writing itself, which only exists in the loss of the real?' (25; cf. Bonn, *Le Roman algérien*, 319–320, 324) After Blanchot, Bonn maintains that 'the solitude of the writer is absolute' (*Lecture présente*, 242).

32 'The death of *all* human communication is one of the obsessive themes of the universe of Mohammed Dib' (Bonn, *Lecture présente*, 155–157, my emphasis) More specifically, and as opposed to more Ishraq-sensitive readings, Bonn claims that the 'ambiguity' maintained in *Cours sur le rivage sauvage* or *Les Terrasses d'Orsol* 'no longer designates another meaning, but really and truly the absence of meaning in this *other side* in which, nevertheless, writing has been chosen to inhabit – to its own *loss*' (*Lecture présente*, 168).

33 Bonn, *Lecture présente*, 82, cf 175, Bonn, *Le Roman algérien*, 319.

34 Adjil, *Espace et écriture* (1995).

35 Adjil, *Espace et écriture*, 9, 11, 33–34, 61, 156–184 See also Regina Keil, 'Des hommes et des arbres. la déterritorialisation du discours identitaire maghrébin', in Bonn, *Littératures des immigrations*, ii, 19–33.

36 Dib, in André Marissel, 'Les écrivains algériens', *Les Nouvelles littéraires*, 13 October 1960, quoted by Déjeux, *Littérature maghrébine de langue française*, 173

37 TL [1994], 43–44, my emphasis.
38 'The work, it seems, constitutes itself in this gap, in this distance', and the great 'task is to fill in the intolerable fault [*faille*]' (TL, 53).
39 Dib, 'Ecrire lire comprendre', *Quinzaine littéraire*, no 665 (1995), 5; cf. TL, 61, 107.
40 Dib, 'Camus', *Simoun*, 31 (July 1960), 57, in Déjeux, *Littérature maghrébine de langue française*, 172.
41 Fanon, *Peau noire, masques blancs*, 148/184tm, 177/218tm
42 Fanon, *Peau noire, masques blancs*, 9/14tm
43 IN, 48. Dib and Fanon further share a refusal of Muslim 'fatalism', an appreciation of the peasantry as the revolutionary class, an appreciation of Algeria's role as 'guide' to decolonisation in Africa and the Third World as a whole (cf. Fanon, *Pour la révolution africaine*, 124–125, 169, 205, 211).
44 Amin, *Le Maghreb moderne*, 90–102.
45 Cf. Nouschi, *La Naissance du nationalisme algérien*, 29, Merad, *Réformisme*, 69–76, 436, Faouzi, 'L'Islam, réformisme et nationalisme', 431.
46 Vatin, 'Puissance d'état', in *Islam et politique au Maghreb*, 251.
47 Déjeux, *Littérature maghrébine de langue française*, 11–12
48 Dib, conversation with the author, 7 May 1996.
49 See especially Bourdieu et Sayad, *Le Déracinement*, 15, 118–119, cf. Ageron, *Histoire*, 62–63; Nouschi, *La Naissance du nationalisme algérien*, 117–118.
50 Bourdieu et Sayad, *Le Déracinement*, 21–23, 141.
51 Bourdieu et Sayad, *Le Déracinement*, 26; cf. 118–119, 156–157.
52 Dib, 'Les Intellectuels algériens et le mouvement national', *Alger républicain* 26 April 1950, in Sari, 'Dib et la Révolution Algérienne', 134–135.
53 Sartre, *Qu'est-ce que la littérature?*, 29.
54 Mohammed-Chérif Sahli, *L'Algérie accuse, le Calvaire du peuple algérien* (1949), in Merad, *La Littérature argérienne*, 69–70.
55 GM, 137. On several occasions in these first novels, the lack of a *patrie* is associated with the lack of a *père* (GM, 22, 35–36, MaT, 39; QSS, 53–55, DSE, 158–159).
56 GM, 52, cf IN, 142–143, 156.
57 GM, 109. The theme is obsessive. cf. GM, 14, 50, 54, 110–111, 127, 135, 152, 170, 173–174.
58 GM, 57. Cf. Khadda, *L'Oeuvre romanesque*, 270–272, 325.
59 GM, 125; 115 Cf. Bonn, *La Littérature algérienne*, 34
60 GM, 115–116 'Omar possessed a marvellous instinct that never betrayed him' (IN, 75), 'little by little his life became an act of defiance [*défi*] in its purest state' (IN, 167).
61 GM, 120, 122, cf. IN, 65–66.
62 GM, 186, my emphasis. *Le Métier à tisser* ends with an equally ambiguous 'resolution' – marked, this time, by the arrival of American soldiers in November 1942 (MaT, 204–205).
63 Khadda, *L'Oeuvre romanesque*, 276.
64 IN, 23. When the despicable landlord Kara 'had decided to get rid [of Comandar], he found himself confronting a rock He realised that he could do nothing against him' (12).
65 IN, 60. When the police arrest two fellahs in a neighbouring village, they can find no place to take them, no limit to their belonging· 'the police led the two men some place where they thought there were the masters But there, in the fields, in the village, in the city, as in the prison. it was the same thing These men were always in their land They were moved from one corner to another, but they remained at home. The police

obviously didn't understand this. There were not from here' (IN, 37).

66 IN, 67, 54, 70–71.

67 As Hamza will argue in *Le Métier à tisser*, after Marx. 'people who have arrived at the point where they are nothing, where they are zero, can only do one thing: […] Lay claim to everything' (MaT, 64–65, cf. EA, 67–68).

68 Feraoun in 1956: 'Camus and Roblès are wrong in speaking out because they are stopping short. It would be a thousand times better if they kept quiet [. .]. Are you Algerians my friends? If so your place is alongside the men who are fighting Tell the French that the country is not theirs, that they have seized it by force. All else is lies and bad faith Any other language is criminal' (Feraoun, *Journal*, 76; in McCarthy, *Camus, A Critical Study*, 301)

69 Cf. Ageron, *Histoire*, 67.

70 IN, 126, cf 137, 151.

71 GM, 152; cf. 50, 156–157, IN, 31.

72 For example, when Dar-Sbitar is searched by the police, 'Omar no longer thought of his hunger, its intensity had dimmed, become distant.. ' (GM, 50).

73 *L'Incendie*, chapter 16. This episode was first published separately as a short story in *Soleil*, January 1950.

74 IN, 188, my emphases These are the last lines of the novel – which ends, then, in the mode of the *tease*.

75 IN, 154. 'Since [Hamid] had been imprisoned in a camp, it seemed as if the voice of a whole people had fallen silent' (MaT, 202).

76 Deleuze, *Cinéma 2*, 356/272 Hakim Madjar, with Lâbane and the mystical Mendiants de Dieu, is perhaps the last of Dib's character to proclaim the existence of a *collective* vehicle of salvation (DB, 201–202).

77 As the 'sensory-motor schema is shattered from the inside, perceptions and actions cease to be linked together'. Actors become 'pure seers, who no longer exist except in the interval or movement', utterly 'helpless', paralysed within a 'pure optical and sound situation' (Deleuze, *Cinéma 2*, 59/41).

78 'Only action pays! […] What we need to do is to hate and to be hard' (MaT, 170, 179)

79 It is true that in this last of the more or less *engaged* novels, Dib includes a Malraux-style 'action' sequence (EA, 38–39; cf. 170–179).

80 Deleuze, *Cinéma 2*, 'Preface to the English edition', xi; *Cinéma 1*, 169/120; see especially EA, 71–72

81 EA, 58–59, 123, 125.

82 Cf. Arnaud, *Littérature maghrébine*, i, 190–191.

83 EA, 87 In a particularly suggestive scene, Dib evokes his passive fascination before the light reflected on a window frame, a scene in which Djamal's functions are reduced to the realm of expression *alone*, an expression beyond deliberation 'Djamal remains immobile, his eyes mid-closed, in stupor. He realises that the mind is never so sharp, so attuned, as in these moments when everything in it is dislocated and in ruins ..' (EA, 132–138).

84 Cf. Deleuze, *Cinéma 2*, 57–59/40–41, 136/103

85 For example, Hamza's neighbour in the café. 'he had disappeared!' (EA, 71). A few pages later, his friend Taïeb Berghoul, 'without explanation, left me standing there and went off' (77). Again, Djamal, in El Hadj's boutique: 'he looks around him nobody! As if the gathered company had dissolved in smoke' (79).

86 See in particular the narrative of Hamid's arrest (IN, 110–121).

87 In his postface to the novel, Dib explains that his aim was to evoke the impact of the Algerian war without falling into the numbing repetition of a flatly realist description

- to suggest, on the model of Picasso's *Guernica*, the 'limitless character of the horror and, at the same time, of the extremely rapid erosion that it produced' (QSS, 189/121).

88 For example, Ismael who 'lost body and soul [..], of him nothing, not so much as a shadow will remain' (148/94), or Ftéma's brother: 'it's as if he'd been swallowed up by the vagina of the earth!' (135/85).

89 Cf Deleuze, *Cinéma 2*, 54/37–58/40

90 Cf. Déjeux, *Mohammed Dib*, 33–35; Arnaud, *Littérature maghrébine*, I, 197–198.

91 QSS, 20/10; cf. NM, 144. The sea begins where the human ends, in a marine becoming-imperceptible. 'The sea lies still, wild-eyed Dark but warm and calm, it surrounds us, seems to watch over us. In its company, I rediscover the original directness of things' (QSS, 68/40; cf. 160–161/103)

92 Badiou, *Beckett: L'Incrévable désir*, 19–22, cf. Deleuze, *L'Epuisé* (1992)

93 His relations with El Hadj consistently illustrate the point (QSS, 56–58/33–35 and *passim*). He runs into the inscrutable Hamdai, likewise, only to feel 'reduced to nothing, flung into the void, after this meeting and these discoveries' (60/35; cf. 15/7). Again, talking to Osman Samed, 'as always they weren't the real words, the ones I had intended to say, that came to my mouth! Others, completely different, came out' (170/109).

94 'This name *nafissa*, which refers equally to the place of residence and to the soul that resides and acts in that place' (QSS, 128/80).

95 QSS, 120/75. At the novel's end, when the narrator appears securely installed in the other worldly realm of the *ville souterraine*, there will be no mention of Nafissa one way or another.

96 Deleuze, *Cinéma 2*, 57/40.

97 QSS, 29/15. The explosion exposes him to a *pure vision*. 'over the fields, in the fiery atmosphere, there danced a lone woman whose incandescence overwhelmed me. I was defenceless against the illumination emanating from her. And I began to float, to rise, prey to the flames. .' (34/18)

98 QSS, 23/12. 'And, as if it were my own body, I sense how the city, in its grip, stiffens' (40/22). Most insistently· 'I understand! *There is no space, or almost none, between us and our city*, we are neither there nor elsewhere, we are ourselves the city, or else it's us' (138/88, my emphasis).

99 'The view of the sun-drenched fields stretching to infinity aroused wild exaltation in me' (QSS, 35/19).

100 'Though but a fraction of the whole, each system, for example, enjoys its own unlimited autonomy, and beyond that, reproduces within itself the configuration of the city [. ,] the whole of the city, the whole of each district – everywhere present and identical. Are you in the centre of a complex? The totality of the others, as well as that of the city, reconstitutes itself around you in its every feature' (QSS, 186/119–120)

101 Bourdieu, *Les Règles de l'art* (1992).

102 Cf Fanon, *Pour la révolution africaine*, 121

103 Abd el-Kader, *Ecrits spirituels*, see esp 119–121, 149, 178. Chodkiewicz notes that Kader's thought is essentially consistent with that of Ibn al-'Arabi. See also Berque, *L'Intérieur du Maghreb*, 520 n. 1; Burgat, *L'Islamisme au Maghreb*, 22–23; Vatin, 'Le soufisme comme révolte', in Gellner and Vatin, *Islam et politique au Maghreb*, 245 ff.

104 Cf. Ben Jelloun, Interview with *Panorama Aujourd'hui* 178 (1984), 30, in Déjeux, *Le Sentiment religieux dans la littérature maghrébine*, 133. Dib himself emphasises the importance, for the cultural environment in which he grew up, of the great

mystics of Tlemcen, Abou Mâdyan and As-Sanoûsi (Dib, conversation with the author, 7 May 1996, Paris, cf Sari, 'L'Ishrâq dans l'oeuvre de Mohammed Dib', 116).

105   Etienne, *L'Algérie*, 120. Gellner stresses the 'inseparable' link between modern Arab nationalisms and 'the advance and victory of Reformism, a kind of Islamic Protestantism' (Gellner, *Nations and Nationalism*, 41).

106   Etienne, *L'Algérie*, 127, 129; cf. Ageron, *Histoire*, 86.

107   *Ech Chiheb*, July 1936, in Nouschi, *La Naissance du nationalisme algérien*, 65.

108   Merad, *Réformisme*, 439–440. 'Ben Badis exhorted his readers to remain themselves, to retain their ties to their history' (85) Cf Nouschi, *La Naissance du nationalisme algérien*, 64 ff

109   Like all French-speaking but non-Arabic-speaking readers, I rely heavily on the monumental work of translation and commentary performed by Henry Corbin, along with the brilliant comparative analyses of his former student Christian Jambet. For Corbin and Jambet – if not for more mainstream commentary on Islamic thought – al-Suhrawardi is perhaps the most significant and most innovative figure of Islamic philosophy (Corbin, *Philosophie iranienne*, 93, Corbin, *Histoire*, 284–285, Jambet, 'Philosophie angélique', *Henry Corbin, Cahiers de l'Herne* [1981], 98).

110   Sari's brief but decisive article of 1976 demonstrates how a great deal of Dib's poetry and shorter fiction in particular can be read as part of a search for 'a sovereign language', adequate to the interpretation of 'signs [...] that rebel against reading' (Dib, *Fomulaires*, 75, *Talisman*, 135, in Sari, 'L'Ishrâq dans l'oeuvre de Mohammed Dib', 110) Her basic argument has been confirmed (though generally not developed) by the great majority of subsequent critics (see for example: Khadda, *L'Oeuvre romanesque*, 301, 305 n 232, Madelain, *L'Errance et l'itinéraire*, 133, 158, 164, Chikhi, *Problématique de l'écriture*, 226–227, Arnaud, *Littérature maghrébine*, i, 241–242). Adjil confirms, without citing al-Suhrawardi, that 'Dib's [Nordic] trilogy was inspired by this oriental theosophy' (Adjil, *Espace et écriture*, 166, 175).

111   Jambet, *Logique*, 218

112   Vitray-Meyerovitch, 'La Poétique de l'Islam', 206

113   al-Suhrawardi (Shaykh al-Ishraq), *Le Livre de la sagesse orientale* §129–130, 112–113.

114   Ibn al-'Arabi, *Futuhat al Makkiyah*, ii, 326, in Corbin, *L'Imagination créatrice*, 330.

115   Mircea Eliade's comparative analyses of 'Expériences de la lumière mystique' demonstrate the ubiquity of the archetype (Eliade, 'Expériences de la lumière mystique', 109–110)

116   Cf Afnan, *Avicenna*, 187–197, Fakhry, *History of Islamic Philosophy*, 157–160; Jambet, 'Introduction', al-Suhrawardi, *Le Livre de la sagesse orientale*, 16.

117   al-Suhrawardi, *Archange*, 431.

118   Tidjâni, *al-kunnâch*, 146, in Berque, *L'Intérieur du Maghreb*, 253.

119   *Qur'an*, 33/72.

120   al-Suhrawardi, *Archange*, 57

121   al-Suhrawardi, *Archange*, 268.

122   al-Suhrawardi, *Archange*, 104.

123   al-Suhrawardi, *Archange*, 101–102, cf. Corbin, *En Islam iranien*, ii, 22.

124   Avicenna, in Corbin, *Avicenne*, 170–171.

125   'Attar, *Le Livre de l'epreuve*, 25, in Madelain, *L'Errance et l'itinéraire*, 11.

126   Jambet, *Logique*, 82. 'The ta'wil [...] resists communitarian imperatives. the ta'wil is irreducibly the act of a subject, alone with "his Lord"' (106, cf Corbin, *Histoire*, 58, 344–348, *Corps spirituel*, 8–9).

127 Jambet, *Logique*, 17; cf. 186
128 Vitray-Meyerovitch, 'La Poétique de l'Islam', 216.
129 Jambet, *Logique*, 188; cf. Corbin, *En Islam iranien*, i, 162.
130 Ibn al-'Arabı, *Les Gemmes de la sagesse*, in Corbin, *L'Imagination créatrice*, 147.
131 Huɪwırı, *The Kashf al-Mahjub*, 367, in Schimmel, *Mystical Dimensions of Islam*, 6.
132 Deleuze, *Différence et répétition*, 332/258.
133 Corbın, *Histoire*, 144
134 Lings, *What is Sufism?*, 25.
135 Bouamrane and Gardet, *Panorama de la pensée islamique*, 140.
136 Baldıck, *Mystical Islam*, 3–4, 44–45.
137 Baldıck, *Mystical Islam*, 42.
138 Cf. Jambet, *Logique*, 130–131
139 Jambet, *Logique*, 131.
140 Jambet, *Logique*, 132
141 See in particular Deleuze, *Cinéma 2*, 268/206, 343/263.
142 Jambet, *Logique*, 232.
143 As Bachelard puts it in a somewhat similar sense, 'the imagination is not, as its ety-mology suggests, the faculty of formıng images of realıty, ıt ıs the faculty of forming images that exceed realıty, that sıng reality. It is a superhuman faculty' (Bachelard, *L'Eau et les rêves*, 23)
144 al-Suhrawardı, *Le Livre des verbes de soufisme*, in *Archange*, 172.
145 Corbin, *Histoire*, 292, my emphasis.
146 Dib, interview with *Combat*, 7 February1963.
147 '*Barzakh*' connotes 'all that is body, all that is screen and interval' (Corbin, *Histoire*, 296).
148 Qotboddîn Shirazî, *Commentaires*, in Corbin, *Corps spirituel*, 154; cf. al-Suhrawardı, *Lu Livre de la sagesse orientale*, §225, §256.
149 Jambet, *Logique*, 118–119
150 Jambet, 'Présentation', *Henry Corbin, Cahiers de l'Herne* (1981), 14, al-Suhrawardi, *Archange*, 272–279.
151 Corbin, *Philosophıe iranienne*, 93
152 al-Suhrawardi, *Livre des Entretiens*, §215, in Corbin, *Spıritual Body*, 124.
153 Remember that Deleuze condemns as '"nonempiricist" every theory accordıng to whıch, in one way or another, relations are derıved from the nature of things' (Deleuze, *Empirısme et subjectivité*, 122–123/108–109; cf. Deleuze, *Différence et répétition*, 3–4/xx–xxı).
154 Jambet, 'Phılosophie angélique', *Henry Corbin, Cahiers de l'Herne*, 101.
155 al-Suhrawardi, *Archange*, 305. The Ishraqı goal, as Corbin summarises, 'to escape the place and the places of thıs world so as to emerge into pure space, where pure space ıs the spiritual. We cannot ask *where* space is' (Corbin, *Philosophie iranienne*, 16)
156 MC, 141 As Lâbane says, 'I am nothing more than a dark chrysalis, empty [. ., o]pacity in full light' (MC, 28)
157 'Naéma dısparue', *Le Talisman*, 73, cf. *Le Talısman*, 136. The narrator of *Le Talis-man* is, through ascesis, 'returned home [...]. I ınhabıt the aır and the light that wıll shine eternally' (*Le Talisman*, 123, 139).
158 Hakım Madjar, in MC, 206, my emphasis.
159 DB, 38, cf. MC, 131.
160 CR, 156; cf. 34, 109. As Chikhi points out, *Cours* 'depersonalises all ways of seeıng and the whole of the socıal, and makes them unıform withın a sıngle language' (Chikhı, *Problématıque de l'écriture*, 246, cf. Bonn, *Lecture présente*, 165–166)

161 CR, 154 The whole of *Cours sur la rive sauvage*, in a sense, develops the situation described in the Sufi parable of the mirror. From the beginning, Iven Zohar knows that it is not only his 'separation' from Radia that keeps them apart; 'not only that. It was also the manifestation of appearance. Will I manage, strengthened by my love, to destroy the mirror which separates me from her?' (CR, 11, cf. SE, 195)

162 NM, 93; cf. IM, 137.

163 Sari, 'L'Ishrâq dans l'oeuvre de Mohammed Dib', 116; Chikhi, *Problématique de l'écriture*, 153, 222–224, 246–247

164 Déjeux, *Mohammed Dib*, 44, 22, Déjeux, *Le Sentiment religieux*, 138–139, Déjeux, *Maghreb, Littératures de langue française*, 45; Khadda, *Esquisse d'un itinéraire*, 35, 75.

165 Bonn interprets Dib's 'obvious theosophic references' as belonging to a 'semantic field close to his preoccupations, certainly, but much more something to be used than translated For once again it's a matter of a meaning, of a reply [to metaphysical questions], and of the trap they entail' (Bonn, *Lecture présente*, 225, n.6). Nothing is less certain. the Ishraqi register is anything but a mere 'champ sémantique'.

166 Bonn, *Lecture présente*, 23, 61, 65, 107, 135, 146, 152, 229–231; cf. Khadda, *Mohammed Dib romancier*, 93; Déjeux, *Mohammed Dib*, 32–33

167 Dib, 'Vega', appended in *Ombre gardienne* (1984 ed.), 67.

168 Cf. Dib, *Omneros*, 67.

169 HB, 43, cf. 23, 142, 154. We know *par ailleurs* that 'waiting is the only thing that's positive [*positif*]' (MC, 43), that 'there will only be an incurable waiting. There will be nothing' (Sohl, in SE, 181; cf. 198–199).

170 HB, 78, my emphasis. 'What began there had no name in fact. It was what never has a name, what defies predictions, undoes calculations' (30). Likewise, Lily refuses to explain the cause of her absolute 'solitude'. She says merely, 'oh! it was, it happened before everything! [...]. "No, before everything else!" This was the most that Habel was able to get out of her on this subject' (121)

171 Deleuze, *Cinéma 2*, 59/41; cf. 169/120

172 Deleuze, *Dialogues*, 49/38

173 HB, 49, my emphasis And Habel. 'above all, don't think you'll be gone on one of those trips from which you come back' (HB, 57). As a rule, in Dib's later work 'whoever goes doesn't come back' (TO, 154).

174 Lyotard, *Le Différend*, 18–19, 129.

175 HB, 132 Azrail, we learn, is 'the angel the other angels do not approach'.

176 HB, 187; Deleuze, *Cinéma 1*, 165/116–117· 'in short, choice as spiritual determination has no other object other than itself' (Deleuze, *Cinéma 1*, 161/114, cf. Deleuze, *Cinéma 2*, 230–232/177–178, Badiou, *Conditions*, 190)

177 HB, 57. Description of this urban nightmare takes up where *Qui se souvient* and *Cours sur la rive sauvage* left off, with 'a city transformed in a vast and solitary stampede of jellyfish', 'frozen in sinister monuments' (70, 71), the space of 'an incommunicable desolation' (17) inhabited by 'monsters in chains' (18).

178 HB, 150, cf. Deleuze and Guattari, *Mille plateaux*, 107/84. It is this aspect of *Habel*, of course, that provides Bonn's reading with some of its most compelling evidence

179 HB, 90, 89, cf. 52

180 From the first of his several encounters with the Vieux, Habel 'had stopped looking for a meaning in all this and, had stopped even wanting to discover one' (HB, 51; cf. 163, 168)

181 Outside, 'the world continues, indefatigable, to go round! But what for?' (HB, 124)

182   HB, 158, my emphasis Dib himself thinks of this extraordinary episode as a 'redemption from evil' (Dib, letter to Déjeux, in Déjeux, *Le Sentiment religieux*, 138).

183   Dib explains that if Orsol is a fictive version of Algiers, 'Jarbher is a composite of Nordic towns [...] whose characteristics were already established before my first stay in Finland' (Dib to Bonn, letter of 28 October 1985, in Bonn, *Lecture présente*, 267).

184   *'He didn't know what he was looking for but he knew he had found it, he knew it but didn't dare admit it in the secrecy of his heart'* (TO, 43, cf. 52).

185   TO, 61. Again, *'he walks on the edge of the darkness of the world because the light has set his flesh aflame, it [the light] is his malediction'* (TO, 9) Such italicised declarations interrupt the 'real' sentence in which they occur without a punctuated break, as if invisible to its syntax.

186   TO, 188–193 In the words Aed strains to overhear in a city square one night, Dib provides an almost programmatic description of what is at stake here, in the logic of a truth which becomes, like al-Suhrawardi's One, opaque in the process of its own expression (see TO, 78).

187   TO, 198, my emphasis Aéd ends the novel 'with dilated eyes, he no longer recognised himself' and can no longer orient himself 'in these places' (205).

188   First 'I whose name is Faïna. I have become silent, but not my voice, [...] the voice that says I and that will continue. The voice that calls me and maintains itself in dialogue only with itself' (11). Then, in the second half, Solh takes up 'a form of speech [*une parole*] that continues all by itself, [.] and speaks only of solitude. Inexhaustible, tireless words' (116).

189   SE, 42, cf. 69, 80. As Solh eventually explains, the Hugo Simberg painting *Saga* represents 'the woman who became she-wolf for love of the Wolf'. Solh is fascinated by 'this woman who abandoned everything, home, children, husband, to follow the Wolf [...]; and you have become, with me, more and more she-wolf' (219–221)

190   SE, 85–86 Adjil notes that the word 'Dib' means 'wolf' in Arabic (Adjil, *Espace et écriture*, 112–114).

191   SE, 106, my emphasis. Solh realises that he must 'give Faïna up to her original element, nature [...] The place of her birth belongs more to the forest [*verdure*] and to water than to people' (207)

192   SE, 189 Faïna: 'I am no longer myself [.] Everything is vanishing so quickly, fading so quickly I am no longer anything'(190, 192)

193   Cf. Khadda, *Mohammed Dib romancies*, 95; Bonn, *Lecture présente*, 84.

194   Secret, from the Latin *secernere*. to separate, put to one side.

195   'Go far in time, Lyyli Belle, far along its rivers [.], its clairvoyant water will confide a secret. It will be for you alone Then *come back'* (IM, 53, my emphasis). Lyyl's father knows that her 'secret will be kept Lyyl will never reveal it. Secret of one heart to another: Lyyl's heart, and the unplaceable heart of the universe' (NM, 153).

196   Ja'far Sâdiq, in Corbin, *Histoire*, 67–68

197   Deleuze and Guattari, *Qu'est-ce que la philosophie?*, 47/45.

198   TO, 206; cf. HB, 12.

199   Derrida, *Donner la mort*, 101–102/108–109.

200   NM, 117; cf IM, 51–53

201   NM, 201. In quasi-Proustian style, Lyyli Belle evokes 'moments, words, images that return in this way, when we thought them lost [.]. They become our story. After having been made all by itself, a story that finds its path in us, and tells itself' (IM, 136).

202   Dib, 'Postface', *La Nuit sauvage* (1995), 246–247 It is worth noting that in the Ismaili tradition, time as such – i e the dimension of Adam's slow return to his originally sufficient self-consciousness – stems precisely from a first, doomed effort to

accede *immediately* to God as *Deus absconditus*. Adam 'seeks to attain the inaccessible Principle deprived of this intermediary "limit" [made up of the First and Second Intelligences], he freezes, then, in a dazzled vertigo [...] and sees himself "surpassed", "made late", fallen backwards from himself. This "delay" introduces in a being of light a dimension that it foreign to it, and that is translated as "opacity"' (Corbin, *Histoire*, 129)

203 Roussia is generally 'absent' (NM, 27, cf. 32, 110, IM, 12, 97–99).

204 NM, 150; cf 166, 170. The most powerful indicator of *dépaysement* is here the father's recurring vision of his own mother dying, far away (NM, 19–20, 71, 76, 114).

205 NM, 59, cf. 105, IM, 140, 144–145.

206 As her father tells her, '"if you want always to look at the light and never the darkness, run always further toward the setting sun because [...] far to the west, is the East The celestial East"' (IM, 58). Such is precisely the movement of Dib's trajectory as a whole. an effort to push the *occident* to its very edge, to the very depths of the nightmare, so as, purified of substance, to slip lightly along the *oriental* divide.

207 Deleuze and Guattari, *Qu'est-ce que la philosophie?*, 200/212, Deleuze, *Le Pli*, 106–107/78

208 IM, 169, cf. NM, 40–41,144.

209 Cf. Michel Henry, *L'Essence de la manifestation*

210 Henry, 'A la recherche d'une phénoménologie idéale', lecture given at L'Ecole Normale Supérieure (Paris), 10 May 1996

211 See especially IM, 30–31.

212 IM, 119, 138 'This is what I'll have to do, me as well. tell stories so as to stay alive' (IM, 144)

213 IM, 165–167. 'I watch, I listen. Because otherwise all will be forgotten' (NM, 38–39).

214 DD, 13. 'Stay there, they told us. You will soon see what you must see' (DD, 25)

215 Forever 'against this fencing *[grillage]*' (37; 41, 69, 73, 115).

216 DD, 69, 71–73 *Iman* is 'the disposition that puts one in a state of faith', *Ihnsan* evokes 'generosity of spirit', and *Islam*, of course, 'surrender in peace' (Dib, conversation with the author, 7 May 1996, Paris). 'Le *Kun*! (*Esto*!) is 'the divine Imperative, unknowable, absolutely transcendent' (Jambet, *Logique*, 109)

217 DD, 116, 117, cf 128–129.

EXCURSUS IV Return to the specific

1 Bourdieu, *Les Règles de l'art*, 467/344.

2 Kant, *Groundwork of the Metaphysics of Morals*, 390–391, 441–443.

3 As Žižek puts it, in a gloss on Kant's moral philosophy: 'the only guarantor of the universality of positive moral norms is the subject's own contingent act of performatively assuming these norms' (Žižek, *The Plague of Fantasies*, 221, cf. Zupančič, *Ethics of the Real*, 94).

4 Marx, 'Introduction', *Grundrisse*, 84, cf. Gramsci, *Selections from Cultural Writings*, 112, Goldmann, *The Human Sciences and Philosophy*, 128.

5 Heidegger, *Being and Time*, §26

6 See respectively. Koestler, 'The Holarchy', in *Janus*, 27, and Mayr, *Toward a New Philosophy of Biology*, 15, Benveniste, 'Les niveaux de l'analyse', *Problèmes de linguistique générale*, i, 119–131, Braudel, *La Méditerranée et le monde méditerranéen à l'époque de Philippe II*, i, 16–17.

7 Cf. Said, *Representations of the Intellectual*, 20–21; Badiou, *L'Etre et l'événement*, 115–117

8 'Each and every word expresses the "one" in relation to the other', and even the most 'individualistic confidence in oneself, one's sense of personal value, is drawn not from within, not from the depths of one's personality, but from the outside world' (Voloshinov, *Marxism and the Philosophy of Language*, 86, 89).

9 Taylor, 'The Politics of Recognition', 34; cf. Bakhtin, 'Appendix II', *Problems of Dostoyevsky's Poetics*, 287.

10 Castoriadis, 'Institution and Autonomy', in Osborne, *A Critical Sense*, 12–13.

11 Levinas, *Totalité et infini*, 79/80; cf. Derrida, *Donner la mort*, 76/78tm.

12 Foucault, *La Volonté de savoir*, 126/95

13 Laclau, 'Politics and the Limits of Modernity', in Ross, ed., *Universal Abandon?*, 61.

14 Foucault, 'Human Nature. Justice versus Power', 171.

15 Césaire, *Letter to Maurice Thorez*, 15.

16 Césaire, *Letter to Maurice Thorez*, 6–7.

CHAPTER 5 Severo Sarduy

1 Baudrillard, *L'Autre par lui-même*, 15, 37 'The whole strategy of seduction is to lead things to pure appearance' (55).

2 Deleuze and Guattari, *Anti-Oedipe*, 37/30, 34/26 'Desire does not lack anything, it does not lack its object It is, rather, the subject that is missing in desire, or desire that lacks a fixed subject, there is no fixed subject unless there is repression' (34/26) These words might almost be taken as a précis of Sarduy's working method as a writer

3 González Echevarría, *Ruta*, 231; González Echevarría, *Celestina's Brood*, 42.

4 Sarduy, 'Locus imaginarius', 9.

5 Sarduy, Interview with Ortega, v.

6 As Baudrillard writes, 'it is not the real that disappears in illusion, it is illusion that disappears in integral [*intégrale*] reality' (Baudrillard, *Le Crime parfait*, 10).

7 Goytisolo, 'Severo Sarduy', 28. Novelist Julian Ríos concurs. Sarduy is the 'eminent protagonist of the new hispanoamerican writing' (Ríos, 'Du grand boom au bigbang', 42).

8 Sollers, 'Sollers Dos', in Ríos, *Severo Sarduy*, 122.

9 Swanson, 'After the Boom', 233.

10 Bustillo, *Barroco y America Latina*, 187, 204, cf. Schwartz, *New History*, II, 207.

11 González Echevarría, *Ruta*, 155, cf González Echevarría, *The Voice of the Masters*, 4, 61

12 Levine, 'Preface' to *Cobra* (COB), vii.

13 According to Raymond Leslie Williams' recent survey, 'Sarduy's writing is the most significant contribution to the Caribbean postmodern and [.] the Latin American postmodern in general' (Williams, *The Postmodern Novel in Latin America*, 98).

14 Cf. González Echevarría, *Ruta*, 153–154

15 Sarduy, interview with Fell, 7 Sarduy writes against *all* 'realism – I include its worst variant· magical realism' (ES, 278/51)

16 Sarduy, interview with Fossey, 10

17 Sarduy, 'Entre les 'arrivés' et l'avant-garde', 14

18 Sarduy, interview with González Echevarría, 41.

19 Lyotard, *Peregrinations*, 41 Lyotard like Sarduy 'dreams of a peregrination among forms freed from the stable point' of the *I* (31).

20 Sarduy, interview with González Echevarría, 45.

21 Sarduy, 'Huellas de Islam', 47 (referring to Jambet's 'Introduction', al-Suhrawardi, *Le Livre de la sagesse orientale*)

22 Sarduy, 'Peintres et machines', 20.
23 Sarduy, 'Deterritorialization', 104.
24 Conversations with Macé, in Macé, *Sarduy*, 46.
25 Conversations with Macé, 88
26 Sarduy, interview with Fossey, 24.
27 'The O of the Other pops up everywhere, behind people and things, as if its little smile were the only bond connecting them. .' (RJ, 14/12, cf. BO (Fr. ed.), 212; cf. Deleuze, *Logique du sens*, 350/301).
28 Sarduy, interview with Kushigian [1982], 18.
29 Artaud, *The Theatre and its Double*, 48, 52; cf. 79.
30 González-Echevarría, 'El primer relato de Severo Sarduy', 142.
31 Prieto, 'Ambiviolent Fiction', 49, 55.
32 Johnston, 'Irony and the Double', 111, 120.
33 Montero, *The Name Game*, 90
34 Barthes, 'La mort de l'auteur', *Oeuvres complètes*, ii, 493–494.
35 González Echevarría, 'Introduction to Volume 2', González Echevarría and Pupo-Walker, *Cambridge History of Latin-American Literature*, 5
36 Mendez Rodenas, *Severo Sarduy*, 137; Guerrero, *La Estrategia neobarroca*, 38.
37 González Echevarría, *Ruta*, 133.
38 Rodríguez Monegal, 'Carnaval/antropofagia/parodia', 405, cf González Echevarría, *Ruta*, 45–46, Guerrero, *La Estrategia neobarroca*, 125–126; Montero, *The Name Game*, 85; Manzor Coats, *Borges/Escher, Sarduy/CoBrA*, 139, Kushigian, *Orientalism in the Hispanic Literary Tradition*, 74, 76, 90–91
39 Kushigian, *Orientalism in the Hispanic Literary Tradition*, 81.
40 Sarduy, 'Toward concreteness' 68.
41 Alzola, 'Verba cubanorum', 12–13. See also Mendez Rodenas, *Severo Sarduy*, 12, 24, 41; Mac Adam, 'Severo Sarduy/Vital Signs', 44; Justo and Leonor Ulloa, 'Leyendo las huellas', 9–10, 24, Johndrow, '"Total" Reality', 448, Sánchez-Boudy, *Tematica*, 20.
42 Barthes, 'Vingt mots-clés pour Roland Barthes', *Oeuvres complètes*, iii, 316.
43 Barthes, 'Plaisir au langage,' *Oeuvres complètes*, ii, 408, cf. Barthes 'Sur La Plage', *Oeuvres complètes*, iii, 699.
44 Barthes, 'Plaisir au langage' in *Oeuvres complètes*, ii, 409. For Barthes, *Cobra* in particular is 'a paradisiacal text, utopian (without place), a heterology through plenitude' (*Le Plaisir du texte, Oeuvres complètes*, ii, 1498)
45 Rivero Potter, *Autor-lector*, 100; Swanson, 'After the Boom', 233, Ghertman, 'Language as Protagonist', 145, Jorge Aguilar Mora, 'Cobra, cobra, la boca obra, recobra barroco', in Ríos, ed., *Severo Sarduy*, 25; cf. Montero, *The Name Game*, 16–17, Ortega, *Poetics* (translation inart of *Relato dela utopia*), 130, 174–175; Ortega, *Relato de la utopia*, 15 The eventual conclusion is that *Cobra* 'says nothing' (Cixous, 'A Text Twister', 28; cf. Sollers, 'La Boca obra', in *Review*, 13, Bustillo, *Barroco y America Latina*, 187, 198, Rodríguez-Monegal, 'Las metamorphosis del texto', 40, Williams. *The Postmodern Novel in Latin America*, 99, Guerrero, *La Estrategia neobarroca*, 158, Rodríguez Monegal, 'Las metamorphosis del texto', 40). It is not surprising that this reading of Sarduy finds negative and occasionally hysterical confirmation in the objections of some critics to his 'elusive avant-garde concoctions', their assumption that 'Sarduy's work may be judged to be external – literally – to contemporary Latin American concerns' (Martin, *Journeys Through the Labyrinth*, 317, Franco, 'The Crisis of the Liberal Imagination', 20–21, Garsha, 'El apogeo de la Nueva Novela', 288; Perez, *Severo Sarduy and the Religion of the Text*, viii).

46 Sarduy, conversations with Macé [1992], 15; cf. Sarduy, interview with Torres Fierro [1978], 65. 'I am a specifically and typically Cuban author' (Sarduy, interview with Dujovne-Ortiz [1980], 38).

47 Sarduy, interview with Seager, 141

48 Sarduy, interview with Fell, 7.

49 Sarduy, 'Deterritorialisation', 104–105; cf. Sarduy, 'Cronología', 12. Montero is certainly right to remind us that 'a hermeneutics based on the metaphor of 'keys' is self-defeating. The text [.] may be charted, not deciphered' (Montero, *The Name Game*, 23). As Rodríguez-Monegal points out, cultural allusions and references are generally confined to the level of 'pre-text' rather than text ('Las metamorphosis del texto', 43).

50 *De donde*'s Dolores Rondón, for example, did indeed live and die in Camaguey, just as its Changhai is based on an actual theatre in Havana; Colibrí's *Casona* is likewise based on a particular Parisian night-club (Conversations with Macé, 88; Sarduy, 'Cronología', 11) *Cobra* was inspired in part by the story of a certain 'Cobra', a transvestite working in the Paris club Le Carroussel, who died in a plane crash over Japan (Sarduy, interview with Torres Fierro, 68).

51 For decades a science reporter on French radio, Sarduy knows that 'in our times, the depository of myth, the decantation or mother [...] of all knowledge, of every figured Idea, is Science [...] Cosmology [is] the true poetry of our time' ('A la sombra del arecibo', 42–43).

52 Sarduy, interview with Rivera [1983], 6. As the Buddhist scriptures say. 'the skill in means of a Bodhisattva consists in this, that he cognises [the] sign, both its mark and cause, and yet he surrenders himself completely to the Signless' (*The Perfection of Wisdom in 8,000 Lines*, 215).

53 Sarduy, 'Cronología', 14

54 Sarduy, interview with Torres Fierro, 66. The phrase recurs in MY, 22/159, and 'Sauro o el pincel púrpura', 51. Sarduy is playing here with a celebrated verse of the *Prajñaparamita* sutras· 'form is emptiness and emptiness is form' (*Heart Sutra*, 81).

55 González Echevarría, *Ruta*, v, cf. 102–107, 116–121.

56 González Echevarría, *Ruta*, 45, cf. 54 'Recuperation for Sarduy [.] takes place through mediations [*mediaciones*]' (*Ruta*, 6), and 'a work consists of the substitution of mediations' (10).

57 For example, 'Son de la loma y cantantes en llano' means [*quiere decir*] that the singers are from the origin and remember it...' (González Echevarría, *Ruta*, 106) Or 'the entire description of the process through which Ktazob "remakes" Cobra [...] signifies the way in which language covers one signified with another [...]. The castration itself is an allegory of the workings of language...' (170). Again, 'Fidel is the Mortal that the protagonists pursue' (128' cf 187, 190), '*Maitreya* is another version of *Paradiso*', '*Maitreya* is *Paradiso*, *Paradiso* is *Maitreya*' (192, 202). González Echevarría's reading of *Colibrí* develops a whole series of allegorical equations For instance 'Colibrí = pájaro = Sarduy' (234); 'La Señora = Dictator = Narrador', 'Casona = Sociedad = Ficción' (238).

58 González Echevarría preserves an emphasis on 'geographic configurations' and the 'American' origin of Sarduy's baroque (*Ruta*, 185, 205).

59 González Echevarría, *Myth and Archive*, 176. Archival fictions stand to the earlier telluric tradition more or as less as Clifford's discourse-based anthropology stands to the participant-observation methods of a Malinowski or Mead (cf. Clifford, *The Predicament of Culture*, 28–34).

60 'This elimination of metadiscourse is systematically carried out in Sarduy [..], by privileging local stories understood as the only possible sum of knowledge'

(González Echevarría, *Ruta*, 251). The application of such postmodern truisms to Sarduy's work is seriously misleading, as sections VI, VII and X of this chapter will show in some detail.

61 González Echevarría, *Ruta*, 249–252.

62 Sarduy, 'L'Ecriture autonome', 3.

63 Sarduy, 'Huellas de Islam...', 48.

64 Sarduy, 'Sauro o el pincel púrpura', 48–49.

65 Sarduy, 'Locus imaginarius', 9.

66 Baudrillard, *L'Autre par lui-même*, 70. 'Everywhere, in every domain, a single form predominates. reversibility' (Baudrillard, *Symbolic Exchange and Death*, 2).

67 Baudrillard, *Symbolic Exchange and Death*, 5.

68 Sarduy's first substantial story, 'El seguro' (in *Carteles* 33, 18 August 1957, 66–67, 107) is a work of social protest that relates how a cane cutter tries and fails to manipulate the socio-economic system that exploits him Cf. González-Echevarría, 'El primer relato de Severo Sarduy', 132, 136–137.

69 Sarduy, 'El torturador', 14. 'El general' relates the vile memories of a decorated (pro-Batista) general while he takes what turns out to be his last shower; gloating over his many victories, he neglects to see a bar of soap lying on the shower floor, cause of 'the most ridiculous of deaths' (5)

70 Sarduy, 'En el salon nacional de pintura y escultura', 3.

71 Sarduy, 'En su centro', 5 – with reference here to Martí.

72 Sarduy, 'Grabados/esculturas', 33, 'the Revolution is above all affirmation of *la nacionalidad*' (33).

73 Sarduy, 'En casa de Mariano', 8.

74 Sarduy, 'De la pintura en Cuba', 18

75 Sarduy, 'ASTA, turismo', 2.

76 Sarduy, 'La taza de café', 16.

77 Sarduy, 'ASTA, turismo', 2. For example, the painting of Marcelo Pogolotti. 'social preoccupations, the reaffirmation of national values, are the characteristic principles of his work' (Sarduy, 'Ambitos de un pintor', 2).

78 Sarduy, 'El salon nacional de pintura y escultura', 3.

79 Sarduy, 'De la pintura en Cuba', 18.

80 Sarduy, 'La taza de café', 16.

81 Sarduy, 'Pintura y Revolución', 14.

82 Sarduy, 'El salon nacional de pintura y escultura', 4

83 Sarduy, 'El salon nacional de pintura y escultura', 2.

84 Sarduy, 'Pintura y Revolución', 14. Cf González Echevarría, *Ruta*, 23–26, 34–35

85 Sarduy, 'Grabados/esculturas', 33

86 Sarduy, 'ASTA, turismo', 2; cf. Sarduy, 'Pintura y Revolución', 14

87 Sarduy, 'Las estructuras de la narración', 17, cf Menton, *Prose Fiction of the Cuban Revolution*, 86.

88 Deleuze, *Cinéma 2*, 41; cf. xi; Deleuze, *Cinéma 1*, 120

89 In José Soler Puig's *Bertillon 166* (1960), for example, the hero Carlos fights against the Americans 'for the poor, for the workers, for the peasants, for the students'; he kills a soldier and is protected by a priest brave enough to withstand interrogation Historians of the Cuban Revolutionary novel 'proper' are divided as to Sarduy's importance. Armando Pereira excludes Sarduy from his recent study, along with Carpentier and Cabrera Infante, as belonging to 'other cultural contexts' (Pereira, *Novela de la Revolución Cubana*, 9). Mendez y Soto, on the other hand, like Menton and Ortega, includes a discussion of *Gestos* and *De Donde* in his *Panorama*

de la Novela Cubana de la Revolución (1977). This characteristically revolution-oriented reading of *Gestos* presents the novel as a description of 'the existential alienation of the individual', and emphasises the atmosphere of police terror and anxiety (*Panorama*, 205–207).

90 As her lover says, 'this is your great opportunity to *act* [*hacer teatro*...]; be careful, you will have to play your part well, *natural* as you say' (GS, 76).

91 Sarduy, conversations with Macé, 22.

92 At least from 1959, Sarduy is familiar with 'Nathalie Sarraute's avant-garde novels', in which 'characters lose their names [...] to be called He or She, or The Man...' ('De la pintura en Cuba', 18). Sarduy agrees with Sarraute, that 'a character does not exist, in reality, except as the catalyst of [collective, anonymous] movements, tropisms' (interview with Torres Fierro, 67). Sarduy believes that Sarraute's *Tropismes* (1939) – a work echoed several times by *Gestos*, beginning with its opening section – was the 'really founding' work of the *nouveau roman* ('Las estructuras de la narración', 17, cf. NI, 26, ES, 311/84)

93 GS, 12–13, 17, 69.

94 See for instance GS, 63–64, 32–34.

95 Segments of especially 'experimental' prose are here clearly marked off from the rest of the text (for instance. GS, 18, 21–22, 28–29).

96 Deleuze, *Foucault*, 91/87 The novel ends on an ambivalent note, with a call to 'turn life upside down' mixed with an apparent decision to abandon the struggle: 'Me too I'm going. To San Lazaro [.], or to the devil' (GS, 138–140).

97 Sarduy, conversations with Macé, 138. 'Painting [. .] allows me to see the small part of reality that I'm able to see [..]. I touch here on something very Chinese – the idea that there is no difference between writing and painting, that they result from the same activity' (138–139, cf. RJ, 22–23/27).

98 Sarduy, 'Des diverses façons de représenter l'espace', 20.

99 Sarduy, conversations with Macé, 88.

100 Sarduy, interview with Mihály Dés, 34.

101 Sarduy, interview with Ortega, iv

102 Sarduy, 'Las estructuras de la narración', 17. Sarduy explains that the major aesthetic reference here is Franz Kline's action painting, which achieves the 'fusion of the sign with its support, of the void and form' (Interview with Torres Fierro, 66).

103 For example, GS, 26–27, see also GS, 33, 100–102.

104 GS, 20. Cf. Johndrow, '"Total" Reality', 448

105 Sarduy, interview with Rodríguez Monegal, 328 Cf. Levine, *Subversive Scribe*, 154–163.

106 Sarduy, interview with Rodríguez Monegal, 318; cf Manzor Coats, *Borges/Escher, Sarduy/CoBrA*, 147; Levine, *Subversive Scribe*, 38, Macé, *Severo Sarduy*, 63–64

107 Interview with Fell, 7; cf Sarduy, 'Un Châtelet de magie noire', 15

108 See Montero, *The Name Game*, 120, cf Guerrero, *Estrategia neobarroca*, 35

109 Sarduy, 'La botérisation de la mode', 379.

110 Deleuze, *Cinéma 1*, 47–49/30–31; Deleuze, *Cinéma 2*, 54–57/37–40

111 Sarduy, 'Las estructuras de la narración', 17

112 Sarduy, 'Rothko', 42.

113 Sarduy, conversations with Macé, 137. 'Rothko is one of the most important people in my life' (Sarduy, interview with Ríos, 21), 'I would like to look behind Rothko's canvasses to know if God is there' (Sarduy, 'Cronología', 12).

114 Sarduy, 'Barroco de la substracción', 53

115 Sarduy, 'Huellas de Islam...', 48; cf. Sarduy, 'Entre les "arrivés" et l'avant-garde', 14

116 Guerrero, *La Estrategia neobarroca*, 11–14.
117 Bustillo, *Barroco y America Latina*, 85; cf. Barthes, 'Plaisir au langage' in *Oeuvres complètes*, ii, 408.
118 Carpentier, *Tientos y diferencias*, 40, 28.
119 Carpentier, *Razón de ser*, 62; cf. Carpentier, *Tientos y diferencias*, 116; Carpentier, *El reino de este mundo*, 13–14
120 Sarduy, interview with Fell, 7; Sarduy, interview with Ríos, 20.
121 Sarduy, 'El barroco y el neobarroco', 173–174.
122 Sarduy, interview with González Echevarría, 44; cf. Paz, *Conjunctions and Disjunctions*, 55
123 Sarduy, 'El barroco y el neobarroco', 167, cf. Sarduy, 'Le Basculement néobaroque', 35.
124 Sarduy, interview with González Echevarría, 42.
125 Sarduy, interview with González Echevarría, 42
126 Deleuze, *Le Pli*, 170/125. As Guerrero observes, Sarduy's is 'a description which invents its object' (*La estrategia neobarroca*, 61)
127 Deleuze, *Le Pli*, 30/20–21.
128 Cf. González, 'Baroque endings', 284 n 18, BO, 151.
129 BO, 209, Sarduy, interview with Rodríguez Monegal, 336.
130 Sarduy, interview with Fossey, 18.
131 Sarduy, interview with Fossey, 16, cf. BO, 209
132 Sarduy, interview with González Echevarría, 44
133 Baudrillard, *De la séduction*, 60.
134 Lezama Lima, in ES, 284/57.
135 Barthes, *Plaisir du texte*, *Oeuvres complètes*, ii, 1523, cf. Sarduy, interview with E.S. [1969], 58
136 'The body without organs is the matter that always fills space to given degrees of intensity, and the partial objects are these degrees, these intensive parts that produce the real in space' (Deleuze and Guattari, '*Anti-Oedipe*, 390/326–327).
137 Sarduy, interview with Rivera, 6
138 Sarduy, interview with E S , 58. Hence 'the object of *Cobra* is the body, and also the subject of *Cobra* is the body' (Interview with Fossey, 11).
139 Sarduy, 'Las estructuras de la narración' [1966], 18, 16. As early as 1966 he is ready to dismiss *Gestos* as a traditional text still stuck in the 'trap of the anecdote, that is, in the trap of historical [presentation]' With *De donde*, Sarduy has realised that the most fruitful approach is 'not diachronic, but synchronic' (18).
140 Sarduy, 'Las estructuras de la narración', 16.
141 Sarduy, interview with Kushigian, 20.
142 Barthes, 'Plaisir au langage', *Oeuvres complètes*., ii, 408
143 *De Donde* is Sarduy's most allusive text. For detailed explication see González Echevarría's critical edition of *De donde* (1993), Barrenechea, 'Sarduy o la aventura textual', 225 ff.; Justo and Leonor Ulloa, 'Leyendo las huellas', 20 ff.
144 Sarduy, interview with Kushigian, 15, my emphasis According to Jorge Mañach's classic study of the subject, the choteo 'has its origin in this impatience of our temperament toward any impediments placed in the way of our free expansion' (Mañach, *Indagación del choteo* [1928], Perez-Firmat, *Literature and Liminality*, 56)
145 Perez-Firmat, *Literature and Liminality*, 74
146 Sarduy, 'Las estructuras de la narración', 20.
147 Sarduy, interview with González Echevarría, 45

148 Sarduy, 'L'Impeccable Itinéraire d'un grand seigneur du baroque', 10

149 ES, 283/56 In 1960, by contrast, Sarduy had believed that 'the Cuban, as a personality, is characterised by the rapid apprehension of the reality that surrounds him, and by his ability to synthesise it [as a coherent whole]' ('Grabados/esculturas', 34).

150 DC, 236/155. Auxilio and Socorro here have a 'philological' rather than a personal coherence (Sarduy, 'Las estructuras de la narración', 19–20)

151 GS, 63. Precise intertextual connections (breadcrumbs, tablecloths, Dolores…) with the earlier novel are explicit (see GS, 135; DC, 94/13; DC, 231/151, GS, 117).

152 Baudrillard, *La Transparence du mal*, 28.

153 DC, 235/154. 'The Chinese world seems to me a world of perception', a 'world of desire' (Sarduy, 'Las estructuras de la narración', 19).

154 Sarduy, interview with Torres Fierro, 67.

155 DC, 108–109/25. The character played by Lotus, the Empress, is nothing other than 'a mirage, a trompe-l'oeil'; 'Ming is pure absence, she is what she is not. There is no water for your thirst. Etc., etc.' (DC, 121/38)

156 DC, 98/18 Again. 'if she entangled him in her champagne locks, if he pricked her with the open brooch of one of his medals [etc..]. we will never know' (DC, 100/19–20).

157 For instance, we are told that *De donde*'s opera director 'looks toward the stage, but *in his reality* he's making his way through battles [..] The Director, stoned, plays on both waves, he's an amphibian of consciousness' (DC, 111/27).

158 Baudrillard, *Symbolic Exchange and Death*, 5

159 Sarduy, interview with Ulloa [1984], 179.

160 Sarduy, 'matière/machines/phantasme/ciel', second [unnumbered] page.

161 SI, 61/98; cf. BO, 215

162 Sarduy, interview with Ríos, 20

163 Sarduy, interview with Kushigian, 16; Sarduy, interview with Pérez Rivera, 6.

164 Sarduy, interview with Rodríguez Monegal, 341.

165 Deleuze and Guattari, *Mille plateaux*, 177/141, Deleuze and Guattari, *L'Anti-Oedipe*, 104/87, *Critique et clinique*, 11.

166 Sarduy, 'Toward concreteness' ('Hacia la concretud'), 62

167 Sarduy, interview with Rodríguez Monegal, 335–336.

168 Sarduy, 'Barroco de la substracción', 54

169 Deleuze and Guattari, *Mille plateaux*, 343–344/280; cf Deleuze and Guattari, *Cinéma 1*, 100/68, *L'Anti-Oedipe*, 334/281.

170 Sarduy, interview with Rodríguez Monegal, 341 The word 'medios' can mean, variously: middle, centre, medium, means, way, medium, environment, milieu.

171 Sarduy, interview with Fossey, 7.

172 Deleuze and Guattari, *Kafka*, 34–35/19. Polar opposites have the same *sense*, as sense 'is indifferent to affirmation and negation', and 'no mode of the proposition is able to affect it' (Deleuze, *Logique du sens*, 46/32)

173 Sarduy, interview with Pérez Rivera, 6. Other examples include the 'minimal art' of Larry Bell, Bob Morris, Donald Judd, and painter Barnett Newman – creators of 'pure geometric forms' – and Sarduy's own radio-play *La playa*, which 'claims to do nothing other than show primary grammatical structures' (Sarduy, interview with González Echevarría, 44).

174 Sarduy, 'Notas a las Notas', 561–562

175 Sarduy, interview with Ulloa, 178, cf. SI, 119–121. Both Paz and Lezama Lima adopt comparable positions, on Tantra and Taoism respectively.

176 Sarduy, interview with Pérez Rivera, 6
177 Quoted in Smith, 'Buddhism', 117.
178 SI, 60–61/98 Sarduy's own first-hand knowledge of Buddhism, and Hinduism, is considerable. 'Yes I have known the monastic life. So the authenticity of my texts exists, what is cited there belongs to the truth of Buddhism' (Interview with Kushigian, 18; cf. conversations with Macé, 73, 131). Here especially, 'Octavio Paz is my guru' (Interview with Ortega, v).
179 Suzuki, Essays, iii, 50.
180 Seng-Ts'an, 'On believing in mind', Conze, Buddhist Scriptures, 175, cf DC, 171–172/88–89.
181 Humphreys, Buddhism, 179–183; cf. Dumoulin, Zen Buddhism, xvii.
182 Watts, The Spirit of Zen, 27
183 Suzuki, Essays, ii, 95.
184 Hui-nêng, Platform Sutra, 150
185 Suzuki, Essays, iii, 31; cf. Suzuki, No-Mind, 20, 54–55, 79
186 Takuan, in Watts, The Spirit of Zen, 52–53.
187 Suzuki, Essays, i, 261
188 quoted in Suzuki, Essays, i, 253–257
189 Smith, 'Buddhism', 136 As Sarduy himself puts it, 'it is a "rule" of Zen that satori cannot come to pass through accumulation, classification or quibblings of knowledge, but on the contrary via an annihilation [.] of science [..., via] an exemption from meaning' ('Un Châtelet de magie noire', 19).
190 Suzuki, Essays, ii, 67, 91.
191 Dumoulin, Zen Buddhism, 253
192 Deleuze, Différence et répétition, 252/195.
193 Miura and Sasaki, Zen Dust, 5.
194 Suzuki, Essays, ii, 109–110.
195 Tai-hui, Suzuki, Essays, ii, 103
196 Dumoulin, Zen Buddhism, 253
197 Gateless Barrier, 221–225
198 Hakuin, Selected Writings, 164; cf. Hui-nêng, Platform Sutra, 110.
199 Suzuki, Essays, ii, 110.
200 Rosen Takashina, in Conze, Buddhist Scriptures, 144; cf. Suzuki, Essays, ii, 105–106.
201 Humphreys, Buddhism, 191.
202 Gyatso, The World of Tibetan Buddhism, 97; cf. Dasgupta, Introduction to Tantric Buddhism, 215.
203 Smith, 'Buddhism', 141.
204 Gyatso, The World of Tibetan Buddhism, 96–97.
205 de Bary, The Buddhist Tradition, 120, 121.
206 Artaud, The Theatre and its Double, 52, my emphasis
207 Dasgupta, Introduction to Tantric Buddhism, 1, Mookerjee and Khanna, The Tantric Way, 13
208 Guhyasamajatantra, in Conze, Buddhist Texts, 223.
209 Mookerjee and Khanna, The Tantric Way, 15.
210 Singh, Tantra, x
211 Saraha, Dohakosha, 55, in Conze, Buddhist Texts, 231.
212 Padmasambhara and Kongtrul, The Light of Wisdom, xiii.
213 Sarduy, 'Por qué el Oriente?', 39
214 Trungpa, The Lion's Roar, 41

215 de Bary, *The Buddhist Tradition*, 118

216 'The Tantric Buddhists stress that no action duly performed with Prajña [...] comes within the scope of our popular code of morality' (Dasgupta, *Introduction to Tantric Buddhism*, 200, 204). Tantra urges 'one to do with all one's might those very things that fools condemn' (Conze, *Buddhist Texts*, 221). Likewise, Hui-nêng's 'Unconscious cannot be held responsible for its deeds [...]. The valuation of good and bad presupposes discrimination, and where this is absent, no such valuation is applicable' (Suzuki, *No-Mind*, 116)

217 *Guhyasamajatantra*, in Conze, *Buddhist Texts*, 223.

218 Paz, *Conjunctions*, 75.

219 *Gandavyuha sutra*, in Suzuki, *Essays*, iii, 88.

220 Deleuze and Guattari, *Mille plateaux*, 317/260

221 Trungpa, *The Lion's Roar*, 45–46, 130.

222 *Guhyasamajatantra*, in Conze, *Buddhist Texts*, 222. One of the earliest Tantras urges us to 'cultivate all sensual pleasures', another advocates 'daily intercourse in out of the way places with twelve year old girls of the Candala Caste [etc.]' (Conze, *Buddhism*, 195; Dasgupta, *Introduction to Tantric Buddhism*, 210)

223 Saraha, *Dohakosha*, 26–29, 35, in Conze, *Buddhist Texts*, 228–229.

224 Mookerjee and Khanna, *The Tantric Way*, 21.

225 In *Maitreya* the monks repeat 'tantric incantations' (MY, 23/159); in *Cobra*, elaborate celebrations of 'the five ambrosias' (CB, 216/122 ff.) refer to precise tantric rituals

226 Paz, *Conjunctions*, 59

227 'Flesh is mental concentration, the vulva is a lotus that is emptiness that is wisdom; semen and illumination are one and the same thing [etc.]' (Paz, *Conjunctions*, 65).

228 Sarduy, 'Por qué el Oriente?', 39.

229 Mookerjee and Khanna, *The Tantric Way*, 18, cf 93, 95–96

230 Tantric 'texts are governed by the same psychological and artistic necessity that caused our Baroque poets to build a language of their own within the Spanish language, the same necessity that inspired the language of Joyce and the Surrealists. the conception of writing as the double of the cosmos' (Paz, *Conjunctions*, 78).

231 Mookerjee and Khanna, *The Tantric Way*, 163.

232 'In Tantra the cardinal principle is that of wealth lavishly spent' (Paz, *Conjunctions*, 78)

233 Deleuze, *Logique du sens*, 98/80; Deleuze, *Différence et répétition*, 293/227.

234 Sarduy, interview with Kushigian, 15.

235 DC, 131/48 There are too many similar examples to enumerate. The most obvious include the Maitreya's repeated and varied refusals to answer conventional questions about the body, the soul, eternity, and so on (many are listed in Kushigian, *Orientalism in the Hispanic Literary Tradition*, 84 ff.). Barthes describes a Buddhist exercise reported by Sarduy. 'the master holds the disciple's head under water, for a long, long time; slowly the bubbles become more and more rare; at the last moment, the master releases the disciple, and revives him when you have desired truth as you have desired air, then you will then know what it is' (Barthes, *Fragments d'un discours amoureux, Oeuvres complètes*, iii, 474). A version appears in *Maitreya*. '"when you need to extinguish desire as you have needed air .."' (MY, 32/165) In *Cocuyo*, Cocuyo will flee a bar, 'searching for the exit like he was searching for air; or the truth' (CY, 170).

236 MY, 66–7/188; cf 22/159, 68–9/190.

237 Sarduy, interview with Kushigian, 16.

238 Sarduy, interview with Kushigian, 17.
239 CB, 61/32 Later 'the Little Bound Maja goes out of orbit, collapses against the sofa' (70/38), before being 'satellised in rotation' (108/60).
240 CB, 85/46. 'Ktazob'. literally, Cut-Cock (Levine, *Subversive Scribe*, 39).
241 CB, 208/118; Sarduy himself uses this English expression (Interview with Kushigian, 15).
242 Sarduy, interview with Rodríguez Monegal, 319
243 CB, 114/64. This is one of Sarduy's several references to this Chinese torture.
244 Artaud, *The Theatre and its Double*, 82–83, 98.
245 CB, 126/70 The description is repeated ten pages later (144/81).
246 CB, 216/122. Cf. Dasgupta, *Introduction to Tantric Buddhism*, 70; Paz, *Conjunctions*, 64–65 The initiation sequence in Cobra maintains clear and elaboration allusions to the Tantric ritual of the five 'M's – referring to the five things prohibited by mainstream Buddhism: *madya* (wine), *mamsa* (meat), *matsya* (fish), *mudra* (beans), *maithune* (sexual union) – along with the sexual ritual of *Asana*, performed collectively in the presence of a corpse (Mookerjee and Khanna, *The Tantric Way*, 185).
247 Levine, *Subversive Scribe*, 37.
248 Sarduy, 'Notas a las notas', 559.
249 CB, 13/5 Ktazob's parody of Lacanian terminology comes complete with diagram (107/60).
250 The Painter's 'dissection' of Pup – 'the body is inscribed in a net [..], and in all directions, forking, interweaving, threads branch outward.. ' (CB, 68/36–37) – recurs with Cobra/the first person narrator as its object (158–159/90) So does the description of Cobra as made-up castrato (143–144/80 and 204/115). Likewise the description of the 'funeral amulet' noted on page 23/10, and rediscovered on Scorpion (138/77). Tiger's words to the barman of page 142/79 'Do you want me to say a word, a syllable, and turn you into a bird?…' are repeated verbatim by a 'monk of the red hat sect' on page 159/90. *Maitreya* is punctuated with the same sort of self-citation.
251 Deleuze, *Francis Bacon*, 37, cf Deleuze, *Cinéma 2*, 28/17.
252 'To be reborn in [the future Buddha] Maitreya's presence is the greatest wish of many Tibetans and Mongols' (Conze, *Buddhist Scriptures*, 237).
253 Sarduy, interview with Ríos, 21–23.
254 Lezama Lima, *Paradiso*, 13, cf. MY, 93/208, 114/221
255 MY, 131/233. It is soon Lady T's turn to take up the 'imitation of her double' (MY, 148/245).
256 MY, 69/190. Likewise Louis Leng· 'he had conceived reality as an empty place, a mirage of appearances reduced to the myth of its interchangeable representations' (120/225)
257 MY, 70–71/191–193; cf. 30/164
258 Garsha, 'El apogeo de la Nueva Novela', 288; cf Rivero Potter, *Autor-lector*, 113.
259 Manzor Coats, *Borges/Escher, Sarduy/CoBrA*, 141.
260 González Echevarría, 'Rehearsal for *Cobra*', 44, *Ruta*, 46, Williams, *The Postmodern Novel in Latin America*, 99, Guerrero, *La estrategia neobarroca*, 72–73, Barrenechea, 'Severo Sarduy o la aventura textual', 221–234; Mac Adam, 'Severo Sarduy, Vital Signs', 44–50, Montero, *The Name Game*, 14, 30–42, 73–88
261 González Echevarría, *The Voice of the Masters*, 31
262 González Echevarría, *Celestina's Brood*, 43, cf. Montero, *Name Game*, 89
263 Sarduy, 'Tu dulce nombre halagará mi oído', 20; conversations with Macé, 47
264 Sarduy, 'Toward concreteness', 63. It is hard to imagine a less Derridian topos

265 Deleuze and Guattari, *L'Anti-Oedipe*, 70/60 Sarduy· 'the entire body is a partial object' (SI, 88/121).
266 Sarduy, 'La botérisation de la mode', 380.
267 González Echevarría, *Ruta*, 99–100; cf. 199, 203.
268 Deleuze and Guattari, *L'Anti-Oedipe*, 352/296. In Sarduy's work, the phallus is merely the tip of a vast, barely submerged erotic surface, lightning rod to a cosmic energy. In the Viswanatha, in Benares, Sarduy sees 'a gigantic lingam, Shiva's symbolic phallus, fount of all energy, all possible action' (RJ, 37/45), and versions of this emblem abound in his own fiction. In *De donde*, we find variants of 'that exposed and over-flowing earthen vessel' of all shapes and sizes (DC, 181/96), from Mustard's, 'small and spiralled like a little screw' (130/48) to the 'porphyry phallus, almost a yard long' that Auxilio steals from the General's apartment (135/54). *Cobra*'s Transformer 'had always had a good aim in puncturing' (CB, 71/38), while Eustachio's 'proportions' evoke 'Ganesa, the elephant god' (CB, 21/9). Totem's phallus is inscribed with 'all of the Buddhist precepts' (CB, 148/83). *Maitreya*'s Leng is the 'lance personified', a 'jade sceptre' or 'stake' (MY, 116–120/223–225). Lady T's chauffeur adds 'massive musculature' (MY, 172/262), a 'vibrant dart' – 'such a generous and touchable contribution' (MY, 176/265)
269 RJ, 33/39. Hinduism and Buddhism, juxtaposed in the two cities of Benares and Sarnath, provide Sarduy 'the two possible images of a single thought. One thought, disguised by the word, conceives reality as pure simulacrum; the other has understood, from the beginning and irreversibly, that the void pierces everything and that the perceptible whole is nothing other than its metaphor or its emanation' (RJ, 37/47)
270 BO, 200. As Baudrillard notes, metamorphosis, strictly conceived, gives rise 'not to individuals, but potential mutants' (Baudrillard, *L'Autre par lui-même*, 46).
271 Sarduy, '*Paradis*· Syllables-Germes/Entropie/Perspective/Asthme', 21.
272 Sarduy, interview with Fossey, 9.
273 CB, 141/79. And *Maitreya* 'beneath their synthetic leopard-skin maxis all of them wore real leopard skins' (MY, 112/219)
274 Sarduy, interview with Seager, 136.
275 Sarduy, 'Toward concreteness', 65.
276 Sarduy, interview with Seager, 129.
277 Sarduy, 'Notas a las notas', 562; cf ES, 266/41.
278 Sarduy, 'Le Basculement néo-baroque', 34. 'It is very important to create a single surface (Interview with Kushigian, 15, 14; cf. CI, 25)
279 Sarduy, interview with Rodríguez Monegal, 323, cf. González Echevarría, *Ruta*, 172.
280 'It is all the same: pure realists – socialists or not – and "magical" realists promulgate and refer to the same myth' (ES, 262/36)
281 Sarduy, interview with Torres Fierro, 68, cf. BO, 197
282 Sarduy, interview with Fossey, 19.
283 Deleuze and Guattari, *L'Anti-Oedipe*, 26/19, 104/87 The schizo lives in a 'absolute proximity [..], this total instantaneity of things' (Baudrillard, *L'Autre par lui-même*, 24–25)
284 SI, 86/120. Sarduy dreams of a 'History in which man and woman would no longer be the more or less conscious producer of events [..], but simply the bearers of costumes, vehicles for fabrics' ('La Botérisation de la mode', 379)
285 'Literature is an art of tattooing' (ES, 266/41).
286 Baudrillard, *L'Autre par lui-même*, 78, 42, my emphasis. Baudrillard's goal is to 'escape from the order [*l'enchaînement*] of meaning so as to throw oneself into a

process of delirious contiguity, into instantaneity and pure continuity' (72). And we know that for Deleuze and Guattari, creative 'metamorphosis is the contrary of all metaphor' (Deleuze and Guattari, *Kafka*, 40/22; cf. Deleuze and Guattari, *Mille plateaux*, 97/77; Deleuze, *Cinéma 2*, 32/21tm, 226/173).

287 Sarduy, interview with Rodríguez Monegal, 321.
288 Sarduy, 'Entre les "arrivés" et l'avant-garde', 13.
289 Sarduy, interview with Kushigian, 19, Sarduy, 'Las estructuras de la narración', 23.
290 Sarduy, 'Le basculement néo-baroque', 34
291 Sarduy, interview with Kushigian, 19
292 Sarduy, 'A la sombra del arecibo', 42
293 ES, 271/45. Ordinary 'metaphor is perfectly compatible with [mere] Galileoism', a pre-baroque preference for the classical stability of the circle over the ellipse (BO, 176).
294 ES, 277/50. For example, Cuba's becoming-India, and vice-versa, in *Cobra*, is a process which eliminates the 'original' independence of its terms.
295 Rousset, *La Littérature de l'âge baroque*, 28 Tantra is another effort to 'act out symbols literally' (Paz, *Conjunctions*, 77, 68, 72).
296 In Deleuze's *Proust et les signes*, metaphor is affirmed only because it is equated, exceptionally, with the figuration of 'original difference', the radical 'spiritualisation' of objects (*Proust et les signes*, 61–65/46–49). Rather than resist univocal differentiation, *this* sort of 'metaphor is essentially metamorphosis' (62/47)
297 CB, 15/5 'The signs of seduction', likewise, 'do not signify, they are of the order of the ellipse, of the short-circuit'; seduction is 'instantaneous, it is not something to decipher' (Baudrillard, *L'Autre par lui-même*, 53–55)
298 Sarduy, 'Un Châtelet de magie noire', 20
299 BO, 150. Alternatively, Sarduy privileges (in Lezama) the intuition of an essential *grey* between the 'excessive antipodal voices' of black and white, obscurity and clarity ('Sauro o el pincel púrpura', 51), Barthes' meditation on 'le neutre' compares (Barthes, 'Le neutre', *Oeuvres complètes*, iii, 887, *Le Plaisir du texte*, *Oeuvres complètes*, ii, 1502; *Roland Barthes par Roland Barthes*, *Oeuvres complètes*, iii, 161, 169, 189).
300 BO (Fr ed.), 24; Sarduy, 'Focus imaginarius', 9.
301 Sarduy, 'Deterritorialization', 104–105; cf. Sarduy, 'matière/machines/phantasme/ciel', first page
302 Sarduy, interview with Pérez Rivera, 6.
303 Deleuce and Guattari, *Mille plateaux*, 342/279
304 Baudrillard, *L'Autre par lui-même*, 36.
305 Caillois, *Méduse et Cie*, 81–82, in SI, 57–58/95.
306 Sarduy, 'Los Travestis', 55.
307 Sarduy, interview with Fossey, 7.
308 Sarduy, 'Le Basculement néo-baroque', 35
309 See in particular Sarduy, '*Paradis*. Syllables/Germes/Entropie/Perspective/Asthme', 22.
310 Sarduy, interview with Ulloa, 176
311 Sarduy, interview with Rodríguez Monegal, 20.
312 MY, 139/239 Serial identity is an important theme in Deleuze's *Logique du sens*.
313 BO, 175, and n. 31, cf. Lacan, *Ecrits*, 537–538.
314 Auxilio and Socorro are also called the Tiny Feet, the So Full of Graces, The Bald Divinities, the Peripathetics, the Painted Ladies, the Neat Ones, the Mistresses-of-the-Grass-of-Immortality The General figures as Peeping Tom, The Spaniard, The

Battle Lover, Medals Galore. Colibri's Japanese rival and eventual lover, is called the 'Oriental', the 'Great Nippon', the 'Ferocious One', the 'Master of Holds', the 'Great Translucent One', the 'Great Lard', and so on. The matron of *Cocuyo*'s *patronato* figures as the All Good, the Very Good, the So Good, the Too Good, Goodness Itself, Goodness in Person, the Always Good, the Good-doer, the Inflexibly Good, the Divinely Good, the Over Good, the Precautionary Good, and eventually the Given As Good.

315 Sarduy, interview with Fossey, 24
316 Sarduy, conversations with Macé, 89, my emphasis.
317 Cf. González Echevarría, *Ruta*, 226, 237; Mendez Rodenas, 'Colibrí', 401.
318 Sarduy, 'Huellas de Islam…', 49.
319 Sarduy, conversations with Macé, 85.
320 In *Maitreya*, for instance, we are asked: 'Was he evading the attack of some giant bird with a sharp beak, or tossing his head against an oncoming wave?' (MY, 17/155); 'Was he a giant from the ocean, who had drifted with the equinoctial tides, too close to the land, like those lashlike intestinal worms that always extend beyond their ends?' (MY, 101/213). When Colibri disappears mid-combat, the narrator is as mystified as anyone 'But what happened? Where is Colibrí? Do you see him. I don't… […]. I know nothing about it […] Did he slip away through a hidden door […]? Did he escape? Fly away? Evaporate […]. Or – final hypothesis, for time is short – […] was he painted into a fresco, through mimetic camouflage?' (COL, 23–24; cf. 56).
321 Sarduy, conversations with Macé, 80.
322 COL, 117, 178; cf Sarduy, conversations with Macé, 80.
323 Sarduy, conversations with Macé, 88. Nureyev represents Sarduy's 'ideal I [yo]' (Sarduy, interview with Sarduy, Fierro, 66).
324 The narrator evokes the 'so Christlike effigy of Colibri' (CI, 18; cf 91), describing him as 'a martyr offering his immaculate body to the arrows of blasphemers' (49).
325 CI, 55; cf. 113, 169–170.
326 CI, 78. For example, he interrupts one suspenseful sequence with 'a blank in the page: the implacable laws of narrative counterpoint compel us to return to the salon' (CI, 121) Later, when Colibri and his newly submissive hunters go to the river, the narrator adds that 'it was not far' – 'first because it's true, and then because the laws of this narrative – already extremely burdened by creepers and entanglements of all kinds, flowery vegetal volutes [*volutas vegetales y floripondios*] – demand it' (CI, 159). Again, should we wonder why Colibri joins in the decoration of fleas, we learn that it is 'because, dear lady, because; because so demands the rigour of the present fiction, programmed down to the tiniest detail; in which nothing, listen to me carefully, nothing, absolutely, has been left to chance (Note of the author of a thesis on Narrative Structures in the Work of Severo Sarduy)' (CI, 60 n. 1).
327 CI, 98; cf. RJ, 17/18
328 Sarduy, conversations with Macé, 91, n. 20 'My first love, as is narrated in *Cocuyo*, was Ada' (Sarduy, interview with Mihály Dés, 32).
329 Sarduy, conversations with Macé, 79.
330 Cf. González Echevarría, *Ruta*, 214–215.
331 Sarduy, interview with Dés, 38, RJ, 84/103.
332 Sarduy, interview with Kushigian, 20, 'Focus on Severo Sarduy', *Review* 72, no 6, p. 24.
333 Sarduy, interview with Ortega, iv. Artaud's theatre of cruelty, likewise, 'acts upon us like a spiritual therapeutics whose touch can never be forgotten' (Artaud, *The Theatre and its Double*, 85).

334 CY, 51. He internalises, in short, the leprosy of his fellow hospice inmates (53)

335 CY, 54 In *Cocuyo*, unlike *Colibrí*, figures of imprisonment dominate the *bestiare* (CY, 61, 62, 108)

336 CY, 84–85. Inversely, confronted with the truth of Ada's fate, Cocuyo prays that it be unreal, a dream. 'my God, make this be an hallucination [..], make it so that none of this is real' (CY, 203). 'if I am to survive', he tells himself, 'I must convince myself that everything I'm seeing and hearing is not real' (CY, 164).

337 Ada is tied and bound as 'prey' to the crones who promise her 'golden earrings', and the first prostitutes Cocuyo sees are distinguished by their earrings, 'which dangle to their shoulders' (CY, 127).

338 CY, 137. He has the same reaction when, broken hearted, he finds Ada in the brothel 'he tried to breathe, but his chest was a poisoned well And his bronchial tubes cut into him like broken glass' (163).

339 In love with an unreachable Ada, cut off from his family, 'insatiable lack [*carencia*] gnawed at him [...] Now absence [*la falta*] ran through everything' (CY, 73). Desire is now generally associated with asphyxiation. 'Ada was the air. And she had disappeared...' (72).

340 Cocuyo's experience evokes the child victims of a bombing described in *Gestos* – 'the children who do not understand a reality which makes their own tremble .' (GS, 46)

341 Sarduy stresses the point by adding an uncharacteristically redundant note (CY, 46, n.1)

342 See for instance CY, 13, 24, 49.

343 CY, 122 Writing also allows the only 'unproblematic' erotic associations in the novel (CY, 123, cf 134)

344 *Matthew* 2/12, in CY, 146, n.1.

345 Bakhtin reminds us. 'the very core of the carnivalistic attitude of the world [is] the pathos of vicissitude and change, of death and renewal. Carnival is the festival of all-destroying and all-renewing time' (*Problems of Dostoyevsky's Poetics*, 102; cf. *Rabelais and his World*, 9, 21)

346 Baudrillard, *Symbolic Exchange and Death*, 5 n.2.

347 DC, 230/150, cf. COL, 51, 117–118

348 Sarduy, 'Sauro o el pincel púrpura', 46.

349 Sarduy, interview with Torres Fierro, 68.

350 Sarduy, interview with Pérez Rivera, 6.

351 Sarduy, 'El barroco y el neobarroco', 176

352 Sarduy died of Aids in Paris in 1993.

353 The poem 'Morandi' ends with the sober line. 'Objects cling to each other. they are afraid' (*Quimera*, 102 [1991], 39).

354 RJ, 12/6–7. Similar boundaries arise in conjunction with the peculiar, defensive sensibility of his navel (RJ, 25–26/31). The instinctual 'life-drive' is here capable of doing something unthinkable in Sarduy's earlier work overriding Eros (RJ, 25/29).

355 RJ, 75/93–94 Fiction appears newly distinct from life or 'reality' 'In a story', he says in *Pájaros*, 'you can delay the worst, defer the unpleasant and even annul, however pertinent it appears, the final denouement' (PP, 51). Not so for the dying writer.

356 Sarduy, 'Deterritorialization', 107–108

357 Sarduy, interview with Fossey, 23.

358 CY, 89, cf. 148, 150 In his own family, Cocuyo is treasured for his 'elocution, his volubility. He was so advanced for his age!' (24).

359 *Pájaros* [birds] have a long-standing presence in Sarduy's fiction '"Pájaro' means

homosexual in Cuba' (Sarduy, interview with Seager, 133, cf. GS, 57; GS, 104, DC, 91/11, DC, 118/34, CI, 129)

360 Sarduy, interview with Ulloa, 178

361 It is of course the discovery of old age, disease and death that breaks the charm of the young Gautama's supremely sheltered and privileged life. 'since I have learnt of the danger of illness, my heart is repelled by pleasures and seems to shrink into itself' (Conze, *Buddhist Scriptures*, 39–40) For 'before long, alas, will this body lie on the earth, despised, bereft of consciousness, useless [.] This body is worn out, a nest of diseases and very frail. This heap of corruption breaks to pieces, life indeed ends in death' (*Dhammapada*, v. 46, 41, 148).

362 See PP, 32, 42, 76.

363 PP, 169. Some comparison with *Colibri* is unavoidable. The energy level of the Casona sinks at times to the levels attained in the hospice of *Pájaros* (CI, 113) – a condition caused, as it happens, by systematic recourse to 'herborism', free distribution of 'leaves' [*las hojas*] (CI, 113), obviously marijuana. By the novel's end, the Casona was 'nothing more than a hospice for *caquéticos patibularios*, who stumble about with glassy eyes: an asylum for frivolous lunatics [*orates ligéros*]' (CI, 169–170). But in *Colibri*, such fatigue is still premised on the basis of an unlimited energy or health. This makes all the difference. The stage is forever set for 'spectacular *revival* [sic]', 'the happy chaos' of old times (CI, 130).

364 The obese Isidro, anatomist and collector of cadavers, remains a specialist in dissection, and favours a strictly 'electro-magnetic' approach; Caiman is inclined to work within 'the primitive purity of the world, its unpredictable multiplicity' (CY, 35).

365 Sarduy, interview with Pérez Rivera, 6, Sarduy, interview with González Echevarría, 44, Sarduy, 'Notas a las notas', 561–562.

366 Sarduy, 'A la sombra del arecibo', 42–43.

367 As one of his poems puts it, 'the wheel owes/its movement/to the central/void, and colour/its fulguration/to whiteness [*blanco*]' (PP, 221)

368 Rosen Takashina, in Conze, *Buddhist Scriptures*, 143. And the Tantras. 'When the mind goes to rest/and the bonds of the body are destroyed,/then the one flavour of the Innate pours forth' (Saraha, *Dohakosha*, in Conze, *Buddhist Texts*, 230).

369 PP, 124–125, cf 188, 189

370 PP, 62. Other reminders from the Sarduyan past arrive in the form of ambulance medics called Auxilio and Socorro, become 'albino twins' (PP, 177, cf 56).

371 'With the nerves of lives', she declares, 'we heal those of people; the roots, which have perceived the murmur of the earth, restore vital energy' (PP, 100).

372 She earns her new name by surviving a terrible car crash (PP, 149).

373 It is essential to remember that 'simulation enunciates the void and death' (SI, 84).

374 Rahubabhadra, 'Hymn to Perfect Wisdom', in Conze, *Buddhist Scriptures*, 170

375 *Dhammapada*, v 179, vv. 87, 91

376 PP, 65–66 Here 'we are all tired, even the birds' (65, cf. 23).

377 Montero, *The Name Game*, 99.

CONCLUSION

1 As Laclau notes, 'I am a subject precisely because I cannot be an absolute consciousness, because something constitutively alien confronts me' – because I exist only in relation to an object, and to other subjects (Laclau, *Emancipation(s)*, 21)

2 Foucault, 'What is Enlightenment?', *Foucault Reader*, 33–34. Foucault explores the

realm of the subject(ed), rather than repeat the (self-)expression of the sovereign Very precisely, 'rather than ask how the sovereign appears on high, [he] seeks to know how, progressively, materially, in reality, subjects are constituted' (Foucault, 'Cours de 14 janvier, 1976', *Dits et écrits*, iii, 179).

3 Foucault, *L'Usage des plaisirs*, 17/11tm

4 Foucault, 'Archéologie d'une passion', in *Dits et écrits*, iv, 605

5 Foucault, 'What is Enlightenment?', *Foucault Reader*, 50. For a more detailed justification of this approach to Foucault, see my 'The Limits of Individuation' (2000).

6 Johnson himself is relatively critical of Morrison. While admiring her 'technical prose mastery', the bulk of his account in *Being and Race* argues that, in violation of Johnson's understanding of 'drama', she *tells* more than she shows, that she fails to fuse 'idea and event'; that her 'fictional universe seems lacking in light and balance', and that she, like 'many black authors', has 'difficulty grasping the rhythm and logic of dramatic scene and plot, the fluid, natural flow of *unmediated* action' (BR, 103, my emphasis).

7 Morrison, 'The Site of Memory',91, 93.

8 Johnson, 'Popper's Disease', SA, 144–145.

9 I adapt these terms from Sabin, 'Postcolonial Individuality' (1994)

10 Naipaul, 'On Being a Writer', *New York Review of Books* (23 April 1987), 7, in Kelly, *Naipaul*, 149

11 Naipaul, *A House for Mr. Biswas* (1961), *The Enigma of Arrival* (1987). Whereas from Wilson Harris's singular perspective, Naipaul's *House for Mr. Biswas* 'never erupts into a revolutionary or alien question of spirit' and serves only 'to consolidate one's preconception of humanity' (Harris, *Tradition*, 40), from the more obviously 'specific' perspective of C L R James, Naipaul's novel was 'the finest study ever produced in the West Indies (or anywhere that I know) of a minority and the Herculean obstacles in the way of its achieving a room in the national building' (James, 'Introduction', in Harris, *Tradition*, 74).

12 Cf Sabin, 'Postcolonial Individuality'.

13 Djebar, *L'Amour, la fantasia* (1985)

14 Sprinker, 'The National Question', 27; cf. Ahmad, *In Theory*, 283

15 Dirlik, *After the Revolution*, 99.

16 Parry, 'The Postcolonial', 16

17 Appadurai, 'Patriotism and its Futures', 412

18 Dirlik, *The Postcolonial Aura*, 166.

19 Aronowitz, *Dead Artists*, ix

20 See Badiou, *Petit Manuel d'inesthétique* (1998) One notable exception is Nick Harrison's reading-centred study, *Postcolonial Theory and the Work of Fiction* (forthcoming, 2002)

21 Freire, *Pedagogy of the Oppressed*, 29.

BIBLIOGRAPHY

General works

This section covers the Preface, Introduction, chapter 1, and the excursuses. Entries on Buddhism and Islam (relevant to chapters 1, 4 and 5) are listed separately at the end of this section.

Adam, Ian, and Helen Tiffin, eds *Past the Last Post. Theorizing Post-Colonialism and Post-Modernism*. Calgary. University of Calgary Press, 1990

Adorno, Theodor *Negative Dialectics* Trans E.B Ashton. London· Routledge, 1973.

Agamben, Giorgio *The Coming Community* [1990]. Trans. Michael Hardt. Minneapolis· University of Minnesota Press, 1993.

Ahmad, Aijaz. 'Imperialism and Progress'. *Mode of Production or Dependency?* Ed. Ronald H. Chilcote and D.C. Johnson. Beverly Hills. Sage, 1983

—— *In Theory. Classes, Nations, Literatures* London Verso, 1992.

—— 'The Politics of Literary Postcoloniality' [1995]. *Contemporary Postcolonial Theory. A Reader.* Ed. Mongia 276–293

—— 'Postcolonialsm. What's in a Name?' *Late Imperial Culture.* Ed. Roman de la Campa London Verso, 1995 11–32.

Amir, Samir *Unequal Development. An Essay on the Social Formations of Peripheral Capitalism.* Trans. Brian Pearce. NY Monthly Review Press, 1976.

Amselle, Jean-Loup *Logiques métisses Anthropologie de l'identité en Afrique et ailleurs* Paris Payot, 1990

Anderson, Benedict. *Imagined Communities* [1983]. London Verso, 1991.

Anderson, Perry. *In the Tracks of Historical Materialism.* London. Verso, 1983.

—— *The Ends of History* London. Verso, 1996

Ansell-Pearson, Keith, Benita Parry, and Judith Squires, eds. *Cultural Readings of Imperialism Edward Said and the Gravity of History.* London. Lawrence & Wishart, 1997.

Appadurai, Arjun. 'Disjuncture and Difference in the Global Cultural Economy' [1990]. *Colonial Discourse and Post-Colonial Theory* Ed. Williams and Chrisman. 324–339.

——. 'Patriotism and its Futures' *Public Culture* 5.3 (1993), 411–429.

Appiah, Kwame Anthony. *In My Father's House Africa in the Philosophy of Culture.* Oxford. Oxford University Press, 1992.

———. 'Is the Post- in Postmodernism the Post- in Postcolonial?' *Contemporary Postcolonial Theory. A Reader.* Ed. Mongia. 55–71.

Arac, Jonathan. *Postmodernism and Politics* Minneapolis University of Minnesota Press, 1986

Aronowitz, Stanley. *Dead Artists, Live Theories, and Other Cultural Problems* London. Routledge, 1994

Arrighi, Giovanni et al. *Antisystemic Movements.* London. Verso 1989

Ashcroft, Bill, Gareth Griffiths and Helen Tiffin *The Empire Writes Back Theory and Practice in Post-Colonial Literature* London Routledge, 1989

Ashcroft, Bill 'English Studies and Postcolonial Transformation'. *The Journal of Caribbean Studies* 13.2 (Summer 1998), 111–131.

Badiou, Alain *Théorie du sujet.* Paris Seuil, 1982.

——— *Peut-on penser la politique?* Paris. Seuil, 1985

——— *L'Etre et l'événement* Paris Seuil, 1988.

———. 'D'un Sujet enfin sans objet' *Cahiers Confrontations* 20 (Winter 1989), 13–22

——— *Manifeste pour la philosophie* Paris. Seuil, 1989.

———. 'L'Entretien de Bruxelles'. *Les Temps modernes* 526 (1990), 1–26.

——— 'Saississement, dessaisie, fidélité' *Les Temps modernes* 531–533. 1 (October 1990), 14–22.

——— Rev of Gilles Deleuze, *Le Pli Leibniz et le baroque Annuaire philosophique 1988–1989* Paris. Seuil, 1990. 161–184.

——— *D'Un Désastre obscur (Droit, Etat, Politique)* Paris L'Aube, 1991

——— *Monde contemporain et désir de philosophie* Reims. Cahier de Noria no. 1, 1992.

———. *Conditions* Paris. Seuil, 1992

——— *L'Ethique Essai sur la conscience du mal.* Paris. Hatier, 1993

——— 'Being by Numbers' *Artforum* 33.2 (1994), 84–87, 118, 123–124.

——— *Saint Paul et la fondation de l'universalisme* Paris. PUF, 1997

——— 'Politics and Philosophy' Interview with Hallward. *Angelaki* 3 3 (1998), 113–133

——— *Abrégé de métapolitique* Paris Seuil, 1998

——— *Petit Manuel d'inesthétique* Paris Seuil, 1998.

———. *Gilles Deleuze 'La clameur de l'Etre'* Paris Hachette, 1997. Trans Louise Burchill Minneapolis. University of Minnesota Press, 2000

——— *Théorie axiomatique du sujet. Notes du cours 1996–1998.* Unpublished typescript, 2000 121 pages

———. *Le Siècle* Paris. Seuil, 2001 [forthcoming references are to the typescript, 144 pages].

Bahri, Deepika 'Once More with Feeling What is Postcolonialism?' *Ariel* 26 1 (January 1995), 51–82.

Bakhtin, Mikhail *Problems of Dostoevsky's Poetics* Trans. Caryl Emerson Minneapolis University of Minnesota Press, 1984.

Balibar, Etienne *On the Dictatorship of the Proletariat* London. New Left Books, 1977

——— 'Has the "World" Changed?' *Marxism in the Postmodern Age* Ed Antonio Callari et al NY Guilford Press, 1995 403–412

——— 'Ambiguous Universality' *Differences* 7 1 (1995), 48–74.

———, and Immanuel Wallerstein *Race, Nation, Class Ambiguous Identities* London Verso, 1991

Barker, Francis et al., eds *Colonial Discourse/Postcolonial Theory.* Manchester Manchester University Press, 1994

Barkow, Jerome H., Leda Cosmides, and John Tooby, eds. *The Adapted Mind. Evolutionary Psychology and the Generation of Culture* Oxford Oxford University Press 1992.

Barthes, Roland *Oeuvres complètes* 3 vols Paris. Seuil, 1993.

Basch, Linda, Nina Glick Schiller and Christina Szanton Blanc *Nations Unbound Transnational Projects, Postcolonial Predicaments and Deterritorialized Nation-States* Amsterdam Gordon and Breach, 1994

Bavley, Stephen. 'Imaginings' *New Statesman & Society* 2.70 (6 October 1989), 46.

Beiner, Ronald Ed *Theorising Citizenship* Albany. State University of New York Press, 1995

Benhabib, Seyla. *Situating the Self Gender, Community and Postmodernism in Contemporary Ethics* Cambridge Polity, 1992

——, et al , *Feminist Contentions A Philosophical Exchange* New York. Routledge, 1995.

Benítez-Rojo, Antonio *The Repeating Island The Caribbean and the Postmodern Perspective* Trans James Maraniss Durham. Duke University Press, 1992.

Benjamin, Walter *Illuminations* Trans. Harry Zohn London. Fontana, 1982

Benveniste, Emile *Problèmes de linguistique générale* Vol. 1. Paris Gallimard, 1966.

Bernabé, Jean, Patrick Chamoiseau and Raphael Confiant *Eloge de la créolité*. Paris Gallimard, 1989

Bertens, Hans *The Idea of the Postmodern, A History* London. Routledge, 1995

Best, Steven and Douglas Kellner. *Postmodern Theory Critical Interrogations*. London Macmillan, 1991

Bhabha, Homi 'Commitment to Theory' *Questions of Third Cinema*. Ed Jim Pines and Paul Willemen London British Film Institute, 1989 111–132.

——. 'Postcolonial Criticism'. *Redrawing the Boundaries The Transformation of English and American Literary Studies* Ed Stephen Greenblatt and Giles Gunn NY Modern Language Association, 1992 437–466.

——. 'Culture's In Between' *Artforum* 32.1 (Sept 1993), 167–168, 211–214.

—— *The Location of Culture* London. Routledge, 1994

—— 'In a Spirit of Calm Violence'. *After Colonialism* Ed. Prakash. 1995 326–343

—— 'Freedom's Basis in the Indeterminate' *The Identity in Question* Ed Jonathan Rajchman London. Routledge, 1995 47–61.

——. 'The Translator Translated' Interview with W.J.T Mitchell *Artforum* 33 7 (March 1995), 80–85.

—— 'Unpacking my Library Again'. *The Post-Colonial Question* Ed. Chambers and Curti 1996. 199–211

—— 'Minority Maneuvers and Unsettled Negotiations' *Critical Inquiry* 23.3 (Spring 1997), 431–459.

—— 'Interview with Olson and Worsham' *Race, Rhetoric, and the Postcolonial*. Ed Gary A Olson and Lynn Worsham Albany. State University of NY Press. 1999 3–39

Blanchot, Maurice *La Part du feu* Paris Gallimard, 1949

—— *L'Espace littéraire*. Paris. Gallimard, coll. 'Idées', 1955 [1988 printing]

—— *Le Livre à venir* Paris Gallimard, coll 'Idées', 1959 [1986 printing]

——. *L'Entretien infini* Paris. Gallimard. 1969

—— *Après-coup*. Paris Minuit, 1983

—— *La Communauté inavouable* Paris Minuit, 1983. Trans Pierre Joris Barrytown NY Station Hill Press, 1988

Blundell, Valda, et al , eds *Relocating Cultural Studies* London Routledge, 1993

Boehmer, Elleke *Colonial and Postcolonial Literature Migrant Metaphors* Oxford Oxford University Press, 1995

Bourdieu, Pierre 'Universal Corporatism The Role of Intellectuals in the Modern World' *Poetics Today* 12 4 (1991) 655–669

——. *Les Règles de l'art Genèse et structure du champ littéraire* Paris. Seuil, 1992 Trans Susan Emanuel. Stanford. Stanford University Press, 1996

—— *Méditations pascaliennes*. Paris Seuil, 1997

——. *Raisons pratiques* Paris Seuil, 1994 Trans Randal Johnson et al. Stanford. Stanford University Press, 1998.

Boyne, Roy and Ali Rattansi. *Postmodernism and Society* London: Macmillan, 1990

Brathwaite, Edward Kamau *History of the Voice The Development of Nation Language in Anglophone Caribbean Poetry* London. New Beacon Books, 1984

Braudel, Fernand *La Méditerranée et le monde méditerranéen à l'époque de Philippe II* Paris. A Colin, 1966

Breuilly, John *Nationalism and the State* Manchester. Manchester University Press, 1993

Brewer, Anthony *Marxist Theories of Imperialism* London Routledge, 1990

Brubaker. Roger *Citizenship and Nationhood in France and Germany* Cambridge Harvard. 1992

Brown, Donald E *Human Universals* New York McGraw-Hill, 1991.

Buell, Frederick *National Culture and the New Global System* Baltimore Johns Hopkins University Press, 1994.

Buhle, Paul *C.L R James The Artist as Revolutionary.* London Verso, 1988

Bürger, Peter *Theory of the Avant-Garde* Trans Michael Shaw Minneapolis. University of Minnesota Press, 1984

Butler, Judith *Bodies That Matter On the Discursive Limits of 'Sex',* London Routledge, 1993

——, Ernesto Laclau and Slavoj Žižek. *Contingency, Hegemony, Universality.* London. Verso, 2000.

Calinescu, Matei *Five Faces of Modernity* Durham. Duke University Press, 1987.

Callari, Antonio, et al , eds *Marxism in the Postmodern Age* NY Guilford Press, 1994

Callinicos, Alex 'Wonders Taken for Signs Homi Bhabha's Postcolonialism' *Post-Ality* Ed. Mas'ud Zavarzadeh et al 98–112

Cavell, Stanley. *A Pitch of Philosophy Autobiographical Exercises* Cambridge. Harvard University Press, 1994

Césaire, Aimé *Discours sur le colonialisme* [1950] Paris Présence Africaine, 1955. Trans. John Pinkham NY. Monthly Review, 1972

—— *Letter to Maurice Thorez* Paris Présence Africaine, 1957.

Chambers, Iain. *Border Dialogues. Journeys in Postmodernity* London Routledge, 1990

——. *Migrancy, Culture, Identity* London Routledge. 1994

——, and Lidia Curti, eds *The Post-Colonial Question: Common Skies. Divided Horizons* London Routledge, 1996

Chamoiseau, Patrick and Raphael Confiant. *Lettres créoles Tracées antillaises et continentales de la littérature 1635–1975.* Paris. Hatier, 1991

Childs, Peter, and Patrick Williams *An Introduction to Post-Colonial Theory* London. Harvester Wheatsheaf, 1997

Chinweizu, et al *Toward the Decolonization of African Literature* Vol 1 Washington. Howard University Press, 1983

Chomsky, Noam *World Orders, Old and New.* London. Pluto, 1994

Chrisman, Laura. 'Inventing Post-Colonial Theory Polemical Observations' *Pretexts* 5 (1995), 205–212.

Clifford, James, ed *Writing Culture The Poetics and Politics of Ethnography* Berkeley. University of California Press. 1986.

—— *The Predicament of Culture. Twentieth Century Ethnography, Literature and Art.* Cambridge Harvard University Press, 1988

—— *Routes. Travel and Translation in the Late Twentieth Century* Cambridge Harvard University Press. 1997

Collier, Gordon, ed. *Us/Them. Translation, Transcription and Identity in Post-Colonial Literary Culture* Amsterdam. Rodopi, 1992

Comrie, Bernard. *Language Universals and Linguistic Typology. Syntax and Morphology* Oxford· Blackwell, 1981.

Connor, Steven. *Postmodernist Culture An Introduction to Theories of the Contemporary* Oxford: Blackwell, 1989.

——. *Theory and Cultural Value* Oxford Blackwell, 1992.

Corballis, Michael C and Stephen Lea, eds *The Descent Of Mind Psychological Perspectives on Hominid Evolution* Oxford. Oxford University Press, 1999.

Corbin, Henry. *Corps spirituel et terre céleste de l'Iran mazdéen à l'Iran shi'ite* Paris Buchet-Chastel, 1979. Trans Nancy Pearson as *Spiritual Body and Celestial Earth* London Tauris, 1990

Critchley, Simon. *The Ethics of Deconstruction* Oxford. Blackwell, 1993.

——, and Peter Dews, eds. *Deconstructive Subjectivities*. NY SUNY Press, 1996

Dance, Daryl Cumber. *New World Adams Conversations with Contemporary West Indian Writers* Leeds Peepal Tree, 1992.

de Alva, J. Jorge Klor. 'The Postcolonization of the (Latin) American Experience. A Reconsideration of "Colonialism", "Postcolonialism", and "Mestizaje"' *After Colonialism* Ed. Prakash. 1995. 241–275

Deleuze, Gilles. *Empirisme et subjectivité*. Paris. PUF, 1953. Trans. Constantin Boundas NY Columbia University Press, 1991.

——. *Nietzsche et la philosophie* Paris. PUF, 1962. Trans. Hugh Tomlinson Minneapolis. University of Minnesota Press, 1983

—— *Le Bergsonisme* Paris. PUF, 1966. Trans Hugh Tomlinson and Barbara Habberjam NY. Zone Books, 1988.

—— *Différence et répétition*, Paris PUF, 1968 Trans. Paul Patton. NY. Columbia University Press, 1994.

——. *Spinoza et le problème de l'expression*. Paris. Minuit, 1968 Trans Martin Joughin as *Expressionism in Philosophy. Spinoza*. NY· Zone Books, 1990

—— *Logique du sens*. Paris Minuit, 1969 Trans Mark Lester with Charles Stivale. NY. Columbia University Press, 1990.

——. *Spinoza philosophie pratique* [1970]. Paris. Minuit, 1981. Trans. Robert Hurley San Francisco City Light Books, 1988.

——. 'Un manifeste de moins'. *Superpositions* [with Carmelo Bene]. Paris. Minuit, 1979 85–131.

——. *Cinéma 1 L'Image-mouvement* Paris. Minuit, 1983. Trans Tomlinson and Habberjam. Minneapolis. University of Minnesota Press, 1986.

—— *Cinéma 2. L'Image-temps* Paris Minuit, 1985. Trans. Tomlinson and Habberjam. Minneapolis University of Minnesota Press, 1989.

—— *Foucault* Paris Minuit, 1986

—— *Le Pli Leibniz et le baroque*. Paris. Minuit, 1988 Trans. Tom Conley. Minneapolis University of Minnesota Press, 1993

——. *Pourparlers, 1972–1990*. Paris. Minuit, 1990 Trans Martin Joughin as *Negotiations* NY. Columbia University Press, 1995

——. *Dialogues* [with Claire Parnet]. Paris. Flammarion, 1996

Deleuze, Gilles, and Félix Guattari. *L'Anti-Oedipe* Paris Minuit, 1972 Trans Robert Hurley, Mark Seem and Helen R. Lane. Minneapolis, University of Minnesota Press, 1977

—— *Kafka pour une littérature mineure*. Paris. Minuit, 1975 Trans Dana Polan. Minneapolis University of Minnesota Press, 1986

——. *Mille plateaux*. Paris Minuit, 1980 Trans. Brian Massumi. Minneapolis University of Minnesota Press, 1986.

——. *Qu'est-ce que la philosophie?* Paris. Minuit, 1991. Trans Hugh Tomlinson and Graham Burchell. NY Columbia University Press, 1994

Derrida, Jacques *Donner la mort*. *L'Ethique du don, Jacques Derrida et la pensée du don*. Eds. Jean-Michel Rabaté and Michael Wetzel. Paris Transition, 1992 Trans David Wills. Chicago University of Chicago Press, 1995.

Dews, Peter *Logics of Disintegration*. London. Verso, 1987

——. *The Limits of Disenchantment* London Verso, 1995

D'haen, Theo, and Hans Bertens. *Liminal Postmodernisms The Postmodern, the (Post-) Colonial, and the (Post-)Feminist*. Amsterdam· Atlanta, 1994

Dirlik, Arif. *After the Revolution Waking to Global Capitalism* Hanover. Wesleyan University Press, 1994

——. *The Postcolonial Aura. Third World Criticism in the Age of Global Capitalism* Boulder, Colorado. Westview Press, 1997.

Djebar, Assia. *L'Amour, la fantasia*. Paris Jean-Claude Lattes, 1985

Docherty, Thomas, ed. *Postmodernism, A Reader*. NY. Harvester, 1993.

Durix, Jean-Pierre *Mimesis, Genres, and Post-Colonial Discourse. Deconstructing Magic Realism*. Basingstoke. Macmillan, 1998

Eagleton, Terry *The Illusions of Postmodernism* Oxford Blackwell, 1996.

—— *Literary Theory An Introduction*. Oxford. Blackwell, 1996.

——. 'Postcolonialism and "Postcolonialism"'. *Interventions* 1·1 (1998–1999), 24–26

Ehrenberg, Alain. *L'Individu incertain* Paris Calmann-Levy, 1995.

Eliade, Mircea *Méphistocles et l'androgyne* [1962] Paris. Gallimard, 'Folio', 1995

Elliott, Gregory 'The Cards of Confusion. Reflections on Historical Communism and the "End of History"'. *Radical Philosophy* 64 (1993), 3–12

Ellison, Ralph. *Shadow and Act*. NY. New American Library, 1966.

Epstein, William H, ed. *Contesting the Subject Essays in the Postmodern Theory and Practice of Biography and Biographical Criticism* West Lafayette. Purdue University Press, 1991.

Fairlamb, Horace L. *Critical Conditions Postmodernity and the Question of Foundation* Cambridge Cambridge University Press, 1994

Fanon, Frantz. *Peau noire, masques blancs* Paris. Seuil, 'Points', 1952 Trans Charles Lam Markmann NY. Grove Press, 1967.

—— *Les Damnés de la terre* [1961] Paris. Gallimard, 'Folio', 1991. Trans Constance Farrington NY. Grove Press, 1991

Featherstone, Mike *Undoing Culture Globalisation, Postmodernism and Identity* London Sage, 1995.

——, et al, eds. *Global Culture Theory, Culture and Society* 7 2–3 (June 1990)

——, et al., eds *Global Modernities*. London. Sage, 1995.

Ferris, Timothy. *The Whole Shebang A State-of-the-Universe(s) Report* NY Simon & Schuster, 1997

Finkielkraut, Alain *Défaite de la pensée* Paris Gallimard, 'Folio', 1987 Trans Judith Friedlander as *Defeat of the Mind* NY. Columbia University Press, 1995

Fish, Stanley. *Is There a Text in this Class?* Cambridge. Harvard University Press, 1978.

—— 'Consequences'. *Against Theory* Ed W.J.T Mitchell. Chicago: University of Chicago Press, 1985.

—— 'Being Interdisciplinary Is So Very Hard To Do'. *Profession* 89 (1989)

—— 'Biography and Intention' *Contesting the Subject*. Ed. William H Epstein West Lafayette. Purdue University Press, 1991.

—— *Professional Correctness. Literary Studies and Political Change* Oxford Oxford University Press, 1995

Flaubert, Gustave *Correspondance*. Vol. 2. Ed. Jean Bruneau. Paris. Gallimard, Pléiade, 1980

Fokhema, Aleid. *Postmodern Characters. A Study of Characterization in British and American Postmodern Fiction*. Amsterdam Rodopi, 1991.

Foster, Hal, ed *The Anti-Aesthetic* Port Townshend. Bay Press, 1983.

—— *Recodings*. Port Townshend Bay Press, 1985

Foucault, Michel. *Les Mots et les choses* Paris. Gallimard, 1966. Trans. Alan Sheridan. London Tavistock, 1970

—— 'Human Nature Justice Versus Power' *Reflexive Water The Basic Concerns of Mankind* Ed Fons Elders. London Souvenir Press, 1974. 135–197.

——. *La Volonté de savoir*. Paris Gallimard, 1976 Trans. Robert Hurley Harmondsworth Penguin, 1981

——. *L'Usage des plaisirs*. Paris Gallimard, 1984. Trans Robert Hurley. NY. Vintage, 1990.

—— *The Foucault Reader*. Ed. Paul Rabinow. NY. Pantheon, 1984

——. *The Final Foucault*. Ed. James Bernauer and David Rasmussen. Cambridge MIT, 1988

—— *Politics, Philosophy. Culture Interviews and Other Writings 1977–1984*. Ed. Lawrence D. Kritzman London. Routledge, 1988.

—— *Technologies of the Self* Ed PH. Hutton et al Amherst. University of Massachusetts Press, 1988

—— *Dits et écrits*. Ed. Daniel Defert and François Ewald 4 vols. Paris. Gallimard, 1994

Fox, Robin *The Search for Society Quest for a Biosocial Science and Morality* New Brunswick Rutgers University Press, 1989.

Frankenberg, Ruth, and Lata Mani 'Crosscurrents, Crosstalk Race, "Postcoloniality" and the Politics of Location' [1993]. *Contemporary Postcolonial Theory* Ed Mongia. 347–364.

Freire, Paulo *Pedagogy of the Oppressed*. Boston Bergin and Garvey, 1976

Gandhi, Leela *Postcolonial Theory. A Critical Introduction* NY Columbia University Press, 1998

Geertz, Clifford. *The Interpretation of Cultures* NY Basic Books, 1973

——. *Local Knowledge Further Essays in Interpretative Anthropology*. NY Basic Books, 1983

——. *Works and Lives. The Anthropologist as Author* Stanford. Stanford University Press, 1988

Gellner, Ernest *Nations and Nationalism* Oxford Blackwell, 1983

—— *Encounters with Nationalism*. Oxford. Blackwell, 1994.

Giddens, Anthony *Consequences of Modernity* Cambridge Polity, 1990.

Gikandi, Simon 'In the Shadow of Hegel. Cultural Theory in an Age of Displacement'. *Research in African Literatures* 27.2 (Summer 1996), 139–152

Gilroy, Paul *Small Acts Thoughts on the Politics of Black Culture* London Serpent's Tail, 1993

—— *The Black Atlantic. Modernity and Double Consciousness* London Verso, 1993.

Giroux, Robert *Désir de synthèse chez Stéphane Mallarmé*. Sherbrooke. Namaan, 1978.

Goldmann, Lucien. *The Human Sciences and Philosophy* Trans. Hayden White and Robert Anchor London Jonathan Cape, 1969.

Gordon, Lewis. *Frantz Fanon and the Crisis of European Man* London Routledge, 1995

——, et al . eds *Fanon A Critical Reader*. Oxford. Blackwell, 1996

Gramsci, Antonio *Selections from Cultural Writings* Ed. David Forgacs and Geoffrey Nowell-Smith Trans William Boelhower Cambridge. Harvard University Press, 1985

Griffiths, Gareth 'Critical Approaches and Problems'. *New Literatures* Ed King 164–177.

——. 'Documentation and Communication in Postcolonial Societies the Politics of Control' *The Yearbook of English Studies* 27 (1997), 130–136

Guha, Ranajit. 'On some aspects of the historiography of Colonial India' *Subaltern Studies* 1 (1982), 1–9

Haber, Honi Fern. *Beyond Postmodern Politics Lyotard, Rorty, Foucault* London Routledge, 1994

Habermas, Jurgen. *The Philosophical Discourse of Modernity* Trans Frederick Lawrence. Cambridge MIT Press, 1987

—— *Postmetaphysical Thinking* Trans William Mark Hohengarten Cambridge. MIT Press, 1992

—— 'Struggles for Recognition in the Democratic Constitutional State' *Multiculturalism* Ed Charles Taylor and Amy Guttman. 107–148.

—— *Justification and Application* Trans Ciaran Cronin Cambridge. MIT Press, 1993.

Hall, Stuart *The Hard Road to Renewal* London. Verso, 1988

—— 'Cultural Identity and Diaspora' *Contemporary Postcolonial Theory* Ed. Mongia 110–121.

—— *Critical Dialogues in Cultural Studies* Ed. David Morley and Kuan-Hsing Chen London Routledge. 1996

Hallward, Peter 'Deleuze and the Redemption from Interest' *Radical Philosophy*, 81 (January 1997), 6–21

—— 'Deleuze and the "World Without Others"' *Philosophy Today* 41 4 (Winter 1997), 530–544

—— 'Generic Sovereignty. The Philosophy of Alain Badiou'. *Angelaki* 3.3 (1998), 87–111

—— 'The Singular and the Specific' *Radical Philosophy* 99 (January 2000), 6–18

—— 'The Limits of Individuation, or how to Distinguish Deleuze from Foucault' *Angelaki* 5 2 (2000), 93–112

—— *Subject to Truth The Philosophy of Alain Badiou*. Minneapolis University of Minnesota Press 2002.

Harper, Philip B *Framing the Margins The Social Logic of Postmodern Culture* Oxford. Oxford University Press, 1994

Harris, Wilson. *Tradition, The Writer, and Society Critical Essays* London New Beacon Publications, 1967

——. *The Womb of Space The Cross-Cultural Imagination* Westport. Greenwood Press. 1983

——. 'The Fabric of the Imagination' *From Commonwealth to Post-Colonial* Ed Anne Rutherford Sydney. Dangaroo. 1992 18–29

——. *The Carnival Trilogy* London Faber & Faber, 1993

Hassan, Ihab *The Dismemberment of Orpheus Towards a Postmodern Literature* [1971]. Madison University of Wisconsin Press, 1982

——. *Paracriticisms Seven Speculations of the Times* Urbana University of Illinois Press, 1975

——, ed *Innovation/Renovation*. Madison. University of Wisconsin Press, 1983.

—— *The Postmodern Turn* Columbus. Ohio State University Press, 1987

Hastings, Adrian *The Construction of Nationhood* Cambridge Cambridge University Press, 1997.

Hegel, Georg W F. *The Phenomenology of Mind*. Trans A V. Miller Oxford: Oxford University Press, 1977.

Heidegger, Martin. *Being and Time*. Trans John Macquarrie and Edward Robinson. NY. Harper and Row, 1962.

——. *Discourse on Thinking*. Trans. J.M. Anderson and E H Freund. NY. Harper and Row, 1966.

hooks, bell. *Yearning Race, Gender and Cultural Politics*. Boston South End Press, 1990.

Hobsbawm, Eric *Nations and Nationalism Since 1780. Programme, Myth, Reality* [1990]. Cambridge Cambridge University Press, 1992.

——. 'He's Back How Marx Bucked the Market' *The Guardian* 20 October 1998, section 2, 1–2

Hoogvelt, Ankie M *Globalisation and the Postcolonial World. The New Political Economy of Development* Basingstoke. Macmillan, 1997

Hutcheon, Linda. *A Poetics of Postmodernism* London Routledge, 1988

——. *The Politics of Postmodernism* London. Routledge, 1989

——. 'Complexities Abounding'. Introduction to special issue on 'Colonialism and the Postcolonial Condition'. *PMLA* 110.1 (January, 1995), 8–12.

Huyssen, Andreas *After the Great Divide Modernism, Mass Culture, Postmodernism* Bloomington. Indiana University Press, 1986.

Jacoby, Russell 'Marginal Returns. The Trouble with Post-Colonial Theory' *Lingua Franca* 6 (September–October 1995), 30–37

Jameson, Fredric. 'Third World Literature in the Age of Multinational Capital' *Social Text* 15 (Autumn, 1986), 65–88.

—— *Postmodernism, or the Cultural Logic of Late Capitalism*. Durham Duke University Press, 1991.

JanMohamed, Abdul R 'The Economy of Manichean Allegory The Function of Racial Difference in Colonialist Literature'. *Critical Inquiry* 12 (1985), 59–87.

——, and Lloyd, David *Nature and Context of Minority Discourse* Oxford Oxford University Press, 1990

Jones, John Paul, ed *Postmodern Contentions* NY. Guilford Press, 1993

Kant, Immanuel. *Critique of Judgement* Trans. Werner S Pluhar Indianapolis Hackett, 1987

——. *Groundwork of the Metaphysics of Morals* Trans. Mary Gregor. Cambridge. Cambridge University Press, 1997

Kaplan, Caren *Questions of Travel Postmodern Discourses of Displacement*. Durham Duke University Press, 1996.

Kedourie, Elie *Nationalism* [1960] London Hutchinson, 1985

Kelly, Richard VS. *Naipaul* NY Continuum, 1989

King, Bruce, ed *New National and Post-Colonial Literatures* Oxford Oxford University Press, 1996

Koestler, Arthur. *Janus A Summing Up*. NY. Random House, 1978

Krishnaswamy, Revathi. 'Mythologies of Migrancy. Postcolonialism, Postmodernism, and the Politics of (Dis)location'. *Ariel* 26 1 (January 1995), 125–146

Kuper, Adam *South Africa and the Anthropologists*. London Routledge, 1987.

——. *The Chosen Primate Human Nature and Cultural Diversity* Cambridge Harvard University Press, 1994

Laborde, Cécile 'From Constitutional to Civic Patriotism', forthcoming in *The British Journal of Political Science* (2001).

Laclau, Ernesto and Chantal Mouffe *Hegemony and Socialist Strategy* London. Verso, 1985

——, ed *The Making of Political Identities* London. Verso, 1994

—— *Emancipation(s).* London. Verso, 1996.

Larochelle, Gilbert. 'Interdependence, Globalisation, and Fragmentation'. *Globalisation and Territorial Identities.* Ed Mlinar 150–164.

Lash, Scott *Sociology of Postmodernism* London· Routledge, 1990

Laurent, Alain *L'Individu et ses ennemis.* Paris. Hachette, 1987

Lazarus, Neil. *Resistance in Postcolonial African Literature.* New Haven· Yale University Press, 1990

—— 'Doubting the New World Order. Marxism, Realism and the Claims of Postmodernist Social Theory' *Differences* 3 3 (1991), 94–138.

—— 'Disavowing Decolonisation. Fanon, Nationalism and the Problematic of Representation in Current Theories of Colonial Discourse'. *Research in African Literatures* 24 4 (1993), 69–98

—— 'National Consciousness and the Specificity of (Post)Colonial Intellectualism' *Colonial Discourse/Postcolonial Theory* Ed. Barker et al. Manchester Manchester University Press, 1994. 197–220

——, et al 'The Necessity of Universalism'. *Differences* 7.1 (1995), 75–145.

—— 'Transnationalism and the Alleged Death of the Nation-State' *Cultural Readings of Imperialism* Ed Ansell-Pearson et al 1997 28–48

—— *Nationalism and Cultural Practice in the Postcolonial World* Cambridge Cambridge University Press, 1999

Leibniz, Gottfried *Philosophical Works* Ed. R S. Woolhouse and Richard Franks. Oxford Oxford University Press, 1998

Lenin, Vladimir. *Selected Works* [single volume edition]. Moscow Progress Publishers, 1968.

Lentricchia, Frank *After the New Criticism* Chicago Chicago University Press, 1980

Levinas, Emmanuel. *Basic Philosophical Writings.* Ed Adriaan T Peperzak, Simon Critchley and Robert Bernasconi Bloomington University of Indiana Press, 1996.

—— *Totalité et infini.* The Hague Martinus Nijhoff, Livre de poche ed., 1961 Trans A Lingis. Pittsburgh. Duquesne University Press, 1969

Lévi-Strauss, Claude *La Pensée sauvage* Paris Plon, 'Agora' ed., 1962.

Lionnet, Françoise *Postcolonial Representations Women, Literature, Identity* Ithaca. Cornell University Press, 1995.

Lohmann, Christopher K. *Discovering Difference Contemporary Essays in American Culture* Bloomington, Indiana University Press, 1993

Longinus *On the Sublime* Trans. James A. Arieti and John M. Crossett NY Edwin Mellen, 1985

Loomba, Ania *Colonialism/Postcolonialism* London Routledge, 1998

——, and Savir Kaul 'Introduction Location, Culture, Post-Coloniality' *Oxford Literary Review* 16 1/2 (1994), 3–30.

Lyon, David *Postmodernity* Buckingham. Open University Press, 1994.

Lyotard, Jean-François *Le Différend* Paris Minuit, 1984 Trans. George Van Den Abbeele Minneapolis. University of Minnesota Press, 1988

——. *Leçons sur l'analytique du sublime.* Paris. Galilée, 1991 Trans Elizabeth Rottenberg. Stanford Stanford University Press, 1994

Mackey, Nathaniel *Discrepant Engagement· Dissonance, Cross-Culturality, and Experimental Writing* Cambridge Cambridge University Press, 1993

MacLeod, Christine 'Black American Literature and the Postcolonial Debate' *Yearbook of English Studies* 27 (1997), 51–65.

Maffesoli, Michel *Le Temps des tribus* Paris. Klincksieck, 1988.

Mallarmé, Stéphane *Oeuvres complètes* Paris. Gallimard, Pléiade, 1950.
—— *Correspondance*. Ed. Henri Mondor. Paris. Gallimard, 1959.
Mandel, Ernest 'The Relevance of Marxist Theory for Understanding the Present World Crisis' *Marxism in the Postmodern Age*. Ed Callari 1995. 438–447
Martine, Brian John. *Individuals and Individuality*. Albany. SUNY, 1984.
Marx, Karl *Capital* Trans. Ben Fowkes Vol 1 NY Vintage, 1977
——. *Grundrisse* Trans. Martin Nicolaus. Harmondsworth. Penguin, 1973
——, and Friedrich Engels, *Selected Works*. NY. International Publishers, 1936
——, and Friedrich Engels, *The First Indian War of Independence 1857–1859* Moscow Progress, 1959.
May, Todd. 'The Community's Absence in Lyotard, Nancy and Lacoue-Labarthe' *Philosophy Today* 37·3 (Autumn 1993), 275–284
Mayaud, Pierre-Noel, ed *Le Problème de l'individuation* Paris Vrin, 1991
Mayr, Ernst. *Toward a New Philosophy of Biology*. Cambridge. Harvard University Press, 1988.
Mbembe, Achille. 'The Banality of Power and the Aesthetics of Vulgarity in the Postcolony' *Public Culture* 4.2 (Spring 1992), 1–30
——. 'Prosaics of Servitude and Authoritarian Civilities' *Public Culture* 5.1 (1992), 123–145
McClintock, Anne 'The Angel of Progress Pitfalls of the Term "Post-Colonialism"' [1992] *Colonial Discourse and Post-Colonial Theory*. Ed. Williams and Chrisman. 291–303.
McGinn, Bernard *The Foundations of Mysticism* 2 vols NY. Crossroad, 1991
McGowan, John. *Postmodernism and its Critics*. Ithaca Cornell University Press, 1991.
McHale, Brian *Postmodern Fiction*. London Methuen, 1989
——. *Constructing Postmodernism*. London: Routledge, 1992
Memmi, Albert *The Colonizer and the Colonized* Trans Howard Grenfield. Boston Beacon Press, 1965.
Mestrovic, Stjepan G. *The Barbarian Temperament: Toward a Postmodern Critical Theory*. London. Routledge, 1993
Meszaros, Istvan *Beyond Capital Towards a Theory of Transition* London Merlin Press, 1995
Miller, Christopher L *Theories of Africans*. Chicago Chicago University Press, 1990
—— *Nationalists and Nomads Essays on Francophone African Literature and Culture*. Chicago. Chicago University Press, 1998
Miller, David *On Nationality* Oxford Oxford University Press, 1995.
Milner, Andrew, et al , eds. *Postmodern Conditions*. NY Berg, 1990.
Mintz, Sidney *The Power of Sweetness and the Sweetness of Power* Deventer Van Loghum Slaterus, 1988
Mishra, Vijay 'Postcolonial Differend', *Ariel* 26 3 (July 1995), 7–45.
——, and Bob, Hodge. 'What is Post(-)colonialism?' *Colonial Discourse and Post-Colonial Theory*. Ed. Williams and Chrisman. 276–290.
Mitchell, W J.T , ed. *Against Theory*. Chicago University of Chicago Press, 1985
—— 'Postcolonial Culture and Postimperial Criticism' *Transition* 56 (1992), 11–19.
Miyoshi, Masao 'A Borderless World? From Colonialism to Transnationalism and the Decline of the Nation-State' *Critical Inquiry* 19·4 (Summer 1993), 726–751.
—— 'Sites of Resistance in the Global Economy' *Cultural Readings of Imperialism*. Ed. Ansell-Pearson et al. 1997 49–66.
Mlinar, Zdravko, ed. *Globalisation and Territorial Identities* Aldershot. Avebury, 1992.

Mohan, Rajeswari 'Dodging the Crossfire Questions for Postcolonial Pedagogy' *College Literature* 19–20.3–1 (October 1992 – February 1993), 28–44

Moharan, Radhika and Gita Rajan, eds *English Postcoloniality· Literature from Around the World* Westport, CT Greenwood Press, 1996.

Mongia, Padmini, ed *Contemporary Postcolonial Theory. A Reader*. London. Arnold, 1996

Montesquieu, Charles de Secondat *Oeuvres complètes* 2 vols Paris. Gallimard, Pléiade, 1949–1951.

Moore-Gilbert, Bart *Postcolonial Theory. Contexts, Practices, Politics*. London Verso, 1997

——, et al , eds. *Postcolonial Criticism*. London· Longman, 1997

Morrison, Toni. *The Song of Solomon* London. Chatto & Windus, 1977.

——. *Beloved* London Chatto & Windus, 1989.

——. *Jazz*. London Chatto & Windus, 1992.

——. 'The Site of Memory'. *Inventing the Truth. The Art and Craft of Memoir* Ed William Zinsser Boston Houghton-Mifflin, 1995, 83–102.

Morton, Stephen. 'Postcolonialism and Spectrality· Political Deferral and Ethical Singularity in the Writings of Gayatri Chakravorty Spivak'. *Interventions* 1.4 (1999), 605–620

Mudimbe, V.Y *The Invention of Africa Gnosis, Philosophy and the Order of Knowledge* Bloomington University of Indiana Press, 1988.

Murray, Stuart *Not on Any Map Essays on Postcoloniality and Cultural Nationalism*. Exeter University of Exeter Press, 1997

Myrsiades, Kostas, and Jerry McGuire. *Order and Partialities Theory, Pedagogy and the 'Postcolonial'*. Albany. SUNY Press, 1995.

Naipaul, V.S. *A House for Mr. Biswas* [1961] NY: Vintage, 1984.

—— *The Enigma of Arrival* NY. Knopf, 1987.

Nancy, Jean-Luc *Une Pensée finie*. Paris. Galilée, 1990

—— *Etre singulier pluriel*. Paris Galilée, 1996.

Natoli, Joseph, and Linda Hutcheon, eds. *A Postmodern Reader*. Albany SUNY Press, 1993.

Nederveen Pieterse, Jan 'Globalisation as Hybridisation' *Global Modernities*. Ed Featherstone et al 1995, 45–68.

——, and Bhikhu Parekh. *The Decolonization of Imagination. Culture, Knowledge, and Power* London: Zed Books, 1995

Newman, Judie *The Balistic Bard. Postcolonial Fictions* London Arnold, 1995.

Norris, Christopher *What's Wrong with Postmodernism*, Baltimore Johns Hopkins University Press, 1990

——. *The Truth About Postmodernism*. Oxford. Blackwell, 1993

—— *Reclaiming Truth Contribution to a Critique of Cultural Relativism* London Lawrence and Wishart, 1996.

—— *Against Relativism Philosophy of Science, Deconstruction and Critical Theory*. Oxford Blackwell, 1997.

Ngugi wa Thiong'o *Decolonizing the Mind The Politics of Language in African Literature*. London· James Currey, 1986

Olaniyan, Tejumola 'On Post-Colonial Discourse' *Callaloo* 16.4 (Autumn 1993), 743–749

Olson, Gary A and Lynn Worsham, eds *Race, Rhetoric, and the Postcolonial*. Albany. SUNY Press, 1999

O'Neill, John *The Poverty of Postmodernism* London Routledge, 1995

Osborne, Peter, ed *A Critical Sense. Interviews with Intellectuals* London Routledge, 1996

Pagden, Anthony 'The Effacement of Difference· Colonialism and the Origins of Nationalism in Diderot and Herder'. *After Colonialism.* Ed. Prakash. 1995

Parry, Benita. 'Problems in Current Theories of Colonial Discourse'. *Oxford Literary Review* 9 (1987), 27–58

—— 'Resistance Theory/Theorising Resistance, or Two Cheers for Nativism' [1994] *Contemporary Postcolonial Theory A Reader* Ed Mongia. 84–109

——. 'Signs of our Times. Discussion of Homi Bhabha's *Location of Culture*'. *Third Text* 28–29 (1994), 1–24

——. 'The Postcolonial Conceptual Category or Chimera?' *The Yearbook of English Studies* 27 (1997), 3–21.

——. 'Liberation Movements Memories of the Future'. *Interventions* 1.1 (1998–1999), 45–51.

Pathak, Zakia, Saswati Sengupta, and Sharmila Purkayastha 'The Prisonhouse of Orientalism.' *Textual Practice* 5 2 (Summer 1991), 195–218.

Pease, Donald E 'National Identities, Postmodern Artifacts, and Postnational Narratives'. *boundary 2* 19.1 (Spring 1992), 1–13.

Pinker, Steven. *The Language Instinct The New Science of Language and Mind* London Allen Lane, 1994.

—— *How the Mind Works* NY. Norton, 1997.

Plotkin, Henry. *Evolution in Mind. An Introduction to Evolutionary Psychology.* London. Allen Lane, 1997

Porter, Dennis 'Orientalism and its Problems'. *The Politics of Theory, Proceedings of the Essex Sociology of Literature Conference.* Ed Francis Barker et al. Colchester. University of Essex Press, 1983. 179–193.

Poulantzas, Nicos *Classes in Contemporary Capitalism.* London. NLB, 1975

Poulet, Georges *Métamorphoses du cercle* [1961]. Paris: Garnier Flammarion, 1979

Prakash, Gyan 'Writing Post-Orientalist Histories of the Third World'. *Comparative Studies in Society and History* 32:2 (1990), 383–408.

—— *After Colonialism Imperial Histories and Postcolonial Displacements.* Princeton. Princeton University Press, 1995

Radhakrishnan, R 'Postcoloniality and the Boundaries of Identity' *Callaloo* 16.4 (Autumn 1993), 750–771

Rajan, Gita, and Radhika Mohanram. *Postcolonial Discourse and Changing Cultural Contexts Theory and Criticism* Westport. Greenwood, 1995.

Ray, Sangeeta. 'Shifting Subjects Shifting Ground, The Names and Spaces of the Post-Colonial' *Hypatia* 7.2 (Spring 1992), 188–201

Renaut, Alain *L'Ere de l'individu* Paris. Gallimard, 1989.

—— *L'Individu.* Paris Hatier, 1995

Robertson, Roland *Globalisation. Social Theory and Global Change.* London· Sage, 1992.

——, and Frank Lechner 'Modernisation. Globalisation, and the Problem of Culture in World Systems Theory'. *Theory, Culture and Society* 2.3 (1985), 103–118.

—— 'Glocalisation Time-Space and Homogeneity-Heterogeneity' *Global Modernities* Ed. Featherstone et al. 1995, 25–44.

Robinson, Douglas *Translation and Empire Postcolonial Theories Explained.* Manchester St Jerome, 1997.

Rorty, Richard. *Philosophy and the Mirror of Nature* Princeton Princeton University Press, 1979

——— *Contingency, Irony and Solidarity* Cambridge. Cambridge University Press, 1989

Ross, Andrew, ed *Universal Abandon?* Minneapolis. University of Minnesota Press, 1988

Rushdie, Salman. *Imaginary Homelands* Harmondsworth Penguin, 1992.

Russell, Charles *Poets, Prophets and Revolutionaries. The Literary Avant-Garde from Rimbaud through Postmodernism*. Oxford Oxford University Press, 1985.

Sabin, Margery. 'Postcolonial Individuality in Naipaul's Indian Narratives'. Talk given at the Whitney Humanities Centre, New Haven. April 1994

Said, Edward W. *Joseph Conrad and the Fiction of Autobiography*. Cambridge. Harvard University Press, 1966.

——— *Beginnings Intention and Method* [1975]. NY. Columbia University Press, 1984

———. 'The Problem of Textuality' *Critical Inquiry* (Summer 1978), 706–725.

——— *Orientalism* [1978] Harmondsworth. Penguin, 1995.

——— *The Question of Palestine* [1979]. NY. Vintage, 1992.

———. *Covering Islam How the Media and the Experts Determine How We See the Rest of the World* NY Pantheon, 1981.

——— 'Opponents, Audiences, Constituencies and Community' [1982]. *The Anti-Aesthetic* Ed Foster 1983 135–159.

———. *The World, The Text and the Critic.* Cambridge. Harvard University Press, 1983

——— 'The Mind in Winter Reflections on Life in Exile' *Harper's Magazine* 269 (September 1984), 49–55.

——— 'Orientalism Reconsidered'. *Cultural Critique* 1 (1985), 89–107.

———. 'Foucault and the Imagination of Power' *Foucault. A Critical Reader* Ed. David Hoy Oxford. Blackwell, 1986 149–155.

——— *After the Last Sky. Palestinian Lives* NY. Pantheon, 1986

——— Interview with Salusinszky [1987] *Criticism in Society.* Ed. Imre Salusinszky. NY. Methuen, 1987 122–148

———. 'Identity, Negation and Violence' *New Left Review* 171 (September 1988), 46–60

———, and Christopher Hitchens, ed *Blaming the Victims. Spurious Scholarship and the Palestine Question* London Verso, 1988

———. 'Representing the Colonized. Anthropology's Interlocutors' *Critical Inquiry* 15 2 (Winter 1989), 205–225

———. 'Media, Margins and Modernity. Raymond Williams and Edward Said' Appendix to Williams, Raymond, *The Politics of Modernism Against the New Conformists* London. Verso, 1989. 177–197

——— Interview with Jennifer Wicke and Michael Sprinker [1989]. *Said A Critical Reader* Ed Sprinker. 1992.

——— 'Third World Intellectuals and Metropolitan Culture'. *Raritan* 9 3 (Winter 1990), 27–51

——— 'Criticism Culture, and Performance An Interview with Edward Said' *Performing Arts Journal* 37 (January 1991), 21–43

——— 'Identity, Authority, and Freedom. The Potentate and the Traveler' [1991] *boundary 2* 21 3 (Autumn 1994), 1–19.

——— *Musical Elaborations*. London Chatto & Windus, 1991.

——— 'Interview with *Radical Philosophy: Orientalism* and After' [1992]. *A Critical Sense.* Ed Osborne 65–86.

——— Interview with Joseph A. Buttigieg and Paul A Bové, *boundary 2* 20 1 (Spring 1993), 1–24.

——— 'Nationalism, Human Rights, and Interpretation' *Freedom and Interpretation* Ed. Barbara Johnson NY Basic Books, 1993 176–205

——. *Culture and Imperialism*. London· Chatto & Windus, 1993.

—— 'Gods That Always Fail'. *Raritan* 13.4 (Spring 1994), 1–15

——. *Representations of the Intellectual* London. Vintage, 1994.

——. *The Pen and the Sword· Conversations with David Barsamian*. Edinburgh: AK Press, 1994.

—— *The Politics of Dispossession. The Struggle for Palestinian Self-Determination 1969–1994*. London· Vintage, 1995

——. 'Cry Palestine' *New Statesman & Society* (10 November 1995), 25–28.

——. *Peace and Its Discontents. Gaza–Jericho 1993–1995* London. Vintage, 1995.

——. 'A Powerless People'. *The Guardian* [London] 25 April 1996, 15.

—— 'Fury of the Dispossessed'. *Observer* 29 September 1996, 23.

—— 'From Silence to Sound and Back Again· Music, Literature, and History' *Raritan* 17·2 (Autumn 1997), 1–21

—— 'Israel–Palestine. A Third Way' *Le Monde diplomatique* September 1998, 6–7

Saint-Sernin, Bernard. *La Raison au vingtième siècle*. Paris. Seuil, 1995.

San Juan Jr, Epifanio, *Beyond Postcolonial Theory*. London. Macmillan, 1998

Sartre, Jean-Paul *Transcendence de l'ego* [1937] Ed Sylvie Le Bon. Paris. Vrin, 1988. Trans. Forrest Williams and Robert Kirkpatrick. NY. Noonday Press, 1957.

——. *L'Etre et le néant*. Paris. Gallimard, 1943. Trans. Hazel Barnes NY Philosophical Library, 1956.

—— *L'Existentialisme est un humanisme*. Paris: Gallimard, 'Folio', 1996. Trans Philip Mairet London. Methuen, 1948

—— *Critique de la raison dialectique* [1960] Vol. 1 *Théorie des ensembles pratiques*. Ed. Arlette Elkaim-Sartre Paris Gallimard, 1985. Trans. Allan Sheridan-Smith London. New Left Books, 1976.

——. *Critique de la raison dialectique* Vol 2 [inachevé] *L'Intelligibilité de l'histoire* Ed. Arlette Elkaim-Sartre Paris Gallimard, 1985.

——. *Qu'est-ce que la littérature?* Paris: Gallimard, 'Idées', 1985

Schnapper, Dominique. *La Communauté des citoyens Sur l'idée moderne de nation*. Paris Gallimard, 1994

Scholem, Gershom G. *Major Trends in Jewish Mysticism* [1941] NY. Schocken Books, 1961.

Schopenhauer, Arthur *The World as Will and Representation*. Trans. E.J.F. Payne. 2 vols NY. Dover, 1966.

Schwarz, Henry, and Sangeeta Ray, eds. *A Companion to Postcolonial Studies* Oxford Blackwell, 2000.

Seshadri-Crooks, Kalpana 'At the Margins of Postcolonial Studies'. *Ariel* 26.3 (July 1995), 47–71

Shohat, Ella 'Notes on the "Post-Colonial" [1993] *Contemporary Postcolonial Theory A Reader* Ed. Mongia. 321–334.

——, and Robert Stam *Unthinking Eurocentrism* London Routledge, 1994.

Siebers, Tobin, ed *Heterotopia. Postmodern Utopia and the Body Politic* (Ann Arbor University of Michigan Press, 1994

Sklair, Leslie *Sociology of the Global System*. London. Harvester Wheatsheaf, 1991.

Slemon, Stephen. 'Post-Colonial Critical Theories' *New Literatures*. Ed King 178–197

——. 'Introductory Note Postcolonialism and its Discontents'. *Ariel* 26.1 (January 1995)

Smart, Barry *Postmodernity*. London Routledge, 1993

Smith, Anthony N *Theories of Nationalism* [1971]. NY. Holmes and Meier, 1983

—— *The Ethnic Origins of Nations*. Oxford. Blackwell, 1986.

——. 'Towards a Global Culture?'. *Theory, Culture and Society* 7 2–3 (June 1990).

Smith, Neil. *Uneven Development. Nature, Capital, and the Production of Space*. Oxford. Blackwell, 1984

Sontag, Susan *Styles of Radical Will*. NY Straus and Giroux, 1969.

Spillers, Hortense, ed. *Comparative American Identities Race, Sex and Nationality in the Modern Text*. London. Routledge, 1991.

Spiro, Melford 'Cultural Relativism and the Future of Anthropology' *Cultural Anthropology* 1 (1986), 259–286

Spivak, Gayatri Chakravorty *In Other Worlds Essays in Cultural Politics*. London. Routledge, 1988.

——. 'Can the Subaltern Speak?' Ed. Cary Nelson and Lawrence Grossberg, *Marxism and the Interpretation of Culture*. Urbana. University of Illinois Press, 1988. 271–313.

—— *The Post-Colonial Critic* London. Routledge, 1990

—— 'Spivak on the Politics of the Subaltern'. *Socialist Review* 20.3 (1990), 85–97

——. 'Poststructuralism, Marginality, Postcoloniality, and Value' [1990] *Contemporary Postcolonial Theory*. Ed Mongia. 198–222.

——. 'Interview with Afsaneh Najmabadi'. *Social Text* 28 (1991), 122–134.

—— 'Reflections on Cultural Studies in the Post-Colonial Conjuncture' *Critical Studies* 3.1–2 (Spring 1991), 63–78.

——. 'Neocolonialism and the Secret Agent of Knowledge' [Interview] *Oxford Literary Review* 13.1–2, (1991), 220–251.

——. 'Acting bits/identity talk'. *Critical Inquiry* 18.4 (Summer 1992), 770–803.

—— 'Teaching for the Times' [1992]. *Decolonization of Imagination*. Ed Nederveen Pieterse and Bikhu Parekh. 177–202.

——. '"What Is It For?"'. *Functions of Postcolonial Criticism'. Nineteenth Century Contexts* 18 (1992), 1–8.

—— 'Interview with Leon De Kock New Nation Writers Conference in South Africa' *Ariel* 23 3 (July 1992), 29–47

——. 'Asked to Talk About Myself' *Third Text* 19 (Summer 1992), 9–18.

——. *Outside in the Teaching Machine*. London Routledge, 1993

—— 'Interview with Sara Danius and Stefan Jonsson' *boundary 2*, 20.2 (1993), 24–51

——. 'Foundations and Cultural Studies'. *Questioning Foundations Truth/Subjectivity/Culture Continental Philosophy* Vol. 5. Ed. Hugh J Sliverman London. Routledge, 1993 153–175

—— 'Responsibility'. *boundary 2* 21.3 (Autumn 1994), 19–64.

——. 'In the New World Order' *Marxism in the Postmodern Age* Ed. Antonio Callari et al. NY Guilford Press, 1994. 89–97

——. 'Response to Jean-Luc Nancy' *Thinking Bodies*. Ed. Juliet Flower MacCannell and Laura Zakarin. Stanford. Stanford University Press, 1994. 32–51

——. 'Supplementing Marxism'. *Whither Marxism? Global Crises in the International Context* Ed Bernd Magnus and Stephen Cullenberg. London. Routledge, 1995 109–119

——, and David Plotke 'A Dialogue on Democracy'. *Socialist Review* 24.3 (Summer 1995), 1–22.

——. 'Love, Cruelty and Cultural Talks in the Hot Peace'. *Parallax* 1 (September 1995), 1–31.

——. *The Spivak Reader* Ed. Donna Landry and Gerald Maclean. London· Routledge, 1996

—— 'Diasporas Old and New. Women in a Transnational World' *Textual Practices* 10.2 (1996), 245–269.

—— 'Setting to Work (Transnational Cultural Studies)' *A Critical Sense*. Ed. Osborne. 163–178.

——. 'Attention, Postcolonialism'. *Journal of Caribbean Studies* 13· (1998), 159–170.

Sprinker, Michael, ed. *Edward Said A Critical Reader*. Oxford Blackwell, 1992

——. 'The National Question. Said, Ahmad, Jameson' *Public Culture* 6.1 (1993), 3–29

Stalin, Joseph. *Marxism and the National and Colonial Question* London. Lawrence and Wishart, 1936

Stratton, Jon. *Writing Sites: A Genealogy of the Postmodern World*. NY. Harvester, 1990.

Suleri, Sara. *The Rhetoric of British India*. Chicago Chicago University Press, 1992

—— 'Multiculturalism and its Discontents', *Profession* 93, (1993). 16–17

——. 'Woman Skin Deep Feminism and the Postcolonial Condition'. *Colonial Discourse and Post-Colonial Theory*. Ed. Williams and Chrisman 244–256.

Taylor, Charles *Sources of the Self* Cambridge. Harvard University Press, 1989

——. 'The Politics of Recognition'. *Multiculturalism. Examining the Politics of Recognition*. Ed. Amy Gutmann. Princeton. Princeton University Press, 1994 25–73

Thieme, John. *Arnold Anthology of Postcolonial Literatures* London Arnold, 1996

Thomas, Nicholas *Colonialism's Culture Anthropology, Travel and Government*. Cambridge: Polity, 1994.

Thompson, E P *The Making of the English Working Class* [1963] Harmondsworth. Penguin, 1980.

Tiffin, Chris, and Alan Lawson, eds *De-Scribing Empire Post-Colonialism and Textuality* London Routledge, 1994.

Touraine, Alain 'The Idea of Revolution'. *Theory, Culture and Society* 7.2–3 (1990), 121–141

Trivedi, Harish. 'Postcolonial or Transcolonial' *Interventions* 1·2 (1999), 269–272.

Varadharajan, Asha. *Exotic Parodies. Subjectivity in Adorno, Said and Spivak* Minneapolis University of Minnesota Press, 1995

Varsava, Jerry A. *Contingent Meanings Postmodern Fiction, Mimesis, and the Reader* Tallahassee Florida State University Press, 1990

Vattimo, Gianni. *The Transparent Society* [1989]. Trans David Webb. Cambridge Polity, 1992.

Veyne, Paul *L'Inventaire des différences*. Paris Seuil, 1976

——. *Comment on écrit l'histoire*, suivi de 'Foucault révolutionne l'histoire' Paris Seuil, 'Points', 1978

Viroli, Maurizio *For the Love of Country. An Essay on Patriotism and Nationalism*. Oxford Oxford University Press, 1995.

Voloshinov, Valentin Nikolaevich. *Marxism and the Philosophy of Language*. Trans Ladislav Matejka and I.R Titunik. Cambridge Harvard University Press, 1986

Wakefield, Neville. *Postmodernism The Twilight of the Real* London. Pluto Press, 1990

Walder, Dennis. *Post-Colonial Literatures in English History, Language, Theory*. Oxford Blackwell, 1998

Wallerstein, Immanuel. *The Modern World System* Vol. 1. NY. Academic Press, 1974

—— *Geopolitics and Geoculture Essays on the Changing World System*. Cambridge Cambridge University Press, 1991

—— 'Post-America and the Collapse of the Communisms' *Rethinking Marxism* 5 1 (1992), 93–100

——. 'Revolution as Strategy and Tactics of Transformation' *Marxism in the Postmodern Age*. Ed Callari et al 225–232

——, and Terence K Hopkins, eds *The Age of Transition Trajectory of the World System 1945–2025* London Zed, 1996.

Warren, Bill *Imperialism, Pioneer of Capitalism*. London. New Left Books, 1980

Waugh, Patricia, ed. *Postmodernism, A Reader*. London Edward Arnold, 1992

West, Cornel. *Keeping Faith, Philosophy and Race in America*. London. Routledge, 1993.

—— *Prophetic Reflections. Notes on Race and Power in America*. Monroe ME. Common Courage Press, 1993.

White, Jonathan, ed. *Recasting the World Writing After Colonialism* Baltimore Johns Hopkins University Press, 1993.

White, Stephen. *Political Theory and Postmodernism*. Cambridge. Cambridge University Press, 1991.

Wierzbicka, Anna *Emotions Across Languages and Cultures. Diversity and Universals* Cambridge. Cambridge University Press, 1999.

——, and Cliff Goddard, eds *Semantic and Lexical Universals. Theory and Empirical Findings* Amsterdam. J. Benjamins, 1994

—— *Semantics, Culture, and Cognition Universal Human Concepts in Culture-Specific Configurations*. Oxford Oxford University Press, 1992.

Wihl, Gary *The Contingency of Meaning. Pragmatism, Expressivism and Deconstruction* New Haven Yale University Press, 1994.

Williams, Patrick, and Laura Chrisman, eds *Colonial Discourse and Post-Colonial Theory A Reader* NY Harvester Wheatsheaf, 1993.

Wilmsen, Edwin N and Patrick McAllister, eds *The Politics of Difference* Chicago. University of Chicago Press, 1996

Wiredu, Kwasi *Cultural Universals and Particulars. An African Perspective*. Bloomington. Indiana University Press, 1996

Wood, Ellen Meiksins *The Retreat from Class*. London. Verso, 1986

——. *The Pristine Culture of Capitalism* London. Verso, 1991

—— 'From Opportunity to Imperative The History of the Market' *Monthly Review* 46 (1994), 14–40

Young, Robert. *White Mythologies Writing History and the West*. London Routledge, 1990

—— *Colonial Desire Hybridity in Theory, Culture and Race* London Routledge, 1995.

——. *Torn Halves Political Conflict in Literary and Cultural Theory* Manchester. Manchester University Press, 1996

—— 'Ideologies of the Postcolonial'. *Interventions* 1.1 (1998–1999), 4–8

Zadworna-Fjellestad, Danuta, and Lennart Bjork, eds *Criticism in the Twilight Zone Postmodern Perspective on Literature and Politics* Stockholm Almquist & Wiksell, 1990

Zavarzadeh, Mas'ud, et al , eds *Post-Ality Marxism and Postmodernism (Transformation 1)* Washington DC. Maisonneuve Press, 1995

Zinsser, William, ed. *Inventing the Truth. The Art and Craft of Memoir* Boston, Houghton-Mifflin, 1987

Žižek, Slavoj, *The Plague of Fantasies* London Verso, 1997

—— *The Ticklish Subject. The Absent Centre of Political Ontology* London Verso, 1999.

Župančič, Alenka. *The Ethics of the Real Kant, Lacan*. London· Verso, 2000.

Buddhism

Agehananda Bharati, Swami *The Tantric Tradition* London. Rider, 1965.

Burtt, E A. *The Teachings of the Compassionate Buddha* NY Mentor Books, 1955.

Chang, Garma C.C. *The Buddhist Teaching of Totality*. University Park Pennsylvania State University Press, 1974

Conze, Edward *Buddhism, Its Essence and Development*. NY Harper Torchbooks, 1959

——, *Buddhism, Its Essence and Development* NY· Harper Torchbooks, 1959

——, ed. *Buddhist Scriptures* Baltimore. Penguin, 1973

Dasgupta, Shashi Bhushan. *An Introduction to Tantric Buddhism.* Calcutta University of Calcutta, 1950.

De Bary, William Theodore, ed. *The Buddhist Tradition* [selected texts]. NY Modern Library, 1969.

The Dhammapada Trans. and ed. S. Radakrishnan. Oxford. Oxford University Press [Indian Branch], 1950.

The Diamond Sutra, The Heart Sutra. Trans. and ed Edward Conze, *Buddhist Wisdom Books.* NY Harper and Row, 1972.

Dumoulin, Heinrich *Zen Buddhism, A History. Volume I, India and China.* NY Macmillan, 1988

The Gateless Barrier. Trans. and ed. Robert Aitken San Francisco. North Point Press, 1990.

Govinda, Lama Angagarikaj. *Foundations of Tibetan Mysticism.* York Beach, Maine Samuel Weiser, 1969.

Griffiths, Paul J. *On Being Buddha, The Classical Doctrine of Buddhahood* NY. SUNY Press, 1994.

Gyatso, Tenzin (The Fourteenth Dalai Lama). *The World of Tibetan Buddhism.* Boston Wisdom Publications, 1995.

Hamilton, Clarence H. *Buddhism. A Religion of Infinite Compassion. Selections from Buddhist Literature* NY. The Liberal Arts Press, 1952.

Hui-nêng. *The Platform Sutra of the Sixth Patriarch.* Trans. Philip B. Yampolsky. NY. Columbia University Press, 1967.

Hopkins, Jeffrey *The Tantric Distinction. An Introduction to Tibetan Buddhism* London Wisdom Books, 1984

Humphreys, Christmas. *Buddhism* Hammondsworth. Pelican, 1951.

Kalupahana, David J. *Causality. The Central Philosophy of Buddhism.* Honolulu. University of Hawaii Press, 1976.

Kapleau, Phil *The Three Pillars of Zen.* NY Anchor Books, 1989.

Lings, Martin. *What is Sufism?* Berkeley: University of California Press, 1975.

The Lotus Sutra Trans. Burton Watson. NY. Columbia University Press, 1993.

Mookerjee, Ajit, and Madhu Khanna *The Tantric Way* London. Thames and Hudson, 1977

Padmasambhava, and Jamgon Kongtrul. *The Light of Wisdom.* Trans Eric Pema Kunsang. Boston Shambhala, 1995.

Paz, Octavio. 'Eva and Prajñaparamita' *Conjunctions and Disjunctions* Trans. Helen R. Lane. NY· Viking Press, 1974.

The Perfection of Wisdom in 8,000 Lines Trans Edward Conze. Bolinas. Four Seasons, 1973.

Robinson, Richard, and Willard Johnson. *The Buddhist Religion.* Belmont: Wadsworth, 1982.

Singh, Lalan Prasad *Tantra, Its Mystic and Scientific Basis.* Delhi. Concept Publishing, 1976

Smith, Huston. 'Buddhism'. *The World's Religions.* San Fraqncisco. Harper San Francisco, 1991. 82–153

Sponberg, Alan, and Helen Hardacre, eds. *Maitreya, The Future Buddha* Cambridge. Cambridge University Press, 1988.

Stryk, Lucien, ed *World of the Buddha, A Reader* NY Doubleday, 1968.

Suzuki, Daisetz Teitaro. *Mahayana Buddhism* [1948]. London. Allen & Unwin, 1981

——. *The Zen Doctrine of No-Mind* [1949]. London. Rider and Company, 1969.

——. *Essays in Zen Buddhism* 3 vols. [1949–1953]. NY: Grove Press, 1961–1971.

Thomas, Edward J. *Early Buddhist Scriptures*. NY. AMS Press, 1935.

—— *The History of Buddhist Thought* [1931]. London· Routledge, 1955

Trungpa, Chógyam. *The Lion's Roar, An Introduction to Tantra* Boston. Shambhala, 1992.

Warren, Henry Clarke. *Buddhism in Translations*. NY. Atheneum, 1963.

The Zen Master Hakuin. *Selected Writings* Trans. and ed. Philip B. Yampolsky NY. Columbia University Press, 1971

Mystical Islam

Abd el-Kader *Ecrits spirituels* Trans. and ed. M Chodkiewicz. Paris. Seuil, 1982.

Addas, Claude *Ibn 'Arabî ou la quête du souffre rouge*. Paris: Gallimard, 1989.

Arberry, A.J. *Sufism, An Account of the Mystics of Islam*. London: Allen and Unwin, 1950

Baldick, Julian *Mystical Islam. An Introduction to Sufism*. London. Tauris, 1989.

Breton, Stanislas. *Le Voyage mystique* Paris Cerf, 1988.

Chodkiewicz, Michel. *Le Sceau des saints*. Paris. Gallimard, 1986.

Corbin, Henry. *Avicenne et le récit visionnaire* [1954]. Berg International, 1979.

—— *L'Imagination créatrice dans le soufisme d'Ibn 'Arabî* [1958]. Paris. Flammarion, 1977.

—— *Corps spirituel et terre céleste. De l'Iran mazdéen à l'Iran shî-ite* [1961] Paris Buchet-Chastel, 1979.

—— *Histoire de la philosophie islamique* [1964, 1974]. Paris Gallimard, 'Folio', 1986

——. *En Islam iranien*. 4 vols. Paris. Gallimard, 1971–1972.

—— *L'Homme de lumière dans le soufisme iranien*. Paris Editions Présence, 1971.

——. *Philosophie iranienne et philosophie comparée* [1977] Paris Buchet-Chastel, 1985

—— *Temple et contemplation*. Paris Flammarion, 1981

——. *L'Homme et son ange* Paris· Fayard, 1983

De Certeau, Michel. *La Fable mystique* Paris. Gallimard, 1982

Eliade, Mircea. 'Expériences de la lumière mystique' *Méphistocles et l'androgyne* [1962] Paris. Gallimard, 'Folio', 1995

Ghazâli. *Le Tabernacle des lumières* Trans Roger de Ladrière Paris. Seuil, 1981.

Ibn al-'Arabi *La Profession de la foi*. Paris. Sindbad, 1985

——. *Traité de l'Amour*. Paris. Albin Michel, 1986

—— *The Meccan Illuminations*. Ed. Michel Chodkiewicz. Paris. Sindbad, 1988

Jambet, Christian *La Logique des Orientaux Henry Corbin et la science des formes*. Paris. Seuil, 1983.

—— *La Grande Resurrection d'Alamût*. Lagrasse. Verdier, 1990.

Jenny, Laurent. *La Parole singulière* Paris· Belin, 1990.

Michel, Jacqueline. *Une mise en récit du silence*. Paris. Corti, 1986

Nicholson, Reynold A *The Mystics of Islam* [1914]. NY. Shocken, 1975.

—— *Studies in Islamic Mysticism* [1921]. Cambridge Cambridge University Press, 1978.

Riffard, Pierre A. *L'Esotérisme*. Paris Laffont, 1990.

Rûmî, Djalâl-ud-Dîn. *Le Livre du dedans* Ed. and trans. Eva de Vitray-Meyerovitch. Paris. Sindbad, 1989.

——. *Mathnawî la quête de l'absolu* Ed and trans Vitray-Meyerovitch. Monaco: Du Rocher, 1990

Schimmel, Annemarie *Mystical Dimensions of Islam*. Chapel Hill. University of North Carolina Press, 1975.

Shah, Idries. *The Sufis* [1964]. NY. Anchor Books, 1971
—— *Les Soufis et l'ésotérisme* Paris. Payot, 1984
al-Suhrawardi, Shihâboddîn Yahya. *L'Archange empourpré. Quinze traités et récits mystiques.* Ed and trans Henry Corbin. Paris Fayard, 1976
—— *Le Livre de la sagesse orientale.* Ed and trans Henry Corbin Intr Christian Jambet Lagrasse Verdier, 1986
Vitray-Meyerovitch, Eva de 'La poétique de l'Islam'. *La Traversée des signes.* Ed Julia Kristeva Paris Seuil, 1975. 195–208
——. *Rûmî et le soufisme* Paris Seuil, 1977.
——. *Anthologie de soufisme* [1978] Paris Albin Michel, 1995

CHAPTER 2 Glissant

André, Jacques. *Caraïbales*. Paris Editions Caribéenes, 1981
Arnold, A. James. 'Poétique forcée et identité dans la littérature des Antilles francophones' *L'Heritage de Caliban*. Ed. Condé, 19–27.
——. Review of *Tout-monde* WLT 69.1 (1995), 205–206.
Baudot, Alain *Bibliographie annotée d'Edouard Glissant* Toronto. GREF, 1993
—— 'Edouard Glissant A Poet in Search of his Landscape' WLT 63 4 (1989), 583–588
Britton, Celia *Edouard Glissant and Postcolonial Theory. Strategies of Language and Resistance* Charlottesville University Press of Virginia, 1999
Burton, Richard 'Comment peut-on être Martiniquais?' *Modern Language Review* 79 2 (1984), 301–312
Cailler, Bernadette *Conquérants de la nuit nue. Edouard Glissant et l'H(h)istoire antillaise.* Tubingen. Gunter Narr, 1988.
—— 'Edouard Glissant. A Creative Critic' WLT 63 4 (1989), 589–592.
—— 'Creolization vs Francophonie'. *L'Heritage de Caliban*. Ed. Condé, 49–62.
Case, Frederick Ivor *The Crisis of Identity Studies in the Martiniquan and Guadeloupan Novel.* Sherbrooke Naaman, 1985
——. 'Edouard Glissant and the Poetics of Cultural Marginalization'. WLT 63 4 (1989), 593–598
Clark, Beatrice Stith 'IME Revisited Lectures by Edouard Glissant on Sociocultural Realities in the Francophone Antilles' *World Literature Today* 63 4 (Autumn 1989), 599–605.
Condé, Maryse. 'Le Roman antillais' *Notre Librairie* 49 (July–September 1979). 63–71
——, ed *L'Heritage de Caliban*. Pointe à Pitre Jasor, 1992.
Corbin, Henry *Clarières du temps* Caracas La Ceiba, 1992
Damato, Diva 'Edouard Glissant et le manifeste *Eloge de la créolité*' HEG 245–254.
Dash, J Michael 'Introduction' to Glissant, *Caribbean Discourse* Trans Dash Charlottesville. University of Virginia Press. 1989, xi–xlv.
—— 'Writing the Body Edouard Glissant's Poetics of Re-membering'. WLT 63 4 (1989), 609–612.
——. *Edouard Glissant* Cambridge University of Cambridge Press, 1995
Degras, Priska 'Name of the Fathers. History of the Name. Odono as Memory'. WLT 63.4 (1989), 613–619.
Gallagher, Mary. 'La Poétique de la diversité dans les essais d'Edouard Glissant' HEG 27–36.
Gikandi, Simon *Writing in Limbo. Modernism and Caribbean Literature* Ithaca Cornell University Press, 1992.
Joubert, Jean-Louis. ed *Littérature francophone* Paris Nathan, 1992

Marinho, Christina de 'L'Intention poétique pour une poétyique de l'intention' HEG 49–54

Mayaux, Cathérine 'La Structure romanesque de *Mahagony*'. HEG 349–363.

Melas, Natalie 'Versions of Incommensurability' WLT 69 2 (1995), 275–280.

Miller, Elinor 'Narrative Techniques in Edouard Glissant's *Malemort*' *French Review* 53 2 (1979), 224–231.

Ormerod, Beverley. *Introduction to the French Caribbean Novel*. London Heinemann, 1985

Pied, Henri 'Eloge de la créolité', *Antilla* 336 (5 June 1989)

Praeger, Michele. 'Edouard Glissant Towards a Literature of Orality'. *Callaloo* 15.1 (1992)

Prigogine, Ilya, and Isabelle Stenghers. *La Nouvelle Alliance. métamorphose de la science*. Paris Gallimard, 1979.

Radford, Daniel. *Edouard Glissant*. Paris Seghers, 1981

Roget, Wilbert J 'Land and Myth in the Writings of Edouard Glissant' WLT 63 4 (1989), 626–631

Rosario Pontes, Maria de 'Edouard Glissant une poétique en quête d'une hiérophanie' HEG. 67–80

Webb, Barbara *Myth and History in Caribbean Fiction* Amherst. University of Massachusetts Press, 1992

Wynter, Sylvia. 'Beyond the Word of Man Glissant and the New Discourse of the Antilles'. WLT 63.4 (1989). 637–647.

CHAPTER 3 Johnson

Baker, Houston A., Jr *Long Black Song*. Charlottesville. University of Virginia Press, 1972

—— *Singers of Daybreak Studies in Black American Literature* Washington Howard University Press, 1974

——. *The Journey Back Issues in Black Literature and Criticism*. Chicago. University of Chicago Press, 1980

——. *Blues, Ideology and the African-American literature A Vernacular Theory* Chicago University of Chicago Press, 1984

—— *Modernism and the Harlem Renaissance* Chicago. University of Chicago Press, 1987

—— *Workings of the Spirit*. Chicago. University of Chicago Press, 1991.

—— *Black Studies. Rap and the Academy*. Chicago University of Chicago Press, 1993

——, and Patricia Redmond, eds. *Afro-American Literary Study in the 1990s* Chicago University of Chicago Press, 1989.

Benesch, Klaus. *The Threat of History. Geschichte und Erzahlung im afro-amerikanischen Roman der Gegenwart* Essen Die Blaue Eule, 1990

——. 'Charles Johnson' Ed Wolfgang Karrer and Barbara Puschmann-Nalenz *The African-American Short Story 1970–1990* Trier Wissenschaftlicher Verlag Trier, 1993. 169–179.

Campbell, Jane *Mythic Black Fiction The Transformation of History* Knoxville University of Tennessee Press, 1986

Crouch, Stanley 'Charles Johnson Free at Last!' *The Village Voice* 27.19 (19 July 1983)

Ellison, Ralph *Invisible Man* NY. Vintage, 1952

—— *Shadow and Act* NY New American Library, 1966.

Fischer, Philip, ed *The New American Studies* Berkeley, University of California Press, 1991

Gates, Henry Louis, Jr *Figures in Black. Words, Signs, and the 'Racial' Self*. Oxford. Oxford University Press, 1987.

—— *The Signifying Monkey. A Theory of African-American Literary Criticism* Oxford. Oxford University Press, 1988.

——. *Loose Canons Notes on the Culture Wars* Oxford. Oxford University Press, 1992

Girard, René. *Mensonge romantique et vérité romanesque*. Paris. Grasset, 1961

Hartman, Geoffrey. *Criticism in the Wilderness The Study of Literature Today*. New Haven Yale University Press, 1980

Henderson, Stephen. *Understanding the New Black Poetry, Black Speech and Black Music as Poetic References*. NY William Morrow, 1973.

Little, Jonathan 'Charles Johnson's Revolutionary Ox-Herding Tale'. *Studies in American Fiction* 19.2 (1991). 141–151

May, H., ed. *Contemporary Authors* 116. Detroit Care Research Company, 1986

Phillips, J.J. review of *The Sorcerer's Apprentice Los Angeles Times Book Review*, 30 March 1986.

Rushdy, Ashraf H.A '"The Phenomenology of the Allmuseri" Charles Johnson and the Subject of the Narrative of Slavery,' *African-American Review* 26.3 (1992), 373–394.

Stepto, Robert. 'After Modernism, After Hibernation. Michael Harper, Robert Hayden, and Jay Wright'. *Chant of Saints* Ed Michael S Harper and Robert Stepto. Urbana. University of Illinois Press, 1979. 470–486.

Weisenburger, Steven 'In-Between', *Callaloo* 7.1 (1984), 153–156

CHAPTER 4 **Dib**

Other works by Dib

Au Café, nouvelles Paris Gallimard, 1956.

Ombre gardienne, poèmes Paris. Gallimard, 1961

Le Talisman, nouvelles Paris Seuil, 1964.

Formulaires, poèmes. Paris. Seuil, 1970.

Omneros, poèmes Paris. Seuil, 1975

Feu beau feu, poèmes Paris Seuil, 1979.

Mille hourras pour une gueuse, théâtre Paris Seuil, 1980.

O vive, poèmes Paris Sindbad, 1989.

La Nuit sauvage, nouvelles. Paris Albin Michel, 1995.

L'Aube Ismael, poèmes. Paris. Editions Tassili, 1996

Interviews with Dib

(partial list. most interview references in the chapter were taken from a file of photocopies held at University of Paris Nord XIII)

L'Effort algérien, 19 December 1952

Les Nouvelles littéraires, 22 October 1953.

Témoignage chrétien, 7 February 1958

Les Nouvelles littéraires, 12 October 1960

L'Humanité, 31 January 1963.

Combat, 7 February 1963.

Les Lettres françaises, 7 February 1963

Arts, 6 November 1963

Le Figaro littéraire, 4 June 1964

Afrique action, 13 March 1967
Les Lettres françaises, 20 March 1968.
La Quinzaine littéraire, 30 April 1968.
L'Afrique littéraire et artistique, no. 18, August, 1971
Coopérateurs de France, 11 August 1973
Les Nouvelles littéraires, 5 February 1976.
Celfan review 2.2 (1983), 20–25.
Dernières nouvelles d'Alsace, 263, 8 November 1992.

Secondary works

Abdel-Jaouad, Hedi 'Review of *Neiges de marbre*' *World Literature Today* 65.4 (Autumn 1991), 750–751
Abu-Haidar, Farida 'Mellowing Protest *Le Sommeil d'Eve* de Mohammed Dib and *L'Honneur de la tribu* de Rachid Mimouni'. *Third World Quarterly* 12.2 (1990), 147–149
Adjil, Bachir *Espace et écriture chez Mohammed Dib La trilogie nordique*, Preface by Denise Brahimi Paris. Harmattan, 1995
Afnan, Soheil Muhsin *Avicenna. His Life and Works*. London. Allen & Unwin, 1958.
Arnaud, Jacqueline *La Littérature maghrébine de langue française* Vol. 1. Paris Publisud, 1986. 161–247
At-Tabyine (Alger) 4 (1992), special issue on Dib.
Bachelard, Gaston *L'Eau et les rêves essai sur l'imagination de la matière* Paris. Corti, 1960.
Badiou, Alain. *Beckett L'Incrévable Désir*. Paris Hachette, 1995
Bamia, Aida A 'Review of *Who Remembers the Sea*' *The Middle East Journal* 41 (Winter 1987), 118–119
Bekri, Tahar 'Une Lecture de la trilogie nordique de Mohammed Dib'. *Littérature de Tunisie et du Maghreb* Paris. L'Harmattan, 1994
Belhadj-Kacem, Nourreddine *Le Thème de la dépossession dans la 'trilogie' de Mohammed Dib*. Alger. Entreprise Nationale du Livre, 1983
Belkaid-Khadda, Naget *Le Discours romanesque de Mohammed Dib*. Alger: OPU , 1983
Bonn, Charles. *La Littérature algérienne de langue française et ses lectures. Imaginaire et discours d'idées*. Sherbrooke Naaman, 1974.
——, ed *Europe* 567–568 (July 1976), special issue on *Littérature algérienne*
—— *Le Roman algérien de langue française*. Paris. L'Harmattan, 1985.
—— *Lecture présente de Mohammed Dib* Alger Entreprise nationale du livre, 1988
—— *Psychanalyse et texte littéraire au Maghreb*, 1991
——, ed *Littératures des immigrations* 2 vols. Paris. L'Harmattan, 1995.
Bouamrane, Chikh, and Louis Gardet *Panorama de la pensée islamique* Paris· Sindbad, 1984.
Bouzar, Wadi *Lectures maghrébines* Alger. OPU, 1984
Cadi, Meriem 'Mohammed Dib. un romancier qui dérange', *Kalim* 6, 39–48
CELFAN Review (Temple University, Philadelphia) 2.2 (1983), special issue on Dib
Chikhi, Beïda *Problématique de l'écriture dans l'oeuvre romanesque de Mohammed Dib* Alger. OPU, 1989
——. 'Le Texte maghrébin entre trace et effacement'. *Quand le roman maghrébin s'interroge sur son écriture* (Actes du colloque de Kénitra, April 1992) Kénitra Publications de la faculté des lettres (1994), 19–30.
Correspondances (Tunis) 21 (1957), special issue on Dib
Daninos, Guy· *Les Nouvelles tendances du roman algérien de langue française* Sher-

brooke. Naaman, 1983.

——. *Dieu en Barbarie de Mohammed Dib ou la recherche d'un nouvel humanisme*. Sherbrooke Naaman, 1985.

Djaider, Mireille, and Naget Khadda 'Pour une étude du processus d'individuation du roman algérien de langue française Feraoun, Dib, Kateb. témoins et/ou écrivains?' *Littérature et poésie algérienne* Alger OPU, 1983.

Déjeux, Jean. 'Regards sur la littérature maghrébine d'expression française', *Cahiers Nord-Africains*, 61 (1957), special issue.

——. *Littérature maghrébine de langue française* Sherbrooke. Naaman. 1973.

—— 'A l'origine de *L'Incendie* de Mohmmed Dib'. *Présence francophone* (Sherbrook, Quebec) 10 (Spring 1975), 3–8

——. *La Littérature algérienne contemporaine* [1975]. Paris. PUF, 'Que sais-je?', 1979

——. *Mohammed Dib, Ecrivain algérien* Sherbrooke. Naaman, 1977.

——. *Situation de la littérature maghrébine de langue française*. Alger OPU, 1982

——. *Le Sentiment religieux dans la littérature maghrébine de langue française*. Paris. L'Harmattan, 1986.

—— *Mohammed Dib* Philadelphia. CELFAN Editions, 1987

——. 'La Passion de l'homme les derniers romans de Mohammed Dib' Ed G. Toso-Rodinis and M El Houssi. *Le Banquet maghrébin*. Rome. Bulzoni, 1991. 83–123.

—— *La Littérature maghrébine d'expression française* Paris. PUF, 1992

——. *Maghreb, Littératures de langue française*. Paris Arcantère, 1993

—— 'Exile et royaume dans la poésie de Mohammed Dib' *Cahier d'études maghrébines* (Cologne) 5 (1993), 12–22

Deleuze, Gilles. 'L'Epuisé' in Beckett, Samuel. *Quad et autres pièces pour la télévision* Paris. Minuit. 1992.

El Nouty, Hassan 'Qui se souvient de la mer de Mohammed Dib'. *Présence francophone* 2 (spring 1971), 142–152

Fakhry, Majid *History of Islamic Philosophy* London Longman, 1983

Feraoun, Mouloud *Journal 1955–1962* Paris. Gallimard, 1962

Fogel, Jean-François and Daniel Rondeau, eds. *Pourquoi écrivez vous? 400 écrivains répondent* Paris. Libération. 1988

Ghani, Merad *La Littérature algérienne d'expression française* Paris. Oswald, 1976.

Henry, Michel *L'Essence de la manifestation*. Paris. PUF, 1990.

Itinéraires et contacts de cultures 10–11, *Littératures maghrébines, Colloque Jacqueline Arnaud*. 2 vols. Paris. Université de Paris-Nord/L'Harmattan, 1989–1990.

—— 20–21 (summer 1996). special issue on Mohammed Dib.

Jambet, Christian, ed *Henry Corbin, Cahiers de l'Herne* Paris Herne, 1981.

Kalim, no 6, *Hommage a Mohammed Dib* Ed. Jacqueline Arnaud and Naget Khadda Alger Office des publications universitaires, 1985

Khadda, Naget *L'Oeuvre romanesque de Mohammed Dib Propositions pour l'analyse de deux romans* Alger OPU, 1983

—— *Mohammed Dib romancier, esquisse d'un itinéraire* Alger OPU, 1986

——. 'Les Terrasses d'Orsol quête mystique du sens et l'écriture de la modernité' *Ecrivains maghrébins et modernité*. Ed Khadda Paris. L'Harmattan, 1994 87–99

——. 'Gide et Dib' *Bulletin de l'Association des amis d'André Gide* 102 (April, 1994). 203–217.

—— 'La Maladie mentale comme medium de la parole interdite dans l'oeuvre romanesque de Mohammed Dib'. *Littérature et maladie en Afrique* Ed Jacqueline Bardolph. Paris. L'Harmattan, 1994. 189–202.

Khatibi, Abdelkebir. *Le Roman maghrébin*. Paris. Maspéro, 1968

———. *La Blessure du nom propre.* Parıs. Denoel, 1974
———. *Le Livre du sang.* Paris. Gallimard, 1979
——— *Maghreb pluriel.* Paris Denoel, 1983.
Lippert, Anne 'Review of *Le sommeil d'Eve*' *International Journal of Middle East Studies* 23.3 (August 1991), 468–470.
Madelaın, Jacques *L'Errance et l'itinéraire. Lecture du roman maghrébin de langue française.* Parıs. Sındbad, 1983.
McCarthy, Patrick *Camus, A Critical Study.* London. Hamish Hamilton, 1982.
Meddeb, Abdelwahab. 'L'Interruption généalogıque' *Esprit* 208 (January, 1995), 74–81.
Merad, Ghani *La Littérature algérienne d'expression française* Parıs. Oswald, 1976.
Sarı, Fewzıa Mostefa-Kara 'L'Ishrâq dans l'oeuvre de Mohammed Dıb'. *Revue de l'Occident musulman et de la méditerranée* 22.2 (1976), 109–118.
Sellin, Erıc 'Revıew of *Le Sommeil d'Eve*'. *World Literature Today* 65.1 (Wınter 1991), 170.
———. 'Review of *Le Désert sans détour*' *International Journal of Middle East Studies* 26 1 (February 1994), 142–143.
Vatin, Jean-Claude, ed , *Islam et politique au Maghreb.* Paris CNRS, 1981
Woodhull, Wınnıfred *Transfigurations of the Maghreb Feminism, Decolonızation, and Literatures* Mınneapolis Unıversity of Minnesota Press, 1993.
Zırem, Youcef 'Mohammed Dıb. l'homme contınuera à souffrır tandıs que les oıseaux chanteront' *Le Quotidien d'Algérie* (Alger) 230 (11 February 1992), 21

Algerian history

Ageron, Charles-Robert *Les Algériens musulmans et la France (1871–1919)* 2 vols. Parıs PUF, 1968.
——— *Histoire de l'Algérie contemporaine* [1964] Parıs. PUF, 1994 ed
Amın, Sahır *Le Maghreb moderne.* Parıs· Mınuıt, 1970
Berque, Jacques *Maghreb, Histoire et sociétés* Alger SNED, 1974
——— *L'Intérieur du Maghreb, XVe–XIXe siecles.* Parıs Gallımard, 1978.
Bourdıeu, Pıerre, and Abdelmalek Sayad. *Le Déracinement la crise de l'agriculture traditionnelle en Algérıe* Parıs Mınuit, 1964
Burgat, François *L'Islamısme au Maghreb. la voıx du Sud* Parıs Karthala, 1988
Etıenne, Bruno *L'Algérıe, Cultures et révolution* Parıs Seuıl, 1977
Fanon, Frantz *L'An V de la révolution algérienne* Paris Maspéro 1959.
———. *Pour la révolution africaine* Parıs Maspéro, 1964
Faouzı, Adel 'L'Islam, réformisme et nationalısme dans la résistance à la colonısation françaıse en Algérıe 1830–1930' *Social Compass* 3–4 (1978), 419–432
Gellner, Ernest 'The Unknown Apollo of Bıskra, The Rıse of Purıtanısm ın Algeria'. *Government and Opposıtıon* (Summer 1974), 277–310
———, and Jean-Claude Vatın, eds. *Islam et politique au Maghreb* Parıs CNRS, 1981
Julıen, Charles-André *Afrıque du nord en marche, nationalismes musulmans et souveraineté française.* Parıs Jullıard, 1972
Le Tourneau, Roger *Evolution polıtıque de l'Afrıque de Nord musulmane 1920–1961* Parıs. Armand Colin 1962
Merad, Alı. *Le Réformisme musulman en Algérıe de 1925–1940* Parıs Mouton & Co 1967
Nouschı, André *La Naissance du nationalısme algérien* Parıs Mınuıt, 1962
Samson, Henri *Laicité islamıque en algérıe* Parıs. CNRS 1983.
Vatın, Jean-Claude *L'Algérie politique, histoire et société* [1974] Parıs Presses de la Fondatıon Natıonale des Sciences Politiques, 1983

Yacono, Xavier. *Histoire de l'Algérie de la fin de la Régence turque à l'insurrection de 1954* Paris Edition de l'Atlanthrope, 1993.

CHAPTER 5 Sarduy

Other works by Sarduy

'Sobre el infierno' [review of Jean Guitton et al. *El Infierno*] *Ciclón* (Havana) 2.1 (1956), 54–56.

'El seguro' *Carteles* (Havana) 33 (18 August 1957), 66–67, 107

'Dos décimas revolucionarias' *Revolución (Nueva generación)*, 13 January 1959, 5

'El general' *Revolución (Nueva generación)*, 13 January 1959, 5

'Las bombas'. *Revolución (Nueva generación)*, 19 January 1959, 15.

'En su centro' *Revolución (Nueva generación)*, 28 January 1959, 5

'Pintura y Revolución'. *Revolución (Nueva generación)*, 31 January 1959, 14.

'El torturador, Cuento Cubano'. *Revolución (Nueva generación)*, 16 February 1959, 14

'Contra los críticos' *Revolución (Nueva generación)*, 16 February 1959, 16

'De la pintura en Cuba'. *Revolución*, 14 September 1959, 18.

'La revolución de un pintor homenaje a Victor Manuel'. *Lunes de Revolución* 29 (5 October 1959), 8–9

'¿Vuelven las figuras?', *Revolución*, 6 October 1959, 2

'Ámbitos de un pintor' [on Marcelo Pogolotti], *Revolución*, 8 October 1959, 2

'En casa de Mariano' *Lunes de Revolución* 30 (12 October 1959), 7–9

'ASTA, turismo' *Revolución*, 15 October 1959, 2.

'En el Salón Nacional de Pintura y Escultura' *Lunes de Revolución* 31 (19 October 1959), 2–4.

'La taza de café' [review of Rolando Ferrer's play, *La Taza de Café*], *Lunes de Revolución* 38 (7 December 1959), 16

'La Bienal de Venecia' *Lunes de Revolución* 65 (27 June 1960), 23

'Picasso expone' *Lunes de Revolución* 72 (15 August 1960), 16–17

'De la pintura in Cuba' *Artes Plásticas* 1 (1960–1961), 16

'Grabados/esculturas' *Artes Plásticas* 1 (1960–1961), 33–34

'La quadriennale de Roma'. *Artes Plásticas* 2 1 (1961), three unnumbered pages

'Peintres et machines' *France observateur* 754 (15 October 1964), 20.

'Pages dans le blanc'. *Tel Quel* 23 (1965), 83–88

'Las estructuras de la narración' [interview with Emir Rodríguez Monegal], *Mundo Nuevo* 2 (1966), 15–26

'Los métodos de un crítico' [interview with Rodríguez Monegal], *Imagen* (Caracas) Suplemento No. 30 (August 1968), 9–16.

'Les dieux et les choses'. *La Quinzaine littéraire* 46 (1968), 18–19

'L'Objet fétiche'. *La Quinzaine littéraire* 55 (1968), 4

'L'Écriture autonome' [review of Gabriel García Marquez, *Cien años de soledad*], *La Quinzaine littéraire* 63 (1 December, 1968), 3–4

'Entre les "arrivés" et l'avant-garde'. *La Quinzaine littéraire* 126 (1 October, 1971), 13–14.

'matière/machines/phantasme/ciel' *Alejandro* [Catalogue of the exhibit of Cuban painter José Ramón Díaz Alejandro]. Paris. Galérie Jacques Debrière 16 February–10 March, 1971. Two unnumbered pages.

'Notas a las notas a las notas a propósito de Manuel Puig'. *Revista Iberoamericana* 37 76–77 (1971), 555–567.

'Un Proust cubain' [review of José Lezama Lima, *Paradiso*], *La Quinzaine littéraire* 115

(1971), 3–4

'El barroco y el neobarroco'. *América Latina en su literatura* Ed César Fernández Moreno. México. Siglo XXI, 1972 167–184.

'Big bang. Para situar en órbita cinco máquinas de Ramón Alejandro' *Plural* (México) 14 (1972), 167–184.

'Todo por convencer'. *Hispamérica* 3 (1973), 39–43

'Des diverses façons de représenter l'espace' [review of Erwin Panofsky, *La Perspective comme forme symbolique*] *La Quinzaine littéraire* 234 (15 June, 1976), 20–21.

'Cronología' *Severo Sarduy*. Ed. Ríos. 5–14

'La desterritorialización (reseña de *Juan sin tierra* de Juan Goytisolo)' *Plural* (first series) 48 (September 1975), 54–57, translated as 'Deterritorialization' *The Review of Contemporary Fiction* 4 2 (Summer 1984), 104–109

'Paradis Syllabes-Germes/Entropie/Perspective/Asthme'. *Tel Quel* 77 (1978), 21–24

'Un Châtelet de magie noire'. Preface to Bertrand Visage, *Chercher le monstre* Paris. Hachette, 1978 15–20.

'Le Basculement néo-baroque' *Magazine littéraire* 151–152 (September 1979), 34

'Hacia la concretud'. *Blanco* (Autumn 1979), 12–19 Trans Amelia Simpson as 'Toward Concreteness'. *Latin American Literary Review* 14 (1986). 61–69.

'Pour un ami indien'. *Tel Quel* 82 (Winter 1979), 57–63

'L'Impeccable itinéraire d'un grand seigneur du baroque' [on Carpentier]. *Les Nouvelles littéraires* 2735 (1980), 10

'Barroco de la substracción' *Point of Contact* (NY) 1–2 (Summer 1980), 53–54

'Los Travestis'. *Point of Contact* 1–2 (Summer 1980), 55–58

'Locus imaginarius'. *Art Press* (Paris) 50 (July 1981), 8–9.

'La botérisation de la mode' *Vogue* (Paris) 619 (September 1981), 378–383.

'Tu dulce nombre halagará mi oído' Ed. Gladys Zaldívar and Rosa Martínez Cabrera. *Homenaje a Gertrudis Gómez de Avellaneda* Miami Universal, 1981 19–21

'Sauro o el pincel púrpura' [1981]. Antonio Saura *Figura y fondo* Barcelona. Libres des Mall, 1987 43–51

'Como una oruga que humedece el gris' *Escandalar* (NY) 5.1–2 (1982), 29–33.

'Un algodón de "Las meninas" para Michel Foucault'. *El Pais* 2645 (27 June 1984), 35

'Huellas de Islam en la literatura española de Juan Ruiz a Juan Goytisolo' *Vuelta* (México) 125 (April, 1987), 47–50

'Homenaje a Arecibo' *Lyra* (Guttenberg NJ) 1 (1987), 10–13.

'Tiempos de Ciclón' [1988], *Quimera* 102 (1991), 35

'¿Por qué el Oriente?' *Quimera* 102 (1991), 39–41.

'A la sombra del Arecibo Mito y novela hoy' *Quimera* 102 (1991), 41–44

'Rothko', *Quimera* 102 (1991), 42

Interviews

Interview with E.S. 'Severo Sarduy. cuerpos y libros' *Primera Plana* 336 (3 June 1969), 58–59

Interview with Emir Rodríguez Monegal. 'Conversación con Severo Sarduy' *Revista de Occidente* 93 (1970), 315–343

Interview with Claude Fell. *Le Monde*, 'Le Monde des livres', 26 September 1970, 7

Interview with Roberto González Echevarría 'Guapachá barroco. conversación con Severo Sarduy' *Papeles* (Caracas) 16 (1972), 25–47 Trans. *Diacritics* 2 2 (1972), 41–45

Interview with Jean-Michel Fossey. 'From Boom to *Big Bang*' *Review* (Winter 1974), 6–12

Interview with Jean-Michel Fossey 'Severo Sarduy. Maquina barroca revolucionaria' [20 February 1975] *Severo Sarduy* Ed Ríos 15–24

Interview with Harold Alvarado Tenorio. 'Con Severo Sarduy en el Café de Flore' *El Mundo* (Medellín), 24 November 1979, 15

Interview with Danubio Torres Fierro. 'Lluvia fresca, bajo el flamboyant'. *La Letra y la Imagen* (Mexico), 6 January 1980, 4–7; reprinted in *Escandalar* 1.3 (1978), 65–68.

Interview with Alicia Dujovne-Ortiz. 'Cuba sí, Cuba no' *Les Nouvelles littéraires*, 13 November 1980, 38

Interview with Dennis Seager. 'Conversation with Severo Sarduy' *Dispositio* 5–6.15–16 (1980–1981), 129–142

'Soy un pintor que pinta con palabras' *El Nacional* (Caracas), 24 October 1981.

Interview with Julián Ríos, *Quimera* 20 (1982), 19–23

Interview with Francisco Pérez Rivera 'Budismo y Barroco en Severo Sarduy'. *Linden Lane Magazine*, (Princeton) 2 1 (January–March 1983), 6

Interview with Julia Kushigian 'La serpiente en la sinagoga' [October 1982], *Vuelta* (México) 89 (April 1984), 14–20.

Interview with Justo C Ulloa 'Señales enviades desde Arecibo. Conversacíon con Severo Sarduy' *Crítica Hispánica* 6 2 (1984), 175–180.

Interview with Julio Ortega 'Severo Sarduy escribir con colores' *Diario 16* 2908 (23 June 1985), 'Culturas', iv–v

Interview with Mihály Dés 'Une autobiografía pulverizada' *Quimera* 102 (1991), 32–38

Other works cited

Alegría, Fernando. *Nueva historia de la novela hispanoamericana* Hanover, New Hampshire. Ediciones del Norte, 1986.

Alzola, Concepçion 'Verba cubanorum El habla popular cubana en *De donde son los cantantes*' *Cinco aproximaciones a la narrativa hispanoamericana contemporanea.* Ed. Gladys Zaldívar. Madrid. Collection Nova Scholar, 1977 11–81.

Artaud, Antonin *The Theatre and its Double* NY Grove Press, 1958.

Bakhtin, Mikhail *Rabelais and his World* Trans Helene Iswolsky. Bloomington. Indiana University Press, 1984.

Barrenechea, Ana María 'Severo Sarduy o la aventura textual' *Textos hispanoAmericanos de Sarmiento a Sarduy* Caracas. Monte Avila, 1978. 221–234

Baudrillard, Jean *De la séduction*. Paris. Galilée, 1979

—— *L'Autre par lui-même*. Paris Galilée, 1987

—— *La Transparence du mal* Paris Galilée, 1990.

—— *Symbolic Exchange and Death* Trans Iain Hamilton Grant London Sage, 1993

——. *Le Crime parfait* Paris Galilée, 1995.

Bush, Andrew 'Literature, History and Literary History A Cuban Family Romance' *Latin American Literary Review* 8.16 (1980), 161–172

——. 'Huellas de la danza gestos primeros del barroco sarduyano' *Historia y ficción en la narrativa hispanoamericana* Ed. González Echevarría Caracas Monte Avila, 1984. 333–342

—— 'On Exemplarity and Postmodern Simulation Robert Coover and Severo Sarduy' *Comparative Literature* 44 2 (1992), 173–193.

Bustillo, Carmen *Barroco y America Latina*. Caracas. Monte Avila, 1988.

Caillois, Roger. *Le Mythe et l'homme*. Paris. Gallimard, 'Folio', 1938.

Carpentier, Alejo *El reino de este mundo* México E D I A PS A., 1949. *Tientos y diferencias* Montevideo Area Editorial, 1967

——. *Razón de ser*. Caracas. Ediciones de Rectoradao, 1976.

Cixous, Hélène. 'A Text Twister' *Review* 74 3 (Winter 1974), 26–31

Deleuze, Gilles. *Francis Bacon Logique de la sensation* Paris. Editions de la Différence, 1984

———. *Critique et clinique.* Paris· Minuit, 1993

Echavarran Welker, Roberto *Margen de ficcion. poéticas de la narrativa hispanoamericana.* Mexico: Joaquin Mortiz, 1992.

Franco, Jean. 'The Crisis of the Liberal Imagination and the Utopia of Writing' *Ideologies and Literature* [Minnesota] 1 1 (1976–1977), 5–24

Garsha, Karsten 'El apogeo de la Nueva Novela hisapanoamericana' Ed Hans-Otto Dill et al *Apropriaciones de realidad en la novela hispanoamericana de los siglos XIX y XX* Frankfurt/Madrid Vervuert Verlag/Iberoamericana, 1994 281–306

Ghertman, Sharon 'Language as Protagonist in Sarduy's *De donde son los cantantes* A Linguistic Approach to Narrative Structure'. *The Analysis of Literary Texts Current Trends in Methodology.* Ed. Randolph D Pope. Ypsilanti Bilingual Press, 1980 145–152

González, Eduardo 'Baroque Endings· Carpentier, Sarduy and some Textual Contingencies' *Modern Language Notes* 92 2 (March 1977), 269–295

González Echevarría, Roberto 'Rehearsal for *Cobra*' *Review* 74.3 (Winter 1974), 38–44.

——— 'El primer relato de Severo Sarduy' *Isla a su vuelo fugitiva Ensayos críticos sobre literatura hispanoamericana.* Madrid J P Turanzas, 1983. 123–144

——— *The Voice of the Masters* Austin University of Texas Press, 1985

——— *La ruta de Severo Sarduy* Hanover Ediciones del Norte, 1987.

——— *Myth and Archive. Toward a Theory of Latin American Literature* Cambridge. Cambridge University Press, 1990

——— *Celestina's Brood Continuities of the Baroque in Spanish and Latin American Literature* Durham. Duke University Press, 1993.

———, and Enrique Pupo-Walker, ed. *The Cambridge History of Latin-American Literature* Vol 2 Cambridge Cambridge University Press, 1996

Goytisolo, Juan 'El lenguaje del cuerpo (sobre Octavio Paz y Severo Sarduy)'. *Disidencias* Barcelona. Seix Barral, 1977 171–192.

———. 'Severo Sarduy' *Quimera* 102 (1991), 28

Guerrero, Gustavo *La estrategia neobarroca. estudio sobre el resurgimiento de la poética barroca en la obra narrativa de Severo Sarduy* Barcelona Mall, 1987.

Johndrow, Donald R. '"Total" Reality in Severo Sarduy's Search for *Lo Cubano*' *Romance Notes* 13 3 (1972), 445–453

Johnston, Craig P 'Irony and the Double in Short Fiction by Julio Cortázar and Severo Sarduy'. *Journal of Spanish Studies Twentieth Century* 5 2 (1977), 111–122

Joseph, Margaret Paul *Caliban in Exile The Outsider in Caribbean Fiction.* NY Greenwood Press, 1992

Kushigian, Julia A. *Orientalism in the Hispanic Literary Tradition In Dialogue with Borges, Paz and Sarduy* Albuquerque University of New Mexico Press, 1991

Lacan, Jacques *Ecrits.* Paris. Seuil, 1966

Levine, Suzanne Jill *The Subversive Scribe Translating Latin-American Fiction.* Saint Paul Graywolf Press, 1991

Lezama Lima, José. 'Confluences' *Review* 74 2 (Autumn, 1974), 6–16

———. *Paradiso* Trans Gregory Rabassa Austin University of Texas Press, 1974

Lyotard, Jean-François *Peregrinations. Law, Form, Event* NY Columbia University Press, 1988

Mac Adam, Alfred 'Severo Sarduy/Vital Signs' *Modern Latin American Narratives The Dreams of Reason* Chicago University of Chicago Press, 1977 44–50

Macé, Marie-Anne, *Severo Sarduy.* Paris L'Harmattan, 1992

Manzor Coats, Lillian. *Borges/Escher, Sarduy/CoBrA. Un encuentro posmoderno.* Madrid. Pliegos, 1996.

Martin, Gerald. *Journeys Through the Labyrinth Latin American Fiction in the Twentieth Century.* London: Verso, 1989.

Méndez Maqueo, Verónica 'Cocuyo. una aproximación a lo dual' *Quimera* 102 (1991), 44.

Mendez Rodenas, Adriana. *Severo Sarduy el neobarroco de la transgressión* Mexico Universidad Nacional, 1983

——. 'Colibri' [review]. *Revista Iberoamericana* 130–131 (1985), 399–401

Mendez y Soto, Ernesto *Panorama de la Novela Cubana de la Revolucion (1959–1970).* Miami: Ediciones Universal, 1977.

Menton, Seymour. *Prose Fiction of the Cuban Revolution.* Austin. University of Texas Press, 1975.

Miranda, Julio C. *Nueva literatura cubana.* Madrid. Taurus, 1971

Miura, Isshu, and Ruth Fuller Sasaki. *Zen Dust. The History of the Koan and Koan Study in Rinzai (Lin-Chi) Zen.* NY. Harcourt Brace, 1967.

Montero, Oscar *The Name Game. Writing/Fading Writer in De donde son los cantantes* Chapel Hill. UNC Dept of Romance Languages, 1988.

Ortega, Julio. *Relato de la utopia Notas sobre la narrativa cubana de la revolución* Barcelona. La Gaya Sciencia, 1973. (The section on Sarduy is partially translated in *Poetics of Change. The New Spanish-American Narrative.* Austin University of Texas Press, 1984)

Paz, Octavio. *Conjunctions and Disjunctions.* Trans. Helen R. Lane. NY. Viking Press, 1974.

Pellón, Gustavo 'Severo Sarduy's Strategy of Irony. Paradigmatic Indecision in *Cobra* and *Maitreya*' *Latin American Literary Review* 11.23 (1983), 7–13

Pereira, Armando. *Novela de la Revolución cubana 1960–1990.* México. Universidad Nacional Autónoma, 1995

Perez, Rolando. *Severo Sarduy and the Religion of the Text.* Lanham· University Press of America, 1988.

Perez-Firmat, Gustavo. *Literature and Liminality. Festive Readings in the Hispanic tradition.* Durham. Duke University Press, 1986

——. *The Cuban Condition. Translation and Identity in Modern Cuban Literature.* Cambridge Cambridge University Press, 1989.

Prieto, René 'The Ambiviolent Fiction of Severo Sarduy' *Symposium* (Spring 1985), 49–60.

Ríos, Julian, ed *Severo Sarduy* Madrid Fundamentos, 1976

—— 'Du grand boom au big-bang', *Magazine littéraire* 151–152 (1979).

Rivero Potter, Alicia. *Autor-lector Huidobro, Borges, Fuentes y Sarduy* Detroit Wayne State University Press, 1991.

Rodríguez Monegal, Emir. 'Sarduy. las metamorfosis del texto' *Narradores de esta América.* Vol. 2 Buenos Aires. Alfa Argentina, 1974 421–445 (References are to the abbreviated version in *Sarduy* Ed Ríos. 1976).

—— 'Carnaval/antropofagia/parodia'. *Revista Iberoamericana* 108–109 (1979), 401–412

Rousset, Jean. *La Littérature de l'âge baroque en France* Paris. Corti, 1954.

Sanchez-Boudy, José *La temática novelistica de Severo Sarduy De donde son los cantantes.* Miami Ediciones Universal, 1985.

——, ed *Diccionario de cubanismos mas usuales.* 3 vols Miami Ediciones Universal, 1978–1986.

Santi, Enrico Mario 'Textual Politics. Severo Sarduy'. *Latin American Literary Review* 16 (1980), 152–160.

Schulman, Ivan. 'Severo Sarduy' *Narrativa y crítica de nuestra América* Ed Joaquín Roy. Madrid Castalia, 1978. 387–404.

Schwartz, Kessel. *A New History of Spanish American Fiction*. Vol. 2. Coral Gables, Florida University of Miami Press, 1971

Sollers, Philippe. 'La boca obra' *Tel Quel* 42 (1970), 35–36, 46–47. Trans. *Review* 74.3 (Winter, 1974), 13–15

Swanson, Philip. 'After the Boom' *Landmarks in Modern Latin American Fiction*. London. Routledge, 1990.

Ulloa, Justo, and Leonor de Ulloa 'Leyendo las huellas de Auxilio y Socorro' *Hispamérica* (University of Maryland) 10 (1975), 9–24.

——. 'Severo Sarduy Pintura y literatura'. *Hispamérica* 41 (1985), 85–94.

Watts, Alan W. *The Spirit of Zen* NYL Grove Press, 1969

Weiss, Judith A 'On the Trail of the (Un)Holy Serpent· *Cobra*, by Severo Sarduy' *Journal of Spanish Studies: Twentieth Century* 5·1 (1977), 57–69

Williams, Raymond Leslie. *The Postmodern Novel in Latin America Politics, Culture and the Crisis of Truth* NY. St Martin's Press, 1995

INDEX

Note 'n' after a page reference indicates a note number on that page

Printed in the United Kingdom
by Lightning Source UK Ltd.
127991UK00001B/250-255/A